THE TWENTIETH CENTURY

THE TWENTIE

TEXTS BY

EDITED BY ALAN BULLOCK

Thames and Hudson · London

TH CENTURY

A PROMETHEAN AGE

ALAN BULLOCK

W.H. McNEILL

HERBERT NICHOLAS

ALISTAIR HENNESSY

HUGH SETON-WATSON

C.P. FITZGERALD

ELIZABETH MONROE

J.D. FAGE

JOHN WILLETT

ANTHONY QUINTON

STEPHEN TOULMIN

JOHN MADDOX

ANDREW SHONFIELD

REINHARD BENDIX

731 illustrations

234 in colour

497 photographs, drawings and maps

Designed and produced by THAMES AND HUDSON, London
MANAGING EDITOR: Ian Sutton BA
ART EDITOR: Ian Mackenzie Kerr ARCA, MSIA
EDITORIAL: Helen Walliman MA, Jennifer Rusden BA, Emily Lane BA
RESEARCH: Georgina Bruckner MA, Sheila Lee BA, Vanessa Whinney BA
MAPS: Hanni Bailey, Shalom Schotten
SPECIAL PHOTOGRAPHY: Philip Gotlop, Eileen Tweedy, John Webb
BLOCKS: Klischeewerkstätten der Industriedienst GmbH und Co, Wiesbaden
TEXT FILMSET in Great Britain by Keyspools Ltd, Golborne, Lancs
PRINTED in Western Germany by H. Stürtz AG, Würzburg
PAPER supplied by Gerald Judd Ltd, London
BOUND by Van Rijmenam NV, The Hague, Holland

0 500 04010 9

FOREWORD

EVERY READER will have his own ideas about the way in which to plan a book dealing with the history of his own times. This is one of the hazards of writing contemporary history. All that an editor can do is to explain the plan on which he himself has chosen to proceed, so that the book can at least be judged in terms of what is intended, not of some other plan.

The series of which this forms the latest volume is an historical series, and the contributors have been invited to treat the 20th century in the same way, writing about it as history. The difficulties involved in this approach are discussed in the introductory chapter. Despite the difficulties, I still believe that it is better to do this than treat the 20th century as a block and fail to distinguish sufficiently between its different periods.

The book is divided into two halves. The first is concerned with events, *l'histoire événementielle*. The scale and complexity of these events led me to decide against attempting to provide a single narrative of world history divided into chronological sections. Instead, after an outline of international developments between 1900 and 1970, to provide the necessary framework, there follows a series of chapters each concerned with the history of the 20th century in a particular area. For the most part, these are geographically defined— Europe, America, the Middle East, the Far East, Africa south of the Sahara—but in one case, that of the Communist World, the definition is political. This superimposing of a political on a geographical pattern corresponds to the historical fact; it seemed better to recognize this, and to treat the Russian Revolution, for example, as an event in two distinct contexts, the history of Europe and the history of the Communist World, even if this meant a risk of repetition and a loss of formal consistency.

The second half of the book is concerned with trends and patterns of development in the most important spheres of human activity, from the scientific and economic to the intellectual and artistic. Here the problem was what to leave out and I can only regret that the limits of an already long book obliged me to omit, for example, an account of the rise of the mass media, entertainment and sport, one of the distinctive features of the 20th century which figures in several chapters but would have been well worth one on its own. Each contributor was encouraged to write about those developments which he himself regarded as the most important and not to sacrifice interest to the effort to be comprehensive. The result is a series of essays each of which surveys its field from an individual point of view which I have deliberately made no effort to reduce to a common formula.

The illustrations have been selected in consultation with the author of each chapter; they are intended to supplement as well as to illustrate the text and to supply their own vivid commentary on the history of the century. In the selection of the illustrations as in everything else connected with the making of this book I wish to record my gratitude and that of the contributors to the staff of Thames and Hudson.

Oxford, 1971   ALAN BULLOCK

Acknowledgements

The illustrations sections have been the responsibility of the publishers, who would like to thank all the authors for their unfailing help and advice in the choice of pictures and wording of the captions, and also the following individuals and institutions for their generous co-operation in the collection of photographs: Miss Marianne Adelmann; Dr Clelia Alberici of Archivio Achille Bertarelli, Milan; the Anti-Slavery Society for the Protection of Human Rights; the Arabian American Oil Company; the Bank of England; British Petroleum; Eric Estorick; J. D. Farmer of the Busch Reisinger Museum, Harvard University; Messrs Stanley Gibbons Ltd; José Gómez-Sicre of the Organization of American States; Bengt Häger of the Dansmuseet, Stockholm; Harrods Store, London; Peter Howe of the Post Office, London; the Imperial War Museum, London; Dr Gerhard Kaufmann of the Altonaer Museum, Hamburg; Krupps of Essen; Marlborough Fine Art, Ltd; Satoshi Nakamura of the Japan Information Centre, London; Siegried Oppenheimer; G. Patrix; A. Rezai; Kenneth Snowman of Wartski's; Richard Tooke of the Museum of Modern Art, New York; Donald Winston.

Thanks are also due to Yale University Press for permission to reproduce the statistical tables on p. 351 and p. 355 and J. B. Condliffe, Esq., for permission to reproduce the map on p. 331. The passage by Jacques Ellul on p. 296 is quoted in Martin and Norman's *The Computerized Society*, 1970. The quotation from *Prometheus Bound* on p. 12 is taken from the translation by H. W. Smyth in the Loeb edition.

CONTENTS

1 A PROMETHEAN AGE

ALAN BULLOCK

PROMETHEUS, 'the forethinker', was the most gifted of the Titans. Athene taught him architecture, astronomy, mathematics, navigation, medicine and metallurgy and other useful arts, all of which he passed on to mankind. When Zeus, angry with the race of men, proposed to extirpate them and withheld the gift of fire from them, Prometheus defied his ban, stole fire (some say lighting his torch at the wheel of the sun), and gave it to mankind.

In revenge Zeus chained him to a rock in the Caucasus and sent an eagle to eat his liver which grew again at night as fast as the bird could devour it by day. Despite his sufferings, Prometheus remained defiant, so combining in Greek mythology the roles of father of technology, friend of mankind and supreme rebel.

Aeschylus made Prometheus the hero of one of his most famous plays, from which these lines are taken:

HEPHAESTUS God though thou art,
Thou didst not quail before the wrath of the gods,
But didst bestow honours upon mortal creatures
Beyond their due. . . .

PROMETHEUS Aye, I caused mortals no longer to foresee their doom.
I caused blind hopes to dwell within their breasts
It was I that gave them fire
From which they still learn many arts.

The earth as no man before 1969 had seen it.

Prophecy and fulfilment:
on these two pages we repeat a few of the pictures which appeared in the last chapter of the previous volume in this series, showing 19th-century predictions of what the 20th would be like, with their modern realizations next to them. The **motor-car,** heralded with naive joy in 1900 (left), has come all too true (below). The **hovercraft** (right), **automated teaching** (below centre), and **prefabricated building** (bottom) were all foreseen with surprising accuracy.

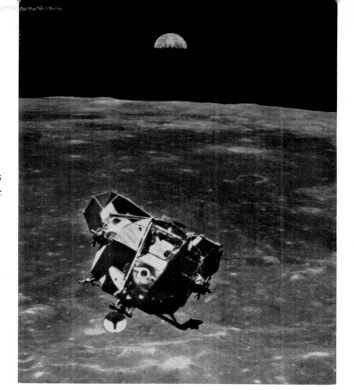

Approaching the moon: the Jules Verne science-fiction (left) and the 1969 reality (right).

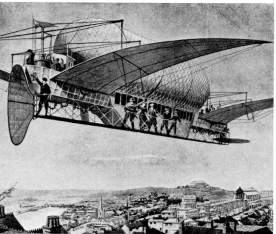

Aircraft were anticipated in principle, though their landing requirements, at the bottom of the earlier picture, were very optimistically estimated.

Television — scarcely less incredible in reality than in fantasy.

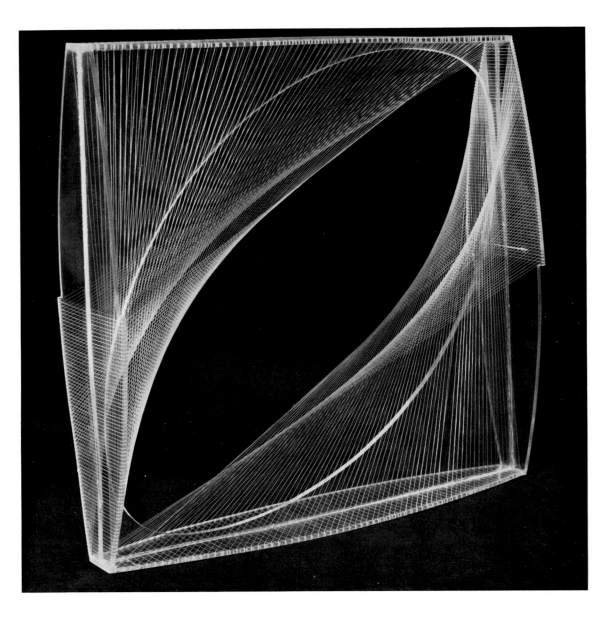

Is this art?

Nobody before 1900 would have thought so. Yet the abstract has become perhaps the most typical of all 20th-century aesthetic forms.

Left: Naum Gabo's *Linear Construction,* 1942–43.

Right: *Composition with Red, Yellow and Blue,* 1921, by Piet Mondrian.

Below: Alexander Calder's *Poisson Rouge, Queue Jaune,* 1968.

The faces of a century give it a peculiarly individual character.

On this page, top row: Einstein, Gandhi, Pope John. Centre: Pavlova, Garbo, Marilyn Monroe. Bottom: Chaplin, Crosby, Mick Jagger.

Opposite, top row: Stalin, Hitler, De Gaulle. Centre: Scott, Lindbergh, Gagarin. Bottom: Edward Prince of Wales, Guevara, Joe Louis.

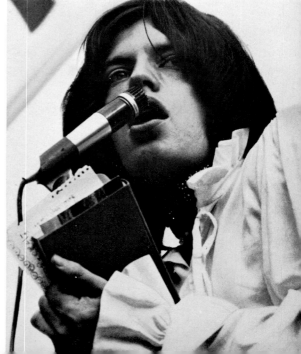

Organized sport
dominates leisure in a way that has no precedent in other centuries. The three events shown here are motor-racing in Belgium, the hurdles at the Mexico Olympics, 1968, and the World Cup, Mexico City, 1970.

This too was done in our century. Graves of the First World War. Belsen. Hiroshima.

The most lasting image of any age is its architecture. Here is the 20th century as two of its architects have left it for posterity. Above: Sydney Opera House, designed by the Danish architect Utzon. Left: Le Corbusier's unexpected masterpiece, the church at Ronchamp, in the countryside of the Vosges.

A Promethean age

ALAN BULLOCK

WRITING A HISTORY of the 20th century presents problems which are not involved, at least to the same degree, in writing about earlier periods. No historian can escape the pull of sympathy towards one side or the other in writing about the conflicts and controversies of the past, but he will almost certainly find it easier to strike a balance and do justice to both sides in writing about the Reformation, the English Civil War or the French Revolution than he will in trying to form an historical assessment of Hitler, Stalin, imperialism or the Cold War. The effort is worth making, indeed essential, for without it our knowledge of the recent past—with the emotional force this exerts in forming people's attitudes—will be based on hearsay, myths ('the Stab in the Back', for instance) and propaganda. But there is no doubt that if a group of Marxist, or Asian or African, rather than a group of Western writers had produced this volume, it would present a very different—though not necessarily more objective—picture. Only with the passage of time will it prove possible to bring these different versions closer together and succeed in establishing common ground between them.

A second objection to the writing of contemporary history, that it is only long afterwards that historians are able to get at the records and penetrate the secrets of governments, seems to me less impressive. There is a time lag, of course, but in modern conditions of publicity few democratic governments succeed in keeping secrets for long; far more news is collected and published from all parts of the world than ever before and in the cases where secrecy is really enforced—e.g. the Soviet Union and Communist China —one may well ask how much more historians will know in fifty or a hundred years' time than they do now. On the other side must be set the unequalled amount of statistical material which enables us already to learn more about economic and social conditions in the 20th century than about those of any previous century, and this over a far wider part of the world than simply Europe and North America.

Much the most serious difficulty in trying to write contemporary history is the lack of sufficient historical perspective, or to put it more plainly knowing what happened in the end. Historians writing of earlier centuries may make great efforts to look at events as contemporaries saw them, but they know perfectly well what happened to the Reformation, the English Civil War and the French Revolution in a way that we cannot yet know about the Russian or Chinese Revolutions, the conflict between Russia and America, or the turmoil in the Middle East. They can see the future of the movements they write about; we cannot, and have to leave our conclusions open-ended and provisional.

This does not of course apply to the earlier half of the 20th century. We know, for instance, that the First World War was followed by a second and that the Germans lost this too; that Hitler's Third Reich lasted only twelve years; that the colonial powers lost their empires, Europe ceased to be the centre of the world and Japan was defeated in her attempt to create a new empire in East Asia. But the 20th century has still more than a quarter of its course to run, and how differently we should assess the international conflicts of its first seventy years if we knew that the remaining years were to see no more major wars, or if on the other hand we knew that the first two wars were to be followed by a third of still greater destructiveness.

Against this ignorance of the future and all that this implies for our historical judgment of the recent past must be set one advantage which contemporaries have always held over later historians of their times. We understand, from our own experience, far more easily than future historians will be able to reconstruct from the surviving evidence, what it has meant to live in the 20th century, what are men's fears and hopes, and how they see the world around them. If a volume like this can make only a provisional assessment of a century not yet completed, it will still, paradoxically, retain a certain value for later historians as a piece of evidence of how a group of Western writers saw the history of the 20th century at the beginning of the 1970's.

The difficulties I have so far described have been common to contemporaries attempting to write the history of their own times since Thucydides' day. There are other problems in writing the history of the 20th century, however, which are not simply those of contemporary history but are likely to remain problems for historians looking back from the vantage point of a later time.

Since the middle of the 18th century there has been a continuous increase in the size of the world's population. Between 1800 and 1900 it is estimated to have risen from 900 million to close on 1700 million. In the 20th century the rate of increase has shot up. Between 1900 and 1970 the population of the world has roughly doubled, from under 1700 to over 3500 million, and is expected to increase by two-thirds again between 1970 and the end of the century. The size of the societies the historian of the 20th century has to describe has therefore become much greater and their life more complicated than those of earlier periods, even of the 19th century.

This increase in the sheer *quantity* of history since 1900 has been accentuated by two other features, the rapidly accelerating rate of change and the emergence of many other parts of the world besides Europe and its overseas settlements into the main stream of historical development.

The first of these hardly needs elaboration. It could already be said of the industrialized West in the 19th century that it had seen greater changes packed into a hundred years than had been spaced out over two or three centuries before. If that was true of the 19th century, it is even more true of its successor, in which social and political change have been speeded up as much as technological.

No doubt earlier generations of historians were myopic in their concentration on the history of Western Europe and the Mediterranean world. But at least in the 19th century it was plausible for European historians to believe that Europe played the central role in world history and that the rest of mankind was only brought in by the expansion of Europe overseas. In the present century this is no longer even plausible, and any history of the 20th century has to take a view of the whole world in a way that was not true of the earlier volumes in the series, which could focus on Europe and treat the rest of the world as peripheral.

The combined effect of these three features of 20th century history—the growth of population, the increase in the rate of technological and social change, the independent development of parts of the world which have hitherto appeared only marginally in history—is to confront anyone trying to discover an historical pattern with a volume of events and evidence out of scale with anything which has gone before. In a hundred years' time historians

25

may have become so accustomed to writing on this scale that they will take the problems it sets for granted and may have worked out with the social scientists ways of dealing with them which we cannot foresee. All that is clear so far is that the difference in scale already begins to make writing the history of the 20th century —even when it has ceased to be contemporary history—look a different sort of undertaking, in kind as well as degree, from writing the history of earlier centuries.

Asa Briggs gave the preceding volume in this series, on the 19th century, a subtitle 'The Contradictions of Progress'. The contradictions were there, all right, but the 19th century still went on believing in progress; the 20th century no longer does, the contradictions have become too glaring, the sense of continuity with the past attenuated.

In fact anyone familiar with 19th-century history must be struck (as Professor Briggs' last chapter brings out) with the extent to which the material conditions of the 20th century's industrialized, urbanized civilization and many of its characteristic ideas and inventions were prefigured in the last twenty years of the 19th. Wherever the break came it was not at the turn of the century, and we are rediscovering the quarter-century before the First World War as a period in which the consciousness, the ways of thinking and feeling, as well as the material conditions of the 20th century began to take shape. My own opinion is that there has never been a break with the past and that people confuse the increasing rate of change (which is undeniable) with historical discontinuity, assuming mistakenly that there was some point at which 'history' ended and the past ceased to be relevant.

Progress however is a different matter from continuity, and any attempt to represent the 20th century in terms of progress and its contradictions would look both old-fashioned and unconvincing. The contradictions of the 20th century need to be expressed in different terms from those of the 19th.

p 14–15 'Futurology' and science fiction were already popular forms of literature in the closing years of the 19th century. Jules Verne wrote his story *From the Earth to the Moon* as early as 1865; another Frenchman, Albert Robida, showed an extraordinary flair in his pictures of life in the 1950s published seventy years before as *Le Vingtième Siècle* and *La Vie électrique*, while H. G. Wells' novels of the future (*The Time Machine*, 1895 and *War of the Worlds*, 1898) still display an originality lacking in his later work. By the 1970s the technological fantasies of the 1880s and 1890s have become commonplace and the transformation of conditions of life by electrical power; by the automobile, the tractor, the aeroplane; by epidemic- and pest-control, to mention only obvious examples, is taken for granted. It is less easy to recognize the transformation which technology has produced in our expectations as much as our living conditions. The fact that we are now beginning to complain about the unwelcome consequences of technological innovation, such as pollution, reflects the extent to which we have come to assume as a matter of course that human beings now have the power to change and mould both the natural and the social environment as they wish and with impunity.

The revolution in expectations which this represents did not begin in the 20th century; it can be traced back to the 18th, even to the 17th century. But it is only in this century that science and technology have provided the means to turn the dreams of earlier ages into fact. Nor is the belief that men now have the technical command of natural forces to sweep away the ancient evils of hunger, disease, poverty and all the suffering they create, any longer limited to a handful of scientists or social visionaries: it has penetrated to every country and every class.

The effect of science and technology in raising human expectations to a height which earlier periods would have regarded as utopian, even blasphemous, has been reinforced by the social and political developments of the century. Down to a time which can be placed somewhere between the French Revolution at the end of the 18th century and the unsuccessful revolutions of 1848, history, in the old sense of *res gestae*, was made by minorities, the majority of mankind enduring life in a harsh obscurity broken only by occasional eruptions of protest in peasant risings or civil war. Only within the past hundred and fifty years have the majority begun to play a continuing and active role in history.

Indeed, one way of writing the history of the 20th century would be to record the successive emergence on to the stage of new groups, each with new demands, from the labour movements of the industrial working classes and the movement for the emancipation of women at the beginning of the century, to the liberation of the ex-colonial territories, the demand of the non-white peoples throughout the world for equality of treatment and opportunity, and most recent of all the claim of youth, led by the student rebels, to a greater share in the decisions which shape society. These different 'groups' are highly disparate in size, character and purpose. Nonetheless they have one thing in common: all have contributed to and at the same time express the unprecedented increase in human expectations—a much higher percentage of the uman race demanding much more and believing that it is possible to provide it —which seems to me perhaps the most striking and distinctive characteristic of the 20th century.

This revolution in expectations has been a frustrated one. Greater changes have been made in a shorter time than ever before in history, but (so far) they have fallen short, both in extent and in results, of what is looked for. Indeed, another way of writing the history of the 20th century would be to take in succession the Grand Illusions which have aroused men's hopes and examine the reasons why the hopes have turned to disillusionment. Yet the striking fact is that, despite all the evidence of frustration and failure, the expectations have been renewed in each generation. The 20th century may be too disillusioned to believe, as the 19th century did, that human progress is a fact, but it still believes that it ought to be— and something more than progress, a social and moral transformation of the human condition which will match the extraordinary success of science and technology in mastering the natural environment.

There are many other characteristics which one could single out as distinctive of the 20th century. For instance, this is the first volume in the series which contains no more than passing references to religion. If one considers the part which religious feeling and controversy played in the past, the growing indifference to a major preoccupation of earlier centuries is striking and, no doubt, is to be related, partly as cause, partly as effect, to the impatient demand for greater satisfactions in man's present life. This may change again (Le Corbusier's superb church at Ronchamp shows how the p 24 religious impulse can find a contemporary form), but up to now the spiritual experience of 20th-century man has found expression in modern art and literature rather than in religion.

Rebelling against any idea of tradition, even their own, refusing to be bound by any convention, avidly in search of the new and the experimental in form, technique and experience, the arts of the 20th century could not possibly be confused with those of any other period. And the audiences to which they speak are very different too, above all they are an urbanized audience. For the age-old balance between country and city has been permanently altered by the movement away from the land to be seen in all countries and the rapid growth in the size and number of great cities, outstripping both planning and prediction, and developing new and constantly changing patterns of life. (In 1900 there were 11 cities with a population of over a million, in 1970 110, thirty-six of them with populations of over 2.5 million, and nine with more than 7 million. On a recent visit to Asia I discovered to my surprise that the capital of Java, Djakarta, has a population of 4.75 million.)

Leaving aside the extraordinary advances in scientific knowledge and technology and new forms of economic organization for discussion later (in Chapters XII, XIII and XIV), one can match the cultural and social changes mentioned in the last paragraph by a group of equally distinctive political changes characteristic of the 20th century. The Bolshevik Revolution of 1917 has some claim still to be regarded as the most important single political event of the century, producing in turn a new form of political action in the revolutionary party, a new form of government in the bureaucratic-totalitarian state and eventually a new division of the world into Communist and non-Communist societies. The alternative form of totalitarianism, fascism, has proved less successful, but Hitler is likely to leave his mark stamped as indelibly on the history of his times as Lenin or Stalin.

Totalitarianism carries the intervention of the state to its logical

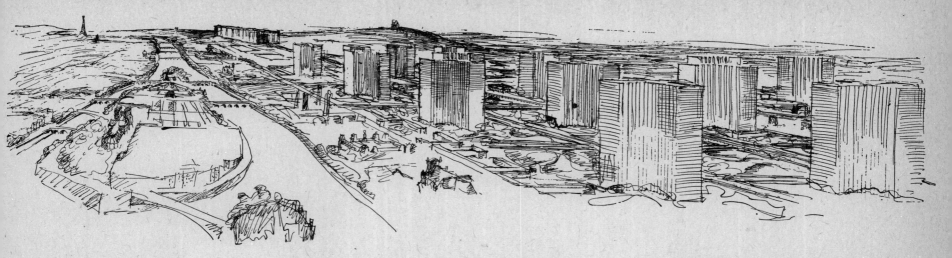

On pages 14 and 15 we have illustrated some 19th-century anticipations of the 20th. The present century is equally fertile in prophecies about the *future. This was Le Corbusier's vision of a new Paris, sketched as early as 1925.*

conclusion (tempered fortunately in practice by inefficiency and corruption); but the growth of the powers of the bureaucratic state in every developed country, irrespective of political attitudes, is one of the major themes of 20th-century history. Even those governments with least faith in the effectiveness of social engineering have been driven to accept methods of planning and control which would have been denounced as despotic a hundred years ago. This increase in the power of the State owes much to war and the need of the industrial nations to mobilize their resources in the two most destructive conflicts in history: until a few years ago most historians would have seen the two world wars and the fear of a third as the centrepieces of 20th-century history.

In short, the history of the 20th century could be constructed around any one of a score of major themes touched on in this introduction, from the growth of world population or the advances of science to technological warfare, the eclipse of Europe or the emergence of the Third World. If I have preferred the revolution in expectations, it is because it seems to me to offer an open-ended pattern capable of accommodating both more of what has already taken place and what may yet be to come. For the revolution is a frustrated one, and the force of this frustration seeking an outlet seems to me more likely than anything else to constitute the dynamic element in the remainder of the century. For this reason I have given the volume the subtitle 'A Promethean Age', calling it after the rebellious Titan who brought fire to men and defied the gods.

This was not the plan to which this book was written: it emerged, as a personal conclusion, only after all the contributions to the text had been received and the illustrations chosen. And the reader who disagrees can forget it and go on to enjoy the rest of the book without bothering about it. But since this introduction was written, as I believe introductions should be, last of all, I will add one further conclusion, again of a personal nature.

There are terrible pages in the history of the 20th century—the world wars, Hitler's attempt to exterminate the Jewish people, the p 22–23 civil wars in Russia and China, Stalin's purges—and an insecurity created by starvation, poverty, fear of unemployment, of violence or of nuclear war which lead many people to regard that history with despair, heightened by foreboding about the future. Much of the literature and art of the century, especially in Europe but more recently in America as well, is stamped with this feeling. Yet when the record is viewed as a whole, there is evident, I believe, as great vitality, as great creativity and as great human achievement as in any century of the past. At all times, at least since 1914, it has been an alarming period in which to live, and perhaps the gap between its dark and its brighter sides is wider, the contradictions more violent than in any previous time. But as a man no longer young who has lived through nearly sixty years of the 20th century, I record my conviction that I would not have wished to be born in any other time and that I know no other century whose history is so extraordinary or fascinating.

Chronology, 1900–1970

	Political Events	Science and Philosophy	The Arts
1900	British Labour Party founded, 1900 Boxer Rising in China, 1900	Rediscovery of Mendel's work on heredity, 1900 Freud, *Interpretation of Dreams*, 1900 Max Planck formulates theory of the *quantum*, 1900 Marconi sends signals across Atlantic, 1901 Weber, *The Protestant Ethic*, 1901	Nietzsche dies, 1900
	Death of Queen Victoria, 1901		
	Anglo-Japanese Treaty, 1902 End of Boer War, 1902	Ford's first plant, Detroit, 1902 Discovery of hormones, 1902	Zola dies, 1902
	USA acquires canal zone in Panama, 1903	G. E. Moore, *Principia Ethica*, 1903 Wright Brothers' flight, 1903	Gauguin dies, 1903 Picasso arrives in Paris, 1903 Dissolution of the 'Nabis', 1903
	Entente Cordiale settles Anglo-French differences, 1904		Strindberg, *The Dream Play*, 1903
	German war against Hereros, 1904–07	Rutherford and Soddy state theory of radioactivity, 1904 Pavlov wins Nobel Prize for work on conditioned reflex, 1904	Loos, Karma Villa, 1904 Chekhov, *The Cherry Orchard*, 1904
	Russo-Japanese War, 1904–05		
1905	Norway becomes independent, 1905	Einstein's *Special Theory*, 1905	Cézanne, *Les grandes baigneuses*, 1905 Cézanne dies, 1905
	Revolution in Russia, 1905	Lenin, *The Tactics*, 1905	Gorki, *Mother*, 1905 *Die Brücke* founded, 1905
	Algeciras Conference, 1906		Otto Wagner's Vienna Post Office Savings Bank, 1905
	Anglo-Russian convention on Persia, Afghanistan, Tibet, 1907	Bergson, *L'Evolution créatrice*, 1907	Reinhardt takes over Deutsches Theater, Berlin, 1905
	Young Turks' rebellion leads to overthrow of Abdul Hamid, 1908–09	Henry Ford manufactures first model T, 1908	'Fauves' at the Salon d'Automne,1905 Ibsen dies, 1906
	Leopold II hands over Congo to Belgium, 1908	G. Sorel, *Reflexions sur la violence*, 1908	*Deutscher Werkbund* founded, 1907 Picasso, *Les Demoiselles d'Avignon*,1907
	Oil discovered in Persia, 1908		Peter Behrens, AEG Turbine Factory, 1908
		Blériot flies the Channel, 1909	Diaghileff brings Russian Ballet to Paris, 1909 Futurist Manifesto, 1909
1910	Japan annexes Korea, 1910	Russell and Whitehead, *Principia Mathematica*, 1910	Stravinsky, *The Fire Bird*, 1910 'Knave of Diamonds' show, Moscow, 1910
	Mexican Revolution begins, 1911 Agadir crisis, 1911 Italy conquers Libya, 1911 Chinese revolution overthrows the Manchus, 1911 Delhi Durbar, 1911	Rutherford and Bohr put forward theory of atomic structure, 1911	Gropius' Fagus Factory, 1911 Strauss, *Rosenkavalier*, 1911 Schönberg formulates the 12-tone scale, 1911 First *Blaue Reiter* show, Munich,1911
	Woodrow Wilson elected, 1912 French protectorate over Morocco, 1912 (March)	Development of electronic valve, 1912 Pathé produces first news film, 1912	Strindberg dies, 1912 Russian Futurist Manifesto, 1912 Thomas Mann, *Death in Venice*, 1913
	First Balkan War, 1912–13 Second Balkan War, 1913	Freud, *Totem and Taboo*, 1913	Stravinsky, *Rite of Spring*, 1913 Proust, *Swann's Way*, 1913 First stories of Kafka, 1913
	Outbreak of World War I, 1914 Battle of Tannenberg, 1914 (August) Battle of the Marne, 1914 (September)	Henry Ford pioneers mass production	Armory Show, New York, 1913 Woolworth Building, 1913 D. H. Lawrence, *Sons and Lovers*, 1913
1915	Gallipoli, 1915 Italy enters the war, 1915 (May) Verdun, 1916 (Feb.–Dec.) Easter Rising in Dublin, 1916 (April) Battle of Jutland, 1916 (31 May–1 June)	Einstein, *General Theory of Relativity*, 1915 Beginning of mechanized warfare	Griffith, *Birth of a Nation*, 1915 Beginnings of Dada in Switzerland, 1915 Joyce, *Portrait of the Artist*, 1916
	Arab revolt against Turkey, 1916 Battle of the Somme, 1916 (July–November) Emperor Franz Josef dies, 1916 (November) America enters War, 1917 (April)		Apollinaire, *Les Mamelles de Tirésias*, 1917 *De Stijl* founded, 1917 Prokoviev, *Classical Symphony*, 1917
	End of Mexican Civil War, 1917 Russian Revolution, 1917 Balfour Declaration, 1917 (Nov.)		Lunacharsky becomes Education Commissar, 1917
	Treaty of Brest-Litovsk, 1918 **Armistice, 1918 (November)** Versailles Peace Conference, 1919	Spengler, *Decline of the West*, 1918–22 Rutherford splits the atom, 1919	Debussy dies, 1918 Satie, *Socrate*, 1918
	Comintern founded, 1919 Amritsar Massacre, 1919 Soviet republics set up in Bavaria and Hungary, 1919	Alcock and Brown fly Atlantic, 1919	Bauhaus founded, 1919 *Cabinet of Dr Caligari*, 1919

Events	Science & Thought	Arts
First assembly of League of Nations, 1920 Russo-Polish War, 1920 Chinese Communist Party founded, 1921 Independence of Southern Ireland, 1921 Treaty of Rapallo, 1922 (April) Mussolini's March on Rome, 1922 (October) Treaty of Lausanne ends war between Greece and Turkey, 1923 (July) Mustapha Kemel elected President of Turkey, 1923 (August) Self-government in Rhodesia, 1923 (October) French occupy the Ruhr, 1923 Inflation in Germany, 1923 Lenin dies, 1924 (January) Dawes Plan, 1924 (July)	Barth, *Commentary on Epistle to the Romans*, 1921 BBC founded, 1921 Rutherford and Chadwick disintegrate the elements, 1921–24 Wittgenstein, *Tractatus Logico-Philosophicus*, 1922 Insulin isolated, 1922	O'Neill, *The Emperor Jones*, 1920 Mendelsohn, Einstein Tower, 1920 Tatlin, *Monument to the Third International*, 1920 'Les Six' formed, 1920 Pirandello, *Six Characters*, 1921 T. S. Eliot, *Waste Land*, 1922 Proust dies, 1922 Joyce, *Ulysses*, 1922 Rivera paints his first mural, 1922 Kafka dies, 1924 Surrealist Manifesto, 1924 Gershwin, *Rhapsody in Blue*, 1924 Shaw, *St Joan*, 1924 Mann, *Magic Mountain*, 1924

Events	Science & Thought	Arts
Locarno Pact, 1925 (October) Death of Sun Yat-sen, 1925 (March) Reza Khan's coup d'état in Persia, 1925 (October) Treaty of Berlin between Germany and USSR, 1926 (April) General Strike in Britain, 1926 Chiang Kai-shek suppresses Communists, 1927 Trotsky expelled from USSR, 1929 (January) Stalin launches First Five Year Plan, 1929 Failure of New York Stock Exchange, 1929	Baird demonstrates television in London, 1925 Quantum mechanics developed by Heisenberg, Schrodinger and Dirac, 1927 Discovery of the red shift, 1928 Penicillin discovered, 1928	Eisenstein, *Battleship Potemkin*, 1925 Chaplin, *The Gold Rush*, 1925 Berg, *Wozzek*, 1925 Neue Sachlichkeit show, Mannheim, 1925 Kafka, *The Trial* published, 1925 Hitler, *Mein Kampf* vol. I, 1925 Scott Fitzgerald, *The Great Gatsby*, 1925 T. E. Lawrence, *Seven Pillars of Wisdom*, 1926 Rilke dies, 1926 Weissenhof Estate, Stuttgart, 1927 Le Corbusier, Villa Savoie, 1928 Mayakovsky, *The Bed Bug*, 1929 Brecht, *Mahagonny*, 1929 Claudel-Milhaud, *Christophe-Colomb*, 1929

Events	Science & Thought	Arts
Young Plan, 1930 Gandhi opens campaign for civil disobedience, 1930 Allied evacuation of Rhineland completed, 1930 Military coup in Brazil; Vargas comes to power, 1930 Statute of Westminster, 1931 Japan invades Manchuria, 1931 Ottawa Agreement, 1932 Election of F. D. Roosevelt, 1932 Hitler becomes Chancellor, 1933 New Deal launched, 1933 World Economic Conference, 1933 Cardenas comes to power in Mexico, 1934 Dolfuss murdered, 1934 Assassination of Kirov leads to Stalinist purges, 1934 (December)	Invention of the cyclotron, 1931 Toynbee, *Study of History*, Vol. I, 1934	Ortega y Gasset, *The Revolt of the Masses*, 1930 Stravinsky, *Symphony of Psalms*, 1930 D. H. Lawrence dies, 1930 Early films of Garbo Bauhaus closed, 1933 Malraux, *La Condition Humaine*, 1933 Socialist Realism proclaimed at Soviet Writers Congress, 1934

Events	Science & Thought	Arts
Stresa conference, 1935 Mao's Long March, 1935 Franco-Soviet treaty, 1935 Anglo-German naval treaty, 1935 Italian invasion of Abyssinia, 1935 Government of India Act, 1935 German occupation of Rhineland, 1936 (March) Blum forms Popular Front government in France, 1936 (June) Outbreak of Spanish Civil War, 1936 (July) Japanese invasion of China, 1937 German Anschluss with Austria, 1938 Czechoslovakia: Munich Agreement, 1938 Mexico expropriates US and British oil properties, 1938 German occupation of Czechoslovakia, 1939 Nazi-Soviet Pact, 1939 **Outbreak of World War II, 1939** Russia invades Finland, 1939	Beginning of radar, 1935 Keynes, *General Theory of Employment*, 1936 A. J. Ayer, *Language, Truth and Logic*, 1936 First jet engine, 1937 Freud dies, 1939	Alban Berg dies, 1935 First Penguin books Federal Act Project, 1935 Golden Gate Bridge, 1937 Picasso, *Guernica*, 1937 Jean Renoir, *La Grande Illusion*, 1937 Exhibition of 'Degenerate Art' in Munich, 1937 New Bauhaus founded in Chicago, 1937 Sartre, *La Nausée*, 1938 Arrest and death of Meyerhold, 1939 Brecht, *Mother Courage*, 1939 W. B. Yeats dies, 1939

Events	Science & Thought	Arts
German invasion of Norway and Denmark, 1940 Defeat of France, Battle of Britain, 1940 Trotsky murdered, 1940 (August) Lend Lease Act, 1941 German invasion of Greece and Yugoslavia, 1941 German invasion of Russia, 1941 Russian counter offensive saves Moscow, 1941 Pearl Harbor, 1941 Battle of El Alamein, 1942 (October) Japanese overrun Dutch East Indies, Burma, Malaya, 1942 Allied landings in North Africa, 1942 (November) Stalingrad, 1942–43 Overthrow of Mussolini: Italian surrender, 1943 Teheran Conference, 1943 Allies capture Rome and land in Normandy, 1944 (June) Bretton Woods Conference, 1944 Russians enter Rumania, Poland and Hungary, 1944	Nylon, artificial rubber and new plastics developed 'Manhattan Project' of atomic research begun in USA, 1941 Explosion of test A-bomb, 1942 Successful application of penicillin and discovery of streptomycin, 1943 Beatrice Webb dies, 1943 German V2 rockets, 1944	Koestler, *Darkness at Noon*, 1940 Hemingway, *For Whom the Bell Tolls*, 1940 Chaplin, *The Great Dictator*, 1940 Orson Welles, *Citizen Kane*, 1941 James Joyce dies, 1941 T. S. Eliot, *Four Quartets*, 1944 J.-P. Sartre, *Huis clos*, 1944

1945

Yalta Conference, 1945 (February) Roosevelt dies (April)
UNO founded at San Francisco Conference, 1945 (April–June)
Mussolini and Hitler die, 1945 (April) German surrender (May)
Potsdam Conference, 1945 (July–August)
Hiroshima and Nagasaki, end of Pacific War, 1945 (August)
Nuremberg Trials Civil war in China, 1945 (October)
  Perón comes to power in Argentina, 1946 (February)
Marshall Plan, 1947 (June) Outbreak of war in Indo-China, 1947
Cominform established, 1947 (October)
OEEC, 1948 (April) Independence of India and Pakistan, 1947 (August)
Communists seize power in Gandhi assassinated, 1948 (Jan.)
Czechoslovakia, 1948 (Feb.) Burma independent, 1948 (Jan.)
  British evacuate Palestine, state of Israel proclaimed, 1948 (May)
Berlin blockade and airlift, 1948–9 Comecon founded, 1949 (Jan.)
NATO, 1949 (April) Communist Republic of China, 1949 (October)
German Federal Republic, 1949 (May) Adenauer elected chancellor
Russia explodes A-bomb, 1949 Indonesia independent, 1949 (Dec.)

Developments of atomic energy to make electricity

Computers begin to be widely used commercially

Keynes dies, 1946

Henry Ford dies, 1947

Max Planck dies, 1947

A. N. Whitehead dies, 1947

Transistor radios, 1948
Invention of LP records, 1948

Britten, *Peter Grimes*, 1945
Bartók dies, 1945
Rossellini, *Rome Open City*, 1945

Messiaen, *Turangelila*, 1946–48

Le Corbusier, Unité d'habitation Marseilles, 1947

Vittorio de Sica, *Bicycle Thieves*, 1948
Abstract Expressionism, 1948
Nervi, Exhibition Hall, Turin

George Orwell, *Nineteen Eighty Four*, 1949
Richard Strauss dies, 1949

1950

Alger Hiss found guilty, 1950 (January)
Schuman Plan, 1950 (May) Outbreak of Korean War, 1950 (June)
  King Abdullah of Jordan murdered, 1951
  Revolution in Egypt brings Neguib to power, 1952
European Coal and Steeel Community, 1952 (July)
Eisenhower elected, 1952 (Nov.) Weizmann dies, 1952
Trial of Slansky and Clementis in Czechoslovakia, 1952 (Nov.)
Stalin dies, 1953 (March) Hammarskjold elected Secretary-
East German rebellion, 1953 (June) General of UNO, 1953 (Mar.)
Beria dismissed, 1953 (July) End of Korean War, 1953 (July)
Malenkov, premier of USSR, 1954 (April)
McCarthy era ends, 1954 Revolution in Guatemala crushed by US, 1954
SEATO established, 1954 (Sept.) Fall of Dien Bien Phu, 1954 (May)
Beginning of Algerian War, 1954 (November)
  Nasser replaces Neguib in Egypt, 1954 (Nov.)

Ventris deciphers Linear B, 1952
Dating by radioactive carbon tests, 1952
Explosion of first hydrogen bomb, 1952 (November)
Wittgenstein, *Philosophical Investigations*, 1953
Hillary and Tenzing climb Mt Everest, 1953 (May)
USSR explodes hydrogen bomb, 1953 (August)
Crick and Watson discover structure of DNA, 1953
Connection between smoking and lung cancer established, 1954
First VTOL aircraft, 1954

Le Corbusier, church at Ronchamp, 1950

UN Building, New York, 1950

G. B. Shaw dies, 1950

David Riesman, *The Lonely Crowd*, 1951

Vilar founds TNP, 1951

Schönberg dies, 1951

First electronic works by Stockhausen, 1953

Matisse dies, 1954
Malraux becomes Minister of Culture, 1954

1955

Malenkov resigns: Krushchev comes to power, 1955
  Baghdad Pact, 1955 (Feb./April)
West Germany enters NATO, 1955 (May)
  Occupation of Germany and Austria ended, 1955 (May)
Summit Conference, Geneva, 1955 (July) Fall of Perón, 1955 (Sept.)
Rebellion in Hungary, 1956 (Oct.–Nov.) Sudan independent, 1956 (Jan.)
Krushchev denounces Stalin, 1956 (Feb.) Riots in Poznan, 1956 (June)
Morocco and Tunisia independent, 1956 (March)
  Suez crisis, 1956 (October)
Treaty of Rome (Common Market), 1957 (March)
  Ghana independent, 1957 (March)
Rapacki Plan, 1957 (Oct.) Desegregation crisis in Little Rock, 1957
EEC comes into force, 1958 (Jan.) Malaya independent, 1957
De Gaulle establishes French 5th Republic, 1958 (May–Oct.)
Cyprus independent, 1959 (Feb.) Cuban Revolution, 1959 (Feb.)
Foreign Ministers conference at Geneva, 1959 (May)
EFTA, 1959 (Nov.) China invades Indian N.E. frontier, 1959

UHF waves developed for use, 1955

Salk vaccine, 1955

Einstein dies, 1955

Neutrino detected, 1956

Sputnik, 1957 (October)

Stereophonic recordings, 1958

Cardinal Roncalli elected Pope John XXIII, 1958 (October)

C. P. Snow, *The Two Cultures*, 1959

Nabokov, *Lolita*, 1955
Beckett, *Waiting for Godot*, 1955
Thomas Mann dies, 1955
John Osborne, *Look Back in Anger*, 1956
Brecht dies, 1956
Sibelius dies, 1957
Vaughan Williams dies, 1958
Grass, *Tin Drum*, 1958
Pasternak, *Doctor Zhivago*, 1958
Nervi and Ponti, Pirelli Building, Milan, 1958
Otto Niemeyer, Brasilia government buildings, 1958–
Mies van der Rohe, Seagram Building, 1958
Frank Lloyd Wright, Guggenheim Museum, New York, 1959

1960

Macmillan's 'wind of change' speech, 1960 (Feb.) Sharpeville (March)
Paris Summit Meeting, 1960 (May) Kennedy elected, 1960 (Nov.)
Congo, Nigeria and French African colonies independent, 1960
OECD, 1960 (November) S. Africa leaves Commonwealth (May)
Krushchev–Kennedy meeting, 1961 (June) Congo civil war, 1961
Berlin Wall, 1961 (Aug.) Hammarskjold killed, 1961 (Sept.):
  U Thant UN Secretary-General, 1961 (November)
Algeria independent, 1962 (July) Jamaica independent, 1962 (August)
Cuba crisis, 1962 (Oct.) Uganda and Tanganyika independent, 1962
GATT: 'Kennedy round', 1963 Kennedy assassinated, 1963 (Nov.)
Franco-German treaty, 1963 (Jan.) Test ban treaty, 1963 (August)
Anglo-US Polaris Treaty, 1963 (April) Kenya independent, 1963
Cultural Revolution begins in China, 1963
  Riots over desegregation in Birmingham, Alabama, 1963
  Beginning of American involvement in Vietnam, 1964
Fall of Krushchev, 1964 (October) Nehru dies, 1964 (May)
N. Rhodesia independent, 1964 (Oct.) China explodes A-bomb

Gagarin, first man in space, 1960
Lasers developed
Introduction of computers on a large scale

DNA code discovered, 1961

Jung dies, 1961

Satellite Telstar, 1962

Vatican Council opens, 1962 (Oct.)

Bishop Robinson, *Honest to God*, 1963

Harold Pinter, *The Caretaker*, 1960
Fellini, *La dolce Vita*, 1960
Boulez, *Pli selon pli*
Hemingway dies, 1961
Solzhenitsyn, *One Day in the Life of Ivan Denisovitch*, 1962

Coventry Cathedral consecrated, 1962

Braque dies, 1963
Cocteau dies, 1963
Aldous Huxley dies, 1963
Hindemith dies, 1963
Saul Bellow, *Herzog*, 1964
Arne Jacobsen, St Catherine's College, Oxford, 1964

1965

Winston Churchill dies, 1965 (Jan.)
  Unilateral independence of S. Rhodesia, 1965 (Nov.)
  India-Pakistan war, 1965
  Communist rising in Indonesia suppressed
  Six Day War, 1967
  Che Guevara killed, 1967
  Sukarno overthrown, 1967
  Nigerian Civil War, 1967
Russian invasion of Czechoslovakia, 1968
  Assassination of Martin Luther King, 1968
Student rebellion in Paris, 1968 (May) Nixon elected, 1968
  Jordanian Civil War, 1970
  Kidnapping of diplomats
  Political hijacking of aircraft

Widespread use of data processing and development of large-scale integration
Molecular biology – the structure of insulin, etc.
Infra-red and X-ray astronomy
Development of very high-strength composite materials, e.g. carbon fibres
Growing social awareness of the environment, noise, pollution, etc.
Cryogenics
Transplant surgery
Genetic control of plant breeding
Lunar landing, 1969

T. S. Eliot dies, 1965

Godard, *La Chinoise*, 1967
Hair, rock-musical, 1968
Solzhenitsyn, *The First Circle*, 1968
Andy Warhol's *Flesh*, 1968
Christo packs his first building, 1968
Exhibition of Cybernetic Serendipity, 1968
Yamasaki, *World Trade Centre*, New York, 1968
Peter Fonda, *Easy Rider*, 1969

1970

President Nasser dies, 1970
De Gaulle dies, 1970

II PEACE AND WAR

The complex web of international relations

W. H. McNEILL

'The age of gentleness and dilettantism is over.
Now we need some barbarians.'

CHARLES-LOUIS PHILIPPE, 1897

Fear of war and the search for peace

have become *leit-motivs* of the 20th century. Few before 1914 could have foreseen that. War, or the threat of war, was part of the accepted practice of international relations, and the numerous treaties and settlements concluded between the great powers were aimed more at benefiting the powers concerned than at avoiding conflict. The experience of the Great War however forced the political leaders to put forward proposals for outlawing war, and the covenant of a League of Nations, at President Wilson's insistence, was written into the Treaty of Versailles.

The League Covenant made provision for the limitation of armaments, the peaceful settlement of disputes, the formation of an International Court of Justice, and the solution of various social problems. The League never succeeded in overcoming the unwillingness of the Great Powers to surrender their freedom of action

in international disputes. Nevertheless, for its first ten years it was an important forum for the discussion of world affairs. The large photograph (opposite) shows the German foreign minister, Gustav Streseman, addressing the Assembly in 1929. Streseman, a great figure at Geneva, made a courageous effort to reconcile Germany with her former enemies and brought his country into the League in 1926. His policy was bitterly attacked by the German nationalists and when he died (less than a month after this photograph was taken) there was no one to take his place.

The League's failure is summed up in John Heartfield's powerful montage, *The Meaning of Geneva* (inset) of 1932. Made as a protest against the Swiss suppression of an anti-Fascist demonstration in which 15 people were killed, it symbolizes the betrayal of peace despite the hopes placed in the League. (1, 2)

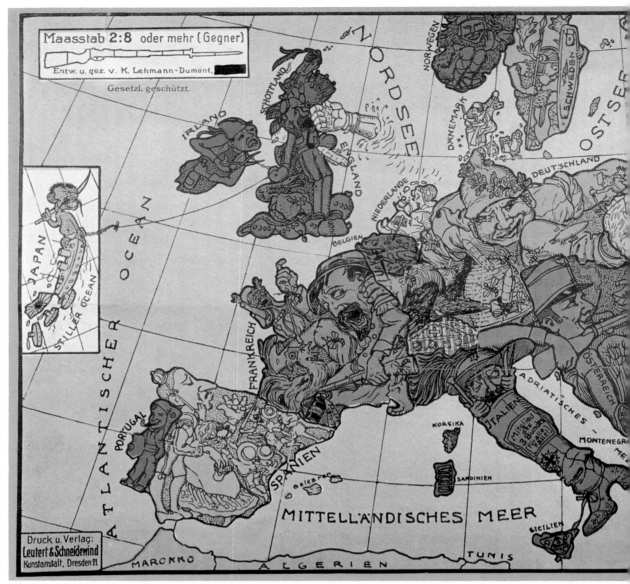

The cult of nationalism, powerfully supported by public opinion, reached a peak in the years before 1914, Britain (above) being among its most blatant devotees. Below: the rival European camps already forming in 1906, Britain, Russia and France on one side, Germany and Austria-Hungary on the other, with the infant Italy hesitating between them. (3, 4)

Russia deserts Germany (left), who has been polishing his boots, and goes off with France — a satirical print from the German periodical *Simplicissimus*. (5)

Anglo-German naval rivalry was one of the major factors leading to war. Germany's expansion of her shipping (above) challenged Britain's supremacy at sea. (7)

The European jungle (left) is a German artist's picture of the situation just after the outbreak of war. The scale (measured by rifle) is 2 Germans to 8 enemies. (6)

On the 'threshing floor' of Europe, Germany and Austria belabour the Allies — Britain, France and Russia — while the rest of the world looks on and learns its lesson: a hopeful view of events from the German side. (9)

The Austrian eagle demands money to carry on the war. War loans became a feature of every belligerent country, with important effects on their economy. (8)

War propaganda could appeal either to a sense of shame (as in the famous British recruiting poster, below) or to military pride. The French example is another war loan poster. (10, 11)

The outbreak of war in 1914 was greeted with enthusiasm in every capital in Europe. Unaware of the ordeal that lay ahead, volunteers crowded eagerly into the recruiting offices. When America entered the war three years later enthusiasm had somewhat diminished. (12, 13)

War placed tremendous strains on the economy, strains beyond the capacity of Russia and Austria-Hungary. At the same time (as shown more fully in Chapter XIII) it was a powerful stimulus to technology. Left: a British shell-factory at the height of the war. Above: German ribbons commemorating the war at sea and in the air. (14–16)

The Western front settled into stale-mate after it became clear that the German offensive of August 1914 had failed. Lines of trenches (right) stretching from the Belgian coast to Switzerland remained practically stationary for four years in spite of massive attacks and the sacrifice of millions of lives. (17)

Verdun (below), one of the strongpoints of the French line, was deliberately selected for attack by the Germans in 1916 in order to draw in and destroy the French armies. By the end of the year each side had lost 350,000 men and Verdun had become the symbol of French resistance. (18)

In the east the success of German arms against Russia totally discredited the Tsarist regime and led to the 1917 Revolution. Below right: the Kaiser inspecting his troops in Galicia. (19)

Gallipoli (bottom) was an attempt by the Allies to by-pass the Western front and strike at the Central Powers from the south. But the costly expedition came to nothing and the bridgeheads had to be evacuated. (20)

The scars of war were left not only on the landscape of northern France but on the consciousness of those who lived through it. Paul Nash's painting of the battlefield (left) is ironically titled *We are Making a New World*. (21)

The new world upon which men placed their hopes was to be forged at the Peace Conference at Versailles. But the victors were too deeply under the spell of the experience which they had just undergone to think straight about the future, and mortgaged the postwar settlement too heavily with the payment of past accounts for it to have much chance of lasting. In this painting (below) by Sir William Orpen, Wilson, Clemenceau and Lloyd George are seated in the centre. The two German delegates, summoned only to receive the victors' terms, are on the near side of the table. (22)

The League proved powerless to avert conflict or control aggression. In 1931 Japan occupied **Manchuria** in clear defiance of the League's ruling. This poster (left) expresses Russian support for the workers of China. Five years later, Mussolini invaded **Abyssinia** (right: a poster identifying the Italian troops with the legions of ancient Rome); the failure of the Powers to apply realistic sanctions against Mussolini meant the effective end of the League. The same policy of 'appeasement', heedless of the protests (below right) of Czechoslovakia, produced the **Munich** agreement which allowed Hitler to occupy the Sudetenland in September 1938. (23–25)

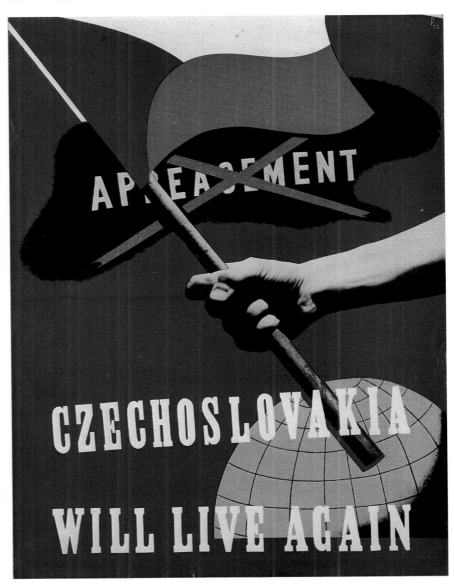

Chamberlain believed (left) that he had achieved peace at Munich by his concessions to Hitler over Czechoslovakia. He and the world soon learned otherwise. In March 1939 Hitler occupied Prague, and by August was pressing his claims to the 'free city' of Danzig (right), which had a majority of German-speaking inhabitants. On 1 September he attacked Poland. Two days later Britain and France declared war. (26, 27)

Warsaw was occupied after a ferocious *Blitzkrieg* which was a foretaste of the power of Hitler's armies. Poland was mercilessly oppressed for the remainder of the war. (28)

Paris fell in June 1940, after a brilliant campaign in which the French and British armies were separated, France forced to capitulate and Britain left to face Germany alone. (29)

Now civilians found themselves in the front line. Above left: French refugees fleeing along the crowded roads in June 1940.

Dunkirk: the evacuation of the British army (below) amounted in fact to a British victory. (33)

Centre: Londoners sheltering in the Underground, winter 1940–41. Above right: shattered Berlin, later in the war. (30–32)

Pearl Harbor: the surprise Japanese attack on the US Pacific Fleet in December 1941 brought America into the war. (34)

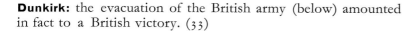

Churchill proved a war-leader of char-ismatic personality, fiercely deter-mined to continue the struggle with-out thought of compromise. The failure of the *Luftwaffe* to destroy the RAF in the Battle of Britain (left), July-September, 1940, was decisive in preventing a German invasion of Britain. (35, 36)

In the desert of northern Africa a series of tank battles decided the fate of Egypt. (37)

Burma: Gurkha troops (above) in the long campaign to defend India against the Japanese. (38)

Italy was invaded by the Allies in September, 1943. Above: the German stronghold of Monte Cassino. (39)

Stalingrad was the turning point in the East. In February 1943 the German Sixth Army was surrounded. (40)

Landings in Normandy (above right), June 1944, forced the German army to fight on two fronts. (41)

Victory in Europe came in April 1945. Right: Russian soldiers raise the red flag over conquered Berlin. (42)

Victory in the Pacific followed in September. Hard won American ad-vances in the Bonin Islands (far right: Iwo Jima) were overtaken by the ex-plosion of the first atomic bombs, forcing Japan to capitulate. (43)

With the issue certain, the future victors met — a secret, anticipatory Versailles — at Yalta (below) in February 1945 to shape the postwar world. The British and Americans had to accept the position Russia had already secured in Eastern Europe. In Churchill's later phrase, an 'Iron Curtain' descended, cutting off the Communist world from the West. (44)

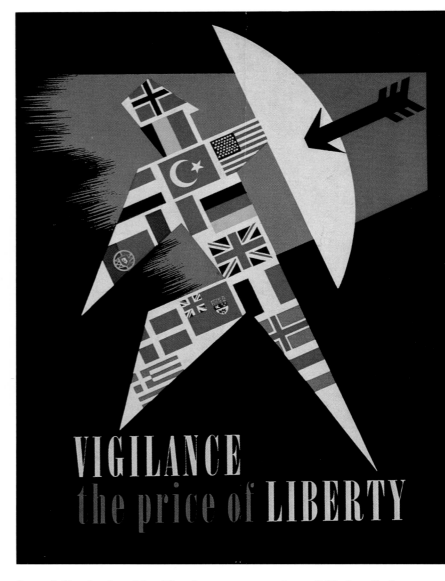

VIGILANCE the price of LIBERTY

NATO (right), the North Atlantic Treaty Organization, was formed in 1949 to recreate a balance of power in a Europe which the Soviet Union would otherwise dominate. (45)

The Warsaw Pact was the Communist answer to NATO. This photograph (below) shows the leaders of Eastern Europe at Bratislava in the summer of 1968, where they met to decide the fate of Czechoslovakia. The front row consists of Kadar, Podgorny, Kosygin, Zhivkov, Svoboda, Brezhnev, Gomulka, Ulbricht, Dubček and Suslov. (46)

The Third World, outside the Communist and Western alliance systems, seeks to preserve its neutrality by avoiding commitment to either side. This poster (below) was produced by the Organization of Solidarity with the Asian, African and Latin American Peoples. (47)

Jornada de Solidaridad con el pueblo Afroamericano/18 de agosto
Day of Solidarity with the Afro-American People/August 18
Journée de Solidarité avec le peuple Afro-américain/le 18 août

يومية التضامن مع الشعب الافروامريكي ۱۸ آب

Korea and Vietnam are symptoms of the tensions that still exist between the two great world blocs. Top: US servicemen patrol the Military Demarcation Line between North and South Korea. Above: a young victim of the war in South Vietnam. (48, 49)

The Middle East has been the third trouble-spot of the postwar years, and is examined in more detail in Chapter VIII. Here an Israeli armoured column passes the Mount of Olives during the Six Day War. (50)

Hopes that the United Nations would be able to play a more independent role in world politics than the League were focussed on the strange, mystical personality of its Swedish Secretary General, Dag Hammerskjold (above: Ben Shahn's portrait, painted after his death in 1961): 'It is very easy to bow to the wish of a big power. It is another matter to resist.' Left: a Yugoslav artist's neat symbol of the hopes millions placed in the UN Organization — 'The End of War, the Beginning of Peace'. (51–53)

The complex web of international relations

W. H. McNEILL

P 34
(3)

IN 1900, as the 20th century dawned, Queen Victoria still sat on the throne and the Royal Navy continued to rule the waves. Yet there were flaws in the *Pax Britannica* that for nearly a century had regulated the world's oceanic relationships. The rising naval power of the United States and of Japan made British predominance in the Pacific impossible; and the naval race with Germany that developed full force in the first decade of the new century called into question Britain's control of seas far closer home. Yet even these important changes were not beyond cure through

p 149
(2)

traditional diplomacy. Thus the Anglo-Japanese alliance of 1902 secured satisfactorily the slender British military presence in the Pacific, and, incidentally, freed the Japanese to attack and defeat the Russians in Manchuria, 1904–05. In Europe, the threat of German power was met by a more radical realignment when Britain settled accounts with its two traditional imperial rivals, France and Russia, to conclude the Triple Entente (1907).

Before 1914: European supremacy

p 34
(4, 5)

The diplomatic quadrille that counterpoised Bismarck's creation, the Triple Alliance of Germany, Austro-Hungary and Italy to the newly concluded Triple Entente of Britain, France and Russia did not seem at the time to carry any particular threat to the pattern of international relations that had been inherited from the 19th century. Struggles among the European powers over the partition of Africa offered precedent for the anticipated conflicts over partitioning of China and Turkey. The clamours of the public press and conferences among diplomats, backed up by the common sense of governments responsible in some degree or other to their subjects, and by the growing economic interdependence of all nations, could be expected to resolve international quarrels in the

p 194
(3)

future as in the recent past with only marginal resort to war. Or so it seemed. For nearly a century, threat and counter-threat, display

p 158
(31)

of force, and, occasionally, the use of European armies and navies on a small scale in some distant part of the globe against 'natives'— but seldom against fellow Europeans—had in fact brought European empires almost to their apogee without provoking major war in Europe itself. The system might be precarious; nevertheless it worked.

Yet the diplomatic precariousness of which men were then aware turned out to be no more than the superficial seething of quicksands that boiled up on every hand in the half-century that followed 1914. Before that time, politics was limited, domestically and internationally, by a series of traditional assumptions and practices that left most economic and social activity alone. Adam Smith and his heirs had analyzed the natural workings of the free market economic system; and because it was believed to be natural—directly based, that is, on an unchanging human nature—deliberate policy could do little but interfere with and prevent the attainment of maximal efficiency. To be sure, governments had always interfered by imposing tariffs and taxes, subsidies and even, in a land like Russia or Japan, by investing directly in armament works and other amenities of industrial modernity. But such departures from regulation of economic activity by free market relationships were viewed as exceptional. They remained marginal to the world's economic structure.

No carefully developed theory sanctified traditional class struc-

tures, agricultural routines, educational patterns, familial, kinship and other social relationships. Indeed, most Europeans and their descendants overseas assumed that all such aspects of society would evolve by degrees towards some imprecisely defined norm and goal of civilization, as the various 'backward', i.e. non-European, peoples of the earth learned of and spontaneously accepted and made their own the obviously superior civilization most perfectly developed in western Europe.

Three regions of the world stood out before 1914 as special cases, where the pattern of progressive development towards liberal European-type society was disturbed by local peculiarities. In most of Latin America (see Chapter V), the directing classes, mainly of European descent, presided over a more complex racial mixture than could be found in other parts of the world. This was not much different from the situation in colonial regions where Europeans governed natives, of whatever physical appearance. What was different was that the directing classes, with their longer experience of living side by side with men of other physical appearance and divergent cultures, were usually not very eager to modernize, liberalize and Europeanize the social scene around them, recognizing, perhaps, that the further spread of western European values and practices might endanger their traditional leadership positions.

In a sense, Japan's remarkable career conformed to and offered one of the most spectacular confirmations of European ideas about the normal course of international affairs. For the Japanese had adopted European technology with remarkable eagerness and success. With victory over China in 1895 and over Russia in 1904–05, Japan entered upon the international scene as a great power in its own right—at least in the remote Pacific area, where the full force of European strength could not, for geographical reasons, be brought to bear.

p 153
(16)

But in another sense, Japan's rise to great power status challenged the prevailing assumptions of European thought even more fundamentally than did the racial mix of Latin America. For the Japanese in borrowing European technique did not borrow the whole panoply of European civilization. In fact, some elements of older Japanese culture that stood at furthest remove from contemporary European views were reinforced and emphasized in the course of Japan's modernization: the divine status of the emperor, for instance, and the mythology of Shinto that surrounded this conception. Japan, in short, offered an example of how a nation with a radically different cultural past could selectively appropriate elements from the European tool kit and, at least in the short run, use the new power such borrowed devices could impart to shore up and defend non-European institutions and ideals.

p 155
(23, 24)

The third region of anomaly from a liberal west European point of view lay much closer home. On the fringes of Europe itself, in Ireland to the west and in the Balkans and Russia to the east, the path of progress was running upon strange and uncharted shoals. Among the Irish, rules of the political and economic game as defined in England had been flagrantly broken. Catholic countrymen counted on Irish shillelaghs more than on English shillings, and preferred heroic patterns of violence and reckless generosity to the niggling stratagems and careful calculations of the market place. Similar archaic values, angrily disdainful of bourgeois caution, also survived in the Balkans. Moreover these survivals from a barbarian past melded by the close of the 19th century with revolutionary political faiths demanding radical liberty, not to say anarchy. In Ireland, the Roman Catholic Church kept such movements pretty well in check; but in the east, heroic, violent and revolutionary gestures appealed powerfully to disenchanted youth—one of whom, Gavrilo Princip, managed to set the world aflame in 1914 by assassinating Archduke Ferdinand, heir to the Habsburg throne.

The revolutionary intelligentsia of eastern Europe had a sounding board among the peasant majority of those lands where the impact of industrialism was just beginning to be felt. Vague though heartfelt peasant discontents, massed and magnified among industrial workers, most of whom had come freshly from the farm, found readier definition through programmes for apocalyptic revolutionary change than in piecemeal and drably practicable programmes of amelioration.

Here then, at Europe's very doorstep, lay a challenge to the limitations upon the political mobilization of human effort tacitly accepted since 1815, when men of the western world had closed the doors upon an earlier revolutionary era. The harsh imperatives of war, unleashed unexpectedly in 1914, reopened doors that had remained closed for a full century, giving expression to the broad range of fanaticism, heroism and violence that the conventions of international life prevailing among the powers of Europe between 1815 and 1914 had kept precariously under lock and key.

War, 1914-1918

p 36
(12-14)
Millions responded to the outbreak of World War I, in August 1914, with a hot surge of enthusiasm. War offered a break from dull routine, an enemy to hate, a cause to defend: scope in short for all the primitive and heroic sentiments bottled up by the European society of the 19th century. Military professionals counted on a short war on the model of 1866 or 1870; and in the first five weeks the Germans came within an ace of defeating the French according to their mobilization plan. But at the Battle of the Marne (September 1914) French reservists arrived in time to penetrate a gap in the German lines. The attacking force drew back, and thereby ruined any chance for a quick victory. In the following weeks hastily constructed field defences developed into a continuous belt of

'*This is our home*'—*the people of northern France return to their ruined villages after 1918; a drawing by T. A. Steinlen.* (1)

trenches and redoubts that scarred the French landscape from the Channel coast to the Swiss border.

Resolutely defended trenches proved all but impregnable. In the years that followed limited breakthroughs were achieved only after fearful expenditure of lives and high explosives. But by bringing up reserves and digging new trenches in the rear, the defenders were always able to re-establish a continuous defended line quickly and at relatively small cost. The resultant stalemate in the west lasted until 1918, despite the loss of millions of lives and the expenditure of millions upon millions of shells. p 37
(17)

In the east, the land frontiers between Russia and the Central Powers were too lengthy and supply systems were too slender to permit the construction of a continuous belt of trenches as in France. Instead, the front fluctuated over several hundred miles, as first one side and then the other mustered manpower and supplies for a major offensive. But here, too, decisive success was not achieved until three long years had passed, and then by revolutionary rather than by strictly military means.

An obvious response to the failure of the initial war plans of 1914 was to seek for allies whose help might tip the balance. The Central Powers attracted Bulgaria (Turkey had joined them almost from the start) for a final and successful assault upon Serbia in 1915. This accession of strength was more than counterbalanced by the entry of Italy into the war on the Allied side in the same year. Rumania (1916) and Greece (1917) later did likewise. As a result of these moves, the Allied forces were able almost to surround the Central Powers. Switzerland, the Netherlands and Scandinavia remained neutral; but systematic control of these nations' imports effectively prevented the beleaguered Germans and their allies from getting access to the outside world through trade with neutrals. p 174
(7)

As the lines were thus geographically drawn tight, the struggle turned into a war of attrition. Surprising resources for waging war were soon discovered. Within each of the principal belligerents the need for more and ever more shells and other equipment soon required drastic and deliberate reorganization of supply and production patterns inherited from times of peace. Germany pioneered, for the British blockade threatened economic disaster to the German war machine almost from the start. France and Britain broke more slowly with peacetime practices since, to begin with, it was easier to increase overseas imports through normal market dealings than to tamper radically with domestic social structures and business interests. But as the dreary war years succeeded one another, manpower shortages became critical for every belligerent state; and shortages of consumer goods, fuel and raw materials provoked massive official intervention in the free market system in order to channel whatever was available more directly into war production.

Rationing and consignment of manpower and scarce goods according to officially determined priorities allowed the nations of western Europe to magnify their military effort enormously. Millions of soldiers and the vast amounts of equipment and supplies they needed were kept in the field, year after year. In the east, the Tsarist administration and industrial plant proved incapable of supplying the Russian armies adequately after 1916. The Habsburg state structure also creaked and groaned under the strains of war mobilization, yet with the help of some essential supplies from Germany, the Austro-Hungarian armies held on until the bitter end.

Intensification of the war effort along these lines fundamentally changed the nature of war and politics as well as of economics. Governments, it turned out, could organize command economies capable of marshalling a hitherto unimagined concentration of resources for fighting a war. In principle, though never quite in practice, the entire nation could be treated like a single firm, in which the management saw to it that every person and every material resource contributed with maximal efficiency to the common goal: victory.

This was a startling and frightening discovery. Limits to political action, assumed until 1914, could no longer be taken for granted. Social engineering could be made to work—at least under some conditions. Logic did not limit the goals of such deliberately radical management to waging war, as Lenin and the Bolsheviks of Russia soon made clear. The fact that the Bolsheviks retained power, despite foreign intervention and civil war meant that war-born techniques of administrative mobilization were carried over into peacetime, eventually to become a new kind of norm for Russian society. In the richer and victorious nations of western Europe, governmental regulation and direction of the economy was associated with shortages, death and desperate strain. Reaction, although very strong in the postwar years, nevertheless turned out to be brief and transitory. For when new emergencies arose, the wartime model lay ready at hand. Needless to say emergencies were not long in coming, but this runs ahead of our story.

Until 1918 German efforts were effectively countered by the Allies' heightened mobilization of their resources. The two sides strained harder and harder merely to maintain the brutal stalemate on the Western Front. Yet there was a limit. In 1918 the German war effort wore down the manpower and other resources of the nation to such a point that continuation became impossible.

Before this ultimate defeat and victory arrived, however, the war changed its character in important ways. The year 1917 was decisive.
p 36 (13) In April, the United States declared war against Germany, and launched an energetic mobilization programme that brought enough armed men to France by the summer of 1918 to tip the balance and help check the final German drive towards Paris. America's entry into the war on the Allied side was, however, counterbalanced by the withdrawal of the Russians in the autumn as a result of Lenin's Bolshevik revolution (November 1917).

These massive shifts of the war's material balance were accompanied by quite new ideological definition of the war's goals.
p 84 (9) President Woodrow Wilson proclaimed that the United States was embarked upon a 'war to end war' and to 'make the world safe for democracy'. This was soon spelled out to mean democratic revolution for all central and eastern Europe. Autocratic and militaristic empires were to yield to governments deriving their just powers from the consent of the governed as attested by free elections. Not only that, President Wilson also intended to abolish war by an equally revolutionary transformation of international relations. A League of Nations would settle future disputes by
p 33 (1) public negotiation and legal process. Should a government defy the League and its decisions, all the League members would be obliged to enforce justice and check aggression by imposing sanctions upon the recalcitrant.

Wilson's vision of a world cleansed of ancient flaws and launched securely upon a liberal and democratic path of progress and of law competed with Lenin's no less revolutionary clarion, that summoned the workers of the world to rise against their capitalist oppressors, overthrow their governments and inaugurate an international dictatorship of the proletariat as a prologue to the social equality and perfect freedom of Communism. The German proletariat, attuned by years of indoctrination to Marxian ideas, was the principal target of Lenin's propaganda; but even the most revolutionary Germans disliked being told what to do by Russians, whom they felt to be less civilized than themselves. As a result, Marxist revolution failed to develop in Germany, even after the last, desperate offensive of 1918 ground to a halt at the Marne river. Hopeless retreat began in August, and in November 1918 the Kaiser abdicated, an armistice was signed, and at long last the guns fell silent on the Western Front. Two days before the fighting ended a new socialist, but scarcely revolutionary, regime came to power in Germany, pinning its faith, at least officially, upon Wilson's principles for the postwar reordering of Europe.

The weakness and impoverishment of the parts of the Russian Empire that remained under Bolshevik control in 1918–19 made Lenin's programme for social renewal less attractive outside Russian borders than might otherwise have been the case. All of eastern Europe followed the German example: nationalist distaste for Russia and the counter-attractions of democratic revolution *à l'américaine* outweighed Marxism-Leninism. This was less true of Asia. There the tiny groups of disenchanted intellectuals who detested and deplored the weakness into which their nations had fallen *vis à vis* the Western world often viewed nationalism, democracy and Communism as different aspects of a single, liberating path towards 'modernity'.

Although professed everywhere in postwar Europe outside of

Doubts that the Treaty of Versailles had solved Europe's problems were voiced at the time, but nowhere more prophetically than in Will Dyson's cartoon in the Daily Herald, 1919. Clemenceau, leading Woodrow Wilson, Orlando and Lloyd George out of the conference, says 'Curious! I seem to hear a child weeping!' It is the generation which will be grown up in 1940. (2)

Russia, Wilsonianism was often honoured in the breach at the peace conference that met in Paris, 1919–20. Yet for all the departures in detail favouring the victors against the vanquished, it still remains true that the Treaty of Versailles with Germany, and the associated treaties prepared for the other defeated powers at the Paris conference, did create frontiers in Europe that conformed in a rough and ready way to lines of nationality. In Asia and Africa, p 38 (22) however, a different principle prevailed. There the spoils were divided among the victors in the good old-fashioned way. France and Britain carved up the Arab lands formerly subject to Ottoman rule, and cheerfully divided up Germany's former African possessions between them. In the Pacific, France and Britain shared former German territories with Japan, Australia, and China. Most of these lands were designated League of Nations 'mandates'. This meant that the administering powers reported to and theoretically derived their powers from the League. But in practice the acquisitions were administered very much like other colonial possessions.

European overseas empires thus reached their maximal extent after World War I; yet even as this landmark was attained, the British Empire, largest of them all, showed definite signs of disintegration. World War I fostered a spirit of independent nationhood in Canada and Australia; South Africa and New Zealand lagged only slightly behind. Their growing independence was acknowledged by giving each of the British Dominions separate membership in the League. But this, ironically, clinched the decision of the United States Senate to reject the Treaty of Versailles in 1920. Suspicious Senators feared a treaty that would commit the country to membership in a League of Nations where British interests were so extravagantly over-represented!

After Versailles

With this decision to repudiate President Wilson's treasured talisman for world peace, the Republican administration that came to power in the United States in 1920 gladly shook off European entanglements. Yet the United States acted quite differently in the Pacific. There, Japan seized the scattered German colonial possessions at the beginning of the war, and took advantage of the European struggle to make far-reaching demands upon China for commercial and other privileges. The Chinese stalled until the war was over; and after 1917 Japanese attention was diverted for a while towards Russian holdings in Manchuria and the Maritime Province. The United States, however, wished to check Japanese expansion—even if it meant restoring the Maritime Province to Russian Communist control.

Confronted by the necessity for a choice between the Japanese and the Americans, British diplomats opted for the latter and, accordingly, declined to renew their naval alliance with Japan that was about to expire in 1922. Instead, an international conference met in Washington to regulate the Pacific and establish naval ratios. This, it was hoped, would head off any future naval armaments race like that between Britain and Germany that had helped to prepare the way for World War I. Within Japan itself, important elements distrusted the military programme for expansion on the Asian mainland. Accordingly, the Japanese Government was able to come to terms with the Western powers, accepting a 3:5 ratio for their navy as against the navies of Britain and the United States whose forces were to be equal. This gave the Japanese superiority in their home waters, and made withdrawal from Russian and Chinese territories on the mainland of Asia acceptable to them.

No sooner had something like stability thus descended upon the Pacific than a new emergency arose in Europe that called the reluctant Americans back to active participation in the tangled affairs of that continent. Italians, discontent with the treaties that awarded them less than the promised and hoped for territories in the Adriatic, came under Benito Mussolini's Fascist government in 1922. He set out—at first without great success—to undermine the Versailles settlement in south-eastern Europe. This the French, with half-hearted British support, were able to cope with.

But Germany was a different matter. Here the French precipitated a first-class crisis in 1923. The Germans had lagged in making reparations deliveries to which the peace settlement bound them. Pressed by difficulties at home, the exasperated French decided to compel the Germans to honour their engagements by invading the Ruhr, with the intention of seizing coal, owed as part of the reparations payments, at the pithead. Almost to a man, the Germans refused to work for the invaders. Runaway inflation and economic paralysis ensued. Communist hopes of revolution, quiescent since 1921, suddenly surged anew as the German economy came to a standstill. This brought the Americans back to the European scene as guarantors of a new financial regimen for Germany—the so-called Dawes Plan (1924). The scheme worked wonders. Within a few months prostrate Germany launched upon a frenetic boom that matched the boom developing at the same time in the United States, and, to a lesser extent, in other nations of Europe and overseas.

The capitalist boom of the 1920s coincided with hard times in Russia. In 1921 the Bolsheviks made peace with Poland, thereby giving up, for the time being at least, the hope of spreading revolution to Germany by sending a missionary army westward. Extreme economic disruption even compelled Lenin to abandon Communist principles to the extent of allowing limited private trading (NEP or New Economic Policy, 1921). Soon thereafter, Lenin was disabled by a stroke, and never entirely recovered. This opened the way for secret quarrels over the succession. The struggle became more open after Lenin's death in 1924. By 1927, however, Stalin had disposed of his rivals and emerged to supreme personal control over the Russian Communist Party and state. He used his new position (pillaging the programme of his defeated 'left' opposition) to announce an ambitious Five Year Plan that would enormously accelerate the industrialization of Russia. The method was essentially the same as that used by the belligerent governments of World War I: mobilization of men and material for the accomplishment of a series of definite tasks, even

'Demagogy' by Alfred Kubin, 1939. The language of Expressionism (Kubin had belonged to the Blaue Reiter before World War I) was well suited to convey the situation of thirty years later. (3)

if this meant diverting resources from the production of consumer goods or other things which a free market would have put first.

The politics of depression

Scarcely had the first Five Year Plan been launched (1928) when financial panic struck Wall Street (1929) and ricocheted quickly throughout the marketplaces of the world. Depression succeeded panic. Millions of men found themselves out of work, while machines stood equally idle on the other side of factory walls. Over-production confronted under-consumption painfully and poignantly; but neither economic theory nor traditional peacetime political practice offered any immediate remedy. Liberal economists, in fact, held that panics and periods of depression were unfortunate but inevitable; they even served a valuable function of eliminating inefficient producers. p 320 (16–23)

This was cold comfort indeed to the unemployed and to bankrupt businessmen. Waiting things out had been bearable when a large proportion of the factory working force still had relatives back on the farm who could help them out; but in the 1920s the rapid migration from farm to factory, that occurred in such key countries as Germany and the United States during the boom, meant that this palliative for bad times was no longer adequate. Political pressures quickly mounted to an intolerable pitch. Not surprisingly, charismatic saviours soon appeared in both Germany and the United States who fell back, fundamentally, upon the same patterns of wartime economic mobilization that Stalin had earlier used for meeting Russia's no less serious crisis.

In Japan, too, the onset of the Depression discredited those who had opposed the military programme of expansion on the Asian mainland. As a result, aggressive military action led to Japanese occupation of Manchuria in 1932. After some delay, the League of Nations censured the aggressor, but Japan had already withdrawn from League membership, and no effective sanctions were ever attempted. Thus, in its first serious test, the League of Nations machinery for keeping the peace failed utterly. In the following years, the task of equipping large Japanese forces on the Asian mainland took up most of the slack in Japan's economy created by the world depression. The army fed upon its conquests, supervising a massive investment programme in Manchuria which was aimed at modernizing and enlarging the flow of military supplies. From 1936, military operations in China proper provided ample oppor- p 39 (23) tunity for the strengthened Japanese army to show its prowess and put its new equipment to the test of battle.

p 62
(17-20)
Hitler, who came to power in Germany in January 1933, cured the German economy of its depressed condition by similarly massive investment in public works and armaments production. The Nazi prescription worked: idle Germans soon got back to work, and had the additional satisfaction of knowing that their nation was again a great power on the European scene. His feat of finding a remedy for the Depression, as much or more than Nazi police and propaganda, secured Hitler's position at home; his foreign policy soon made rearmed Germany a real and immediate threat to the world balance of power that had emerged from World War I. The Nazi movement was also an ideological challenge to both the Wilsonian and the Leninist political ideals, mingling naive racialism, brutal anti-Semitism, venomous nationalism and irresponsible obedience to a charismatic leader with idealistic appeal to self-sacrifice on behalf of the nation.

p 85
(13-17)
In spite of many new programmes of public service launched by President Franklin D. Roosevelt's New Deal, the United States responded to the Depression less drastically and less efficaciously than did the Germans or the Japanese. Yet here, too, when the Democrats returned to power in 1933, much New Deal legislation was clearly modelled on the experience of mobilizing the nation's resources in World War I. The New Deal did not, however, revive American concern for Europe. On the contrary, as the danger of a new war mounted, the US Congress passed legislation intended to ensure American neutrality in any future European struggle.

This left France and Britain as the only industrially powerful supporters of the *status quo* in Europe. But neither of these nations responded at all successfully to the Depression. Civil strains within France called the stability of the Third Republic seriously into question; and in Britain distaste for economic mobilization was exceeded only by distaste for war itself. Under these circumstances, the first impulse of the British Government was to meet the new German threat by redressing Germany's just grievances against the Versailles settlement. If that should fail to appease Hitler, the British were prepared to try to deflect his expansion eastward against Russia, where another dictatorship, unfriendly to Britain, had existed ever since 1917.

This policy ran up against criticism from those in Britain who adhered to the League and the ideal of collective security. A
p 39
(24)
critical test came in 1933-34 when Italy attacked Ethiopia. The French and British governments realized all too well that if they applied sanctions and prevented Mussolini from winning victory in east Africa—as they could have done easily by closing the Suez Canal to Italian shipping—they would drive the Italians into Hitler's arms. Consequently the two victors of World War I hemmed and hawed. Eventually when Mussolini's victory over Ethiopia was clearly in view they agreed to impose largely fictitious sanctions against Italy. Such meddling failed doubly, alienating Mussolini and impelling him to form an alliance—the Rome–Berlin Axis—with Hitler in 1936, and discrediting the principle of collective security and the League at the same time.

The French tried to bring Russia into the balance by concluding an alliance with the Communists in 1935; but neither government trusted the other. Russia's efforts to breathe fresh life into the League of Nations by joining that body in 1934 got nowhere, largely because the Communist parties of Western Europe, acting as spokesmen and champions of Russian interests, aroused intense distrust of Stalin's real motives. Leaders of all the governments of Europe wondered whether Stalin only wanted to stop Hitler, as his diplomats at the League of Nations declared, or secretly planned to export revolution, once the overthrow of Fascist dictatorships had opened the way for Communism, as Party ideologues in the West
p 64-5
(29-31)
freely proclaimed was sure to happen. Civil war in Spain (1936–39) fanned such fears, for Communists from all of Europe rallied to the support of the legitimate Spanish Government so effectively that it soon seemed a Loyalist victory would mean Communist power in Spain. Once again the French and British governments found themselves in a false position: officially committed to non-intervention while winking at large-scale Italian, German and Russian participation in the Spaniards' internecine struggles.

Mutual distrust among his potential opponents allowed Hitler to

win a rapid series of diplomatic victories in the late 1930s. He remilitarized the Rhineland in open defiance of the Versailles treaty in 1936 and concluded the 'Axis' pact with Mussolini in the same year. Japan, meanwhile, had invaded China and pushed steadily
p 154
(22)
down the China coast sealing off Chiang Kai-shek's Nationalist regime deep in the interior. In 1937 Germany and Japan, followed by Italy signed the Anti-Comintern Pact. This was more symbolic than anything else, proclaiming a largely fictitious solidarity among the three prime disturbers of the world's peace.

As World War II approached with all the forseeable fatality of a Greek drama, the greatest industrial power of the world simply looked on from across the Atlantic. Self-righteous disapproval of the folly and inveterate duplicity of Europeans—whether German, French, British or Russian—completely dominated American public attitudes between 1920 and 1939. Equipment at the disposal of the American armed forces was soon rendered obsolete by the rearming Germans; and the manpower of the US army remained trifling compared to any of the world's major military establishments. As a result, in the 1930s the New World did next to nothing to redress the shifting balance of the Old.

In 1938 Hitler resumed his triumphant advances, occupying Austria in the spring and wringing agreement from the uncertain French and British governments at Munich for his take-over of the German-speaking regions of Czechoslovakia in the fall. When he
p 63
(24)
transgressed these Munich agreements in the following spring, Britain and France belatedly attempted to form a countervailing alliance system. But Russia was deeply distrustful and preferred to come to terms with the Nazis through the Ribbentrop-Molotov Pact of August 1939. Unilateral British guarantees to Poland and Rumania were an ineffectual gesture at best to counter this sharp shift in the diplomatic alignment of Europe.

War renewed, 1939-1945

With Stalin's benevolent neutrality assured, Hitler lost no time in attacking Poland on 1 September 1939, thereby beginning World
p 40
(28)
War II. As required by their undertakings towards Poland, France and Britain declared war against Germany on 3 September. In contrast to the popular mood of 1914, no one welcomed the new war, not even in Germany. Mobilization in Britain and France proceeded morosely and according to plan, but Franco-British war plans no longer called for attack as in 1914. A long war of attrition was taken for granted. Above all, the military and political leaders of the Western democracies were resolved never again to risk the bloodshed of mass assaults on defended positions which had proved so futile in World War I.

The Germans also eschewed the tactics of World War I. They harked back instead to their 19th-century ideal of a war so carefully planned as to assure victory after only a short campaign. New *Blitzkrieg* tactics, centring upon the use of massed columns of tanks to penetrate far behind enemy lines, and of airplanes to paralyse enemy movement on the ground deep in the rear, proved dramatically successful against the Poles. In six weeks the war was over; Poland lay utterly defeated and partitioned into a German and a Russian sphere. Russian occupation of Lithuania, Latvia and Estonia soon followed; but when the Russians demanded territory and bases from the Finns they met a dogged resistance. The Finns' success in holding the Russians at bay for the long weeks of the so-called 'winter war' (1939–40) seemed to prove beyond doubt how weak the Russian colossus really was when it came to the test of battle.

In spring 1940 the Germans struck anew. They ancitipated a Franco–British move to aid the Finns by occupying Denmark and Norway in early spring. Then in May 1940 the German *Blitzkrieg* struck France and the Low Countries. Once again, Hitler's soldiers proved brilliantly successful. By 22 June 1940, ten days after Italy had hastily entered the war in order to be in at the kill, France
p 40
(29)
surrendered. Only Britain remained; but German planners had not prepared in advance for crossing the English Channel, and efforts to improvise during the summer and autumn of 1940 came to naught when the German air force proved unable to drive the RAF
p 41
(35)
from the skies over England. Without air superiority, the risks of a Channel crossing were all too obvious. Hitler, whose long-term aims had always included expansion to the east, decided to leave

49

Britain on one side for the moment and isolate her by first defeating her only potential ally on the European continent, Russia.

A preliminary campaign into the Balkans to rescue the Italians from an embarrassing stalemate in a war with Greece, launched by Mussolini in October 1940, delayed the German assault on Russia slightly. But once the German advance began, on 21 June 1941, it looked as though yet another decisive victory would quickly come to Nazi arms. The Russians lost vast armies, and retreated across hundreds of miles. But they never quite lost the will to resist, even when Russia's two largest cities, Moscow and Leningrad, both came within range of German guns. This stubborn resistance foiled German plans. Cold weather arrived in November, making field operations all but impossible for the German troops, whose clothing and equipment were not designed for sub-zero fighting. Accordingly, on 8 December 1941 Hitler reluctantly announced the suspension of the German offensive until spring. The German army thus suffered its first serious setback—a setback enhanced by a Russian counter-offensive, launched in the depth of winter, that compelled the Germans to draw back from around Moscow.

The Russian winter offensive was spearheaded by troops newly arrived from the Far East. They were withdrawn from that exposed frontier when Stalin knew (through a well placed spy) that the Japanese had refused German suggestions for an attack on Russia's Far Eastern Provinces, deciding instead to push southward towards supplies of oil needed for their industrial war machine. There is therefore more than a symbolic coincidence in the fact that less than twenty-four hours before Hitler announced the suspension of the German offensive against Moscow, the Japanese

p 40
(34)

had attacked the US Fleet at Pearl Harbor, sinking all the battleships the Americans then had in the Pacific by means of a sudden assault from the air. This was shortly followed by Japanese landings in the Philippines and in Malaya; successes there led to Japanese occupation of Indonesia, Burma, and islands of the south-west Pacific during the ensuing six months.

The Japanese attack, followed on 11 December by Hitler's declaration of war against the United States, brought the Americans headlong into the war. President Roosevelt had already gone a long way in stretching official neutrality, seeking to bolster up British resistance to Hitler by every possible means short of war. After the collapse of France, British mobilization for the struggle had for the first time become thoroughgoing: calculations of postwar balance of payments and trading positions, which had hampered an all-out effort at first, were thrown to the winds. A

p 41
(35, 36)

new prime minister, Winston Churchill, breathed fire and determination into the British people for the climacteric Battle of Britain —a battle which never really came, because the RAF proved so much stronger than the Germans expected.

After Pearl Harbor, fully effective trans-national strategic co-operation between Britain and the United States became possible. A series of top-level wartime conferences between Churchill and Roosevelt, with their military and other key advisers and technical experts, co-ordinated economic as well as military effort as between the two nations. The Russians stood apart. Stalin's deep suspicion of all capitalist states led him to keep secret many of the statistical data upon which detailed strategic and industrial co-ordination had to rest.

The achievements of the Grand Alliance, as Churchill dubbed Great Britain's wartime relationship with the United States and Russia, stand out in sharp contrast to the failure of their opponents to concert strategy or anything else. To be sure, the victorious Nazis did conscript most of continental Europe's available resources for the German war machine; but as long as Mussolini retained any sort of independent power he tried to conduct a separate war in North Africa and the Balkans. The failure of co-operation between Germany and Japan was even more striking. The Japanese never declared war against Russia, thus maintaining the Pacific theatre of operations as a separate enterprise from the European war. Neither Mussolini's attack on Greece in 1940, nor Japan's attack on the United States in 1941, was announced to the Germans ahead of time; Hitler reciprocated by keeping all of his major strategic moves secret from his supposed allies until after the event.

From December 1941 until the end of the war, the United States

was the only nation in a position to direct its manpower and supplies at will either towards the Pacific and the Japanese war or towards Europe and the German war. Roosevelt early accepted the strategic principle of Germany first. This coincided with both British and Russian priorities, and permitted the three great powers to wage war together, though only the British and Americans can be said to have waged war in common. Nevertheless, Lend Lease supplies to Russia, delivered despite great difficulties via the North Atlantic and Archangel, provided the Red Army with essential supplies. By the end of the war, for example, almost all the trucks and most of the food used by the Russian soldiers came from the United States.

As for the British, with them the Americans were able to arrange joint commands in all the principal theatres of war. A very exact and far-reaching mobilization plan allowed the two English-speaking nations to achieve maximum striking power at the moment of the climactic invasion of Normandy in June 1944. These Anglo-American feats of co-ordinating economic and strategic effort far surpassed the rudimentary trans-national co-operation achieved in World War I. War production in Britain, the United States and throughout the wide regions of the world accessible to these two powers, was keyed to proposed strategic enterprises. Logistical planning achieved remarkable precision. By the end of the war, for example, all but one of the US Army divisions, planned in 1942, had been committed to combat overseas.

p 41
(41)

Even more remarkable, and a sign of things to come, was what may be called the invention of deliberate invention. The Germans did rather well here, producing during the course of the war such new weapons as jet planes and the V1 and V2 self-propelled bombs. The Americans, with British participation, invented a far more terrible weapon: the atom bomb. In addition, innumerable new devices were designed and produced to fit specifications of desired performance; and in some cases, these performance characteristics were defined by intended strategic or tactical uses. This reversed what had always before been assumed to be the normal relationship of invention and use. Instead of waiting for an invention to occur and then seeing what changes it might permit in familiar ways of doing things, the new approach asked first: What do we wish to be able to do? And then: How can we get the tools and weapons that will let us do what we wish?

A vast acceleration of the inventive process proved possible when skilled technicians and scientists set to work to devise means for achieving definite, limited but previously unattainable ends. If the central significance of World War I was its demonstration of how society as a whole could be twisted and turned to serve deliberately assigned goals, the central significance of World War II may well prove to be the invention of deliberate invention.

As the United States harnessed its human and technical resources to the tasks of waging war, the balance between the Axis and the Allies slowly shifted in favour of the latter. Nothing within the power of the Germans and Japanese allowed them to match the manpower and productive capacity that was now aligned against them. The shift became apparent on the battlefields in the waning months of 1942, when the second German offensive in Russia petered out in the ruins of Stalingrad on the Volga. Simultaneously, local victories in the Pacific (Guadalcanal) checked the Japanese advance, while British and American offensives from both ends of North Africa began to outflank Hitler's *Festung Europa*.

The Russians wanted much greater diversion of German strength from their front than the North African campaigns brought. Yet when a Russian counter-offensive proved able to capture the remnants of an entire Germany army trapped in Stalingrad (February 1943) and when, next summer, the German counter-stroke (July 1943) proved incapable of doing more than denting the Russian lines for a few weeks, it became clear that Russia was unlikely to collapse after all. It therefore proved possible for Churchill, Roosevelt and Stalin to lay plans for the final drive against Hitler in relative harmony at Teheran (November 1943).

p 41
(40)

Thereafter, as victory approached, harmony between the principal allies came under increasing strain. President Roosevelt, like Wilson before him, hoped to transform international relations by establishing a truly effective international body that would perpetuate into peacetime the sort of co-operation that had been achieved among the Allied powers during the war itself. He sought

'Further retreat is impossible', announced Berlin radio in September 1944. It was the classic German predicament of war on two fronts. The cartoon is from an English newspaper. (4)

to profit from Wilson's errors by getting such a body set up before volatile American public opinion had time to draw back into an isolationist frame of mind. Accordingly, Roosevelt pushed hard for a treaty to establish the United Nations while the war was still p 44 in progress. This was achieved at the San Francisco Conference, (51) May–June 1945, just after Roosevelt's death.

The prospects of peace

Roosevelt thought that Russian participation in the United Nations was as important as American participation: only so could the new international body keep peace effectively and escape the futility that had so sadly beset the League of Nations. To attain this goal, territorial and other concessions to Stalin seemed eminently worthwhile. Stalin and Churchill, on the other hand, tended to think in terms of spheres of influence, and the division of Europe between the advancing Russians coming from the east, and Anglo-American forces coming from the south and west. For a long time Roosevelt put off facing hard decisions. In particular he refused to consider Poland's future and arrangements for administering conquered p 42 Germany, until German collapse was near at hand. At the Yalta (44) Conference (February 1945) verbal formulae were found to disguise growing differences between the Russians and the Anglo-p 88 Americans; at Potsdam (July–August 1945), after Germany's (24) surrender, *ad hoc* decisions regulating the administration of Germany and plans for defeating Japan were agreed to.

But these superficial successes in concerting Allied policy soon ran into heavy weather. To be sure, Russia entered the war against Japan as Stalin had promised; but by then Japanese resistance was at an end, and the United States no longer wished to share the victory. Moreover, before the Pacific war came formally to a close, on 2 September 1945—five years and one day after Hitler had invaded Poland—difficulties had multiplied in Europe, where Russian ideas of 'free and democratic' governments accorded ill with British and American definitions of these terms.

At first, the major difficulty was in Poland, where democratic piety conflicted with vital Russian security interests. Among the Poles, anything resembling free elections was certain to return a keenly anti-Russian government to power—a fact that made nonsense of the phrases of the Yalta agreement to which American and British diplomats kept harking back. That agreement had called for a Polish government both democratic and friendly to Russia; and when the Western powers pointed out how dubiously democratic the Polish provisional government was, the Russians, not unnaturally, interpreted their scruples as a thinly disguised effort to stir up anti-Russian sentiments among a people living at Russia's very gates and in territory that had been the highway for German invasion in 1941.

In view of Russia's profound exhaustion from the war and America's possession of a new master-weapon, the atom bomb, such behaviour must have seemed ominously threatening to almost every Russian, from Stalin down. Ironically, Stalin's countermeasures soon convinced the Western public that Russia was ruled by a sinister and aggressive dictatorship, not significantly different from the Nazi tyranny itself.

By 1946, the question of how to administer Germany eclipsed the Polish issue. The Russians wished for reparations—at once and in kind; the British and Americans began to fear that massive withdrawal of reparations would so embitter and impoverish the Germans as to promote Communist revolution—or, at least, make the task of importing food to feed them an impossibly heavy burden for the Anglo-American occupying powers.

Other friction points arose in Turkey and in Iran, where the Russians proposed to establish advance defences like those the Red Army had created in liberating eastern Europe from the Germans. From the Russian point of view, the two Western powers kept on meddling in their east European sphere of influence by asking the Russians to allow their nationalist and capitalist enemies to organize politically and participate freely in elections. The Russians did experiment with coalition governments in the east European countries that fell under their control. They even allowed comparatively quite free elections in Hungary, with the result that Communists (the only dependable element from a Russian point of view—and not all of them were really to be trusted) came close to being excluded from government.

Greece offered the Russians a chance for counter-attack. There p 133 British troops had helped to return the royal government-in-exile (27) to power by overcoming Communist-led resistance forces in a brief, sharp struggle (December 1944–January 1945). The Russians stood by passively at the time, hoping, perhaps, that the Western powers would exercise similar restraint when it came to the Russian turn to take a high hand in putting governments of their choice into office in such countries as Poland and Rumania. When the Western powers failed to take the hint, Stalin probably decided to unleash the Greek Communists. At any rate, with enthusiastic support from the Yugoslav and Albanian Communist governments, a new guerrilla movement arose in Greece, beginning in the spring of 1946. Its leaders claimed to represent the democratic will of the Greek people against the 'monarcho-fascist' regime fastened upon the nation by the imperialist British. The claim had just enough colour of truth to hurt the public image of Britain's new socialist government.

In spite of these signs of the wearing out of the wartime alliance, peace treaties with Italy, Hungary, Rumania, Bulgaria and Finland were eventually drawn up and duly ratified (February 1947). But by the time that the touchier questions of peace with Germany and Japan came up for deliberation, relations among the victors had so degenerated that agreement became impossible.

A new balance of power

Until 1947 Great Britain took the lead in trying to counterbalance Russian power on the European continent. This proved costly, and in the early months of 1947 the British Government decided it would have to withdraw from Greece and reduce other overseas commitments. This confronted the United States with a fateful decision. American planning for the postwar world had been premised on the assumption that American troops would soon come home and leave the task of policing the world to the United Nations. This vision of the future now seemed utopian. What to do? President Harry S. Truman decided to use American power to check Communist aggression, arguing that if aggression were not stopped, the world of law envisaged by the UN Charter would never come into being. Accordingly, in March 1947 he asked the United States Congress to appropriate funds for aid to Greece and Turkey. In the course of his speech he casually enunciated what came to be called the Truman Doctrine: 'that it must be the policy of the United States to support free peoples who are resisting attempted subjugation by armed minorities or by outside pressures'. Truman did not say 'anywhere in the world'; that implication of the new policy was only gradually drawn when Communist victories in Asia persuaded the American public and government of the reality of a world-wide Communist conspiracy for world domination.

Until 1950 Europe remained the critical theatre. In June 1947, George C. Marshall, US Secretary of State, proffered massive American credits to assist European economic recovery on condition that the European governments get together and draw up an overall plan for the rational use of such credits. The Russians p 322 at once scented a trap: the 'Marshall Plan' would simply enslave (24)

Europe's economy to American capital. Accordingly, all the East European governments had to withdraw. When some of them proved reluctant, the Russians felt compelled to impose more reliable regimes—in the case of Czechoslovakia by means of an untidy *coup d'état*. This put Eastern Europe under out-and-out Communist governments for the first time. In the West, however, international consultation speedily defined effective uses for American credits, with the result that by 1952, when the programme came to an end, Western European economies had achieved and surpassed prewar levels. As for Greece, a public quarrel (1948) between Stalin and Tito, the Communist leader of Yugoslavia, had the effect of crippling the Greek Communist forces. This made the final victory for the royal government, backed by American aid, relatively easy.

In Eastern Europe, three-, four- and five-year plans on the Russian model also led to economic stabilization and substantial growth by 1952. But these lands started from a lower base level, and Russia could not afford to advance credits as the United States did so successfully to the richer lands of the West. This limited the pace of East European economic development. Moreover, the Tito–Stalin quarrel of 1948 precipitated a round of ugly purges in Communist Party ranks. 'Titoists', that is, Communists who declined to follow Stalin's leadership at whatever cost to local interests and/or Marxist ideology, were brought to trial. Many suffered execution for fictitious crimes. Such actions diminished the appeal of Communist doctrines all round the world at a time when capitalist-pluralist society was showing unprecedented resilience in Western Europe and North America.

Germany was the place where the shift in fortunes as between the Communist and the pluralist worlds was most acutely felt. The German surrender terms had put Berlin under four-power administration; and it was relatively easy for Germans from the Russian zone to cross into the Western portions of Berlin. As such flights gathered momentum, they became a profound embarrassment for the Communists. In June 1948, the Russians tried to cure this running sore by compelling the Western powers to withdraw from Berlin. They shut off access by road, but the Western powers countered with an improvised airlift that dramatized the situation to the entire world.

For the next eleven months West Berlin was supplied by air, and a nervous Europe wondered whether some clash along the Berlin airways would set off World War III. Preparedness seemed the only rational policy with such an acute danger at hand. Conse-

p 42
(45)

quently, the United States, Canada and the nations of Western Europe signed the NATO Treaty in April 1949, setting up a common, supra-national command and supply system to guard against Russian attack. The first NATO commander was General Eisenhower, the former commander-in-chief of the Anglo-American armies that had landed in France in 1944. His return to the scene of World War II victories emphasized the fact that NATO amounted to a peacetime adaptation of the pattern of Anglo-American strategic co-operation that had achieved such striking successes in World War II. It involved an extraordinary limitation of traditional state sovereignty, which could never have been institutionalized without the urgent threat the Berlin blockade—and Communist victories in Asia—created in the minds of Americans and Europeans in the years 1947–49.

Ideologies and atomic weapons
In postwar Asia, as we shall see in Chapter VII, sharp contrasts prevailed. Britain, France and the Netherlands retired, with varying degrees of reluctance, from their old empires. In China

p 132
(22)

the Communist victory of Mao Tse-tung (October 1949) forced Chiang Kai-shek to retreat to Formosa, still claiming to be the legitimate ruler of all China. Some American diplomats believed that Russia and Communist China would soon quarrel despite a common Marxist language, and thought that no harm would come to American interests if the United States recognized the new Chinese regime and waited upon results. This policy was discredited in June 1950 by the outbreak of war in Korea. That land, part of the Japanese Empire since 1910, had been divided by the terms of Japan's surrender into an American zone in the south and a Russian zone in the north. The boundary was arbitrarily drawn at

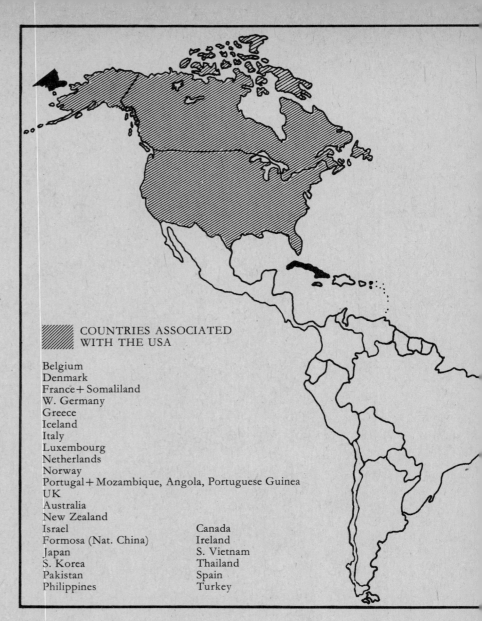

COUNTRIES ASSOCIATED WITH THE USA

Belgium
Denmark
France + Somaliland
W. Germany
Greece
Iceland
Italy
Luxembourg
Netherlands
Norway
Portugal + Mozambique, Angola, Portuguese Guinea
UK
Australia
New Zealand
Israel
Formosa (Nat. China)
Japan
S. Korea
Pakistan
Philippines
Canada
Ireland
S. Vietnam
Thailand
Spain
Turkey

The three worlds of 1970. (5)

the 38th parallel of latitude. Each occupying power set up a government claiming the right to rule all Korea; and soon after Russian and American troops withdrew, the Communist North Koreans tried to make good their claim, arms in hand. What part Stalin and the Chinese Communists may have played in this decision cannot be stated, though it is clear that the Russians supplied the North Korean army with new equipment on a scale to make the venture seem assured of easy success.

From an American point of view, however, North Korea's attack seemed to prove beyond all reasonable doubt that there was indeed a world-wide Communist revolutionary plot, directed from Moscow. The Berlin blockade, the coup in Czechoslovakia, the guerrilla war in Greece all fitted in as part of the pattern revealing itself in Asia. Stalinist aggression, Americans soon decided, was not fundamentally different from Hitler's, and would have to be stopped at once lest greater threats arise later on when world Communism had become even stronger.

As it happened, when the Korean War began the Russians were boycotting the United Nations Security Council to indicate their disapproval of the refusal of that body to unseat Chiang Kai-shek's government and recognize the Chinese Communists in his place. The Security Council was therefore able to act speedily, censuring North Korea and instructing members of the United Nations to take whatever steps might be necessary to punish aggression. The United States Government emphatically concurred, and despatched American troops from occupation duty in Japan to hold a bridgehead in southernmost Korea. United Nations (mainly US) forces later launched a counter-offensive and turned the tables completely. Not the South Korean but the North Korean Government and army was soon in danger of collapse. This provoked the massive intervention of Communist China. Taken by surprise, American troops were forced to retreat in disorder until a front eventually established itself close to the original line of demarcation at the 38th parallel.

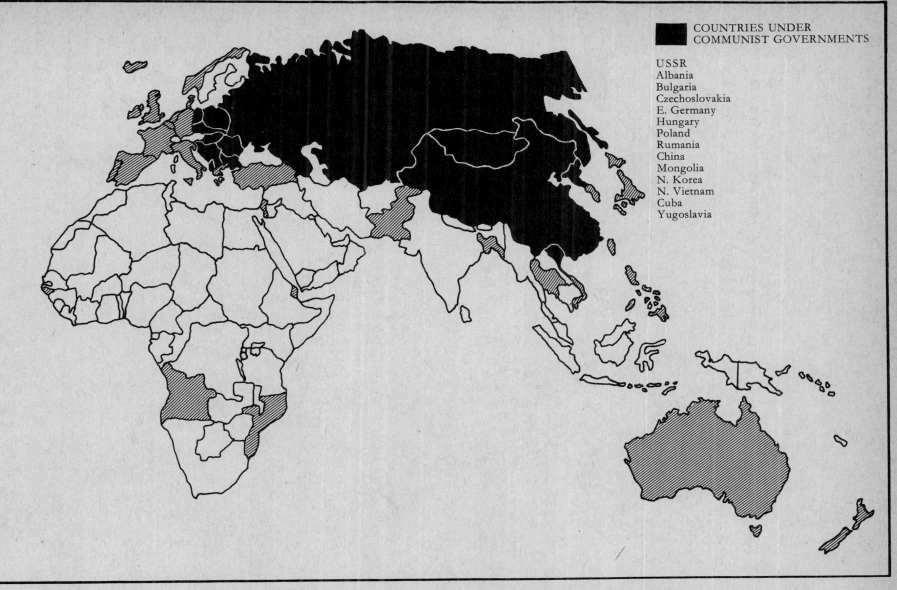

This tumultuous course of events in the Far East roused intense reactions within the United States. Accusations of Communist treason in high places were freely bandied about. This seemed to some the only adequate explanation of how American policy in the Far East could have gone so completely awry. Alliance with Chiang Kai-shek committed the United States to supporting his claim to rule all China. A corollary excluded the Chinese Communists from the United Nations as usurpers and aggressors who could not be trusted to honour the principles of the UN Charter. As military stalemate set in, the Korean War became intensely unpopular in the United States. In 1952 a new Republican administration, headed by General Eisenhower, came to power. Success at the polls rested in large part on Eisenhower's promise to end the fighting in Korea. After long months of bargaining, truce was finally concluded in 1953.

p 88
(25)
p 43
(48)

American public debate over the stalemate in Korea turned largely upon whether or not to use atomic weapons as a short cut to victory. An important reason why such weapons were not used was that in September 1949, long before American experts had predicted the possibility, the Russians exploded their first atomic warhead. American bombing of China and North Korea might, thus, invite Russian counter-attack, and realize the apocalyptic vision of an atomic World War III. Yet, from an American point of view, not to use A-bombs meant allowing Chinese numbers to nullify US technical superiority.

The resulting tense frustration in the United States was exacerbated by public trials both in Britain and America of spies who had transmitted information to the Russians about atomic techniques. It was easy to conclude that treason had made Russia's atomic success possible, and in doing so, had endangered America's security at home and abroad. Fear of treason in high places mounted to new heights, until the leading red-hunter, Senator McCarthy, discredited himself in 1954 by reckless and unfounded accusations against high officers of the US Government.

The fact that from 1949 onwards the Russians, too, had an atomic arsenal at their disposal raised a new kind of problem for the two great powers. Scientists had long realized that far more powerful explosions could be produced. Instead of resting content with explosive fission of a uranium isotope, fusion of hydrogen nuclei could, given high enough temperatures and pressures, be induced. This reproduced *in parvo* and on earth the reaction sustaining the sun's radiation. Those who understood the potential power thus resting within man's grasp were appalled and alarmed at what fallible human hands might do with hydrogen weapons. Yet if one side pressed ahead, could the other afford to hold back? And if the Russians proceeded in secret could the Americans risk finding themselves outclassed in atomic weaponry? The decision was to go ahead. The two governments must have reached the same conclusion at nearly the same time. At any rate the Americans' first successful tests of the hydrogen 'thermonuclear' reaction occurred in November 1952, followed in August 1953 by a similar Russian experimental blast.

Radically new inventions like the H-bomb offered the prospect of attaining overwhelming advantage; failure to compete threatened disaster. In both America and Russia military planners therefore set out to design complex new weapons systems. Deliberate invention came to be harnessed on an unprecedented scale to a new, secret, highly technical armaments race. Patterns pioneered in World War II were thus translated into peacetime. Lesser powers—even the British—soon had to drop out, for costs were astronomical. Yet the consequence for the two nations that could afford it was an enormous acceleration of technological advance across a wide spectrum of endeavour. For communications systems, delivery systems, production systems, training and educational systems—in short almost any aspect of the modern industrial process—were relevant to the military tasks of constructing, using and controlling generations of new and complex weapons systems that began to sprout luxuriantly from designers' drawing boards.

Many fateful, secret decisions quickly devolved upon the leaders of what President Eisenhower once called the 'military-industrial complex'. It seems clear, for instance, that early in the 1950s the

American Government decided to concentrate on producing atomic explosives in small packages, for tactical use on future battlefields. At the same time, the Russians put major resources into building big rockets that would be able to deliver atomic warheads from Russian soil anywhere on the surface of the globe. The result, by 1957, was dramatic Russian superiority in the field of rocketry.

p 135
(33)

When Sputnik, the first artificial satellite, was launched from Russian soil in October 1957, all the network of airbases the United States had constructed around the Communist periphery seemed suddenly obsolete. What could a slow-poke airplane do against intercontinental missiles? Even America's possession of atomic-powered submarines, capable of launching atomic warheads from resting places on the ocean floor, did not seem a really adequate counter to the new Russian capability. Hence the United States launched a crash programme to develop rockets superior to Russian models, with the result that by 1969 it became possible to send men to the moon and back.

The secret and uncanny development of the arms race after 1950 transformed the realities of international life without changing outward forms. As the two rival Great Powers developed an arsenal of weapons whose destructive power surpassed ordinary human imaginations, the practicability of all-out war as an act of policy faded rapidly away. Yet mutual fears and the extreme technical difficulty of policing the observance of any agreement that might be reached prevented any effective limitation upon the arms race. Moreover, vested interests in old and new weapons systems arose in both Russia and the United States. This made what seemed on the surface to be merely technical decisions and choices into political acts of great significance for internal as well as for external affairs.

Unanswered questions

In the 1950s and early 1960s Africa and the Middle East became areas of international tension as, in the first, the old colonial powers handed over to indigenous governments and, in the second, the new state of Israel failed to conciliate Arab hostility. These developments are covered in Chapters VIII and IX. The Suez crisis of 1956 was complicated by the fact that it coincided with the outbreak of popular resistance to Communist governments in Hungary and (less violently) in Poland. After initial hesitation, the Russians sent Red Army troops into Hungary to put down the rebellion. The United States stood quietly by, doing nothing to aid the peoples of Eastern Europe to throw off Communist rule. This was the more surprising since prominent spokesmen for the Republican Party, then in office, had talked of rolling Communism back; and no more promising opportunity could easily be imagined than that which came, and was passed up, in the autumn of 1956.

p 182
(35)

p 136
(35)

American inaction was certainly governed in large part by the fear that thermonuclear war might be unleashed by intervention in the Russian sphere. Six years later the Russians demonstrated exactly the same restraint when they backed down in the Cuban missile crisis. In this case, the Russians had begun to erect rocket-launching pads in Cuba, close enough to the American mainland to bring most American cities within reach of intermediate range missiles. When the United States Government discovered what was afoot, President John F. Kennedy announced that the US Navy would intercept Russian vessels bringing rockets and other vital equipment for the rocket sites. After a few tense hours, the Russian ships turned back.

The effects of these two episodes upon Cold War alignments was very disruptive. Nuclear weaponry, through the very excess of its power, had become an implausible threat, whether against friend or foe. Both super powers had demonstrated that they would not risk war to aid a third party, even one clearly on their side of the ideological fence. This implied first, that the satellite and allied states could not really count on support in time of need, and, second, that they could afford to defy their erstwhile patrons and expect no really effective retaliation. International alignments therefore quickly lost the simplicity of the Cold War era. France pulled away from any but distant co-operation with the United States, seeking instead to build a strong and fully independent European power-centre under French leadership. An independent French atomic capability was part of this policy; so was the European Common Market, launched in 1957. The remarkable early success that came to the Common Market gave substance to such a hope, although up until 1970 the Western European cluster of nations had not succeeded in attracting any Eastern European states into its embrace, as French plans for Europe's future envisaged.

p 323
(27)

In Asia, an even more spectacular rift took place in 1960 when the Communist Chinese quarrelled with the Russians and proceeded, in the years that followed, to build an atomic capability of their own, and to wage a global war of words against both the capitalist-imperialists of America and Europe, and the corrupt deviationists of Russia who, according to Mao Tse-tung, had recklessly betrayed Marxist principles ever since Stalin's death in 1953—if not before.

The fierceness of Red Chinese rhetoric was fed by events in Vietnam, one of the successor states into which French Indo-China had been divided in 1954. According to an agreement reached at Geneva in 1954, Vietnam itself was split between a Catholic regime in the south and a Communist regime of north; but this was provisional, pending elections that would establish a single government for the whole land. The United States was not a party to this agreement, and American agents soon decided that appropriate support for the anti-Communist government of the south could head off the Communist victory which a free election in any near future seemed likely to assure. Elections were therefore postponed; American advice and material aid was assigned to the task of strengthening the government of the south. When the impatient northerners organized guerrilla warfare and started to send 'volunteer' units to the south, American involvement escalated to match the new challenge. By 1965 full-scale war, involving more than half a million American soldiers was the result; a war that soon became even more unpopular than the Korean War had been a decade and a half before. Both the Chinese and the Russians sent military supplies and offered moral support to the Vietnamese Communists; and the spectacle of aggressive American action almost at their southern doorstep seemed to confirm the Chinese Communist diagnosis of the imperialist thrust inherent in capitalist societies.

p 43
(49)

p 89
(32)

Yet the Russians had difficulty in accepting such a view. The United States had not been aggressive in Europe and it was not hard for Russians to detect points of common interest between themselves and the Americans in such matters as restricting the spread of atomic weaponry, or in limiting the obstreperous behaviour of each other's lesser allied states. Yet Marxian doctrine made out-and-out agreement with the Americans distasteful. American commitment to democratic ideology had an exactly similar effect, making a deal with the dictatorial Communist regime of Russia seem a betrayal of principle. Nevertheless, by 1970 the ideological glitter of Leninism and of Wilsonianism had lost the newly minted brightness of 1917. The new terrors and imponderable consequences of an ever renewable weapons revolution fundamentally altered the behaviour of the two world rivals, without providing them with a new vocabulary or a popularly acceptable set of guide lines for international conduct.

III ECLIPSE,
DIVISION - AND RENEWAL

The place of Europe in world history

ALAN BULLOCK

'Will Europe become what she is in reality,

that is, a little promontory of the continent of Asia?

Or will Europe remain what she seems to be,

that is, the precious part of the terrestrial universe,

the pearl of the sphere, the brain

of a vast body?'

PAUL VALÉRY, 1919

Europe before the Deluge

was supreme in its material progress and cultural continuity. Apart from the USA and Japan, European interests effectively ruled the whole world. The internal tensions which were to bring that rule to an end between 1914 and 1945 already existed but had not yet burst out in conflict. The power of Great Britain, France, Germany, Austria-Hungary and Russia still seemed secure, and scarcely less so the power of the privileged classes within those countries.

Great Britain (top) was a liberal and constitutional state, but power was concentrated in the hands of an oligarchy of rank and wealth of which the monarch, Edward VII, was the living symbol. This invitation to his coronation was issued in 1902.

France (left): the cover of the satirical magazine *Assiette au Beurre* for 14 July 1901 sums up its view of the political development of the Third Republic without need of words. The revolutionary idealist has turned into a fat and self-satisfied bourgeois.

Germany's ruler, the Kaiser Wilhelm II (centre) reflected in his own personality the brash and aggressive behaviour of a nation which sought to compensate for its late arrival on the scene by vigorously asserting its claims in all directions. This card marks his twenty-fifth jubilee in 1913.

Russia (right) experienced in 1905 the first shock of the earthquake that was to convulse her in 1917. Defeat by Japan sparked off a spontaneous revolt of workers and peasants. *The Flag*, of which this is the cover of the first number, chronicled its brief success.

The Habsburg Empire's dissolution had been freely predicted ever since Franz Josef ascended the throne in 1848. His celebration of his sixtieth jubilee in 1908 (bottom) encouraged the illusion that the Empire would survive the crises of the 20th century as it had those of the 19th. (1)

LONDON

ST PETERSBURG

KING EDWARD HEARTILY BIDS YOU
WELCOME TO HIS CORONATION
DINNER, ON JULY 5TH. 1902.

14 Juillet par   1888   1913   steinlen

789
901

RF

ЗРИТЕЛЬ

ГОДЪ I.   ЕЖЕНЕДѢЛЬНО.   1905.

N° 15

1848   1908

60

Zum
60
jährigen
Regierungs
Jubiläum
unseres Kaisers
Franz Josef

PARIS

WIEN

When the crowned heads of Europe met for Edward VII's funeral in May 1910 they were in a sense assisting at their own. It was to be the last such gathering. From left to right: the King of Norway, Ferdinand of Bulgaria, Manoel of Portugal, Kaiser Wilhelm II, King George I of Greece, Albert of the Belgians, and (sitting) Alfonso XIII of Spain, George V of England and Frederick VIII of Denmark. A socialist cartoon of about the same time (above right) sees the time coming when they would all be trying to pawn their crowns and finding no takers. Below: the values for which the pre-war landed gentry stood — elegance, courtesy, culture, taste — are caught in Sargent's portrait of the Sitwell family, painted in 1900. (2, 3, 4)

The middle and lower classes continued to benefit from the long period of peace and prosperity that characterized the second half of the 19th century. Above: Bonnard's *Terrasse Family* (subtitled *L'après-midi bourgeois*) makes no pretensions to the Sitwells' gentility but their enjoyment of life is evident. Below: the working class in England and Germany — at leisure in Sickert's *Gallery at the Old Bedford* and at work in *Before the Shift* by Gotthardt Kuehl, showing miners waiting their turn at the pit. (5, 6, 7)

The Great War ended Europe's old way of life but left many of its tensions unresolved. Germany was the key. Defeat had come unexpectedly, bringing political revolution and economic chaos. The terms of the Treaty of Versailles were bitterly resented. 'Shall this misery go on?' asks the poster below, pleading for a 'just peace', while moralists like the artist Otto Dix (right) pointed to crippled ex-servicemen begging in the streets. (8, 9)

'Hands off the Ruhr!' — a poster of 1923, protesting against France's occupation of the Ruhr to enforce payment of reparations. Right: George Grosz's *Pillars of Society*, the priests, businessmen and politicians of the twenties who put their own interests before those of Germany. (10, 11)

Competing for power in Central Europe were the socialists, the Communists, encouraged by the October Revolution in Russia and confident that it would spread, and a variety of middle-class and right-wing parties. The disastrous inflation of 1923 and 1924 made the struggle all the more desperate. Right: an election poster on behalf of the Democrats, promising a cure for inflation. (12)

Communism won a brief triumph in Hungary in 1919 under Béla Kun — this poster (below) carries the slogan 'Forward Red Soldiers'. But within a few months the revolutionary movement was defeated. (13)

Communism lost its best known leaders in Germany when Karl Liebknecht and Rosa Luxemburg were assassinated in January 1919. This etching by Käthe Kollwitz expresses the mourning of the German workers. (14)

Communism or 'Hitler our last hope' (right) was the choice that seemed to be facing Germany in the first years of the thirties. Fear of Communism was a major factor in Hitler's victory. (15, 16)

Gegen eine neue **Inflation**
ür Reichseinheit und Republik
ür Loslösung von unseren Feinden

Rettung bringt die O.D.P.

Wählt Deutsch-Demokratisch

1. MAI KAMPFMAI

Für den 7-Stunden-Tag und 40-Stunden-Woche!
Für Arbeit und Brot! Für den Sieg des Proletariats!

Maikomitee Bezirk Sachsen, KPD Bezirk Sachsen, KJVD Bezirk Sachsen

Unsere letzte Hoffnung: HITLER

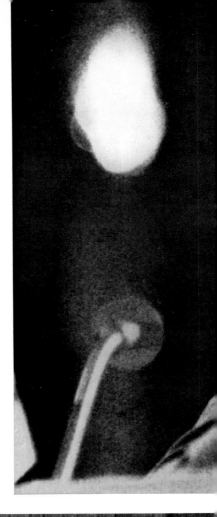

The dictators, Mussolini and Hitler, were both able to offer simple solutions to problems that had baffled the liberal and socialist parties. They could also enlist dissatisfied ex-soldiers whose taste for violence and national pride were equally frustrated. During the early twenties (left), when the Nazi party was a relatively insignificant group, Hitler modelled himself on Mussolini (below right) even down to such details as the Roman insignia on his banners. As an orator he surpassed his model, largely because his belief in his own mission was more fanatical. Hitler's opportunity came during the Depression. He promised to restore the country's prosperity, to protect it from Communism, to tear up the Treaty of Versailles and to make Germany once again a great military power. All these promises he kept. (17, 18, 23)

National Socialism was an apt enough description of Hitler's programme. He could appeal equally, and with apparent consistency, to the conservative business man in the name of nationalism and to the worker (above) in that of socialism, ready to smash 'International High Finance'. (19)

Nazi deputies in the Reichstag in 1930 appear in uniform in the chamber — a typical act of aggressive showmanship. (20)

The scapegoats, upon whom the Nazis unloaded responsibility for all Germany's ills, were the Jews and the Communists. Left: a poster of 1937 showing the Jew as moneylender, slavedriver and master of Russia. Right: Communists being arrested after the Reichstag fire of 1933, Hitler's excuse to suppress the whole party. (21, 22)

Hitler's successes were unbroken from 1933 to 1939 and were achieved without involving Germany in war. In 1936 he re-occupied the Rhineland, in March 1938 announced the *Anschluss* with Austria, and in September won agreement at Munich to the German annexation of the Sudetenland (above). (24)

Nazi mass rallies, with their elaborate ritual and skilful techniques of crowd psychology, were a key element in Hitler's rise and were imitated by totalitarian regimes all over the world (see Chapter XV). In Spain the Falangists (below) employed similar methods to express a Spanish version of Fascism. (25, 26)

The defeated Left could do little to oppose the dictators. The Russian-dominated Comintern consistently underestimated the threat, seeing more danger in the rival socialist parties than in Fascism, with the result that during the crucial years 1931–33 the two largest German parties of the Left were bitterly divided. This painting (right) of a German Communist meeting in 1932 is by Hans Grundig. (27)

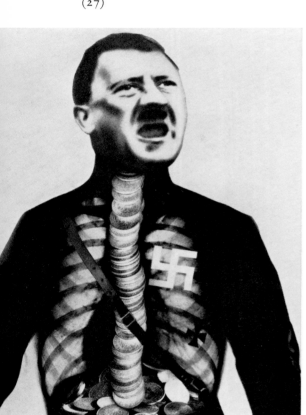

The deadly accuracy of John Heartfield's photomontages has already been noted in the previous chapter. This one, called *Adolf the superman swallows gold and talks tin*, was published in 1932. In 1933 Heartfield moved to Prague and continued to produce works of prophetic insight and power. In 1938 he fled to England. (28)

Conflict in Spain broke out in July 1936. The issues were deeply involved with Spanish history, but in the eyes of the rest of the world they quickly resolved themselves into Fascism versus Democracy. The poet Federico García Lorca was killed at an early stage in the war and became a martyr of the Left. This painting by the Italian sympathizer Renato Guttoso (right) is not a representation of his death but is dedicated to his memory. (29)

World opinion was strongly anti-Fascist. The Western democracies, however, pursued a policy of non-intervention, and Stalin used the struggle for his own ends. But left-wing idealists from all countries came to the aid of the Government, forming the famous International Brigades. The poster reproduced right was issued by one such group, calling attention to Fascist brutalities and pointing to Germany (the swastika and the word *Kultur*) as the allies of Franco. Spanish artists abroad did much to arouse public feeling. Picasso painted *Guernica* and Miró contributed posters (below) with the message that the creative power of free Spain would eventually astonish the world. (30, 31)

When war came 'resistance' took on a new meaning. Organized guerrilla groups in the occupied countries hampered the German military machine and prepared the way for the allied armies. Underground Communist parties were among the most active of such groups, partly because they saw in the war an opportunity to seize power when it was over (see Chapter VI). But they were by no means alone. Right: a French Resistance poster printed in London. Far right: hatred of Nazism in America was intensified by such events as the destruction of the Czech village of Lidice in revenge for the murder of a Gestapo general by the Resistance. (32, 33)

Ruin: the Second World War was the most destructive in European history. Poland, western Russia and Germany lost most of their industries and urban centres; large areas of northern France were reduced to rubble; Britain and Italy also suffered heavily. The whole continent was dependent on outside aid to escape starvation. In 1945, when Ben Shahn painted his *Italian Landscape No. 2* (below), the damage seemed almost irreparable. But the sense of common misfortune gave impetus to the realization that Europe was after all an entity, and that the best chance of survival was to co-operate. In 1948 a Dutch competition for a poster expressing this idea produced some striking images (right). European federation was never a real possibility, but such organizations as NATO and the Common Market (see Chapter XIV) have shown that co-operation between nations can work on a military and an economic level. (34, 35)

Recovery came more quickly than most economists expected. Rotterdam had been the first West European city to know the effects of *Blitzkrieg*, when it was obliterated by German bombers in May 1940 with the loss of over 25,000 lives. That event was commemorated by Zadkine's monument (right), perhaps the most expressive symbol of suffering to have emerged from the war. Yet within ten years Rotterdam had become a model of architectural and economic regeneration. (36)

Reconciliation: as the postwar world resolved itself into opposing blocs whose scale dwarfed earlier European rivalries, the old enemies gradually drew closer together. De Gaulle's meeting with Adenauer in Bonn in September 1962 (below) marked a new era in relations between France and Germany, based largely on Schuman's plan for industrial co-operation. (37)

In the east the Soviet grip on her satellites made contact with Western Europe slow and difficult. Various initiatives in this direction were firmly suppressed, but in 1970 the West German Chancellor, Willy Brandt met Gomulka, first secretary of the Polish Communist Party (below), to sign an agreement recognizing the Oder-Neisse line as the German-Polish frontier. (38)

Political division during the last 25 years has prevented Europe from enjoying the fruits of her unprecedented economic prosperity. In 1951 the subject of *The Unknown Political Prisoner* was proposed for an international sculpture competition. It was a theme that had as much meaning after the War as before, and it evoked a powerful response. This entry (left) is by the Italian artist Luciano Minguzzi. Its spiky, menacing forms are echoed ten years later by the barriers (below) built by the Russians in Berlin as part of the Berlin Wall. (39, 40)

The place of Europe in world history

ALAN BULLOCK

In 1900 Europe stood at the height of her power and prestige. Geographically insignificant, the smallest but one of the seven continents, the inventiveness, energy and aggressiveness of her peoples had given her a primacy which had lasted so long that most Europeans simply assumed it would continue indefinitely. This was the classic age of imperialism with the European Powers' partition of Africa as its centrepiece. Only two nations outside Europe enjoyed real independence, the Americans and the Japanese. The rest of the world was either parcelled out between the rival European empires or under the rule of governments too feeble or corrupt (or both) to withstand European economic penetration or political pressure.

Europe dominated the world economically as well as politically. Britain, Germany and France between them commanded sixty per cent of the world market for manufactured goods, and between 1900 and 1910 Germany virtually doubled her steel, iron and coal producing capacity.

To Europe's political and economic power must be added her cultural supremacy. Paris, Berlin, London, Vienna, Rome were the cultural centres of the world. This supremacy was based not just on an unbroken tradition, centuries old, which made her cities and towns a unique museum of the past, but on a continued vitality which other ancient cultures such as China's had lost. The twenty years before 1914 were one of the most creative and innovatory periods in European history, not only in the arts but also in science (e.g. the start of the 20th-century revolution in physics) and the study of man and society (Freud, Max Weber, Durkheim).

There was, of course, another side to the picture. The United States was rapidly overhauling Europe's economic and technological lead; the Japanese defeat of Russia in 1904 showed that a non-European people could master Western technology well enough to stand up to Europeans in war. Even without the two great wars in which the European nations destroyed it themselves, Europe's uniquely favoured position in the world would not have lasted out the 20th century. But Europe's hegemony was not overthrown by external enemies: it was destroyed by its own internal quarrels.

This 'Europe' of which we have been speaking as the centre of the civilized world was not at all identifiable with the continent as it was defined geographically. Large parts of Europe did not share in the material progress and prosperity of the leading nations. The three southern projections of Europe—the Iberian peninsula; Italy below the industrialized north; the Balkans and Greece— certainly did not, nor did the greater part of Eastern Europe, where a peasant population continued to live in a traditional preindustrial society, a century and more removed from conditions of life in the urban centres of Western and Central Europe.

Many of those who lived in the cities, too, would have considered themselves excluded, for Europe was still a stratified society governed by class distinction with an undisguised and gross inequality between rich and poor. The poor who thronged the overcrowded slums of the big towns and industrial districts were a lower order of humanity and treated as such, valued only as the necessary pool of labour, always in surplus, on which the social as well as the economic system depended.

By 1900 some of the workers had learned to organize and to protest: there were frequent strikes in the next fourteen years, some of them violent, and social problems began to figure more frequently on the agenda of politics. Yet one must beware of reading too much into the history of the 1900s from hindsight. In the parliamentary countries of Western Europe this was the golden age of radicalism, but a radicalism which was still very much concerned with completing a 19th-century programme of *political* reform, the extension of the franchise and anti-clericalism, a radicalism still individualist rather than collectivist in its outlook. It is only in the light of what was to follow after the war that one can see the foundations of the welfare state being laid before 1914. In the greater part of Europe, even where it was disguised by parliamentary institutions as in Germany and Austria-Hungary, the imperial prerogative and class rule were still what counted. True, there was fear of revolution, but up to 1914 no serious revolt against the existing order had taken place except in Russia, where the loss of the Russo–Japanese War was followed by the confused outbreak of 1905. Even there, the most vulnerable regime in Europe, once it recovered its nerve, was well on the way to recovering its power as well by 1914. Certainly no European government hesitated to go to war for fear that its subjects would refuse the call to arms or turn their weapons against their own rulers—and they were right.

The war of 1914-18

The imperialist competition between the European Powers had not led to war. But it contributed powerfully to creating a new temper of aggressive nationalism in Europe, giving it a racist as well as a messianic character, producing a crude philosophy of social Darwinism ('survival of the fittest') and above all popularizing it.

Between 1900 and 1914 every one of the European governments responded to the public mood and to its own distrust of the other Powers by spending greatly increased sums on armaments. With armaments went a search for diplomatic and military 'understandings', which a series of crises (Morocco, 1905; BosniaHerzegovina, 1908; Morocco again in 1911) hardened into rival alliances. France and Russia confronted the Central Powers of Germany and Austria-Hungary, with England trying to maintain a free hand but reaching understandings with France and Russia which Germany's challenge to her naval power prevented her from ever reaching with the Central Powers. With each successive crisis the politicians felt their room for manoeuvre reduced. In 1913, with Austria and Russia threatening to intervene on opposite sides in the quarrels of the Balkan States, the Great Powers succeeded in reviving the Concert of Europe and imposing a settlement. But when a further crisis was precipitated by the Sarajevo assassination a year later, the political leaders failed to produce a solution in time to avoid war and seemed to lack not only the skill but the will to find one.

The feeling that war was inevitable had been steadily growing. The prospect, however, evoked little of the widespread horror which it was to in the 1930s. The use as well as the threat of force was an accepted part of the system of power politics which all states practised and, before the actual experience of 1914–18, few

p 318-9
(4-15)

p 57
(1)

p 254-5
(18-24)

p 153
(16)

p 34
(3)

p 34
(4, 5)

p 34 (7)

even among the soldiers had any idea of what a modern technological war would mean. Hardly anyone believed the war would last for years; and no one dreamed that, when it was finally over, the Europe they had known would be gone for ever. The crowds who cheered the declaration of war in every European capital did so, not out of some collective death urge, but out of ignorance.

The subsequent dispute about war guilt confused moral with political issues. All the Powers were prepared to contemplate war as an instrument of policy, had armed to the limit in readiness for it and, once it began, let nothing stand in the way of their efforts to defeat the enemy. From a moral point of view, there was little to choose between them. But leaving aside questions of *moral* responsibility, there is no doubt that the unification of Germany and the extraordinary growth in German power which followed it had a profoundly disturbing effect on the rest of Europe. Bismarck realized this and recognized limits to German expansion: his successors did not. The most powerful groups in prewar Germany—industrialists and bankers as well as the military and naval leaders—thought in terms of war and annexations which would establish a German hegemony in Europe. It was the combination of this frame of mind with the power to carry it out which alarmed the other Powers and led to war.

p 36–7
(12–20) Although there were campaigns in other parts of the world, the fighting in Europe and its sea approaches overshadowed everything else, a war of movement in the east, a war of attrition in the west. Between 10 and 13 million men were killed, 20 million wounded. In addition to the loss of life on the battlefields, each side tried to break the resistance of the civilian population by cutting off supplies and starving them into submission, the object of the Germans' unrestricted U-boat campaign and of the British blockade. In the end, as many more again—including millions of women and children—died from these causes as were killed in action.

p 38
(21) The material destruction was much less than in the Second World War, although a great part of northern France looked as if it could never be cultivated or inhabited again. But the psychological shock was greater, for the men and women thrust into this experience were totally unprepared for a prolonged and systematic destruction of human life on a scale never known before. The result, felt long after the fighting had ended, was a loss of security in everything that had been taken for granted or relied on, a spiritual as well as a social crisis of confidence reaching into the depths of men's consciousness and affecting in some degree the entire population of the continent.

p 128
(7–10) The crack came first in the east, where the Tsarist regime, totally discredited by the inefficiency with which it conducted the war, gave way to a Provisional Government which in turn succumbed to a revolutionary seizure of power by the Bolsheviks

(October 1917). The Russian armies disintegrated and the Germans seized their opportunity to dictate terms (Brest-Litovsk, March 1918) which deprived Russia of large areas in Eastern Europe including the Ukraine.

The Germans, however, although relieved of the need to continue fighting on two fronts, were unable to achieve the break-through in the west (spring 1918) on which their High Command had staked everything. With the United States now in the war and able to p 36
(13) reinforce the Western Front with fresh supplies of men and material, the French and the British had the promise of victory if they could hold out: the Germans had nothing except the prospect of defeat, however long postponed.

The end came suddenly. The German Army, although outnumbered and in retreat, was still undefeated in the field, the Allied leaders preparing for a final campaign in 1919, the German people still unaware of how serious their country's situation had become, when Ludendorff, in the name of the High Command, abruptly demanded that the German Government seek an armistice. Once the news got out, the spell was broken: crews of the German High Seas Fleet mutinied on 3 November; four days later revolution broke out in Bavaria; on the 9th the Kaiser abdicated and a republic was proclaimed in a desperate effort to hold off revolution in Berlin. On the 11th, the Armistice was signed, but signed by a German civilian (Erzberger) not by a soldier, and in circumstances which were capable later of being twisted into the myth of the 'Stab in the Back' of the undefeated German Army.

Years of disorder, 1918-23

The old Europe broke up in a welter of disorder which lasted for years after the peace treaties were signed. The habit of violence was not easily dropped and the experience men had been through turned many towards extremism.

The Russian example was vividly before men's eyes. There, with a superb disregard for Marxist theory, for the democratic rights of the Constituent Assembly or for the losses involved in signing the Brest-Litovsk Treaty, Lenin had concentrated on one thing, the seizure of power. But even Lenin would not have believed the Bolsheviks could hold on to power in face of civil war, famine, Allied intervention and the collapse of the Russian state, if he had not counted on the revolution spreading to the rest of Europe.

The key was Germany: if Germany could be captured for the p 60
(8–12) revolution, this could be the break-through Lenin was looking for. Between January 1919 and the autumn of 1923, the German Communists made several attempts to capture power. All failed. The republican leaders, pushed into power when the Kaiser abdicated, held their ground in face not only of attacks from the Left but from the Right (the Kapp Putsch, 1920), in face even of the peace terms imposed by the victorious powers and bitterly resented by the German people. When a choice had to be made, the majority of the German workers turned down revolution in favour of reform by constitutional methods.

The same pattern repeated itself throughout the European working-class movement. When the Russian leaders forced the issue at the 1920 congress of the Communist International by demanding acceptance of the 'Twenty-One Conditions' and the expulsion of the 'reformists', every European socialist party split, the majority voting in favour of reform and against revolution. After the tumultuous years of 1919 and 1920 the revolutionary tide steadily receded: the tragedy was that the quarrel between the Communists and the Social Democrats left the socialist and working-class movement permanently divided, to the ultimate profit of those who were enemies of both. Italy pointed the way: there, Mussolini took advantage both of the fears raised by talk of revolution and of the divisions which destroyed the effectiveness of the Left, to stage his so-called 'March on Rome' in October 1922 and go on to establish the first of Europe's Fascist regimes.

While the postwar tide of disorder was still at its height, the Peace Conference met in Paris early in January 1919 to draw up a p 38
(22) settlement for the new Europe. The Russians were not represented (though very much present in the delegates' minds), nor were the defeated states: the Germans were only summoned to receive the Allies' terms.

The Habsburg empire, which had weathered five hundred years

Radical left-wing movements before 1914 fought an unequal battle against the forces of law and order—Félix Vallotton's 'The Anarchist'. (1)

Europe in 1914. The shading indicates those countries which joined in the fighting against the Central Powers (Germany and Austria-Hungary) and their allies (Turkey, Bulgaria). (2)

of history, had already followed the empire of the Tsars into oblivion. The Czechoslovaks, the South Slavs, and the Poles had not waited for the Peace Conference to establish provisional governments and stake their claims; Rumania had occupied Transylvania. The treaties of Saint-Germain and Trianon simply recognized the facts: Austria was reduced to Vienna and its German-speaking provinces, but forbidden to take the logical step of union with Germany; Hungary suffered the severest territorial losses of any of the defeated nations.

This part of the peace settlement was in rough accord with President Wilson's views and promises on national self-determination; the clash between his doctrinaire liberal approach and the sceptical Clemenceau's concern with security came over the conditions to be imposed on Germany. The German Reich was left intact but reduced in area both in the West (Alsace Lorraine) and the East (West Prussia, Poznan, Upper Silesia).

The Treaty of Versailles can be justly criticized, not because it was too harsh (certainly not by comparison with the German terms at Brest-Litovsk) but because it failed to carry out either of the policies which could be adopted towards Germany and stultified both. It was too lenient if it was meant to hold Germany down permanently; too humiliating if it was meant to bring a democratic Germany into the European community. The result was a policy of half-measures severe enough to discredit the new republican regime but not to check the revival of German nationalism which throve on the 'injustice' of the Versailles *Diktat*.

Wilson consoled himself for the concessions he had to make with his hopes of the League of Nations. But America's withdrawal from the League, on top of Russia's absence, left it with little chance of becoming the universal association based on voluntary co-operation and the moral force of world opinion which Wilson envisaged. The French, left without the treaty of guarantee proposed by the Americans and the British, tried to turn the League into an organization to provide security (by which they meant enforcing the terms of the peace treaties), but the British were unwilling to commit themselves to an effective system of collective security, and so the League like the Versailles settlement fell between two stools.

The Peace of Paris brought the war to an official end, but fighting continued in Eastern Europe. Until the end of 1919 the Allies persisted in their policy of supporting the anti-Bolshevik forces in the Russian civil war, entirely without success. The Poles, demanding the restoration of their 18th-century boundaries, refused to accept the line proposed by Curzon and the Allies for their eastern frontier; they attacked the Russians, occupied most of the Ukraine and were then driven back by the Red Army to the outskirts of Warsaw before being saved by French military aid. On their other frontier the Poles' fought the Germans for the possession of Upper Silesia. The League intervened to impose a partition, but this no more satisfied the Poles and Germans than the frontier fixed by the Treaty of Riga (1921) satisfied the Poles and the Russians. The double threat to Poland's existence which precipitated the Second World War was already evident.

The possibility of such a threat, a combination between Germany and Russia, the two pariah powers, was suddenly made real by the secretly negotiated Treaty of Rapallo (1922), restoring diplomatic and economic relations between Berlin and Moscow to the anger and alarm of Paris and London: it continued to haunt Europe throughout the inter-war years.

The French were left by the Americans and the British to provide for their own security against a revival of German power. Believing that the peace treaties must be upheld in their entirety, the French built up an alliance system with the Poles and the Little Entente of Czechoslovakia, Rumania and Yugoslavia. This gave an illusion of strength only so long as Germany and Russia remained weak. The French policy of enforcement brought them into conflict with the Germans, which was to be expected, but also with the British who no longer believed in a threat from Germany and had become exasperated by the French obsession with security.

The quarrel came to a head—and the limits of enforcement were clearly shown—in January 1923, when the French marched troops into the Ruhr to secure pledges for the payment of reparations. The Germans met coercion with passive resistance, a bitter struggle in which the German state as well as the economy came near to dissolution and the value of the mark collapsed, until in September a new German chancellor, Stresemann, showed courage in reversing this disastrous policy. Unexpectedly, as 1923 came to a close, there appeared a chance that it might see the end of Europe's postwar disorders. One effect, however, could not be made good. The newly appointed Finance Minister Schacht succeeding in stabilizing the German currency, but not before the savings, and with them the remaining security, of millions of Germans, particularly in the middle classes, had been wiped out. This was a social revolution which bit far more deeply than the political changes of 1918 and powerfully assisted that 'radicalization' of German society of which the Nazis were to be the beneficiaries.

p 33 (1)

Recovery, 1924-29

Nonetheless, the years 1924–29 were the nearest Europe came to stability between the wars. Once inflation was ended and a procedure at last agreed for the payment of reparations (the Dawes Plan, 1924), German industry recovered its old drive and by 1928 was again second only to the USA in industrial production: despite the loss of Upper Silesia and the Saar it had increased its productive capacity by 40% over the prewar figure. The French astonished everyone by the speed with which they rebuilt their devastated areas. In 1925 Britain restored the gold standard and the following year Poincaré succeeded in stabilizing the franc.

Economic recovery was matched by a new and more reasonable spirit in international relations, the work of Briand, Stresemann and Austen Chamberlain. In October 1925 agreement was reached at Locarno between France, Belgium and Germany on a mutual guarantee of their common frontiers underwritten by Britain and Italy. Germany was admitted to the League of Nations and given a permanent seat on its Council; Allied control of German disarmament was brought to an end; foreign supervision of the German economy was lifted by the Young Plan, and the Allied evacuation of the Rhineland was brought forward to June 1930.

All this was an improvement on the early 1920s, but it did not restore the position Europe had held in the world before 1914. Her share in the world's trade was less; the leadership in technological development had fallen into American hands; in place of an average rate of growth of over 3% between 1870 and 1913, industrial production grew by little more than 1% in the 1920s; her investments overseas were reduced and she was heavily in debt to the United States. Of the five European states which had ranked as Great Powers before 1914, only two, Britain and France, could still be counted as such. For the first few years after the war France had taken a bold lead in European affairs, but the withdrawal from the Ruhr and the adoption of a more conciliatory policy towards Germany were recognition that she had over-reached her strength.

The British and French had redistributed the German and Turkish empires, but the revolt against imperialism was already beginning: against French rule in Morocco, against British in India. Sensitive to the growing nationalism of the white colonies, Britain started the conversion of her empire into the British Commonwealth when she formally recognized the independence of her overseas dominions (Statute of Westminster, 1931). This was a far-sighted policy but it confirmed the change in the relationship between Europe and the rest of the world.

Although the two Western powers had preserved their democratic institutions intact (the failure of the General Strike in 1926 marked the defeat of the militants in the British Labour movement), their government and business leaders left the impression of being on the defensive, anxious to perpetuate or restore the past rather than to face new problems. The lost generation of younger men weighed heavily on the consciousness of both nations. The old self-confidence had gone and with it the capacity for new ideas. It was characteristic that the British ruling class should congratulate itself on restoring the gold standard as a symbol of the soundness of British credit when (as Keynes and the trade union leader Bevin pointed out) its main effect was to add to the difficulty of expanding British exports. The stagnation of Britain's staple industries (coal, shipbuilding, textiles) and an unemployment figure which never fell below a million were a standing reproach to government and business alike.

The German economic recovery was real enough but it was precarious, dependent on a flood of American short-term loans, and thus vulnerable to any recession in the United States. The Weimar constitution was a democratic masterpiece, but the coalition governments which it produced lacked authority and failed to reconcile a great many Germans to the break with the authoritative traditions of the Empire or the responsibility which they laid on the republic for the defeat of 1918 and the Versailles *Diktat*. Stresemann had refused to conclude an Eastern Locarno which would mean accepting Germany's postwar frontiers with Poland and Czechoslovakia, and in April 1926 he balanced his acceptance of Locarno by a new treaty of friendship with Soviet Russia. His policy of *Erfüllung* ('fulfilment' of the Versailles terms)

as far as Germany's western frontiers were concerned, put him in a stronger position to press for peaceful revision which would enable Germany to resume her natural place as the most powerful nation in Europe. But this was not enough for the nationalists, who denounced Stresemann as a traitor and demanded not the revision but the repudiation of Versailles. If German prosperity ever foundered, the Republic was likely to find itself under violent attack from extremists on the Right as well as the Left—where the Communists despite their quarrel with the Social Democrats continued to attract working-class support.

Recovery was in any case limited to the western half of Europe. The fragmentation of the Habsburg empire and the nationalism of the successor states left the eastern half (with the exception of Czechoslovakia) still chronically impoverished, in some cases (Hungary, for example) worse off than before. Southern Europe was the same, burdened with an immemorial poverty which the 20th century had so far failed to change. In such circumstances, democracy meant no more than corruption and frustration: in one country after another it was abandoned, either openly or under concealment of a royal dictatorship (e.g. Alexander of Yugoslavia, Carol of Rumania), for a more authoritative form of government at least halfway to Fascism: after Mussolini, Primo de Rivera in Spain; Pilsudski in Poland; Salazar in Portugal; Metaxas in Greece.

Paradoxically, the 1920s which proved so checkered in Europe's political and economic history were as brilliant a decade in the arts, literature and science as any in her history. The originality which had marked the years 1900–14 now found full expression, and an audience as well, in the freer more open postwar society of Western Europe. Paris had never attracted more writers, painters and their hangers-on, and Berlin in the days of the Weimar Republic rapidly became a legend. The paradox however is only superficial. The culture of the 1920s which gives the decade so much of its character in retrospect was that of a minority even in the handful of cities where it flourished. And underneath the brilliance of the performance there was evident a deep anxiety about the future of a Europe which could not forget the nightmarish experiences it had lived through since 1914.

The watershed, 1930-33

In 1929–30 the nightmare began again. The Depression which started with the collapse of the New York stock market in October 1929 was the most severe in the history of modern capitalism. The rapidity with which its effects spread to Europe showed how dependent on the United States Europe had become: the recall of American loans and the drying up of the supply removed the underpinning of the whole Central European recovery. In Germany unemployment mounted until it passed six million, and this figure does not take account of those on part-time work, or of dependants. With these added, half the population was in need. In Britain with a smaller population the *official* figures at their peak were over three million. The Depression hit farming as much as industry: European agriculture had been suffering from world over-production, falling prices and the dumping of surpluses since 1926. Particularly hard hit were those countries like Hungary, Poland and the Balkan States which depended on agricultural exports to finance their imports. Governments rushed to put up tariffs or provide other protection for their own producers. The cumulative effect was to reduce trade even further: between 1929 and 1933 the volume of world trade shrank by two-thirds.

The political effects were quick to follow. In Britain the economic crisis broke the Labour Government. For the next nine years Britain had a Conservative Government under a National ticket: its policies were hardly more enterprising or imaginative than before the Depression. It followed the abandonment of the gold standard by abandoning free trade as well in favour of imperial preference, a formal recognition that the self-regulating system of international trade on which Britain's role as the world's banker and workshop had rested was gone for good. If there was recovery after 1933 little of it was due to Government policy, and recovery was still not much more than a return to the limited prosperity and limited depression of the 1920s with an unemployment figure stabilized at a million and a half.

p 320 (16–20)

French experience was different but not much more encouraging. The Depression hit France later than other European countries (1932). Its effects were sharpened by the Stavisky affair, a political scandal which threatened to become a crisis of the regime. In February 1934 right-wing and patriotic organizations attempted to storm the Chamber of Deputies and were only stopped by gunfire. The danger from the Right was exaggerated and French democracy survived, but it was no more capable than the British of finding adequate answers to the problems of the thirties. The most promising departure of the decade, the rally of the Left which produced a Popular Front government supported by Socialists, Radicals and Communists under Blum's leadership (1936), ended in disillusionment a year later.

The one part of Europe where democracy mastered the problems created by the Depression was Scandinavia, where the nearest approach to a successful social democracy anywhere in the world was strengthened rather than weakened by the experience. In the rest of Europe the trend set more strongly towards authoritarian government and was given a powerful impetus by the Nazis' capture of power in Germany.

Since March 1930, when the Coalition Government had split on the measures to be taken in face of the Depression, Germany had been governed by a conservative administration under Brüning (1930–32). Neither Brüning nor his successors, Papen and Schleicher, could secure a majority in the Reichstag and were forced to rely on the emergency powers of the President. Unemployment grew steadily worse throughout 1931 and 1932, and the Government became more and more isolated from the mood of the country. The cumulative experience of defeat, civil disorders, inflation, and an even worse plunge into economic disaster had produced in a great number of Germans a pent-up force of despair, anger and insecurity which was there for the taking by an extremist party. What the situation called for and what Hitler provided was a radicalism of the Right, revolutionary not conservative in character, but drumming up nationalist frenzy and offering a universal scapegoat in the Jews. On this platform the Nazis leaped from nowhere to become the second party in the Reichstag in September 1930, and went on winning more votes for another two years.

p 62 (17–23)

Yet Hitler became Chancellor on 30 January 1933 as a result neither of an electoral victory—he never won a clear majority in a free election, and actually lost votes in the last election (November 1932) before he took office—nor of a revolutionary coup d'état. He took office as part of a back-stage deal with Papen and other conservative politicians who congratulated themselves that, in return for the mass support which Hitler would bring them, they had offered him no more than three seats in a coalition Cabinet in which they would control the real power. It was the miscalculation of the century. Once in office, Hitler launched a revolutionary take-over which left the rest of the Cabinet helpless.

After that the success of the Nazi programme of public works and rearmament in relieving unemployment, plus the restoration of German national pride by a series of successes in foreign policy unmatched since the Unification, won for Hitler a greater measure of genuine popular support than any other government in Europe. For a minority whose judgment had not been corrupted by the propaganda of success, it was an oppressive and corrupt regime, but the majority of the German people were content to be swept along in the powerful tide of national feeling which Hitler had harnessed.

Hitler regarded the Western democracies as relics of a past age. Some of those who hated Nazism most came to the same conclusion and turned to Communism as the only effective alternative. Russia, which had become remote during the 1920s, moved back into the centre of the European picture in the 1930s.

At the time of Lenin's death the Revolution had virtually come to a standstill. Four years later, in 1928, Stalin resumed the initiative, with a campaign to force through the collectivization of agriculture. When the more independent peasants—the 'Kulaks'—objected, he broke their resistance by force: the final cost in human lives has been estimated at five million. Collectivization was far from being a success; and agriculture remained the chief weakness of the Soviet economy. But this did not shake Stalin's belief that it was only by such methods, ruthlessly enforced, that a real break could be made with the past and a new pattern imposed on Russian society.

p 129 (14)

Stalin applied the same methods to the forced industrialization of Russia. The Five-Year Plans ran into every sort of difficulty and, with their obsessive concentration on heavy industry at the expense of the consumer industries, left the Soviet economy unbalanced and the standard of living of the Russian workers desperately low. Drastic purges, involving several million people, followed the assassination of Stalin's deputy, Kirov, in December 1934. But the break-through had been achieved: insulated from the Depression which hit the rest of Europe, Russia emerged at the end of the 1930s as a major industrial power, with an overall production only surpassed by the USA and Germany, and the elimination of privately owned industry and commerce. Unlike Hitler whom he defeated and outlasted, Stalin left something more behind, a Russia which he had bludgeoned but transformed.

p 128 (12)

Outside the Soviet Union the example of Communism in action attracted many with left-wing sympathies in Western Europe. Disillusioned with the inability of democratic institutions to provide effective answers to the problems of a capitalist society, they saw in Soviet Russia a country which had broken with its past and was being remade in a new and more equal pattern, without the watered-down compromises of reformist socialism. Their enthusiasm was increased by the fact that the Communist International, after disastrously mistaken tactics in Germany in

'*The Autograph Collector*'—*David Low's satire on Anthony Eden's appeasement policy, 1933. Hitler and Mussolini build up their armies; Britain puts her faith in treaties. (3)*

face of the Nazis, had now been converted to a policy of rallying all the forces of the Left in a popular anti-Fascist front. The new tactics were endorsed by Moscow which, alarmed by the growing power of Nazi Germany, emerged from its isolation to enter the League of Nations (1934) as the advocate of collective security, and signed treaties of mutual assistance with France and Czechoslovakia (1935). The news of the purges in Russia disturbed but did not destroy the hopes which the Left in Western Europe still placed in Communism as the pattern of the future and in Soviet Russia as the one reliable opponent of Nazi and Fascist aggression. They were to be renewed with even greater enthusiasm in the course of Hitler's war.

The dictators and the Second World War, 1933–45

p 63
(24–26)
The thirties were the decade of the dictators, years indelibly associated with Hitler and Mussolini and with the raucous propaganda of Nazism and Fascism as the irresistible 'wave of the future'. By the end of the decade Hitler overshadowed his Italian partner, but in the middle thirties the Mediterranean and Mussolini were the centre of attention rather than Central Europe, and Mussolini's attack on Ethiopia the test case for collective security. The strength of European support for the League was shown by the wave of indignation which greeted the news of the Hoare–Laval agreement to hand over two-thirds of Abyssinia to the Italians.

p 39
(24)
But Britain and France refused to impose the one form of sanctions which would hurt Italy, an embargo on oil. By May 1936 the Italians had occupied Addis Ababa and the failure of sanctions, largely due to the reluctance of Britain and France to act with decision, had killed the League.

Nothing could have suited Hitler better. He had already got away with the remilitarization of the Rhineland (March 1936). Now, without lifting a finger, he saw the idea of collective security, which might have been turned against Germany, discredited; and Mussolini quarrelling with Britain and France and driven to look to his fellow dictator in Germany for support. Hitler was able to derive equal profit from the second Mediterranean episode, the Spanish Civil War, which broke out (July 1936) almost exactly as the campaign in Ethiopia ended.

p 64–5
(29–31)
This was the one occasion during the century when Spain, once the greatest of the European powers, emerged from her isolation. For the Spaniards themselves the civil war was rooted in their history, a further chapter in fierce and bitter feuds of their own, but to many outside Spain it appeared as the opening chapter in the European civil war between the anti-Fascist Popular Front of the Left, the working classes led by the intellectuals, and the reactionary forces of the Right. Nothing, in fact, marked the Second World War more distinctly (or added more to its confusion) than this double character, of an ideological and at the same time a national conflict. In 1938–39, however, it was still far from certain that any of the Great Powers would oppose Hitler's and Mussolini's ambitions. The French, whose own social and ideological divisions were sharpened by divided sympathies over the Spanish war, increasingly left the initiative to the British, and the British

p 40
(26)
Government now led by Neville Chamberlain (from May 1937) was profoundly distrustful of the Left and Russia, and preferred to look for a settlement with Hitler and Mussolini which would avoid war.

Hitler well understood the divided state of Europe, and by the end of 1937, with Germany's economic strength restored and her rearmament under way, he was ready to take advantage of it. His first move, the annexation of Austria (March 1938) was hastily improvised. The gamble succeeded, however, and greatly increased Hitler's confidence: neither Britain nor France showed any sign of intervening and Mussolini, swallowing his anger at Hitler's failure to consult him, sent his congratulations.

The next target was obvious: Czechoslovakia, under Masaryk and Benes the one successful example of democracy in Central or Eastern Europe, and the ally of both France and Russia. Munich,
p 63
(24)
however, did not satisfy Hitler. His real objective had always been not the Sudetenland but the destruction of the Czechoslovak state, and within six months he used the excuse of a declaration of independence, which the Slovak separatists were prodded into making, to move into Prague and declare Bohemia and Moravia

a German protectorate (March 1939). Even before that he had tabled fresh demands, this time on Poland.

At long last the British Government was forced to recognize the threat to Europe's peace and its own interests. But the ill-judged guarantee which Chamberlain offered the Poles did not deter Hitler. He was confident that, when the crisis came to a head, the British and French would hesitate to go to war to stop him as they had the previous autumn, and his confidence was strengthened by signs during the summer of 1939 of a change of policy in Moscow. After four years in which the Russians had taken the lead in urging joint action to check Hitler, Stalin was disillusioned with the West and concluded that Russia would have to look after herself. This was Hitler's opportunity and he took it with both hands. While the British and French, reluctantly converted to the need of common action with Russia, could not meet Stalin's price, Hitler asked only for her neutrality and was ready to accept—at other people's expense—everything Russia demanded in return. With the Nazi–Soviet Pact in his hand, Hitler was more than ever sure that the West would not risk war for the sake of Poland or that, if they did, he could crush Poland before their intervention became effective. This time the first gamble failed to come off, but after twenty-four hours' hesitation his confidence in the second held and on September 1st he launched his troops in an all-out effort to destroy the Poles before the West could move.

Once again the German urge to expand and dominate, this time consciously manipulated by Hitler, had led to war. After the First World War the other Powers were held to blame because they had been prepared to go to war to prevent Germany achieving her object: in 1939 they were blamed because they had been reluctant to do so. In the 1930s there was a widespread horror of a European war which had not existed before 1914. Hitler knew this and exploited it. Even Mussolini hesitated when the crunch came; Hitler did not. He took the risk of war and, when the gamble came off and the Poles were overwhelmed before Britain and France
p 40
(28)
were ready to move, he doubled the odds and attacked in the West. By doing so he deliberately turned a limited into a general European war.

The crushing defeat of France, the victor's entry into Paris and
p 40
(29, 33)
the British Army's evacuation from the continent were triumphs which the German Army had never been able to achieve in 1914–18—and now brought off at a fraction of the cost. If Hitler had been willing to halt at this point he would have eclipsed even Bismarck in fame. No external necessity compelled him to extend his conquests. The British, recovering their courage and national
p 41
(36)
unity under Churchill's leadership, might defy him but were powerless to challenge his mastery of the continent; the Russians, having secured their former frontiers in Eastern Europe, were anxious to avoid a clash; the United States was still neutral; the majority of the German people would have been relieved to risk no more and enjoy the hegemony they had at last achieved. But it was not in Hitler's nature, nor in that of the movement he had created, to know when or indeed how to stop. Hitler and the Nazis were adventurers who had captured power first in Germany, then in Europe, but had neither the desire nor the ability to turn that power to constructive purposes.

June 22, 1941, the day on which the German Army invaded Russia, has a good claim to be regarded as the most fateful date in the modern history of Europe. If the Germans had succeeded in overthrowing the one Communist state in the world and bringing the resources of Russia under their control, the whole pattern of the rest of the century would have been changed. Their failure was hardly less momentous in its consequences for Europe, for it brought the Russians to the Elbe, left half the continent under Communist rule and opened the way to the emergence of the Soviet Union as one of the two super-powers of the postwar world. It was fortunate for Europe that, in December 1941, Pearl Harbor brought the USA as well as Russia into the
p 40
(34)
war, and that Roosevelt gave victory in Europe priority over the war in the Pacific—another of the crucial decisions in Europe's 20th-century history.

The Germans systematically stripped Russia and the other countries they occupied and forced millions of men from Western as well as Eastern Europe to go and work in Germany in conditions

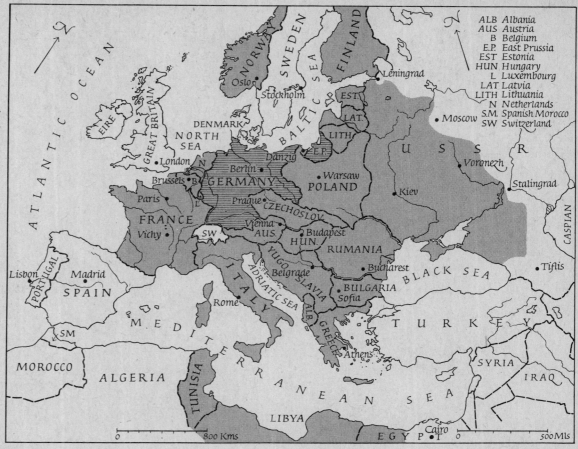

European frontiers in 1938. Shading shows the greatest extent of Hitler's empire in 1942, including territory controlled by Italy. (4)

of slave labour. Eastern Europe felt the full brunt of Nazi racist policy. In the Ukraine, where an intelligent policy would have followed the German example of 1918 and set up an independent Ukrainian state, the population was treated with the same brutality as in Poland: the Ukrainians, like the Poles, were Slavs, *Untermenschen*, not human beings at all. Early in 1942 Hitler secretly ordered the 'final solution' of the Jewish problem and in the next three years SS detachments under the command of men like Eichmann carried out the systematic extermination of some five million Jews, a crime without parallel in European history.

p 132 (24)
In these circumstances, the Resistance attracted increasing numbers who might otherwise find themselves deported to work in Germany. The political outlook of the Resistance tended towards the Left, an advantage skilfully used by the Communists who were better trained for clandestine activity and guerrilla warfare than other groups and gained great prestige from the part they played in the Resistance in countries as far apart as France and Greece.

p 41 (38, 40)
While the Russians steadily fought the Germans back, at terrible cost to both sides, from the Volga to the Vistula, the British and Americans had cleared North Africa, invaded Italy and in the summer of 1944 made their long awaited landing in the West. The last-minute attempt by the German Resistance to kill Hitler on 20 July 1944 failed. The forces now in the field against him left Hitler with no rational hope of avoiding defeat, but rather than admit that he was beaten he preferred to see Germany destroyed.

p 41 (42)
By the time the Russians forced their way into the ruins of Berlin and Hitler committed suicide (30 April 1945) it looked as if she had been. Three years after the German armies had dominated the whole of Europe they had suffered the most crushing defeat in history.

The Cold War, 1945–53

The Second World War was the most destructive of all wars and, although it was far more of a world war than the first, the heaviest burden again fell on Europe. The scale of the losses makes the statistics meaningless: between 25 and 30 million dead, double that number uprooted from their homes, hundreds of towns in ruins, thousands of square miles lost to cultivation. For several years after the fighting stopped many parts of Europe lived on the verge of starvation, with inflation and the black market rampant. Poland, Yugoslavia, Italy and the Ukraine were only kept going with aid from UNRRA, Germany and Austria with help from the occupying powers.

Yet within a decade Europe made a more permanent recovery than after the First World War. This is the more surprising since, from the beginning, the continent was divided down the middle, and has remained so ever since with great obstacles to trade and communication across the barrier, and the threat at times of open, not just a cold, war between the two halves.

Distrust between Russia and the Western Powers, more than once turning into open hostility, goes back to the 1917 Revolution. Only Hitler's attack on Russia had thrown them together, and even during the war there were far more difficulties between the Allied leaders than was allowed to become known. These difficulties grew as the tide turned in favour of the Allies and were papered over, not removed, at the three summit conferences, Teheran (1943), Yalta and Potsdam (1945). At the end of the war, the Soviet Union annexed 190,000 square miles of territory in Eastern Europe (a territory the equivalent in size of Spain) and moved Poland's western frontier in compensation to the Oder and the Western Neisse. The Russians sought to extend their power over the whole of Eastern and part of Central Europe as far west as the Elbe, setting up Communist-controlled governments which they could rely on. The Western Powers regarded this as simply exchanging one form of totalitarian government for another and feared that, if the Russians remained in control of so large a part of Europe, this would mean a permanent alteration in the balance of power, leaving the Soviet Union as the dominant power on the Continent with no European nation capable of providing a counter-weight. Thus, once the common interest in defeating Hitler was removed, an escalation of suspicion and counter-suspicion, action and counter-action was set in motion, culminating in the Berlin blockade of 1948–49. Germany remained, even in defeat, the central issue in European politics, as it had been after the First World War.

p 42 (44)
p 88 (24)

Determined to avoid the mistakes made then, the Allies had insisted on unconditional surrender, acknowledged no German government as successor to Hitler and divided the country into four zones of occupation. Once they attempted to go on and define a common policy, however, they ran into sharp disagreement. While the argument continued, each of the occupying powers began to organize its zone in accordance with its own views.

The same pattern appeared in the two halves of Europe. In the West, the Americans helped the European governments to stimulate economic recovery and so restore confidence through

p 323
(24)
the Marshall Plan and the Organization for European Economic Co-operation. On the other side of the Iron Curtain, as it now came to be called, Stalin tightened up political control first in Russia, then in Eastern Europe by forcing out non-Communist ministers like Nagy in Hungary and Mikolajczyk in Poland, harassing and suppressing their parties.

In 1947 the split became an open one. In March, President Truman stepped in to promise American support to Greece which was faced with the Communists' renewal of civil war. In the summer, the Russians rejected the offer of American economic aid under the Marshall Plan and sharply called the Poles and Czechs to order for showing interest in it. In the autumn the Cominform was set up to establish greater conformity of the satellite regimes to Moscow's line, and in February 1948 the Communists seized power in Czechoslovakia.

Stalin's blockade of Berlin not only failed to force the Western powers out of Berlin, thanks to the airlift and the staunchness of the Berliners, but committed them to maintain Berlin as a Western island in the middle of the Soviet zone, a commitment which was to prove a major obstacle to any future settlement. The Russians suffered a no less serious defeat inside their own camp when their expulsion of the Yugoslav Communist Party from the Cominform (June 1948) misfired and strengthened instead of weakening Tito's position.

Stalin could not reach Tito, but elsewhere he could stamp on any sign of deviation from the total submission he demanded. In the last years of the ageing tyrant's life his suspicion became insatiable, and between 1948 and 1953 Eastern Europe went through the same experience of the purge as Russia in the 1930s. Amongst those executed were some of the most prominent of the Communist leaders—Rajk in Hungary, Kostov in Bulgaria, Slansky in Czechoslovakia. Shortly before he died (March 1953) there were signs that he was about to extend the purge to Russia itself, with the same anti-Semitic overtones as in Eastern Europe.

The divided continent, 1953–70

By 1953 the Cold War had reached stalemate: this was the year the Soviet Union exploded its H-bomb and so produced a more equal 'balance of terror'. The new rulers in the Kremlin appeared eager to break with Stalinist policies abroad as well as at home. They restored relations with Tito; signed the treaty with Austria after ten years' deadlock (1955); invited Adenauer to visit Moscow; and took part in the first summit conference since Potsdam—at Geneva (1955). Further evidence of a retreat from Stalinism came in Khrushchev's famous speech (February 1956) to the 20th Congress of the Soviet Communist Party—delivered in secret but soon widely known—and in the ousting of Molotov as Foreign Minister. These changes were widely welcomed in Western Europe where there was a strong feeling that Stalin's death marked the end of an epoch and that a *détente* was now possible.

The difficulty for the Soviet leaders was to know how far they could go in relaxing Stalin's methods, either in the Soviet Union or in the Soviet empire, without losing control. Revolt in Hungary, which had to be suppressed by open force (1956), and near revolt in Poland showed what could happen. The so-called 'thaw' stopped short of the point where the Soviet position in Europe might be brought in question.

The Hungarian revolt interrupted but did not end the Russian attempt to draw the Western Powers into negotiation. In 1957 the Polish Foreign Minister, Rapacki, proposed a plan for a demilitarized zone in Central Europe and in January 1958 Bulganin suggested another summit conference. Hopes of a settlement between East and West reached a new climax with Khrushchev's visit to the USA in 1959: 'the spirit of Camp David' matched 'the spirit of Geneva' in 1955. After the fiasco of the Paris summit conference (1960), these hopes rapidly gave way to an atmosphere of crisis, with Khrushchev threatening to force the Western Powers out of Berlin. The West however, although divided, was not so amenable to pressure as Khrushchev seems to have expected.

p 68
(40)
He over-reached himself on Berlin (the Wall hastily erected in 1961 was a confession of failure) and had publicly to back down over Cuba in 1962.

During the 1950s the rivalry between the USA and the Soviet

p 136
(35)

p 68
(40)

Union had become much more of a global conflict. After the sealing off of Eastern Germany by the Berlin Wall (1961), Europe ceased to be the main area of confrontation and was replaced by Asia and later the Middle East. This reduced the tension in Europe and encouraged hopes of a local, purely European *détente*. De Gaulle tried to mobilize this feeling in support of a French initiative to make a European settlement with the Russians without the Americans; the Russians themselves tried to take advantage of it by proposing a new European collective system to replace both NATO and the Warsaw Pact.

The quarrel between Russia and China, and the split in the Communist world also produced effects in Europe. Albania became a client state of the Chinese, and Rumania took advantage of Russia's preoccupations to follow a line of its own in foreign policy and trade. When the Czechs, however, started on a liberalizing policy, the Russian attitude hardened. Khrushchev's successors had called a halt to de-Stalinization in the Soviet Union and in 1968 they used force to snuff out the Czechoslovak experiment.

Neither de Gaulle's failure, however, nor the demonstration in Czechoslovakia that the Russians had no intention of abandoning their control of Community Europe ended the search for a European *détente*. It was taken up by the German Social Democrats in the late 1960s and in 1970 produced a Soviet–German and a German–Polish treaty recognizing the Oder–Neisse line as the western frontier of Poland. How substantial these agreements would prove to be and whether they would lead to a normalization of relations across the Iron Curtain were questions left to the 1970s to answer.

p 67
(38)

The West organizes itself

The split in Europe affected the western half as much as the eastern, but in a very different way: its most important result was to commit the United States to Western Europe's recovery and defence.

The West had the great advantage of being liberated by the Americans and British, neither of whom wanted to stay. There were great hopes, nourished by the experience of the Resistance, of a new beginning, at least of radical reforms and, to start with, the now powerful French and Italian Communist parties joined with the socialists and the Christian Democrats (MRP in France) to put them into effect. In France, the tripartite ministry carried through a programme of nationalization, founded the welfare state and gave France a unique planning organization under Jean Monnet. The hopes of the Liberation, however, soon died; the split in international relations was matched by an internal split, the Communists were pushed out of both the French and Italian governments in May 1947, and there was a swing away from the Left towards more conservative policies. The same year France began a disastrous colonial war in Indo-China (1947–54) which was immediately followed by that in Algeria (1954–62).

p 158
(36)
p 183
(41–43)

In Britain the remarkable degree of mobilization which had been achieved during the war—both of people and of the economy—had produced a much more equal society with 'fair shares' for all. It was the desire to see this continued which led the British electorate to reject Churchill in 1945 in favour of a Labour government, and Labour under Attlee's leadership proceeded to carry out a permanent if quiet revolution which the Conservatives never attempted to reverse, the establishment of a welfare state. But Britain had suffered major economic losses in the war and, although helped by an American loan, her economy threatened to break down in the severe winter of early 1947. France and Italy were in no better situation, the Germans in much worse.

At this point, the United States, alarmed at the prospect of a general collapse which might open the way to the western as well as the eastern half of Europe coming under Communist rule, produced the offer of the Marshall Plan, which ranks with Lend Lease as an imaginative and far-sighted act of policy. In contrast to Russian policy, American power was used to encourage European initiative and restore not only its economy but self-confidence as well. In 1949, following the same pattern—in this case, the efforts of Britain, France and Benelux to organize their own defence in a Western European Union—the USA agreed to join in an enlarged alliance for mutual defence, the North Atlantic Treaty Organization, thereby supplying the missing counter-

p 42
(45)

weight to the Soviet Union and creating a new European balance of power.

The Atlantic framework in which the postwar recovery of Western Europe took place suited the British, whose wartime experience as well as their commitments to the overseas Commonwealth made them conscious of their separateness from the Continent, but it did not satisfy some of the ablest men in the other countries of Western Europe, who wanted a purely European and federalist organization in addition.

In May 1950 Robert Schuman, the French Foreign Minister, put forward the most original suggestion of the postwar period: a project drafted by Monnet for a European Coal and Steel Community (the Schuman Plan) which would pool the heavy industries and eliminate tariffs in the core nations of Western Europe as a first step towards their economic and political integration.

The plan had another strong attraction: it offered a way of containing the revival of German power which Frenchmen were already beginning to fear. The separate development of Western Germany, on which the British and Americans had embarked in default of Four-Power agreement on a common policy for the whole of Germany, could only succeed with German co-operation, first in economic matters, but also, inevitably, in political as well.

Adenauer skilfully made use of the American and British need to win German support in their contest with the Russians, but was wise enough to recognize the fears which the rebirth of a German state was bound to arouse. He therefore welcomed the Schumann Plan which would bring the German steel and coal industries under a common European authority with the French. It was a fortunate coincidence that at this crucial stage the representatives of France, Germany and Italy—Schumann, Adenauer, and de Gasperi—should all be Christian Democrats with a deep attachment to a common Catholic conception of European civilization. Britain remained aloof, but Monnet for one did not give up hope that, if the Schumann Plan succeeded, the British would eventually come in.

This promising pattern of development was almost destroyed by the outbreak of the Korean War (June 1950). Fear that a divided Europe, and in particular a divided Germany, would suffer the same fate as divided Korea and become the battleground for a third world war between Russia and America created a near panic and led to a widespread demand for Europe to declare neutrality—'*ohne mich*'. At the same time the American Government, bearing the brunt of the fighting in Korea, began to insist that Western Europe could not be defended unless the Germans were armed for their own defence, a prospect which repelled many others besides the French.

The Western alliance, however, although subjected to heavy strain, did not break up or abandon its programme. A NATO headquarters was set up outside Paris with an American commander, Eisenhower, as a guarantee of the United States' commitment to Europe; the German Federal Republic with its capital in Bonn was recognized as an equal partner, and the Coal and Steel Community began operations from headquarters in Luxembourg. By the date Stalin died, the quarrel between East and West which had threatened to paralyse Western Europe had, in fact, produced the opposite effect: the American commitment to Europe which had been refused after 1918; a strong impetus to Western unity; a quicker and, as it turned out, more secure economic recovery than after the First World War.

The two Europes

Twenty-five years after the end of the war, then, there was still no European settlement comparable to that of Vienna in 1815 or Paris in 1919, yet paradoxically this non-settlement lasted longer and proved more stable than the settlement of 1919. In 1955 West Germany was admitted to NATO; the same year the Russians put their military arrangements in Eastern Europe on a more permanent basis with the Warsaw Pact. Between the blocs were the two traditional neutrals, Sweden and Switzerland, both examples of successful democracy. To these Austria was added in 1955. There remained Finland, a democratic anomaly within the Soviet sphere of influence, and Yugoslavia, a Communist anomaly outside it.

p 42 (46)

After 1945 Europe's importance had declined so drastically that de Gaulle's cherished atomic bomb (left) and Britain's 'do-it-yourself' satellite (right) were matters for derisive comment in 'Die Zeit'. (5, 6)

The contrast between the backward eastern and the more advanced western halves of Europe is one of the stock themes of European history, but the present line of partition lies a good deal further to the west. No one ever thought of Leipzig, Dresden or Prague as belonging historically to anything other than Central Europe. In the late 1960s, if the population of the Soviet Union west of the Urals was counted in, there were 278 million on the eastern side of the division, 330 million on the west. But the peoples of the satellite states—Poles, East Germans, Hungarians, Czechs, Rumanians—certainly still regarded themselves, and were regarded by the West, as Europeans in a sense that was no longer true of the Russians. If this definition of Europe, stopping at Russia's western frontier, was accepted, then under a quarter of its 458 million people lived in the six countries behind the Iron Curtain (100 million) and three-quarters outside it.

The achievement of Communist Europe was to carry out a social revolution, eliminating private property and the old ruling classes—although establishing Djilas's new ruling class in their place—and to start on the industrialization of the historically backward areas of eastern and south eastern Europe.

Its failure was failure to win the willing co-operation of the mass of the people (except in Yugoslavia) or to reconcile Communist rule with anything like the personal freedoms enjoyed in the West, and most important of all failure to free itself from the heavy-handed control of the Russians and work out its own pattern of development. The success of Communism as a social and economic system remained compromised and frustrated in Eastern Europe for the same reason as in Soviet Russia itself, its inability to free itself from the consequences of the methods by which the Communist Party secured and maintains its power. The difference was that national feeling which in Russia could be drawn on to strengthen the regime, worked the other way in Eastern Europe. Corroboration of this was the fact that the Communist government which enjoyed the greatest degree of popular support was the Yugoslav, which succeeded in harnessing national feeling, thanks to the Russians' miscalculation. The same conclusion could be drawn from the popularity which the Communist government in Rumania gained from asserting its national independence.

The great achievement of Western Europe was a rate of economic growth which, beginning in the early 1950s, soon went far beyond recovery from the war and produced an extended period of prosperity in the 1950s and 1960s without precedent in European history. In 1960 with 3% of the world's land surface and 9% of its population, Western Europe produced a quarter of the world's industrial output and accounted for 40% of the world's trade. The rate of growth, of course, was not uniform: it varied from country to country (the British, for example, coming well down the table), and from year to year. There was a falling off in the 1960s, especially in the middle years, and growing anxiety about inflation, the 'technological gap' between the USA and Europe and the extent to which the leading growth industries were in the hands of American companies. But doubts about the future could not detract from the extraordinary achievement of the 1950s and 1960s and the consequent rise in living standards.

For, by contrast with earlier periods of European economic growth, the material benefits were much more widely shared. Western Europe in the 1960s was still far from satisfying those who

p 322–3 (26, 29)

wanted an egalitarian society, but by comparison with the 1920s, leave alone the 1900s, there was far less unemployment and poverty, much greater equality, greater social mobility and greater social freedom. One reason for this was that the European version of 'the affluent society', unlike the American original, was combined with the welfare state. Thus in Western Germany, where economic recovery had been achieved under the slogan of a market economy, almost 17% of the Gross National Product in 1967 was spent on social services. The comparable figure in the rest of the EEC was 14% to 15%, in the UK and Denmark 11%—and in the Soviet Union 10%. For all the imperfections and tensions of its society, it could be argued that Western Europe came nearer to working out a viable compromise between individual freedom and social responsibility than either Communist Russia or capitalist America.

The incomplete union

Western Europe's political could not match its economic recovery. American aid was given without an attempt to establish anything like the Russian system of control in Eastern Europe, but American power and Western Europe's dependence on it could not be disguised and were not easily accepted by nations like the French and the British which were still conscious of the role they had once played as Great Powers. Europe had lost its old autonomy, it was divided between two alliance systems which were not only hostile to each other but world-wide in scope. Europeans felt, for the first time in their history, that they could become involved in war and see their countries turned into battlefields in quarrels originating outside Europe and as a result of decisions in which they had no voice.

The change was underlined by the end of the European empires. European rule in Asia and Africa could not survive the shocks of the Second World War and the powerful stimulus this had given to nationalist movements. Germany and Italy had already lost their colonies; now Britain, France, Holland and eventually Belgium lost theirs too. Economically, the metropolitan countries soon recovered from the loss, but the process put a heavy strain on their powers of adaptability, especially for the older generation and for particular groups—white settlers, colonial administrators, army officers, businessmen—who saw their livelihood and position in society destroyed. Through the 1950s French life was deeply disturbed and the 4th Republic fatally weakened by the effects of the Indo-China and Algerian wars, and the emotional revulsion which many Englishmen and Frenchmen felt against this forced retreat from imperial greatness found expression in the attempt to call a halt at Suez (1956).

In 1955, the attempt to create a wider power base in Western Europe had been resumed. Reverting to Monnet's economic approach after the blind alley of EDC, the six countries of the original Schuman Plan agreed at Rome in 1957 to set up a European Economic Community. Britain was invited to join but refused, preferring to set up a simple free trade association with the three Scandinavian countries, Austria, Switzerland and Portugal. This was a much more disastrous mistake on Britain's part than the refusal to join the Schuman Plan. For within five years, the EEC emerged as the world's greatest trading power, and Britain, holding aloof, failed to keep up with the economic growth of the EEC countries.

p 323 (27)
p 322 (25)

The transition from an economic to a political community, however, proved more difficult. Ironically, the chief opposition came from France, the country which had supplied much of the driving force behind the European idea, but which had also wrecked the EDC and now in de Gaulle (French President 1958–69) provided a supreme exponent of traditional nationalism. De Gaulle did everything he could to block the development of the Community and vetoed Britain's application to join in 1963—a change of attitude on the British part which might have been a turning point for the Community. De Gaulle claimed for France the leadership of Western Europe—hence his desire to keep Britain out of the EEC and the obstructionist attitude he adopted towards NATO, which included both the United States and Britain. France lacked the strength to sustain such a role: in practice, de

Gaulle's grand design amounted to a series of gestures and nothing more, but it caused much confusion in European politics which the French exploited to the full. Only after his retirement (1969) could the British renew their application to join the Community, and the EEC itself resume the attempt to add political to economic integration.

De Gaulle thought of himself as restoring France to a great role in the world, but his real achievement is more likely to appear that of rescuing France from the role she was unable to play out in North Africa and restoring her confidence after the demoralizing experience of the Algerian war. His other achievement was to set the seal on the effort from both sides to replace the historic enmity between France and Germany with a degree of co-operation which, after all that had gone before, must surely rank as one of the outstanding features of this period of European history. p 67 (37)

Even more surprising, in spite of periodic scares about the revival of Nazism and the potentially explosive issue of a divided Germany, was the fact that the Federal Republic easily outlasted its famous predecessor of the 1920s, the Weimar Republic, proving economically stronger than Britain, politically more stable than either France or Italy.

All the West European governments benefited from the long period of prosperity, and in the mid 1960s there was much talk of 'the end of ideology' and consensus politics. Political extremism, whether of the Left or Right, made little headway, the mass votes of the French and Italian Communist parties were sterile, and by comparison with the 1920s and 1930s, the 1950s and 1960s (with the exception of France before de Gaulle took power) were a period of political stability.

At the end of the 1960s there were signs that this might be coming to an end. The novelty of affluence had worn off; expectations had outstripped the ability to meet them; and no government appeared able to solve the problems of the new industrial society—from overcrowded cities and pollution of the environment to inflation, industrial strife and the poverty of those left out. This was one common source of discontent, the failure of the affluent society to live up to expectations: the other, strongly felt by the young, was the hollowness of its success, a disillusionment with material prosperity and a revolt against the constrictions of a technological civilization, the banality and triviality of its culture. Both currents merged in a growing impatience with the *immobilisme* of consensus politics and a preference for protest and direct action. How far this would create a new pattern of politics in Western Europe in the 1970s was a question no one could yet answer.

The fact that the first seventy years of the 20th century ended with so many issues unsettled—the future of the Communist regimes in Eastern Europe, the chances of a settlement which would end the division of Europe or, more realistically, at least reduce the barriers between the two halves, the prospects of a European federation being created in the West—in short, the uncertainty of Europe's future, should occasion no surprise. Uncertainty about the future is something Europe shares with every other part of the world. And if the line had been drawn earlier in the century, in 1919, for instance, in 1940, or in 1947, the same would have been true then.

Between 1914 and 1950 the peoples of Europe experienced such an accumulation of disasters and horrors that anyone might have expected them to lose any confidence or capacity for recovery. Between the wars it looked as if they had, and the worst was still to come in the second war and its aftermath. If one thing seemed certain at the close of the Second World War it was the end of Europe. And of course it is true that the old Europe, the Europe of the 1900s with its unique position in the world, has gone for ever. But between the end of the 1940s and the end of the 1960s this heterogeneous collection of peoples crowded into the smallest but one of the continents showed a capacity to recover from the war and to go on and create a new Europe which upset every prediction. This is too short a period on which to base conjecture about the rest of the century but it justifies the conclusion that, if Europe's circumstances have been transformed in the seventy years since 1900, her peoples have not lost the vitality and energy which made Europe great in the first place.

IV AMERICA: IDEAL AND REALITY

The rise of the USA to world power

HERBERT NICHOLAS

'It's a complex fate, being an American.'

HENRY JAMES

American growth

rested largely on the movement of population from Europe. The tide of immigration, which by 1900 had pushed the 'frontier' to the Pacific, continued to flow until 1914. In that decade and a half the rate was about one million per year. This photograph, *Steerage* (opposite), taken in 1907, is one of Alfred Stieglitz's evocative studies of New York life, and reflects the influx of the 'New Immigration' from southern and eastern Europe. These im-

migrants were, for the most part, poor, but they were independent and ambitious, and the society they created was pluralist, tolerant and mobile. It valued liberty, self-sufficiency, free-enterprise and material success; it distrusted state interference and involvement with Europe. The First World War and the Depression shattered much of that philosophy, but it remained—and remains—an important element in American opinion. (1)

Two Americas existed side by side in the early years of this
century. One was the America of factories and great cities, already
acquiring a harsh poetry of its own. John Sloan's *Six O'Clock*
(top) shows New York in the evening rush-hour, the 'El'
blazing with lights above the busy street. The lower picture, *The
Holy Name Mission* by Reginald Marsh, takes us to a later and
less prosperous New York, during the Depression of 1931. (2, 3)

Rural America — hard-working, traditional, honest — was the inevitable contrast to the degenerate big city, a contrast that appears repeatedly in literature and fairly often in painting. J. S. Curry's *Kansas Baptism* endows a small-town Baptist ceremony with nostalgic simplicity. (4)

'Manchester Valley', Pennsylvania (below), by Joseph Pickett, looks at the rural scene with the innocent eye of the self-taught countryman. Genuinely 'primitive' artists were now acquiring a new value because they seemed to preserve qualities that eluded the more sophisticated. This landscape, with its fast-flowing river, its railway and handsome middle-class houses, was painted about 1916. (5)

The aggressive optimism of the early years was incarnated in Theodore Roosevelt (left). Devoted to outdoor life and sports, he brought an image of physical toughness into politics, whether he was fighting financial monopolies, mine owners, despoilers of the countryside or the policies of Woodrow Wilson. (6)

Jazz expressed another side of America's mood. Emotional, uninhibited, improvised in a syncopated style new to European ears, it was the voice of the poor and the blacks. (8)

Slapstick and splendour for the whole world were provided by Hollywood's film industry. Left: the Keystone Cops. Below: the immense Babylon scene from Griffith's *Intolerance*. (7, 10)

Woodrow Wilson succeeded Taft in 1912. His extensive schemes for reform in the fields of tariffs, trusts, banking and working conditions were overtaken by the First World War, in which, after first pledging to keep America neutral, he was forced to adopt an increasingly hostile attitude to Germany. At the Peace Conference of 1919 his 'Fourteen Points' had more influence in Europe than in his own country, which refused to ratify his settlement or to join his cherished League of Nations. (9)

Film could also comment on America past and present, as in the parade of Klansmen in Griffith's *Birth of a Nation* (above) or the gangster movies of stars like Cagney (below). (11, 12)

F. D. Roosevelt was elected in the dark days of the Depression on a programme — the 'New Deal' — of reform and revival (left: a cartoon of his inauguration in March 1933). During the ensuing 'Hundred Days' he succeeded in restoring financial confidence and in organizing large-scale schemes of public works such as the Norris Dam (below) in the Tennessee Valley. As the country's leader in World War II (above) he achieved the unprecedented success of re-election for third and fourth terms. (13, 14, 17)

Reality inevitably made fiction look pale. Above: an assembly of the Ku Klux Klan in 1915 to admit new candidates. Below: Al Capone, king of Chicago for a decade. (15, 16)

Houses were re-thought from new points of view, utilizing space, light and clear clean lines unhampered by tradition. Frank Lloyd Wright's Robie House (top) of 1909 was a pointer to the future. Philip Johnson's Leonhardt House, near New York, nearly fifty years later, takes the same ideas even further. (19, 20)

Architecture consolidated the brilliant achievements of the beginning of the century (see p. 210) in the towering skyscrapers which became such a typical expression of American confidence. The Woolworth Building, finished in 1913, combines technical virtuosity with a crowning flourish of Neo-Gothic. (18)

(see p. 210)

Engineering problems have generated new architectural forms. One of them, pioneered by Buckminster Fuller, is the geodesic dome. His USA Pavilion for the Montreal Exposition (above) of 1967 is made up of thousands of identical prefabricated parts (steel hexagons and triangles) which can if necessary be dismantled and re-erected. (22)

Airports are one of the few architectural types for which the 19th century offers no precedent. Eero Saarinen's TWA Building at Kennedy Airport, New York (below), uses huge interconnected concrete vaults in a vividly expressionist way to convey something of the excitement of air-travel. (21)

A triumph of American technology between the wars was the Golden Gate Bridge, San Francisco. It was completed in 1937, with a central span, held by cable suspension, of over three-quarters of a mile. The highway takes six lanes of traffic. (23)

Truman took over the presidency after Roosevelt died suddenly in 1945, and attended the Potsdam conference (left, with Attlee and Stalin) at which the shape of the post-war world was largely decided. It was a world in which America had to shoulder more burdens than she ever contemplated before 1941. (24)

Eisenhower's attractions to the voter were his patriotism, his transparent honesty and his independence from partisan politics. He succeeded in disentangling America from the Korean War, but his Secretary of State, John Foster Dulles, was less successful in his attempts to combine alliance policies with 'brinkmanship'. (25)

The colour question reached a crisis during the Eisenhower years, when the Supreme Court ruled that racial segregation in State schools was illegal. At Little Rock, Arkansas (above), troops had to be called in to enforce the decision. The Negro civil rights movement began by relying on peaceful rallies (addressed, above right, by Martin Luther King) and 'freedom rides' in buses (right), but later lapsed into violence. (26, 28, 29)

Senator Joe McCarthy crystallized a nation-wide anti-Communist neurosis. In this photograph (left) he covers the microphones in order to exchange confidences with his assistant investigator Roy Cohn. His campaign rested on suspicion, slander and fear and came to an end only when he challenged the army itself. (27)

Kennedy represented the hopes of a younger generation, though he barely had time to fulfil them. His stand over civil rights, his programme of social welfare, and his firm but not inflexible attitude towards Russia won him a devotion which created a Kennedy legend. (30)

Johnson's achievements tended to be credited to Kennedy, who had only initiated them, and his 'escalation' of the Vietnam War in 1964, popular at first, became by 1968 an insuperable obstacle to his re-election. (31)

A mood of protest swept the country in the mid-sixties, continuing into the seventies. Many causes were combined, often in a confused and confusing way — hostility to the war in Vietnam, the civil disabilities of coloured minorities, urban misgovernment and bad housing, student dissatisfaction with their universities or with the world in general. This demonstration takes place against the background of the United Nations Building. (32)

A language of protest evolved in the form of Pop, which owed its attack and its imagery not to 'art' as it had hitherto been understood but to the brash vulgarity of commerce, like these signs in Times Square. (33)

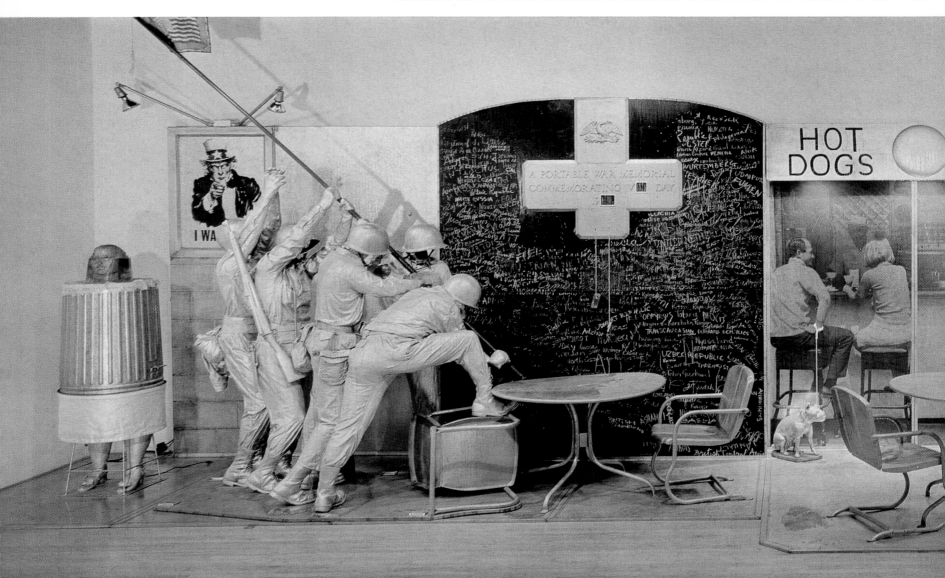

'My fascination with images', wrote Robert Rauschenberg, in a statement which may or may not be intended to be helpful, 'open 24 hrs is based on the complex interlocking of disparate visual facts heated pool that have no respect for grammar... It is extremely important that art be unjustifiable.' Above: Rauschenberg's *Axle*, 1964. (34)

'The Portable War Memorial' is easier to interpret and has been explained at length by the artist, Edward Kienholz. It takes the cliché images of patriotism — Kate Smith singing *God Bless America* (a gramophone is concealed in the dustbin), Uncle Sam, a famous wartime photograph of marines planting the flag on Iwo Jima (see p. 41)... and sets them in the context of a tawdry café with hot-dog stand and Coca-Cola machine (this actually works). His avowed purpose, however, is not cynical but idealistic. (35)

91

It was an American who in 1969 first stood on the surface of the moon, a crowning technological triumph made possible by vast expenditure and an immense organization of skills and expert knowledge. The contrast between the lavishly expensive 'space-race' with its dubious long-term benefits and the pressing needs of a still imperfect society was drawn with emphasis by the government's critics. But whatever its scientific usefulness, the moon-landing remained a source of national pride and a symbol, an event which gives the 20th century a unique place in the history of mankind. (36)

The rise of the USA to world power

HERBERT NICHOLAS

THE UNITED STATES in the 20th century was fortunate in escaping the cataclysms which afflicted most societies, young or old, Western or non-Western. It continued to live under its 18th-century constitution and 19th-century party system with little change in their forms and not much more in their functioning. It remained a pluralist society, of diverse ethnic origins, various (but not warring) faiths, individualistic, mobile and democratic, its economy marked by relative abundance and devotion to the precepts (and in some degree the practice) of 19th-century liberalism. By 1900 it had filled out its North American *lebensraum* and had acquired minor properties in the Pacific and the Far East; seventy years later these still represented the utmost limits of its territorial ambitions.

Yet the country which escaped revolutions and had only a small and brief tenure of empire did not escape involvement in the two world wars or the contagion of the world-wide economic depression that fell mid-way between them. Though its boundaries remained unchanged, its power and influence rose to heights unparalleled. The growth in its military, economic and industrial strength made it, by 1945, the greatest power in the world. A people, which as late as the 1930s was essentially isolationist, was, by 1945, accepting burdens and responsibilities across the face of the globe. And the revolution in communications, physical and psychological, which American skills had in large part promoted, intensified America's involvement with the outside world at the same time as it heightened, at every point, their awareness of each other. The pattern of life thus established combined to a remarkable degree uniformity and diversity. A nation of nations, the United States was also a culture of cultures. Yet indubitably, well before mid-century, it had created a style of its own as distinctive and independent as that of any of the national cultures of Europe, while in certain fields, particularly architecture, it led the world.

Two Americas

The United States of 1900 was a country which had only just been fully settled, where 'the frontier' still held its romantic significance as a term denoting the point where the white man's settlements left off and nature or the Indian began. And when free land was exhausted 'the frontier' as a symbol of American society, open and opportunistic, retained vitality. Even the depression of the twenties did not entirely shatter the dream. In 1900, for an America where sixty per cent of the population was still living on farms or in small towns, the ideal of a democracy of small property-owners still had meaning. The America of Mark Twain's Missouri or Sarah Orne Jewett's *Country of the Pointed Firs*, communities of Anglo-Saxon Protestant tradition and Victorian morality, retained an appearance of living in an age of innocence while at the same time being adventurous and dynamic.

Yet this America was already fading fast. The other America, of great cities and large-scale industry, was already the effective repository of power and control, already the greatest industrial power in the world. She made as much steel as Britain and Germany combined, was the leading producer of copper, was just about to overtake Britain's output of coal, extracted and consumed more oil and natural gas than the rest of the world put together and, of course, not only produced most of the world's cotton, but, by

1900 was manufacturing more cotton textiles than any other country except the United Kingdom. True, Henry Ford had yet to produce his Model T, but by 1919 there would be six million cars on the American roads. Meanwhile the railroad, and its newfangled adjunct, the electric streetcar, kept America moving.

To a disproportionate degree this urban and industrial America was peopled by the products of the New Immigration, the non-English-speaking, non-Protestant overplus of central, southern and eastern Europe. Between 1900 and 1920 over sixty-five per cent of the fourteen and a half million immigrants came from these regions, writing a chapter as much of European history as of American, providing their homelands sometimes with a safety valve sometimes with a new focal point for frustrated nationalism. In American towns they created a chequer-board of ethnic diversity, a proletariat divided by sharp barriers of speech, religion and tradition. They were a labour force, a social problem, a conglomerate of the uprooted, an infusion of the unpredictable. Though their 'alienism' shocked Henry James, revisiting his 'American scene' from Europe, though their numbers strained that potent agency of assimilation, the American school system, the surprising thing is how little overt resistance their presence evoked until the slump after World War I gave xenophobic prejudice an economic edge. Then came the closing of the gates and the immigrant quota loaded in favour of the older racial stocks.

The cities of this America were an exciting, crowded, unplanned but intermittently handsome setting for this blending of Old World and New. In Boston the romanticism of H. H. Richardson, in Chicago the steel frame pioneering of Dankmar Adler and Louis Sullivan and the radical innovations of Frank Lloyd Wright, in New York the Caracallan splendours of the Pennsylvania Station and the Gothic fantasy of the Woolworth Building—these were the architectural excitements of the New World townscape of the 1900s. And the life that surged beneath them was attracting a new kind of artistic response—the Hogarthian realism of John Sloan, the graphic vitality of George Bellows, the brilliant and sensitive camera eyes of Alfred Stieglitz and Edward Steichen. Naturalism dominated the literature of city life—the *exposé* literature of Frank Norris and Upton Sinclair, fictionalized newspaper reporting, and the deterministic tragedies of Stephen Crane and Theodore Dreiser.

p 86 (18)
p 82 (2)
p 81 (1)

The prewar presidencies: Roosevelt to Wilson

The two Americas, town and country, native and immigrant, found common cause, as the century opened, in an aggressive optimism, in part an adaptation of the Manifest Destiny of the 19th century, in part an infection from European imperialism. The easy triumphs of the Spanish-American War left America supreme in the Caribbean, expansive in the Pacific, impatient to link her two oceans by an American-controlled isthmian canal (realized in 1914) and oscillating repeatedly between a 'White man's burden' solidarity with Britain and a resurgence of rivalry with the ageing mother figure. In Asia she insisted on equality of treatment with other imperial powers, demanding an 'open door' in China, negotiating spheres of influence with Japan, conducting a 'civilizing mission' in the Philippines. In the Caribbean she insisted simply on hegemony, 'taking' Panama, colonizing Puerto Rico, establishing a protectorate over Cuba.

p 86
(6)
Theodore Roosevelt incarnated the mood—cowboy, historian, 'rough rider', big game hunter, nature-lover, politician, moralist, chauvinist and showman, serving his decade as a combination Ernest Hemingway, Billy Sunday, Baden-Powell, Kaiser Wilhelm and Rachel Carson. After the long reign of faceless *laissez-faire* presidents he reasserted America's sense of national and public duty—crudely, sometimes incoherently, as when he dogmatized about 'bad trusts' and 'good trusts', certainly jingoistically, waving the fleet at Japan and appointing himself policeman south of the Rio Grande, but also disinterestedly, in his campaign to end America's long rape of her natural heritage of woodland, wild life, mineral resources and scenic beauty. Politically reincarnated as the 'Bull Moose' candidate for a third term in 1912, he ended up as the champion of a 'New Nationalism' far more coherent than his own performance in office, which accepted bigness in business and government and sought to harness it to the pursuit of national efficiency, Hamiltonian means to Jeffersonian ends.

For all his popularity and dynamism Roosevelt had committed the unforgivable crime of 'bolting his party'. He failed at the polls, and the brand of progressivism to which the electorate gave their endorsement was the 'New Freedom' of Woodrow Wilson—Jeffersonian means to Jeffersonian ends, the revitalizing of competition, the policing of over-powerful interests, the preservation of peace and American neutrality. Wilson, like Roosevelt, was a

p 84
(9)
moralist and a muscular Christian, a reformer on top and a good bit of a conservative beneath, a firm believer in the potency and propriety of presidential leadership. But Wilson's moralism was blended of Calvin, Gladstone and Cobden. Where Roosevelt was a jingo, Wilson was an internationalist. Where Roosevelt had enthusiasm, Wilson had dedication, the single-mindedness not merely of a crusader but, if need be, of a martyr.

Initially it was on the domestic front that Wilson scored his triumphs—reducing the tariff, curbing the trusts, overhauling the nation's banking system, ameliorating the working conditions of farmers and labour. In his first four years he achieved something of the same order of social advances that marked the early years of the prewar Liberal governments in Britain. He had no such ambitious programme in foreign policy and his first term's mishandling of relations with Mexico, San Domingo and Haiti suggested that he had little to offer except crude Yanqui moralism and interventionism, clumsily conducted.

The coming of the European war, however, projected him on to quite another stage. He saw it initially not merely as a cataclysm to be avoided but also as an opportunity and obligation to project a positive pacifism by an America which could maintain a disinterested mediatory role. The vision crumbled before the realities of a conflict in which both sides violated Wilson's standards of international law. But, while the British command of the seas enabled them to respect most American susceptibilities, the German reliance on the U-boat led her to flout them. Although at one stage in the diplomatic argument Wilson seriously contemplated intervening against Britain, in the end the rigidity of German diplomacy, coupled with the stark revelations of the Zimmermann telegram, turned him irresistibly against the Central Powers. Already the Allies were using America as a supply base and a good deal of the American economy was geared to the Allied cause. But it was not these considerations, nor yet the strategic implications of a German victory, that weighed with Wilson. He took America to war on the highest idealistic motives, 'for democracy', for 'a concert of free peoples'. It was magnificent, but it was costly. It left the American people ignorant of the relations between ideals and reality, a prey, in the inevitable slump of peace, to every nostrum and demonology that quacks or fainthearts might propagate.

World involvement

The war itself was notable as the first example of a decisive American intervention in the affairs of Europe. But though for Americans it involved a great feat of organization—four million men under arms, over two million shipped to Europe, with comparable outpourings of munitions and supplies—the traces it left on a population who knew war only as something 'over there' were remarkably evanescent. Casualties were light, civilian hardships

comparatively few, the institutions of a wartime socialism—War Industries Boards, etc.—unoppressive and strictly 'for the duration'. Economically it left labour with a somewhat stronger base, and farmers in a flush of prosperity. In spite, or perhaps because, of its idealism it coarsened the nation's moral fibre; hyperpatriotism, xenophobia, enforced orthodoxy and more than usually bitter party rivalry were the order of the day. It converted Wilson's very limited intervention in Russia into a rallying cry for an all-out attack on 'Red Communism' at home. At Versailles Wilson fought from a less high-minded national base than he was willing to admit. This does not diminish the majesty of his effort or the value of his ideals. Without his Fourteen Points, the Versailles settlement would have been far worse than it was. Without his dedication, the League might never have got off the ground. But it helps to explain not only why Europe was unwilling to give him all he wanted but also why America was even less willing to be the beneficiary and underwriter of his designs for a world settlement. Not the least tragic of the Wilsonian ironies is that, in the end, his intrusion into the stream of history affected Europe, for better or worse, more than it affected the United States. Furthermore—a footnote irony as it were—when the Senate came to reject Wilson's peace, it was the transatlantic aftermath of Europe, the old homeland grudges of German-American, Irish-American and Italian-American which helped to sway the vote.

p 38
(22)

The decade that followed the peace and the Wilsonian collapse saw the dominance of all the elements of American life which the critics of majoritarianism and a business culture most deplored: the cult of 'availability' which propelled a small-town newspaper proprietor like Warren G. Harding and his 'Ohio gang' to the White House: the dessicated counting-house puritanism which enabled Calvin Coolidge to preside happily over a 'noble experiment' that made the American city safe for the gangster at the same time as the countryside was at the mercy of the Ku Klux Klan. But the middle class which deplored the scandals and the crime (and kept the bootleggers in business) was insensitive to the baneful consequences of fusing business and government when it took the form of the Fordney-McCumber Tariff of 1922 (which gave the president the power to alter rates of customs duty if necessary to protect American products against foreign competition) or the even worse Smoot-Hawley Tariff of 1930 (which raised import duties still higher), or the unabashed mercantilism of the Merchant Marine and Jones-White Acts which cosseted and cushioned an incurably ailing shipping industry. It was inevitable that such a mentality should view the problem of the Allied war debts in the Coolidge terms of 'They hired the money, didn't they?'. Thus the $10,000 million legacy of a wartime partnership persisted into the 1930s to poison opinion on both sides of the Atlantic and to block the creation of any sensible economic relationship between a creditor America and a debtor Europe.

p. 85
(16)
p. 85
(15)

There was indeed a paradox running through America's relations with Europe in the twenties. The USA, which had reneged on Versailles, adhered to a book-keeper's philosophy over war debts, raised sky-high tariffs while pumping out private loans, bolted the once open door upon the immigrant—this homeland of the dollar embodied all that was provincial, irresponsible, banal and insular, whether viewed from London, Paris or Geneva. But Americans themselves recoiled from this travesty of their national ideals, sometimes as expatriates fleeing to a less philistine Europe—Hemingway, Eliot, Pound, Getrude Stein—sometimes as critics and flagellants at home—Sinclair Lewis, Dos Passos, O'Neill. To European ears, however, it was the freshness, the power, the American-ness of these voices, by comparison with the tired muses of Europe, that gave them a kind of appeal which even their much read American forebears had lacked. Nor was this all. The America which was hounding the Negro through the Klan was also embracing and exporting his blues and his jazz. As Jonny in Křenek's *Jonny spielt auf* put it:

> *Da kommt die neue Welt*
> *übers Meer gefahren mit Glanz*
> *und erbt das alte Europa*
> *durch den Tanz.*

('Here's the new world, come across the sea in splendour, to take over old Europe with a dance.')

At the same time Hollywood was purveying celluloid dreams and entertainment not merely to all America but to all the world. By 1920 the cinema was America's fifth largest industry and whether it drew on American talent, like D. W. Griffith, or processed immigrant genius, like Chaplin or Garbo, equally it made its products into the mass folk art of the 20th century speaking a language, of pictures, which all could understand.

p 84
(11)
p 20

The diplomacy of the twenties reflected an uneasy combination of nativism, isolationism, guilty conscience, idealism and parsimony. The generally poor relations with Japan at the war's end combined with anxiety over the Anglo-Japanese alliance to force Hughes, Harding's Secretary of State, to reconsider American commitments in the Pacific. The result was the only successful disarmament conference of the inter-war years, from which came the Washington Naval Treaty of 1922 and the London Naval Treaty, extending it, of 1930. The core of the agreements was the establishment of Anglo-American parity, at the price of considerable scrapping of American naval construction, and acceptance by Japan of an inferior strength. The 5:5:3 ratio was made palatable by the Anglo-American willingness to halt fortifications between Singapore and Hawaii. At the same time the Anglo-Japanese treaty was allowed to lapse. Thus Japan got a free hand in the Far East, Anglo-American strategic amity was restored, the American taxpayer rejoiced and Manifest Destiny turned homeward. In 1927 Hughes's successor, Kellogg, made a characteristic contribution to the diplomacy of inflated idealism by promoting his Peace Pact renouncing 'recourse to war'. But the Senate that ratified this inexpensive gesture could not be induced to adhere to the World Court—nor, of course, could Republican Presidents contemplate recognition of revolutionary Russia.

The end of prosperity

The harshest critics of the twenties could hardly deny the reality of the economic progress which was the idol of the decade. The immediate postwar boom brought in its wake a proportionate slump, but by 1922 this deflation had run its course and from then until 1929 almost all economic graphs pursued an upward course. Two sets of figures demonstrate the change. National income, which in 1921 was $59·4 thousand million, by 1929 was $87·2. Real income per capita, which in 1921 was $522, by 1929 was $716. Business, no doubt, was the disproportionate beneficiary, but high wages spread the gain, if not universally, certainly widely. Labour's real wages rose 25% in the decade. This owed more to a Henry Ford-like managerial philosophy of high wages for increased productivity than it did to any ability of organized labour to hold industry to ransom. So much was clear from the decline in the strength of the trade unions, absolutely and relatively, from 12% of the labour force in 1919 to 7% in 1929. The concentration of business, smiled on by Republican administrations indifferent to anti-trust obligations, was not matched by any comparable movement on labour's side. Eight thousand mergers in business had as their counterpart a collapse of the steelworkers' union and a total failure to organize the great new automobile industry.

Prosperous America was urban America. In 1920 America had ceased to be predominantly a country of countrymen. By 1930 56% of its inhabitants were living in towns of over 2,500 population. Yet the substantial rural minority that persisted was having to make do on a declining share of the national product. The fat years of war were followed by the withdrawal in 1920 of the government's support price for wheat. Productivity remained high, but consumption at home, and still more abroad, fell catastrophically. Prices fell simultaneously. The value of farm products, which in 1919 had totalled $21·4 thousand million, by 1929 was down to $11·8. Small wonder that the only serious manifestation of political insurgency during the decade came out of the rural Middle and Far West—La Follette's Progressive candidacy in 1924, which carried only one state, Wisconsin, but ran second in eleven other states and polled 16·5% of the popular vote, the second largest third-party vote between the Civil War and the present day.

The collapse in 1929 of the impressive, if unevenly distributed, structure of American prosperity has in retrospect assumed the dimensions more of a myth or symbol than of an event in the annals of political economy. This is not altogether surprising. The onset of the Great Depression, severe as its direct economic consequences were, remains a watershed in American development primarily because of the shock it administered to the American psyche. Far more than in Europe the bolt fell out of a sky not merely clear but positively smiling, and against a set of euphoric expectations more tenaciously held and more widely diffused than in any other country in modern times. The Crash came after Coolidge, handing on the torch of Republican self-satisfaction to Hoover, had asserted that things were 'absolutely sound' and Hoover, accepting the succession, envisaged a 'future bright with hope'. Economists, industrialists and bankers indulged and stimulated similar illusions up to the very eve of 24 October, 1929, when the first earthquake shock was felt—and indeed at frequent intervals after, when successive tremors intensified the havoc. And the frenzy of stock-market speculation which finally broke in the crash was not the result of mere get-rich-quick contagion. It was promoted by Wall Street and what a subsequent generation identified as Madison Avenue—advertising and salesmanship, the twin handmaidens of prosperity.

p 320
(16–19)

p 320
(19)

Subsequently 'objective' weaknesses in the economy were identified as causal factors as well. The growth in productivity made possible by business efficiency and technological development had gone into profits rather than being passed on in wages or prices. A decline in government spending and a deflationary fiscal policy intensified the resulting imbalance. By 1929 five per cent of the population absorbed about a third of all personal income. The surpluses in the hands of the big corporations relieved them from the restraint of the banks while the rigidity induced by trustification caused rigidity in the whole structure of wages and prices. And the banks, custodians in theory of sound business practice were neither strong enough to sustain their independence nor honest enough to abstain themselves from playing the market with their depositors' funds.

Once the Crash broke, its progress into the Depression was headlong. Two sets of figures tell all that is needed:

p 321
(23)

Unemployment 1929	1·5 million	Bank Failures 1929	642
1930	5 "	1930	1,345
1931	9 "	1931	2,298
1932	13 "	1932	1,456

Hoover had no answers commensurate with the scale of the problem; he was held prisoner within his own scale of values. The root cause of America's ills lay not at home, but in Europe. Unemployment could not be relieved by federal action, because 'doles' were demoralizing. But the Reconstruction Finance Corporation could relieve necessitous corporations. No doubt it was virtuous to refuse the exservicemen their 'bonus' but it was politically suicidal to order General MacArthur to drive them, with bayonets, out of Washington.

No doubt any Democrat could have beaten any Republican candidate for the presidency in 1932. A party, a class, a philosophy were hopelessly discredited. But in nominating Franklin D. Roosevelt the Democrats were fusing, in a unique way, two streams of progressivism—the Republican tradition of his namesake and relation ('F.D.R.' was both a kinsman and nephew by marriage of 'T.R.') and their own Wilsonianism ('F.D.R.' had been Assistant Secretary of the Navy from 1912 to 1920). Toughened by his own triumph over a crippling attack of polio, seasoned by his experience in fighting the Depression as Governor of New York State, assisted and promoted by a singularly devoted personal following who succumbed to his charm and believed in his idealism, Roosevelt swept to victory without difficulty and faced the consequential avalanche of responsibility with fearlessness and gaiety.

p 85
(13, 14)

The preposterous constitutional provision which required four months to elapse between presidential election and inauguration left a 'lame duck' Hoover to watch helplessly while the disintegration of the nation's banking system proceeded apace, moderated, if at all, only by the emergency action of state governors. By inauguration day, 4 March, four-fifths of the states had suspended all banking operations. The New York Stock Exchange had closed its doors. In truth, 'the money changers had fled from their high seats in the temple'. Business America was on its knees.

At the time and subsequently there was a disposition in some quarters to see the America that Roosevelt confronted on 4 March as balanced on the edge of revolution. This might be so, for certainly the situation was desperate enough. Yet what in retrospect seems most striking is the quietness of the desperation, the stunned orderliness of the millions of Americans who saw their hopes, their security, their very livelihood vanish like a desert mirage. This was the most traumatic experience the country had suffered since the Civil War, yet hardly a shot was fired in anger or protest—save those from suicidal hands. What would have happened without a Roosevelt to calm and reassure, to insist that there was nothing to fear but fear itself is anyone's guess. What is certain is that the hour brought forth the man.

The New Deal

f 1   He offered leadership and action—not a programme, but an affirmation. He was a commander-in-chief, exploiting every resource of his presidential office and his personality—taking the nation into his confidence in 'fireside chats', forcing legislation through an emergency Congress with the warning that if they did not act he would. Within a fortnight he had the economy moving again; at the end of a hundred days Congress had re-written the socio-economic pages of the statute book. Relief had the first priority—Roosevelt did not fear a 'dole', but his aim, even at the cost of 'boondazzling' was wherever possible to provide work as well. Recovery came next—the Agricultural Adjustment Act (AAA), which guaranteed farm incomes and restricted overproduction, and the National Industrial Recovery Act (NIRA) which sought simultaneously, by a system of 'codes' for business, to increase production, spread employment, raise wages, reduce hours and encourage trade unionization. The banks were put under stricter Federal Reserve discipline and a Securities Act policed the stock market. Financially, inflation was deliberately pursued, even at the price of wrecking the World Economic Conference and abandoning all hope of international stabilization. But in 1934 a reversal of tariff policies was put under way by the passage of the first of a series of Reciprocal Trade Agreement Acts.

Inconsistency never bothered Roosevelt, and his New Deal contained elements of every reformer's nostrum. Its attitude to bankers and contempt for 'sound' money went back to populism. Its belief in organization and ignoring of anti-trust principles went back to T.R.'s New Nationalism—as did its frank insistence on national recovery before international economic co-operation. Its concern for the 'little man' and labour derived from the forms of Wilson's first term and the social experiments of progressive states like Wisconsin. Its low tariff objectives went back to the Cobdenite tradition of the New Freedom. But it supercharged this amalgam with a mystique of its own—best exemplified in its most visible

p 85   memorial, the TVA (Tennessee Valley Administration) with its
(17)   poetry of dams and power plants, rural electrification and Apalachian ballad-singing farmers, combining regional planning with

local participation, and provided with its own demonology by the relentless hostility of private electric power interests. Almost equally symbolic of the New Deal's willingness to ignore shibboleths and try everything were the Federal Theatre Project, and the Federal Writers Project for the unemployed members of these professions, while the Federal Art Project at one time seemed to have as its goal the covering of every square yard of United States Post Offices with the productions of out-of-work mural painters.

The headlong pace of the Hundred Days could not last. Nor did it need to. But though the country was on its feet again, unemployment persisted and business, convalescent, fought back against insurgent labour. So, in what is sometimes dubbed the Second New Deal, emphasis shifted. The Wagner Act (1935) threw comprehensive legal protection around unionism and stimulated the growth of the more militant and enterprising CIO (Committee for Industrial Organization) to break away from the American Federation of Labour, forcing total union membership up from three million in 1933 to eight million in 1939. In return labour recognized Roosevelt as their friend, notably under John L. Lewis, the melodramatic maestro of the United Mineworkers, who aligned labour decisively behind the Democratic Party in 1936—an alignment that, with minor deviations, has persisted since. Meanwhile the Social Security Act of 1935 brought the USA into line with other advanced industrial societies by establishing a national contributory system of pensions and unemployment insurance.

The novel role for government, and in particular for the federal government, implied in all this legislation inevitably raised constitutional questions which called for decision from the Supreme Court. The time-lag of checks and balances had resulted in a Court whose membership continued to reflect the mentality of a previous age—a 'horse and buggy age' in Roosevelt's opinion. As case after case came up, the Court, on a conservative reading of the Constitution and a liberal interpretation of its own role, struck down the NIRA (though not until the codes had exhausted their usefulness), the AAA and both federal and state control of hours and wages. Roosevelt, encouraged by his landslide re-election of 1936, gave battle. He both won and lost—won, because the Court underwent a change of heart and membership, sufficient to bring it into line with the goals of the New Deal; lost, because his indirect and devious tactics failed to convince Congress, indeed broke the solidity of the New Deal coalition, so that he lost both his Supreme Court 'packing' bill and his dominance over the party. The lost legislative territory was re-conquered (notably by a second AAA and a Fair Labour Standards Act) and deficit spending *à la* Keynes finally won through as New Deal orthodoxy. But the reforming *élan* was gone, unemployment climbed up again and conservative detestation of 'that man' became the conventional ethic of millions of middle-class Americans who, five years before, had felt a quickening of hope at the mention of his name.

To say this is not to deny the reality of a New Deal or Roosevelt 'revolution'. It was not a revolution of extremism; Huey Long, the neo-populist dictator of Louisiana, Dr Townsend with his share-the-wealth scheme of old-age pensions, Father Coughlin with his Catholic-Fascist 'Union for Social Justice', all petered out or suffered absorption into the Democratic stream. The American Communist Party, whatever its underground significance (generally exaggerated), remained a pathetic mockery of Marxist hopes and analysis. Even the socialism of Norman Thomas (its perennial presidential candidate) remained an essentially academic exercise. Politically and economically Roosevelt was a conservative-liberal who saved American capitalism by reforming it. But certain things were never the same again. America, for better or worse, was henceforward a welfare state. In future, in fact and symbol, Washington was the capital of the country. White House and Capitol Hill, not Wall Street or Pittsburgh or Detroit, would decide. And government henceforth would mean, in inescapable degree, experts, even intellectuals. The 'Brains Trust' was, in one form or another, there to stay. This went beyond politics and administration. After 1933 (perhaps after 1929) America was never to be so philistine, so Babbittish again.

Moreover the New Deal's positive achievements, standing out in stark contrast to the inertia of Britain, the decline of France,

Roosevelt's 'New Deal' of 1933, besides revitalizing the economy, was also seen as the first serious attempt at social welfare, bringing some of the fruits of prosperity to the poor. (1)

For the offices of the Johnson Wax Company at Racine, Wisconsin, Frank Lloyd Wright built a series of spacious rooms all based on combinations of circles supported on concrete columns like mushrooms. In this section, *1* is the entrance lobby; *2* the main offices; *3* the perimeter balcony; *4* the executive penthouse; *5* a lecture room; and *6* the parking area. (*2*)

the headlong rush into barbarism of Germany, produced a new creative American nationalism in place of the centuries' old dependence, in part or whole, on Europe. In literature it was the heyday of William Faulkner, E. E. Cummings, Robert Frost and Eugene O'Neill, in painting of Georgia O'Keefe, Reginald Marsh, Charley Sheeler, Ben Shahn and Edward Hopper—diverse talents, but united in drawing their inspiration and their style from the observation of America. The abstract mobiles of Alexander Calder affirmed no less emphatically a New World inspiration. In architecture the thirties were the decade of Rockefeller Center, the first and still the best skyscraper group, and at the other extreme of inventiveness the Johnson Wax buildings of Frank Lloyd Wright. Even so, it was not extravagant to claim that the fullest statement of the American aesthetic was to be found in structures that were not architecture at all—the great suspension bridges of the thirties—the George Washington in New York and the Golden Gate in San Francisco.

European, and especially British, liberals, sick with appeasement in the face of Fascism, saw in the Roosevelt of the thirties a clear-eyed enemy of the dictators, restrained from more positive action only by the difficulty of dragging an isolationist American public along the path which duty and interest behoved them to tread. A careful and cooler study of Roosevelt's policy during the prewar years suggests rather that, for all his clear vision, he shared in large measure those conflicting and paralysing sentiments which animated most Americans—of sympathy for the democracies and dread of involvement in another world war. He acquiesced in the illusions which induced Congress to think it could legislate American neutrality; he acquiesced, as Hoover had done, in Japanese aggression on the Asiatic mainland; he pursued a 'good neighbour' policy in Latin America and 'multilateralized' the Monroe Doctrine; and he welcomed, as most of his fellow-countrymen did, the appeasing settlement of Munich. But when war came, in September 1939, he made no pretence of impartiality; he secured revision of the Neutrality Act to permit the Allies to buy supplies on 'cash and carry' terms, and, in 1940 when the cash ran low, he devised 'Lend-Lease' as a device to continue 'all aid short of war' without arousing the odious association of war debts. His shrewd strategic sense, even more than his sympathies, enabled him to educate a 'continentalist' America into an awareness of their stake in British survival. The step-by-step tactics of the destroyers-bases deal, Lend-Lease, the occupation of Greenland, the extension of aid to Russia, the 'shoot on sight' order and the convoying of allied merchantmen seem in retrospect to have their logical conclusion in war. But it is doubtful whether Roosevelt had any such grand design: when war came, it struck from the East in the form of the Japanese raid on Pearl Harbor.

World War II: 'the arsenal of victory'

Though spared invasion or even aerial bombardment, America felt the impact of World War II in every corner of her national life. She fought still under the disadvantage, for purposes of public morale, of it being a war 'over there', but she fought as a united people, whose last vestiges of isolationism had been blown away in the smoke of Pearl Harbor. From the beginning the USA assumed the leadership of the wartime coalition. Over sixteen million men and women were in uniform and American forces saw service on every battle front except the USSR's. In the appalling calculus of war Americans came off lightly compared not merely with the Russians but with their other principal allies, thanks largely to the excellence of their medical services and the intensive mechanization of their forces. The weight of American material, produced both for the USA and her allies ('the arsenal of victory'), was stupendous—almost 300,000 aircraft, over 85,000 tanks, more than eight million tons of naval shipping and fifty-five million tons of merchant marine, to list only the most obvious items. This was made possible by the mobilization of the country's under-employed economic resources, including the seven million men and women whom all the peacetime efforts of the New Deal had still left unemployed. The gross national product rose from $91 thousand million in 1939 to $166 in 1945. As a result the country was able to enjoy butter as well as guns. Workers' incomes doubled and great movements of labour brought the poor, whites and Negroes alike, from traditionally deprived areas like the South, into a new affluence in centres like Detroit or Los Angeles. Despite a good deal of administrative chaos and in-fighting in Washington, valid priorities for production and consumption were generally established, not only for the USA itself, but also with her principal allies, conspicuously Great Britain. The Combined Production and Resources Board represented as unprecedented a pooling of sovereignties in the economic field as the Combined Chiefs of Staff did in the strategic. But perhaps the most remarkable demonstration of the pooling of Allied efforts was the 'Manhattan Project' which drew on the electric power resources of the TVA and the scientific skills of every country, including America's refugees from Fascism, to fashion the atom bomb.

For the strategy of the war, reliance was placed at the summit, on meetings of the leaders, always of Roosevelt and Churchill in a remarkable partnership, but sometimes expanded, as at Teheran and Yalta, to include Stalin. Below them, but not including the Russians, were the combined Chiefs of Staff, an essentially Anglo-American instrument, which, despite the strong claims on national pride of the Pacific front, loyally adhered to the Roosevelt-Churchill 'Atlantic First' strategy. Two Americans in particular, George C. Marshall as Chairman of the Joint Chiefs of Staff and Dwight D. Eisenhower as Supreme Allied Commander in Europe, personified in a remarkable degree this fusion of national loyalties in a common cause. Down to the invasion of France, British and American strategies in Europe were remarkably well harmonized in a common recognition of Hitler as the main enemy and a common desire to postpone the assault on 'fortress Europe' until overwhelming strength would guarantee minimal Allied losses. Subsequently a diversion of emphasis became increasingly apparent, with Churchill concerned to anticipate the threat of a victorious Russia by advancing the Allied presence as far as possible into Central Europe and Roosevelt willing to accept Russian undertakings at something more like their face value, in the conviction that in direct personal diplomacy he could bring Stalin into the comity of nations. Yalta represented the high point of this Rooseveltian tactic and illusion.

In the Pacific theatre American forces held an overwhelming predominance and although a formal structure of combined command existed there and in South-East Asia this really was America's war, and Admiral King, the United States naval commander-in-chief, and General MacArthur, Supreme Allied Commander in the Pacific, saw that it remained so. In a remarkable series of amphibian operations, the American forces beat back the Japanese from island to island across the Pacific to their homeland

p 82
(3)

f 2

p 87
(23)

p 40
(34)

p 42
(44)

p 41
(43)

97

and were preparing for the final and, as it was anticipated, costly assault when the invention of the atomic bomb made possible the holocausts of Hiroshima and Nagasaki and the Japanese surrender. Roosevelt, dead within two months of Yalta, saw·neither in Europe nor in Japan the victory which his genius had done so much to win. After twelve years in office, an unprecedented tenure, and the enjoyment of extraordinary power both in peace and war, he left behind him an America triumphant over both her economic and her military foes, transformed from a posture of dispirited insularity into a position of invincible world supremacy.

The transformation was, of course, too sudden to be immediately absorbed by the American people themselves. Their first reaction, as after World War I, was to bring the boys back home, end all wartime controls and obligations, from rationing to Lend-Lease, and return to business as usual. At first sight it might have appeared as if Roosevelt's successor, Harry Truman, the ex-haberdasher from Missouri, was type-cast for such a national mood. But he quickly revealed qualities of courage and forthrightness which America and the world grew to respect. Undaunted by Russian spinosity, he followed through on Roosevelt's neo-Wilsonian dream of a United Nations Organization, brought into being at San Francisco and ratified by the United States Senate by eighty-nine votes to two. And although the war, following on eight years of New Deal reforms, had left the business-minded middle class with a distaste for 'Washington' and especially for Democrats, it had also created a new government-oriented American 'establishment' recruited from both parties and running the occupational gamut from Wall Street to the universities, which recognized America's new world role and accepted its implications. Thus there was never any serious question but that an American occupation force would stay in Germany and Japan while the new security structure of the United Nations was being erected.

Cold war

Unfortunately it became swiftly apparent, as Yalta had indicated, that the consensus necessary for this structure did not exist. The Russian exploitation of the revolutionary situation which they found in postwar Europe was, in American eyes, an attempt to subvert all war and postwar agreements and to foist Communism on nations that the Allies had fought to liberate. The crunch came initially in Germany in the form of a failure to agree on occupation policies. Soon it extended to the whole Russian treatment of her East European satellites. But it only made its full impact felt in the USA with the collapse of the British underpinning of Greece and Turkey in March 1947. From this moment followed two years of intensive re-vitalization and re-orientation of American foreign policy and military attitudes—the transition from the postwar to the full acceptance of the cold war. It involved acceptance for an indefinite period of American leadership of and responsibility for the free world and a recognition of the USSR as an opponent as menacing as Hitler, though lacking his maniacal fury, and capable, in George Kennan's phrase, of being 'contained' by a passive but militarily alert alliance of the West.

Since the Communist threat lay as much in subversion as aggression, a restoration of Europe's shattered economies was recognized as an absolute priority. General Marshall, recalled to service in the novel capacity of Secretary of State, lent his name to the grand design of the Marshall Plan which, though ostensibly pan-European in its offer of economic assistance, assumed, in a sense, its true character as a defence against Communism when Russia refused for herself and denied to her satellites all participation in its operation. Peculiarly American in its large-minded deployment of the nation's vast economic resources and in its emphasis on the full co-operation of its beneficiaries in its execution, the Marshall Plan undoubtedly marked a turning point in European history. By comparison, the establishment of NATO, far-reaching though it was, was only the provision, in essence, of an American guarantee to a Europe which had already taken the basic decision in favour of collective resistance. For the United States, however, NATO had a significance which Marshall Aid lacked. For the first time in peace, the United States was accepting a commitment to the defence of European boundaries, was entering for an indefinite future upon one of those entangling alliances

p 88 (24)
p 322 (24)
p 42 (45)

which the Founding Fathers had always deplored. Yet the Senate accepted it by a vote of eighty-two to thirteen.

With this commitment to the long-haul strategy of the cold war went an unprecedented expansion and reinforcement, in peace, of the American military establishment. In 1947 the National Security Act overhauled the machinery of government to provide, through a National Security Council, a body hitherto unknown in Washington, a kind of equivalent to the Defence Committee of the British Cabinet, and also to set up, in the form of the Central Intelligence Agency (CIA), an organization which combined the collection of intelligence with the conduct of undercover para-military operations. In the huge funds at its disposal and its virtual freedom from public scrutiny the CIA constituted a new, doubtfully healthy and certainly undemocratic element in American government. The unification of the armed services under a single Secretary of Defence was a logical corollary of changing armaments and tactics, though it took longer to achieve than to enact. A return to conscription was required to maintain a level of forces adequate to America's new needs; though it was operated on a selective basis with wide and generous provision for exemption, its establishment in 1948 for an indefinite period marked a new (and to earlier generations unthinkable) phase in American evolution. Finally the development of new military technologies, most dramatically but by no means exceptionally exemplified in nuclear weapons, brought into a close relationship with and frequent dependence upon the military a vast range of industrial operations and a very large segment of the scientific community. To a degree unmatched in any other democratic country the USA found itself creating an interfusion of the military and civilian sectors of its life in what was still ostensibly peacetime. Significantly it was an ex-soldier President, Eisenhower, who felt obliged, on laying down his office in 1961, to warn the nation against 'the acquisition of unwarrantable influence . . . by the military-industrial complex' in an America which was spending more on military security than the net income of all its business concerns. So far, in a generation, had the country travelled from the America whose 'business was business'.

In Europe in the 1940s American strength and diplomacy, in company with Britain and the free parts of the Continent, succeeded in holding the line. In the Far East things went differently. Though a triumphant MacArthur maintained a dramatic proconsulship in an occupied Japan devoted to the renunciation of war and emulation of American technology and democracy, on the mainland things fell apart. Chiang Kai-shek revealed himself to be, not, as Roosevelt and American public opinion had wishfully believed, a great national leader, but an autocrat who, despite repeated American urgings, would neither introduce the reforms indispensable to his and his people's salvation nor, despite American urgings, compromise with the Communists. His collapse and flight to Formosa created in the USA a degree of shock and indignation incomprehensible unless the convergence of three disparate factors is recognized—China's long-standing role as a recipient of American philanthropic and missionary benevolence, America's long-cherished illusions about the status of the Chiang Kai-sheks, and finally the value to the Republican party of an issue with which to belabour a Democratic administration 'soft on Communism'. Even so, it is not out of the question that the new Chinese regime might have been recognized had not the Korean War broken out within six months to etch deeper the image of Mao as a ruthless aggressor.

The promptness of Truman's reaction to the challenge of aggression in Korea revealed afresh his resources of decisiveness and courage, while the mobilization of United Nations endorsement for what was *de facto* an American military operation with token allied support demonstrated the diplomatic skill of his Secretary of State, Dean Acheson. In the field General MacArthur displayed no lack of dash or determination; what was lacking was moderation in the hour of victory. By pressing into North Korean territory he provoked a rebuff which cost him dear (his dismissal at the hands of the President) and his troops even dearer, as they had to beat a retreat in sub-zero weather south of the thirty-eighth parallel. Truman resisted the dual pressures to withdraw completely and resort to atomic weapons, but the inconclusive prolongation of the war was a sore trial to American nerves and patience. To suffer over 50,000 dead and 100,000 wounded in a war which could not be won was a new and frustrating experience which bit deeply into the national consciousness.

The Truman-Eisenhower years

The good fortune that gave America a Democratic and liberal President in the year after World War II prevented the full flowering of the reaction which was perhaps a natural consequence of the strains of war and the new insecurities of peace. In most of his attempts to provide a 'Fair Deal' sequel to the New Deal, Truman was frustrated by a House of Representatives which went Republican in 1946 and a Senate which went the same way in 1948, but he was able to hold the line on full employment and social welfare and to eliminate, for Negroes, the hitherto legal elements of segregation in government service and in the armed forces. Congress, alarmed at trade union militancy, passed the Taft-Hartley Act over his veto in 1947, but although (or because) it outlawed the closed shop and imposed a cooling-off period in major strikes, the Act inflicted no lasting damage on the trade union movement. What Truman, despite his own notable re-election victory in 1948, could not control was the paranoiac obsession in Congress and elsewhere with the menace of 'godless Communism' inside the USA. The USA, of course, continued to be unique among Western industrial states in its failure to sustain a socialist party of any size, but its Communist Party was minute to the point of absurdity. It was no doubt true that a Communist underground had existed in the New Deal and had had some success in infiltrating the administration before and during the war, but the extent and intensity of the public hysteria was quite out of proportion to the threat. The Hiss case was the American Dreyfus affair, with the difference that the accused's conviction gave the victory to the opposite party. It also provided the launching pad for a young Richard Nixon's rise to national office. The sustained harrying of Communist Party officials under the wartime Smith Act, prohibiting conspiracies to overthrow the government by force, was upheld by the Supreme Court, while the McCarran Internal Security Act virtually excluded Party members and fellow-travellers from the United States. However all this took place within the provisions and to some degree the safeguards of the law. The campaign of vilification, of 'guilt by association',
p 88 (27) conducted by Senator Joseph McCarthy, with the acquiescence of a supine legislature, ran its course almost unhampered by legal or political resistance until 1954. It permanently damaged segments of the administration, in particular the State Department, debased the language of public debate, silenced free expression in large areas of American life and damaged the nation's reputation for liberty and fair dealing around the globe.

It was the need to re-affirm the values of liberal America against this kind of nativist reaction that gave Adlai Stevenson's nomination as Democratic candidate in 1952 an epochal quality. It was the success of his eloquence and integrity in this task that redeemed his posture in the electoral context against the overpoweringly
p 88 (25) popular figure of 'Ike', Dwight D. Eisenhower. But it was also true that after twenty years of tenure of the White House the Democratic Party had discharged its immediate historical function and was due, if not overdue, to make way for its opponents. Certainly the Republicans, soured and impatient after long years in exile, could not have returned to office under a more healing and less partisan father figure than the ex-soldier who, at SHAEF and SHAPE, had personified American large-heartedness and good-feeling. To restore the Republican party to a sense of responsibility for the nation, to enable them, in office, to accustom themselves to a government of welfare at home and involvement abroad—this was the task, and on the whole the achievement, of the Eisenhower years.

It began, appropriately enough, in the Pacific, the Republican ocean. Elected in part on a pledge to bring peace in Korea, Eisenhower did eventually, by mid-July, bring the peace talks to the point of armistice, accepting (and imposing) the prewar thirty-eighth parallel frontier and committing American arms and aid for an indefinite period to maintain the independence of the Republic of South Korea. 'Containment' was thus established as a

'Don't be afraid—I can always pull you back!'—John Foster Dulles' foreign policy as seen by a cartoonist in January 1956. (3)

substitute for victory in East as well as West. Unfortunately Eisenhower's Secretary of State, John Foster Dulles, obsessed in equal degree by legalism and anti-Communism, found difficulty in accommodating the language of policy to the realities which, in the main, he recognized in common with his presidential master. His vocabulary of crusade with its talk of 'liberating captive peoples', 'instant and massive retaliation', 'rolling back' Communism, and 'unleashing' Chiang Kai-shek, was better calculated to confuse and alarm America's allies than to intimidate her enemies. For some time America seemed to hover on the edge of hostilities with mainland China on the shores of the China Sea, but the net result was more of a containment of Chiang in Formosa than any real action against Peking. Again, on the French collapse in Indo-China, Dulles conveyed a vivid impression of eagerness to commit American forces, restrained only by British refusal to co-operate; the net result was estrangement from Eden, American abstention from the Geneva Settlements of 1954 and the impatient construction of a South East Asia Treaty Organization (SEATO), a paper mis-application of NATO, with few or no roots in the area, dependent entirely on America for unity and strength. Japan, now independent but uncertain of its destiny and status, was preserved as a bastion of American security in the Far East by the Treaty of Mutual Co-operation and Security of 1960 which permitted American tenure of military bases but only narrowly escaped shipwreck on the shoals of Japanese neutralist sentiment.

In Europe similarly Dulles's language outran his behaviour; neither the riots in East Germany nor the rising in Hungary provoked him into the error of living up to his words. In Europe the attempt to bulldoze the European Defence Community (EDC) into existence by talk of 'agonizing reappraisal' of America's European commitment failed altogether, but the Eisenhower charm at least exploited the thaw which followed the death of Stalin to produce a temporary accord at the 'summit' meeting at Geneva in 1955. Unfortunately the *imbroglio* of Suez revealed how the structure of America's alliance system had become weakened at its heart, with Britain and France, frustrated by Dullesian legalisms and ambiguities, taking independent and covert action in the Middle East, thereby exposing themselves to defeat and rebuke at the hands of the United States and the United Nations. For America the consequence was to accelerate the obligation she had long evaded, of implicating herself in the security of this divided area, by the enunciation of an Eisenhower 'Doctrine' promising aid to

Middle East countries threatened by Communism. France drifted into a Gaullist *je m'en fiche*-ism, necessitating in consequence a re-emphasis on Anglo-American solidarity, reflected in the British-American missile agreement (a riposte to the Soviet *Sputnik*), and creating in its turn fresh problems for the NATO alliance. Tension with the USSR persisted despite Eisenhower's assiduous cultivation of personal relations with the Soviet leaders; it was a sad, ironic commentary on his efforts that the Paris 'summit' conference of 1960 should go on the rocks ostensibly on the grounds of the Soviet interception of the CIA's U.2 spy plane. Even so, and despite the failure of so many initiatives, it could be fairly said that when Eisenhower retired in 1961 he left his party and his country better set on the road to peaceful co-existence than he had found them.

At home the Eisenhower years largely reconciled the Republicans to the gains and practices of the New Deal—high employment, social security, the budget as an instrument of economic control, 'big' government. But the most notable reform came about by legal, not political, action, when the Supreme Court in 1954 reversed a fifty-eight-year-old rule which permitted segregation of blacks and whites in state schools. In demolishing this bastion of white supremacy in the South the Court ushered in a social revolution, provoking 'last ditch' white resistance in states such as Arkansas and Mississippi, arousing Northern liberal 'invasion' of the South through the various civil rights organizations, and stimulating Negro militancy on all the fronts, from education to the ballot box, on which their legitimate rights had so long been denied. In the fifties and sixties this long-delayed self-assertion by a minority now twenty million strong became a dominating feature of the American scene. Their northern migration, away from poverty or persecution, continued until they formed huge Negro 'ghettoes' (significant term) in every large city, over-crowded and barren of every kind of communal facility, breeding grounds for crime and social disintegration. A philosophy of non-violence which fitted the country-based protest movement of Southern blacks, largely collapsed in the urban North even before the assassination of its most notable exponent, the Reverend Martin Luther King, in 1968. Militantly anti-integrationist creeds and styles found favour in the North as migration and peaceful agitation brought little or no improvement in the Negroes' condition. Black power replaced the civil rights movement as the dominating influence, and physical force acquired a new respectability. In 1967 nearly 150 cities experienced civil disorders; in Detroit forty people died, in Newark twenty-six. In 1968 the assassination of Martin Luther King provoked riots in 125 cities; in Washington, by this time a predominantly Negro city, the flames of destruction were within sight of the White House.

Linked, of course, to the Negro protest were the vast socio-economic changes of postwar America. While, for the middle class, affluence and mobility encouraged a positive cult of the family and an exodus to suburbia and exurbia beyond, the centre of the American city deteriorated, its decline accelerated by the motor car and the freeway. Agriculture occupied an ever smaller proportion of the population, 5·5% in 1967—a third fewer than in 1914 out of a population twice as large. Urbanization accelerated. By 1960 under 30% of Americans lived in communities of 2,500 or less. In agriculture and in industry fewer hands produced more. Between 1950 and 1960 the gross national product rose from $284 thousand million to $500 while the population rose from 151 million to 179 million. This affluence, the wonder of the world, was very widely diffused. Even so, poverty, often in acute forms, persisted to a degree that most Americans failed to realize. In the 1960s there were some 30 million or so classifiable poor, of whom about half lived in acute deprivation. In part this was due to a reluctance to allow the new affluence to find a public outlet; too much went into consumer satisfactions, too little into raising the often appallingly low level of common services and public life.

p 88
(26, 28)

p 88
(29)

Kennedy and after

The accession of John F. Kennedy to the presidency in 1960 was hailed as a new dawn largely because his 'New Frontier' programme called for a vigorous attack on all these problems, led by a wealth of talent recruited, in 'Brains Trust' fashion, from every walk of American life. But the dawn turned into common day with Congress's refusal to co-operate and it took his successor, Lyndon Johnson, a throw-back in many ways to the earlier reform tradition of the New Deal, to secure the passage of a civil rights bill, of an 'anti-poverty' programme and above all perhaps of 'Medicare', a limited scheme of medical insurance for the elderly—all features of what he called his 'Great Society' programme. The Johnson achievement was remarkable, not least as a demonstration of what could still be accomplished by a politician of genius within the limitations of the traditional American politics of consensus. But it too ground to a halt, with the swift collapse of that consensus in the America of the sixties.

Although the assassination of Kennedy in Dallas in 1963 was directly the work of an isolated psychopath, yet, in a larger sense it was expressive of the disruptive forces which seemed at times to be tearing America apart—the forces caught in the American paintings of the period, the abstractionism of a Pollock or the 'pop' art which satirized the affluent society. In such an America it was not only Negroes who were militant. There was a white 'backlash', represented in a quasi-respectable form by Senator Goldwater who won the Republican presidential nomination in 1964. His trouncing at the hands of Johnson forced extremist elements in 1968 to gather around the independent Southern racist, Governor Wallace of Alabama, who, although a poor third to Nixon and Humphrey, yet secured 13·5 per cent of the vote. But in some ways the most remarkable manifestation of domestic dissent occurred on college campuses, notably Berkeley and Columbia, where youthful alienation from the America which was at the peak of its power and prosperity showed itself in every form, from the 'beat' writings of Jack Kerouac to sit-ins, riots and the burning of draft cards.

Perhaps there was justice in the contention of violent youth that theirs was only a reflection of the legalized violence of the American state. In 1961 even the liberal Kennedy allowed the CIA to launch their filibustering 'Bay of Pigs' operation against Cuba. In 1965 Johnson intervened in San Domingo with 24,000 troops to frustrate a left-wing revolt. In 1962 the Soviet attempt to use Cuba as a missile base was only frustrated, after an 'eyeball to eyeball' confrontation which kept the whole world holding its breath, by Kennedy's realism, restraint and resolution. Unfortunately in the great, continuous, unresolved confrontation of the sixties—Vietnam—comparable qualities were not displayed. American involvement began in Indo-China almost insensibly under Eisenhower and continued under Kennedy but was still of modest dimensions until Johnson in 1964, on the basis of an incident in the Gulf of Tonkin, secured congressional authority to 'resist aggression'. In 1965 the bombing of North Vietnam commenced and United States combat units were involved to a total of 180,000 men. In 1966 bombing was intensified and troop totals rose to 380,000. 1967 saw anti-war protests and demonstrations sweep the country as the American commitment reached a total of 486,000 men. Small wonder that in 1968 the wave broke. After American casualties surpassed the figure reached in Korea and Senator Eugene McCarthy's anti-war candidature showed obvious signs of success, Johnson threw in his hand, announcing simultaneously that he would not stand again and that he would seek peace talks with Hanoi. The talks led nowhere and McCarthy lost the Democratic nomination to Hubert Humphrey, in a year made doubly bitter by the assassination of Robert Kennedy, President Kennedy's brother. But the heart had gone out of the war. 1969, the year which saw America put a man on the moon, also saw her begin her withdrawals from South Vietnam. Had the world's leader over-reached herself in the hour of her greatest technological triumph?

p 89
(30)

p 89
(31)

p 90
(33)

V LATIN AMERICA
IN SEARCH OF ITS FUTURE

The struggle for a new identity

ALISTAIR HENNESSY

'The great civilizations began around the tropics,
and the final civilizations will return
to the tropics.'

JOSE VASCONCELOS

The unending struggle

between freedom and oppression has given Latin American history a unity which is perhaps more apparent than real. As an ideological dogma it passed easily into the pictorial language of the post-Revolutionary mural painters. This huge fresco, for instance, by Juan O'Gorman links together foreign conquest, religious persecution and capitalist exploitation. Always it is the people of Mexico who suffer, but who eventually triumph. At the top stretches the land of the Aztecs, with its volcanoes and lake city, its warrior culture and human sacrifice. In the centre: the arrival of Cortes,

leading to slavery. At the bottom, in spite of the 'Utopian' efforts of the church, the fight for liberty is already producing its martyrs.

The mural is over forty-five feet high, and the building in which it is painted, originally a church, is now a municipal library. After the suffocation of Soviet art under Stalin, Mexican mural painting has been almost the only serious style to emerge in the 20th century that is both wholly committed politically and genuinely popular. History is presented in terms of extremes—light against darkness, idealism against greed, virtue against vice. (1)

Foreign investment before 1914 opened up the industrial potential of Latin America, but deprived her of most of the profits. Early railways (right) were built to serve the needs of exporters rather than those of the continent itself. (3)

Rubber: in 1910 nine-tenths of the world's rubber came from South America. The industry had been developed by British and North American companies, and it was their shareholders who benefited. (2)

The Panama Canal (right), built with United States interests in mind, was nevertheless a powerful stimulus to Latin American trade. (4)

City growth is an indication of economic progress. Manaus, in the central Amazon basin, rose on the booming rubber industry. When that industry collapsed after 1918 in the face of competition from East Asia, the town lost its reason to exist. Its great opera house (left) and public squares survive as the ghosts of former splendour. (5)

Population has flocked to the burgeoning capitals, but their development has followed a pre-industrial pattern. Most have a modernized centre, then 19th-century suburbs where the old wealthier classes lived, and then an outer ring of apallingly primitive slums. In Rio de Janeiro (right) the three strata can be seen side by side. In La Paz (far right), the mountain capital of Bolivia, the slums spread outwards like an overgrown peasant village. (6, 13)

On the land life was, and is, hard and slow to change. Above: Bolivian women sorting tin-ore by hand in 1954 and (below) a farm-labourer in Chile in 1938. (7, 8)

The new wealth of Latin America comes from her mineral and agricultural resources: **steel** (top left), processed at the huge works of Volta Redonda, Brazil; **grain** (top right) exported from the silos of Buenos Aires; **oil** (lower left) from the rich oilfields of Venezuela; and **copper** (lower right) at El Salvador, Chile. (9–12)

Away from the towns, where life becomes increasingly 'international modern', Latin America displays an astonishing diversity of cultures and traditions. Candido Portinari's *Morro* (above) shows a Brazilian village affected by proximity to the town, the high-rise blocks creeping steadily nearer. (14)

Religions, or superstitions, often traceable to pre-Christian origins, retain their power over wide areas. Left: a Voodoo ceremony in Haiti. Right: Peruvian Indians in the old Inca village of Ollantaytambo carry their images in procession. (15, 17)

Rural Honduras (above) is portrayed with naive charm by J. A. Velasquez. With its neat fields and Baroque church, this might easily be the countryside of Spain or Portugal. (16)

'Peasant mother' (right) by Siqueiros, amid the desert cacti of Mexico, seems to look back to the Aztec past. (18)

Six years of civil war had to pass before Mexico could establish a stable democratic republic. President Porfirio Díaz (top left) had ruled the country for thirty-four years. It was an efficient rule, based on organized corruption. In this satirical portrait by Siqueiros he sits with his feet on the Constitution, surrounded by capitalists and society women.

By 1911 the opposition was too strong to be suppressed. Popular unrest in the country produced the guerrilla leaders Emiliano Zapata in the south and Pancho Villa in the north. In this photograph (above) they are seen together—Zapata, with his long moustache, in the centre and Villa, in uniform, on the right. Right: peasant soldiers, the 'Zapatista', as seen by the mural painter Orozco.

The man who claimed to lead the new movement was Francisco Madero (left, entering Mexico City), who replaced Díaz in 1911. (19–22)

'Madero has unleashed a tiger' said Díaz; 'let us see whether he can tame it.' Madero, in fact, fell from power and was murdered in 1913. For four years Villa, Zapata, Huerta and Carranza fought it out. Carranza emerged as the strong man, and the constitution established in 1917 is still the basis of the Mexican Republic.

The huge murals of Rivera, Orozco and Siqueiros have hammered home the lessons of the war. Right: Marx instructs the workers and points forward to the promised land, while the corrupt powers of society, the army and the church gather their ill-gotten wealth. Below: Carranza, idealized by Camarena into a mighty ruler; he was in fact a fragile and unimpressive figure. Below right: a photograph of irregular troops defending a position. (23–25)

The old order, with its connotations of European superiority and the imperial past, is reflected in the public buildings erected before the First World War. The three photographs on the left show (top) the Parliament Building of Montevideo, Uruguay, the Palace of Fine Arts, Mexico City, and the Chamber of Deputies of Santiago, Chile. (26–28)

 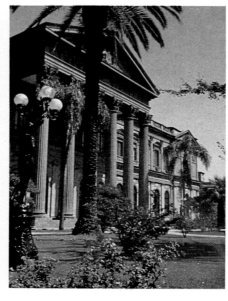

New forms in modern architecture embody the spirit of postwar Latin America. Boldest of all urban experiments has been the foundation of Brasilia, six hundred miles in the interior of Brazil. Planned by Lúcio Costa in 1959, it was begun the following year and is still under construction. This view (below) shows the arcade of the Supreme Court in the foreground, with behind it the buildings of the Senate and House of Representatives, all designed by Oscar Niemeyer. (29)

Like an opening flower, Niemeyer's Cathedral of Brasilia (above) proclaims its faith in modern technology as well as in the Church (South America is the most staunchly Catholic of all the continents). The ribs are of concrete, the walls of glass. Brasilia's superb situation, by a huge artificial lake, and the spacious monumentality of its planning, make it a symbol of confidence in the future, but many of the problems of present-day living remain unsolved. Beyond the public buildings and apartments of government officials, a vast shanty-town of slums has grown up to house the poorer classes for whom little provision was made in the original scheme. (30)

The prestige architecture of the Simon Bolivar Centre, Caracas (right), serves as living propaganda for the regime, as well as meeting the practical needs of the Venezuelan capital. Like the Rockefeller Center, New York, it consists of civic buildings linked by imaginative planning. (31)

Conservative oligarchies have managed to retain power despite revolutions in many Latin American countries. Above: the Colombian artist Fernando Botero's satirical group *The Presidential Family*, which includes a general and a bishop as well-fed as the president.

Right: three presidents whose populist regimes have provided strong leadership at the expense of liberal democracy: Estenssoro of Bolivia (top), kept in office partly by American aid; Perón of Argentina (centre), who with his film-star wife Eva resisted all attempts to depose him for over nine years; and Vargas of Brazil (bottom), 'the Father of the People', who held power from 1930 until his suicide in 1954. (32, 34–36)

Three races meet in a street of La Paz — European, Negro and, in the foreground, native Indian. (33)

Left-wing opposition culminated in the Cuban Revolution. Fidel Castro (right) has emerged as an independent Communist with genuine support from the people and a genuine programme of social reform. (38)

Castro speaks both for the young intelligentsia and for the traditionally pious sector of the Cuban population for whose benefit this montage was produced (right). His rule, dating from December 1958 when his guerrillas overthrew the dictator Batista, began as a protest against corruption. Its effect has been massive nationalization and close economic links with Russia. (39)

Cuba as the liberator of the rest of Latin America was the prophecy of José Martí (above), from whom Castro and his followers have derived much of their inspiration. In the romantic figure of Che Guevara that prophecy almost achieved incarnation. (37)

Guevara's features make the backcloth against which Venezuelan students flourish banners bearing the image of the other hero of the left, Ho Chi Minh. Below: the slogan 'Workers and peasants with Cuba' painted on a national monument in Colombia. (40, 41)

'The end of the old order' by Orozco sums up the mood of revolution in Latin America. In the background the old world crashes in ruins, unlamented. Worker and peasant give it one backward glance before setting forward to build the future. (42)

The struggle for a new identity

ALISTAIR HENNESSY

In 1900 the Uruguayan writer José Enrique Rodó published *Ariel* which was to become one of the most influential books in 20th-century Latin America, reprinted in over thirty editions. In it a philosopher exhorts his pupils—the uncorrupted younger generation in whom lies the hope of the future—to follow in the paths of spiritual idealism and to resist the temptations of materialism. Although it was not Rodó's intention to write an anti-American tract this is how many of his readers interpreted it, seeing in the antithesis between the spirituality of Ariel and the materialism of Caliban the opposition between South and North America.

The 19th century had closed with a striking illustration of North American power by the defeat of Spain in the 'glorious little war' and the final dissolution of the Spanish Empire. Much though the demise of Spanish power might be welcomed in South America, United States intervention was widely regarded as the opening of a new phase of expansionism—a view confirmed in 1903 when a United States protectorate was established over Panama. Geographical proximity underlined the immediacy of the United States threat and criticism of Europe was always inhibited by the preference of the Latin American élite for European aristocracy rather than North American democracy, but there was a deeper, more nagging doubt. North American successes were the realization of the American dream, and however brash the new Manifest Destiny, its outspoken confidence highlighted the gulf between aspiration and achievement in its southern neighbours.

The utopianism of the early Spanish Empire had been revived in secularized form by Bolivar during the Emancipation Movement at the beginning of the 19th century. But his vision of a federated union of republics which would realize the yearnings for El Dorado and an earthly paradise and which would embody the messianic hopes of the New World collapsed in civil war and political anarchy. Once independent, the new states developed nationalist attitudes, destroying hopes and frustrating collective endeavour even if in the tenuous search for their separate national identities, complicated by overlapping loyalties—to the *patria chica* or the region, to the nation state and to the concept of Latin America—the hope that unity could be achieved once again has never been entirely abandoned.

The weakness of Latin America, divided into twenty independent republics, was Europe's and the United States' opportunity. In no other part of the world before 1914 was the concept of 'informal empire' more applicable than to Latin America. The 'new imperialism' of European powers from the 1870s onwards intensified the process as their investments rose in all sectors of the Latin American economy, plantations, public utilities, gas and electricity, urban transport, cattle companies, meat packing houses, and mines. Economies based on the *hacienda*, and limited to local markets, now became enmeshed in the international economy. Thus the periodization of Latin American history no longer follows its own inner logic as in the early years of independence but increasingly reflects that of Europe. The First World War, the Great Depression and the Second World War are nodal points of 20th-century Latin America. Imitators rather than innovators, neither the separate countries of Latin America nor the continent as a whole have impinged on world consciousness in the 20th century until the Cuban Revolution galvanized world interest.

p 110
(27–29)

The land and the people

A widely shared culture, a common colonial legacy, similar religious experience and language gives to Latin America a deceptive impression of homogeneity which can obscure the wide differences between countries—in population and racial composition, in illiteracy rates, in educational standards, in stages of economic development and even within the same country, as in the Brazilian contrast between São Paulo's ultra-modernism and primitive jungle Indians.

p 106–7
(14–18)

At the opening of the 20th century the majority of the population lived in the countryside, either in small towns or on isolated *haciendas*. These were usually self-sufficient landed estates owned by absentee landowners, managed by bailiffs and worked by debt-peonage labour. Surplus production was mostly sold or bartered in local markets, but in the early decades of the 20th century the opening of the Panama Canal and the Great War stimulated demand to which *haciendas* responded by expanding at the expense of neighbouring Indian lands. Throughout Andean America and in Mexico innumerable revolts were evidence of increasing rural distress, but only in three countries have peasant grievances passed from the stage of rural revolt to full-scale revolution—in Mexico after 1910, Bolivia after 1952 and Cuba after 1959.

p 104 (4)

A sparse population, difficulties of communication and geographical intractability determined the settlement pattern in which the centres of finance, government and commerce were either ports or near to them—Rio, São Paulo, Montevideo, Buenos Aires, Santiago de Chile, Lima, Guayaquil, Caracas. Communications radiated from these centres; few railways penetrated the interior. The return on railway capital was insufficient to attract Latin American investors, but foreigners were prepared to take the high risks involved—as they were with oil prospecting later. Without foreign capital and skills there would be even fewer railways than there are today, but these lines were constructed with the profits and utility of the foreign companies in mind, not the needs of the country. Thus the lines fanning out from Buenos Aires were built to convey cattle and wheat as quickly as possible to Buenos Aires or the huge grain port of Rosario rather than to link together isolated settlements on the pampas. In Mexico most of the 12,000 miles of track built by the US companies (in association with mining interests) in the railway-building boom at the beginning of the century had been constructed with a view to carrying crude ore to smelters in the United States. In Chile alone (where railways were internally financed) did railways play a constructive role in nation building.

p 104 (3)

Shipping companies were also foreign owned as only 10% of trade was carried on between Latin American countries. Similarly air transport was pioneered, and owned in the 1920s, by Germans and Americans.

Immigration was another important factor in the economic expansion accompanying political stability. Nevertheless it never provided the self-generating momentum of an expanding frontier as it had in the United States. Brazil has only received 5 million immigrants in comparison with the United States' 40 million. Current arguments over population control carry little conviction with many Latin American intellectuals so long as the heartland of the continent remains virtually empty.

Before the 1870s immigration had either been involuntary, as in the case of imported African slaves (slavery was abolished in most Latin American countries at the time of independence but in Cuba not until 1886, and in Brazil in 1888), or by indentured Chinese labour, imported to work on Cuban sugar plantations or in the guano islands off Peru. Early schemes to attract voluntary immigrants had had little success. Political instability and the pre-empting of land by large landowners deterred potential immigrants and many who did come before the 1870s found reality very different from the alluring promises of colonizing agents. But as the cattle and wheat revolution in Argentina gathered momentum a flood of immigrants from southern Europe turned it into a largely immigrant country. By 1910, nearly 75% of the adult population of Buenos Aires had been born in Europe.

In Brazil, slavery deterred immigrants in large numbers until after its abolition, although the expansion of coffee cultivation in São Paulo from the 1870s began the demand for free labour. By the 1920s the single state of São Paulo produced nearly 75% of the world's coffee based on cheap migrant labour from Europe. The energy of the Italians combined with the drive of the Paulistas turned São Paulo into the Chicago of the southern hemisphere, a vast megalopolis with one of the fastest growth rates of any city in the world.

Immigrants tended to concentrate in the metropolitan centres. Unlike the United States, there was no cheap or free land to lure them into the interior. In some areas, however, notably Brazil's most southern state, Rio Grande do Sul, or in the upriver states of Santa Fé and Corrientes in Argentina, or in southern Chile on the edge of sodden rain forests, pioneer communities were established, often employing European mixed-farming techniques, but these were exceptional in a continent of large semi-feudal landholdings. Only highly motivated groups went further afield, like the Welsh in Patagonia on the Mennonites in the Chaco desert. Nor was there much migration into the interior by Latin Americans themselves.

p 110–11 (29, 30)
Recent years have seen an expansion of settlement from the Andean region into the jungle of the Amazonian basin, and it is in Brazil—where, in 1960, the new capital of Brasilia was built 500 miles inland to attract settlers into the interior—that there is a recognizable frontier movement comparable to that of the 19th-century United States and which is now posing, in an acute form, the problem of how to save primitive Indians from extinction. In the late 19th century drought in the north east of Brazil had drawn thousands into the Amazon basin to become tappers in the rubber boom of the pre-1914 years. But this was short-lived and, although at its height in 1910 some 90% of the world's rubber came from Amazonia, the industry was killed by Far Eastern competition. The

p 104 (5)
huge opera house at Manaus, visited at the time by the greatest singers from Europe, stands as a mute memorial to one of the most spectacular booms of modern history but one which brought little lasting benefit to a region which is still the largest undeveloped and unsettled area in the world.

Not only immigrants from abroad, but increasingly migrants from the interior, escaping from rural poverty, limited educational and economic opportunities and inequitable tenancies, helped to expand the metropolitan centres. This is one of the most striking phenomena of contemporary Latin America. By mid-century 34% of Argentina lived in Greater Buenos Aires, 32% of Uruguay lived in Montevideo, 26% of Chile in Santiago and 20% of Mexico in Mexico City which has grown from a modest 150,000 in 1910 to become the second city of the American continent with over 8 millions to-day.

Cities

Cities are the visible mark of Latin America's progress. By 1910 Buenos Aires was the largest city south of the Equator, the Paris of the southern hemisphere. It had a cosmopolitan air with its Jewish minority, anglicized suburbs and English-style public schools which could offer the mores and veneer of English upper-class culture but without the intellectual discipline of the academically prestigious French *lycées*—an explanation perhaps why Paris rather than London still remains the European intellectual capital of Latin America.

Few Latin American cities, can be strictly described as industrial

cities. Buenos Aires with its miles of wharves, *abattoirs* and meat packing houses spawned a militant urban working class which often took to the streets, competing with Barcelona in the violence of its strikes (anarchist influence was strong among Spanish immigrants), but, in general, urban labour is mostly employed in public services. Industrial complexes like São Paulo or Mexico City have been unable to absorb the masses of migrants flooding in from the countryside—even less so as industry becomes capital rather than labour-intensive. Latin American cities, therefore, present many of the features of the pre-industrial city with enormously expanded service sectors, thinly disguised unemployment and huge slum accretions, the *barriadas* of Lima, *callampas* of Santiago, *villas miserias* of Buenos Aires, the *favelas* of Rio, different names for similar phenomena which produce the sub-cultures of marginal slum-dwellers—the culture of poverty as popularized by Oscar Lewis in *The Children of Sánchez* and Buñuel's film *Los Olvidados*.

p 104–5 (6, 13)

To the outsider it is puzzling why these cities with their sharp extremes of poverty and wealth, have not exploded in revolutionary violence. There have been sporadic outbursts of which the most striking case was the *bogotazo* in 1948, when the centre of Bogotá was burnt down, but apart from the Buenos Aires of Perón no Latin American city can be called revolutionary. The most militant industrial workers tend to be miners, such as the Trotskyist tin miners in Bolivia or the Communist copper miners in Chile where concentration in isolated communities has created a sense of class solidarity. In the cities, the politics of the slums tend to be of the boss type—a carry-over perhaps of residual admiration for the *patrón* of rural society; an atavistic throw back to the uncomplicated allegiances of rural culture. It is the impermeability of marginal societies to impersonal political appeals as well as the density of their social structure which makes it difficult for the middle-class radical politician to win their confidence. The efforts of rural immigrants are concentrated on earning a precarious living and trying to slot themselves into existing society rather than attempting to overthrow it.

p 105 (12)

Rulers and ruled

The burgeoning of cities, which has now given Latin America one of the world's highest urbanization rates, has increased the size and importance of the middle classes. But the significance of the 'rising middle class' is difficult to determine. It does not bear many similarities to the bourgeoisie of Northern Europe or North America, generating its own ethos and secure in its economic and political power—except, that is, for Mexico where one of the visible achievements of the Revolution since 1910 has been to create an identifiable middle class familiar to Western industrial societies. Elsewhere the middle classes are often distinguished by psychic insecurity and economic uncertainty. In conditions of galloping inflation (such as few Latin American countries have escaped) private capital may be exported and land and real estate become favoured forms of investment. During the Cuban Revolution the Urban Reform Law crippled the *rentier* middle class and was an important factor in accelerating the exodus of this group.

Retarded industrialization and financial and technical control by foreign firms have been a brake on the emergence of an independent middle class. The surprisingly large proportion of industries in the hands of immigrants gives an insight into the behaviour patterns of creoles whose ambitions tend to be focussed on the professions and government service. The strategic importance of universities in the political culture of Latin America can be related to a middle-class concern with job opportunities. With the exception of Cuba, educational systems are still geared to the humanities: law and medicine remain the prestige professions. Students, drawn overwhelmingly from the middle classes, are taught to manipulate concepts and abstract arguments which are given higher priority than disciplines involving mastery over nature. From the 1890s the increasing professionalization of the military provided another opening for the sons of the middle class who valued its prestige as well as the security it offered when alternative openings were restricted.

Over-expanded bureaucracies also provided a haven for unenterprising and insecure middle classes, as happened with the expansion of state agencies in the depressed 1930s. But these

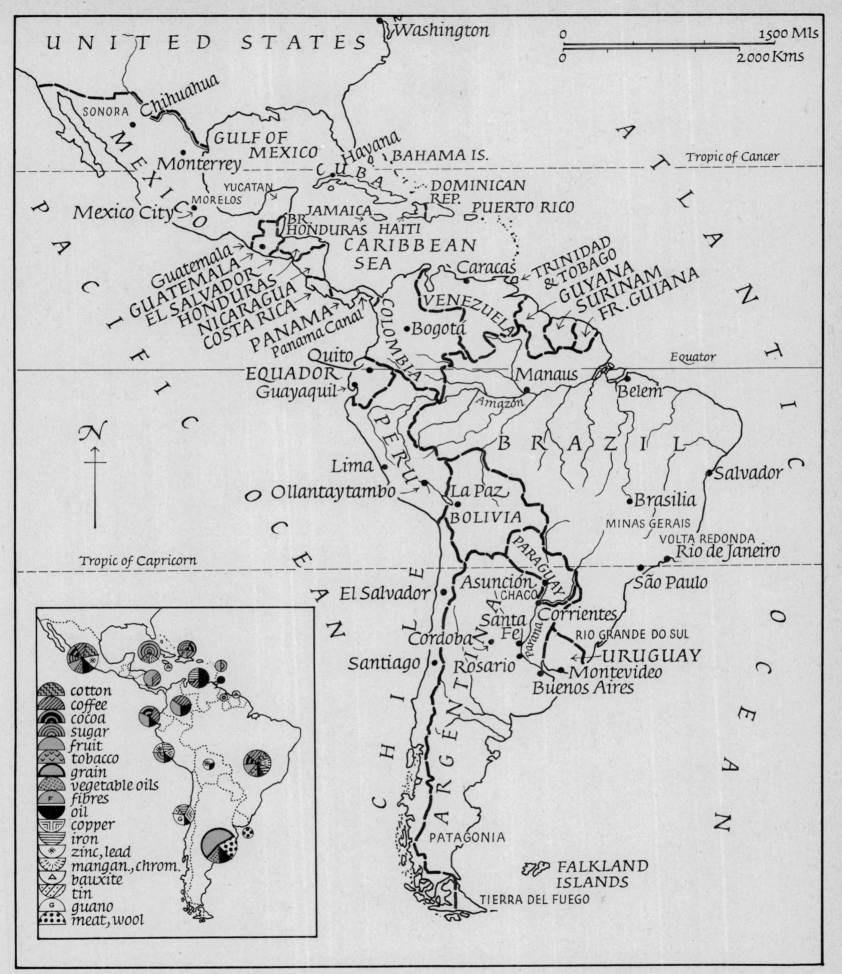

Latin America. The inset map shows the principal natural resources. (1)

bureaucracies tend to operate with personal rather than impersonal norms. Advancement often depends on personal contacts, operating either through the extended family system or the *compadre* system of god-parenthood. The popularity of family businesses as against corporations reflects a dislike of impersonalism which is one of the distinctive traits of Latin American culture.

Politically, this is expressed in *personalismo*—the loyalty given to the person of a political leader, rather than to a set of abstract principles. Thus the importance of the individual politician's personality and of the skills with which he can build up a following. The cultivation of father-figure imagery—as in Getúlio Vargas's self-description as 'O Pai do Povo' (The Father of the People) in Brazil—humanizes the considerable powers vested in Latin American presidents and serves also perhaps as a psychological substitute, in a continent where a high illegitimacy rate has produced many fatherless families.

p 112
(36)

117

The question of social class in relation to political power leads to a parallel but more fundamental question, that of race. The visible prosperity of Argentina, Chile, and Uruguay which under the great reformer Batlle y Ordóñez (president from 1903 to 1907, and again from 1911 to 1915) became a welfare state, was widely attributed in the opening decades of the century to their being overwhelmingly European in racial origin. Such also was the explanation for the prosperity of São Paulo and Rio Grande do Sul with their large immigrant populations whereas the predominantly negro north east or mestizo north were (and still are) depressed areas. The north east, centre of sugar and cotton from the 16th century, had been in decline since the discovery of gold and diamonds in Minas Gerais in the 18th century moved the economic centre of gravity south and inland. But the social problems of the new Brazilian republic after 1889 were attributed to the legacies of slavery and to degeneracy caused by miscegenation rather than to the economic consequences of declining sectors in the economy or to the environment of the drought-ridden back-lands. Gobineau's views on race had been formulated partly under the influence of a stay in Rio, and pseudo-scientific racial theories and social darwinism conditioned Brazilian intellectuals to think that their country's future was blighted. This was heightened by the classic account by Euclides da Cunha in *Rebellion in the Backlands* (*Os Sertões*) of the suppression by the army in 1897 of the rising of the cowboys under their messianic leader, Antonio the Counsellor. A ten-month campaign to crush poverty-stricken mestizos was not an auspicious start to the new republic.

Similarly, the backwardness of the Andean countries was attributed to the deadweight of their predominantly Indian population. The vogue for racialist interpretation tallied with Spencerian and Comtian Positivism which was the current 'development ideology' of the pre-1914 era, and nowhere was it held more enthusiastically than in the Mexico of Porfirio Díaz between 1876 and 1910. Although of Indian extraction himself, Díaz's government was impeccably creole. European ideas, fashions and experts were extolled whilst indigenous art and culture were deprecated. Indian labour fuelled an industrial and commercial revolution from which the creole élite and foreign investors benefited. Ironically, the period before Díaz—the Reforma associated with Juárez the great Indian president—had undermined the social and economic basis of Indian livelihood. Indian communal lands as well as Church lands were considered a brake on progress, but the subsequent sale of land only swelled the large estates and increased the holdings of foreigners who, by 1910, had come to own between one-fifth and one-seventh of all land in

p 108 (19)

Mexico. Indians deprived of their commons became a landless proletariat as the sugar plantations of Morelos and the henequen plantations of Yucatán expanded in response to increasing demand.

The Mexican revolution

The Mexican Revolution was the dominant event of the first half of the century although the repercussions have not been so widespread internationally as those of the Cuban Revolution later. The Revolution erupted as a consequence of tensions within a developing economy in which the Mexican middle class had not been given a big enough share of either political or economic power, and in which many traditional *haciendas* were unable to compete with the new commercially oriented estates of the Porfirian élite and those foreign landowners who owned a fifth of Mexico's land in 1910. Francisco Madero the Revolution's first leader was a diminutive, soft spoken spiritualist whose land-owning family from north Mexico had made a fortune in distilling brandy—an odd gentle figure to usher in one of the most destructive revolutions of modern times. He was an old-fashioned liberal influenced by the moralistic politics then in vogue across the border who believed that political reform would be sufficient to regenerate Mexican society. Failing to appreciate the peasants' land-hunger he forfeited Zapata's support when he rejected the use of armed action against landowners. Madero's assassination in 1913 revived his waning popularity, giving him in death a greatness which had eluded him in life. His death was the signal for a bitter conflict between regional *caudillos* to fill the power vacuum—Obregón and Calles from Sonora in the north-west, Villa from Chihuahua in the north and Carranza from Coahuila in the north too—all states which were open to influences from across the border and where there was greater social mobility than in the tightly controlled central region round the capital. For four years campaigns ebbed and flowed along the railway lines; Mexico City was entered and re-entered by rival armies. Finally, in 1917, a constitution was framed in which are expressed the principles of the Revolution (but as a programme for future implementation not as a codification of existing fact): agrarianism; Indianism; socialism; nationalism; anti-clericalism and presidential non-re-election.

An unusual feature in Mexico is the way in which the social myth of the Revolution found pictorial rather than literary expression. Seeking inspiration in the neglected Indian past and drawing on an extraordinarily rich tradition of popular art, a school of muralists, the most famous of whom are Rivera, Orozco and Siqueiros produced a revolutionary art without parallel anywhere. Painters rather than writers constitued the revolutionary vanguard.

p 108 (22) f2

p 108 (20)

p 108 (20)

p 107 (18) p 108-9 (23, 24) p 114 (42)

Francisco Madero and his wife entering Mexico City on his election to the presidency in November 1911—an engraving by J. G. Posada. (2)

The Twenties: a new identity

The Great War broke the spell which European culture had cast over Latin America since independence. After the holocaust many intellectuals felt that Europe had forfeited its right to be leader of world civilization. They were still responsive to the latest avant-garde expressions of poetry and art but now there was a conscious search for other sources of inspiration. This was expressed in three forms of cultural nationalism.

Firstly, the Mexican Revolution stimulated *indigenista* thought, especially in the Andean countries with their large Indian population and visible remains of pre-Spanish civilizations. Indigenous traditions could provide a new cultural identity and an escape from spiritual subjection to Europe. In Peru Haya de la Torre and, more profoundly, Carlos Mariátegui, and in Bolivia Franz Tamayo regarded the Indians as the foundation of nationality. In Mexico, José Vasconcelos argued that Latin America could make a unique contribution to world culture through its fusion of races. In Brazil the writings of Gilberto Freyre mark a swing away from the pessimism of the early years of the century to an acceptance of the positive value of miscegenation. The publication of his *Masters and Slaves* in 1933 recast Brazil's self-image by enabling Brazilians to come to terms with their African heritage. In Cuba, the work of Fernando Ortiz explored the African elements in Cuba's culture although his significance was not fully appreciated until after the revolution.

Secondly, there was a re-evaluation of the Spanish legacy and a recognition of the cultural unity of the Hispanic world, stimulated by the great renaissance of poetry, literature and philosophy in Spain with the writings of the 'Generation of 1898'. No Spanish thinker since Independence had exerted a comparable influence to Ortega y Gasset (and through him of German philosophy) and Unamuno. Until the Civil War, Spain was to remain the centre of the Spanish publishing world, where the reputations of Latin American writers were made and lost.

Thirdly, the Bolivarian ideal of continental unity was revived as the need to find a means of combining against cultural and economic imperialism became more urgent with the United States' intervention in the Caribbean and Central America—in Haiti between 1915 and 1934, in the Dominican Republic between 1916 and 1924, in Nicaragua between 1912 and 1933, in Panama with its protectorate of 1903 as well as the annexation of Puerto Rico and the inhibiting Platt Amendment to the Cuban Constitution of 1901 which permitted the Americans to intervene if public order was threatened.

The continental ideal was most forcibly expressed by the University Reform Movement which began in the Argentinian University of Cordoba in 1918. Originally an attack on the old, colonial style university, unrelated to the needs of modern society, it reaffirmed Bolivarian ideals, envisaging rejuvenated universities as the means by which corrupt and stagnant societies could be transformed by students acting as the shock troops of revolutionary change. The movement struck a responsive chord among students elsewhere and within a decade it had spread to every Spanish American country. In Cuba Venezuela and Peru students spearheaded attacks on the dictatorships of the 1920s.

The explicit anti-imperialism of the Reform Movement attracted the attention of the Communists, although the pretensions of bourgeois students to be a revolutionary élite clashed with Marxist orthodoxy. Communist ideas and the influence of the Russian Revolution, largely filtered through the French Left, had only a limited impact as Communism seemed yet another derivative ideology. But it is not surprising that Communism should have made its deepest impact in Cuba, partly because the weakness of the indigenous traditions had left a cultural vacuum, but also because it was the first country to be exposed to the full blast of US economic power as banks took over bankrupted sugar concerns in the postwar recession. Even outside Cuba it is still noticeable that immigrants unresponsive to *indigenista* traditions, were prominent among founder members of Communist parties as they had been among socialist parties earlier.

The 1920s were the seed-bed of modern nationalist ideas in Latin America, but there was little political innovation apart from the student movement and some expressions of military reformism; in

Another Posada engraving showing a peasant hanged by Government troops during the Mexican Revolution. (3)

Brazil, where a rising of radical young army officers in 1924 failed, and in Chile, where under Colonel Carlos Ibáñez, who became president in 1927, soldiers ironically provided the impetus to social change in the country which had the longest record of civilian government. But the rise of student and military politics was a symptom of the failure of the middle classes to prevent the old ruling groups from re-establishing the prewar relationships with foreign powers.

In the 1920s, as in the 1820s, Latin America seemed an El Dorado for the foreign investor. 10% was a normal return on private capital. Oil corporations could get a 50% return and mining corporations 20% or more. Two thousand million dollars of private investment and three thousand million dollars of bonds floated in European and US money markets indicate the extent of Latin America's dependence on foreign investment. In 1929 prosperity evaporated as markets collapsed and the flow of foreign money dried up. Within a year Latin American's exports had declined by 40%. Imports were cut to a third. In most countries moratoria were declared on public debts and, as demand for primary products declined, there was massive unemployment; two-thirds of the miners in Chile, the most hard hit country, were thrown out of work and as bureaucracies were slashed, white collar unemployment became a major social and political problem.

p 104 (2)

With the loss of foreign markets, industrialization and self-sufficiency was the only alternative. Hence in the larger countries—Mexico, Brazil, Argentina, Colombia, Chile—the 1930s saw a policy of enforced industrialization, in which the state took the initiative, much as in some European industrial development in the 19th century. Even before the stimulus of the Second World War, manufacturing output had doubled, so that in 1939 (unlike 1914) there was an infrastructure on which import-substitution industry could be based, with a strong emphasis on heavy industry and capital goods. The Second World War thus speeded up an industrial process into which Latin America had initially been forced by the Great Depression.

The thirties: the Depression and its consequences

Although the political and social framework within which these economic developments took place varied from country to country, economic insecurity and political instability in the early 1930s provided opportunities for the military to intervene everywhere except Mexico.

Not even Argentina was exempt, the most highly developed of all Latin American countries and one of the richest in the world by the 1920s, thus confounding those observers who believed that military intervention was a consequence of a retarded economy coupled with the absence of a large middle class.

In Argentina the middle class was large and, through the Radicals, had been in power since 1916, but in this time it had been fattening in the pastures of patronage. A small-minded party, much in the tradition of their European (and Chilean) namesakes, they had failed to restructure the political system—even the much vaunted university reform was unable to create institutions consonant with the needs of Argentinian society. The Radicals failed too to inaugurate social policies, and—even more serious—they used the armed forces for political purposes. They could scarcely complain therefore when their own lack of moral fibre and economic incompetence brought army intervention in the wake of the Great Crash of 1929. Unlike the Brazilian radical officers of the early 1920s or Colonel Ibáñez in Chile, however, the Argentinian army was a front for the old oligarchy and until 1943 the conservative landed interests remained in power. Some industrialization occurred, but to extreme nationalists the Roca-Runciman treaty in 1933 (by which Britain took Argentinian agricultural and cattle products in return for British manufactured goods and coal) sacrificed the industrial needs of the country to the landed interest. It was within the army that extreme nationalism found its most forceful expression in secret societies where officers such as Colonel Perón, influenced by Italian Fascism, argued for industrial self-sufficiency as the prelude to establishing Argentinian hegemony in South America.

p 112 (35)

In contrast to Argentina where the response to economic crisis was to restore the land-owning oligarchy to power, in Brazil a military coup in 1930 ushered in the fifteen years' populist dictatorship of Getúlio Vargas. The 'Old Republic' of 1889–1930 had been dominated by the two states of São Paulo and Minas Gerais. But the economic crisis had bankrupted their policies, which depended on coffee exports and a valorization scheme by which coffee planters were protected by government subsidies against price fluctuations. Vargas, who came from the rich cattle country of Rio Grande do Sul, represented not only regions hitherto excluded politically but also rising industrial and professional groups as well as the urban proletariat of the growing industrial centres.

p 112 (37)

In the smaller, more backward countries, such as those of Central America, economic crises strengthened the hold of the traditional landowners. Elsewhere, where there was a growing middle class and a nascent working class, traditional ruling groups were forced to accept alliances with them. But common to most of Latin America was the weakness and inability of any group to make fundamental changes in the social structure. This was as true of the conservative reaction in Argentina as of the populist dictatorships of Vargas in Brazil or Batista in Cuba, or of the Popular Front in Chile.

Mexico alone in the 1930s is an exception, as Cárdenas (1934–40) revitalized the Revolution by redistributing more land to peasants than all his predecessors combined. There could be no doubt of Cárdenas' sympathies when he identified Mexico's revolution with the policies of the Spanish Republic: Mexico was the only country to support the Republican government throughout the war and into the years of exile. It has also benefited from the exodus of Spanish intellectuals who have made a substantial contribution to all aspects of Mexican intellectual life.

Mexico's diversified economy had helped to save the country from the worst consequences of the Depression, and the existence of a broadly based official party, representing workers, peasants and the middle classes, gave Cárdenas an advantage possessed by no other country, enabling him to revivify the Revolution by implementing the agrarian clauses of the Constitution and by nationalizing the oil industry in 1938—the one outstandingly successful nationalist act of the 1930s. By 1940, therefore, Mexico was uniquely placed to take advantage of the economic opportunities offered by the outbreak of the Second World War.

After World War II

The economic boost experienced by Latin American countries under the impetus of the war threw up social groups which could no longer be contained within restrictive political systems.

The first stirrings of a new independent spirit came from Argentina where, in ten years of ultra-nationalistic dictatorship between 1945 and 1955, Perón made an unsuccessful bid to seize the leadership of Latin America and to establish it as an independent force in world affairs. Peronism grew out of Argentinian conditions. Unlike Italian Fascism, for which Perón had considerable admiration, it was not a response to economic collapse. Perón's initial successes were due to being able to buy his mass following by redistributing the economic surpluses accumulated during the war. His main support rested on an alliance between newly arrived rural migrants (one million of whom flooded into Buenos Aires between 1947 and 1954), organized labour and the army. Although new industrialists welcomed an economic nationalism which would protect them from foreign competition, the middle classes generally were anti-Peronist. In spite of his hostility to landowners there was no substantial agrarian reform and on Perón's fall the structure of society remained much as it had been ten years earlier. Perón bequeathed a legacy of a run-down economy, a demoralized middle class, and hostility between army and unions which is still the major factor in Argentinian politics.

p 112 (35)

In spite of aspirations to continental hegemony and the exaggerated claims for the ideology of 'justicialism' as a Third Position—neither capitalism nor communism—Peronism's impact outside Argentina was limited: the attempt to establish a continental labour federation received little support. In 1952 a revolution in Bolivia was hopefully welcomed by Peronists as the first in a chain of continent-wide revolutions, but the Bolivians needed no prompting from outside and the influence of Peronism is debatable. Bolivia's revolution stemmed from the disastrous defeat suffered at the hands of Paraguay in the Chaco War of 1932–35. Whereas in

Going to the polls in the 1938 elections in Uruguay. Though the smallest of the South American states, Uruguay has the highest standard of living, partly due to its relatively stable constitutional government ever since the reforms of Batlle y Ordóñez in the second decade of the century. (4)

Cuba as a pawn in the Cold War, by the South American cartoonist Aldor. The 'Greeks', Khrushchev and Mao, climb into the Trojan Horse (Castro) in order to enter the Kennedy fortress. The presidents of (from left to right) Mexico, Colombia, Venezuela, Peru, Chile and Uruguay are depicted as defenders of the fortress, but the Brazilian ex-president Quadros and the President of Ecuador have surreptitiously opened the gate. (5)

p 112
(34)

p 113
(41)

victorious Paraguay the dislocation of war resulted in a military authoritarianism from which it has still not escaped, for Bolivia the defeat was the germ of the social revolution of 1952. Younger officers, angered at civilian incompetence and influenced by Nazi ideas, had initiated a series of proto-revolutionary regimes in the 1930s and 1940s, but the Revolution of 1952 was the work of the middle classes under the leadership of Paz Estenssoro and the MNR (*Movimiento Nacionalista Revolucionario*) together with militant tin miners. After the success of the initial coup in the capital, La Paz, Indian peasant risings widened the area of conflict and forced the government to inaugurate a radical agrarian reform programme which gained it peasant support in the intractable conflict with the tin miners that followed.

The Bolivian Revolution has been unusual in Latin America in that it has been the only successful social revolution to have occurred in one of the poorer undeveloped countries. Elsewhere revolution has failed, as in Guatemala in 1954 when the ten-year-old revolutionary regime was overthrown with CIA aid. Where revolution has succeeded, as in Venezuela and Cuba, it has been in the most developed countries. In both countries dictators were overthrown in 1958 but the similarity stops there. In spite of their reforms, the failure of the Venezuelans to carry out radical structural changes invited invidious comparison with Cuba. Venezuela has since been plagued with the problem of pro-Cuba guerrillas and urban terrorists, drawn mainly from students, who have been critical of the government's refusal to break with the United States which has greater investments in Venezuela than in any other Latin American country.

The Cuban Revolution

In Cuba the revolt against Batista was not a mass revolt but one led by a small group of middle-class revolutionaries working to a moderate reformist programme. Experience of living with and being dependent on peasants in the Sierra Maestra converted Castro to the need for a more fundamental social transformation than he originally planned. The widening of his programme, especially by agrarian reform and the nationalization of major industries, alienated much of the Revolution's middle-class support but this was compensated for by the support of the rural and urban masses and later by the Cuban Communist Party. However, the Communists failed to take over the revolution and in fact were purged and harnessed to it. Although useful as a link with Moscow and for their organizational expertise, the old Communists have no real power and indeed their bureaucratic mentality is seen as one of the major threats to the Revolution's progress.

The momentum of the Revolution has been sustained over a long period by the enthusiasm of the younger generation, by Castro's own personal rule and by his refusal to institutionalize the Revolution. But in addition, there are historical and cultural factors unique to Cuba. No other Latin American country has a comparable revolutionary tradition stretching back into the middle of the 19th century in the struggle against Spanish rule. This tradition is constantly invoked to create a sense of continuous revolution—first against Spain and then against United States influence and dictators at home. One important consequence of the long revolt against Spanish rule is that Cuba, unlike other Latin American powers, emerged at independence with a strong concept of nationhood.

p 113
(38, 39)

121

p 113
(37) This is embodied in the life and writings of José Martí and it is from him that Castro has derived the messianic notion of Cuba as the liberator of the rest of Latin America from economic servitude. The second factor is the 'visibility' of Cuba's sugar culture. Cuba's dependence on sugar is so complete and the rhythm of economic and social life so bound up with the sugar harvest that it is possible to achieve a very high degree of mass mobilization in activities such as cane-cutting with which national survival can be equated.

ff The precarious balance of the Cold War has made Cuba dependent on Russian economic and technical support without which the island could not have survived. Absence of a flourishing scientific sub-culture and the exodus of many Cuban technicians meant that Cuba's survival has depended on this foreign support. But the emphasis—unique in Latin America—on technical and scientific education is gradually reducing this dependence and is ultimately designed to create a surplus for export to the rest of Latin America so that when other revolutions follow, as Cubans believe they must, Latin America will be able to generate its own technocratic and scientific élite without which any revolution in the Third World must be driven into the arms of a foreign power.

p 113
(40, 41) The Cuban Revolution gave an impetus to reform mongering and to revolutionary exegesis throughout the rest of the continent. The Alliance for Progress, launched in 1961, is the best example of the former. Conceived as a 'partnership in development' between the United States and Latin American countries, it was based on the premiss that a healthy middle class was the best insurance against revolution and that, once sufficient capital had been pumped into the system, economic progress, impelled by the middle class, would acquire a self-generating momentum. But the middle classes did not respond to external stimuli as the planners had anticipated and the Alliance has had only a limited success; it has neither stimulated the expected economic expansion nor has it contributed to political stability.

The corresponding revolutionary shibboleth has been the guerrilla mystique based on Cuban experience but also on the assumption that, as both the middle class and urban working class have proved incapable of fulfilling a revolutionary role, revolutionaries must look for change to the peasants as the untapped source. The failure of countless rural guerrilla movements, climaxed in Guevara's death in Bolivia in 1967, has exposed the weaknesses of this view and thrown the Left into disarray. On one side it has gained a more sympathetic hearing for the orthodox Russian view that armed revolution is premature under existing conditions. On the other it has led to a bewildering kaleidoscope of left-wing factions: Trotskyism has taken on new life and Castroist, Guevarist and Maoist solutions are furiously canvassed, especially on the campuses. One practical consequence of rural failure has been an outburst of urban terrorism which may be a sign for the future. If the expectations of the children of rural migrants in the cities are not satisfied the cities, rather than the countryside, may become the battlegrounds of the future.

The threats from the revolutionary Left, combined with the failure of civilian politicians and the flaccidity of reformist parties, have left a political vacuum which the military have been quick to fill. In 1964 a junta came to power in Brazil and Bolivia, in 1966 in Argentina and in 1968 in Peru. The motives for intervention vary in each case but, in Peru at least, the military's claim to be acting as a nationalist revolutionary force bears some relation to its actions.

A further response to the Cuban Revolution can be seen in new attitudes within the Catholic Church aware that Latin America has the largest concentration of Catholics in the world. The rise of Christian Democrat parties is one reflection of this new mood in which the Church has shifted from an intransigent position as defender of the *status quo* to cautious reformism and in some cases to extreme radicalism. Although Christian Democracy as a political movement is non-confessional, its philosophy is derived from liberal Catholic social thought with an emphasis on communitarianism. However, there is a contradiction between the radical implications of this philosophy and the dead weight of those who support the Christian Democrats for the negative reason that they are non-Communist. The tension is particularly apparent between Catholic student groups and party leaders. However, Christian Democracy is a significant movement in that it seeks political and social solutions within the Latin American cultural tradition.

The Cuban Revolution has acted as a spur to change but it is unlikely to become a model: conditions in the rest of Latin America are too different and few Latin Americans would wish to exchange one form of dependence for another. But neither do they want to perpetuate their client status as producers of primary products for the industrial West. If the widening gap between Latin America and the developed world, caused by deteriorating terms of trade and a spiralling population growth, is to be narrowed, it is recognized that there can be no solution in national isolation and that co-operation between Latin American states must increase. The Pan American Union had been founded in 1889 as a forum for discussion and for resolving intra-American disputes, but the Organization of American States is now suspect due to the membership of the United States. From the early 1960s other forms of co-operation have been developed in the field of economics, education, military affairs, in the creation of common markets, free-trade associations and regional groupings aimed at rationalizing economic development and increasing the size of markets so as to compete more effectively with foreign industries. But the setback to the Central American Common Market, the most promising of these new organizations, caused by the 'Football War' between El Salvador and Honduras in 1969, demonstrated just how near the surface nationalist rivalries lie.

A century and a half of independence has built up a complex of attitudes and interests which may take decades to overcome. But although political and economic problems seem intractable and solutions may appear repressive or, in comparison with Cuba anaemic, there is justifiable optimism based on an aroused awareness of the continent's enormous potential. An important factor here has been the re-discovery of Latin America by the outside world. Crises within North American society have encouraged a reassessment of the values of Latin American culture. Gradually, as outsideers become aware of the sophistication and vitality of this culture as shown in its contributions to the modern world in fields as varied as football, race relations, art, architecture, music, the dance and literature, that self-confidence which ebbed away during the years of informal empire is flowing back. Cultural influence is no longer a one-way process: not only can Europe and North America draw sustenance from what Latin America has to offer, but the experience of a hundred and fifty years of experiments in independence can offer both an example and a warning to the emerging Third World.

VI THE COMMUNIST WORLD

Soviet Russia and its progeny

HUGH SETON-WATSON

*'Lenin's methods lead to this : the party organization
at first substitutes itself for the party as
a whole; then the Central Committee substitutes itself
for the organization; and finally a single
dictator substitutes himself for the Central Committee.'*

LEON TROTSKY, 1904

The Bolshevik victory

of October 1917 made Russia the first, and for long the only, Communist state in the world. Communism as a moral idea had been preached throughout history. As a political programme it dates from Marx and Engels' *Communist Manifesto* of 1848. The fact that it triumphed first in Russia was by no means inevitable— indeed, according to orthodox Marxism, it should have come first to the advanced industrialized states of the West. By 1914 Russia was certainly ripe for revolution, but only two of the revolutionary parties were Marxist, and only one had the ruthlessness and the leadership to turn theory into practice.

In the montage shown opposite, the portrait of Lenin is by the Russian artist El Lissitsky, made some years after Lenin's death in 1924. The process of idealization has not been allowed to go too far. The large picture behind it shows the attack on the Winter Palace in Petrograd. The monarchy had been ended by the revolution of February, 1917, and for six months the various reforming parties, ranging from the right-wing Cadets to the left-wing Mensheviks and Bolsheviks, wrangled over the form of government that was to succeed it. Finally in November (October according to the old Russian calendar), the Bolsheviks under Lenin and Trotsky, and with the general support of workers and soldiers, seized power by force. The taking of the Winter Palace, where the Provisional Government was in session, marks the symbolic beginning of Communist rule. (1, 2)

The **Tsars had ruled** an empire more deeply divided by race and class than any other in Europe, but one in which their own power had been absolute. Concessions forced by the revolution of 1905 had been rendered politically null. By 1911, the fifteenth anniversary of his coronation, Nicholas II seemed to be as firmly seated on the throne as any of his predecessors. To mark the occasion the court jeweller, Carl Fabergé, made this gold Easter Egg (right) with miniature paintings by Zuiev showing notable events of his reign. The three visible here are the unveiling of a monument to Peter the Great at Riga, Nicholas' coronation in Moscow, and the removal of the remains of the sainted Serafim Sarovski. To left and right are portraits of the imperial family. (3)

Jews in Russia formed one of many minority groups within the Empire, along with Poles, Ukrainians, Georgians, Armenians and Asian peoples. Both Jews and Moslems suffered from religious discrimination, and remained secluded in their own communities. Many of the intelligentsia, however, were Jews. Above: *The Sabbath*, an early work by Marc Chagall, painted before he left Russia for France. The orthodox family sits inactive as the slow minutes tick away. (4)

'**Peasants in church**' by Malevich looks at the rural population who formed the vast majority of Russians. The painting dates from 1910–11, when many Russian artists were using themes from peasant life and folk-art. Just before the Revolution Malevich went over to an extreme form of abstraction which he called Suprematism. (6)

The proletariat made up a small, but politically the most significant, section of the population. In 1905 they had staged a revolution in St Petersburg many of whose features, such as the formation of workers' soviets, foreshadowed 1917. Brodsky's *Red Funeral 1906* (below) commemorates those killed in the fighting. (5)

The spontaneous rising of the people of Petrograd against the monarchy in February 1917 took everybody (including Lenin) by surprise. At first it seemed likely that a middle-class liberal regime would take over, but among the factory workers and soldiers demands for more radical change began to gain momentum. Here (left) a soldier harangues the crowd from the balcony of Tsarskoe Selo, the Tsar's former palace outside the city. It was from such elements that the Bolsheviks recruited their support. Below: Bolshevik Red Guards being organized in one of the factories. Lenin (seen, right, in Moscow two years later) returned from exile in April and within a few months was able to achieve the final seizure of power. (7, 8, 10)

Communist success in Petrograd did not automatically give them the whole of Russia. It took three years of civil war and a whole series of campaigns — in the east, the Ukraine and Poland — before the Whites were defeated. In that struggle the Red Army was created by Trotsky (above right, inspecting troops in 1919). Left: an anti-Bolshevik poster showing Red troops plundering a village during the war. (9, 11)

Forced industrialization became the programme of the thirties under Stalin. Five-year plans (right) were rushed through in four, those who were slow in co-operating being branded as in league with the Catholics, big business or the social democrats. (12)

The making of the new Russia compressed the horrors of a whole industrial revolution into one decade and cost the lives of millions of men and women. Vast schemes were set in motion when almost no resources were available but human labour, and this was exploited with complete ruthlessness. New hydro-electric stations on the Dnieper (right) were begun in 1929 to provide power for the new industries. Within a decade Soviet production had trebled. (13)

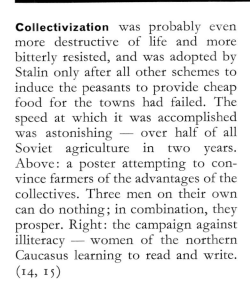

Collectivization was probably even more destructive of life and more bitterly resisted, and was adopted by Stalin only after all other schemes to induce the peasants to provide cheap food for the towns had failed. The speed at which it was accomplished was astonishing — over half of all Soviet agriculture in two years. Above: a poster attempting to convince farmers of the advantages of the collectives. Three men on their own can do nothing; in combination, they prosper. Right: the campaign against illiteracy — women of the northern Caucasus learning to read and write. (14, 15)

ЛЕНИНА ПОБЕДИЛИ МЫ В БОЯХ ЗА ОКТЯБРЬСКУЮ РЕВОЛЮЦИЮ.
ЛЕНИНА ДОБИЛИСЬ МЫ РЕШАЮЩИХ УСПЕХОВ В БОРЬБЕ ЗА ПОБЕДУ
О СТРОИТЕЛЬСТВА.
АМЕНЕМ ПОБЕДИМ В ПРОЛЕТАРСКОЙ РЕВОЛЮЦИИ ВО ВСЕМ МИРЕ

(Сталин. Политический отчет ЦК XVI съезду ВКП(б).)

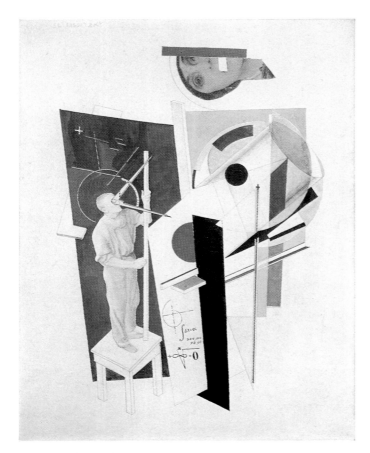

For a few years after the Revolution Russia could claim to be among the leaders of modern art. Artists who, like Tatlin and Malevich, welcomed the advent of Communism, saw themselves in new roles as citizens. Art, said Mayakovsky, was to be 'a living factory of the human spirit — in the streets, in the tramways, in the workshops and the workers' homes'. 'Constructivism' was declared the aesthetic of the new society. Tatlin's *Monument to the Third International* is shown on p. 139. An illustration by El Lissitzky (above left), of 1922, shows the artist at work on it. (16)

By the mid-twenties the propaganda element was already beginning to dominate Soviet art. Industry is idealized in Deineka's *New Constructions,* 1926 (above), agriculture in Gregoriev's *Peasants* (left), painted in 1923. From the point of view of international Communism an interesting artist is Heinrich Vogeler, a German sympathizer who went to Russia after the Revolution and settled there. His rousing appeal *For Increased Production in Karelia* (right) ▶ combines scenes in what is now the Karelo-Finnish Republic with slogans in Russian and Karelian. (17, 18, 20)

The poet laureate of the Revolution, Vladimir Mayakovsky, designed this drop-curtain (left) for his own, un-performed, *Mystery Play* of 1919. It was to have been a 'heroic, epic and satirical portrayal of our era'. (19)

World revolution, so confidently expected in 1918, failed to materialize. Communist parties in the West were either crushed by Fascism or failed to win a substantial following. It was only later — in China, in Yugoslavia and elsewhere — that the same conditions as in Russia brought about the same consequences.

In China the Communist Party dates from 1921, but Stalin's advice to co-operate with the Kuomintang nearly brought it to disaster. Communist soldiers during the late twenties (above left) fought a long battle for survival, and only after their heroic part in the war against Japan was Mao Tse-tung (above right) in a position to oust Chiang Kai-shek. (21, 22)

The Comintern, the Third Communist International, suffered from the fact that instructions from Moscow were increasingly geared to Russian, as distinct from Communist, interests, and underwent confusing changes of direction. This poster, issued to mark the 14th anniversary of the October Revolution greets the oppressed peoples of the world, prisoners of imperialism, in the name of the working class. (23)

Yugoslavia followed the same pattern of 'heroic Communism' as Russia and China: defeat of the governing class by an outside invader and the identification of Communism with patriotism. Tito (left, with his wartime staff in 1944) alone of the Balkan leaders was strong enough to maintain a position independent of the Kremlin. (24)

Liberation from the Germans in 1945 was for many countries only a prelude to another kind of subservience. Right: Soviet tanks being welcomed in the streets of Prague. In Czechoslovakia the Communists emerged at the free parliamentary election of 1946 as the largest single party. They ruled in a comparatively democratic fashion until 1948 when they took over power by force, becoming thereafter more and more dependent, politically and economically, upon Russia. Communists also forcibly seized power in Poland, Hungary, Rumania and Bulgaria. (25)

France and Italy both support large Communist parties, whose members take part in coalition governments, but have not been able to win majorities. Above: Maurice Thorez of France, sitting in the centre. Right: Palmiro Togliatti of Italy, once secretary of the Comintern. (26, 28)

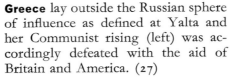

Greece lay outside the Russian sphere of influence as defined at Yalta and her Communist rising (left) was accordingly defeated with the aid of Britain and America. (27)

133

May Day Parades in Moscow are colourful exercises in the art of political encouragement. In this view (opposite) we are looking down Red Square with the Kremlin and tomb of Lenin on the right, St Basil's on the left. In the centre are a Sputnik and a space-rocket, symbols of Russia's technological triumph. (33)

'Socialist Realism' was adopted as the required style in all the arts by Stalin in the thirties. Only two qualities were now acceptable: political orthodoxy and comprehensibility by the people. Where originality was dangerous the inevitable result was a monotonous reliance on stereotypes, such as the colossal monument *Worker and Kolhoznik* (right) by V. Mukhina, glorifying agricultural labour. Even more explicit ideological lessons are taught in the poster reproduced below. The working classes march forward to the future, heartened by such slogans as 'Down with capitalism, the regime of slavery, poverty and hunger!' On the left are the Western nations, on the right, 'the heroic Red Army of China' fighting against the imperialist menace of Japan, America, Britain and France. (29, 30)

The grandiose architecture of the Stalinist years looks back to the Tsars. Left: Moscow University. Above: Moscow's gift to Warsaw, the Palace of Culture and Science. (31, 32)

Revolt among the peoples of Russia's empire in Eastern Europe has been a recurring feature of postwar history, most notably in East Germany, 1953 (top left), Hungary 1956 (centre) and Czechoslovakia 1968 (bottom). In each case the demand for greater freedom was seen as a threat to Russia, and force was used to restore the status quo. (34–36)

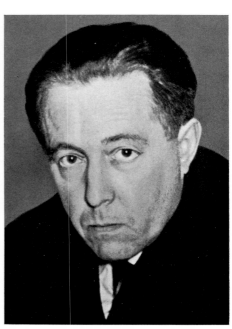

Voices from inside Russia after Stalin's death were able to criticize the regime indirectly, though still liable to persecution. Both Boris Pasternak (top) and Alexander Solzhenitsyn (above) won Nobel Prizes for books which were banned from publication in their own country, but suffered no worse punishment than the threat of exile if they left Russia. (37, 38)

Soviet Russia and its progeny

HUGH SETON-WATSON

BELIEFS that human possessions should be held in common, movements to achieve this state of affairs, and institutions which at least partly embody this principle, can be found far back in history, in the organization of primitive tribes, in the official doctrines and the heresies of the great religions and in the collective life of monastic orders and brotherhoods. The development of secular ideas of a communist type was greatly accelerated during the European Enlightenment of the 18th century, and in the second half of the 19th the claim was made that Karl Marx had placed socialist and communist theory on a scientific basis. Twentieth-century communism, as a powerful political movement and as a system of government, is the work above all of Vladimir p 125 Ilyich Ulyanov (1870–1924), better known as Lenin. A devoted (1) disciple of Marx, he also owed much to the example and teaching of earlier Russian revolutionaries, especially to the writer N. G. Chernyshevsky (1828–89), the Jacobin exile P. N. Tkachov (1844–86) and the People's Will group which carried out the assassination of Tsar Alexander II in 1881. Lenin was a pioneer of the social democratic movement in Russia in the 1890s, and from 1903 onwards he built up his own faction, the elitist and conspiratorial party of the Bolsheviks. When the Russian monarchy collapsed in March 1917, Lenin had his great opportunity. In the chaos of the next eight months, while the armed forces and the civil machinery of government disintegrated, orders could neither be given nor obeyed, peasants seized the land, workers tried to take over factories and intellectuals dreamed of an imminent reign of peace and virtue, Lenin outmanoeuvred all his liberal and socialist rivals. A brilliant revolutionary tactician, he chose his moment, seized power in November 1917 with very little bloodshed, organized a new political and military system based on his disciplined Bolshevik cadres, fought and won from 1918 to 1920 a civil war which cost millions of lives, and emerged with his party, now renamed Russian Communist Party, sole ruler of the former empire of the Tsars. (When Russia was renamed Union of Soviet Socialist Republics in the 1920s the Party took the name All-Union Communist Party, and after the Second World War it was renamed Communist Party of the Soviet Union—CPSU, by which initials it will be called in the following pages.)

The paradox of Russian Communism

It is an important historical paradox that the first victory of revolutionaries professing Marxist socialism, which insists on the leading role of the industrial working class, should have been won not in industrial England (which Marx studied and knew well) or in industrial Germany (which possessed the oldest and most numerous workers' movement inspired by Marx's ideas) but in overwhelmingly agricultural Russia. The main subsequent victories of Communists were also won in industrially backward countries— China, Yugoslavia, Indo-China and Cuba—while Communist hopes of industrial western Europe and North America were disappointed in the following half-century.

p 127 In Russia in 1917 the vast majority were peasants. Despite some (6) progress since 1905, agriculture was primitive and rural education had only just begun. The peasants had been heavily taxed by governments which put hardly any resources back into the improvement of farming. Overpopulation was a serious and growing cause of poverty in large parts of the country, and the presence of large estates belonging to noble landowners stimulated class hatred among the millions who had too little land to support their families. In the towns a predominantly unskilled industrial labour force and huge numbers of casually employed urban poor lived in material and moral misery: wages were kept low by competition for unskilled jobs by peasant boys and girls pouring in from an overpopulated countryside, and the immigrants uprooted from village society found themselves in an inhuman anonymous agglomeration which had no new values to offer them. The third social group disaffected from the Russian old regime was the intelligentsia, men and women of contemporary European education and outlook who found themselves tragically isolated both from their own people and from its rulers. The Tsars and their advisers insisted on upholding autocratic government, refused to grant the political liberties of modern constitutional states, and either rejected or obstructed social and economic reforms. Finally, it must not be forgotten that more than half the population of the Russian Empire were not Russians at all, but Poles, Ukrainians, Balts, Georgians, Armenians, Tatars, Central Asian Turks and Iranians, and members of scores of smaller peoples. Religious discrimination against Jews, Moslems and members of schismatic p 126 or sectarian communities, derived from the Orthodox Church, (4) was a further cause of bitterness to millions.

Russian autocracy forced a large and talented minority of the educated class into revolutionary action, as there was so little hope of achieving reform through legal channels. A much larger part of the educated class, though not engaged in any revolutionary action, at least felt no loyalty to the regime. Revolutionary leadership in the late 19th century came overwhelmingly from the intelligentsia: the revolutionaries took their ideas from European socialism, and learned the lessons of organization and action from the bitter realities of Russian political life. By 1900 they had a substantial following among the workers and the urban poor and were winning sympathy among the peasants. Military defeat by Japan threatened collapse of the political system, and there were not only massive strikes but also large-scale peasant revolts. The Tsar's governments were able to crush the revolts, and they also introduced reforms in political institutions, agriculture and education which gave some hope of peaceful social and political progress. However, these did not suffice to remove revolutionary feeling. The war of 1914 brought worse military defeats, and in 1915 and 1916 a phenomenon occured for which no more precise expression can be found than that the ruling cadres lost their nerve and proved quite unable to govern. The successors of the Tsar, the liberals and socialists, had little real will to power, and they found that the machinery of government itself, which was supposedly at their command, was rapidly falling to pieces.

The Bolsheviks' victory in November can be explained by p 128 saying that Lenin alone of the political leaders had the will to (7, 8) power and knew how to seize it. But the November Revolution was only the beginning of the story. The victory in three years of p 128 civil war can only partly be explained by the superiority of Bolshe-(9, 11) vik military and civil discipline over that of their conservative or 'White' opponents. It was also due to the fact that the workers, the peasants and the non-Russian peoples at least felt that they had something to hope for from the Bolsheviks and everything to fear from a White victory which was expected to bring the landowners and the bureaucrats and the old army officers back to power. The Bolsheviks were also greatly helped by the fact that their most dangerous potential foreign enemy, the Germans of William II and Ludendorff, were defeated by the Western powers, and that though the British and French governments disliked the Bolsheviks heartily and gave material aid to the Russian Whites, it was inconceivable that they could mobilize their war-weary subjects to fight a war in Russia.

Variant patterns of revolution

The same social forces—primitive peasants, exploited urban poor and a disaffected intelligentsia—faced similar opponents—a bureaucracy serving a dictatorial regime averse to real social reform—and won victory in similar conditions of war—defeat and collapse of the state machine—in the two countries where Communists achieved power by their own efforts later in the century: China and Yugoslavia.

p 154
(18–22)

p 132
(21, 22)

In China it was a long process. Brief successes in the early 1920s led to disaster and massacre of Communists in 1927. There followed a decade in remote provinces, with the epic Long March to the north-west and the establishment of the territorial base in Yenan. Then came years of successful guerrilla war against the Japanese invaders, in which the Communists mobilized on their own behalf the patriotic feelings of the Chinese people whom Chiang Kai-shek's Kuomintang had disappointed. The final stage was a civil war of three years which began with heavy fighting but ended with the complete disintegration of the military and civil apparatus of the enemy. In the first stage the workers of a few great cities formed the decisive mass base of the Communists, but after 1927 this was supplied by peasants. The Chinese civil war of 1946–49 resembles the Russian civil war of 1918–20 in many respects, especially in the demoralization of the Whites and in the wavering and ineffective help given to them by the Western powers. China in the 1940s, like Russia in the 1920s, was too remote and too little known for it to be possible for Western parliamentary governments to mobilize their subjects, war-weary and patriotically self-satisfied after victory over well-known and powerful enemies.

p 132
(24)

In Yugoslavia there was a long period of brave but almost hopeless underground struggle against dictatorship, but the decisive phase came after the Germans had destroyed the old Yugoslav state in 1941. The cadres of the underground Communist Party consisted partly of workers and partly of intelligentsia, but the mass support which brought them victory came, as in China, from the peasants. As in China, their main appeal was to patriotic struggle against the foreign invader and his domestic agents. Especially important in the Yugoslav case was the appeal to members of the different nations of Yugoslavia—Serbs, Croats, Slovenes and Macedonians—to unite in a common struggle on a basis of equality. The old regime had stood for Serbian domination, and the domestic agents of the Germans were either Serbian or Croatian extreme nationalists, while in Macedonia there was substantial support for Bulgarian extreme nationalism. The Communist argument, that these extreme nationalisms only served the German invaders, was at first unpopular, but the behaviour of the Germans and the extreme nationalists, together with the heroic example shown by the Communists in action, gradually won millions of Yugoslavs over to the Communists' People's Liberation Army, and this was a major factor in their victory. The factor of remoteness from the international power centres, mentioned in the Russian and Chinese cases, also has a certain parallel. The Germans were prevented from using against the Yugoslavs sufficient forces to crush them, because they were engaged on the great battle fronts of the Second World War. As for the Allied Great Powers, especially the British, they regarded the Yugoslavs as allies, and gave them a certain amount of material support. When the war ended, each of the Allied Great Powers found itself in turn in conflict with the Yugoslavs, but by this time the Communist Government was so firmly entrenched that it could be dislodged by nothing short of invasion, which was impossible for fundamentally the same reasons as in the Russian and Chinese cases.

The success of the Communists in Indo-China closely resembles the Chinese and Yugoslav cases. The difference is that, though they achieved victory comparatively quickly in North Vietnam, their struggle to take over the whole country was resisted first by French and then by American military power on a major scale, and was still continuing in 1970 after a quarter of a century. The Albanian victory in 1943–44 closely resembled the Yugoslav, and was indeed largely facilitated by Yugoslav advice and material aid. In Greece between 1942 and 1944 a similar movement developed and achieved similar success, but was twice defeated by superior military force—by British troops in 1944 and by the Greek army, supplied from American sources, in the civil war of 1946–49. In Hungary in 1919 Communists for a time held power. The social forces on which they relied, and the struggle for power which they conducted, rather closely resemble those of Russia in 1917. Once in power, they were able for a short time to enlist patriotic emotions on their behalf by fighting against the Czechs and Slovaks who laid claim to what had been northern Hungary. However, the regular army of another neighbouring state with claims on Hungarian territory, Rumania, proved too strong for them, and military defeat led to the collapse of the Communists and counter-revolution.

p 133
(27)

p 61
(13)

The Communist parties of Western industrial countries have from time to time won substantial electoral victories and have gained the support of powerful trade unions, of large sectors of the working class, and of many intellectuals, but they have never been within sight of power by their own resources. The German party was outwardly impressive between 1921 and 1933, but missed such opportunities as came its way, especially in 1923 and 1932. In Czechoslovakia in the 1930s the Communists had, as in Germany, a powerful minority of the working class but made no bid for power. In France the Communists were strong in the early 1920s and again at the time of the Popular Front in 1935–39. Their greatest success came during the Second World War, when they were extremely active in the resistance movement, and emerged as the strongest single party, but proved unable to achieve power either by constitutional or by violent means. The same applies to the Italian party, which also achieved immense prestige by its resistance record, emerged as the second strongest party after the war, but was also unable to attain power.

p 133
(26)

p 133
(28)

Whereas the Yugoslav and Albanian Communists won power by their own efforts, those of Poland, Hungary, Rumania, Bulgaria and East Germany were put in power in 1944 and 1945 by the conquering Soviet army. The case of Czechoslovakia is more complicated. Between May and December 1945 the Soviet army was present in Czechoslovakia, and enabled the Czechoslovak Communists to build up for themselves a powerful position in key sectors of the state machine. At a general election, held in May 1946 in conditions of comparative liberty, the Communists emerged as the strongest single party, with 40% of the votes. For nearly two years they shared in a coalition government with other democratic parties, and during this time, with certain exceptions, democratic liberties were preserved. In February 1948, however, the Communists provoked a crisis with their allies and seized power by force. A constitutional appearance was preserved by the fact that the President entrusted them with the formation of a new government, and that they had in fact sufficient additional parliamentary support from the socialists to give them a bare parliamentary majority, had they needed it. In view of the decisive help given to them earlier by the Soviet authorities, and the fact that the timing of their seizure of power appeared to have been decided in Moscow, it is difficult to say whether the Czechoslovak Communists should be considered to have taken power by their own efforts or not.

The last important victory of Communists before 1970, in Cuba, is also a complicated case. The Cuban revolution of 1959 was the work of Fidel Castro and his small guerrilla force, which had for some years fought a brave action in the mountains. It was, however, also due to the widespread hostility of the Cuban middle classes to the Batista regime, and to the loss of nerve and paralysis of will that afflicted the dictator and his officials. Castro's movement was not Communist. Only some time after he was installed in power did Castro declare himself a Marxist-Leninist and displace the leaders of the existing Communist Party in a personal take-over

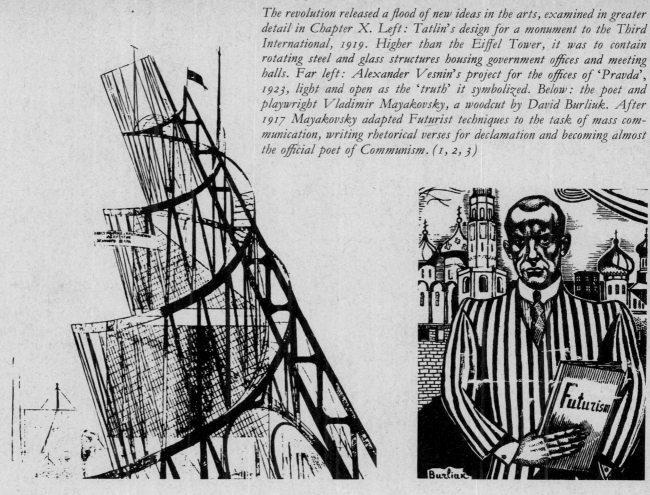

The revolution released a flood of new ideas in the arts, examined in greater detail in Chapter X. Left: Tatlin's design for a monument to the Third International, 1919. Higher than the Eiffel Tower, it was to contain rotating steel and glass structures housing government offices and meeting halls. Far left: Alexander Vesnin's project for the offices of 'Pravda', 1923, light and open as the 'truth' it symbolized. Below: the poet and playwright Vladimir Mayakovsky, a woodcut by David Burliuk. After 1917 Mayakovsky adapted Futurist techniques to the task of mass communication, writing rhetorical verses for declamation and becoming almost the official poet of Communism. (1, 2, 3)

bid unique in the history of Communist movements. As Cuba is discussed more fully, in its Latin American setting, in Chapter V, no more will be said here either of the Cuban Revolution or of the regime which emerged from it.

Looking back over fifty years of Communist revolutionary activity a few points may be emphasized. First is the role of disaffected intelligentsias in underdeveloped societies. No crude attempts at quantification are likely to be helpful, but one may say that the revolutionary propensity of the intelligentsia has been definitely correlated with the extent of the cultural gap between the educated élite and the mass of the people, and with the extent of dictatorship and repression exercised by the rulers and the bureaucrats. Russia, in which these two phenomena were maximized, is the classic example. Secondly, the urban poor and unskilled industrial workers of a society in an early stage of industrial development have been far more promising revolutionary material than the skilled workers of a highly industrialized society: this is best illustrated by the different attitudes of workers in Russia and in Germany in 1918. Thirdly, the ability of revolutionaries to enlist massive support among the peasants has largely depended on their ability to present themselves as patriots defending the people against foreign invaders or exploiters: China, Yugoslavia and Indo-China are obvious cases, but even in Russia this factor played some part in the civil war, in so far as the Bolsheviks were able to persuade many Russians that the Whites were agents of foreign powers. Finally, though the skill, the heroism and the sufferings of Communist leaders and supporters in the fifty years from 1917 onwards were beyond doubt, it is arguable that their successes were due as much to the vulnerability of enemy power as to their own merits. The state machine in underdeveloped societies appears outwardly formidable, but it is insecure. It is like a block of cast iron placed vertically on the shoulders of its subjects: like cast iron, it is brittle, and a powerful external shock can shatter it. The state machine in advanced industrial societies is linked horizontally with various levels of the social pyramid, and it is made of more flexible material. These observations must, however, be taken as a comment on the years 1917–70, not as a prophecy for the future. It is perhaps possible that methods of urban guerrilla warfare may be devised which can shatter the state machine of advanced industrial societies. What is less unlikely is that the ruling cadres of ·

such societies may be affected by so drastic a loss of nerve and paralysis of will that, like the Russian ruling cadres under Nicholas II, they allow power to slip from their hands.

Russia: the structure of absolutism

The political institutions introduced by the victorious Russian Communists were called soviets. These were originally revolutionary councils of workers in the factories, of soldiers in garrisons or fighting units, and of peasants in villages, which sprang up, under the leadership of the various socialist parties, in the revolutionary months. Lenin at one time claimed that these were the most genuinely democratic bodies yet known in history, and that they were as characteristic of the age of socialism as parliaments were characteristic of the age of bourgeois democracy. The new Russian state became known as Soviet Russia, and later as the Union of Soviet Socialist Republics. The implication was that the essential nature of the Soviet state was determined by the fact that its organs of government were soviets.

p 128 (8)

This is not true. From the November Revolution onwards the soviets were dominated by Communists. In the civil war, the presence in the soviets of some socialist parties other than the Bolsheviks was for a time tolerated: the last of these were not removed until 1922. Thereafter the soviets at all levels from the village up to the Supreme Soviet—the formal equivalent of a national parliament under the Constitution of 1936—were composed of CPSU members or of allegedly 'non-Party' representatives appointed by the Party. At 'elections' only one candidate presented himself. The soviets were in fact no more than the formal framework through which Communist Party rule was exercised.

The Communist Party even before 1917 was autocratically ruled by Lenin, although argument was permitted and even at times encouraged. The principle of 'democratic centralism'—that the Party members could freely discuss policy until the leaders had taken a decision but must then obediently carry out the policy—would be accepted by many parties that were not Communist. However, the 10th Congress of the CPSU in March 1921 passed a resolution which was a historical landmark. It prohibited 'factionalism', or the formation within the Party of any group standing for a particular policy. Thus, an individual Party member was entitled to put his ideas before the Party leaders, but if he joined with even one other member he was guilty of factionalism. Of course this resolution did not prevent factions from arising in subsequent years, but it gave the leaders formal justification for suppressing them.

After Lenin was made helpless by illness in 1922 (he died two years later) a struggle for power developed, which was won by p 21 Joseph Vissarionovich Djugashvili (1879–1953), better known as Stalin. His main strength was his control of the Party machine, and especially of the means of appointing persons to executive power, through his position as General Secretary. He showed himself a brilliant tactician, well able to play his rivals off against each other and to choose the moment to strike. He first combined with G. E. Zinoviev and L. B. Kamenev against the great military leader of the civil war and Lenin's closest colleague in the epic days, L. D. Trotsky. When this battle had been won, Stalin combined with the right wing of the Party, whose main spokesman was N. I. Bukharin, to defeat Zinoviev and Kamenev. These two, belatedly reconciled to the now powerless Trotsky, were defeated by the end of 1927. Two years later Stalin turned against Bukharin. He reversed Bukharin's policy of favouring the peasants, and introduced forcible collectivization of agriculture.

p 129 The object of this vast revolution was not so much to improve (14) the output of agriculture as to set up a machinery of coercion capable of extracting cheaply from the peasants as large a proportion as possible of whatever was produced. The peasants' objection was not so much that they preferred private ownership of their land to membership of collective farms (though this was probably true) as that they resented having the product of their labour seized at prices which barely enabled them to keep alive. Essentially, Stalin was continuing the policy of the last Tsars, of paying for industrial and military power by squeezing the peasants, while putting very little of the revenue back into the improvement p 129 of agriculture. Collectivization was accompanied by forced (13) industrialization at breakneck speed. Machinery, skilled labour and managerial efficiency were extremely scarce in Russia, but unskilled manpower and raw materials were abundant. The result was that millions of peasant sons and daughters were mobilized, at miserable wages and in appalling living conditions, at the new mines, factories and construction sites: a job that could have been done by one skilled worker with a machine was done by five or ten or more pairs of bare hands. The horrors of the early industrial revolution, which had dragged on for decades in England or Germany a century earlier, were concentrated into one decade in Russia. The achievement was tremendous, but it cost the lives of millions of men and women and many more millions of livestock, besides permanently undermining the health of still larger numbers of workers and peasants.

These horrors caused discontent, and Stalin, though now victorious, feared conspiracies within the Party. When S. M. Kirov, the Party leader in Leningrad, was murdered in 1934, former supporters of Trotsky and Zinoviev were arrested in large numbers. Between 1936 and 1939 the process of arrest escalated at a frantic speed. Stalin was not content to arrest those who had genuinely supported his rivals in the past: he sought now to eliminate anyone who could conceivably threaten his position in the future. Two-thirds of the Central Committee of the CPSU, half the army officers from the rank of major upwards and most persons holding key posts in the management of civil government and industry were swept away. Government propaganda worked up a hysterical fear of treason and sabotage. The population was constantly urged to be vigilant, and this meant that citizens, and especially Party members, were expected to denounce those around them. As the denunciations poured in, the public prosecutors and police officials were obliged to act even when it was clear to them that the accusations were absurd: any official who dismissed a case would be denounced by his colleagues as an agent of the traitors and saboteurs. The mechanism took over from those who had set it in motion. It could be stopped only by Stalin's order, and this was given in the first half of 1939. The last wave of arrests consisted primarily of policemen. The cost in human lives of three years of this Great Purge cannot be exactly estimated. In addition to the hundreds of thousands who were executed, and the millions who perished from slow undernourishment and overwork in the inhuman forced labour camps directed by the police throughout the vast country, there were millions more whose health was ruined or whose families were broken up for ever.

An important but underrated aspect of the Soviet Union was its colonial character. The proportion of non-Russians was a little smaller than in the empire of the Tsars because Poland and Finland became independent after the First World War, but it remained almost half the population. The fact that in the 1960s most non-Russians had a much higher birth-rate than Russians meant that they would probably exceed the Russians in the 1970s. The non-Russians, of whom the most numerous were the Ukrainians, Belorussians, Volga Tatars, Central Asian Turks and the peoples of Transcaucasia, were never given the chance to choose between independence and enforced membership of the Soviet Union. Lenin proclaimed the right of self-determination, but he interpreted it in such a way that wherever Bolshevik arms prevailed the non-Russians were forced into subjection. Georgia, which attained independence in 1918 and became a well organized social democratic republic, was simply invaded by the Bolsheviks in 1921. In the 1920s the non-Russians gained some advantages. They were subjected to the same Communist Party dictatorship as the Russians, but at least they were allowed to use their own languages in public affairs, and local persons were largely recruited to local office: neither of these things had been true under the Tsars. However, in the periods of crisis—collectivization of agriculture, forced industrialization and the Great Purge—the non-Russians suffered even more than the Russians. Inevitably, the discontent arising from these convulsions took nationalist forms: whereas Russian sufferers blamed the Government or the Communists, non-Russians blamed 'the Russians'. Equally, Russian Communist officials tended to see in non-Russians who resisted them, national rebels and agents of foreign powers. Resistance to collectivization was strongest, and deaths from famine were proportionately most numerous, among the Ukrainians and the Kazakhs; the Purge fell with special severity on Ukrainians, Tatars and Central Asians. During the Second World War, the German invaders found willing helpers among some small Caucasian peoples and among the Crimean Tatars: when the Soviet army returned, these nations were deported from their homes to distant parts of the empire. After the war Soviet spokesmen continued to denounce 'bourgeois nationalism' among the non-Russians, and from time to time there were arrests and punishments for this offence.

At the end of the 1960s the situation of the non-Russians in the Soviet Union was complex and contradictory. Fifty years of the Soviet regime had brought enormous progress in industry and in education, and the general standard of living had substantially improved. It remained true that the non-Russians had never been allowed to decide whether they wished to remain in the Soviet Union, or to choose the independence which had been successfully claimed by so many small states in Asia and Africa. In the terms of the familiar dilemma of United Nations anti-colonialist spokesmen, the Soviet leaders had refused the non-Russians 'self-government', but maintained that they had provided them with 'good government'. Evidence from the Soviet Union showed that there were tendencies towards absorption in Russian culture, but also tendencies to maintain distinct non-Russian cultures. The evidence was inconclusive. For example, it was not clear whether, in the Ukrainian capital of Kiev, the immigrants from the Ukrainian countryside were becoming absorbed in a Russian working class, or on the contrary were Ukrainianizing the existing labour force. There were undoubted signs of Ukrainian nationalism among the educated class: how much popular support it had, no one could tell. In Central Asia the Asian and Russian elements in the cities worked side by side, but they did not mix socially or intermarry. Whether greater prosperity and better education made them grateful to their Russian 'elder brothers' or increased their impatience to be rid of Russian rule, no one could tell.

The system of government operating in the last years of Stalin's life was marked by the greatest concentration of power yet seen in human history. It may be advisable not to use the word 'totalitarianism', which has associations with the European Fascism of the 1930s and with American polemical literature of the 1950s—

although the claim to total power over all his subjects was of the essence of Stalin's rule. Perhaps the truth can be better expressed simply by saying that all political, economic and spiritual power was concentrated in the same hands. Economic power included not only ownership and control of industry but a coercive mechanism which through the collective farm management extended right down to the individual peasant—a mechanism never previously achieved in any agricultural system. Spiritual power included not only the negative practice of prohibiting the expression of any ideas distasteful to the ruler, but also the positive imposition of new moral criteria. The final source of all morality—with no reservations whatsoever—was the leadership of the CPSU, the authorized interpreter and exponent of Marxist-Leninist science, and this in practice meant Stalin. What Stalin said was the law and the prophets. Soviet citizens were entitled to no private lives independent of the supreme ruler's will. The purpose of art and literature was to glorify the supreme ruler and to work up popular enthusiasms for his purposes. The whole structure was cemented by a 'cult of personality' which equalled and probably surpassed the adulation of classical oriental despots or the deification of Roman emperors. It would however be wrong to believe that the claim to total power was really effective. Individual Russians conformed, often with enthusiasm, but their private lives and their family loyalties still preserved a great deal of autonomy. The nightmare of the complete atomization of society, of the reduction of every individual to the status of a helpless pawn facing the immense resources of the omnipotent state, remained a nightmare.

After Stalin's death there were great changes. In the subsequent struggle for power, N. S. Khrushchev won first place by 1955 and strengthened his position still further in 1957 by the defeat of the 'anti-Party group' of surviving veterans of the Stalin era. But he never attained, nor indeed is it likely that he desired, the pre-eminence of his former master. In 1964 he was overthrown by a majority in the Central Committee of the CPSU, and he was then allowed to live peacefully in retirement: two facts which truly formed a landmark in Soviet history. His successors, First Secretary L. I. Brezhnev and Prime Minister A. N. Kosygin, showed no desire to exalt themselves into charismatic leaders.

During the Khrushchev era the forced labour camps were almost completely dismantled, the powers of the security police were used much more sparingly, writers and artists were given greater liberty of expression provided that they left politics alone, some conciliatory gestures were made towards the non-Russians, more consumer goods of better quality were offered to the public, real wages appreciably increased, and the peasants were given better prices for their goods and some of the social services which had hitherto been available only to townspeople. Yet the essential nature of the regime, the concentration of all political, economic and spiritual power in the same hands, remained. The power was exercised more humanely but the machinery of power, including the whole apparatus of terror and indoctrination, police dossiers and informers was still there, and the claim of the Party leadership to infallibility was not relinquished.

The Soviet Union was now one of the world's two greatest powers. Between the world wars, Russia had been only a potential Great Power. Soviet spokesmen had poured forth clouds of revolutionary rhetoric, breathing fire and slaughter against the capitalist world, and the hatred had been reciprocated by the capitalist rulers in the 1920s and with much greater venom by the Fascist dictators of the 1930s. The cause of revolution, however, p 132 (23) made little progress; the Communist International (Comintern) set up in 1919 as a general staff of world revolution, proved a most ineffective instrument. Equally, it cannot be said that Soviet attempts at traditional diplomacy were markedly successful: the alliance of 1935 with France ended ingloriously at Munich in 1938, and the alliance of 1939 with the Third Reich served mainly to blind Stalin's eyes to the German danger until Hitler was ready to attack. However, the tremendous military achievements of the Soviet army in the Second World War, in which without doubt it made the greatest single contribution to victory, increased Soviet prestige, and brought a hundred million Europeans under Soviet rule. In 1970 the Soviet Union was still behind the United States in the nuclear and missile arms race, but it was catching up. From

A Chinese paper-cut celebrating the period of close Russo-Chinese friendship in the decade after World War II. (4)

the mid-1950s onwards Soviet influence in Asia and Africa grew, immensely helped by the ignominious failure of the Anglo-French invasion of Egypt in 1956. In the early 1960s Latin America began to appear a promising field: the setback in the Cuba confrontation of October 1962 did not do lasting damage. The odium attaching to the United States government throughout the world, and especially among its own citizens, as a result of the Vietnam war, was also of immense advantage to the Soviet Union. In the mid-1960s the Soviet leaders began to commit themselves heavily to the Arab side in the conflict with Israel, and Soviet naval forces increased steadily in the Mediterranean and even in the Indian Ocean.

China: contrasts and parallels

The great disappointment was China. The victory of Communism in a country of seven hundred million people brought more trouble than profit. The Soviet-Chinese conflict developed slowly f 4 from the mid-1950s onwards. The Chinese Communists probably still resented the bad advice given to them by Stalin in 1927, his underestimation of Mao Tse-tung in the 1930s and his friendly relations with the Kuomintang in the 1940s. They also objected to the relatively small amount of economic aid which the Soviet Union offered them once they were in power, to Soviet refusal to supply them with atomic weapons or help them make their own, and to Soviet failure to give them any support in their attempts to recover Formosa. Relations became even worse when Khrushchev visited Eisenhower in the United States, and when the Soviet Union showed towards Chinese-Indian hostilities in 1962 a neutrailty which was not far short of support for India. In the 1960s came open polemics between the two governments. The Chinese accused the Soviet leaders of betraying the revolutionary cause: the whole Soviet regime was degenerating, under the leadership of 'modern revisionists' who were rapidly turning into bourgeois. Chinese spokesmen began to talk of the territories taken from China by the Tsars under unequal treaties. It is true that they did not ask for the return to China of the Far Eastern provinces taken in 1858–60, but the repeated reference to these historical grievances understandably alarmed Soviet observers. During the 1960s there developed on both sides a mood of bitter hatred. The original causes of disagreement now became less important than the fact that each side regarded the other as an enemy. Once hatred has developed between two ideological dictatorships it becomes more formidable than hatred between traditional secular states: the ideologists and the propaganda apparatuses take over, public hysteria is worked up and becomes a new factor in the situation. By the end of the 1960s the Soviet Union was the main supplier of arms to India, its presumed defender against China, and in many parts of the world pro-Chinese Communist groups bitterly attacked the parties loyal to Moscow. Even in Vietnam there was no effective co-operation between Russia and China. In March 1969 there was fighting between Soviet and Chinese forces on the frontier of the Ussuri river in the Far East, and later in the year there were clashes in Sinkiang and on the Amur.

The Chinese regime was at first closely modelled on the Soviet. p 160 (39, 40) In 1955 collectivization of agriculture was carried out with little resistance from the peasants and without disastrous economic consequences. Possibly emboldened by this success, which contrasted remarkably with Soviet experience in the 1930s, Mao decided, in his 'Hundred Flowers' campaign of 1957, to encourage open expression of opinion, even if it were critical. The result was disappointing: it revealed that there was still much discontent with the regime, especially among intellectuals. Rigid controls were clamped down again, and more radical economic policies were introduced.

It was at this point, in 1958, that Chinese internal policies began to diverge widely from Russian. The Government announced a 'Great Leap Forward' in industrial production, and the establishment of People's Communes. The Communes were intended to transform the people's way of life, reducing private and family life to a minimum, regimenting as far as possible the whole lives of men and women alike. Rapid industrial production was to be achieved not so much, as in the Soviet Union in the 1930s, by mobilizing vast numbers of children of peasants in new industrial centres and construction sites, as by organizing great numbers of small-scale units—diminutive metal-works in farmers' backyards, and the like. Enormous energy was put into the campaign, but the economic results were very poor, with maximum dislocation and minimum extra output. At the same time extravagant ideological claims were made: on the basis of People's Communes, China would achieve Communism in the near future, thus rushing ahead of Soviet Russia which had been ruled by Communists for forty years yet was still only in the long process of transition from socialism to Communism. This claim, however, was modified by a Resolution of the Central Committee of the Chinese Party of 18 December 1958, and the decision of Mao in November 1958 to give up his post as Chairman of the People's Government appeared to be an indication that he himself was under serious criticism.

For the next four years Mao remained in the political background. The deterioration of relations with the Soviet Union brought him back into active leadership. Convinced that Soviet society was degenerating rapidly and reverting to capitalism, he felt that China must be protected from a similar danger, and that this could only be done by a reaffirmation of the heroic virtues of the revolutionary era. In September 1962 he launched a campaign for a Socialist Education Movement for this purpose. Meeting with little support from within the existing political hierarchy, and seeking better models from his own revolutionary experience, he found the solution in the ethos and discipline of the armed forces. In the summer of 1964 he pressed for action to train 'heirs to the revolution' and put forward the army as a model for Chinese society. Marshal Lin Pao, the outstanding commander of the civil war, was built up by propaganda as Mao's second-in-command and eventual successor. In the summer of 1965 Mao announced a Great Proletarian Cultural Revolution. This reached its climax between the summer of 1966 and the end of 1967. During this period Mao incited the mass of the population against the existing Party leadership and against the intellectual élite, using the army to provide a minimum of cohesion.

The striking force of the Cultural Revolution was the Red Guards, formed principally from students and adolescents. Schools and universities were shut down. Crowds of adolescents began by humiliating and terrorizing their teachers and taking over the premises of schools, colleges and various other public bodies. War was declared on the old culture of China, and works of art were symbolically destroyed in public. Soon more powerful persons were attacked: prominent leaders of the Party in Peking and in the provinces were denounced on placards and posters and in many cases publicly assaulted. The Red Guards were swollen by millions of workers and peasants. Hundreds of thousands of persons travelled round the country to demonstrate, terrorize and make propaganda, or poured into Peking to proclaim their love for Mao and their hatred for the 'capitalist-roaders' in the Party high command. In January 1967 a mob for a time took over the city of Shanghai. Co-operation between the army and the Red Guards frequently broke down, and there was also fighting between rival groups of revolutionary enthusiasts. During 1968 order was slowly restored, and in April 1969 the 9th regular Congress of the Chinese Communist Party was held. Of the members and alternate members of the Central Committee then chosen, only a fifth had been elected at the 8th Congress in 1956.

The Cultural Revolution recalls inevitably the Great Purge of 1936–39 in Soviet Russia. In both cases the supreme leader des-

troyed the leadership of the Party, including a majority of persons who had loyally followed him. In both cases a grotesque campaign of mass adulation raised the leader to a semi-divine status: the differences between the two campaigns amount to little more than the differences between Russian and Chinese styles of rhetoric. In both cases the whole machinery of the Party, the civil government and the management of the national economy were disrupted, reducing each country to extreme weakness. However, the two cases differ no less than they resemble each other. In China the army was not attacked: in Russia the army was deprived of about half its officer corps. In Russia many hundreds of thousands were executed or done to death by inhuman privations, and millions more were wasted for years in forced labour of dubious value, and released with their health ruined: in China there were some casualties in fighting, but they do not seem to have been numerous, and there appear to have been no mass executions or mass imprisonments. In Russia the whole grisly process was carried through by a section of the regular coercive apparatus— the security police: in China it was the work of millions of ordinary citizens, called in and incited to violence by the leader himself. Though the aim was to reinforce the power of an ageing autocrat, the method did enable vast numbers of Chinese workers and peasants to express their rage against some of those who had despised and exploited them for so long. Thousands of innocent persons, officials or teachers or managers, suffered undeserved violence or insults, and the frenzied hatred of the mob for the glories of China's past civilization was a terrifying spectacle, yet there was an undoubted element of poetic justice in the story. Participation of the people, overthrow of bureaucracy and rejection of mandarin superiority were notions that awoke enthusiasm from persons very unlike Chinese peasants, in the Boulevard Saint-Michel or within sight of the Bay Bridge. Though China's material power dwindled rapidly, the Chinese myth won supporters throughout the world.

Central Europe

The Soviet conquest of Central Europe in 1945 was followed by the establishment of a Soviet empire in these lands. The new governments proceeded rapidly to copy both the political institutions and the social and economic policies of the Soviet Union. Their economic resources were made available to their Soviet masters. Such valuable products as Polish coal and Czech uranium ore were sold to Russia at artificially low prices. In the three states formerly allied to Germany (Hungary, Rumania and Bulgaria) 'joint companies' were set up, which soon had a dominant position in Rumanian and Hungarian oil, and in air and sea transport in all three countries. The claim to reparations enabled the Soviet Government pitilessly to exploit the industrial resources of East Germany. In all the most important positions of control in the economy—the police, the armed forces and the civil administration —there were 'Soviet expert advisers' who were essentially colonial officials. Teaching in schools and universities was based on Soviet models, and an essential feature of education and of the whole mass-media network was unlimited flattery of the Soviet Union, the Russian people, and those aspects of the Russian past and of Russian culture which were designated for the purpose. The history of the Central European nations was rewritten to suit the purposes not so much of Marxism as of the Stalin myth and of Russian chauvinism. Inevitably this policy of denying the national identity, and suppressing the culture, of at least ten nations with long historical memories and proud traditions aroused resentment. This could not in fact be completely suppressed, but exploded in varying degree in the next quarter-century.

The first conflict was with Yugoslavia. Though the Yugoslav Communists were at first more drastic in their methods and more determined to impose the full Soviet blueprint on their subjects than any other Communist leaders, and though they were unshakeably loyal to the Soviet Union in foreign policy, they were unacceptable to Stalin precisely because they had won their own victory, and so could not be counted on as his abject servants. This was the basic reason for conflict, though there were also a number of practical matters of internal and foreign policy on which the two governments disagreed. In June 1948, on Soviet instructions, the Cominform (or 'Information Bureau' of eight ruling and two Western Communist parties, set up in 1947 as a less ambitious successor to the Comintern, dissolved in 1943) expelled Yugoslavia from its ranks. The Soviet Government and its Central European satellites launched a massive propaganda campaign against Yugoslavia, but this stopped short of military action. The survival of the Yugoslav Communist Government was due essentially to the same cause which had brought about the conflict: Tito possessed his own armed forces, police and state machine, and he commanded not only the devoted loyalty of most Communists but also a certain more or less admiring assent from millions outside the Party. The few persons who preferred Stalin to Tito were made harmless without much difficulty. The breach subsequently proved a blessing for the Yugoslav Communists. In the following twenty years they had their difficulties and their failures, but the trend away from Soviet models unmistakably promoted a more efficient economy and greater cultural and personal liberty.

The breach with Yugoslavia was followed by the imposition on the Soviet-dominated countries of a Party purge, whose methods and style recalled those of the Soviet purge of 1936–39 though its scale was much smaller. In 1949 and 1950 the victims were those leading Communists considered liable to 'nationalism', that is, to a tendency to put their own countries' interests before those of the Soviet Union. In 1951 and 1952 the scope was widened, and it was notable that blows fell with special severity on Communists of Jewish origin. The two parties which suffered most from the purge were the Czechoslovak and the Hungarian. In both countries about half the members of the Central Committee of the Party disappeared, while some of the most eminent were put on public trial and executed or sentenced to long terms of imprisonment. It was in these two countries too that the methods of torture and humiliation most closely approached those of the Soviet Union. In Bulgaria and Rumania too the purge was doubtless brutal, but it had much fewer victims, and in Poland it was both smaller and milder.

The new course in the Soviet Union after Stalin's death was reflected also in Central Europe. The first upheaval was a revolt in the Czech industrial centre of Plzen in May 1953: for a whole day the city was in the hands of the workers. Much more serious was the p 136 (34) rising in East Berlin and other major cities of Soviet-occupied Germany on 17 June. Both were of course repressed, but advice from Moscow favoured concessions. In July the new Hungarian Premier, Imre Nagy, introduced a programme of reforms, and a similar policy was adopted in Czechoslovakia. Khrushchev's public reconciliation with Tito during his visit to Belgrade in 1955, and his secret speech to the 20th Congress of the Soviet Communist

Party in February 1956 accelerated the trend. In June 1956 the workers of the Polish industrial city of Poznan took over the town. In the autumn of 1956 a similar crisis occurred at the same time in Poland and in Hungary. In both countries pressures for reform within the Communist Parties centred on outstanding leaders who were in opposition to the dominant group—in Poland on Gomulka, the chief victim of the purge in 1950, in Hungary on Nagy, who after two years of reforming policy had been removed from the premiership by the chief Stalinist Mátyas Rákosi. The results, however, were different in the two countries, because the two dominant groups reacted differently.

In Poland the Stalinist incumbent, Edward Ochab, decided to give way to the feeling in the Party and in the country, to call Gomulka to power, and to present a united front of the Party leadership towards Moscow. Thus the Polish Party never lost control of power, and Khrushchev and his colleagues, visiting Warsaw, decided that they must do business with the new leadership. The result was that the worst forms of Soviet economic exploitation of Poland were ended, and the Polish Party obtained effective internal sovereignty. In the subsequent decade Gomulka used his power as he saw fit. He made concessions to the Catholic Church, and put an end to the partial collectivization of agriculture which had started in the 1950s. On the other hand he relentlessly deprived the urban educated élite, which had in fact organized the movement that brought him to power, of such liberties as it briefly won during the crisis in October 1956. In foreign policy he became the most loyal ally of the Soviet Union. Both to please his Soviet patrons and to minimize the steady decline of his popularity in Poland, he used the whole propaganda apparatus of the regime to maximize hatred of West Germany. This propaganda had some of the aspects of the anti-semitic propaganda of Hitler's Third Reich. The Germans for Gomulka's subjects, like the Jews for Hitler's, were above all a scapegoat to divert hatred from nearer home, and whatever they might do or not do, they were held up as objects of loathing.

In Hungary the Stalinist incumbent, Ernö Gerö, who succeeded his close friend Rákosi in July 1956, refused to yield to pressure, ordered his police to fire on demonstrations of students and workers, and when this was ineffective, lost his head and appealed to the Soviet army. After a few days' fighting, in which the Hungarian p 136 army joined the Hungarian workers in fighting the Soviet army, (35) there was an armistice. Nagy had now been made Premier, but was unable to keep power in the hands of the Communist Party: he had to make a coalition government with the resuscitated Social Democratic and Small Farmers' Parties. Hungary was rapidly turning into a multi-party democracy like neighbouring Austria.

'Lenin, on the ruins of an ideal'—a cartoon first published in Holland, after the crushing of revolts in Eastern Europe had caused many Western Communists to lose faith in Russia's ideological leadership. (5)

In a desperate bid for international support in the face of a growing threat of further Soviet intervention, Nagy declared Hungary neutral: the neutrality of Austria, which the Soviet Union had recognized, was his model. This action only aggravated his offence in Soviet eyes. Helped by the fact that international attention was monopolized by the Anglo-French expedition to Port Said, the Soviet army invaded in force on 4 November 1956. Invasion was followed by executions of workers and soldiers, and two years later Nagy and the commander-in-chief of his army, General Pál Maleter, were also executed. However, the Hungarian Revolution was not without its effects. The new party leader, János Kádár, a former associate of Nagy and victim of torture under Rákosi, was able, after convincing the Soviet leaders of his loyalty to the Soviet Union and of his determination to preserve the Communist Party's dictatorship, to introduce a number of reforms. At the end of the 1960s Hungarians enjoyed greater personal and cultural liberty, and their economy was better managed, than those of any country of the Soviet camp.

The Soviet-Chinese conflict of the 1960s gave the Central European Communist leaders the chance of demanding a price for their loyalty to Moscow, or even of manoeuvring between the two Communist giants. It was the Rumanians who made best use of the opportunity. The immediate cause of Rumanian-Soviet conflict was economic. Khrushchev attempted to increase the co-ordination of the economies of the countries belonging to the Comecon (or Council for Mutual Economic Aid, founded in 1947, for many years rather passive, but to some extent reactivated in the early 1960s). This may have been desirable on general economic grounds but had the disadvantage, from the Rumanian point of view, that specialization by each country according to existing resources would mean slower progress in Rumania's industrialization. This the Rumanian Government publicly refused to accept, in 1962. Behind the economic conflict lay other resentments. Rumanians had suffered especially from what may be called cultural Russification. At Soviet behest, the links with the Latin countries, France and Italy, which had been of primary importance to educated Rumanians ever since the foundation of the modern Rumanian state, had been virtually destroyed, and attempts made to exaggerate the Slav element in Rumanian language and culture, and to portray the Russians, traditional oppressors of Rumania, as their main benefactors. All this was bitterly resented as an attempt to deprive the Rumanians of their culture and their national identity. The resentment was felt no less inside the Communist Party than among the people at large. From 1962 onwards the Rumanian Government made successful efforts to increase its economic and cultural links with Western Europe and the wider world. In foreign policy, while repeating their loyalty to the Soviet Union, Rumanian spokesmen studiously refrained from denouncing the Chinese. In internal affairs the grip of the Communist Party was not relaxed, but undoubtedly there was a steady increase of freedom in the non-political sphere.

In 1968 Czechoslovakia experienced a revolutionary crisis. For some years cultural and personal freedom had increased, and this had been used, especially by writers and especially in Slovakia, to press for reforms. In January 1968 Antonín Novotný, for many years leader of the Communist Party, was forced from his post. In the next months there was a rapid upsurge of liberty in all parts of the country. The Communist Party did not lose political control, and its leaders, headed by the new First Secretary of the Party, Alexander Dubček, proclaimed their loyalty to the Soviet Union, thus hoping to show their innocence of the two sins which had brought about the ruin of Imre Nagy in Hungary twelve years earlier. However, the Communist Party itself was changing so rapidly, both in policies and in personnel, that it seemed doubtful to Communist leaders in Moscow and in neighbouring countries— especially to the unpopular and ageing tyrants Ulbricht in East Germany and Gomulka in Poland—whether it was a Communist Party any more, and whether Czechoslovakia could be called 'socialist' (in the orthodox Soviet Empire sense) any more. A meeting of the Politburos of the Soviet and Czechoslovak Parties at Černa, on the Czechoslovak side of the border with the Soviet Union, in early July, and a subsequent meeting of the leaders of all the Soviet camp Communist parties in Bratislava, appeared to have

p 42
(46)

brought agreement. However, either these meetings were deception manoeuvres or the Soviet leaders changed their mind. On 21 August 1968 the Soviet army invaded Czechoslovakia, together with token forces from East Germany, Poland, Hungary and Bulgaria (but not from Rumania). During the winter of 1968–69 an equivocal situation existed in Czechoslovakia. The invading forces abducted the Czech and Slovak leaders, but the passive resistance of a united people, especially of the young, forced the Soviet leaders to temporize. They released Dubček and his colleagues, and for a time it seemed that, though Soviet military forces were to stay, some of the liberties won in 1968 might be preserved. The Soviet leaders, however, slowly and efficiently pursued their aims of subjection and humiliation of the Czechs and Slovaks, reimposition of terror, refalsification of history, redegradation of national identity and vengeance against the 1968 leaders. Whether Dubček would be spared the fate of Nagy remained in 1970 an open question.

p 136
(36)

At the end of the 1960s it was clear that the Russians were hated in Central Europe as never before in history. The last remnants of pan-Slav romanticism, which survived longer among the Czechs than anywhere else, were destroyed in August 1968. After a quarter of a century of Communist rule the difference between the Russians and their nearest neighbours was greater than it had been when Russia was Communist and its neighbours feudal or capitalist. In 1939 Rumania had had an upper stratum of Western-educated French-speaking Europeans, but the Rumanian peasants, backward and impoverished and barely educated, had been much closer in life and outlook to Russian peasants (whether *muzhiki* ruled by a Tsar or *kolkhozniki* ruled by Stalin) than to their own upper stratum. By 1970 the Rumanians had become a largely urbanized and well educated, if still poor, European nation. The Rumanian masses had entered Rumanian culture, and this culture was European. The material progress achieved by the Communist Government had widened the gulf between Rumanians and Russians. Rumania belonged now not to Eastern Europe but to Central Europe. How far these considerations applied to Bulgaria was not clear: evidence was conflicting. That they applied to Poland, Hungary and Czechoslovakia could not be doubted.

f 5

Socialist Realism and the Russian folk tradition are happily combined in the work of Vladimir Favorsky. This linocut of 1961 is entitled 'We Will Achieve Disarmament'. (6)

Ideology, power and the state

There was plenty of evidence that the old Marxist-Leninist faith had lost much of its hold over Russians. To some of the elderly shamans of the Agitprop Department of the Central Committee of the CPSU the sacred doctrines retained their ancient power, but for most administrators or managers they were no more than cant phrases to be recited on ritual occasions, for most workers and peasants they were a dreary set of incantations prescribed by the powers that be, and for young intellectuals who took ideas seriously they were fit for the drastic rethinking which the apparatus of power existed to prevent.

Yet it would be wrong to argue that 'ideology' had ceased to play any part in Soviet society or in the mentality of Soviet policy-makers. There remained an ideological amalgam served up to the Soviet public in school, university, press, radio, place of work and public meeting. This was not Marxism, nor even Leninism if by that is meant the ideas of the historical personage Vladimir Ilyich. It was a compound of residual Marxist clichés, Russian chauvinism and cultural philistinism. In style if not in content it closely resembled the outlook of the triumphant capitalist class in Western Europe and North America at the end of the 19th century. There is the same half-conscious belief that all moral and aesthetic standards should conform to the convenience and the prejudices of the dominant class, the same belief that the future belonged to them, the same contempt for 'lesser breeds without the law'. To members of the Soviet upper stratum (whether one calls it, in the phrase first used by the Yugoslav Communist heretic Milovan Djilas, 'the new class', or prefers some such description as 'state bourgeoisie') what was important and valuable in residual Marxism-Leninism was not the content of its theories—of which most had but the most imperfect grasp—but its claim to be 'scientific'. Marxist-Leninist science had predicted the future course of human history and Soviet policy was based upon it. The prevalence of such views was an immense source of strength to the Soviet leaders, and they did not underrate it. They were themselves affected by these beliefs, and they had a direct collective interest in propagating them.

There was evidence however in the late 1960s that the orthodox amalgam was not universally accepted. The critical tradition of the Russian intelligentsia still survived, and in the 1960s a few men and women showed extraordinary courage, not only protesting against perversion of justice in the courts and brutality in the concentration camps and asking that the liberties listed in the 1936 Constitution should be observed, but also defending the cause of the persecuted Crimean Tatars and protesting against the invasion of Czechoslovakia. These few heroes were punished by the Government, but less severely than in Stalin's time, and there was evidence that the younger generation as a whole was less prepared to be cowed by the authorities.

Nevertheless there were also strong reasons to believe that those features of Russian government and society which for centuries have disheartened both native and foreign observers, remained strong: contempt for law, admiration for brute force, a belief that political oppression is something like the weather—beastly and unchangeable—hysterical hostility to foreigners (which may be combined with exquisite courtesy and hospitality to individuals) and an impenetrable and all-pervasive self-righteousness. It may indeed be argued that the docility of the Russian people has been the greatest single instrument of tyranny in human history: this vast nation of suffering slaves and brave soldiers has provided its rulers with unequalled opportunity to enslave others. Russian soldiers gave their lives to stop Napoleon, Ludendorff and Hitler, though the masters who sent them to fight all three had scourged and exploited them without mercy. After fifty years it seemed that the main effect of the convulsions and bloodshed, the messianic hopes and moral passions of the Russian Revolution had been to replace a decadent élite, no longer able to command obedience or even to give orders, by a vigorous élite, of unlimited ambitions and with a profound understanding of the mechanism and psychology of power. The prize for which these élites had contended was control of the most powerful instrument yet devised for the regimentation and the humiliation of man, the Russian state. For seven hundred years the outstanding feature of this state has been the obsession with power of its rulers, a power

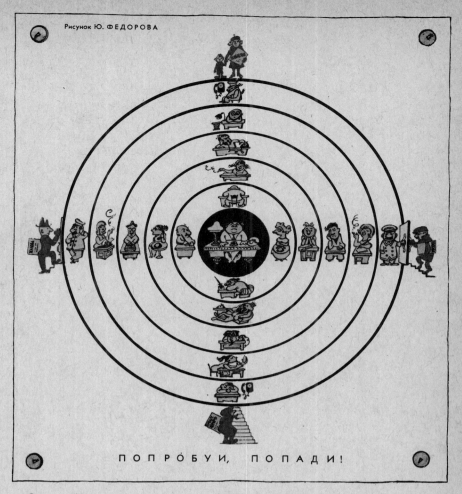

Soviet self-criticism: a cartoon from 'Krokodil' satirizing the evils of centralization and bureaucracy. Ordinary citizens have to penetrate five circles of officials before arriving at the man in the middle. (7)

empty of all other considerations. Chaadaev in his 'Philosophical Letter' of 1836 made a diagnosis that has never been bettered: Russia belonged neither to West nor to East, it had no culture, it formed 'a lacuna in the intellectual order'. Chaadaev admittedly exaggerated: there was a Russian culture, centuries old and derived mainly from Orthodox Christianity. However, this Russian culture was ignored or repressed by the holders of power, at least from the 14th century onwards. In the 19th century Russia experienced a magnificent new flowering of culture, but this too was ignored or repressed by the holders of power. Chaadaev later said that Russia would have some great lessons for the human race. Russia in 1917, and later, undoubtedly provided tremendous lessons for the human race, but the emptiness of power, the persecution of culture, the lacuna in the intellectual order remained. Some might argue against this that the Revolution itself was a triumph of Russian culture, because the revolutionaries were among the most brilliant products of that culture which the men of power had despised yet had failed to repress. Yet this is only a small part of the truth. After 1917, once the revolutionaries were in control, they too became men of power, and they too were affected by the emptiness of power. The new élite went through a hard school. For those who were still in power in 1970 the most testing time of all had been the Purge of 1936–39. Brezhnev, Kosygin and their contemporaries had risen rapidly, and remained on top, because they had proved their consummate ability as denouncers of innocent men.

In the 1960s the combination of men of power with docile masses seemed as strong as ever in Russian history. The men of culture were also there, and from their ranks it was likely that a few revolutionaries were being formed. Yet it was difficult to see how a situation could arise which would give them a chance to act.

Communism and co-existence

In 1970 'the Communist world' was little more than a phrase, covering at least three distinct groups. There was one super-power ruled by a Communist Party, the Soviet Union, with its two colonial empires—one within its borders, stretching from Bessarabia to the Pacific and composed of some 120 million non-Russians, the other to the West and composed of over a 100 million Europeans, living private and cultural lives quite different from those of the Russians, yet in the last resort available for Soviet purposes when required. There was another power of potential super status, yet still materially weak, China. There was a movement of opinion, strong among a section of the most educated young people of Western Europe and both North and South America, which believed in some purer and semi-anarchical form of Communism. Most of these young people rejected with loathing the Soviet regime, condemned the invasion of Czechoslovakia and felt that Brezhnev and his kind had betrayed the Revolution, yet at the same time they repudiated all West European and American policies of defence, whether military or diplomatic or propaganda, against Soviet power. Many of them were attracted by some aspects of Chinese Communism, at least as they interpreted it, and still more so by Cuban. They admired Che Guevara as a martyr of the revolutionary cause, and they professed admiration for guerrilla warfare as a means of revolutionary struggle. In their minds the revolutionary struggle within advanced industrial societies was indissolubly linked with the struggle of the peoples of Asia and Africa and Latin America against poverty, backwardness and exploitation by the rich nations.

Soviet orthodoxy, Maosim and utopian Communism differed profoundly from each other, but all three had one cause in common, the struggle of the North Vietnamese Communists and the Vietcong to drive the Americans out of South-East Asia and to impose their rule on Indo-China.

These three forms of Communism also competed for the allegiance of Communist parties throughout the world, of which the most potentially important were the French and Italian, each capable of mobilizing millions of votes and impressive trade-union support, yet both still far from power. Soviet domination of the French Party was only superficially affected by intellectual defections after the events in Hungary in 1956 and in Czechoslovakia in 1968. The Italian Party contained a wider range of opinion and a number of factions, some of which expressed and maintained strong opposition to Soviet policies. The utopianism of the young exercised some disintegrating influence on both parties. Chinese influence was small in European Communist parties but significant in those of Latin America and of Asia, especially perhaps in Bengal.

The Soviet Government in 1970 faced four hostile forces outside its boundaries: the governments of the United States, China and the West European NATO countries, and the peoples of Communist-ruled Central Europe.

In Western countries much was heard of the theory of 'convergence' of the capitalist and socialist, and especially of the Soviet and American systems. There was a widespread desire to 'end the cold war'. American and West European politicians longed to persuade themselves that the Soviet Union was a satisfied power, a natural ally of the United States against the irresponsible adventurist revolution-mongering of the Chinese. A longer-term view was that the Soviet Union and the United States had a common interest in the struggle against poverty, overpopulation and pollution. This view was eloquently echoed in an essay by an outstanding Soviet scientist, Academician A. D. Sakharov. He argued that the difference between 'capitalism' and 'socialism' was a matter of minor significance in comparison with the duty of the two super-powers to co-operate for world peace and progress.

There was, however, little reason to believe that the Soviet Government shared the views either of Sakharov or of Western optimists. The Brezhnev doctrine of limited sovereignty, issued after the invasion of Czechoslovakia, laid down that whenever 'socialism' is in danger in a 'socialist country', the other 'socialist governments' have the right to give help, whether or not this help

has been requested. It was made clear that it was for the Soviet Government to decide whether 'socialism' was in danger, and what kind of 'help' was suitable. Soviet spokesmen continued to emphasize that the conflict between 'capitalism' and 'socialism' was the basic reality of world politics, that 'peaceful coexistence' applied only to the diplomatic and military spheres, and that 'ideological coexistence' (that is, free discussion about opposed political views between the peoples of Communist and non-Communist countries) was absolutely impermissible. As for Vietnam, it was certainly arguable that Soviet interests were best served by an indefinite prolongation of the war. Even a clear victory for the Vietnamese Communists would be less advantageous. There was indeed no serious reason for thinking that Soviet hostility to the United States and the West had diminished since 1945. What had diminished was the willingness of the Western public to face so depressing and boring a state of affairs. The old anti-Communist orthodoxy of the 1950s was largely replaced in the 1960s by a new orthodoxy which maintained that 'the cold war' was a reactionary policy initiated by the Western powers against a relatively blameless Soviet Union, and that peace and co-operation were to be had for the asking.

The immediate threat of China to the Soviet Union in 1970 did not seem large. China had produced atom bombs and satellites, but remained militarily and industrially far behind the two super-powers. However, Chinese territorial claims on the Russian Far East, and Chinese intrigues in Central Asia were possible dangers for the future, and already in the 1960s fear of China caused an increasing involvement of the Soviet Union in the affairs of the Indian subcontinent, from which it could expect little but trouble. Meanwhile, the posture of ultra-revolutionary purity adopted by the Chinese, and their repeated denunciations of the Soviet Communists as traitors to the revolutionary cause, created rage in Moscow. Most important of all was a growth of mass hatred of China in Russia, something approaching a mood of hysterical obsession with the 'yellow peril', an irrational terror of the swarming millions which formed more than a quarter of the population of the globe.

If the danger from China, indefinable yet terrifying, was steadily growing, if some sort of a drastic reckoning with the Chinese would be necessary in the longer term, this must alter the perspective in which the Soviet leaders saw Europe. Would it be possible either to reach an understanding with the West, or to finish off Western Europe, before the Chinese danger reached its climax? The Soviet attitude to Western Europe was largely determined by its own relationship to Central Europe. The peoples of Central Europe were more aware than ever before that they belonged to European culture, and not to the Russian cultural world. This awareness was not confined to small intellectual élites, as it had been in the first decades of the century: it now extended much deeper. As long as Western Europe remained free and prosperous, its attraction to the peoples of the Soviet Empire would remain irresistible. The Soviet army had suppressed revolts and heresies, but there would probably be others and the cost of crushing them would grow. The existence of free and prosperous Western Europe was thus a perpetual menace to Soviet security.

Would a weakening of the West's will to defend itself tempt the Soviet rulers to believe that they could, before they had to face the Chinese menace, impose a settlement by force or threat of force on Europe which would deliver the rest of the continent into their hands? Or would the West's resolution last long enough for fear of the Chinese to force the Soviet Union to agree to a European settlement on European, not on Soviet, terms? As the seventies opened, it seemed that the fate not just of the Communist but of the Western world as well would turn on the answer to these questions.

VII ASIA AWAKENED

China, Japan, Indonesia and India

C.P. FITZGERALD

'The major challenge to traditional ethics,

customs and institutions was Western thought

in the guise of ideas like liberalism, democracy and science . . .

The shift from liberalism to socialism may be explained

in terms of the need to industrialize rapidly,

humiliating defeats, and authoritarian political heritage.'

PROFESSOR CHOW TSE-TUNG, 1960

Two problems

faced the nations of Asia at the beginning of the 20th century: freedom from imperialist rule and the modernization of industry and society. In India, the proudest possession of the British Empire, industrialization began early. By 1900 it had more railways and a more efficient administration than any other country in Asia. The story of 20th-century India, therefore, centres on the political struggle to achieve home rule. In 1911, the year of the Coronation Durbar of King George V and Queen Mary (upper picture, opposite), British domination seemed fixed and permanent. It was the first—and was to prove the last—occasion when a reigning Emperor visited India. It also marked the removal of the capital from Calcutta, a British creation, to Delhi, the old capital of the Mogul Empire—a gesture, however empty, to conciliate Indian nationalists.

In Japan, the situation was reversed. Here there was no problem of national sovereignty. Nor did the country need to undergo an internal revolution such as shook China for forty years. By taking what she needed from Western technology, but leaving her social structure intact, Japan was able to transform her whole economy in a miraculously short space of time. Victory over Russia in 1905 triumphantly vindicated such a policy. In the following year an Anglo-Japanese alliance was concluded, confirming Japan in her influence over Manchuria and Korea, and Prince Arthur of Connaught, a grandson of Queen Victoria, was received by the Emperor (lower picture). Already the Japanese contingent have adopted Western dress and ceremonial conventions. Japan was the only country in Asia to be recognized as modern, and therefore 'civilized', by the European powers. (1, 2)

The British Raj gave to India a measure of stability, and to its upper classes a way of life which replaced that which they would otherwise have inherited. Lord Curzon, Viceroy from 1899 to 1905 (right, with the ruler of Hyderabad and party), saw no likelihood of change: 'Congress is tottering to its fall, and one of my great ambitions is to assist it to a peaceful demise.' Meanwhile, a future President of Congress and Prime Minister of India, Jawaharlal Nehru (far right, with his family) was about to go off to public school and university in England, from which, like many other Indians of his class, he would return determined to play a role in the future of his own country. (3, 4)

Industry remained primitive (above right: an engineering workshop in 1926) and was not helped by inadequate transport facilities. Because of the bad roads and lack of road vehicles, expansion of the railway system was a profitable venture and 6,000 miles of track were added during Curzon's viceroyalty. Above: the railway station at Shelabagh, Baluchistan. (5, 6)

Five Indians in six live on the land, but agricultural methods generally remain backward, due to fragmentation of property, old-fashioned techniques and lack of capital. Right: threshing wheat in Manipur. (7)

After the First World War, Britain could no longer ignore Indian claims to self-rule. But the more extreme members of the Congress Party such as Gandhi and Nehru (right, with his daughter Indira Gandhi, herself to become Prime Minister in 1966) pressed for more rapid progress. In 1930–33 a series of Round Table conferences were held in London (below: Gandhi and Ramsay Macdonald at the 1931 meeting). The Second World War accelerated the process and full independence came in August 1947. Bottom: jubilant crowds surround Lord and Lady Mountbatten in New Delhi on Independence Day. (8, 9, 10)

Partition was unavoidable, given the hostility between Moslem and Hindu communities. Even so, bloodshed was widespread and eleven million people migrated. Those shown here are Hindu refugees from West Pakistan. (12)

Steel production is one sector which has greatly expanded since Independence. Between 1955 and 1965 output rose from 1,700,000 to 4,600,000 tons. Below: women workers at the Durgapur steelworks in Bengal. (11)

六月廿八日團民頑棄出隊中央奄成

民頑棄出隊經英法陸軍隆英法陸軍與國之兵與兩國開仗我國蟲兵軍門標下統帶從中央攻麼戰多時未分勝員云

圖戰麼民團與軍陸法英

In China, disillusionment with the corrupt and ineffective Manchu dynasty, aggravated by China's defeat by Japan in 1895, was translated into hatred of the foreigners who were carving up the country into 'spheres of interest'. The Boxers, a nationalist secret society which soon gained popular support, massacred thousands of foreigners, until a hastily assembled international military expedition (above) intervened. (13)

Rebellion against the Manchus broke out in 1911, when a section of the imperial army at Wuchang mutinied (above). The dynasty fell. Sun Yat-sen returned from America to head the new republic but was forced to give up the presidency to a right-wing general, the first of a series of 'war-lords' who dominated the country for a decade. (14)

The Japanese invasion of Korea in 1895, in which China was defeated, both fanned Chinese discontent with the dynasty and encouraged Japanese imperialism. Right: European reporters behind the Japanese lines. (15)

152

Japan's victory in the Russo-Japanese War of 1904–05 (above: Japanese woodcut of the Battle of Tsushima, the first military defeat of Europeans by Asians) enhanced Japanese prestige abroad and stimulated nationalist feeling at home. Below: Samurai working land which they were given in return for military service. (16, 17)

153

China's first president, Dr Sun Yatsen (left), living mostly abroad, had worked for a revolution since 1895. But his programme, embodied in the 'Three Points'—nationalism, democracy and socialism—was vague and his party, the Kuomintang, failed to provide effective leadership for the country. (18)

Under Chiang Kai-shek (right), who succeeded to the leadership of the Kuomintang after Sun's death in 1925, the party turned increasingly to the right, and the army became the real organ of power. In July 1926 he began a military advance from the south and by July 1928 had occupied Peking. China was once more united under relatively firm rule. (19)

Communist support had been vital in the early years of the Kuomintang. In 1926 the southern city of Canton was practically controlled by Communist workers (above: strike-breakers being tried). But by April 1927 Chiang Kai-shek was strong enough to break with them. Tens of thousands were massacred. The survivors formed a state within the state, against which Kuomintang forces (above right, photographed about 1929) waged a prolonged battle. (20, 21)

Invasion by Japan submerged the Civil War in a larger national struggle, in which the Communists co-operated with Chiang. Right: Japanese occupy Peking, July 1937. (22)

154

Japan's revolution was technological rather than political. The ease with which the country, on the surface at least, adopted a Western way of life is apparent in these photographs of two emperors—Yoshihoto (left) in 1915, wearing traditional costume, and his son Hirohito, photographed in 1957 (right). Japan's material strength stood in sharp contrast to the confused state of China in the twenties and thirties and the weakness of the European colonial powers after the German victories of 1940. The temptation to take advantage of the situation and make a bid for control of the whole of eastern Asia proved irresistible. (23, 24)

Health and strength, athletic prowess and military might: the combination seen here in a photomontage of 1938 is familiar from Fascist and Nazi propaganda, upon which the rulers of Japan in many ways modelled their image. (25)

Japan lost the Pacific War when the atomic bombs exploded over Hiroshima and Nagasaki in 1945. Right: the Japanese delegation arrives on board the *Missouri*. Surrender was complete, universally observed and without severe disadvantages. By co-operation with the American occupying force, Japan was soon able to resume her triumphant economic progress. (26)

Modern Japan welcomed the world—
especially the capitalist world—to the
International Exhibition at Osaka
(above). Beyond the flags of the
nations rises the strange 'symbol' of
the exhibition, like a creature from
another planet. (27)

Physical renewal has always been a
feature of Japanese culture. The ancient city of Osaka (left) was practically rebuilt after 1945 and since
then its traffic has outgrown its road
system. The solution has been to build
raised motorways over the old streets
and above the rivers. Nagasaki (right)
rose from its ruins to become one of
the leading shipbuilding centres of
the world. Here a ship is being completed at the Mitsubishi Heavy Industries Yard. (28, 29)

The trouble-spot of postwar Asia has been the South East, where the withdrawal of the colonial powers left chaos and disunity. The Dutch had imposed an unreal cohesion upon the very disparate cultures of Sumatra, Java, Borneo and Celebes, but gave their inhabitants no political responsibility. Above left: a Dutch governor of Samarang, Central Java, in 1904 and (centre) Dutch Indonesian troops after crushing a rebellion in 1901. Nationalist movements gained strength in the twenties, recruited mostly from the ranks of the Western-educated. Achmed Sukarno, a young engineer, began to organize resistance to the Dutch in 1927. He suffered imprisonment and exile between then and 1942, when he was released by the Japanese. In 1945 he and his party proclaimed the new republic of Indonesia (this photograph was taken in 1949), but faced with breakaway movements in the Moluccas, Sumatra and Celebes, he used force to maintain unity and abandoned any pretence of democracy. (30–32)

The French colonies left the most permanent legacy of disaster. 'Indo-China' was ruled from Saigon by a French governor (left). A medal, struck in 1937 (above), comemmorated its fiftieth anniversary. After the war the French attempted to re-impose their rule (right) but were defeated by the nationalists in May 1954. At the Geneva Conference of 1962 it was divided into four independent states—Laos, Cambodia, North and South Vietnam, all under right-wing governments except the Communist North Vietnam. (33–35)

Malaysia was born amid the clash of nationalists, Communists and colonial power. After a state of emergency that had lasted since 1945, the British handed over power in 1957. In the federal capital of Kuala Lumpur (right) a grand military parade marked the occasion. (36)

SOUTH VIETNAM

With the help of friendly nations, South Vietnamese soldiers are fighting and winning this war against the Viet Cong.

Government troops display captured Viet Cong flag and weapons.

把仇恨集中在枪膛里
消灭美国侵略者

War in South Vietnam, seen variously as invasion from the north or as civil war between Communists and government, was prolonged by American support for the latter until complete stalemate resulted. The Communist poster on the right is captioned: 'If the enemy refuses to get out, annihilate him'. (37, 38)

China's Communists seemed to be in an even worse position in 1945 than in 1937. Japan was defeated, but Chiang Kai-shek's regime was recognized by both America and Russia and was receiving massive aid from the former. Yet in four years Chiang had thrown away his advantages and had been forced to retreat, beaten and discredited, to Taiwan (Formosa). Mao proclaimed the People's Republic of China on 1 October 1949. Stamps commemorating the occasion (right) stress unity, industrialization and ties with Russia. (39)

China today is politically as monolithic as Soviet Russia, but is distinguished by the fact that it rests on peasant rather than proletarian foundations. Mao Tse-tung's personal supremacy was enhanced by the Cultural Revolution, when he seems to have appealed from the 'Old Guard' to the youth of China (below) who are encouraged to see him as an infallible and almost superhuman figure. (40)

China, Japan, Indonesia and India

C. P. FITZGERALD

ASIA is a very wide term, covering many diverse peoples and countries, but for the general reader it is usually not inclusive of the Russian territories of northern Asia, while the Middle East has had such close associations in history and culture with Europe that it forms a separate entity. Asia, therefore, in this chapter will mean China and Japan, the countries of South East Asia, India and Pakistan. What characterized almost all of these countries is that at the beginning of the century they were either under European rule or heavy pressure—some having only just escaped with independence—and that in the course of the first half of the century they one and all repudiated the authority of Europe and became involved in differing kinds of revolution, the underlying purpose of which was the 'Search for Wealth and Power' as Yen Fu one of the first acute Chinese writers of the late 19th century defined it. Wealth and power were to be sought for the community as a whole, not for individuals nor a single class. The Asian peoples saw that they had lost these desirable qualities to Europe through the decay of their own institutions as well as through the assaults of the Western nations. They must rebuild, and to rebuild they must pull down.

Thus the 'Revolt of Asia', as some writers began to call it as early as the twenties of the century, is the great theme of this age: it took many forms, not only political independence, but also social change—sometimes violent—cultural transformation and economic and industrial revolution. Different countries tried varying systems to achieve these aims, but the apparent gap between, say, capitalist Japan and Communist China should not obscure the fact that the primary aim in both countries was the modernization and rejuvenation of a society long bound by outdated conventions and a rigid social system confined by limited economic development. It proved, everywhere, impossible to eliminate one outmoded institution without undermining all the others. If ancient political forms were changed, so too must the social system be altered, and therefore its economic base called in question, its values challenged. If the political framework was retained, the forces of change at work in the economy and in society profoundly altered the character and operation of the political system. It thus came about that where European political control was established it became identified with the conservative forces opposed to change, the very opposite result of the high expectations with which the generation of Macaulay had embarked on the great imperial adventure. In the countries under foreign rule the first objective was to oust the foreigner from control; how independence should be used to further other goals was often given much less consideration.

China: forty years of revolution

It is probably therefore no accident that the two countries which never came under direct European government, China and Japan, should exhibit, each in their very different ways, the maximum social and economic transformation, since the political struggle for independence from foreign control was for them only a minor aspect of their problems. Both had suffered limitations upon their sovereignty imposed by force in the 19th century; both freed themselves from these constraints, Japan nearly half a century before China. But for both the real problems were social, economic and internal.

The change in China was delayed; at the beginning of the century the country was still ruled by the Manchu dynasty, far gone in decline, its prestige dimmed, its authority challenged by an active revolutionary movement. Since it appeared to embody all the antique institutions which the younger generation believed to be keeping China backward and weak, these institutions were also to be attacked and challenged, and if possible replaced by others more in accord with modern needs. It proved relatively easy to get rid of the Manchu dynasty; much more difficult to find an alternative system of government to replace the imperial system which had endured for more than two thousand years. The reformers who had hoped to modernize the monarchy, partly on the model of what had been done in Japan, had been discredited by failure to overcome the extreme reactionary element in the Court led by the Empress Dowager and Regent, Tz'u Hsi. When their brief moment of power in 1898 was ended by the virtual imprisonment of the Emperor Kuang Hsu, whom they had inspired with reforming zeal, reform of the monarchy was a forlorn hope. The revolutionary element which also traded upon the antipathy to the Manchus felt especially in south China, captured the younger generation and set as its goal the establishment of a democratic republic. The overthrow of the dynasty in 1911–12, accomplished with slight opposition, seemed to foreshadow a very rapid programme of change and modernization in China. This did not occur: the revolutionary leadership consisted of young, largely expatriate students who had spent years in exile in Japan and were very ignorant of the true disposition of power within the country.

p 152 (14)

China became from the first years of the Republic involved in a series of military dictatorships—the first ending in an abortive attempt to set up a new dynasty—which led to a breakdown of central authority, increasing disorder in the countryside, civil wars between military satraps, and a further decline rather than recovery in her national status among the powers of the world. After ten years the revolution seemed to have accomplished nothing, except the destruction of most of the old institutions—but without replacing them with viable or desirable alternatives. A president who was the helpless tool of the general in power for the moment, an army divided against itself, a degenerated bureaucracy filled, not with successful examination candidates, as in the imperial age, but by nepotism and corruption: these were the only substitutes for the imperial system which had so far appeared. The economy was stagnant, since investment in any place other than the foreign controlled Concessions in some of the great port cities was hazardous and unprofitable. There was, indeed, one very active movement in the new society: the growth of higher modern education, associated with strong new currents in literature, usually inspired by ideas derived from the European Left. The cultural transformation was rapidly outstripping political change and economic development; inevitably, it was first felt in social attitudes and conventions.

In the twenties, the Western visitor to China and Japan was often struck with a great and significant contrast. In Japan all was orderly—indeed regimented—clean, modern, efficient; in China the same aspects of life were chaotic, insanitary, antique and inefficient. But in Japan women were still treated as inferiors, walking behind their husbands or brothers; social change was much less in evidence. In China women of the educated class were claiming and receiving an equality almost beyond that which contemporary Europeans granted. Social change in other ways was evident and rapid, uncontrolled and often ill-directed, but dynamic. Since the Chinese could feel no satisfaction from the achievements of their government, they had no respect for it and no loyalty towards its forms and personnel. In Japan the restored monarchy had presided over the modernization of the country and led it to high international status. It was possible for modern men to accept some of the myths associated with the Throne in view of the obvious and real achievements of the governments over which the emperor presided. Thus revolution in Japan was not a requisite for further progress; in China it was essential.

From the very first the revolutionary movement in China had been radical: the goal of a republic rather than a constitutional monarchy was, in 1911, in Asia, extreme. Outside the American continents there were only two republics, France and Switzerland. After World War I and the Russian Revolution, parliamentary democracy, which had lamentably failed in China, was discredited. The Party Dictatorship was now the fashion, at first inspired by the Russian Communist Party, then, on the Nationalist side, deriving fresh inspiration from Fascist Italy and later Nazi Germany, and on the other side leading to the foundation of the Chinese Communist Party. The original revolutionary movement bifurcated, at first working in harmony to overthrow and destroy the military dictators and satraps, then coming, in 1927, to an open and final breach.

p 154
(18–21)
p 132
(21, 22)

In 1926, one year after its founder and leader, Dr Sun Yat-sen, had died, the Nationalist Party in China, acting in alliance with the small but growing Communist Party (founded in 1921) launched a military campaign which with sweeping success and strong popular support overthrew the military dictatorships and satrapies in the southern half of China. The conquest of the north was certain to follow, and did follow, in 1928: but before that year, in 1927, the Nationalist or Kuomintang Party had quarrelled with the Communist Party, and the two rivals, at first so unequal in power and resources, were to fight for twenty-two years until the ultimate and total triumph of the Communist Party in 1949.

It was this contrast which from this period onward involved China in more acute and acrimonious foreign relations both with her neighbour, Japan, and with the powers of Europe. China was still backward economically; therefore she remained weak militarily; and the equation of power as read in the West meant that, as long as these conditions lasted, social and political transformations were not to be held in esteem or consideration. In China the view was different, partly itself a transformation of the old ethical Confucian teaching that Form was insignificant and Content all that mattered. The Form of Chinese government and society might still be confused and retarded, the Content, the ideas which moved within it, the solutions groped for, discarded, or devised, were of great significance. When theory was right, order would evolve from it; to the Western observer—particularly the Anglo-Saxon—only when Order was established could theories be applied. In practical terms this meant that China claimed her lost sovereign rights as due to her without regard to internal inadequacies of law or administration. The Western powers argued that rights could only be yielded when law and order justified their relinquishment. There are very deep and ancient divergences in the cultures of the two parts of the world which explain this modern disagreement; the important point was that the Chinese culture proved too strong to compromise easily with this aspect of Western modernization, and had to struggle through to its own solution.

Japan posed a different problem for China. A country of ancient Chinese civilization, modified and adapted to Japanese life, it was fundamentally similar. It was the Empire modernized, with all the authoritarian ideas of the Empire, and the ambitions of a dominant military caste. The Manchu Empire, three hundred years before in its early vigour, had exhibited the same characteristics. The Chinese knew what that meant—military conquest and rule by a privileged, alien élite. They had not driven out the Manchus to put the Japanese in their place, therefore there was ultimately no possible compromise. So long as Japanese imperial ambitions were directed to conquests upon the mainland, China was bound to be

her enemy. The question of whether a better relationship would be established if China had an orderly government and a developing economy did not arise; in so far as these possibilities seemed real, they militated against Japanese ambitions. From 1931, when the Japanese seized Manchuria, there were only two possible future developments: either China would succumb to Japanese encroachments and in effect lose her independence, or the situation would deteriorate into a disastrous war. The second eventuality was by far the more probable, and proved to be the fact; it was made inevitable by the development of the Chinese internal revolution which precluded the alternative. Few foreign observers and, it would seem, no influential Japanese understood this. p 39
(23)

Thus one of the great events of Asian history in the 20th century, World War II, began in that continent some two years before it broke out in Europe and some four years before its later development, the Pacific War, broke out in December 1941. On 7 July 1937 the Japanese forces stationed, under treaty, in the vicinity of Peking attacked the Chinese garrison of a small town. Thus began a war which ended eight years later with the surrender of Japan and the total evacuation of all her forces and nationals from any part of China. Many millions of victims were claimed by that war, and among the casualties was the Nationalist Government of China, which appeared briefly to be among the victors at the end of the war. It was in fact fatally degenerated, corrupt and out of touch with the movement of national opinion; on the other hand the Communist Party had taken the lead in organizing the guerrilla resistance to the Japanese occupation, and had enormously enlarged its following and the territory it controlled. It was no longer, as in 1935–37, a small armed insurrection defying the power of a massive, if poorly organized, central government; in 1945 the two parties faced each other, still unequal in military power, but almost on a par in the areas they really controlled and the population on which they could draw. Attempts at mediation undertaken by the US Government, which in the postwar period had inherited all that remained of European influence and succeeded Japan as ruler of the eastern seas, failed to avert a final civil war. p 154
(22)

Whether this was also inevitable can be disputed. It may be that if the US had not become during the war so heavily committed to the Nationalist Government of Chiang Kai-shek, he would not have relied on America to back him in an all-out attempt to destroy the Communist movement. As it was, he could not believe that America would not intervene with decisive power to win his war; he would not, therefore, listen to the Americans when they warned him to reform his government before it collapsed. Although his forces were four to five times the strength of the Communist

Chiang Kai-shek's regime is represented by the Communists as a cruel exploitation of the peasantry. This woodcut shows an eviction for unpaid rent. (1)

armies, and equipped with US weaponry, although the Nationalists had an airforce, also US trained, and the Communists had no aircraft at all, none the less in three years, from July 1946, when open large-scale civil war broke out, to 1949, when the Nationalist forces withdrew to Taiwan, the regime of Chiang Kai-shek had encountered total military defeat. This result had nothing to do with the machinations of Moscow nor the treason of US diplomats as was so long believed in some circles. The Russians, who had occupied Manchuria at the Japanese surrender, were mainly concerned to strip that province of all its industrial equipment, not to retain it. When they had taken what they could move, they withdrew, leaving the countryside to the Communist guerrillas, and the cities to be taken over by Nationalists flown in to occupy them. Subsequently all such cities were surrounded and forced to surrender to the Communists. But this had nothing to do with the USSR.

The final turn to the Chinese Revolution, which after nearly forty years brought a Communist Party to power, was the consequence of forces operating within Chinese society, reacting to outward pressures, such as the Japanese invasion, but essentially moved by the transformation of Chinese society in the long course of the revolution. The economic changes which seemed, to the West, so essential a preliminary to the social changes, did not in fact become large-scale until after the Communist Government had restored peace and order. It was the social change, the decay of the old gentry class, erstwhile scholar gentry and officials, the rise of political consciousness among the peasant masses (for which the rigours of the Japanese invasion were largely responsible), the failure of the small merchant middle class to provide a viable effective alternative 'bourgeois' leadership to the old gentry—these were the factors which had been operating for many years within Chinese society, largely unremarked by outside observers, which made a victory for the Communist Party possible. That Party won also because it had adapted its methods and ideas to the realities of the Chinese social situation. Ignoring the more doctrinaire precepts of Marxism, the Chinese Communist Party was

p 160 (39, 40)

founded on peasant support and attuned to meet peasant demands. Industrial workers, rare enough in prewar China, and not open or energetic supporters of the Communists during the civil war, could be brought into the movement when it was victorious. China's story in the 20th century is not unintelligible, but it must be understood in Chinese terms, and not in European stereotypes which do not fit.

Japan and the 20th century

Early in the 20th century Japan became the one Asian country which was recognized as modern (and therefore as 'civilized'), and which, by successful wars, achieved the status of a Great Power. All extraterritorial rights and concessions, which Japan had had to grant to foreign powers in the previous half-century, were abandoned; Britain concluded the Anglo-Japanese Treaty of Alliance (1902) and thus set the seal on Japan's claim to full equality with any other nation. No other Asian nation had obtained the alliance on equal terms of any European power. In the last forty years of the 19th century Japan had undergone a very far-reaching industrial and political transformation, guided by the highly competent but authoritarian statesmen who had contrived in 1869 the abdication of the last Tokugawa Shogun and the restoration of the hitherto secluded emperor, Meiji. In the eighties the Japanese were already asserting their influence in Korea, still a Chinese tributary kingdom, and in 1895 they defeated the Manchu Empire in a brief war fought in northern Korea and southern Manchuria. Japan acquired a predominant position in Korea, which in 1910 was annexed outright. Japan had also obtained as part of the peace terms the lease of the Liaotung peninsula in Manchuria with the two ports of Lushun and Talien-wan (later known to the West as Port Arthur and Dairen). China, however, by invoking the secret aid of Russia and France, was able to force Japan to renounce this acquisition, which the Chinese then had to grant instead to Russia. This manoeuvre was the first cause of the Russo-Japanese war of 1904–05, in which Japan defeated imperial Russia in Manchuria (Chinese territory though it was) and obtained the Liaotung ports as well as a dominant position in

p 149 (2)

p 152 (15)

p 153 (16)

Democracy came to Japan in the 20th century. This cartoon from 'Jiji' in 1918, when only one in thirty-five had the vote, expresses agitation for an extended franchise. Yet Japanese social traditions remained basically intact. (2)

the southern half of Manchuria. These two wars founded the Japanese overseas empire. Formosa had also been annexed following China's defeat in 1895.

Japan thus entered the 20th century as a formidable power, locally dominant in eastern Asia. At home modernization had made great progress; the country was well served by a railway system, although not so well provided with roads, which before the motor age were considered unimportant. A large and growing merchant marine carried on trade with all parts of the world; Japanese industry, especially textiles, was modern and run on very economical lines. This indeed, was the major complaint that foreigners had to make against Japan. Her goods were too cheap, and undercut the products of other nations. The reasons were that, while the material aspect of the economy and society had been rapidly modernized, the social side remained largely unchanged. Japanese factory labour in the textile industry was recruited from peasant girls in very large numbers, who were paid very little, housed in dormitories owned by the companies and kept under a strict surveillance. Labour troubles were unknown, industry had an infinite supply of cheap workers, and the Japanese peasantry, accustomed to centuries of feudal subservience, were as ready to obey their new masters the industrialists as they had been docile under their former rulers the feudal Samurai and Daimyo.

Political life also had more an outward appearance of modernity than an inner core of progress. The former feudal lords had surrendered their status in return for becoming peers in a new aristocracy, which was strongly entrenched in the Upper House of the Diet. The Diet itself, brought into being by the Constitution of 1889 promulgated by the emperor as an act of his imperial free will, first convened in 1890. It expressed, often tumultuously, the aspirations of the rising industrial class, but was in effect controlled by the strong bureaucratic government, which, acting in the name of the emperor, remained in all essentials supreme. Particularly the armed forces, navy and army, were beyond the control of elected politicians. They were responsible only to the emperor, their ministers in the Cabinet were appointed by the Throne, could not be dismissed by the prime minister, and were serving officers on the active list. The Diet could talk, could hold up supply for a year, but could always be dissolved and was soon manipulated by a sophisticated system of rewards and corruption. The Japanese people, content with the removal of the servitudes of their former feudal masters, encouraged to indulge chauvinistic patriotism, with

The bureaucracy kept control in Japan, but did not inhibit Westernized industry and Westernized banking (above) from developing with astonishing ease. (3)

the road open for the talented to climb to affluence and some degree of power, seemed happy to revere the emperor whose status was nearly divine, and support a policy of imperial expansion and ambition.

It can be argued that the oligarchs who really ruled Japan diverted internal opposition by encouraging imperialist chauvinism; but the internal opposition was as yet formless and dispersed. Not every Japanese profited from the new society, which displayed some at least of the ugly aspects of an industrial revolution. But capitalism was then the almost unchallenged road to modernization: as in China modernization was the goal which united the nation beneath all faction and class conflict, but the unity of Japan was much more clearly manifest in its secure and stable institutions than that of China, which ran in effect counter to decaying and inefficient institutions. Thus Japan surged ahead; her economic *f 3* development, her military power, her prestige in international affairs and above all her dominant position in the eastern part of Asia, concealed certain lags in social change and a repressive internal police-dominated state.

For the oligarchy, which by the early 20th century was in its second generation and no longer led by the exceptionally competent men of the Meiji Restoration but increasingly by military figures, the goal of ambition, and also the potential fear for the future was China. China had overthrown her decadent alien dynasty, she was embarked on a revolution, chaotic and confused, but unpredictable in its outcome. On the analogy of previous history, after a 'period of confusion' which might last half a century, China would be reunited by a new strong regime (probably not a new dynasty in the modern age) and would at once realize her latent strength, which must far exceed that of Japan. It also seemed more than probable, and increasingly so, that the new regime when it finally gained control would be of a Left political complexion, whether Communist or not, and in any case inimical to the ideas and to the institutions of imperial Japan.

Whether as some would claim, the Japanese military hierarchy worked consciously and consistently to forestall this development and substitute their own conquest of China, or whether they followed a more opportunist policy—intervening for the profit of Japan when the chance occurred, holding off when there was no such opening, taking into consideration the probable hostility of other powers, but trying to secure Japanese commercial and economic domination in vital areas—is perhaps a question of degree rather than of motivation. Japanese military leaders would not have renounced any real chance of conquering China; they were ultimately to make the fatal attempt. Japanese diplomats and industrialists were not so convinced of the possibility, or perhaps of the desirability, of such an outcome. Many modern Japanese could see, by the twenties and thirties, that the trend in Asia was running against the colonial empires of which their own was the latest. Nationalism was a rising tide; Japan's own example was an inspiration to other peoples. The choice seemed to lie between Japan as the leader of the Nationalist revolt of Asia against the

West, or the Japanese empire of the Far East, an anachronism in the eyes of the rising generation of Chinese and other Asian peoples. In the end the Japanese leaders tried to combine these opposite roles, and failed in both.

The last imperialist

Japan had tried to impose an almost protectorate status on the early Chinese Republic during World War I, by presenting the Twenty-One Demands to the President, Yuan Shih-k'ai, whom in any case they disliked as a previous opponent in Korea. Only the less obnoxious of these demands were accepted, and Western disapproval forced Japan to withdraw the others. In return Japan obtained the former German Leased Territory of Tsingtao in the Chinese province of Shantung, as her share in the spoils of the Versailles Peace Treaty. This decision sparked off the May 4th Movement in China (1919) a violent nation-wide and student-led demonstration of protest against the corrupt warlord government which had signed away the national territory to Japan. It became a landmark in the development of the Chinese Revolution on nationalist lines. When, a few years later, the Chinese Nationalist Party swept the warlords' government out of power, Japan also tried ineffectively, to hinder the March to the North (1928). Three years later, when it became clear that the new Chinese Nationalism was about to infect Manchuria, Japan's especial preserve, the Mukden Incident (October 1931) was staged by which Japan swiftly seized all of Manchuria, drove out the Chinese forces and administration, and a short time thereafter proclaimed the country as the new and 'Independent state of Manchoukuo', soon to become an 'empire' with the dethroned Manchu emperor, P'u Yi, as titular monarch.

The virtual Japanese annexation of Manchuria, at which the League of Nations protested ineffectively, and which the Great Powers accepted with bad grace, was both the first major step in the policy of conquering China, and at the same time a possible limited alternative to that policy. To his chagrin the Emperor P'u Yi was discouraged from hoping that his restoration in Manchuria was a first step to his restoration to the Dragon Throne of China. But it equally proved almost impossible to limit Japanese expansion to the ample confines of the three Manchurian provinces. Their population was overwhelmingly Chinese, very largely immigrants from the adjacent provinces of North China. To the west the region merged with Inner Mongolia, also a goal of rapid and extensive Chinese immigration and settlement. The Chinese people, even their government, preoccupied as it was with its internal struggle against the Communist armed insurrection, refused to recognize the loss of Manchuria. In the years that followed 1931 there were other and serious conflicts with China. In 1932, at Shanghai, the Japanese attempt to repress nationalist demonstrations resulted in large-scale fighting which devastated part of the International Settlement and saw a Chinese army hold up the Japanese in that area for three months. This was an unpleasant indication of the rising quality of Chinese military power and of the growth of nationalist and patriotic support. The Japanese also added the Inner Mongolian province of Jehol to Manchoukuo, and in 1935 forced the Chinese to concede to them so predominant a position, backed by increased military garrisons, in the Peking-Tientsin area of Hopei province, adjoining Manchuria, that this region was almost withdrawn from Chinese authority, except for local officers subservient to Japan. Step by step, ineluctably, Japan was drawn into the vast region of China for which there is no interior frontier, no limited regions to be detached, no other solution than total conquest or total withdrawal. The Mongol invaders had met the same problem in the 13th century, the Manchus in the 17th century. These nations moved in *en masse* and became a ruling élite class. Could the Japanese follow such a precedent, or must they aim at a new, huge colonial empire administered by expatriate officials, dubiously supported by Chinese puppets?

The weakness of the Japanese imperial policy was that this overriding issue was never faced; action was spasmodic, motivated by opportunity: at home it increasingly failed to muster that loyal support which the early stages of imperial expansion had evoked. The industrialists were now aware that Japanese imperialism

P 39
(23)

roused not only Chinese national resentment, involving boycotts and loss of markets, but also the fears and hostility of Western peoples. It was becoming too obvious that Japan would not stop at China; the rich colonial empires of the Western powers lay at her doorstep, virtually undefended in the face of Japanese power. The Japanese navy, never too close comrades of their military colleagues, saw the island world of the South Seas as a more profitable field for imperial expansion than vast, inland, cohesive China. Also it was an enterprise in which the navy must play the major role, whereas in China the sailors had little scope for their ambitions. Within the army itself the Young Officers were restive, and occasionally violent. They came from relatively poor families, and realized that the burden of empire building fell heavily on the rural peasantry. They disliked their aristocratic leaders, felt contempt for their hesitations and complacencies, believed that these oligarchs both concealed the truth from the emperor, and truckled unduly to the demagogues of the Diet, who represented another disliked class, the industrialist and financier. In the thirties the pressures of these discontents, and the consequences of imperial expansion both shook the power of the older aristocratic rulers and weakened, finally destroyed, the rather undeveloped and flawed structure of Japanese parliamentary democracy.

P 155 (25)

The example of Fascist Italy and Nazi Germany was present in the minds of the Young Officers, not as a model to be copied exactly, for they felt that Japan was a unique polity governed by a divine emperor, very different from the republican form of Nazi Germany or the Italian constitutional monarchy. The idea that power should be taken from a narrow élite of high-born people and from a parliament of self-seeking demagogues or their moneyed backers, and held by dedicated, pure minded officers devoted to the Emperor and the Nation owed something to these European prototypes, if also based on Samurai traditions native to Japan. Finally they were convinced believers in Japan's 'Divine Mission' to rule at least the Far East, and perhaps a wider world in due time. They wanted, therefore, all-out policies of conquest and occupation, not only in China. Their terrorist attacks on senior officers and statesmen, such as the occasion when in 1932 they assassinated the prime minister, Inukai, culminated in the Tokyo Rebellion of February 1936 (one week after a general election had shown the continuing strength of the parliamentary parties with the mass of the people). On this occasion 1,400 men of the First Division in Tokyo occupied many of the principal public buildings and slew or wounded many prominent people. For three days it seemed that the Young Officers might seize power in Japan. The firmness of the emperor supported by the last of the Elder Statesmen, Prince Saionji, rallied other sections of the army and the revolt was suppressed by force.

The consequences of this event were that although the Young Officers lost authority and influence, the army as a whole gained more power. It alone could be relied upon to restrain its wilder elements. But it was far from united. The various factions around prominent generals and separate commands continued to jockey for position and to try to influence policy. The result was that although from the outside, particularly from China, Japan's militarists appeared to be a ruthless band of dedicated conquerors seeking opportunity for further expansion, in Japan itself the truth was that the army was worried by the danger of Russia—the great Communist power—joining with China if the situation in that country went too far for peaceful compromise. Although the Tokyo-Berlin Axis gave Japan the reassurance of a friend in Europe, it was not at all apparent how German power could operate in the Far East. Moreover, Germany was not wholehearted about Japanese ambitions in China, and ready, as 1939 was to show, to come to temporary accommodation even with the USSR.

Japan at war, 1937-45

The Chinese did not at the time believe it, but it is now clear that the outbreak of the Sino-Japanese War in July 1937 (called the China Incident so that both sides could avoid the legal inconveniences of admitting a state of war) was in reality accidental. The Japanese army in the north China area was nervous of the growing hostility of the Chinese people, and fearful of the consequences of the truce and peace settlement negotiated between Chiang Kai-shek and the Communist Party following the Sian Mutiny in December 1936. This seemed to portend united Chinese resistance to further Japanese encroachment. The consequences of a clash which could easily have been settled were further Japanese action, the seizure of the city of Peking, and then an escalating war which proved impossible to confine or conclude. p 154 (22) The Japanese army still lacked either an overall plan of operations in China or a unified command. The army in Manchuria was a separate entity, so was that in north China; when the war spread to central China a new command was formed. Each set up its own puppet Chinese regime. The Government in Tokyo was unhappy with this system, but lacked the determination either to make peace with the Chinese Government, or to control and unify its own armed forces. The war proceeded by a series of expedients, the hope that the capture of this or that large city—Nanking, the capital; Wuhan, the middle Yangtze city to which the Chinese Government withdrew; or Canton, the loss of which cut off the Chinese from the sea—would bring the Chinese to capitulate or at least to acknowledge defeat and sue for peace. It was a vain hope: apart from the force of opinion which was for resistance to the end, Chiang Kai-shek judged that the further Japan went the more she would antagonize the West and ultimately force America to enter the war. Once America was China's ally the war would eventually be won; no one, he judged, could defeat the USA.

It must for ever remain unknown whether, had the Sino-Japanese conflict not widened into the Pacific War, Japan would have achieved her purpose in China. An adverse factor which had certainly been underestimated was the rise and spread of the guerrilla resistance led by the Community Party. After the initial Japanese victories had forced the Nationalist armies and Government to withdraw into the almost inaccessible west of China, the main activity and preoccupation of the Japanese occupying forces in eastern and northern China was the sustained attempt to crush the guerrilla movement. Although this was carried on with ruthless violence—the 'Three Alls': 'Kill All, Burn All, Loot All'—it failed. Japanese field officers, unlike their superiors, realized that this policy was mainly effective in driving the Chinese peasantry to desperation and into the arms of the Communist Party. The protection which the Communists could give in 'liberated areas' became the only hope of the rural population. By the end of the war the Japanese had difficulty in keeping the main railways working, and their forces were confined to garrisons in large cities. The countryside over a vast area had slipped out of control. Such a situation could have endured for years, but was ended by the atomic bombs on Hiroshima and Nagasaki and the evident fact that Japan had lost the wider Pacific War.

The empire which had seemed so strong and which had been expanded so rapidly after Pearl Harbor till it comprised all South East Asia, proved unable to withstand the concentrated power of the USA. Command of the sea was lost, Japan could no longer meet the air attacks, and the armies came to be isolated in the regions they had conquered. Invasion of the homeland itself was imminent. It is now known that the decision to surrender, after tentatives for a less complete capitulation had been made and rejected, was opposed by powerful reactionary circles, even to the point of an attempted but abortive, *coup d'état* on the eve of the surrender. The emperor made his famous broadcast requiring his forces to surrender; it was an act of great courage and statesmanship, which gave the Throne a new prestige just when it was about to relinquish direct executive power to the occupation forces and accept a new constitution which made the emperor a constitutional monarch with very limited authority. The extraordinary fact is that this command was obeyed without question p 155 (26) by the armies throughout the Far East, and no attempt was made by the formerly independent-minded commanders to resist or frustrate it. The Japanese people had long been known for their discipline and their readiness to obey the imperial commands; on this supreme occasion they fully justified their reputation.

The occupation of Japan is another very exceptional event in the history of nations. There was no internal resistance to the presence of foreign troops, something which Japanese tradition held to be unthinkable. The occupation authorities, in effect the forces commanded by General MacArthur and very largely American, behaved with scrupulous discipline and made continuing efforts to restore the shattered cities and prostrate economy. Opinions may differ as to whether the new constitution, which renounced the right to wage war or maintain armed forces, was not a document too idealistic for the contemporary world; but although the provision about armed forces has been circumvented, with American encouragement in more recent years, it remains a fact that the main provisions of this imposed constitution are in force and seem acceptable to the great mass of the Japanese people. When the occupation ended, the Japanese did not at once modify this instrument, and have created and maintained a system of government which is broadly in conformity with that which the occupation inaugurated and hoped to establish. The system is parliamentary democracy under a constitutional emperor who reigns but does not rule. Parties of the Right, representing business and wealth have successively provided the governments, but the Socialist opposition, although not yet in sight of a majority, slowly grows stronger, and is effective in checking extreme Right-wing policies.

p 156-7
(27-29)
p 339
(6)

Helped by massive American aid, and by the boost to the economy provided by the Korean War, Japan has made a phoenix-like recovery from the ashes of fallen empire. Her industry rivals any in the world, her economy is strong and growing, her national life orderly and her cities rebuilt. Japan, in fact, in spite of the disastrous essay in world imperialism, is still the most modernized country in Asia, and the archaic features of society which persisted under the empire have passed away with it. These impressive results have been achieved under the capitalist system, both before the fall of the empire, and since. Thus Japan is an alternative example of how modernization can be brought about, a challenge to the Communist plan, even though within Japan the Communist Party has a considerable following and makes a strong appeal to young intellectuals.

South East Asia: aftermath of colonialism

Japan and China were never colonial countries in the sense that they were annexed and governed by foreign powers. Chinese may stigmatize the prewar regime of the Treaty Ports and Concessions as 'semi-colonialism', but the accent must be on the 'semi': the weakness of that system was precisely that, while restricting the sovereignty of the Chinese state, it substituted no authority of its own. South East Asia, with the single exception of Thailand, then known as Siam, was on the contrary entirely under European colonial rule at the beginning of the century, and for the most part this foreign domination had been imposed for many years previously, in some cases for centuries. Dutch rule in what is now Indonesia dated from the 17th century, the Spanish had been even longer in the Philippines.

The British had begun their penetration of both Burma and Malaya in the early 19th century, and the French had been expanding their authority in Indo-China since the middle of the 19th century. Nowhere in the world did colonial empires appear so enduring, so well established, and, it seemed, so accepted by their subjects. In reality this last condition varied very much from one country to another. The last embers of old-style resistance to foreign conquest were hardly stamped out before the new nationalism began to rise in its place. In Vietnam the French never were at ease; conspiracy, uprisings, and clandestine nationalist movements never ceased to strive for the expulsion of the foreign rulers. The Burmese, after the rather late extinction of the old monarchy in 1885, were resentful and unwilling British subjects, the more so as the incorporation of their country as a province of the Indian Empire—with which they felt no affinity—was deeply resented. The Dutch had to contend, especially in northern Sumatra, with sustained resistance from a fanatical Muslim population, and were covertly opposed by large elements in Java also. The Spanish, till, at the end of the 19th century, they were ousted from the Philippines by the USA, had often met with rebellions and uprisings, especially in the Muslim southern islands. Here the US was to find no ready welcome either, and was forced to conduct what others would have described as a 'colonial war' to reduce the rebellious

sultans. Malaya was in many ways a 'new country' when Raffles founded Singapore in 1819. Malacca was an ancient settlement, which had been captured by the Portuguese in 1511 and taken from them by the Dutch in the 17th century. British control was established following the settlement of the Napoleonic Wars. The interior of the country was but lightly inhabited and ruled by weak Malay sultans established on the rivers. Chinese tin mining, which had started in the late 18th century, rapidly increased and became a major factor both in the economy and in the politics of Malaya in the 19th. The turmoil which resulted from this new immigration both of men and money brought about British control from the 1870s onward.

At that time the Chinese merchants welcomed British rule; the Malay sultans were preserved in wealth and some residual power by the colonial overlord. No one was seriously opposed to the restoration, or rather the creation, of law and order, and a prospering, expanding economy. There had never been a Malayan nation; the earlier history of the country had been one of association in a provincial role with empires based on Sumatra or Java. Whether because nationalist movements were too weak to shake the colonial authority, or because no such coherent movements existed among a population of diverse ethnic origin, the colonial powers remained firmly in control, nor did they modify the direct form of administration to any appreciable extent. Governors in Council, with a few native representatives nominated by the governor himself, were the general rule throughout the colonial world. The control of the country was entrusted to expatriate officers from the European home country, supported by a police force similarly officered, and a garrison, usually mainly of European troops, in the larger cities.

Another aspect of colonial rule was the disassociation which it tended to impose upon neighbouring countries formerly linked by cultural relations founded upon a common religion. Burma was a Hinayana Buddhist country; so are Cambodia and Laos, as also Thailand. But the former was a British colony, the others French protectorates, and Thailand independent. Education in the modern subjects, languages and law, tended to be based on the culture of the colonial power, or in the case of Thailand, on the culture of the power felt to be most friendly, in this case Britain. Students went to London, Paris and Leiden, and returned with no contact with their fellow Buddhists or Muslims in countries under a different colonial power. Even today many educated Thais, Burmese and Cambodians speak English or French; very few can speak the languages of their close neighbours, which are not even taught in their universities. There can be no doubt that this localism, fostered, partly unconsciously, by colonial rule, opened both an economic and an educational opportunity to the large communities of Chinese immigrants who in many of these countries dominated the economy and controlled such industry as had developed. Chinese were everywhere Chinese; they may not have spoken the same dialects, but they wrote and read their own language in their own script, which few others could read, and they established their own Chinese schools.

It was not until the 20th century was past its first two decades that any serious internal challenge was presented to colonial rule, and even then it was more a distant threat than an actual menace. The first nationalists were, almost without exception, the students who had gone abroad to study in European universities. This educational advantage which the European colonial powers often imagined would create an élite favourable to their rule and loyal to the 'home' country, had the opposite effect. In London, Paris or elsewhere students met others from other colonial countries, or from China and Japan. They learnt the doctrines of nationalism as fast as they qualified in Western literatures and sciences. The new higher education was seen, and became, the best weapon of the rising nationalism. Many such young men were very able, often rather more so than their colonial rulers. They felt frustrated at their exclusion from real power or influence. Making money, an obvious substitute, was too often the monopoly of the Chinese. Thus as soon as any form of political association or party was permitted to exist it became a focus for nationalism and a potential anti-colonial movement.

In every one of the colonial countries of South East Asia the

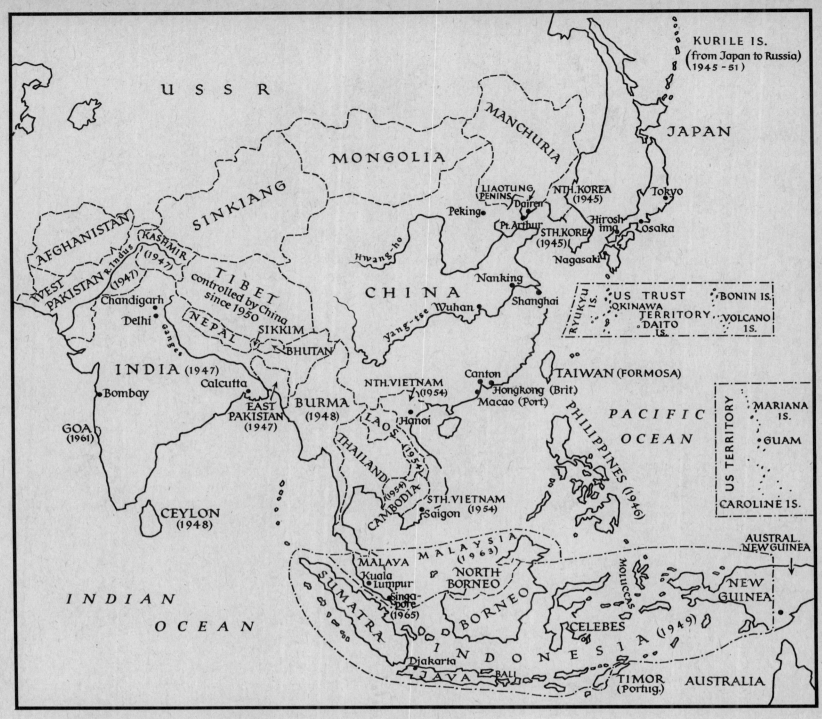

Asia in the 20th century, with the dates of independence of former colonial territories. (4)

pattern of development and of the composition of society had differed, in part as a consequence of indigenous situations, in part as a result of colonial policy. In Indonesia—or the Netherlands East Indies as they were then called—Dutch rule had imposed a kind of unity upon peoples and islands of diverse origin and history. Java and Sumatra had ancient and refined civilizations originally of Hindu derivation, later (except in Bali) overlaid by Muslim conversion. Borneo, except for a coastal fringe, was primitive. Celebes and the eastern islands, racially quite distinct from the western Java and Sumatra, were the original 'spice islands', and had been ruthlessly exploited since the 16th century, first by the Portuguese, later, in a more restrained manner, by the Dutch. In late colonial times the Dutch recruited their colonial army largely from this part of the Indies, particularly Amboina. In Burma the trade of the country, and much of the clerical profession also, had fallen into the hands of Indian immigrants since the British conquest. This, too, was a grievance to the Burmese, which was one day to be harshly discharged. Vietnam was systematically exploited by French rubber and mining interests, and governed, often to a very low administrative level, by expatriate French civil servants. Malaya had a multi-racial society running throughout the colonial period—and since—at about 50% Malays, 40% Chinese and 10% Indians and Ceylonese. Singapore had an overwhelming 80%

Chinese population, and Penang was also predominantly Chinese populated. Land was held by Malay aristocrats who leased it only to Malay peasants. Business, industry and commerce, at their highest level British, were otherwise in the hands of the Chinese.

Independent Thailand was very largely under the economic domination of foreign interests for its international trade, and equally in the hands of the Chinese for its domestic trade and industry. An absolute monarchy until 1932, it had been ruled by two successive monarchs of unusual talent and strength of character, King Mongkut and his son Chulalangkorn, whose careful policy and cautious modernization had preserved the country's independence between the rival empires of Britain and France. After the American conquest, the Philippines were soon granted a large measure of self-government, since American policy did not seek to set up a colonial empire but was interested in economic development. Being a country which the Spaniards had found primitive in the 16th century, the Philippines had developed a hybrid culture, Spanish and Catholic but also Asian and native. It had a society more resembling that of the former Spanish American domains than that of any country in Asia. This society was now granted democratic political forms on the American pattern, with the promise of full independence when maturity was attained. It was inevitable, given the fragmentation both of

p 158
(30, 31)

p 158
(33, 34)

political control and the cultures and peoples of the colonies themselves, that the movement for independence and revolution, common to all, should develop unevenly and in an unco-ordinated manner. One may speak of the anti-colonial revolution of South East Asia as a useful collective term, but it was in reality a series of parallel but unconnected movements particular to each country.

New nations, new dilemmas

The Japanese invasion and temporary conquest of every one of these countries in 1941–45 imposed upon them a unity they had never known and for the first time subjected all to the control of a single overlord power. It also utterly destroyed the myth upon which colonial power had been built: white men could be defeated by Asians; why only by Japanese? Clearly the answer was because Japan possessed the arms and the organization to achieve this result. If the Asian countries themselves acquired the arms and formed the necessary cohesive organization, under whatever banner, they could do the same. So, under the cover of Japanese occupation, all the nationalists of South East Asia set this as their goal. In some countries they worked at first ostensibly with the Japanese, to gain power locally and, if Japan won the war, to keep in favour with the new dominant nation; if Japan lost, as soon appeared more probable, to establish a position of political and if possible military strength which would make the return of the colonial authority impossible. The Burmese National Army, formed under Japanese auspices, switched sides when Japan began to lose the war. In Indonesia, the nationalist movement played on both sides, some leaders visibly co-operating with the Japanese, others carrying on clandestine resistance. Both groups worked in concert, to make the best of any eventuality. The Philippinos came down more decidedly on the American side, for America could be trusted to fulfil her promise of independence after the war, while Japanese domination held no such prospect. In Vietnam the nationalist movement, coming under mainly Communist direction, opposed the Japanese occupation, but prepared even more ardently to resist French reoccupation. In Malaya the situation was more ambivalent. The Chinese population suffered bitter persecution under the Japanese rule, for Chinese would not co-operate with the invaders of their home country. Some, under Communist leadership, carried on a guerrilla resistance in the jungle. The Malay rulers tended to co-operate with the Japanese, to keep their thrones.

Japanese plans for South East Asia reflected these varying conditions. They proposed a three-tier system, if they never were really able to carry it out. Burma, the Philippines and parts of Indonesia, with Vietnam, were to be independent nations, under Japanese protection. Other areas were to be protectorates not so autonomous. It was proposed to unite Sumatra with the Malayan peninsula as 'Mahamalaya'. Singapore and less advanced places in Borneo, were to become outright Japanese colonies. All would be members of the East Asian Co-prosperity Sphere, which it was hoped would reconcile them to the hard facts of Japanese military control and

political supervision. Co-prosperity never materialized under the unfavourable conditions of a losing war. Shared misery and hardship was the lot of the South East Asian peoples. Yet their attitude to Japan and her occupation remained somewhat two-faced. Only the Chinese wholeheartedly welcomed the return of the British colonialists in Malaya, and even among them there was the hard core of the Communist Party, which accepted the British as preferable to the Japanese, but was equally opposed to their continued power.

Elsewhere, in Burma, in Indonesia, in Vietnam, the nationalists, whether also Communist or not, attempted, at the surrender of Japan, to set up governments which could deny the colonial powers' claim to sovereignty and resist their return. In the Philippines the devastated country was ready to accept American reconstruction and the promise of speedy independence, but there was also a Communist opposition in arms which long disputed power. Except in Vietnam, where the struggle against the returning French widened out into the later Vietnam War, the return of the colonial powers was either brief or abortive. The Dutch, in spite of two 'police actions' failed to crush the nationalist movement in Indonesia, and were induced by lack of strength and the disapproval of the major Western powers themselves, to abandon their position, reluctantly and by stages, until Indonesia became completely independent in 1949. The British in Burma, after the Japanese army had surrendered and been repatriated, accepted that the permanent reduction of Burma to colonial or even to dominion status within the British Commonwealth was no longer possible. Burma became completely independent in 1948 and ceased to be a member of the Commonwealth. Various attempts at constitutional reform in Malaya met with local difficulties. The first proposal, the Malayan Union, satisfied Chinese aspirations to a fuller citizenship but was rejected by the Malays who awoke to a full political consciousness as a result of this agitation. The separation of Singapore from Malaya was resented and deplored by its Chinese population, who feared both for their trade and that they would remain under colonial authority. The next proposal, which conceded much to Malay demands and sentiment, failed to please the Chinese. The Communist Party then took to the jungle once more and started the 'Malayan Emergency' as it was euphemistically called, in fact an armed terrorist insurrection. It was clearly nowhere possible to return to the old ways and undisputed European rule.

The Malayan Emergency was only brought to an end, or mainly p 159 (36) driven beyond the frontier, when Britain agreed to immediate independence for the whole country, which was made possible by political agreement between Malays and Chinese, overtly formed to make a British withdrawal possible. Subsequently the two communities have not managed to achieve an equitable or stable relationship; Singapore was virtually driven out of the new Malaysian Federation (which was formed to include the former British colonies in North Borneo) and became an independent city state. The riots between the two races in Kuala Lumpur, the capital of Malaysia, in 1969 resulted in the suspension of the democratic constitution and the formation of an authoritarian regime, intended to be temporary and in fact under Malay control. The impending withdrawal of British military protection from Malaysia and Singapore poses new problems for both countries.

Thus all South East Asia had gained independence from colonial rule. In some countries, such as Vietnam, this was followed by a p 159 (37, 38) still more violent struggle with American intervention on behalf of one side of the civil war. In others, such as Indonesia, internal tensions between Communists and Muslims have led to bloody massacres and repression. In Burma an endemic civil war between the Communists and the government has continued for twenty years. The Philippines have not found it easy to operate an American-style constitution without corruption and inefficiency. What can be said is that all these peoples will and must settle their future for themselves; the proposed withdrawal of America from Vietnam only puts the seal on a process which had already occurred elsewhere. The colonial era is dead and cannot be revived under any guise of military assistance, protection against Communism, or regional defence. The European is not wanted in these countries as a soldier nor administrator, he is still welcome as a trader and an expert.

p 158 (32)

A street in Hanoi, dominated by war posters and marching troops. (5)

The British in India: a drawing published in 'Punch' in 1903, when Edward VII succeeded as Emperor. (6)

India: unity and division

The British Indian Empire was a polity on the scale of China, but it had no such historical foundation as the empire of the Manchu Dynasty. It included not only Hindu and Muslim areas, but also Burma which was Buddhist and had had a long separate history as an independent kingdom. There were tribal areas in the north-west and north-east which had never submitted to any Indian regime. Within the borders it was a patchwork of princely states, some very large and some very small, and British-administered provinces of varying ethnic character. The most obvious aspect of unity was the British Raj itself; underlying that, in most of India, was the Hindu religion in its many aspects and local forms. In opposition to it was the Muslim community, once dominant under the Mogul empire which the British had replaced and finally destroyed. By the beginning of the 20th century this structure was showing signs of stress and warning voices were soon to be speaking of the 'Lost Dominion'.

The Congress Party, which was ultimately to lead the campaign against British rule and had been founded as far back as 1885, drew support from the middle class which had, since about the same period as the foundation of the Congress, rapidly expanded its modern character by means of large-scale education in the Western manner. The government of India, British in effect, was rather slow to recognize the consequences of this development, which meant an ever increasing demand for Indian participation in government at all levels. Economic development in the Indian Empire had been directed on lines which should not seriously compete against British interests but which would facilitate

political control. Railways and roads covered the sub-continent; factories and industries of the modern type were less conspicuous. Indian agriculture, still carried on in ancient ways, also bore a heavy burden of rent due to a landlord class whose social position was secured through the working of the caste system. The British Government had never sought to reform the basic character of Indian society, except to suppress such customs as the suicide of widows, and such sects as the Thugs who practised ritual murder. The aim of the British was to keep the peace and prevent racial and religious riots between Hindu and Muslim. Democracy and its ideals were held up in the schools and universities as the highest form of political life; but very little progress had been made in introducing democractic methods into the day-to-day government of India.

p 150 (5, 6) p 150 (7)

There was a latent conflict in respect of political advance between the administrators in India—men who had risen through the Indian Civil Service, an élite body of carefully selected candidates—and the political leaders in the home country, especially those of the Liberal Party. Indian civil servants did not believe that the introduction of political reform would either benefit the mass of the people, or lead to stability and contentment, which were their aims. Politicians in England realized that the movement of world and nationalist opinion could not be thwarted indefinitely; it might be necessary as one of them put it, to 'disturb the pathetic contentment of the Indian masses'—a view which was not welcome to the men on the spot. The first political reform in 1909 was associated with the names of Morley, Secretary of State for India in the ruling Liberal Government, and Lord Minto, the Viceroy. Lord Curzon, his successor, was more dedicated to the continuation of British rule and, if possible, its further expansion. He considered that a step such as the removal of the capital from Calcutta—the old centre of British influence and power under the East India Company—to Delhi, the old capital of the Mogul empire and earlier regimes, would conciliate Indian nationalist opinion. The change was carried out in 1911 and publicized by the Durbar held in that city to mark the accession to the throne of King George V, as Emperor of India. This magnificent and extravagant ceremony marked, perhaps, the high point of the British Indian Empire, which in many ways, even to the title (in Persian) of the monarch seemed to be a revival of the pomps of the Mogul emperors.

p 150 (3)

p 149 (1)

Gandhi's unusual techniques of persuasion puzzled other nations beside the British. This cartoon showing him at the conference table in 1931 is from the German periodical 'Simplicissimus'. (7)

Within four years World War I disturbed this prospect. Indian troops were extensively used in the Middle East, East Africa, and in France; Indian national consciousness was aroused and stimulated to demand further and much more significant political changes. As in other parts of the world, the sympathies of the reformers were for democratic forms of government, and monarchy whether native or foreign made little appeal to the new educated class. The aftermath of the war brought to India a tide of unrest and disturbance which weakened the British Raj. The Muslims were aroused by the fate of Turkey, and the threat, as they saw it, to the largest and most powerful Muslim country left independent in the contemporary world. Unwise and ruthless acts of military repression, such as that which occurred at Amritsar in the Punjab in 1919, gave Indian nationalist leaders their opportunity. Above all it was Mahatma Gandhi, who had already emerged as an Indian nationalist leader among the Indian community in South Africa and had returned to India in 1915, who now organized a nation-wide 'non co-operation' movement. This activity and its results led to the transformation of the Congress Party from a middle-class nationalist party into a mass movement aiming at independence.

Throughout the inter-war period the Congress Party, led by Gandhi, dominated the political development. The first non co-operation movement certainly failed to overthrow the British Raj, but it very largely discredited it, not least among the British Left. The second movement, launched in 1930, and continuing for more than a year, obtained world-wide publicity, which was generally unfavourable to British rule and sympathetic to the Congress Party. Indian students and intellectuals abroad acted as persuasive and intelligent propagandists, exemplifying their claim that Indians could and should be counted as the equals of any other people, and therefore entitled to govern themselves. This was an argument which Western liberals found very difficult to deny, and for which very many of them had great sympathy. Non-violence, Gandhi's technique of agitation, was effective in discrediting and hampering a regime which was not prepared to use brutal repression, but it was not always observed by the followers of the Congress Party. It also was not able to overthrow the British Raj. It did force the pace of reform, and in 1937 provincial autonomy was granted, although the Central Government remained under predominant British control.

The consequences of provincial autonomy were not all that had been expected. Under democratic voting procedures the Congress Party won seven out of the eleven provincial governments; but the Congress Party was overwhelmingly representative of the Hindu majority, and its local political leaders did not respond to Muslim expectations for a share of power. Thus the Congress rule in the provinces in the years before World War II created, or rather activated, the Muslim-Hindu antagonism, which had been a constant if politically latent feature of Indian society. Congress was not enthusiastic about the participation of India in the war, and

the check which it imposed on the road to independence. The offer of a postwar constitution which would have meant the establishment of Congress rule in India under a residuary British sovereignty was rejected in 1942. Congress opted for the 'Quit India' policy. The British responded, in wartime, by the arrest of Congress leaders. The Muslim community had now found its leader in Jinnah, who came out for the partition of the Indian Empire and the creation of Pakistan, a Muslim state. The immediate postwar years were racked with the contest of Muslim and Hindu, for or against Pakistan and partition. The question of whether the British should go or stay was now secondary; the British were ready, indeed anxious, to hand over: the problem was, to whom.

The partition became inevitable; it was not easily nor peacefully performed, and was sullied by the massacres which both sides perpetrated upon those trying to flee to the country of their co-religionists. Full independence for both countries was proclaimed on 15 August 1947. Mahatma Gandhi had attempted with noble courage to stay the massacres, and his example was valuable; still more so, for the cause of communal peace, was his death on 30 January 1948 at the hands of a Hindu fanatic. The nation was shocked and contrite; extremist groups lost support and influence. Political leadership of the Indian Congress, and now of the Indian Government, passed to Nehru, who was for many years to head the government of India and create its distinctive foreign policy of non-alignment. This was shaken, if not wholly destroyed, by the developing quarrel with China from 1962 onward, and to some degree by the continuing dispute over Kashmir with Pakistan, an issue left over from the partition of the Indian Empire. India has been able to maintain its democratic system of government, almost alone among the postwar states of Asia. There has been considerable economic development, but the problems of population growth and modernization of agriculture are still pressing. The Congress Party has held power since independence, but in recent times has shown signs of loss of support and factional disagreement. On the other hand, no rival political party has yet emerged with any prospect of winning power by parliamentary means.

The dominant trend in Asia in the present century has been disclosed in the series of political movements, sometimes revolutionary, sometimes reformist, but all consciously directed to the two aims of modernization and national independence. The Asian peoples have seen a connection between these two objectives which is not a logical necessity. An economy and a social system could be 'modernized', that is industrialized and made more democratic and just, without national independence. Equally a nation could achieve political independence without any significant modernization. In practice, the Asian peoples have decided that the two aims must be attained together and are inseparable. The fact that most of the former colonial powers and imperial regimes were unwilling to accept this view and tended to oppose its fulfilment was the major cause of the conflicts in Asia during the last half-century.

f 1 p 151 (9)

p 151 (12)

p 151 (10)

p 151 (8)

p 338 (4)

VIII   THE TURBULENT MIDDLE EAST

The end of Western dominance

ELIZABETH MONROE

*'Independence is a prize that must be seized.
It cannot be handed down as a gift from one people
to another.'*

JA'FAR EL ASKARI, 1936

Mecca, the heart of Islam,

brings Arabs from every nation together in unity. In spite of political rivalries, the spiritual bond is still strong—a more potent factor than the Church in the Christian West, because Islam is a way of life and, for the Arabs, God-given in their language.

Every devout Moslem hopes to make the pilgrimage to Mecca once in his lifetime. About 200,000 people each year manage to go, staying about a month, at one stage in tents outside the city, and carrying out the lengthy ritual requirements. The ceremonies focus on the Ka'ba ('cube'), a stark, windowless building. Built into it is a black stone the holiness of which predates the Prophet Mohammed. It is covered by a large embroidered black cloth, changed annually during the pilgrimage season.

Mecca was in the Ottoman Empire and till 1916 was controlled from Istanbul (in 1908 a railway was built as far as Medina, but never actually reached Mecca). After the Arab revolt of 1916 against Turkey it became independent, and was later a subject of contention between its Sharif, Hussein, and Ibn Saud, the *de facto* ruler of Eastern Arabia, until the latter captured it in 1924. Today it is the capital of the Saudi Arabian province of Hejaz. Modern technology, including air transport, has transformed the pilgrimage into a highly organized and lucrative industry. But its spiritual significance remains unchanged. As every Moslem turns to face Mecca while he prays, so all acknowledge the supra-national link that it represents. (1)

Three decaying empires were by 1900 all that remained of Islam's once splendid conquests. In **Persia**, Shah Muzaffer Uddin (below) exercised a precarious rule over his multi-racial Empire, fearful of internal opposition and foreign interference. (2)

Turkey: in 1909 Sultan Abdul Hamid (below), faced with the loss of most of his Christian territories in Europe and with rising hostility to his regime both there and in Asia, was deposed by a newly elected National Assembly. (4)

Morocco had for decades been an object of imperial ambitions to France, Spain and Germany. In 1912 the French deposed its Sultan and obtained the accession of his more accommodating brother Maulay Yusuf (above). French troops (below) advanced to Fez and the country was declared a French protectorate. It adjoined Algeria where Frenchmen had long predominated (bottom) and whence they sent in white troops. (3, 5, 6)

The 'Young Turks' who then took over the government were responsible for Turkey's alliance with Germany in the First World War. Above: the German battle-cruiser *Goeben* which slipped past the British blockade and entered Istanbul in August 1914. Below: Enver Pasha (on the right), who led the revolt of 1908 and in 1914 became Minister for War. (7, 8)

Britain encouraged an Arab revolt against Turkey organized from Cairo and Khartoum. Colonel T. E. Lawrence (above) played a famous part in it, relying largely on promises to create an 'Arab nation' after the war. But first steps in this direction were thwarted by Great Power greed at the Paris Peace Conference. Thus, though the Syrians proclaimed Sharif Hussein's son Feisal their king in 1920, French bayonets were too much for him and, lacking further British support, his kingdom ceased to exist. Bottom: King Feisal in London with Allenby, the British general who had taken Damascus in 1918, and Lloyd George. (11, 12)

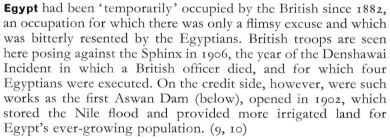

Egypt had been 'temporarily' occupied by the British since 1882, an occupation for which there was only a flimsy excuse and which was bitterly resented by the Egyptians. British troops are seen here posing against the Sphinx in 1906, the year of the Denshawai Incident in which a British officer died, and for which four Egyptians were executed. On the credit side, however, were such works as the first Aswan Dam (below), opened in 1902, which stored the Nile flood and provided more irrigated land for Egypt's ever-growing population. (9, 10)

Slow to change and deeply rooted in tradition, the Islamic way of life had a picturesque appeal to Western artists but cleavage to it retarded modernization and social change until after the Second World War. Below left: by 1907 **Cairo** had grown to be the largest city in the Arab world, with a population of 655,000, of whom 46,000 were Europeans. **Luxor** (below right), nearly five hundred miles further up the Nile, lived mainly on the tourist traffic to its ancient ruins. Both these sketches date from 1913. (13, 14)

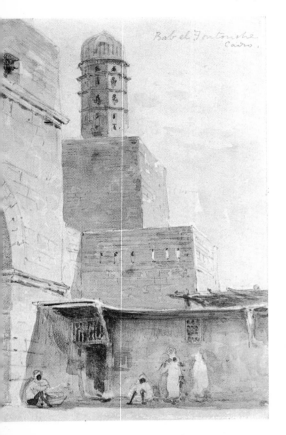

Jerusalem has a unique history as a centre of three religions. Above: a drawing of 1909 shows it to be a stone-built hill-town, containing Holy Places that include the Moslem Dome of the Rock, the Christian Church of the Holy Sepulchre and (left) the Jewish Wailing Wall, painted in 1932 by Marc Chagall. (15, 16)

Kut el Amara on the Tigris was in Ottoman times a mud-built town typical of desert plains where no stone is available. In 1915–16, a retreating British army was surrounded here by the Turks and forced to surrender. Mud towns are soon rebuilt as this picture (1919) shows. Today, Kut is in Iraq and the site of a barrage that controls the spring Tigris flood, and supplies summer water to farmlands downstream. (17)

Muscat, capital of Oman, lies on the Indian Ocean and Oman was till a coup d'état of 1970 the most traditional and backward-looking of the states of Arabia. Muscat's grand bazaar (below) is typical of markets all over the Moslem world, where small traders compete, each trade in its own narrow alley. Oil has now been discovered inland and a young Sultan has set out to catch up with his neighbours. (18)

The 'Near East Problem' was born
when Turkey had been defeated and
the fate of her possessions had to be
settled. The hopes of Arab nationalists, and in particular those of Sharif
Hussein and his family, had been
cruelly disappointed when Feisal was
expelled from Syria. Feisal was thereupon offered the throne of Iraq and
his brother Abdullah the Amirate of
Trans-Jordan. This photograph (right)
shows Churchill in Jerusalem in 1921
hurrying away after the settlement,
while Lawrence continues the discussion with Abdullah (the grand-
father of the present King Hussein of
Jordan). (19)

Jewish hopes had been raised by the
Balfour Declaration of 1917, by which
Britain officially supported the idea
of a national home for the Jewish
people in Palestine. Above: scenes
of enthusiasm near the Mount of
Olives when earlier Jewish settlers
greet the arrival of the Zionist Commission in Jerusalem in April 1918.
(20, 21)

Independence for Egypt was uni-
laterally declared by Britain in 1922
under King Fuad (above, opening
Parliament in 1936), the son of the
last Khedive and the father of King
Farouk. But it still fell short of the
demands of nationalists; British troops
stayed on and anti-British demonstrations continued. (22)

Turkey herself submitted to the loss
of her empire but not to the dismemberment of her homeland. When the
victorious allies proposed to hand
over part of Anatolia to Greece,
Mustafa Kemal formed a revolutionary army, defeated the Greeks
and abolished the Caliphate. As president, Kemal (right), who took the ▶
name of Ataturk, 'Father of the
Turks', led the modernization of
Turkey and the fight against illiteracy.
(23)

Oil, which makes the Middle East of such crucial importance today, was first exploited in Persia and thereafter slowly in Arab lands. Until after the Second World War it was entirely financed by foreign companies who spent years prospecting for it and building up the industry. Right: the first discovery in Iraq, October 14th, 1927; oil gushes uncontrollably 140 feet into the air. Below: Persian workers being paid, in the very early days before 1914. (24, 25)

Thirty-inch pipelines were later installed to carry inland oil direct to the Mediterranean and Europe. They do so to ports in Syria, Lebanon, Libya, Tunisia and Algeria. Here (right) a tanker has connected its hoses to the sea lines from the tank farm at Tripoli in Lebanon, which stores oil piped from Kirkuk in northern Iraq. (26)

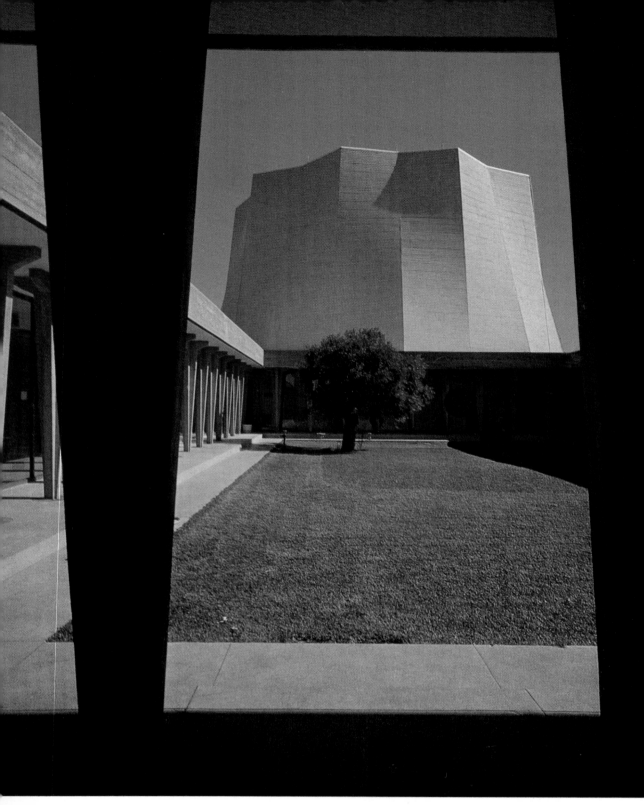

Persia's oil still forms its greatest natural asset. Between 1951 and 1954 a government under Mussadiq attempted to divert the profits from it into Persia's own economy by nationalizing the foreign-owned companies. It failed because the industry depended too much on the sales network and the carrying trade, neither of which were in Persian hands. The nationalized companies now run only internal distribution. This pipeline is near Gach Saran. Most pipelines are buried but in Persia the short distance to the sea, coupled with internal security, enables oil companies to lay surface lines. (28)

Modern technology began to transform the Middle East with dramatic suddenness during World War II; though foreign capital and foreign expertise were still essential, motor transport, air lines and transistor radios began to open eyes to new worlds. Israel, with advantages in know-how, has taken the lead. Alone of Middle Eastern countries she has been able to develop atomic power. The nuclear reactor at Rehovot (above), designed by the American architect Philip Johnson, was built in 1961. Offices and research rooms form a central court, shut off from the outside world. (27)

In Saudi Arabia's airport at Dhahran (right) pre-stressed concrete is used to create a neo-Islamic style; the design, however, is by the Japanese-American architect Yamasaki. (29)

Two high dams, one of concrete, the other rock-filled, are both ambitious feats of engineering that symbolize modernization. Above: the Farahnaz Dam, south of Teheran, was named after the Shah's daughter and opened by him in May 1967. It provides both irrigation water for areas near Teheran and drinking water for the capital, and was built by a British firm. Left: building the High Dam at Aswan, Egypt. The withdrawal of Western funds to pay for this project was the immediate cause of Nasser's nationalization of the Suez Canal. The dam was eventually built with aid from Soviet Russia and opened in 1964. This photograph shows ancient and modern methods side by side. Egyptian labourers wrestle with granite blocks while behind them mechanical grabs from Russia lift twenty tons at a time. (30, 31)

The promised land of prewar Zionism became for many Jews their last hope of refuge from Nazi persecution. By 1939 the flood of immigrants was swollen beyond British-imposed quotas by illegal immigration. As Jewish numbers grew, clashes between Jews and Arabs became fiercer. Above left: illegal immigrants landing in 1939. Centre: the *Theodor Herzl* arrives in Palestine, carrying refugees from Central Europe. Above right: one of Jerusalem's main streets in 1948, blocked with barbed wire to create a British security zone; this area the Jews christened Bevingrad to show their hostility to Britain's Foreign Secretary. (32, 33, 34)

The state of Israel was proclaimed on May 15th, 1948, the day the British mandate expired, by David Ben Gurion (right), soon to be elected its first prime minister (the portrait is that of Herzl, the founder of modern Zionism). Its foundation was the signal for a concerted attack on Israel from Syria, Iraq, Jordan and Egypt. (35)

Arab hostility to the new state planted in their midst was implacable. Egypt's King Farouk confidently issued stamps (above left) showing his victorious army on the march. But in fact Israel resisted the invaders on all fronts. In 1952 Farouk was deposed by a military revolution nominally headed by Colonel Neguib, seen (above centre) standing next to the real leader, Gamal Abdel Nasser. Two years later Nasser negotiated an agreement (right) by which Britain evacuated the Suez Canal zone, and in July, 1956, now president, announced its nationalization (above right). (36–39)

The Algerian revolution began when the Arabs, despairing of ousting the *colons* from their positions of power by negotiation, formed the Front de Libération Nationale, the FLN (above), and resorted to violence. The *colons* and the French army fought back. De Gaulle's proposal of self-determination in 1960 provoked violent settler demonstrations (above left) when the general himself visited the country soon afterwards. But a referendum held in January 1961 resulted in a decisive endorsement of his policy (left: Arabs voting 'Oui'). In spite of terrorism and atrocities, de Gaulle's policy prevailed, and Algeria became independent in 1962. (40, 41, 42)

Like the shattered statue of its builder, Ferdinand de Lesseps (right), Anglo-French authority over the Suez Canal had been destroyed by Nasser's stroke. This was a truth which both governments found hard to accept. In collusion with Israel, they launched an invasion of the Canal area in November 1956. French troops (far right) are seen landing at Port Fuad. 'I do not intend to fight,' said Nasser, 'I intend to stand back and wait for world opinion to save me.' This is exactly what happened. More specifically, the flight from the pound forced the British to withdraw their men (below right). (43, 44, 45)

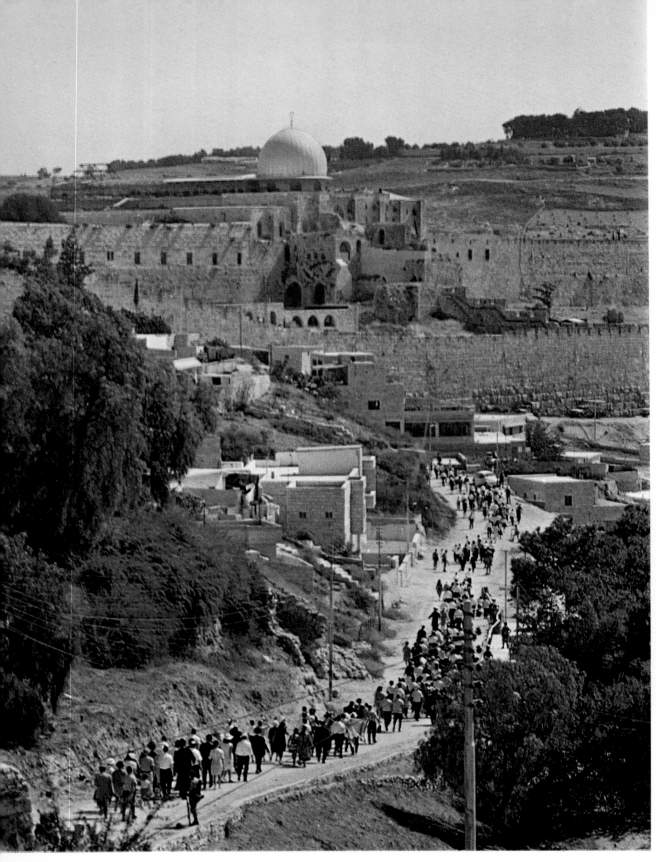

Israel and its Arab neighbours had clashed twice — once in 1948 after the proclamation of the state of Israel, again in 1956 during the Suez Affair. In June 1967 came the third and most decisive conflict so far: the Six Day War. Its immediate cause was the closure by Egypt of the Strait of Tiran, Israel's vital outlet to the Red Sea. The Arab states, amid a crescendo of propaganda, were threatening the complete extinction of Israel. Israel acted first. In a swift and well organized campaign the forces of Egypt, Jordan and Syria were defeated. The Israelis occupied a small part of Syria, all Jordanian territory west of the river Jordan and the whole peninsula of Sinai. Left: Jews make their first pilgrimage to the Wailing Wall, closed to them since 1948 in the Jordanian sector of Jerusalem. Below left: Israeli soldiers look across the Canal to Egypt. (46, 47)

Arab refugees cross the Jordan by the damaged Hussein Bridge. Arab reaction to further loss of territory and a new wave of refugees stimulated the creation of a Palestinian Arab guerrilla movement (below), which has divided Jordan and led to a civil war in 1970. (48, 49)

184

The end of Western dominance

ELIZABETH MONROE

THE CHRISTIAN YEAR AD 1900 was the Moslem year AH 1318. Twelve centuries after the Arabs' great conquests that spread the faith of Islam from Asia to the Atlantic, the lands they had converted consisted of three independent but decayed empires—the Ottoman, the Persian and the Moroccan—and several European dependencies, of which the largest were Algeria and Tunisia, run by France, and Egypt, run by Britain. Far to the south, the British held a colony, Aden, and their navy kept the *pax Britannica* in the Persian Gulf.

Three Moslem empires

p 174 (2-4)

Each of the three empires was ruled by an autocrat—the Caliph of all Islam at Istanbul, the Shah-in-Shah ul Islam at Teheran, and the Sultan of Morocco in the Maghreb, or west. Each exercised power that was absolute in theory, but in fact limited by the inaccessibility of far provinces and the turbulence of many tribes. Each ruled peoples consisting of a tiny minority of courtiers, great landowners and tribal or merchant rich, and a vast mass of poor peasants and nomads whose chief comfort came from Allah. In the settled areas His word was conveyed to them by a mullah to whom the faithful turned for counsel. Mosque and market were the chief source of news, but only for men; women lived in seclusion, and few except soldiers and pilgrims moved far from home.

Each empire was multiracial. The Shah ruled over Kurds and Azerbaijanis who spilled over into Turkey and Tsarist Russia; the Sultan of Morocco over Berbers whose ancestors had founded great dynasties; and the Sultan of Turkey over large religious as well as racial minorities—Christians in Armenia, the Levant and the Balkans, and Jews in compact city communities everywhere from Constantinople to Baghdad.

The lands under European management were exceptions to this medieval scene. Algeria's coastal plain was peopled with French settlers, the *colons*, and in Egypt the British, imposingly represented by Lord Cromer, had given the most sophisticated of the Arabic-speaking peoples good government but not self-government. The major difference between British and French handiwork was that the latter conceived their best export to be their language and educational system, whereas the British set more store by law courts, dams and drains.

Each of the three imperial rulers lived in seclusion for fear of assassins. By making himself difficult of access, each also hoped to minimize an alarming curb on his power, which was that exercised by foreigners. On his borders lived predators—rival great powers who were always contending for influence over him. Their immediate purpose was usually to keep one another at a distance and avoid general war, but all were wont to pursue their policy at his expense. Britain and France, for instance, struck a bargain in 1904 whereby the first was to have a free hand in Egypt provided that the second could have one in Morocco; in 1905 several powers staged a joint naval demonstration in the Aegean in order to force the Sultan to accept foreign officers to command his gendarmerie; in 1907, out of shared fear of Germany, Britain and Russia signed a truce about competition in Persia and divided it into spheres of influence, and in 1910 they jointly instructed the Persians that any advisers hired abroad must come from minor

p 174-5 (5, 6, 9)

powers; in 1906 and again in 1911, France and Germany nearly came to blows over rival claims in Morocco. And all the while Europeans honeycombed the three empires with concessions and monopolies. Europeans even aspired to their actual lands; in 1908-09 Austria-Hungary annexed two of Turkey's European provinces; in 1911 Italy, declaring one of the most unjustified wars in modern history, conquered the Ottoman province of Libya, and in 1912 France advanced to Fez and declared a protectorate over Morocco. All European memoirs of the period implicitly reveal the extent to which these moves were made without a thought for Islamic dignity or local culture. By European standards the values that mattered were administrative efficiency, and keeping chaos at bay in unstable areas.

p 174 (3, 5, 6)

Naturally there were objectors to this bullying by foreigners. These were mainly angry young men who saw Paris as the city of enlightenment, though some of the soldiers among them preferred Berlin. All were ashamed at the subservient and corrupt ways of officials, the sale of assets to foreigners, and the obscurantism of mullahs. What they wanted to discover was the secret of Western power. Most reckoned that it lay in education and in rule by parliamentary democracy, and were cheered when neo-orthodox theologians began to preach, usually from Egypt, the doctrine that Islam and modernism were compatible.

But their opposition to their ruler had to be secret. He was well equipped with police and spies; therefore they met in secret societies; these knew little of one another until, in 1905, an electric flash lit up their activities. Generated by the Japanese victory over Russia, it dispelled the notion that Asians were permanent inferiors, and quickened opposition to tyranny. Revolution broke out in Persia in 1906; simultaneous unrest in Egypt was written off by Lord Cromer as religious fanaticism; the Young Turks overthrew Sultan Abdul Hamid in 1908-09. Both the Persian and the Turkish revolutions were greeted as the dawn of liberalism, but from this standpoint both were failures. By 1908 the Shah was using his Russian Cossack brigade to bombard Parliament, and by 1912 the Young Turks, even before their defeat in war by first the Italians and then the Balkan Christians, were preaching Ottomanization, or jobs for the Turks. Arab secret societies thereupon began to plan autonomy within the empire on Austro-Hungarian lines, and to consult French friends in Syria and British ones in Egypt as to how to get it.

p 174 (8)

The impact of the War

The World War of 1914-18 swept away much of this oriental scene. It kindled nationalist hopes that were to lapse, for the foreigners did not go away. But it brought material changes such as the introduction of the combustion engine; by 1918 motor transport was carrying men and ideas from town to town, and between pockets of dissatisfaction.

The powers at war did as suited them in the Moroccan and the Persian empires. The first became, with Algeria and Tunisia, an accessible source of manpower for France. Persia was invaded both by Russian and by British troops in order to ward against a German-Turkish drive into Asia and soon disintegrated into tribal and political chaos. The Turks, by contrast, behaved as befitted an imperial people, and gave a good account of themselves.

p 174 (7) After momentary hesitation they plumped for the German side, when two German cruisers, the *Goeben* and *Breslau*, evaded the British navy and sought refuge in the Bosphorus. The first results of their declaration of war were a British landing at the head of the Persian Gulf to defend a British-run oil field in south Persia, and the British declaration of a protectorate over Britain's former fief in Egypt. Undaunted by these setbacks, the Turks threatened the British colony at Aden, threw back a British force that over-reached itself in Mesopotamia and captured a substantial British garrison at Kut; they kept Russia at bay in north Persia and eastern Turkey and, stiffened with Germans, threw the British out of Gallipoli. Less successfully, they made two attacks on the Suez Canal, but they pinned down in Egypt upwards of 150,000 British troops to defend the lifeline from India to France.

The Turks' successes did not deter their enemies from laying plans for the dismemberment of the Ottoman Empire. The Tsar was to have Constantinople. Britain and France promised one another spheres of influence in the Arab lands, while Palestine, being important to three faiths, was to enjoy a regime of which all three approved, or so the Allies said in 1916. Simultaneously, and with some misgivings about the effect on Moslem opinion in

p 175 (11, 12) India, the British decided to encourage Arab revolt against the Turks. To lead it, the British in India would have preferred Ibn Saud, a ruler in east Arabia. But London and Cairo chose the Sharif Hussein of Mecca, to whom they promised an 'Arab nation'.

Lloyd George, however, had another idea in mind. He wanted a British Palestine. He thought, as others had done before him, that it would be a useful buffer between the French (who wanted to restore links with Syria and the Christian Lebanon that dated from the Crusades) and the British base on the Suez Canal. The biblical significance of the Holy Land fired his imagination, and he hoped to install there a westernized community that would serve as a British ally. This was the Zionists, secular Jews who, under the leadership of Weizmann and Sokolow, wanted at least a national home and at most a state in a land that had once been Jewish. Some of his cabinet colleagues with experience of Moslem India questioned the wisdom of promoting this aim, but were overruled on the grounds that grateful Jews would be an asset, would attract the support of American Jewry for the Allies, and might even keep Russian Jewry interested in continuing to fight.

p 178 (20, 21) The British promise to the Zionists, called the Balfour Declaration after the Foreign Secretary who signed it, was given on 2 November 1917; it came too late to affect Lenin's seizure of power in Russia. It is difficult to reconcile it with subsequent promises about freely chosen national governments made by the British and French in order to keep pace with President Wilson's Fourteen Points, or the gospel of self-determination on the basis of which the Americans came into the war.

p 178 (19) Beating the Turks proved simple by comparison with dividing the Ottoman spoils. Egyptians, Arabs, Jews, Armenians, Kurds —all reckoned that they deserved attention. Their chagrin, and particularly that of the well-educated Egyptian *Wafd*, or delegation, was immense when no one from the area except the Sharif's son Feisal was admitted to the Peace Conference. Nearly all saw their best chance of independence in the disinterestedness of the Americans, and most, if they had to have a foreign mentor, said that President Wilson would be their first choice. But when Congress repudiated him, this hope was dashed, and they were left to the mercy of imperialism.

War's aftermath

Two territories only evaded this grip. One was Persia. Shorn of a Russian counterweight to British influence, it became a hotbed of warring tribes and factions; but it avoided the British dictation that London thought would be good for it, by using well-tried means of slipping out from under the net. The second area was the Arabian peninsula. Here the British reckoned that involvement in the rivalry between the Sharif and Ibn Saud would be profitless. Elsewhere, Turkey, reduced to Anatolia and Constantinople, seemed due for dismemberment by competing Greeks, Italians and Frenchmen, and in the Arab lands the British and French were at odds as to how much authority to give to the Sharif's family in fulfilment of the promise of an 'Arab nation'.

The British armies held a thin line running all the way from Cairo and Constantinople to Baku and Basra; at one moment it was possible to travel from Teheran to the Bosphorus via the Caucasus and sleep in a British mess every night. But they were dangerously overstretched. By 1919 riot and rebellion of a kind that a war-weary nation was in no mood to handle had broken out against them.

Except at two points, however, the British were too powerfully entrenched to fail to get their way. Their first setback was in Syria. True to their promise to the Sharif, they had installed his son Feisal as king, but the French willed otherwise. Syria and Lebanon were their promised sphere of influence, and to them Feisal was a British stooge. They took no notice of his election as King of a Greater Syria (which included Lebanon and Palestine) by an Arab congress of 1920, and took advantage of the withdrawal of British troops to attack and dethrone him. Britain's second setback was in Turkey. Here a general with a good war record, Mustafa Kemal, was aghast at the support that they were giving to Greek claims on Smyrna and its hinterland; he therefore raised the standard of Turkish nationalism in Anatolia. In no time, he had rallied a Turkish national army. The French, the Italians and the Bolsheviks, quick to sense the solidity of his backing, left him free to drive the Greeks into the sea. The British withstood him in isolation. They averted war with him at Chanak chiefly thanks to the good sense and restraint of their general on the spot.

Elsewhere all good nationalists were in despair, for Western paramountcy continued, and seemed too mighty to be worth opposing. The only change was that it had new labels. One was 'mandate', meaning in Western eyes control subject to supervision by the new League of Nations, but to Arabs military supremacy that amounted to colonial rule. The ex-Ottoman mandates were shared between Britain and France—Palestine, Transjordan and Iraq for the one, Syria and Lebanon for the other. The British tried to make amends for the humiliation that the Sharif, now King of the Hejaz, and his sons had suffered over the promise of an 'Arab nation' and over Feisal's discomfiture at Damascus; they placed Feisal on the throne of Iraq and made his brother Abdullah Amir of Transjordan. In their own eyes, they had fulfilled their obligation. But disillusioned Arabs thought otherwise; to them *f1* the new frontiers drawn by foreign hands were an offence against the former unity of Greater Syria, and the promise to further Jewish immigration into Palestine began to be seen by them as a breach of faith. The double problem of respecting Arab rights as well as promoting Jewish immigration was to baffle London for a generation.

p 179 (22) For Egypt, the new label was independence, but this was a misnomer, for Britain refused to withdraw her garrisons. The Khedive became a king, and the *Wafd* a parliamentary party, but Britain reserved the right to protect the Suez Canal, the large foreign communities in Egypt, and the Anglo-Egyptian Sudan, which was in name a condominium but in fact a British dependency. If the British failed to see the obnoxiousness of this arrangement to Egyptian nationalists, the Egyptians failed to see its advantages to a weak and covetable country until, in 1936, Mussolini's adventurous conquest of Ethiopia caught them between his Libyan and his Ethiopian pincers and sent them scurrying into an Anglo-Egyptian treaty of alliance. Its terms, which made Egypt eligible for membership of the League of Nations while preserving the British Suez Canal base, were to stand Britain in good stead in World War II. So was a treaty of Iraqi independence signed in 1930, that was likewise limited, since it afforded Britain air bases and a virtually exclusive right to supply Iraq with foreign advisers.

The important international feature of the mandate system was the League's insistence on maintaining the open door for trade. Invoking equal rights for all comers, the Americans were able to gain a share in oil production in Iraq, and in 1929 to join in an agreement whereby, within a red line drawn on a map, major companies of four nationalities agreed that all should participate in prospecting. The company in Persia was British, and that in Saudi Arabia was American. In the realm of oil production, competition was less fierce than is generally imagined; it was cut-throat only over marketing. Because the Middle East became known in the second half of the century to contain 60% of the world's proven oil reserves, people think that its oil wealth is of long standing. They forget the years of outlay spent by the companies on drilling dry holes, and the small royalties they paid to local landlords while they recouped their losses. The British company that discovered oil in Persia in 1908 paid no dividend until 1917; Iraq, where a gusher was first discovered in 1927, could not export in quantity until pipelines reached the Mediterranean in 1934, and the oil of Arabia and Kuwait, though discovered before World War II, could not be exported until after it for lack of shipping and pipe. Except in Persia, the bonanza did not start until the 1950s; in Libya and Algeria it began ten years later. Before the boom, the area's main sources of export revenue were Egyptian cotton, Persian carpets and Iraqi dates and barley. Only French North Africa produced mineral raw materials—phosphates and iron ore. Territories that lived on agriculture, and largely on cash crops destined for export to Europe, were vulnerable to collapses of world prices. Most of the Middle East earned less and ate less during the slump of the 1930s than it had done before World War I.

Frustrated nationalism

An early symptom of the head of nationalist steam that was building up was the rise to power in Persia of a successful military dictator. Reza Khan had been an officer in the Shah's Cossack brigade. In 1921 he set out to reduce anarchy to order; by 1925 he had proclaimed himself Reza Shah, and by 1932 felt well enough entrenched to cancel the British oil company's concession, though, for lack of Persians able to work it, he was obliged later to agree to new terms that gave him a larger share of the company's earnings. As before, the Arabian peninsula was the only point at which Arabs exercised a similar degree of independence. No one interfered when in 1924–25 Ibn Saud harnessed a movement of puritan desert Arabs—the Wahhabis—struck at his old adversary the former Sharif, conquered Mecca and founded the single kingdom of Saudi Arabia.

Elsewhere, Egyptian and Arab nationalism fermented without result. The prop once afforded by Islam was shaken when Mustafa Kemal abolished the Caliphate in 1924. Chagrin found expression in romantically pessimistic poetry. Yet another cause for despair was that parliamentary democracy, which had for so long been thought the key to success, turned out to be a perpetuation of the rule of the landowning rich, who either bullied or bought their way into all seats except those in major towns. The nationalists of the 1920s had been liberals; those of the 1930s were becoming socialists.

In Algeria, proximity to France, trade with France and the French system of education produced some nationalists who aspired to be Frenchmen. Elsewhere, the reaction to Western dominance was to copy Western practices of government and business, but to resent dependence on Europe. Anti-Western movements and parties abounded; in the main they followed local leaders, and so tended to perpetuate the foreign-drawn frontiers of which they complained; but some drew their membership from more than one territory—for instance the *Etoile Nord Africaine* in the Maghreb, and the Moslem Brotherhood based on Egypt. These were a foretaste of the desire for Arab unity that was to gain momentum during World War II. In the 1920s no one territory had the strength to help another to rebel against Western might. Throughout that decade, therefore, the British were able to shrug off the consequences of their double undertaking to Jew and Arab. They were lulled into complacency because few Jews arrived, and because the Arabs felt so depressed and unsupported that they resisted their fate only intermittently; they boycotted, rather than combatted all British suggestions for working jointly with the Jews.

In 1933 an event far outside the area transformed this scene. Hitler's rise to power and the Nazi policy of anti-semitism that followed it stimulated active Arab resistance, and projected the Palestine problem into the centre of world affairs. Soon worldwide opinion was pressing the British to stop rationing Jewish immigration. Sheer humanitarianism dictated a British response, and by 1935 the rate of admission was such that, if maintained, it

p 182
(32, 33)

An Egyptian comment in 1930 on the 'neutrality' which John Bull has declared in Palestine, Iraq, and Egypt and on which he hypocritically asks God's blessing. (1)

would produce a Jewish majority in Palestine before mid-century. The Arabs understandably rebelled, and from 1936 to 1938 almost continuously made the country unsafe for isolated Jewish settlements and for travellers. For the first time, some help came to them from outside. Guerrillas crossed from Syria, and the Arab kings, summoned by the British in the hope of counterbalancing the influence of world Jewry, tendered comfort and advice. In 1937 a British Royal Commission proposed that half a loaf would be better than no bread, and suggested partition of Palestine into two states, with a new mandate drawn up for the Jerusalem area. But both Jewish and Arab opposition was such that partition would have needed enforcement, and the British, hampered as they were by the worsening situation in Europe, were in no mind to enforce it. They therefore dropped the proposal, and watched while the Jews began to organize self-defence and to engineer illegal immigration. Finally, after Hitler had raped Czechoslovakia and war in Europe seemed inevitable, they made a move to secure their sea and air passage to India and their Middle Eastern oil supply. In May 1939 they issued a White Paper that fixed a limit to Jewish immigration for five years, and thereafter made it subject to Arab consent. This document left the Jews in a fix. 'We shall fight the White Paper as if there were no war,' they said, 'and the war as if there were no White Paper.'

The young generation of Arabs and Persians admired the Nazis; older men in responsible positions feared them once they had signed a pact with Soviet Russia. Yet even at the darkest hour of the war for Britain, when the Mediterranean was impassable and the Germans were winning in Crete and Libya, only Iraq rebelled, and only two prominent Arabs, the Mufti of Jerusalem and Rashid Ali of Iraq, went to Berlin to help Hitler. Their puny efforts were more than offset by active military help given by the Amir Abdullah and by Palestinian Jews and Arabs.

World War II

The war greatly quickened the pace of economic and social changes some of which had germinated before it began. Until the Allied landings in French North Africa took place in 1942, the three French dependencies there were starved of goods and work, but behind the British lines light industries mushroomed and military purchases filled the pockets of entrepreneurs. Inflation followed, and widened the gap between rich and poor. Yet the latter had seen new sights and chances of better jobs, and social aspirations began to grow. By the 1950s transistor radios had become a first buy, and were soon helping to spread new social

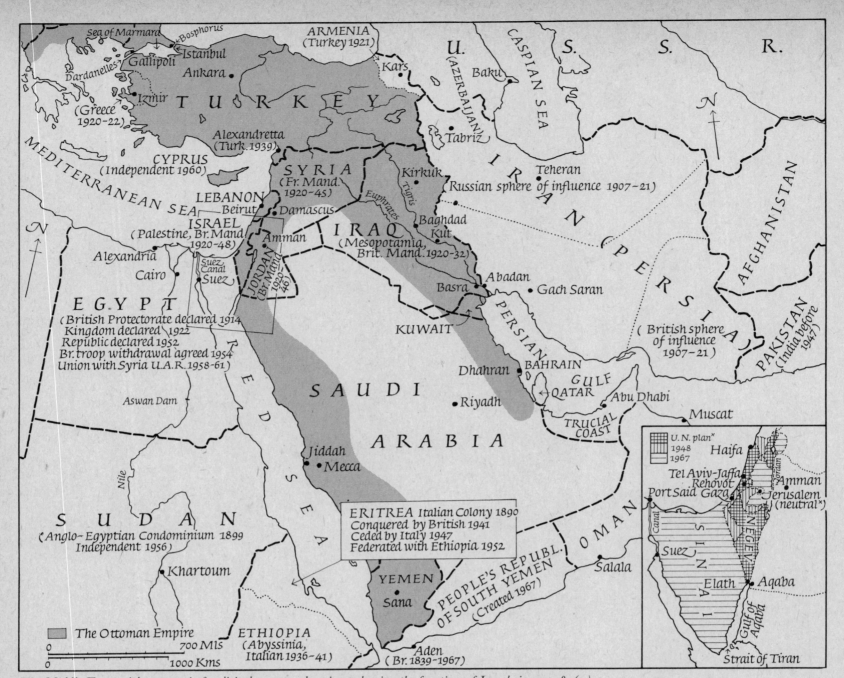

Sea of Marmara
Bosphorus
Dardanelles
Gallipoli
Istanbul
Ankara
Izmir
(Greece 1920-22)
ARMENIA (Turkey 1921)
Kars
U. S. S. R.
CASPIAN SEA
Baku
(AZERBAIJAN)
Tabriz
Teheran
Russian sphere of influence 1907-21
T U R K E Y
Alexandretta (Turk. 1939)
MEDITERRANEAN SEA
CYPRUS (Independent 1960)
SYRIA (Fr. Mand. 1920-45)
Kirkuk
Euphrates
Tigris
LEBANON
Beirut
Damascus
Baghdad
Kut
ISRAEL (Palestine, Br. Mand. 1920-48)
Amman
IRAQ (Mesopotamia, Brit. Mand. 1920-32)
I R A N (P E R S I A)
AFGHANISTAN
Alexandria
Cairo
Suez Canal
Suez
JORDAN (Br. Mand. 1920-46)
Basra
Abadan
Gach Saran
(British sphere of influence 1907-21)
PAKISTAN (India before 1947)
E G Y P T
(British Protectorate declared 1914
Kingdom declared 1922
Republic declared 1952
Br. troop withdrawal agreed 1954
Union with Syria U.A.R. 1958-61)
KUWAIT
Dhahran
Riyadh
BAHRAIN
QATAR
Abu Dhabi
GULF
Muscat
TRUCIAL COAST
Aswan Dam
S A U D I
A R A B I A
RED SEA
Jiddah
Mecca
S U D A N
(Anglo-Egyptian Condominium 1899
Independent 1956)
Khartoum
Nile
ERITREA Italian Colony 1890
Conquered by British 1941
Ceded by Italy 1947
Federated with Ethiopia 1952
YEMEN
Sana
PEOPLE'S REPUBL. OF SOUTH YEMEN (Created 1967)
O M A N
Salala
ETHIOPIA (Abyssinia, Italian 1936-41)
Aden (Br. 1839-1967)

The Ottoman Empire
0   700 Mls
0   1000 Kms

U. N. plan 1948 1967
Haifa
Tel Aviv-Jaffa
Rehovot
Port Said
Gaza
Canal
Suez
S I N A I
N E G E V
Elath
Aqaba
Amman
Jerusalem (neutral)
Gulf of Aqaba
Strait of Tiran

The Middle East, with a resumé of political events and an inset showing the frontiers of Israel since 1948. (2)

and political gospels to mass audiences. Even Moslem women began to peep out from seclusion and to envy their Christian counterparts—Copts, Assyrians, Maronites—who were getting jobs in shops and offices.

Political upheaval was marked only where the chance of getting rid of Great Power intrusion seemed promising. In the north of Persia (now called Iran), where the Soviets broke their promise to go and fostered an Azerbaijani separatist movement, the Iranians successfully invoked the help of the new United Nations Organization in getting rid of them. (Turkey, in which they claimed bases and territory, disposed of their claims on its own.) In Syria and Lebanon, the nationalists mustered British help in forcing the Free French to grant them independence. In Palestine, immediately Hitler had been driven from Africa and the Jews began to learn of the scale of his gas chambers, they turned on the British for their inability and consequent refusal to rescue European Jewry from death. They switched their political pressure from London to New York, and organized private armies some of which began to kidnap and murder British victims even before the war was over.

The concept of Arab unity gained momentum from wartime experiences and grievances. Now that Islam had become, for educated Arabs, less a religion than a culture, Moslem and Christian Arabs began to think as one. An Arab League, blessed by the British, sprang into being, but was quickly appropriated by the Egyptians as an instrument for increasing their importance. This League had a weakness, which was that all its aims were negative: Out with the French! Out with the British bases! Down with the Zionists! For a generation, most of its members had had no

experience of evolving constructive policies, and for lack of practice made no such plans now. The League helped to turn the French out of Syria and Lebanon, and thereafter concentrated on criticizing the British and the Jews in Palestine—a topic on which all its members thought alike.

It had great hopes of an end, at last, to foreign domination of Egypt, because the new Labour Government in Britain was ready to negotiate a British military departure. But within two years this hope had proved vain. For in Palestine the British foreign secretary, Bevin, after fruitless attempts at compromise between Jew and Arab, punctuated by open battle between them, had handed the problem to the United Nations. Simultaneously, Egyptian over-confidence in proclaiming the unity of the Nile Valley and, consequently, denying the right of the Sudan to self-determination, had led to defeat of the case against Britain that Egypt presented at the United Nations, and to the breakdown of Anglo-Egyptian negotiations. The British forces that left Palestine were able to settle back into the Canal Zone base.

But they were not as all-powerful as they once had been. In 1947 Bevin had to avow to the Americans that the British could no longer be the reservoir of financial-military support to Greece and Turkey in their struggle against Communist encroachment. President Truman at once took on the job. His undertaking of March 1947 was the turning point that brought the Americans on to the Middle Eastern scene under the banner of anti-Communism. By 1948 they were supplying arms and aid to Iran also.

For both powers, the Palestine problem was now not so much a dilemma as a vicious circle. In their eyes the crying need of the times was the rehabilitation of Western Europe. For this, the oil

p 182 (34)

of the Middle East was a necessary ingredient, and its production and transit westwards were vital. Yet the fountain-heads and supply routes belonged to Arabs. Simultaneously, Jewish immigration was building up, both by permission and illegally. Partition was a possible answer to the problem of Jewish numbers, and the United Nations proposed it; most Jews now favoured it, but the Arabs were against it, and no power or group of powers was ready to enforce it. The British, unwilling even to protect the lives of United Nations umpires, left on 15 May 1948 in disillusionment and ignominy, leaving the two communities to fight the solution out.

From Israeli independence to Suez

p 182 (35) Immediately, Israel declared itself an independent state. In indecent haste, Truman and Stalin competed to be the first to recognize it; the first, to please American Jews; the second, hoping to sow discord between Britain and America. The Arab League,

p 182 (36) undismayed at the volume of support for Israel, rushed forces to the aid of the Palestine Arabs, but could not agree on unity of command. Israeli courage and ingenuity, as well as the clumsiness of opponents fighting individually, led to a resounding Israeli victory and to a huge exodus of Arab refugees. These, poor and unwanted in most of the rest of the Arab world, sowed bitterness and resentment broadcast. The only tales of Arab glory were that of Abdullah's Arab Legion, which held on to the Old City of Jerusalem, and that of a last stand by an Egyptian outpost at Falujah, where a colonel called Nasser was a hero.

The Middle East was still run by kings, shahs and pashas, and on their lips for the next few years, the magic word was planning —planning to harness rivers, found clinics, schools and housing estates, and improve industrial and agricultural techniques. They hoped thereby to keep the rising tide of socialism at bay. They had the money for the job thanks to the war debts owed by Britain,

p 179 (24–26) or to oil revenue, or to loans from the charitable United States. But only at the hands of dictators did the plans come to fruition. In Turkey, Mustafa Kemal had paved the way by means of étatism, or state management of investment and industry; in Kuwait an all-powerful sheikh changed life for all, high and low; in Iraq, virtual dictation by a prime minister, Nuri Pasha, produced an effective Development Board. But elsewhere plans were replanned every time the government changed hands, and little or nothing emerged from the reams of paper.

By 1950, therefore, there were major causes for nationalist chagrin and mortification, and people were more vocal about it because of the mass media at their disposal. They criticized the bombast and incompetence of leaders who had overcalled their hands in the Palestine war. They voiced disappointment at the lack of quick results in the field of development and welfare. And they gave full rein to their prime grievance—continuing Western dominance, symbolized by the British bases, by Anglo-American efforts to recruit allies against Communism, and by the new and supposedly Western outpost, Israel, into which Jews were flowing endlessly thanks largely to the bounty of the citizens and Government of the United States. For the North Africans, the indignity was French insistence on embodying them in a French Union.

p 180 (28) For the Iranians (who saw no harm in Israel) it was the presence on their soil of an oil company in which the British Government held a majority of the shares.

This accumulation of grievances touched off a chain of nationalist and socialist reactions. In 1949, a military revolt in Syria set off a series of coups and countercoups that were to last for years. In 1951, disgruntled Palestinians murdered Abdullah of Jordan, and the Iranians first nationalized and then expelled the British

p 182 (37) oil company. In 1952, Egyptian officers staged a bloodless Egyptian revolution that dismissed King Farouk and carried Nasser to power. In 1953, the French banished the Sultan of Morocco for

p 183 (40–42) co-operating with the nationalists, and in 1954 the Algerian Liberation Front began the eight years of bloody revolt that led to civil war not only between themselves and the French but between French *ultras* and French moderates.

By 1955, nationalist morale was rising. Transistors were buzzing with triumphs. Egypt's new men had recognized the right of the Sudan to decide its own future. The British had withdrawn their

troops from the Canal Zone (a move to which even Churchill grumpily assented once the hydrogen bomb had been fully tested). The Arab oil states were richer than before thanks to a new fifty-fifty sharing of proceeds with the companies, and to their taking up the markets lost by Iran during its three-year experiment in total oil nationalization, in the course of which Western oil companies had teamed up in order to baulk it of markets. The biggest triumph of all was scored by Egypt's Nasser. Incensed, as were all members of the Arab League, at the West's arrangements for rationing arms between the Arabs and Israel, and irritated at its readiness to arm states, including Iraq, that joined pacts directed against Communism, he bought arms from the Soviet bloc. At one bound in 1955, the Soviets leapt over the barrier of anti-Communist states erected against them by the British, Turks and Americans, and entered Middle Eastern power politics.

Western dominance was challenged, but not wrecked. No Arab state was Communist, and most were linked by force of habit to traditional Western suppliers. They hoped for, and obtained, supplies from both sides of the Iron Curtain. But Nasser's arms deals with Russia caused a scare, and in the course of it the Americans, incensed at his flirtations with Russia and China, cancelled an offer to finance a project on which he had set his heart—a high dam at Aswan to generate power and irrigate new land. Several p 181 (31) parties besides America's Dulles had their knife into Nasser. The French were enraged by his export of arms to the Algerian rebels; the British resented the audience he commanded for his criticism of their policy of weaning one Arab state, Iraq, from the Arab League's policy of non-alignment, and the Israelis condemned his denial of passage to their ships through the Suez Canal and his restriction of their sea and air passage through the Strait of Tiran —their exit to the Red Sea. When, in reaction to Dulles' blow about the Aswan Dam, he nationalized the French Suez Canal p 182 (38) Company and began to run the Canal himself, he seemed to all three to have 'his thumb on our windpipe'. At first separately, but soon in p 183 (43) collusion, France, Israel and Britain laid plans for toppling him before it was too late.

In the eight years since independence, the Israelis had transformed their state. They had pounded their private armies into a national army. They had reclaimed waste land, admitted a million immigrants, taught them all Hebrew, and used copious American and French aid to buy arms as well as industrial implements. If someone would guarantee them air cover, they were keen to attack Egypt. Secretly, the British and French promised this cover, to be followed by their own seizure of the Suez Canal.

The plan worked. It won military prestige for Israel because, given the promised air cover, Israel had routed the Egyptian army, captured much of Sinai and reopened the Strait of Tiran hours before the Anglo-French capture of the Canal was due to start. But it ended in a minor setback for France and a major disaster for Britain. Heedless of American, Russian and United Nations warnings, these two powers pressed on with seizing the p 183 (44, 45) Canal. They stopped only because an alarming flight from the pound sterling caused the British to desist. The adverse balance sheet from Britain's point of view was loss of American confidence, closure of the Canal by Nasser's blockships, the temporary Arab application of an oil boycott, and loss of contact with all important Arab leaders except those in Christian Beirut and conservative Baghdad. This last they were to lose in the aftermath. Two years later Nuri Pasha and his king were murdered partly because of their loyalty to Britain at a time when she was the ally of Israel. The most important outcome of the second Palestine war was the establishment by a virtually unanimous United Nations of a force to man the frontier and hold open the Strait of Tiran. It was accepted by Egypt, though not by Israel, in return for Israeli withdrawal from all captured Egyptian territory. The Egyptians, therefore, were able to count their defeat a victory.

The end of imperialism

Except at Aden and a few points on the Arab shore of the Persian Gulf, the era of British imperialism was over. But that of Great Power influence was not. The American Sixth Fleet lay in the offing, ready to help anti-Communists such as Israel or Lebanon, while the post-revolutionary states, Egypt and Syria, began to mortgage their exports to pay for arms from the Soviet Union; after the 1958 revolution Iraq did likewise. In North Africa, France continued to try and defeat the independence movements. Within them, a heavy overlay of French civilization had exposed the nationalists to strains unknown farther east. Algiers had the third biggest French university, and any Moroccan or Tunisian cabinet contained many ministers with higher degrees from France. All educated men felt the pull of Paris as well as that of the Arab League, or of Mecca. By 1956, the French had been obliged to concede independence to both Tunisia and Morocco, but in Algeria they were still at grips with a problem they had created for themselves by pursuing two incompatible policies—simultaneously assimilating the Moslems to themselves while educating them in techniques of self-government. Inevitably, Moslem aspirations led to revolt against the million French *colons* who, like whites elsewhere in Africa, wanted to cling to minority privileges. In the civil war of 1954–62, the Algerian Liberation Front was helped not only by fellow Arabs but by the follies of French *ultras* who fought their own countrymen as well as the Arabs rather than admit that they had failed to make Algeria part of France. By the time that Algerian independence was negotiated in 1962, most *colons* had fled, leaving their cars, factories and farms to looters. Algeria was politically free, but economically a ruin.

Once Nasser had ousted Britain and was a beneficiary of both Soviet and American aid, he vested all his Arab admirers with dignity and seemed capable of balancing on a pinnacle of non-alignment. The Syrians, fearing the spread of Communism, asked to unite with Egypt, and Nasser formed the United Arab Republic. But these new strengths brought new problems. One was how to organize political power. Another was how to handle economic and social dilemmas including a population explosion.

An unprecedented increase of births over deaths began during World War II, chiefly thanks to disease control; thereafter it grew so rapidly that at least 50% more people lived in the area in the mid-sixties than did so in the mid-forties; the highest rates of growth were in Turkey and Syria, Egypt and Morocco. Only in compact and forward-looking Tunisia was there any sustained effort to cure rural prejudice against birth control. In these conditions, how was even an autocrat to judge which came first —expenditure on the health and education of a population nearly half of which was under fifteen? Or on goods that show—housing, drinking-water, consumer requirements? Or on prestige enterprises such as steel works? Or on expensive but invisible infrastructures such as flood control and up-country dams?

Choices

Every country must make these choices, but in much of the Middle East they were hampered by constant political upheavals. The most successful reforms were those carried out in countries with continuity of government—land reform under Reza's son Mohammed Reza Shah, family planning and the abandonment of conservative Islamic practices in Bourguiba's Tunisia, or slum clearance in Nasser's Cairo. No scheme succeeds overnight; outside every city, from Istanbul to Cairo and Casablanca, huge shanty towns drew attention to the flow citywards of under-employed and unemployed peasants.

The Arab states soon fell to quarrelling between themselves; the quarrels were the sharper because they were tinged with envy created by the uneven distribution of revenue from oil. The military dictators of Iraq and Egypt could not agree, and Syria, incensed by Egyptian bossiness, in 1961 split off from Nasser's UAR. Algeria quarrelled with Morocco over frontiers, and, everywhere, socialist regimes tended to pit themselves against hereditary rulers. This pattern crystallized into a civil war in Yemen in which Nasser, by participating on the republican side, succeeded in polarizing the Arab world that it was his aim to unite.

But greater than the loss of influence that Nasser suffered through fruitless interference in Yemen was the ground he lost through inept handling of the Arab quarrel with Israel. By 1967, the United Nations force had held his frontier covered for ten years; guerrilla attacks on Israel, to which the Israelis replied occasionally but massively, were taking place only from Jordan and Syria. The Great Powers, who were all selling arms to their

ideological favourites, grew nervous lest these should cause a third Palestine war; the Americans warned the Israelis against using their power, and the Soviets warned the Egyptians against the bombast to which the Arabic language easily lends itself. But Nasser was sensitive about his loss of leadership. When, in May 1967, the Syrians called for help, he jettisoned his theory that Arab unity must precede any battle with Israel, and tried a piece of brinkmanship that was to prove excessive. He asked the United Nations force to leave his soil, he reinforced Sinai and, heedless of experience, closed the Strait of Tiran.

The Israelis reacted at once; within six days they had won their third war, captured much ground in southern Syria and Jordan, including all Jerusalem, reopened the Strait of Tiran and reached the east bank of the Suez Canal. While they remained there the Canal was closed to the world's shipping, and Egyptian civilians could for the first time see Israeli might face to face.

p 184 (46, 47)

Israel's third overwhelming victory altered the balance of local power; indeed it rendered the Israelis physically strong enough to flout their foreign sponsors and go it alone. They had proved their courage and efficiency three times over; they owned a nuclear reactor; yet they had preserved their image of a small David beset by a Goliath represented by superior manpower. But their very success brought drawbacks of which the worst was the classic dilemma of the victor—whether to surrender gains and preserve the homogeneity of their state, or to retain territory populated by vengeful Arabs. One result of Egypt's discomfiture was that the Egyptians began to rely increasingly on Soviet support; another was that initiative in confronting Israel passed to ex-Palestinian guerrilla groups who began to constitute a political entity of a kind that, when dispersed as refugees, they had never done.

p 180 (27)

p 184 (48, 49)

The scene in 1970 was vastly different from that in 1900. People were far more literate and more socially conscious, better fed and healthier, better armed and less pacific, better equipped with communications but no better united. Though the hereditary rulers—the Shah, kings, sultans—would now and then combine to worst republicans and Communists, both groups were equally often torn by personal rivalries. Yet seven decades of nationalism and revolution had endowed the area with some notable leaders. Excluding men whose life-span is not over, those most deserving of remembrance are first, Mohammed Abdu, the Egyptian theologian who paved the way for nationalism by preaching that men could reconcile Islamic purity with modern behaviour. Next, Mustafa Kemal Ataturk, who rallied a defeated army, generated pure Turkish nationalism, defeated foreign domination and native conservatism, and promoted Turkey's entry into Europe and NATO. Next, Chaim Weizmann, who, in contrast to many Israeli leaders, had the gift of seeing into Western, and notably British, minds and shaping his course to allow for their point of view. Next, Ibn Saud of Arabia, who by a combination of sagacity and puritan virtue of an Islamic kind forged the warring tribes of Arabia into a respected nation. Next, Sultan Mohammed V of Morocco who, by quiet recalcitrance, defeated French attempts to baulk his support for nationalism, and who died in 1961 as both political and religious leader of a mourning nation. Lastly, Gamal Abd el-Nasser of Egypt, who by force of example showed the Arabic-speaking world how to get rid of Western dominance.

p 179 (23)

But neither nationalism, nor revolution, nor the influence of such men eliminated the dependence of weak and quarrelsome countries upon outsiders rather than upon one another. Atomic power had changed the nature of the discrepancy between great and small, but the gap between them remained constant; a foreign fleet, once British but by 1970 Soviet, still dominated Alexandria harbour. Perhaps Iran, thanks to forging self-confidence through social prowess, stood a better chance than its neighbours of playing an independent role. Elsewhere, even two new and unimagined elements had not altered the degree of dependence on foreigners: the one, the economic power enjoyed by the states endowed with oil resources, but not used in unison until 1971; the other, the central presence of an inexorable newcomer, Israel. Yet for all Israel's strength, acumen and ability to withstand Arab resistance, it remained a transplanted organ within a body with a latent capacity for working at one. Can it render itself assimilable, instead of rejected?

p 173 (1)
p 183 (40–42)
p 180 (29)
p 181 (30, 31)

IX EMERGENT AFRICA

The dangerous legacy of imperialism

J.D. FAGE

'*We are going to put an end to suppression of free thought*
and make it possible for all citizens fully to enjoy
the fundamental liberties set down in the
Declaration of the Rights of Man.'

PATRICE LUMUMBA, 1960

Africa's past

is a more potent factor in determining her present than appears on the surface. Not only are African artists and thinkers turning to cultural links that lead back beyond colonialism, but even when ideas and institutions are copied closely from European models, the ways in which they are interpreted and the values that animate them may be totally alien to Europe.

Pre-colonial chiefs and kings, for instance, often ruled by a sort of 'consensus' system—discussion between head-men leading to general agreement. This is neither 'despotism' nor 'democracy' in the European sense, nor does it harmonize easily with European formulae for decision-making. The result is that in many countries where parliamentary government has been introduced, it has failed to function as it would in Europe, and single-party rather than double- or multi-party states have been the rule.

Kingship in early 20th-century Africa is symbolized by this throne of glass beadwork from Cameroun. It was made for King Njoya of the Bamum people. Every Bamum king had a new personal throne. The two-headed python stands for royalty. Purely African as it is in design and conception, the two guards at the feet carry European rifles. (1)

The ethics of colonialism rested on the 'export' of European civilization, a concept in which philanthropy co-existed with exploitation. Above: a German propaganda postcard. (2)

German troops set out for South West Africa in 1904 to suppress the rebellion of the Herero. It involved a full-scale war which dragged on for over two years. (3)

The 'King's Own' rifles on parade in Northern Rhodesia. It was only by the enrolment of vast numbers of African troops that the colonial powers could organize and enforce their rule. Such troops were also used to fight in wars between European countries, both inside and outside Africa. (5)

France gave something of her national character to each of the African territories that she once ruled. These Senegalese scouts were photographed in July 1913. (6)

One white missionary (left) provides a token schooling for the children of a whole Congolese village. Even by 1950 very few Africans had any opportunity of secondary education. (4)

Christian missions were often the first form of European penetration and may be destined to outlast all the others. Above: Catholic mass celebrated in Mugera, Urundi. (7)

On state occasions, the sense of European superiority was expressed without inhibition. This is the opening of Takoradi Harbour, Gold Coast, in 1928. (8)

Degrees of exploitation varied widely, the worst example being that of the Congo, which until 1908 was the private empire of King Leopold of the Belgians. Left: ivory being collected by the king's agents about 1905. (9)

The confrontation with Europe is expressed most directly in art, where one can see new experiences being partially assimilated with indigenous traditions. The five examples of sculpture shown above and right all date from the early years of the century and originate from what is now the Congo. Above left: Kaiser Wilhelm II of Germany. Centre: a European civil servant, in soapstone. Above right: Father Bittremieux, a missionary who spent most of his life in Africa, in wood and glass. Right: wooden figures of a cyclist and an early motor-car with two passengers. (10–14)

The Congo today preserves much of the vigour of its traditional art. This wooden panel (below) is by the contemporary sculptor F. Berquin. In a village setting that, significantly, is wholly pre-colonial, a chief receives the offerings and homage of his people. (15)

A Yoruba king commissioned this entirely traditional door (right) for his royal palace, and the sculptor, Areogun of Osi, died as recently as 1954. The panels show Yoruba daily life or events from history, carved in hard wood (to resist termites) with a variety of tools: axe, adze, knife and chisel. Not all of them can be satisfactorily explained. At the top a woman is apparently having some altercation with two soldiers. In the centre a cyclist dextrously smokes a pipe and waves a fan; while at the bottom a cavalry officer is seen, wearing a sword and holding a large pistol in his right hand. The smaller figures at the sides are musicians playing *dun-dun* drums or, in one case, a horned flute. (16)

Modern Africa was born during the decade 1955–65, when over twenty-five states achieved independence. Left: an early election in Nigeria, conducted with typical enthusiasm in a country which, as this cowherd outside Ibadan (below) bears witness, is still only partly of the 20th century. (17, 18)

The new nations were defined not by ethnic communities but by the accidents of colonial occupation, a fact which added to the internal tensions following independence. In Nigeria, the attempted secession of the Ibos led to a protracted civil war (below) in which millions suffered. (19)

Ghana's problems were constitutional. Six years after independence it had become a monolithic one-party state dominated by Kwame Nkrumah. Elected president in July 1960 by a devoted following, he fell from power in 1966, accused of corruption. (20)

White domination has become the firm policy of those parts of Africa where minority settler governments were in power at the time of independence—South Africa and Rhodesia. It is a policy that depends on apartheid laws (below) and, if necessary, force. Below right: Sharpeville, 1960. (21, 22)

African unity, although hoped for by almost every black African statesman, has proved difficult to achieve in practice. The Organization of African Unity, with its headquarters in Addis Ababa, exists to promote this ideal, made explicit in its stained-glass window shown here. Portraits of the leaders of free Africa surmount a globe of the continent (African-ruled states coloured black) and their national flags. (23)

The same spirit of pride and resolution animates the designs of commemorative stamps issued to mark the achievement of independence. (24)

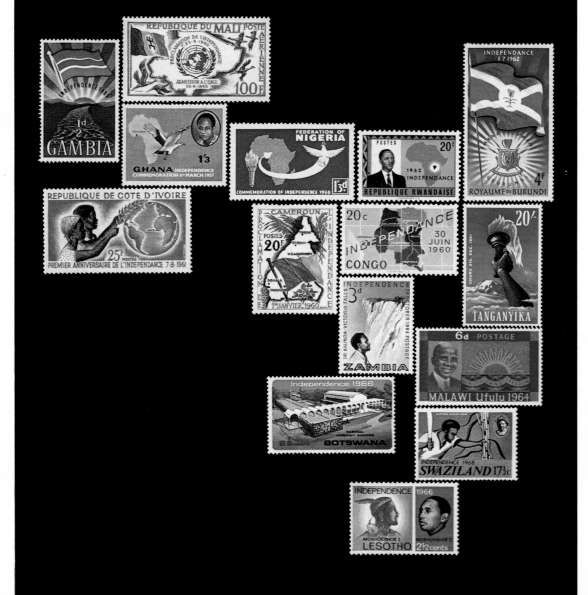

The dangerous legacy of imperialism

J. D. FAGE

FOLLOWING upon some twenty years of intense European competition and conquest, virtually the whole of sub-Saharan Africa spent the first sixty years of the 20th century under colonial rule. But it would be a mistake to view the history of this period in Africa solely in terms of the policies and actions of the European ruling powers.

The colonial interlude

It is now evident, for example, that the colonial period of African history was an extremely short one. For most Africans, it could be encompassed within little more than two generations, within a single life-span even. But during the last twenty years or so, historians have become more aware than ever before that Negro Africans have a traceable historical record extending over many centuries. The story of human society in Africa has had its ups and downs, but essentially it is much the same as that of human development anywhere, a story of progressive achievement onwards from the revolutionary discoveries of how to grow food and to use metals. And in Africa this knowledge came from much the same sources and at much the same times as that which sparked off the development of society elsewhere in the Old World.

The colonial period in Africa must then be seen as something of an interlude in a very much longer span of African development. This is not to belittle the importance of this interlude. It was colonization from Europe which first brought much of Negro Africa into full contact with the rest of the world, and which has made Africa a matter of interest and concern to all mankind. Equally, no one could dispute the strength of European influence in forming the states, governments, economies and modes of life and thought of present-day Africa.

But it would be misleading to continue from this and to build an essay on 20th-century Africa solely around enquiries into the African policies of the individual European colonial powers and into the activities of their official and unofficial agents on the continent, with the role of the Africans being seen merely as one of reaction to these policies and activities. It would be quite wrong to accept a dialectic in which the only active principles were the alien, colonial ones. Recent research has demonstrated, for example, the importance of active, indigenous African principles of thought and action in some of the early responses to colonial conquest—for instance in the Shona rising in Rhodesia in 1896–97 and in the Maji-Maji movement in German East Africa in 1905–07 —and also that there can be significant continuities between such early resistance movements and modern mass nationalisms. It is in fact evident (and historians at least should not find it surprising) that behind the 20th-century Western forms that clothe so much contemporary expression and action in Africa, distorted if not wholly concealed by the terminology with which political scientists, economists and even sociologists attempt to analyze and explain such expression and action, there are African men and women, whose values are to a considerable extent formed by their own African experience and history.

p 193 (1)
p 196, 7
(10–15)

It seems then that two things are desirable for an essay on black Africa in the 20th century. First, instead of trying to assess and compare either what the individual British and French, Portuguese and Belgian colonial regimes did (or thought that they were doing) in Africa, or what their particular reflections were in particular territories such as Ghana or Senegal, Angola or the Congo, it is advisable to try to see what were the general principles of European control in Africa that were of universal significance to its peoples. Secondly, it seems desirable to try and assess what the several major groups of African peoples made of these principles in the light of their previous historical experience.

Cultural imperialism

The first essential characteristic of European empire-builders in Africa was their belief that European culture was vastly superior to any culture that could be found in Africa, not only technically, but also spiritually and morally. It followed that they had no hesitation whatsoever in imposing their rule upon Africans.

p 194 (2)
p 195 (8)

It seems possible indeed to explain the onslaught of European imperialism in Africa at the close of the 19th century almost on the simple ground that never before or since has there been so wide a gulf of understanding between the two cultures. In the previous four centuries in which Europe had been in contact with Negro Africa, whatever the views of stay-at-home *philosophes*, Europeans who had actually known African societies had found little difficulty in coming to mutually acceptable terms with them. Whether we look at 16th-century accounts of Portuguese adventure in and around the Congo and Zambezi valleys, the writings of 17th-century Jesuit missionaries in Ethiopia, the 17th- and 18th-century books of Dutch traders to the Gold Coast and Benin, or even some of the accounts of the kingdom of Dahomey written by 18th-century English slavers, we find African societies being described and discussed in terms applicable to human society in general. They were seen to be different, often very different, from European society, but this did not seem to mean that they were necessarily inferior.

This early tradition of looking at Africa was never wholly extinguished. Indeed it illumines the works of many of the great 19th-century European explorers of Africa, perhaps reaching its peak in the five volumes of Henry Barth's *Travels and discoveries in North and Central Africa*, published in 1857–58. The popular authors, however, were those who accepted and pandered to, or who indeed inspired beliefs in the innate moral and material inferiority to European civilization of African peoples and cultures. Sir Richard Burton is a notable example. At the end of his *Mission to Gelele, King of Dahomey*, published in 1864, for example, he wrote that 'the Negro, in mass, will not improve beyond a certain point, and that not respectable'. Or we may note the conclusion of the politically motivated French explorer, Captain L. G. Binger, after his visit to the Mossi kingdom of Wagadugu in 1888, that 'if the European should ever come here, he should come as a master, constituting the upper class of society, and should not have to bow his head before native chiefs, to whom he is infinitely superior in all respects'.

Such opinions flowed naturally enough from the supreme self-confidence of 19th-century Europeans. The technological and economic strengths of their civilization were so manifest that the inferiority of all other peoples and their cultures could practically be assumed. Medical men and missionaries shared in this assumption, even though the first should have had scientific and the second Christian reasons for believing in the equality of the species. In 1897, for example, the head of the medical service of the British colony of Lagos could write that 'no native of West Africa is fitted for any position of trust or independence, as he is sure to prove unreliable the moment he escapes control'. Similarly, most missionaries believed that European control was essential if Christianity were to be implanted in Africa. Almost everywhere by the end of the 19th century, missionaries had come to doubt whether control of the church could be entrusted to the African pastorates they had initially worked so hard to create. (This, of course, provided a notable incentive for the growth of African separatist churches, especially perhaps in the settler colonies and the Congo, where European attitudes were most rigid.)

Aftermath of the slave trade

But there is also a particular reason why Negro African society was thought to be so inferior. Some of its most notable achievements were regarded as intrinsically evil, on the ground that they were based on the immoral institutions of slavery and slave-raiding and, in the case of such major West African kingdoms as Benin and Ashanti, also of human sacrifice. Missionaries joined with explorers, proconsuls and traders in regarding the major African political systems simply as bloodthirsty tyrannies which had to be swept away before Africa and its peoples could progress. The outstanding missionary of the era and, in the popular mind, the greatest of the explorers, David Livingstone, was quite specific in demanding European colonization to eradicate such evils.

The origins of this abnormally sharp contrast that was drawn between the new, shiny, white Christian crusaders and the old, dark, black Africans of slavery and 'juju', are to be explained by a sense of guilt arising from earlier centuries when the dominant and only really profitable European connection with Africa had been the slave trade, when Europeans themselves had been the most immoral exploiters of African slavery and superstition, and when slaves, debased humans whom they (and western European civilization alone) ranked with cattle, had been the only Negroes most of them ever met with.

It was not until well into the colonial period that Europeans seriously thought to investigate the actual place and role of the slave in *African* society. Then an anthropologist like R. S. Rattray could reveal (in Ashanti) a complex social balance involving many distinct categories of what was commonly termed 'slavery', in many of which, however, a man's social rights and opportunities seemed almost to outweigh any limitations on his freedom. Equally, at first no one considered the religious doctrines involved in sacrifice, or the practical advantage to African rulers of using it to dispose of social undesirables. Thinking that Africans had no history, Europeans could not conceive that what they branded as slavery (but which they might often just as well have termed 'serfdom' or 'clientage') might not be a moral aberration, but an element in processes of mobilization by which Africans were advancing from simple kinship concepts of organization to political statehood, and from subsistence economies to the production of economic surpluses and organized foreign trade.

It was not appreciated that moral distortions in African attitudes to slavery might often actually be due to the insatiable demand for export slaves developed by European society in the Americas (and also, to some extent, by some Asian countries). Equally it was not understood how much Europe's sudden about turn to its 19th-century crusade against the slave trade and slavery had done to weaken and subvert some of the African kingdoms which were economically and politically dependent on serfdom.

The European conquest

European political rule thus entered Africa after nearly a century of economic and political turmoil and disruption associated with the suppression of the export slave trade. In such circumstances, p 194 (2–6) military action may have been inevitable. Certainly the use of force to conquer Africans evoked little or no feeling of guilt among Europeans. Military service was still viewed as a useful and romantic career for upper and lower classes alike. Moreover campaigning in Africa was usually referred to not as a war, but as 'pacification'.

'Pacification' continued well into the 20th century—into the 1920s, certainly, for territories such as Niger, the southern Sudan and Somaliland. But it attracted little notice in Europe unless things went badly wrong, as they did for the Italians at Adowa in 1896, for the British in Rhodesia in 1896–97, or in the German war p 194 (3 against the Hereros in 1904–07. The last two of these wars were technically only 'rebellions', and the battle of Adowa, at which 8,000 Italians were killed and which caused the postponement of Italian designs on Ethiopia for forty years, was really wholly exceptional.

More normally, the cost of the conquest to Europe was minimal, both in men and money. The enormous self-confidence of the Europeans, together with the great superiority of their weapons, meant that the forces engaged were never large. Moreover Europeans themselves formed only a small part of them. Thus in the early 1900s, Lugard imposed British rule over some 250,000 square miles and perhaps ten million people in northern Nigeria with a military establishment of only some 3,000, and all but some 150 of these were Africans. African soldiers cost far less to equip and to maintain in the field, especially in tropical conditions inimical to Europeans, and there was no call to publish the names of their dead in the home newspapers. France would never have acquired her vast West African empire without her *tirailleurs sénégalais*, while the quite mythical belief that the Bahr-el-Ghazal would form a good recruiting ground helps to explain European competition for this territory.

Bearing in mind that, as well as fighting on both sides in the original wars of colonial conquest, African soldiers and auxiliaries saw service in some numbers in both world wars, the loss of African lives in wars for which Europeans were responsible cannot have been insignificant, especially since Africa was by and large a thinly peopled continent in which adequate supplies of manpower were essential if starvation, disease and death were to be kept at bay. This was not simply a question of casualties in combat. In 1915–18, from Kenya alone, about 190,000 men were impressed to serve as carriers for the campaign in German East Africa, not far short of 10% of the *total* population. Of these, nearly 24,000 were known to have died, many more were invalided, and a considerable number were never accounted for. The absence of so many able-bodied young men from the family farms undoubtedly contributed to the 100,000 deaths thought to have occurred in Kenya during the famine and 'flu epidemic of 1918. The losses caused by other campaigning in Africa, for example during the conquest of the Congo, can usually only be guessed at, but were presumably comparable.

From such tragedies, bitter harvests could be stored away for the future. In Kenya, memories of the carrier corps undoubtedly influenced African attitudes to European settlers' demands for labour, and labour grievances were second only to land grievances in leading ultimately to Mau Mau. Equally it has been shown how African nationalist movements in Tanzania and in Rhodesia in the 1950s and 1960s have in part drawn on emotions stemming from the Maji-Maji rising and the Ndebele and Shona rebellions.

The few and the many

Having at length conquered their African colonies, the Europeans next had to govern them. Except for the highland territories attractive to European settlers in southern and—to a lesser extent— eastern Africa, there were very few Europeans on the ground. Malaria control and inocculation against yellow fever made service in the tropics somewhat less unattractive than it had been in the 19th century, but the colonial powers were slow to establish permanent corps of civil administrators. It was generally understood that the cost of governing African colonies should not place a burden on the home governments and taxpayers. Outside southern Africa, with its mineral resources, there was little prospect of raising an effective revenue other than by duties on trade. But at the beginning of the 20th century, the foreign trade of all Africa between the Sahara and the Zambezi was worth only about £20,000,000 a year. This was hardly impressive for an area about sixty times the size, and containing twice the population of Britain (whose foreign trade was then about forty times as great).

The resources available to support any colonial administration were thus exiguous. The British administration in what is now Ghana, one of the most prosperous territories, had an average of only about £600,000 to spend each year in the 1900s, and little more than twice this in 1911–20. Its revenue did not top the £10,000,000 mark until 1947, and was then not much more than £2 per head of population. At about the same time, the enormous federation of French West Africa, with about 17 million people spread over about 1,800,000 square miles, commanded an annual revenue of only about £20,000,000.

It followed, first, that the European colonial administrations were on a very small scale. Having conquered his northern Nigerian empire, Lugard began to govern it with a civil establishment of only 200, giving a ratio of European rulers to African subjects of something like 1 to 50,000, including technical officers, and at any given moment one third or more of this strength would be away on leave or sick leave. Even as late as the end of the 1930s, nearly four million people in Ghana were controlled by only 842 British officials, of whom only 191 held military, police or properly administrative appointments.

Secondly, these administrations were initially built up on an essentially *ad hoc* basis, by recruiting from the few Europeans who already had some kind of African experience. These included commercial men, explorers, big game hunters and even some missionaries, but it was the soldiers, professional or amateur, who had conducted the conquests, who tended to predominate. For the governorships of colonies, some professional military experience remained a useful qualification in official eyes until at least the end of the 1920s. Thus in Africa colonial administration was commonly begun, and its traditions were largely set, by amateurs, and especially by the soldiers who had been the conquerors.

Such men tended to be authoritarian, and also somewhat conservative in their concepts of the role of government. Government to them was essentially a matter of officials collecting the taxes and keeping the people in order—and not only the black people. There was always a clear distinction of status between the p 195 (7) administrators and other Europeans—the traders, the missionaries, the government technical officers even, sometimes also the settlers—even if membership of the same European clubs meant that the gulf was never as great as that between white man and black man. But Lugard would limit Christian missionaries in northern Nigeria on the ground that they would arouse trouble among his Moslem subjects; scant notice was taken of non-official European opinion in German colonies before about 1908; and in the Belgian Congo, right up to independence, Europeans had no more political rights than Africans.

Of course at first there was not really enough revenue to do more than maintain law and order, to ensure that the taxes were collected, and to maintain the minimum public services necessary to achieve these limited aims. Nevertheless the concept of the duties of government in Africa remained remarkably limited and static for many years. Roads and railways, postal, hospital, sanitary, veterinary services, and many other things besides, were all obviously needed, and only government could really provide most of them. But there was a tendency to think that they were needed as much as anything to help government rule more effectively. The idea was very slow to gain acceptance that Africa needed to be developed so that its people could lead better lives, could themselves become more efficient and wealthy, and so provide government with more revenue with which even more could be done. Joseph Chamberlain thought and spoke in this sense at the British colonial office during 1895–1903, and Albert Sarrault at the French colonial ministry in the 1920s, but little was actually done before the 1940s. Until then, the sponsorship of active programmes of economic and social improvement by colonial governments had really only been seen in colonies such as Rhodesia and Kenya, where European settlers were sufficiently organized and politically powerful enough to influence policy (and where the larger part of development was to the settlers' benefit), and in the Gold Coast. In the latter colony in the 1920s there was both exceptional affluence due to the growth of African cocoa-farming, and also an exceptional governor, Sir Gordon Guggisberg, who, though a soldier, was also both a colonial and a technocrat (he was a Canadian-born Royal Engineer).

Education without equality

Since white men with training and experience were so few and so expensive in relation to the exiguous resources of the colonies, the European administrators shared their control of Africa with large numbers of Africans. The role of the European, in business as well as government, was essentially managerial. Just as the conquest depended on an African rank and file, so the business of colonial control and exploitation would have been impossible without hosts of African acolytes: policemen; clerks, messengers, and storekeepers; nurses and dispensers; carpenters and miners, telegraphers, platelayers and engine drivers; brokers, agents and petty traders—there is no end to the list. All of this employment was in some degree educative; to permit of much of it being done with some efficiency, formal systems of education were needed. All colonial governments found it advisable to inspect and supervise, and often to organize, supplement or take over, the schools that had been started by Christian missions. Appreciable p 194 (4) numbers of teachers were needed, and teaching became one of the most prestigeful of professions open to Africans.

European attitudes to what they were doing here varied. The Belgians, terrified by the excesses of Leopold II's personal regime p 195 (9) that had ruled the Congo until 1908, insisted that everything done in the Congo must be rigidly controlled from Belgium. However good their primary education, their health services, their housing for Africans, the whole system was limited simply to providing more efficient African auxiliaries. In British Africa, a not dissimilar attitude prevailed in those colonies where the local legislatures came to be dominated or controlled by representatives of white settlers. Thus when, in the early 1950s, the settlers succeeded in getting their Federation of Rhodesia and Nyasaland, embracing an African population of about six millions, although about 550,000 Africans were attending schools of some kind, only 300 were receiving any kind of secondary education. The French and the Portuguese were logical in that they laid down certain minimum standards which could qualify Africans for civil equality with Europeans, but this did not mean that they provided many facilities for Africans to reach these standards, or that any large numbers of them did so, or that, if they did, they were admitted into the higher echelons of colonial control. In 1937, for instance, out of some 15 million Africans in the eight colonies of French West Africa, only some 80,500 had achieved the status of French citizens, and only 2,500 of these had qualified by merit. (The remainder qualified by the accident of their being *originaires* of four towns in one colony, Senegal, to whom citizenship had been granted wholesale in 1879, when formal colonization had hardly begun.)

Bearing in mind the universal European condemnation of indigenous African achievements in the pre-colonial past, it would have been reasonable to expect a warmer welcome for those Africans who, through education or employment, had achieved recognized levels of acculturation to Western society. In practice, such Africans were almost invariably distrusted and cold-shouldered, condemned as 'trousered niggers'. If they were to be admitted on their merits to positions of power, it was all too easy to envisage a time when control of Africa and its resources would have slipped out of European hands. There was a manifest need to secure adequate returns from a speculative and immediately not very rewarding investment, and the mechanisms of control designed to this end—whether administrative, commercial or settler—had developed very distinct self-interests. Whatever the ultimate ideal, European dominion in Africa would be maintained for as far into the future as man could see.

The south and east: settler domination

This was patently obvious in southern, central and eastern Africa. By the late 19th century, Europeans had had two centuries in which to entrench themselves in the extreme south. Their hold here had been consolidated by two accidents. First, they were in a part of Africa which, for strategic reasons, Britain desired to supervise, and they were able to appeal to an early 19th-century tradition of British anti-colonial sentiment which believed that self-government must inevitably be given to settler communities. (This tradition was still influential as late as 1923, when self-government was granted to the settlers of Southern Rhodesia. It was this which meant that, although in African interests Britain could dismantle the Federation of Rhodesia and Nyasaland, Southern Rhodesia, like the Republic of South Africa, had passed beyond her effective control. The unilateral declaration of settler independence in 1965 simply made the fact explicit.) Secondly, the accident of great mineral discoveries provided the foundations for the only full-scale industrial revolution in Africa, and led to a revolutionary expansion of the numbers and, still more, the power of the settlers.

Rhodesia emerged as a natural extension of the South African system of settler control, and so extended the base from which, at the very end of the 19th century, a most self-confident movement of conquest and settlement could very rapidly be extended to areas which had hitherto had remarkably little contact with Europeans. African mechanisms of government and economic life which had developed in almost complete isolation from the rest of the world were either swept aside, or became fossilized in total subservience to European authority. Only in Uganda and Malawi (Nyasaland), where missionaries and education had preceded conquerors, governors and settlers and, temporarily only, on the former boundaries of European settlement in the extreme south, was there any appreciable compromise with African society. Elsewhere European education for Africans was slow to get off the ground and, as has been seen, *de facto* if not always *de jure*, its products were being trained only for subordinate roles. In the settler territories, principally British and Anglo-Dutch, but also including Portuguese Mozambique and Angola, the eastern Belgian Congo, and, for a time, German East Africa, there was no place at all for the acculturated African except in the most servile roles.

The west: conflict and compromise

European colonial attitudes in western Africa were not essentially dissimilar, though it proved ultimately to be extremely significant that here they were neither dominated nor reinforced by the ideology of autonomous settler sub-imperialisms. But the point from which formal colonial action started was very different, and it was possible for a significant African reaction to gain strength relatively quickly.

In West Africa, indigenous political and economic growth had not occurred in isolation from the rest of the world. West Africa had been in communication with Mediterranean Africa from the earliest times, and by the 19th century the whole of its Sudanic belt was firmly part of the world community of Islam. Further south, in the Guinea coastlands, mutually profitable commercial relations with western Europeans dated back to the 15th century. There had thus been centuries of dialogue with foreigners, from which West Africans had gained much, both strengthening confidence in their own political and economic institutions and learning how these might be adapted to changing world conditions. They had created major empires and kingdoms like Mali or Benin, which had inspired the respect of early visitors from North Africa or Europe. They had evolved a rich urban life, with towns and cities matching in size and social complexity, in craft products and organization, even sometimes in artistic achievement, those of pre-industrial Europe. They had mined for export, and had developed crops and marketing mechanisms specifically for international trade. They had responded eagerly first to Moslem, and then to Christian patterns of education and scholarship, possessing their own Arabic historical chronicles by the 16th century, and, in the 19th century, secondary schools and even a university institution some years before territories like Rhodesia or Kenya had become European colonies. In the 19th century, indeed, they had produced a growing stream of doctors, lawyers, civil servants, educators, clergy and authors who had shared equally with Europeans in initiating change, and who had for the most part been treated as equals by them.

In many parts of West Africa, contrary to what happened elsewhere in the continent, there had been no sudden, traumatic shock of European conquest. Often, indeed, there had been processes of infiltration in which the early agents of the colonial order had been as much black as white. Especially in the areas which evolved into British colonies, for most of the 19th century there

had been no formal or informal position of colonial power or influence—businessman, bishop, chief justice, or even governor—which might not be filled by a man of African descent. Where there had been conquest, as for example in the Fulani emirates of northern Nigeria or in Ashanti, resistance had sometimes been slight, at least initially, simply because the Africans had been slow to appreciate the seriousness of the Europeans in this new role.

Thus when, at the turn of the century, formal and exclusively white systems of European political and economic control were suddenly instituted, there was both an articulate sense of considerable African achievement in the past to which an historical appeal could be made, and also a specific class of acculturated Africans who, suddenly excluded from all positions of power and influence, could organize to do political battle with the Europeans.

The pace and the emphases of the political confrontation were not wholly the same among the English-speaking and the French-speaking Africans. This was not simply the result of differences between British and French colonial policies and action. There was also the underlying fact that the British colonies tended to correspond with those parts of West Africa where, at the beginning of serious colonial involvement, the African economies (and often, therefore, the political structures also) were most advanced and successful, and where, therefore, early European—largely British—trading and missionary activities had been most prosperous and stimulating, and had produced the greatest further economic and social advances.

There was however one contrast between the two colonial policies, which was of some significance. The French obsessions first with assimilation, and then with the idea that the colonies and the mother country formed a single, organic community, however imperfectly these may have been applied, meant that until at least the mid-1950s, the major field of expression for African critics or opponents of their colonial system lay less in local than in French politics.

On the other hand, the British concept of colonies as separate entities capable of considerable autonomous development provided their larger numbers of acculturated Africans with local forums for political expression (including local legislative councils and a local press). It also at first seemed to offer the hope that, as British policy progressed, there might be increasing recognition in the individual colonies for African aspirations. But then, following Lugard's pioneer example in northern Nigeria, the British adopted the concept of 'indirect rule'. They came to believe that, in so far as it was necessary to seek the co-operation of African subjects, this should be sought through the traditional rulers of their pre-colonial communities. It was not until about the 1920s that the African *évolués* appreciated that this involved a diminution of status for the traditional rulers. Men whom the whites had once termed and treated as kings, and with whom the *évolués* had often been willing to work to resist or to modify British pressures, were now only 'chiefs', agents of the British administrations, and deriving such power as remained to them from those administrations and not from their own peoples. (There had never been much doubt that this was the position of African chiefs under the French system.) The *évolués* then went on, correctly, to question whether this British encouragement, however limited, of the leaders of the old pre-colonial communities could really bring about the larger, colony-wide, communities that were needed in 20th-century conditions, and which were in fact a declared goal of British policy.

It was not, therefore, until about the end of the 1930s that the British West African *évolués* began to be convinced of their need to mount a direct challenge to the perpetuation of the colonial regime. The smaller and rather less powerful French-speaking group moved to the same position a little later when they began to have serious doubts as to the genuineness of French beliefs in assimilation or in a multi-racial *Francophonie* in which colonial subjects would become citizens with the same rights as those of the mother country. These doubts were occasioned by essentially external events. First, during 1940–42, the French administration in West Africa had been associated with the government and ideology of the Vichy regime in France. Secondly, when the colonial administration had switched to the rising star of de Gaulle, and more liberal concepts of empire had been embodied in the first draft

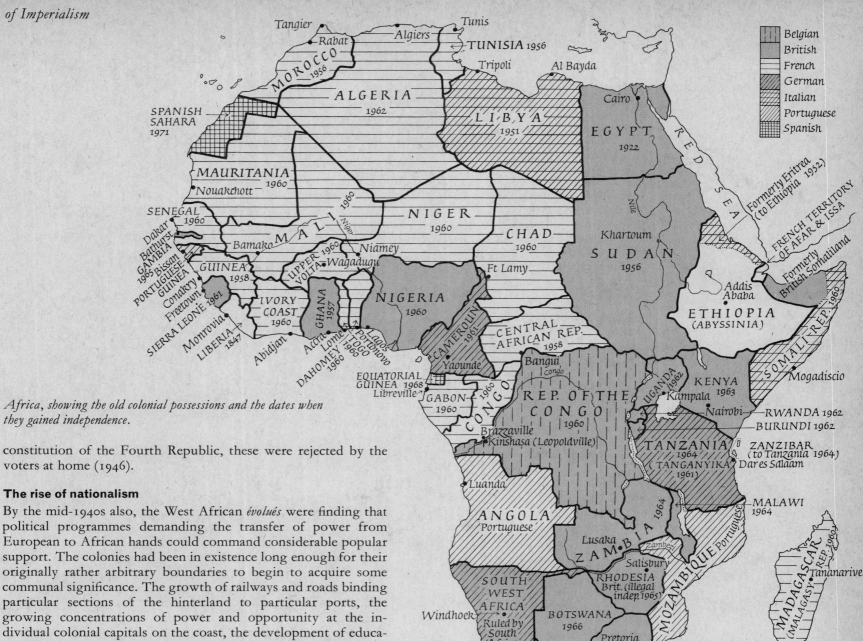

Africa, showing the old colonial possessions and the dates when they gained independence.

constitution of the Fourth Republic, these were rejected by the voters at home (1946).

The rise of nationalism

By the mid-1940s also, the West African *évolués* were finding that political programmes demanding the transfer of power from European to African hands could command considerable popular support. The colonies had been in existence long enough for their originally rather arbitrary boundaries to begin to acquire some communal significance. The growth of railways and roads binding particular sections of the hinterland to particular ports, the growing concentrations of power and opportunity at the individual colonial capitals on the coast, the development of educational and mass communication systems directed from these capitals, all meant that there were more and more senses in which men were thinking of themselves as Ghanaians or Nigerians, Guineans or Togolese.

This did not necessarily mean that they were as yet ceasing to think in terms of their old ethnic unities. The 1940s, indeed, saw a lively pan-Ewe movement aiming to unite the Ewes of Ghana and Togo. After Nkrumah and his nationalists had begun to take over power in Ghana in the 1950s, they faced for a time a bitter opposition centred round the local nationalism of the Ashanti. But Europeans have probably over-emphasized 'tribalism' as a divisive force in West Africa. The massacres of Ibos in northern Nigeria in 1966, which precipitated the secession from the Nigerian federation of the essentially Ibo state of Biafra, were not occasioned by Hausa-Fulani enmity for Ibos simply as strangers. They also reflect the excessive class conservatism of Hausa-Fulani society, buttressed and even enhanced by British indirect rule, and its atavistic rejection of penetration by educated, thrusting, increasingly successful and wealthy individualists from the south, among whom Ibos happened to predominate.

Ibo experience in fact exemplifies another vital aspect of the changes that were providing *évolué* politicians with something approaching a mass following. While, from one point of view, the old ethnic communities were being built up into larger units by the growth of the colonial administrations, educational and communications systems and economies, from another the same forces were beginning to dissolve them into series of individuals. By firmly joining West Africa to Europe and to world markets, colonial rule had greatly enhanced the growth of cash economies which had already been developing for some time, most markedly in the coastlands. Instead of cultivating communal lands essentially for subsistence, farmers were increasingly developing individual plots for the production of cash crops such as cocoa, coffee, palm

oil, and groundnuts. The profits were available for investment in property, in all sorts of manufactured imports, and above all, perhaps, in education, which was increasingly appreciated as the key to further social and economic advance. The consolidation of colonial rule and of European trading power also provided increasing opportunities for wage-earning employment, and thus further enhanced the demand for education.

The spread and the intensity of this economic and social revolution were by no means uniform. Thus, by and large, the new class of individual money earners was less significant in the French territories than it was in the British colonies, where the successful exploitation of cash crops for world markets had most swiftly expanded, and where the spread of education tended to be wider. It was also much more in evidence in the coastlands than in the hinterland, and for the same reasons. This explains why the Ibos, with an expanding population, a shortage of good land, a long acquaintance with the value of overseas markets and of imported goods, and a remarkable investment in education, found so much to attract them to entrepreneurial and skilled jobs in northern Nigeria (and elsewhere besides).

In its coastal strongholds, especially in southern Ghana and southern Nigeria, the new class had shown a very early awareness of its economic interests and strengths. In southern Ghana, for example, actions to boycott European merchant houses and to

p 198
(19)

hold up crops for export can be traced to as far back as the 1860s and 1870s. By the 1930s and 1940s, together with strikes of wage-earners, these were becoming formidable weapons for the expression of economic discontents. It was clear, therefore, that in the right situation there could also be powerful support available for political agitation. The two world wars, the great depression of the 1930s, and the difficulties experienced in world trade immediately after 1945, combined to provide such a situation.

The sprint to self-government

Appreciable numbers of West African soldiers were sent to fight outside their homelands, even outside Africa, and so gained considerable new experience and confidence at times when weaknesses and divisions in European society were all too evident. The first war gave birth to the League of Nations and its colonial mandates system. On the European side there was thus at least a latent sense that the administration of colonies could be a terminable trust, while on the African side expectations were raised that ultimately colonial peoples might be allowed to exercise the right of self-determination. All these things were taken a stage further in the war of 1939–45, which produced the Atlantic Charter and the United Nations. The latter's Trusteeship Council provided an international platform on which colonial discontents might be publicly displayed. The Pan-African movement, hitherto essentially a movement of New World Negro intellectuals, seized its opportunities, and, at its 1919 congress in Paris and, above all, at its 1945 congress at Manchester, became a new international focus and spur for African politicians seeking colonial freedom.

Both wars appreciably weakened the confidence of Europeans in the rightness of their system and the superiority of their civilization. If first Germany and then Italy could be robbed of their colonies on the plea that they were not fit to be entrusted with them, the remaining colonial powers needed to look more closely at the ends and achievements of their own regimes in Africa. The appalling economic disaster of the early 1930s further weakened European self-confidence. It also led both Britain and France to begin to question whether they had done enough to develop their colonies—as much in the interests of their own consumers and workers as in those of the African peoples. By the end of the 1930s, they were beginning to move towards a new colonial orthodoxy which involved active programmes of investment in colonial economic and social development. Such programmes were greatly stepped up by new needs for colonial raw materials and markets, and to conserve and to win foreign exchange, occasioned first by the Second World War and then by the subsequent world shortages of vital commodities and goods.

In West Africa the later 1940s and the early 1950s were a period when new dynamic colonial policies were evident on the economic and social fronts. It was also a time when the exports of African producers were commanding remarkably high prices, but when there were great shortages of imported goods, both the consumer goods desired by the indigenous producers and the capital goods needed to implement the much-hampered development programmes. The expectations of the money-earning class, swollen by the producers' boom and by the ranks of the returned soldiers, were exceptionally high, but their rewards were universally disappointing. This was particularly so in the political field, where such changes as had been initiated by the British and French policy makers quickly seemed quite inadequate.

New nationalist political leaders like Azikiwe and Nkrumah emerged who, in the most developed, and hence the most frustrated areas, were able to mobilize large-scale discontent into effective political parties. The French were initially able to hold their position by repressive measures. But in southern Ghana and in southern Nigeria, both the social revolution and British policy had already gone too far for this to be really practicable. India, Burma and Ceylon had already been freed from colonial strings. There was thus no real wish, no will even, to repress colonial nationalism when it appeared in West Africa. By 1949, Britain had accepted the desirability of co-operating with the West African

nationalist leaders in programmes of devolution which were to lead rapidly to self-government and independence.

Ghana's independence, accepted as a goal in 1950 and achieved in 1957, together with the promise that the other British West African territories would quickly follow, meant the beginning of the end of formal European dominion for almost all Africa. Indo-China was more of a warning to the French than Malaya had been for the British, and even before a comparable colonial war in Algeria had brought the fall of the Fourth Republic, the return of de Gaulle, and a rapid shift to decolonization, the French had abandoned their old imperial concepts in tropical Africa. Spurred on by African politicians like Houphouët-Boigny, who were able to exploit the divisions and weaknesses in French domestic politics, by 1956 they were already recognizing colonial claims to autonomy. Four years later, all the French territories had formally gained their independence. p 199 (20)

p 199
(20)

The rapid and relatively straightforward way in which West Africans had secured independence from colonial rule provided a powerful inspiration for a new generation of black African politicians elsewhere in the continent, and such men were actively encouraged by new pan-African organizations established on African soil by men like Nkrumah. It was no longer necessary to seek outlets for east and central African discontents only in separatist messianic churches and prophet movements. Despite the much lower levels of economic and educational advance and of political experience, it was now possible to float and to secure wide support for nationalist political parties throughout east and central Africa. Just as important, it was possible to secure rapid recognition for the demands of these parties, not only from a United Nations in which former colonial territories now formed an important element, but also from the colonial rulers themselves. In the advanced countries of western Europe, decolonization was now as fashionable as imperialism had been two generations earlier.

p 198
(17)

p 200
(23)

In the inward-looking society of Belgium, indeed, decolonization suddenly became more popular than ever imperialism had been. In 1960 it was abruptly decided that the anti-colonial wind had become so strong that the best method of preserving Belgian interests in the Congo was to recognize its independence. It was supposed that, since no Congolese had been trained for administrative or managerial roles, an independent Congo would still in fact depend on Belgians. But the Congolese army had other ideas, and so precipitated a crisis in which not only European investments in the country but its whole future were gravely at risk.

With Spain also joining the anti-colonial band-waggon, the only colonial power in Africa to enter the 1970s was Portugal. The rulers of this poor and backward country, insulated from the mainstream of international thought and discussion, were still prepared to fight to defend an anachronistic quasi-Roman concept of overseas 'provinces' on African soil. Since Portugal's two principal colonies, Angola and Mozambique, lay at the gates of southern Africa, she thus provided a by no means insignificant shield and encouragement for the entrenched settler communities of South Africa and Rhodesia.

p 199
(21, 22)

With these exceptions, the struggle for independence from white political control was a matter of history as early as the end of the 1960s. In fact there had hardly been a struggle at all: the principle of the right of black Africans to political freedom had been conceded almost as soon as the issue had first been raised, in Ghana in 1948–50. Marxists and cynics would say indeed that the political issue was not a real issue at all, and that the Western powers had no call to deny political independence, since the economies of the new African states were still all too dependent on their capital and trade. Certainly a major preoccupation of the new African rulers everywhere was how to secure the foreign trade and capital needed to improve the living standards of rapidly increasing populations without compromising their political independence. If they could not do better than the colonial rulers had done, usually in much less critical conditions, they were only too likely to be rejected by the very people whose intrinsic dislike of foreign rule had occasioned their rapid rise to power.

p 200
(24)

X CHAOS AND ORDER

The arts in pursuit of new forms

JOHN WILLETT

'What shall I think tomorrow?'

GEORGE GROSZ, 1920

Ceaseless experiment

has been the most obvious characteristic of 20th-century art, as compared with the art of the past. At no previous period have changes in style been so rapid, or the overthrow of accepted standards so marked. In this respect, at least, the arts have run parallel with the society and technology that produced them, but in other ways the two paths have diverged. Only in areas like Latin America or the Communist world (as we have already seen in Chapters V and VI) did the arts maintain a direct social involvement. In Western Europe and America, during the first two thirds of the century, the artist became increasingly isolated, and his work harder and harder for the ordinary man to understand.

Paradoxically, this development began in part with the artist's rediscovery of popular culture, either his own or that of other races. Looking outside the stale academic tradition of Western painting, outside even the experiments of the Impressionists and Post-Impressionists, he found inspiration in European folk-art, in the sculpture of Negro Africa and Polynesia or in the stylized patterns of China and Japan.

One of the most vigorous of such folk-cultures was that of Russia, and the man chiefly responsible for introducing it into Western Europe was Diaghileff. His *Ballet Russe* was in fact a highly sophisticated enterprise combining talents from many fields, but its main impact came from its boldness, its colour, its effect of 'barbarity' and passion, its uninhibited rejection of ordinary canons of taste, and these in turn came from the elements of Russian popular art that it was able to exploit. The detail shown opposite is part of the drop curtain painted by Natalia Goncharova for *Le Coq d'Or*—produced by Diaghileff in Paris in 1914 with music from Rimsky-Korsakov's opera, choreography by Fokine, and Karsavina as prima ballerina. Goncharova was one of a group of Russian painters who launched a 'new Primitive' style, basing their designs on Siberian embroidery, peasant woodcuts and even pastry and gingerbread figures.

The period before 1914 saw the beginning of almost all the major movements in the arts up to the middle of the century. It also saw a new cross-fertilization between the arts, of which the conjunction of painting, music and dance in Diaghileff's ballet was among the most exciting instances. Paris between 1900 and 1914 was the centre of an artistic ferment. The story of 20th-century art is the story of the artist's conquest of all the unexplored tracts of human experience that now opened up ahead of him. Picasso, asked the question, 'What is art?' replied 'What isn't?'. (1)

A setting for experiment was provided by architecture which, in its deliberate break with the past and its emphasis on functionalism, followed a more consistent line of development than the other arts. Adolf Loos, in Vienna, declared war on ornament and designed buildings in a bare rectangular style that was to be influential in the coming decades. Right: his Karma Villa, Switzerland, of 1904–6. Far right: a step in the same direction by Henry Van de Velde, the Kunsthochschule, Weimar, of 1911, subsequently the Bauhaus. (2, 3)

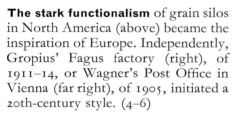

The stark functionalism of grain silos in North America (above) became the inspiration of Europe. Independently, Gropius' Fagus factory (right), of 1911–14, or Wagner's Post Office in Vienna (far right), of 1905, initiated a 20th-century style. (4–6)

Architecture and engineering, using steel and concrete, came together to produce new forms. Below: the Republic Building, Chicago, by Holabird and Roche, of 1905. Below right: Salginatobel Bridge, by Robert Maillart, an artist in the mathematics of tension and stress. (7, 8)

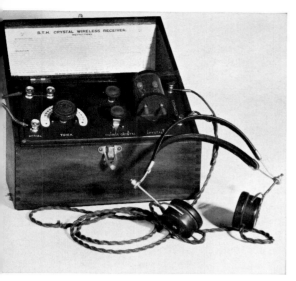

Technology gave art new languages and new media of expression. The first wireless sets (above) and gramophones (centre) were used to transmit and record already existing material; only in time did they generate their own art form. Film, on the other hand, had a liberating effect on the imagination from the start. Above right: one of the earliest experimenters in cinematic fantasy, Georges Meliès, in his own film *The India-Rubber Head.* (9–11)

The camera also made good its claim to be more than a mere recorder. Painting began to revolt against photography, while the latter started to establish its own pictorial style. *In the Bois de Boulogne* (right) by Lartigue recalls the world of Bonnard. (12)

In the theatre producers and designers broke away from realistic conventions to create freer, more symbolic effects. Above: Gordon Craig's set for Ibsen's *The Vikings*, and (right) Max Reinhardt's production of *The Miracle* (1911), using an open arena to draw the audience into the action. (13, 14)

Painting after Cézanne tended to break up into distinct 'schools' or 'movements', each preoccupied with a particular method and a particular technique, and resting on elaborate theoretical foundations. Most European painting up to 1945 can be seen as a development from one or other of these pre-1914 movements, which originated in Paris and spread to the rest of Europe.

The Fauves (wild beasts), led by Matisse, developed the Synthetism of Gauguin by using continuous areas of light, bright colours for largely decorative effects. 'Composition,' said Matisse, 'is the art of arranging in a decorative manner the various elements at the painter's disposal for the expression of his feelings.' The feelings that he expressed are in fact predominantly those of pleasure in the world of the senses. *Nasturtiums and the Panel 'Dance'* (left) features the artist's own large frieze of dancing figures now in the Hermitage. André Derain applied the same principles to townscape in his *Westminster Bridge* of 1907 (below left). (15, 16)

The Cubists developed the structure found in late Cézanne by superimposing several viewpoints and making more or less impersonal objects into neutral coloured facets. Cubism was invented by Picasso and Braque, whose *Violin and Jug* (above) was painted in 1910. (17)

'Les Demoiselles d'Avignon' (1907) by Picasso was probably the most influential painting of the whole period. The basic conventions are those which evolved into Cubism, but it also bears witness to Picasso's study of other cultures. The three figures on the left look back to early Spanish art, the other two to Negro masks. (18)

Expressionist portraits share a certain tense nervousness, though a master like the Austrian Oskar Kokoschka catches equally the individuality of each sitter. Above: his portrait of the painter Carl Moll (1913), one of the founders of the Secession movement in Vienna. (20)

Expressionism placed the greatest emphasis on the emotional content of a painting. It was essentially a German movement, and was seen by Worringer, its chief theoretician, as characteristic of Northern, as opposed to Classical, art: 'Actuality, which the Gothic man could not transform into naturalness by means of clear-sighted knowledge, was overpowered by this intensified play of fantasy and transformed into spectrally heightened and distorted actuality.' The wide variety that could be included under the term is illustrated in these three paintings.

Above: Kirchner's *Artist and his Model*, of the Brücke, or Dresden, school, produced its effect by its deliberately harsh outlines and jarring colours.

Right: with the Russian-born Kandinsky, Expressionism approached the abstract, for he believed that lines, shapes and colours had emotional content in themselves, apart from what they represented. *Fugue*, of 1914, illustrates his application of musical structure to painting. (19, 21)

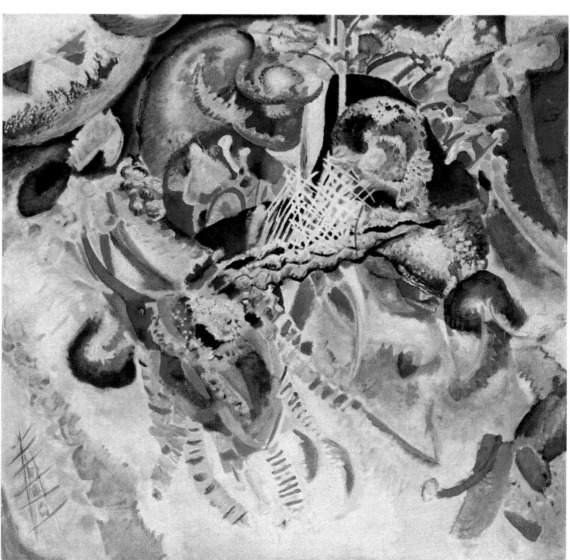

214

The Futurists in Italy tried to establish a closer relationship between art and life, rejecting nostalgia and proclaiming, in the words of Marinetti, that 'a roaring motor-car, which runs like a machine-gun, is more beautiful than the Winged Victory of Samothrace', and that 'universal dynamism must be rendered as dynamic sensation; movement and light destroy the substance of objects'. Carrà's *Funeral of the Anarchist Galli* (above) uses a contemporary political event, reflects its violence in the violence of its colour, and, following Marinetti's formula, concentrates on movement at the expense of form. (22)

Cubism in action: Marcel Duchamp's *Nude Descending a Staircase* can be seen as a combination of Cubist and Futurist techniques — the first giving it its analytic geometry, the second its sense of movement in time. (23)

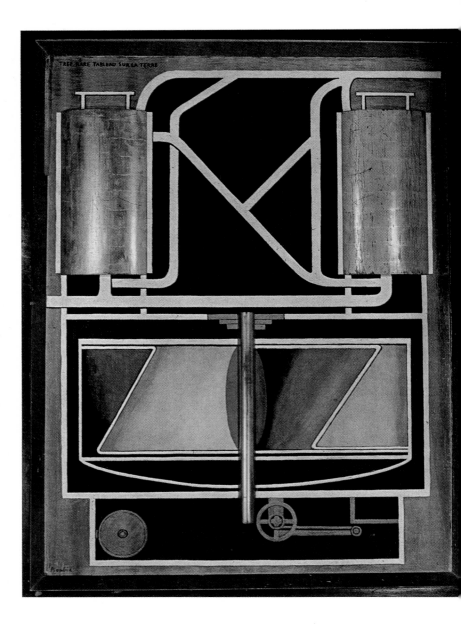

'I could not see the reason', wrote the independent Dadaist Kurt Schwitters, whose *Blue Bird* is shown above, 'why old tickets, driftwood, cloakroom tabs, wires and wheel parts, buttons and old rubbish found in the attic and in refuse dumps should not be material for painting just as good as the colours made in factories.' (24)

The 'metaphysical' De Chirico created a new kind of landscape with the haunting eternity of a dream. (26)

Against a lunar background the Paris Dadaists and their friends mingle with figures from the past (right). Max Ernst sits on Dostoyevski's lap. (27)

Dada and Surrealism were both reactions against the rule of the intellect. Neither movement was confined to painting. The Dadaists, by flouting every kind of convention, whether aesthetic or moral, were in fact demanding a radical re-examination of all standards. Evolving out of their Parisian wing, the Surrealists explored the newly-discovered regions of the unconscious, producing works whose symbolism was not the less powerful for having no single connotation.

'The omnipotence of the dream, the belief in the superiority of certain forms of association hitherto neglected, the disinterested play of thought' were three of the defining characteristics of Surrealism according to its precursor Apollinaire. Yves Tanguy's *Through Birds, through Fire but not through Glass* (right) conjures up strange living shapes emerging from the mind when the restraints of consciousness are relaxed. (28)

An arrangement of pipes, tanks and wheels form a futile but intriguing machine (left). The Dadaist Francis
◀ Picabia makes no concession to logic in the title he gave it: *Very Rare Picture on the Earth.* (25)

The commercial possibilities of the new styles were soon realized. A. M. Cassandre (in 1927) and Salvador Dali (as late as 1969), in their posters for French Railways, draw freely on the resources of Surrealism. (29, 30)

A wider public than the one which followed the fine arts could enjoy the theatre and its new offspring, the cinema. After 1918 the silent film rapidly outstripped every other art form in the universality of its appeal and the rate at which it developed. 'Film stars' came to be one of the 20th century's archetypes, half-real, half-fictitious personalities who somehow focussed the mass emotions of audiences upon themselves. No following was more devoted than that of Rudolph Valentino (left), who died in 1926, aged thirty-one. (31)

Buster Keaton raised silent comedy to an unsurpassed level of invention. Groucho Marx and his brothers succeeded in combining farce with verbal humour. (32, 33)

Naturalism was rejected in the theatre as decisively as in painting. In Moscow, Meyerhold's system of bio-mechanics (above: Mayakovsky's *Bath-house*) reduced actors to automata. (34)

Reality recreated: Eisenstein's *Battleship Potemkin* brought to life an incident in the Russian revolution of 1905 so vividly that it has almost replaced history. (37)

Constructivist décor appeared in the West with Diaghileff's *La Chatte*, by Pevsner and Gabo. Brecht exploited the theatre's artificiality to convey social messages (below: *Mahagonny*). (35, 36)

Wright's 'Night Mail' (above) transformed prosaic English life into poetry, while L'Atalante (below) by Jean Vigo captured the industrial desolation of Northern France. (38, 39)

Josephine Baker brought a new exoticism to Parisian revue. The Negro impact on the world of entertainment was a phenomenon of the twenties and thirties. (40)

Paul Whiteman (above centre) adapted Negro music to the popular dance band, while **Gershwin** (right) tried to graft it on to the Western classical tradition. (41, 42)

Imagination in the cinema reached a peak in the German Expressionist films of the twenties. Above: *The Cabinet of Dr Caligari* by Robert Wiene. (43)

The Western is one of several Hollywood film types each with its own strict conventions, though used differently by different directors. Above: Ford's *Stagecoach*. (46)

Realism and fantasy: Vertov's *Man with the Movie Camera* was among the earliest Soviet documentaries. *L'age d'or* (below) united the talents of Dali and Buñuel. (44, 45)

The animated cartoon (Mickey Mouse as the Sorcerer's Apprentice) and the **musical** (Fred Astaire in *Top Hat*) both reached full popularity in the thirties. (47, 48)

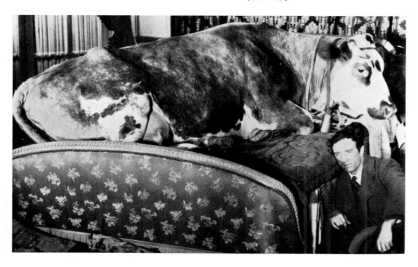 

Modernism in fashion: after 1914, and especially during the twenties, the pioneer experiments of the early years began to win acceptance at a smarter level, leading to that strange amalgam of tastes that is now known as the Jazz Age. Probably the most important link between avant-garde painting and the public was the ballet. Diaghileff used a drop-curtain by Picasso (left) for *Parade* in 1917. The music was by Erik Satie. (49)

'Les Six' (below) were a group of composers, united by a respect for Satie (who died in 1925), and whose aesthetic principles were largely formulated by Jean Cocteau. This painting of the group with some friends by the academician J. E. Blanche shows Germaine Tailleferre, Milhaud, Honegger, Jean Wiener (a pianist), Marcelle Meyer (also a pianist), Poulenc, Auric and Cocteau. Durey is missing. Below right: Milhaud's negro ballet *La Création du Monde* was performed in 1923 with sets and costumes by Léger. (51, 54)

A domesticated Fauve was Kees van Dongen, a Dutch painter who adapted the brilliant colours of Matisse to witty social portraiture: *Montparnasse Blues*. (50)

The endlessly versatile Jean Cocteau (left, a portrait by Modigliani) epitomized the Parisian intellectual life of the twenties and thirties. Artist, poet, novelist, dramatist and critic, he began his career as scenario-writer for Diaghileff and ended it as the producer of such lyrical films as *Orphée*. (52)

Rococo and ragtime came together in the wildly eclectic *Les Biches* of 1924, with music by Poulenc and costumes (below) by Marie Laurencin. (53)

Western music underwent transformations comparable to those of the visual arts.

Claude Debussy (below) forms the link between the 19th and 20th centuries. Concerned to unite all the arts into a single experience, he evolved an Impressionist style of composition, stressing colour and mood more than the melodic line. (55)

Alban Berg followed Schönberg in rejecting traditional harmony altogether and adopting the twelve-note system; he was the first to introduce it into opera in *Wozzek*. The portrait (left) is by Schönberg. (56)

Arnold Schönberg (below) was the inventor of twelve-note, or serial, music, in which the order of the notes, rather than their harmonic relationships, becomes the basis of composition. (57)

Igor Stravinsky (below), the most influential of all 20th-century composers, moved from the extreme romanticism of some of his early ballet scores for Diaghileff to a later Neo-classical austerity. (59)

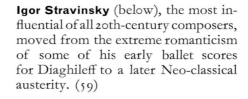

Béla Bartók (above) was by training a concert pianist. While he introduced bold innovations, he remained more traditional in technique, making considerable thematic use of Hungarian folk-music. (58)

Serge Prokofiev also worked with Diaghileff for a time but returned to Russia and evolved a style, strongly classical in inspiration, which was original without being technically revolutionary. (60)

Literary traditions remained basically intact, though enriched by new attitudes and insights.

James Joyce brought a new psychological realism to the novel. In *Ulysses* he analyzes a wide spectrum of Dublin life — intellectual, sensual and banal — in a brilliant variety of techniques. (61)

T. S. Eliot (portrayed by Wyndham Lewis) freed English verse from its artificial romanticism and made it express a wholly 20th-century anxiety. His own solutions tended towards a mystical religious faith. (62)

Thomas Mann retained the form of the long 19th-century novel but transformed it into an allegory of modern man in society, reflecting the agony of Germany's intellectual and artistic life. (63)

Franz Kafka (above) and **Bertolt Brecht** (right) were both preoccupied with man confronted by authority. Where Kafka saw isolation and defeat, Brecht preached involvement and struggle. (64, 65)

André Gide, one of the most characteristic voices of the 20th century, spoke for the demolition of conventional taboos — religious and moral — and the free realization of individual happiness. (66)

The doctrine of function was institutionalized in the Bauhaus, a school founded at Weimar in 1919 to unite the teaching of all aspects of design. The director was Walter Gropius, whose Fagus factory has been illustrated earlier (pl. 5). Oscar Schlemmer taught sculpture and theatre but also painted — the *Bauhaus Stairway* (left) is his. Kandinsky, Klee, Feininger and Breuer all belonged to the Bauhaus, which in 1925 moved to Dessau, in 1930 to Berlin, and was closed by the Nazis in 1933. A selection of typical Bauhaus designs is shown below. On the wall: posters by Dexel and Bayer, a photograph of the Dessau building by Gropius, and a table-cloth by Albers. In front: furniture by Marcel Breuer. (67, 68)

The clear lines of Le Corbusier's early houses reflect the same aesthetic principles as De Stijl and the Bauhaus, though he belonged to neither. Below: the Villa Savoie at Poissy, designed in 1927. (71)

In Holland a group of designers known by the name of their magazine, *De Stijl*, promoted a strict 'Neo-plasticist' discipline of bare geometry, straight lines and primary colours. In painting its greatest exponent was Mondrian, in architecture Gerrit Rietveld, whose Schröder House, Utrecht (above and below) of 1924 was prophetic of the thirties. (69, 70)

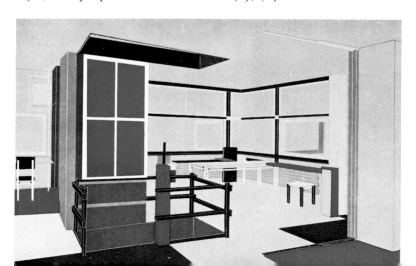

Out of German functionalism came the 'International Style', the steel-frame and glass-wall architecture brought to classic perfection by Mies van der Rohe. Mies succeeded Gropius as director of the Bauhaus in 1930 and emigrated to America in 1937. His Lake Shore Apartments, Chicago (above) were built between 1948 and 1951. (72)

A reaction against logic and clarity after the war led many architects back to a form of Expressionism in which concrete is moulded into new and disturbing shapes that are close to abstract sculpture. Le Corbusier's second style, exemplified in his government buildings at Chandigarh in India, was a potent influence in this direction. (73)

Artistic continuity from the prewar years to the atomic age was assured in painting, as in architecture, by the survival of most of the leading figures (including Picasso, Matisse, Braque and Léger) who now experienced a period of renewed vitality. One of the prevailing tendencies was towards a cool, geometrical abstraction such as the English artist Ben Nicholson had evolved in the thirties. His *April 1959 (Paros)* (below) is a subtle essay in tonal and formal relationships.

The works of Matisse's old age show a parallel fondness for abstract shapes, though the sense of pattern and range of colours were still essentially the same as in his earlier paintings. He decorated the interior of a chapel of Dominican nuns at Vence, and turned finally to compositions made of large cut-out pieces of coloured paper. *The Snail* of 1953 (below), for instance, has a gaiety and simplicity which appealed strongly to the new generation. (74, 75)

Abstract expressionism, or 'action painting', the first major artistic tendency to emerge from the United States, carries the emotive energy of Kandinskyan Expressionism to a new pitch. Feeling is communicated through the act of putting the paint on canvas. 'The painting has a life of its own,' said Jackson Pollock, its most influential exponent. Pollock's paintings, however, are not random gestures, but records of aesthetic activity; utilizing to the full the unplanned effects of accident and instinct, they still rely on rhythm, movement and the organizing human mind. Right: *One*, painted in 1950. (76)

Colour relationships in a calmer, more mystical setting characterize the work of the American Mark Rothko (far right: his *Orange Yellow Orange* of 1969). More subtle and intellectual than Pollock, Rothko imposes such severe limitations on his art that it can never make wide contact with mankind in general. (79)

Postwar sculpture reflects a variety almost as rich as painting. The humanist tradition, however, persisted and was strengthened by the achievement of Henry Moore. Moore's work is concerned with the human figure, relating it to the shapes of nature, to bones and mountains eroded by weather. He was among the artists to contribute to the UNESCO head-quarters building in Paris in 1957 (above left). The work of Germaine Richier (right: *Water*) is humanism of a more highly charged kind. (77, 78)

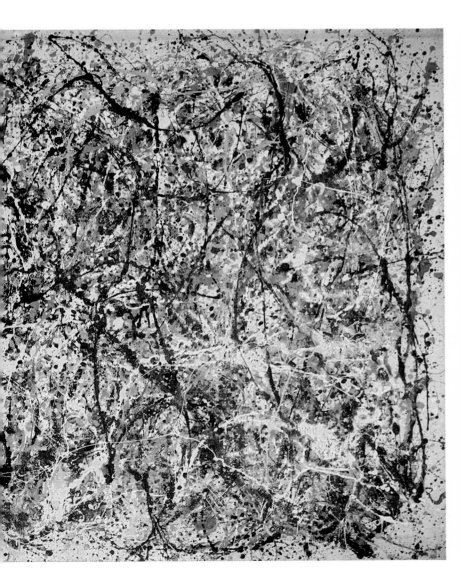

The arrival of Pop in the fifties was in some ways an attempt by serious artists to bridge the gap that appeared to separate them from ordinary people's interests, by using everyday visual clichés, advertisements and commercial products. The result, however, required (like Dada) a high degree of sophistication to be seen as 'art' at all. Some artists meticulously reproduced real objects, others used the objects themselves, often defaced or distorted. Roy Lichtenstein took the technique of the printed comic-strip and presented it, with minute variations, for aesthetic consideration. The original comic, he has said, 'intends to depict and I intend to unify'. *Whaam!*, which is over thirteen feet long, was painted in 1963. (80)

Repetition, boredom, the deadening effect of familiarity, go to the maknig of Andy Warhol's hypnotically monotonous art. A picture of a Campbell's soup tin is silk-screened on to canvas and endlessly multiplied. (81)

The giant woman, *Hon*, built at Stockholm by the kinetic sculptor Jean Tinguely and Niki de Saint-Phalle, who has been called 'a religious fetichist and mythologian', is a sort of cross between Pop and prehistory. In this view we are looking from the top of the head towards the enormous breasts. The way in, naturally, is on the other side between the legs. Drinks are provided in the knees. (82)

'**Typhoo Tea**' by David Hockney is a variation on a Pop theme rather than a Pop painting. Hockney was among the first to bring popular imagery of this kind into British art. (83)

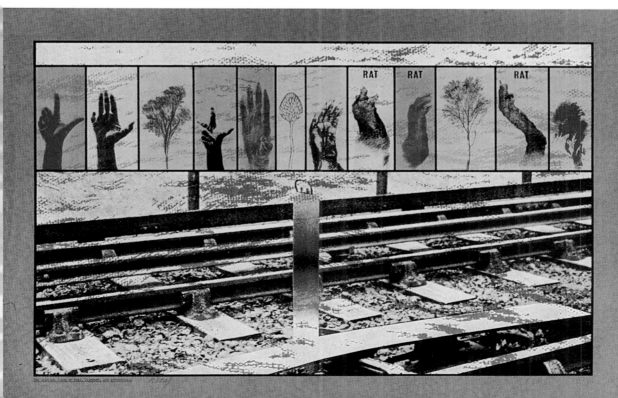

In the private world of everyday things, magazines, postcards, souvenirs, the paraphernalia of a painter's work, Peter Blake finds the material for art. The banality of the subject-matter is made interesting by his sense of pattern and his playing with the conventions, so that we do not know, for instance, whether the children are meant to be real or themselves part of the montage. (84)

'**Cultural Value of Fear**': R.B.Kitaj is a highbrow artist using certain Pop techniques. His works are self-conscious enigmas containing layers of meaning and allusion which hardly expect to be deciphered at a glance. (85)

229

The truly popular art of the 20th century remained until the war the cinema. 'Picture palaces' built in its prewar Golden Age are now the showpieces of 'Art Deco'. Above: the New Victoria, London. (86)

Classical music gained new devotees in the postwar years, largely through broadcasting and the longplaying record. The new hall of the Berlin Philharmonic by the former Expressionist Hans Scharoun is moulded to the needs of acoustics. (87)

The Beatles managed to preserve their charm amid all the techniques of the mass media — recording studio, film and finally, in *The Yellow Submarine* (above), animated cartoon. (88)

Television commercials (above right, four frames for Mann's Beer) are in many countries the backbone of the latest of the mass media. (89)

The paperback revolution began in England with the first Penguin Book (Maurois's *Ariel*). Now most of the greatest literature is cheaply available in every civilized country. (90)

Other arts still exist in a rarefied atmosphere to which state subsidy, big business, and the economics of tourism all contribute. **Herbert von Karajan** (right) did much to make the Salzburg Festival a major event. The more intimate Aldeburgh Festival of **Benjamin Britten** (centre) makes a more selective appeal. **Karlheinz Stockhausen** (far right) wins still fewer to follow him into the world of electronic sound. (91–93)

'West Side Story' by Leonard Bernstein introduced serious drama and dance technique to the fashionable musical. (94)

The Royal Ballet made London the centre of ballet after the war: Fonteyn in *Symphonic Variations* choreographed by Frederick Ashton. (95)

At Bayreuth Wieland Wagner, influenced by Appia and Craig, substituted universal symbolism for the old realistic décor. (96)

The new realism of postwar Italy: Rossellini's *Open City*. (97)

Samuel Beckett helped to introduce a new timeless absurdity. Below: a scene from *End Game*. (100)

The 'new wave' combined realism with wit: Godard's *Alphaville*. (98)

The happening (below: Yves Klein's 'Painting Ceremony') has become a new form of theatrical experience.(101)

Swedish film was established by works like Bergman's *Seventh Seal*. (99)

The open stage is being welcomed for bringing actors and audience into immediate contact. (102)

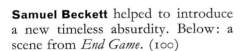
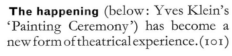
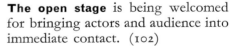

Op art, a fashion of the sixties, makes its appeal direct to the eye, excluding both intellectual and emotional content. It was largely the invention of the Bauhaus-trained Hungarian Victor Vasarely whose *Vega Jon* is shown above. In such paintings the eye is stimulated to a sense of movement — sometimes to the point of dizziness — which brings them close to kinetic sculpture, another popular contemporary movement. (103)

From the cerebral patterns of Op or serial art to completely programmed painting by computers (left) seems no very long step. The computer can subject any given design to endless variations, either in accordance with a programme, as here, or at random. (104)

The arts in pursuit of new forms

JOHN WILLETT

To THE pessimist who looks at the world around him, our century's claim to have produced a great civilization is bound at times to seem hollow. But in one respect at least it can rank among humanity's great periods, for it has seen an extraordinary efflorescence over the whole area of the arts. Not since the late 16th century have there been such transformations in painting, music, architecture and the theatre, while literature, if its central tradition has been less radically interrupted than theirs, has likewise pushed out into all kinds of new areas. Moreover where once the technical advances that shaped the arts were few and far between—such inventions, for instance, as those of oil paint, movable types, equal temperament in music, or the pianoforte—over the past seventy years the speed of innovation has been such as to throw up a whole wealth of new materials and media of which one at least, the film, has established itself as a major new art. While these developments were being absorbed into the mainstream of the various arts, there was an equally radical change in our culture's diffusion and the size of its public, leading to a shift in the arts' whole role. A Victorian reader of Jules Verne might have foreseen the first landing on the moon, but he would be entirely baffled by a Mondrian, or a piece of electronic music, or a television commercial. The distance travelled has been so much greater; and it has been travelled not to a single self-evident target but simultaneously in a thousand unexpected directions.

The setting for experimental art

At the beginning of this century, the creative artist could feel—if he was open-minded and sensitive enough—a number of powerful forces thrusting at and through him. There was a spirit of revolt against the materialist complacency of the previous decades and the authoritarian mores, both social and political, on which it reposed. At the same time there was a relatively new sense, originating with the early French socialists, of a creative minority forming an avant garde way out in front of their society and to some extent cut off from it. There was a general speeding-up of communications, leading to an influx of more or less exotic works: Japanese graphics, Russian and Spanish music, Scandinavian plays, the novels of Tolstoy and Dostoyevsky, the poems of Whitman and Tagore. There was a new scientific concern with the study of primitive peoples, which interacted with the synthetic barbarism preached by Nietzsche to turn men's eyes (or ears) to even remoter sources: to the cultures of India, Africa, South America and Polynesia, or to European and Russian folk art. There were new techniques of reproduction (e.g., half-tone) to help inform the artist, and new methods of construction (e.g., steel and concrete) to challenge the architect. There was a blurring of traditional frontiers between the arts—as in the synaesthetic doctrines of the Symbolists or the music-dramas of Wagner—and a semi-social, semi-ethical concern with handicraft which sprang largely from the socialist principles of William Morris and went with a drive to extend popular awareness of the arts. There was a new mysticism, operating largely outside the orthodox religions and often with oriental elements, and at the same time a pulsating new life of machines and cities which academic artistic conventions seemed too feeble to express.

The point where these forces fused is easy enough to locate

p 209 (1)

geographically: it was Paris. Other countries had their own artistic revolutions, or contributed to the general movement, while even in Paris many of the key figures came, like Picasso in 1900, from elsewhere. But right up to World War II it was there that the vital ideas and groupings were for the most part launched or decisively acclaimed, and the whole process was rooted in the development of French literature and the visual arts in the second half of the 19th century. In country after country the modern movement can be dated from the first awareness of certain pioneering French ideas. And this meant that our sense of that dating was for a long while slightly confused. Even within France modernism was felt to be a movement of the 1920s, which was when its principles became intellectually acceptable and fashionable enough to make a real impact on society. Now that we are remoter from it, and judge by the works themselves rather than by their reception, we see that the heroic period was around 1910: the last years of Edward VII's (and the Hohenzollerns' and the Habsburgs') reign.

What gave the movement its all-embracing framework was an architectural revolution more comprehensive than anything since the Renaissance. This not only provided the other arts with fresh settings but set out to transform the entire physical surroundings of our daily life, particularly in towns and cities. In France, it began when men like the Perret brothers and Tony Garnier came to realize that the new materials of the engineers—as seen in the Eiffel Tower (1889) or the concrete industrial buildings of François Hennebique—were ripe for use; a few years later the French-Swiss Robert Maillart built a series of bridges which showed that they could be handled with simplicity and elegance. To the latter's example can be added the impact of the massive grain silos of North America and the wide-windowed steel-frame buildings of Adler and Sullivan and other Chicago architects. The way was open for a new architectural aesthetic which would substitute mass, truth to function and freedom of planning for the old Beaux-Arts concept of period style and surface ornament. As a German critic put it in 1907:

p 210 (9)
p 210 (4)

> A small circle of artists began wondering whether it was exactly dignified for somebody whose home was lit by electricity and heated by steam to surround himself with forms engendered by a long-departed generation.

Among them were Berlage, architect of the severe new brick Stock Exchange at Amsterdam, and the pugnacious Viennese Adolf Loos, whose attitude can be summed up in the title of his best-known lecture: 'Ornament and Crime'.

Europe's first truly modern buildings went up around 1905: Otto Wagner's Post Office Savings building in Vienna, with its plain glass and iron vault; and a house built by Loos on the Lake of Geneva, whose flat roof, big windows and severely rectangular details would have seemed 'advanced' in England thirty years later. The centre of the modern architectural movement now shifted to the German-speaking countries, where it was to remain right into the 1930s. For it was the Germans who actually put the new aesthetic to work, most notably with the founding of a Deutscher Werkbund of architects and designers in 1907. What gave this body its particular impetus was a social conception of architecture and industrial design inherited from England, thanks

p 210 (6)
p 210 (2)

Expressionism was essentially a German movement, the two main groups being 'Die Brücke', formed in 1905, and 'Der Blaue Reiter'. Left: the manifesto of 'Die Brücke' by one of its leaders, Ernst Ludwig Kirchner, proclaiming faith in a new generation and new forms of expression. Right: book-jacket for the 'Blaue Reiter Almanac' (founded in 1906) which contained major essays by Kandinsky and Marc. (1, 2)

in part to Hermann Muthesius's attachment to the German Embassy in London to study it. The Garden City movement, the ideas of Morris and Ruskin, the unpretentiousness of the domestic architecture of the 1890s were all transported into Germany, where industry was younger and more dynamic than in England, and the socialist movement stronger and more all-embracing. German industrialists and (until their downfall in 1918) petty rulers engaged such men as the Belgian Henry van de Velde (Morris's most brilliant successor as an all-round artist-craftsman-designer) and Peter Behrens, who became design chief of the great AEG electrical company about 1908. In 1911 Behrens's pupil Gropius built the Fagus shoe-last factory at Alfeld, a cleanly-detailed iron-and-glass-walled building that was like a leap straight into the middle of the century. Three years later he built the show factory for the Werkbund exhibition at Cologne, where van de Velde built the theatre. This confrontation of the new industrial age with the last of Art Nouveau was echoed in the accompanying discussions, where the Belgian spoke up for the old artistic individualism against the principles of standardization and prefabrication put forward by Gropius and others.

Fauves, Cubists, Expressionists and Futurists

Before World War I there was no common aesthetic linking architecture and the other visual arts; indeed the incongruity between modern art and its setting was often striking—as it sometimes is even today. None the less one can see a similar concern with simplification and structure in the twofold pictorial revolution which followed the pioneering work of Gauguin and Cézanne, those great isolated artists who died respectively in 1903 and 1906. What was new here—and quite distinct from the passionate Expressionism stimulated by the example of Van Gogh—was the sense that the picture itself was the central matter of art, not its 'likeness' to nature, or its realist or humanitarian theme, or its symbolic content, or its capturing of effects of colour or light. Before anything else the canvas was, as the young Maurice Denis put it in 1890, 'essentially a flat surface covered by colours assembled in a certain order'. This principle lay at the root of both the main Parisian schools. The Fauves under Matisse's leadership, who got their nickname at the Third (1905) Salon d'Automne, took it to mean that they should develop Gauguin's flat surfaces and arbitrary use of colour, and exploit every element of a representational painting for decorative and expressive ends. The Cubists, whose characteristic interest in solid, angular or broken forms sprang rather from the 1904 and 1907 Cézanne retrospectives at the same Salon, saw it more as an encouragement to turn the canvas into an analytical or (later) synthetic structure, where colour and representational allusions played a much more subordinate role. In both

cases, however, the painters were now setting down their own shapes rather than those of their subjects. In the former the shapes were curved, flat and brilliantly coloured. In the latter they were sharp-cut, three-dimensional and, initially at least, more or less monochrome.

These two new tendencies, soon to be carried all over the globe as foreign artists and collectors reported back from Paris and the pictures themselves started to travel (e.g., to Matisse's Berlin show of 1907, or to the London Post-Impressionist Exhibition of 1910, or into the Shchukin and Morosov collections in Moscow), were spontaneous ones, starting without any kind of formal programme or adhesions, and they were connected by personal friendships, so that men like Braque and Derain could move from Fauvism into the Cubist camp, and in due course away from either. They shared a common interest in primitive, and specifically negro art, for which Gauguin's two spells in the South Seas had obviously paved the way, though it was Vlaminck who claimed to be the first collector of Negro carvings (from 1905). The Negro influence was strongest of all in Picasso's immediate pre-Cubist phase, a transition from the delicate quasi-humanitarian sentimentality of his early twenties, and particularly in that pivotal masterpiece of 1907 known as *Les Demoiselles d'Avignon*. Even for the Cubists this influence was not purely formal, since it coincided with their discovery of Henri Rousseau, a retired *douanier* in his sixties whose ambitious yet amateurish paintings set the fashion for a serious interest in naive art. But away from this relatively sophisticated Parisian circle it stood for a good deal more: for directness of expression, rooted in mysterious submerged or unconscious powers such as could also be sensed in pictures by children and madmen or mystically absorbed from the cosmos. In German Expressionism, from 1910 onwards, this concern with emotional intensity fused with the Fauve influence (very visible in the early work of Kirchner and Pechstein) and the example of such disturbed artists as Van Gogh and Munch to make a third powerful school, whose more symbolist Munich branch, called *Der blaue Reiter* after a book published in 1912, was already pursuing Kandinsky's concept of musical significances and a mystically-tinged synaesthesia towards pure non-figurative painting.

Expressionism originated in the restlessness of a few young men in Dresden and took its savagery largely from resentment at the rigid and authoritarian elements in Imperial German life. In the visual arts it long had little international standing, no doubt because apart from the Swiss Paul Klee it never produced a painter with the sensuousness and concentrated skill that was common to the Parisians—though its brilliant graphic work is another matter. But within its area of influence, which came in time to cover most of central Europe, it was an all-absorbing force which

p 210 (3)

p 210 (5)

p 212 (15, 16)

p 212-13 (17, 18)

p 215 (23)

p 213 (18)

p 214 (19–21)

f 2

p 249 (1)

sucked up every other new tendency since Fauvism (Cubism, Futurism and Delaunay's near-abstract Orphism), digesting them and turning them into its own form of dionysiac energy. Another distinctive feature—and one which was to give it a more important social role than any other 20th-century artistic movement—was its extension from 1910 onwards to cover all the arts. Where Fauvism was a purely pictorial school, and Cubism a movement of painters and sculptors with the odd writer ally (like Cendrars and Apollinaire), Expressionism was so predominantly an attitude of mind that poets, playwrights, designers and even musicians like Schönberg could all be classed under that heading. There was a recognizably common approach, to be seen in their preference for morbid themes and their emotive use of formal fragmentation and distortion.

Futurism, the fourth of the main prewar movements, likewise came to embrace all the arts, but it was a more artificially whipped-up affair in which the kind of nationalistic showmanship identified with d'Annunzio was taken over by the poet F. T. Marinetti as a means of activating and promoting an Italian avant garde. For three years after the first appearance of the movement's manifesto in the Paris *Figaro* in 1909 it seems to have had no influence outside Italy, where it was essentially a noisy and iconoclastic proclamation of the modern spirit, coupled with aggressive patriotism of a militaristic kind. The handful of Neo-Impressionist Milanese painters who adhered in 1910, publishing their own manifesto in favour of the depiction of modern urban, technological life in its most dynamic forms, at first hardly lived up to this programme. But when it came to showing in Paris and competing with the Cubists on their own ground they worked out distinctive new ways of conveying the effects of movement and the simultaneity of different events: most impressively of all in Boccioni's few sculptures. This first Futurist exhibition made a considerable impact not only in Paris (notably on Apollinaire and Delaunay) but in the many other cities which it visited, above all Berlin; and it was followed by a Technical Manifesto of Futurist Literature which opened the way to pure sound poetry and the staccato arrangement of bare verbs and nouns.

Literature and the performing arts

Outside all such groupings there were a number of highly original individuals who generated no Isms and issued no manifestos. This applied even in painting—a solitary artist like Bonnard, for instance, was producing beautiful pictures that made no sudden leaps or dramatic breaks with the past, yet were quite unlike anybody else's—and far more so in literature, whose basis is after all a much more direct relationship between writer and reader, conducted in private and largely unaffected by adhesion to groups. In the prewar years the biggest and, in the long run, most revolutionary books were not those that made technical innovations but those that took the existing tradition a stage further, bringing it into line with the life of the time and the evolution of men's judgment and interests. Conrad's novels, the fantasies of Chesterton, the stories of Thomas Mann, Schnitzler and Gorky, the poetry of Valéry, Rilke, Blok and Hofmannsthal all fall under this head, as does Proust's great work which began appearing in 1913. At the same time there was a class of literature which, while orthodox enough in outward form, seemed to have made a sharp jump forward in its moral and social ideas; this was the case most strikingly with the short novels of André Gide (giving its programme to the *Nouvelle Revue Française* which he helped found in 1909), though it also held good for the early works of D. H. Lawrence, whose vitalism, like Gide's new morality, derived ultimately from Nietzsche. Even with Kafka, whose first book of stories appeared in 1913, the originality lay primarily in the richness and desperate quality of his imagination, and its contrast with the sober formal economy of the prose. Of all these writers only Lawrence and Gorky were not from middle-class (bourgeois) families, and even they became to some extent assimilated into the professional literary world. A completely plebeian book like the house-painter Robert Tressell's *The Ragged Trousered Philanthropists* (finished just before his death in 1910) was so rare as to be something of a landmark.

Those revolutionaries who transformed the face of European

p 222
(57)

p 215
(22)

p 223
(63)

p 223

p 223
(66)

p 223
(64)

'Exotics' Theatre' by Paul Klee. The drawing was made in 1922, when Klee was teaching at the Bauhaus, Weimar, and is partly an allusion to the experiments in theatrical technique that were being made there. (3)

poetry around this time likewise took some of their dynamism from Nietzsche, whose influence was strong throughout Futurism and Expressionism. They used the free verse of Laforgue and Gustave Kahn (which Marinetti had been propagating even before the launching of Futurism), the imagery of Rimbaud and Baudelaire and the sweeping global rhetoric of Whitman to express their vision of the modern world. In this their immediate precursor was the Belgian Verhaeren, whose treatment of urban and industrial themes seemed to reflect the principles of the Neo-Impressionists (such as Maximilien Luce) and his own compatriot the sculptor Meunier. The humanitarianism and sense of collective enthusiasm which inform such writing were taken up by Jules Romains, whose faith in the anonymous mass, largely shared by the Abbaye group of younger French poets, inspired his short-lived doctrine of Unanimism. It influenced a number of German Expressionist writers too, though their movement was characterized also by a marked morbidity, and the eye which they cast on the urban life around them tended to be colder (as with Gottfried Benn) or more sardonic. With Pound in England, again, and with Apollinaire and Cendrars in France itself, that slightly synthetic warm-heartedness was quite lacking. Here the Polish-born Apollinaire, with his almost archaic simplicity, his random use of allusions, his Whitmanesque invocations and his cosmopolitan range, not only became a lasting avant garde myth but evolved a form of French poetry that is still with us. In 1912, the year of his most famous long poem *Zone* (and of the equally cosmopolitan Cendrars's first big poem), he flirted briefly with the Futurists, whose concept of 'liberated words'—i.e., words and phrases scattered across the page in quasi-graphic arrangement—linked up with his own *Calligrammes* as *f 4* forerunners of today's Concrete Poetry. At the same time it pointed the way via the Germans Stramm and Schwitters to a poetry of more or less meaningless sounds, helping to form the chopped and jerky prose style characteristic of many Expressionist stories and plays.

In the theatre, while Shaw was continuing to cram his brilliant wit and acute social comments into a wholly conservative dramatic form, the more enterprising playwrights were busy breaking that form up into a shifting sequence of scenes in which the other arts played a role more equal to that of the dialogue. The later work of Strindberg, Maeterlinck's plays of the 1890s, Synge's *Riders to the Sea* and the massive dramas of Paul Claudel, combining the language of Whitman and Rimbaud with a mystically-flavoured Catholic traditionalism: such plays formed a bridge between Symbolism and the new 'theatrical theatre'. There were two fresh factors here: first the spread to Germany and Russia of the French *chansonnier* or highbrow cabaret, with its songs and sketches; and secondly such new technical devices as spotlighting, the cyclorama

235

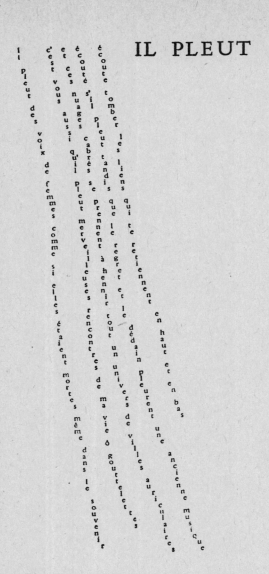

IL PLEUT

'Il pleut', one of the poems in Apollinaire's collection 'Calligrammes' (1918) in which words are arranged on the page to convey a visual impression. (4)

The arts

The Russian ballet played a crucial part in the purely musical revolution too, since it commissioned Stravinsky's three early masterpieces—*The Firebird*, *Petrushka* and *The Rite of Spring*—and put them before a much larger audience than normally went to concerts. The last of the three was performed in 1913, when the composer was thirty, and caused one of the greatest scandals in the history of music, even though its highly artificial primitivism was not all that far from the ideas of Gauguin and Nietzsche. By Western European standards, in fact, Stravinsky was himself something of an exotic, with his fierce and complex rhythms, his discordant harmonies and his use of Russian folk tunes; but then those standards were still strongly identified with the German Romantic school—Brahms having died in 1897 while Mahler and Strauss were just reaching the height of their powers. Like the even more nationalistic Béla Bartók, then still almost unknown, Stravinsky owed much to that astonishingly original composer Debussy, whose 'impressionism' is of less relevance in this connection than his independence of traditional harmony, his ear for popular rhythms (*Golliwog's Cake Walk* was written three years before Irving Berlin's *Alexander's Ragtime Band* of 1911) and his elegant and economical late chamber works. Meanwhile the German school, again somewhat under Debussy's impact, was generating its own avant garde in the shape of Arnold Schönberg and his disciples Berg and Webern, late Romantic rebels against the traditional concept of key. Often associated with Expressionism because of their sombre themes and Schönberg's contribution to the *Blaue Reiter*, this Vienna-based group combined an interest in formal patterns (such as canons and inversions) and Mahlerian subtleties of orchestration with a heavily symbolist choice of vocal and operatic texts. The twelve-note system towards which they were already heading was not a conscious preoccupation before, at the earliest, the end of 1914.

f 5

p 222
(59)

p 222
(57, 56)

f 2

1914: Art and war

Subconsciously anticipated in certain works of German Expressionism, the shock of World War I jolted and interrupted many of these trends, and set yet others going. Many of the chief innovators were swept off, sometimes for the full four years, into the armed forces or internment, often with traumatic effects; of the Parisian Cubists, for example, only neutral subjects like Gris and Picasso could develop more or less undisturbed. Irreparable losses were suffered, particularly by the Expressionists, though Boccioni and Sant'Elia, Gaudier-Brzeska and Wilfred Owen likewise left lasting gaps in their respective countries and movements. Within Europe the barriers came down: people were shut in their countries, or shut out of them, and in many cases cut off from the places where they had done most of their work. Thus van de Velde had to leave Germany for good; the chief Cubist dealer Kahnweiler left

Stravinsky composing 'The Rite of Spring' and shocking the bourgeoisie, by Jean Cocteau, 1913. (5)

and the revolving stage, which made possible a correspondingly plastic and fluid form of production. The turning-point came about 1905, when Reinhardt took over the Deutsches Theater in Berlin and Meyerhold's Studio was set up as part of the Art Theatre in Moscow: Gordon Craig's *Art of the Theatre* appeared that year, immediately preceded by Ernst Fuchs's *Die Schaubühne der Zukunft*, which emphasized the need for closer contact between stage and audience, and the relevance of Japanese methods. A year later the third great anti-Naturalist theoretician, Adolphe Appia, joined forces with his fellow-Swiss Jaques-Dalcroze, who had devised the new synthesis of music and movement known as Eurhythmics.

p 211
(13, 14)

Stylization (which spread to Paris with the opening of Copeau's Théâtre du Vieux-Colombier in 1913), the breaking down of the 'fourth wall' (Meyerhold was playing with ideas of production in the round as early as 1907), the shaping of stage space by platforms and steps, the choreographing of crowd movements, finally the dominant role of the director (as demanded by Craig): all this required a more skeletal form of dramatic text, such as began to be written by the German Expressionists even before 1914. At the same time there were the makings of a new alliance between the stage and the avant garde painters, prefigured in the work of Bonnard, Vuillard and their friends for Lugné-Poë's Théâtre de l'Œuvre in the 1890s, as in the production of Alfred Jarry's farce *Ubu Roi* at the end of 1896. When, in 1909, Diaghileff brought the Russian ballet to Paris he not only took his audiences' breath away to a degree that permanently changed the Western attitude to the dance; he also showed how all the arts could be brought together to collaborate within the theatre at an advanced level. Perhaps the most daring of all productions of the prewar theatre took place in 1914: Meyerhold's staging of two plays by Blok in the Tenishev Academy in St Petersburg, with open scene-changes, a trestle stage and the audience seated in a semicircle around it.

236

France; Kandinsky and Chagall went back to Russia. Such new traffic in ideas as did take place was very largely across the Atlantic; the Diaghileff ballet, for instance, travelled widely in North and South America, while Duchamp and Picabia, establishing themselves in New York in 1915, had a lasting effect on that city's attitude to the modern movement. At the same time there was a quite new and increasingly commercial traffic in cinema and jazz music, which only began seriously to enter the world of the arts about this time. For many people the war was above all the period of Chaplin's unforgettable short comedies, culminating in 1918 in the war film *Shoulder Arms*.

p 221 (54) There was surprisingly little direct reflection of people's experience—or even observation—of the fighting. Léger, for instance, who later felt that his years as a sapper and stretcher-bearer decisively altered his attitude to his fellow-men and to the portrayal of reality, scarcely referred to it in his paintings, while even the Futurists, who had begun as apostles of war (in days when the enemy were the Austrians or the Arabs), depicted it as any newspaper reader could have done. In the whole of European poetry the front-line verses of Owen, Isaac Rosenberg (another casualty), Siegfried Sassoon and Herbert Read have an exceptional place; almost the only thing like them is the odd poem written by Georg Trakl before his death on the Galician front. Even the war novels which became so common a decade later were slow to appear, the only one of importance to be published at the time being Barbusse's *Le Feu*. There was one interesting scheme of state-sponsored art, which led to the commissioning of Wyndham Lewis and other advanced painters as British 'war artists'. Another influential piece of government policy was the German encouragement of a separate Flemish culture in occupied Belgium. Whereas the Belgian cultural revival at the turn of the century had been conducted in the French language, a new Flemish Expressionist movement now began to evolve.

There were those who went on pursuing the researches begun before the war, particularly in the neutral countries: Switzerland and Holland. Just forty at its outbreak, Schönberg published nothing for the next eight years, but worked to establish a unifying principle which would govern both the structure and the harmony of his compositions. In Italy Giorgio de Chirico joined with the ex-Futurists Carrà and Morandi to evolve a mysterious treatment of urban spaces and dummy-like figures which they termed 'metaphysical'. In Paris the core of the Cubist movement now disintegrated; already in 1914 Picasso was starting to work in a much prettier, more speckly and decorative style, and the following year he began varying such experiments with classical, almost academic portraits and drawings. Braque returned seriously wounded in 1915, never to resume the strict sobriety of his Cubist pictures. In Holland, however, Piet Mondrian, who had been feeling his way from Cubism towards total abstraction before leaving Paris, now established his lifelong style of strictly rectangular flat surfaces, painted in primary colours and defined by solid black bars. With the painter-poet Theo van Doesburg, an outstanding avant garde *animateur* some ten years younger, he founded the review *De Stijl* (1917) which established a comparably rigorous aesthetic for sculpture, furniture, typography and architecture. This interacted with the influence of the strong horizontal emphasis in Frank Lloyd Wright's houses of a decade or so earlier (which Berlage had helped to make known in Europe just before the war), and with the country's relatively normal situation, to produce such notable housing schemes as J. J. P. Oud's in Rotterdam, well in advance of anything done in France or even Germany for several years.

p 216 (26)

p 17

p 86 (19)

p 222 (59) p 223 (61) The other main centre of activity was Switzerland, where Busoni and Stravinsky had settled and the isolated and dedicated James Joyce arrived in 1915. Stravinsky, some of whose works of this period reflect the influence of American ragtime, was occupied with such smaller works as the chamber opera *Renard* (1915) and the highly original entertainment called *The Soldier's Tale* (with spoken text by the Swiss writer Ramuz), both of which were designed to be played on a trestle stage and to be economically feasible under wartime conditions. Joyce, whose *Portrait of the Artist as a Young Man* appeared in 1916, with its remarkably modern dialogue and attitudes and shifts of level and angle, was

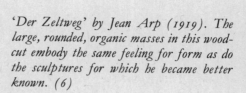
'*Der Zeltweg*' by Jean Arp (1919). The large, rounded, organic masses in this woodcut embody the same feeling for form as do the sculptures for which he became better known. (6)

then deep in *Ulysses*. Also in Zurich in the same year a group of much younger men, most of them fugitives from the war, came together around the newly formed Cabaret Voltaire under Hugo Ball, who had worked in the Munich theatre and contributed to Expressionist periodicals. Their movement of total contemptuous protest against the war, and against every other accepted idea or institution including art itself, was a mixture of several different elements: Futurist-style showmanship (as practised by the Rumanian Tristan Tzara), deep spiritual malaise (Ball), a purist art refined from Cubism (by the Alsatian-born Arp, who arrived from Paris in 1915), plus a desire to tease the stodgy and Germanophil Zurich public, all topped off with a formidable sense of fun.

Dada, a name which they picked as meaningless (and hence mystifying), soon spread into Germany, where Raoul Hausmann, the satirical draughtsman George Grosz and the Herzfelde brothers turned it into a still sharper weapon of attack against everything to do with the war and the society that supported it. There was already a similar but much less purposeful trend in France, where Apollinaire's late play *Les Mamelles de Tirésias* and the Cocteau-Satie-Picasso ballet *Parade* (1917) recalled the provocative nihilism of *Ubu Roi* some twenty years earlier. This linked with the work of Duchamp and Picabia in the United States, as they now moved away from the fine painting of Duchamp's *Nude descending a staircase* with its quasi-Futurist rendering of movement, through some inconclusive attempts to make a new notation out of mechanical, literal and mathematical elements, into the total non-art of the 'ready-mades'. In 1918 Picabia came over to Zurich, and with his return to Paris, drawing Tzara in his wake, the power centre of Dada shifted to that city. By then all its main features had been formed. The Futurists' love of mixed manifestations and shock effects had been taken over, largely stripped of its element of self-advertising (for men like Hülsenbeck and Grosz believed in deflating *everything*, including themselves). Sound poetry and free typography, likewise part of the Futurist programme, had been taken a stage further. The experiments with nonsense and absurdity made (well after Lear and Carroll) by Jarry and Christian Morgenstern had been given a fresh kick. The collage technique introduced by the Cubists around 1912 had been adapted to a wider range of materials and used in Berlin to make the first photomontages.

p 215 (23)

Yet Dada remained marginal to the main events of the war by comparison with another movement which grew up in Switzerland around Romain Rolland and the refugee Expressionists. This was much more seriously political, and it brought a number of writers into a position close to the views of the minority (or anti-war) Socialists whose Russian section under Lenin had been established in that country since September 1914. That month Rolland, whose massive prewar novel *Jean-Christophe*, with its Franco-German setting, had been conceived as 'an arch over the Rhine', issued his pacifist appeal *Au-dessus de la mêlée* in the hope that such eminent literary figures as Thomas Mann, Gerhart Hauptmann, Verhaeren, Romains and Georges Duhamel would help him build some kind of moral-intellectual third force. At first his efforts fell very flat, most of his would-be allies apart from Hermann Hesse preferring

Symbol of the 'State Bauhaus' (designed by Oscar Schlemmer), the aim of which was to teach design suitable for the age of mass production. (7)

to side with their respective armies, though a few younger men like Pierre-Jean Jouve and the Belgian engraver Frans Masereel came to join him, and Gorky's letters were a strong support. From about 1916 on, however, an increasing number of the younger Expressionists began to make their way over the German frontier, bringing with them an important anti-war journal in the shape of René Schickele's *Die weissen Blätter*. No group of intellectuals anywhere was so keenly against the war as this dominant humanitarian wing of Expressionism, and the result was a great deal of passionate and rhetorical poetry which was very unlike what came from the Allied side of the trenches.

The art of revolution

The artistic sides of the Russian and German Revolutions had more in common than is often allowed, and until it became clear that there would be no Bolsheviks to take the latter over the two seemed to their participants like aspects of a single massive revolt. Particularly in Russia the first four or five years of the Soviet Revolution were an astonishing period in the arts. Anatoly Lunacharsky, whom Lenin at once made Commissar for Education, had been in touch with Rolland's circle and had learnt to understand Cubist painting in Paris, and under him the small Russian avant garde was now given official commissions and jobs. Meyerhold became head of the Theatrical Department; Kandinsky and Rodchenko were put in charge of picture purchases for the museums; the Constructivists Gabo, Pevsner and Tatlin became professors in Moscow; Chagall, Lissitzky and Malevitch in Vitebsk. Two of the most important decisions were taken by Lenin himself: the institution of what he termed 'propaganda by monuments'—i.e., the erection of giant public statues—and the creation of a Soviet film industry as the best way of reaching the masses. There were decorated propaganda trains, mass pageants with texts by men like Mayakovsky, and poetry readings (books still being in short supply); in 1918 Lissitzky designed the Central Committee's banner for the first May Day parade. Aesthetically the immediate effect of all this was to force the growth of Constructivism, a form of abstract art somewhat akin to that of *De Stijl*, but with an added flavour of machinery and engineering. In
p 139
(2)
Moscow in 1920 Tatlin made his (quite unrealizable) Constructivist project for the headquarters of the new Third International. The State Institute for Art and Architecture, or Vkhutemas was founded under N. A. Ladovsky, anticipating much that became common in Western art teaching forty years later; the first Constructivist Exhibition was held; and there was a classic production of Verhaeren's *Les Aubes* by Meyerhold, with Cubist settings.

The German Revolution of 1918 likewise gave an established footing to the modern movement, particularly in the visual arts and the theatre. Artists like Pechstein made posters and pamphlets for the new Republic; Schmidt-Rottluff designed its improved German eagle; Kokoschka, Barlach and a number of lesser Expressionists were appointed to professorships or made members of academies. Theatres changed directors, notably the former Imperial Theatre in Berlin, which became a headquarters of Expressionist production under Leopold Jessner. Gropius, who had meanwhile fallen under the influence of the utopian Socialist architect Bruno Taut, was given van de Velde's job at the Weimar Applied Art School, together with the new regime's authority to
f 7
fuse it with the Fine Art School and rename the whole thing 'State

Bauhaus'. In January 1919, however, the suppression of the Spartacist revolt in Berlin came as a shock to all those who could not forget that the ruling Majority Socialists had supported the war, while a number of Expressionists were prominent in the brutally repressed Munich Soviet which ended with the imprisonment of the poets Toller and Mühsam and the murder of Gustav Landauer, Whitman's anarchist translator. Thus although the 1918 Revolution helped to spread the Expressionists' ideas right across Germany, giving them a position apparently stronger than that of any other part of the international modern movement, it also introduced them to the sad compromises and betrayals that come with the conversion of ideals into reality, and, nastier still, to certain special characteristics of the new German Right.

Modernism in fashion

It was only after the war that the modern movement became intellectually and (in the smart sense) socially acceptable, and actually penetrated into ordinary people's homes and clothes and ideas and leisure entertainment. The process had perhaps begun in Paris with *Parade*, which not only established the name of Cocteau,   p 220
together with the witty, popularly based music which he was   (49)
advocating, but marked the start of Diaghileff's collaboration with   p 221
Picasso and other members of the Paris avant garde. Those French   (52)
critics who before the war had had little use for the austerities of Cubism now began to write approvingly of its artists; dressmakers like Poiret and Chanel followed their lead; the ex-Fauve Van   p 220
Dongen became a society portraitist. Only occasionally did   (50)
Diaghileff, from his base at Monte Carlo, turn back to the Russian tradition, as in Stravinsky's severe and powerful *Les Noces* (1923) with its sets by Goncharova. *Les Biches* of the following year, with   p 221
chic sets by Marie Laurencin and music by the amiably eclectic   (53)
Francis Poulenc, was much more typical. For this was already the heyday of jazz-modern decoration and the debased modernist architecture of Robert Mallet-Stevens: a style known as Arts Déco 25, after the Paris Exposition des Arts Décoratifs of 1925.

Within this slightly parasitical evolution there were genuinely new threads, particularly among such younger composers as Honegger and Milhaud whose work had something of the elegant modern classicism of Ravel and the new, economical Stravinsky. These two in particular were a good deal more serious than Cocteau's sponsorship of their group 'Les Six' might suggest;   p 220
Milhaud's real literary affinity was with Claudel, several of whose   (51)
works he set, besides writing the negro ballet *La Création du Monde*   p 221
(1923), with its strong jazz rhythms and small orchestra of soloists,   (54)
to a story by Cendrars. All the same, the softening-up of Cubism, the return of Picasso and Derain to academic and neo-classical styles of painting, and the emergence of the Ecole de Paris—a heterogeneous collection of mainly central European artists with no distinctive formal programme—all suggested a creeping superficiality. And this formed a devitalizing background for the newly imported Dada movement, which now became a basically literary affair, a kind of anti-art for anti-art's sake quite lacking its earlier impetus. The whole Paris Dada period, from Tzara's   p 216
arrival in 1920 and the first public manifestations right up to 1924,   (27)
was in fact a prelude to Surrealism, remarkable mainly for the early work of the German Max Ernst and for Picabia's ballet *Relâche*, which had music by Satie and an interval film called *Entr'acte* by the young René Clair. As the poet André Breton came to take the movement over it became a forcing-house for some of his own pet concerns, such as the revival of Lautréamont, the practice of automatic writing (i.e., the setting down of whatever comes into one's head, in chance order), and the subjection of art to dreams. Succeeding Tzara as its leader (and with the German wing now more or less merged in Constructivism), he annexed the term 'surrealism' coined in quite a different context by Apollinaire seven years earlier, and in 1924 published his Surrealist Manifesto which virtually refounded Dada on the basis of his own ideas.

Though in theory Surrealism, as a romantic, pseudo-Freudian doctrine of interior imagery and subconscious association, could apply to any art, in practice it was literary, and Breton's magazine   p 217
of 1919 from which it sprang was rightly called *Littérature*. Its   (28–30)
relevance to painting was above all that it allowed Breton to claim as Surrealist any artists of whom he approved, from Uccello

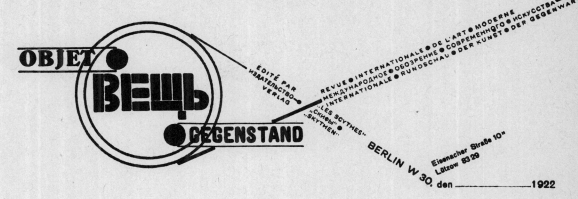

Letterhead for the magazine 'Vesch' by El Lissitzky, the Russian pioneer of modern typographical design. (8)

onwards, including those like Klee and Picasso who at no point believed in this label. Gradually, however, Surrealism in painting became defined by a kind of case-law of minor experiments made by Ernst, Masson, Miró, Magritte and (from 1929) Salvador Dali. Ernst's collages of old engravings, Miró's (and even Arp's) biomorphic forms, Dali's precisely-painted distortion and decomposition of symbols against an endless horizon: in fact, *any* kind of startling or disquieting juxtaposition and allusion, or use of chance textures and elements, or return to childhood and its nightmares, came to be seen as Surrealist. The amazing thing was that, despite its lack of true formal innovation, this last major Ism of the modern movement had such exceptional staying power, surviving World War II to provide some kind of inspiration to artists even today. Whether this was because or in spite of Breton's disciplinary tactics, which led to quasi-religious expulsions and excommunications (among others of the actor Antonin Artaud), is not at all clear. But Surrealism canalized the 20th century's largely stifled romanticism, and it also gave us a new view of many interesting aspects of the 19th's, as for example the creepier paintings of Gustave Moreau and Burne-Jones.

'Art and technology: a new unity'

The main rival tendency, much less organized and scattered over several movements and countries, got its first impetus when the Swiss painter-architect Le Corbusier settled in Paris in 1917 and joined the artist Ozenfant in a campaign to drag Cubism back to the strait and narrow path still being pursued by Léger and Gris, with intermittent contributions (like *The Three Musicians* of 1921) from Picasso. Their two-man school of Purism was admittedly short-lived: a severe, near-abstract Cubism based on a neutral selection of common domestic objects, somewhat as in the much more subtle art pursued for many years in perfectionist isolation by Morandi in Bologna. But the magazine *L'Esprit Nouveau* which they founded in 1920, together with Corbusier's revolutionary *Vers une archi-*

Le Corbusier's drawing illustrating the 'Modulor', the scale of proportions, based on the human body and the mathematics of the golden section, to be used for creating buildings of ideal proportions adapted to human use. (9)

tecture (1923) and its successors, brought their ideas into a common perspective with the more abstract and rationalist art of *De Stijl* and the Constructivists, as well as with Arp's sculptures and Corbusier's own extraordinary architectural genius. In this whole complex, which has never been given a specific name, a great many of the key architectural ideas came from Corbusier: the adoption of a steel and concrete skeleton to allow free planning, with the walls carrying no weight; the roof garden; the careful fixing of proportions by a geometry akin to that of the Renaissance artists; the segregation of road traffic from public open spaces and paths; and the use of high tower blocks to restrict urban sprawl and clutter. It was a programme in which everything down to the curvature of a lavatory wall was at once highly rational and informed by a personal visual aesthetic derived from his own painting. *p 224 (69, 70) f 6*

From 1924 on, when Corbusier built a house in Paris for his collector Dr Raoul Laroche, he was exemplifying these ideas in some of the century's finest buildings, of which the Villa Savoie at Poissy (1928–30) is perhaps the most famous. But whereas the French establishment was against him, rarely allowing him to work on big public jobs, in Germany the way for a more widely accepted architecturally aligned aesthetic was being cleared by a brief pincer movement on Gropius's Bauhaus. This school had set out in a largely utopian, Expressionist, mystically orientated spirit, and for all its admirable interdisciplinary programme its relations with architecture and industry were alike left vague. In 1922, however, a mixed band of Dadaists and Constructivists moved briefly in on it, led by Van Doesburg and including the Hungarian Moholy-Nagy, their organ being the Russo-German magazine *Vesch* of which Lissitzky and Ehrenburg edited three issues from Berlin. A year later Moholy became Gropius's right-hand man, introducing fresh techniques like photography, and teaching the use of space, materials and textures on the lines of the Vkhutemas school in Moscow. Kandinsky too, who had joined the staff in 1922 on leaving Russia, was now painting in a much more geometrical abstract style. The school's new slogan was 'Art and Technology—a new unity!', and the machine aesthetic of the Constructivists and *L'Esprit Nouveau* naturally followed. *p 224 (71)* *p 224–5 (67, 68)* *f 8*

In itself this aesthetic was not new, since Marinetti (for one) had loudly proclaimed the beauty of machines, arguing that a racing car was a better sight than the Victory of Samothrace. What appealed to him however was not their clean elegance of design so much as their power and noise, while to Marcel Duchamp, who in 1913 had stood fascinated by a ship's propeller and decided that art could no longer compete, the interest was to some extent the way in which machinery worked and moved. After the war, which brought people into unexpectedly intimate contact with such things, their metallic precision seemed to fit Cocteau's *Rappel à l'ordre* and the rhythmical, clearly orchestrated music that embodied it, while their large-scale functioning appeared, in works like Honegger's *Pacific 231* or Prokofiev's ballet *Le Pas d'Acier*, to synthesize a whole new technological world. The art of the 1920s is full of similar examples, of which Léger's film *Ballet mécanique* (1923) is one of the more striking. In the new Soviet theatre, for instance, Meyerhold trained his actors in 'biomechanics' and for *Le Cocu magnifique* in 1922 turned the stage into a mass of rotating machinery; a year later the young Sergei M. Eisenstein, who had trained as an engineer, staged a play in a Moscow gasworks. Around this time *p 218 (34)*

Eisenstein wrote an article in the Constructivist magazine *Lef* putting forward his quasi-scientific theory of 'montage of attractions', which used the analogy of Dadaist photomontage to present the theatre director as a form of engineer, assembling his production from preselected components.

The return to order

'The lesson of the machine,' wrote Corbusier, 'lies in the pure relation of cause to effect'; and again, in a famous passage from *Vers une architecture*: 'machinery contains an economy factor which determines choices. The house is a machine for living in.' This recognition came at a crucial turning-point in the modern movement, whose whole basis everywhere—practical as well as ideological—seems to have changed decisively with the return to order (of one brand or another) four or five years after the end of the war. Thus in Russia the less revolutionary-minded artists and writers started re-emerging on returning from abroad, and the need for government subsidies to the modernists became less urgent. In 1922 Mussolini seized power in Italy, turning the refurbished Futurism of the 1920s into a semi-official movement. In 1923 the German currency stabilization cut short the boom on which Expressionist theatre, publishing and the art market had depended. With Dada at an end and neo-classicism flourishing in France it was as if the whole experimental period were now over.

But this was not so much a reaction against the modern movement as a shifting of its energies to another, less individualistic plane. The process can be most clearly seen in Russia and Germany, where the avant garde now found that it had been much too optimistic about its relationship with the new regimes. In 1921 a split occurred within Constructivism between the 'pure' artists like Gabo and utilitarians like Rodchenko who felt that the movement should be centred on engineering and practical design, and were prepared to go into industry themselves. By the end of 1922 Gabo, Pevsner, Chagall and Kandinsky had all returned to Western Europe, while Tatlin and Malevitch were finding it increasingly hard to work. There had been a succession of disasters among the poets too, death, emigration or other causes silencing Blok, Chlebnikov, Tsvetaeva, Gumilev, Yesenin and Akhmatova. None the less, from the beginning of serious rebuilding in 1925, the Soviet architects played an active and original part in the modern movement, summoning Corbusier (Centrosoyuz Building, 1929) and other Western functionalists to work with them, and relating the new aesthetic to their country's quite equally new social aims and conditions. The theatre flourished, Meyerhold in particular staging a remarkable production of Mayakovsky's *The Bed Bug* in 1929, with music by the twenty-two-year-old Shostakovitch and sets by Rodchenko. Above all, the Soviet cinema now emerged, p 218 (37) with Eisenstein's *Potemkin* in 1925, as a collective art form which mixed brilliant photography, original montage, realism of detail and revolutionary impetus of feeling to make a new and compellingly forceful impression.

In Germany the death of Expressionism around 1922 was followed by a similar transformation under the functional-sounding label of 'new matter-of-factness' or *Neue Sachlichkeit*. Prefigured by certain works of Dadaism and by the near-'metaphysical' paintings of Oscar Schlemmer, this concept is associated with an exhibition held under that title at Mannheim in 1925, which featured a number of post-Expressionist painters (notably Beckmann, Grosz and Dix) whose work combined sober realism with social comment or 'metaphysical' stillness. The title was an apt description of much more than that, however: the drily atonal early music of Hindemith; the satirical 'utility' poetry of Tucholsky and Erich Kästner; the advertising graphics of Schwitters and Lissitzky; the dispassionate war novels of Remarque and Renn. It stood for a return to unpretentiousness and impersonality after the excesses of Expressionism, and it had not only an unfamiliar wit but a strong functional p 223 (65) streak. Brecht bore its stamp, with his early efforts to align art and sport, his penchant for jazz and cabaret and his increasingly p 218 (36) austere interest in the collective rather than the individual. Even the establishment of the twelve-note system with Schönberg's Piano Suite of 1924, for all its Symbolist ancestry, reflects a comparable intellectualism and belongs to the same stock of ideas, so that the première of Berg's *Wozzeck* a year later now seems as

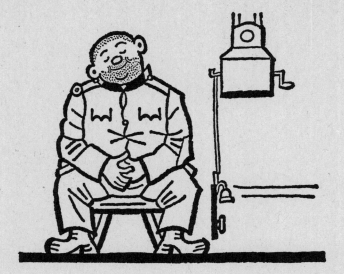

Schweik, the anti-hero of Hašek's satirical novel about life in the Imperial Austrian Army during the First World War. (10)

characteristic of Berlin in the 1920s as the Brecht-Weill *Threepenny Opera* (1928) or the documentary theatre of Piscator, with its original use of film and new mechanical devices. The whole complex was embraced by the curriculum of the Bauhaus, where it was Gropius's particular achievement to combine the example of outstanding individual artists (such as Klee) with a Constructivist school of design, a severely beautiful group of new buildings, an awareness of modern industry and a pervading sense of social responsibility.

Much the same process of consolidation can be seen in literature, where the large-scale novel now flourished, often in the hands of former avant garde poets like Werfel or Jules Romains. In several countries the 1920s saw the publication of 20th-century masterpieces, such as changed the face of writing everywhere. They were of many sorts: *Ulysses*, with its verbal fireworks, its mixture of styles and levels, has been a challenge to writers ever since, and so have the precisely imagined posthumous novels of Kafka, which he himself wanted to be destroyed. These, however, like Eliot's p 223 *The Waste Land* (perhaps the decade's greatest and most influential (62) single poem), belong before the turning-point, in the era of individual technical experimentation. But Ernest Hemingway's stories and novels, culminating in *A Farewell to Arms* in 1929, headed a whole influential new school of American fiction which included Faulkner, Fitzgerald, Wolfe, Sinclair, Dos Passos's montage-like *Manhattan Transfer* and the tersely economical crime stories of Dashiell Hammett, and which collectively put the United States for the first time on the cultural map as a fertile new source of ideas, forms and language. The same period saw the publication of Mann's *The Magic Mountain*, Forster's *A Passage to India*, the ageing Svevo's ironic *The Confessions of Zeno*, the softly impressionistic novels of Virginia Woolf and the greater part of *A la recherche du temps perdu*, as well as the main plays of Pirandello and O'Neill. Soviet prose likewise struck a most fertile patch, despite such exemplary works as Gladkov's *Cement* (1924), with Olyesha's *Envy*, Babel's short stories, the imaginative fantasies of Pilnyak and Zamyatin, and the satires of Zoshchenko and Ilf and Petrov. And it is difficult to conceive of a finer comic novel appearing this century than the Czech Hašek's massive unfinished *Schweik*, with its *f 10* unsuspectedly precise documentary background and permanently subversive message.

The true individuality of the 1920s is to be found in the changes effected in the relations between the arts and the society around them. Here the outstanding development was the use of more or less functionalist architecture for mass housing in Germany. Following the Dutch example, the city of Vienna had adopted the principle of wholesale replanning with its Socialist housing programme of 1923, but little use was made there even of such established pioneers as Behrens and Loos, and none at all of the younger moderns. In 1925, however, the rebuilding of Frankfurt began under the city architect Ernst May, and by the end of the decade one-eleventh of the population had been rehoused in modern-style buildings. The same year Bruno Taut, now an orthodox functionalist, became chief architect of the very active GEHAG housing society in Berlin, while in 1927 Corbusier and other leading innovators collaborated under Mies van der Rohe's direction to build the Weissenhof estate for the Werkbund at Stuttgart. The whole physical setting of German life was in such ways brought nearer to the social-aesthetic programme of *L'Esprit Nouveau*, as well as that of Gropius, who himself designed flats or housing estates for a number of cities. It became, for the first time in any country, an appropriate setting for the other modern arts.

The new audience

This was not the only change in the cultural framework. For the audience was at the same time growing, thanks partly to the conscious social and educational policy pursued in such revolutionary states as Russia and Germany, where museums now actively promoted modern art, and partly to the spread of new forms of mechanical reproduction: the records, radio and cheap coloured prints, bringing Caruso's voice, Paul Whiteman's band and the Van Gogh *Sunflowers* into so many homes. A crop of musical or operatic festivals sprang up: Salzburg (1921), Donaueschingen (1921), the International Society for Contemporary Music (1922). Moreover whole new arts were starting to flower, first and foremost that of the cinema, where René Clair's early comedies, the abstractions of Richter and Eggeling and the documentary 'Kino-Eye' of Dziga Vertov (a contributor to *Lef*) all showed in their different ways that films were not just a vehicle for popular narrative or the promotion of worldwide mythical figures such as Douglas Fairbanks, Rudolph Valentino and the dog Rin-tin-tin. Chaplin's masterpiece *The Gold Rush*, made in the same year as *Potemkin*, was certainly one of the most brilliant and memorable works of art of the decade, in whatever medium.

Similarly photography itself was at last beginning to be used creatively in the hands of artists like Lissitzky, Moholy-Nagy and the American Man Ray, who had come from the Dada or Constructivist camps and were not too fussy about 'fine' art. An even lower branch of art to develop with the new reproductive techniques was jazz music, whose principal medium of communication became the ten-inch 78 r.p.m. gramophone record. Originating primarily in New Orleans and Chicago, a phenomenal generation of semi-literate instrumentalists, both black and white, now went to the recording studios to give performances of the greatest expressiveness and originality, often burning themselves out in the process. These virtuosi, however, such as Louis Armstrong, Bix Beiderbecke (d. 1931), Frank Teschemacher (d. 1932) and the pianists Earl Hines and Fats Waller, scarcely left their mark on a 'jazz age' dominated rather by the big dance bands and by composers of hit songs like Gershwin, Cole Porter and Irving Berlin. Only the music of Duke Ellington, whose band took shape around 1928, formed a bridge between the two. Like theirs, his music has lasted where the great contemporary successes are now nothing but nostalgic memories.

In these and other ways there were in the 1920s the beginnings of a new breaking-down of established class barriers in the arts.

f 11

p 219 (41)

p 219 (44)

p 218 (31)

f 12

p 219 (42)

Music reached enlarged audiences through the gramophone record. His Master's Voice was one of the pioneering record companies. (11)

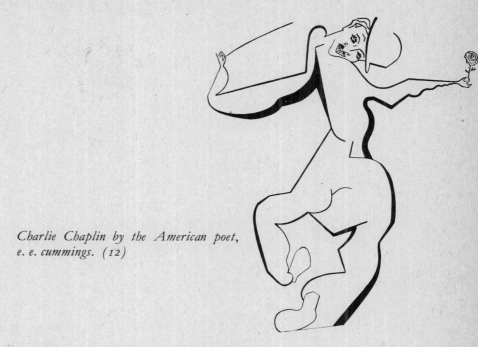

Charlie Chaplin by the American poet, e. e. cummings. (12)

Highbrows brought up on the traditional hierarchy of genres now began to appreciate and themselves adopt many features of what had been thought lowbrow, popular and vulgar. Thus Stravinsky, Milhaud, Eisenstein, Brecht, Weill and Ernst Křenek were among those who borrowed elements from the music-hall and from (big-band) jazz; sport became a matter for art (Honegger's *Rugby*, 1928); Eliot introduced plebeian elements into *Sweeney Agonistes* and *The Waste Land*; and the crime thriller, with Edgar Wallace as its most prolific master, became intellectually respectable, besides constituting the principal new English literary genre. Returning the compliment, Cole Porter wrote a ballet and Gershwin his 'symphonic' *Rhapsody in Blue* (1924): two composers who subsequently studied with Ravel. Linked with this process—which itself reflects the age's wider social awareness of the arts—was a simultaneous breaching of the race barrier, to be seen for instance in Cendrars's *Anthologie nègre* of 1920, the *Revue nègre* of 1925 which made Joséphine Baker's name, Paul Robeson's success in O'Neill's *The Emperor Jones*, and Křenek's first 'jazz opera' *Jonny spielt auf* (1927), with its black hero. This trend went very much further than the Cubists' earlier curiosity about Negro sculpture, and pointed the way to a new attitude of equality, if as yet only in the cultural field.

p 219 (40)

The thirties: the arts fight for life

In 1929 the Nazi ideologist Alfred Rosenberg founded a Militant League for German Culture to combat all such tendencies. There were demonstrations against the modern arts, including a near-riot at the première of Brecht and Weill's opera *Mahagonny*, and the whitewashing of Schlemmer's murals in the old Bauhaus building at Weimar by the new head of the school there, another racially-minded theorist called Schulze-Naumburg. In Russia a new policy of party management of the arts began with the resignation of Lunacharsky in that year. Eisenstein was summoned by Stalin and told to change the ending of his new film *The General Line*, while a year later, after the banning of his satirical play *The Bathhouse*, Mayakovsky killed himself for motives that are still unclear. In the Museum of Modern Western Art, formed from the old Shchukin and Morosov collections, it was thought wise to label the exhibits to show 'the fundamental contradictions of bourgeois society as reflected in its art'. In both these countries the reaction against the modern movement was to continue right through the 1930s, with drastic and demoralizing effects on the arts throughout the world. For there was a double polarization here which put many artists in an irresolvable quandary. On the one hand the Nazi menace and the threat of war forced them into a new political awareness and made them co-operate with the Communists in their anti-Fascist organizations of 'intellectuals'. On the other, Nazis and Communists proved to be equally philistine, dangerous and dictatorial where the arts themselves were concerned, and almost identical in their condemnation of artistic experiment.

p 218 (36)

p 218 (34)

'We felt young and surging with the creative energy of a new Renaissance,' wrote Eisenstein of his work on *The General Line*. 'And we saw a perspective of boundless new possibilities in the future.' It was this sense of confidence that was now destroyed, as the arts' new social setting in central and eastern Europe quickly crumbled, leaving the artist to organize himself politically or not at all. Further experiment other than for political ends could only be carried out in some kind of ivory tower, marginally to the life of the time and largely by members of the older generation: among English-speaking writers, for instance, by Joyce, Virginia Woolf and Gertrude Stein, with Samuel Beckett (*Murphy*, 1938) as one of the rare young exceptions. In Paris few new artists of importance emerged; and apart perhaps from Olivier Messiaen the younger

p 231 (92)

composers everywhere (like Françaix, Khrennikov and Britten) were far less startling than their predecessors. The positive importance of the 1930s for the modern movement thus lay rather in the spreading of its past achievements, techniques and conventions to countries such as the United States and England which had so far remained largely outside it. Part of this was undoubtedly due to the German emigration after 1933, followed by a lesser exodus of European artists and intellectuals around 1939. Thus the United States in particular came to acquire the services, often permanent, of men like Stravinsky, Schönberg, Bartók, Milhaud, Hindemith, Weill, Brecht, Piscator, Léger, Ernst, Dali, Mondrian and Beck-

p 225 (72)

mann, not to mention Gropius, Mies van der Rohe and a good part of the Bauhaus staff. However, there was also a considerable catching-up by native talent, particularly in the visual arts in England, where newcomers like the painters Nicholson and

p 227 (77)

Sutherland, the sculptors Moore and Hepworth and the architect Maxwell Fry began working within the continental Cubist-Constructivist tradition, which they now extended in their own way.

In Germany (and the countries absorbed by her) the reaction was first and foremost against any art with non-Aryan, Communist or anti-militarist associations, then against the cultural apparatus set up by the Weimar Republic and the persons who staffed it, and finally against all new formal discoveries as such. On the more 'positive' side the Nazi party set out to encourage whatever seemed heroic, optimistic, consciously German, easily intelligible and affirmative of life. It purged schools and academies, allowed its student supporters to carry out a ceremonial book-burning in Berlin (10 May 1933), drove most exponents of the modern movement into exile and gradually silenced those who remained—even such supporters of the regime as Nolde and Benn—by forbidding them to exhibit or publish, or even in some cases to work for themselves. All the arts were brought under Goebbels's Propaganda Ministry, which took control of the media, setting up a *Reichskulturkammer* with seven chambers in which everyone concerned with the arts, including journalists and booksellers, was compulsorily organized. Censorship could be exercised on the initiative of Party, Ministry, the Reich Youth Leader and Rosenberg's largely lunatic office. Then came a new drive starting in 1936 (when Lissitzky's abstract gallery in Hanover was demolished and Benn forbidden to write) and culminating in a grand purge of the museums the next year, together with a Degenerate Art Exhibition in Munich which coincided with Hitler's opening of a new Party-style House of German Art there. Roughly 17,000 pictures of all kinds, including masterpieces by Gauguin and Van Gogh, were removed from the public collections in this way, two-thirds of them being in due course sold or stolen and the remaining 5,000 burnt.

The Russian procedure was based on different outward assumptions, but proved to be remarkably similar in its methods and results. In 1932 the Party abolished the existing cultural organizations—of which the most important were either modernist, like the influential architects' group OCA, or aggressively 'proletarian' —and set up new monolithic Unions of Soviet Writers, Architects, Composers and Artists. The fundamentally aesthetic character of this change was marked by the choice of a massive piece of wedding-cake architecture (by Iofan, Gelfreich and Rudnev—fortunately never built) for the projected Palace of Soviets in Moscow, in preference to the designs submitted by Corbusier and members of OCA. In 1934 the new doctrine was presented at the first Congress

of Soviet Writers under the name 'Socialist Realism', a blanket formula devised in discussions between Stalin and Gorky, who had returned from exile in 1928 and now presided over the congress. What this Ism entailed, above all in arts like music and architecture where the question of realism scarcely arose, was left vague in theory, though it was made clear enough from the first that the enemy was 'formalism'. The proof of the pudding lay in the practical measures taken between 1936 and 1938: transfer of all cultural matters to a new state Committee on Art Affairs; attacks in *Pravda* on Shostakovitch, Eisenstein and Meyerhold; closure of Meyerhold's and Okhlopkhov's theatres; suppression of Eisenstein's film *Bezhin Meadow*; removal of foreign and modern pictures from the walls of the galleries, and so on. Tretyakov, Babel and Pilnyak were among the writers shot as traitors in the political purges of those years, on evidence since recognized as false. Meyerhold was arrested in 1939 and killed, seemingly on no other pretext than his public disagreement with the new policy.

Nobody felt the ambiguities of this situation more strongly than the German anti-Nazi exiles, whose learned interpreter of Socialist Realism, Georg Lukács, confined himself to literature and never sought to explain why the same 19th-century visual conventions were being simultaneously imposed in both countries. The Germans were also the chief victims of the new Soviet suspicion of everything 'alien', among those to die in the camps being the widow of Mühsam, who had himself been killed in a Nazi camp in 1934. Elsewhere the difficulty of accepting such coincidences of policy caused the Left to close its eyes to them, though the ensuing uneasiness runs like a recurrent flaw through the apparent consensus of creative artists in the democracies that Fascism must be stopped. Only the Surrealists seem openly to have admitted the dilemma, publishing a statement against Stalinism in 1935 and subsequently becoming associated with the Trotskyite opposition; yet their actual work was unpolitical, with an increasing influence on such commercial fields as window-dressing and advertising design. Apart from them, and from the non-political Abstraction-Création group around Mondrian, Kandinsky and the Constructivist exiles, the main effort of the French intelligentsia in the 1930s was canalized through the Communist-run Association d'Ecrivains et Artistes Révolutionnaires founded in 1932, together with its journal *Commune* and the related international meetings to defend culture against Fascism, in which older humanists like Gide, Heinrich Mann and E. M. Forster appeared alongside the Communists. Whether or not this whole wing of the Popular Front campaign was politically effective it was felt to be so, and from its convictions and its commitment (most passionate in the case of the Spanish Civil War) came the decade's outstanding works of art: the novels of André Malraux, Brecht's plays written in exile and the strongly expressive paintings of Picasso's fifties, whose climax was the huge monochrome *Guernica* for the Paris International Exhibition of 1937.

Much else fell into the same context: the films of the short-lived Jean Vigo (*L'Atalante*, 1934) and of Jean Renoir (*La Grande Illusion*, 1937), for instance, or the solid novels written by Aragon

p 218 (39)

after he left the Surrealists in 1932. Men like Malraux, Toller and Lorca, who was shot by the Spanish Nationalists in 1936, became legends of the time. In England too a coherent anti-Fascist movement grew up around such new institutions as the Artists' International Association, the GPO Film Unit under John Grierson (who had worked on the American version of *Potemkin*), the Group Theatre, the Euston Road school of painting and John Lehmann's magazine *New Writing*, whose first issue appeared in 1936. Apart from the work of the Catholic novelists Evelyn Waugh and Graham Greene, and the more surrealistic Dylan Thomas, most of the distinctive English contribution to the arts of the mid-century originated here, though there was also a separate development of some importance in the establishment of a native ballet after Diaghileff's death in 1929. The prevailing mode was realist, as could be seen from Isherwood's and Orwell's camera-eye writing or from the documentary film movement, though even this had its imaginative offshoot in the abstract films of Len Lye. There was also a new school of poetry which used the phrases and imagery of contemporary industrial society. Auden, Spender, Day Lewis and later MacNeice were its leaders: men between twenty-five and thirty at the outbreak of the Spanish War, an event which became central to the whole movement.

In America too there were new groupings on the Left, privately initiated like the Group Theater, which applied the realistic Stanislavsky 'method' for social ends, or Communist-inspired like the New York Congress of American Writers of 1935. Under the New Deal, Roosevelt in 1935 included Federal Art, Writers', Music and Theater Projects with his Works Progress Administration for the relief of unemployment. While the writers thus patronized slogged away at such worthy but unexciting tasks as the compilation of guidebooks, and fifteen WPA orchestras supplied music to the masses, both Art and Theater projects broke new ground. For the former was born in the shadow of the Mexican political painters Rivera, Orozco and Siqueiros, who had executed a number of socially conscious murals for US capitalist institutions while in exile from their own country. They influenced Ben Shahn, who had acted as one of Rivera's assistants, while unknown artists called Pollock, de Kooning, Guston and Rothko were among those engaged to do murals in the Mexican tradition. As for the Theater Project, its best-known production was that of Marc Blitzstein's Brechtian *The Cradle Will Rock* (1937) by the young Orson Welles, but it also evolved a new form of lecture-cum-sketch in the Living Newspaper, of which Joseph Losey was one of the directors.

The same years of crisis were the 'golden years' of Hollywood, which had been booming ever since the arrival of sound in 1928. Whole new genres now popped up like lucrative mushrooms alongside the classic Westerns, romances and costume films of the silent era: the gangster film featuring such actors as James Cagney, Edward G. Robinson and Paul Muni; the first spectacular musicals like Astaire's dancing films or the succession of Broadway Melodies; the Mickey Mouse and Silly Symphony cartoons of Walt Disney; and the wisecracking comedy whose unforgettable masters were the four Marx Brothers. Into this flourishing mélange of art and industry, dominated by a very strange set of largely unlettered tycoons, came first the emigré directors from central Europe, such as Stroheim, Lubitsch and Fritz Lang, then Odets, Welles, Franchot Tone and other products of the new left-wing theatre, lured by the colossal rewards.

Culture in an atomic age

Except in those countries where an underground resistance to Nazism and Fascism developed, the war against Germany took away the arts' political function and broke their international links. It was not in itself the occasion of major original work, and its immediate impact on poets and novelists was altogether less startling than that of 1914–18 or even the Spanish War. Partly this was because its outbreak came as less of a shock, partly because the shock when it came, in the shape of Auschwitz and Hiroshima and the mass bombing of Germany, was too great for any imagination to cope with; the ensuing view that such events made nonsense of literature was borne out by the fact that the outstanding books to issue from the war, like Carlo Levi's *Christ Stopped at Eboli*, or Primo Levi's *If this was a man*, or Inge Scholl's *The White Rose*, were accounts of first-hand experience which no novelist could match. Most of Malraux's *La Lutte avec l'Ange* was destroyed by the Gestapo and never rewritten; Evelyn Waugh's trilogy, for all its brilliance, only fitfully came within range of its subject; German 'inner emigrants' like Erich Kästner, when they surfaced, found nothing much to say. While Cyril Connolly's magazine *Horizon* preached 'pure' literature from the rump of Bloomsbury and British critics rummaged desperately for war poets there was an outburst of imaginative genius on a much lower level: in the wartime radio show ITMA and Nat Gubbins's Sunday column 'Sitting on the Fence'.

What the war did was radically to rearrange the setting within which the arts operated. Thus in England a new appetite for the arts developed, leading to a measure of state patronage à la WPA whose results included not merely such works as Moore's shelter drawings, but the growth of the Old Vic under Laurence Olivier into something like a national theatre, and the discovery of a vast audience for our ballet. In France, whose four-year exposure to German ideas surely had some bearing on the importance subsequently attached there to Heidegger, Husserl, Kierkegaard and

Kafka, the prime anxiety once political scores had been settled (exile of Céline, suicide of Drieu La Rochelle) was to re-establish Paris as the world's cultural capital. Unfortunately, the renewed vitality of such ageing masters as Picasso, Matisse and Corbusier was not quite enough to ensure this, while the new Existentialist generation of Sartre and Camus, with their good resistance record and earnest concern with 'commitment', were a bit too long-winded and too formally conservative to recreate the prewar level of excitement. In Germany the splitting of the country made for a certain cultural competitiveness on both sides of the Elbe, but the overwhelming problem was how to pick up the threads after the Nazi defeat: something that the West Germans in due course guiltily responded to by a new, solemn and largely uncritical enthusiasm for the avant garde arts. Something of the same kind happened in Italy, where there was an omnivorous wish to catch up; though here the spirit of liberation due to the break with Fascism inspired a belated minor renaissance, typified in Roberto Rossellini's resistance films and the (Guernica-influenced) paintings of Guttuso.

In the USSR, however, the leaders emerged from the war determined not merely to maintain Socialist Realism against all 'alien bourgeois influences', but to tighten it up (as was done in Zhdanov's pronouncements of 1947–48, which criticized the bourgeois and formalist tendencies of Shostakovitch, Prokofiev, Zoshchenko, Akhmatova and others) and impose it in the countries now within their sphere. With Stalin's death in 1953 this doctrine underwent a mild relaxation, called the 'Thaw' after a gently probing, quite mediocre novel of that name by Ehrenburg which appeared in 1954; within the Soviet Union, however, nothing like a return to pre-Stalinist conditions ever took place, though at least it became possible once more to see or read some of the more revolutionary works: e.g., Meyerhold's writings on the theatre. As a result, although it was once again Soviet policy to draw the world's left-wing artists and writers into large meetings and movements on the prewar pattern—this time in aid of 'peace'— the Russian example after 1945 became singularly discouraging. For the alternative now was not the even more objectionable aesthetic ideology of the Nazis but the very different attitude prevailing in America. There not only was it plain that the exiled leaders of the modern movement had found it feasible to work but a positively stimulating indigenous centre was forming in New York, which by the mid-1950s was widely felt to have taken over Paris's old role, at least in the visual arts.

It is true that the hunt for un-American activities, before and during McCarthy's reign of modified democratic terror, led to attacks on various men of the arts for their pro-Soviet or pro-Spanish Republican conduct in the 1930s, particularly those of a certain prominence in films—Chaplin, for instance, who has lived abroad ever since. But with the campaigns of the Congress for Cultural Freedom, an organization likewise formed on the 1930s pattern, but with rather different political affiliations and backed by American money, support for experimental art came to be accepted as part of the 'free world's' creed, to a degree where anybody questioning the value of its achievements was regarded as suspiciously unorthodox. Ever since the early 1950s neither the Soviet Government nor any individual Communist Party has been able to command much support for the old kind of international meeting, while the very notion of a 'committed' art, for all its appeal in a disorientated age, has been open to the accusation that it leads to aesthetic servitude. None the less there were still situations where the arts assumed a political role, as in Poland (with Adam Wazyk's 'Poem for Adults') and Hungary (with Lukács, Déry and Hay) in 1956 or Czechoslovakia (with the Thousand-Word Manifesto and the activities of the Writers' Union) in 1968. In England it was possibly the foundation of the English Stage Company and its search for new plays, rather than the bald political events of the former year, which helped to reveal the new generation of playwrights that started with John Osborne and Arnold Wesker; certainly the notion of 'Angry Young Men' which became associated with them and one or two novelists quickly became as meaningless as it was silly. But the writers of the dominant Gruppe 47 in West Germany, whose master is Günter Grass (*The Tin Drum*, 1955), have an emphatic commitment in their concern with their country's and parents' guilt, while the French intellectual

p 107
(18)
p 108-9
(20, 33)
p 114
(42)
p 226-7
(77, 79)

p 219
(46)

p 219
(47, 48)

p 230 (90)

community in 1960 published the Manifesto of the 121 in favour of Algerian independence, and many American writers have gone on record against their country's intervention in Vietnam.

In all such highly industrial countries there has been a change in the arts' social function. To a greater or lesser extent it has become recognized that even in a capitalist economy the old kind of private patronage is now inadequate to keep the arts going. In America the gap has been filled by the growth of independent foundations, with their grants, gifts and fellowships, stimulated by tax concessions that make it relatively painless for the very rich to subscribe. In England two semi-autonomous state bodies were founded after the war: a Council of Industrial Design and an Arts Council, whose first major tasks were the establishment (largely under Keynes's p 231 (94) influence) of a new Royal Opera and Ballet, and the holding of a Festival of Britain in 1951. The latter's impact on our visual surroundings was decisive; English architects and designers became as advanced as any, while London's development into the musical and (with the National Theatre and Royal Shakespeare companies) theatrical capital of Europe can be laid largely at the Arts Council's door. In France the first notable achievement was the setting up of a regional theatre network in the 1950s under such men as Roger Planchon (Villeurbanne) and Jean Dasté (Saint-Etienne); later came de Gaulle's Napoleonic (III) appointment of Malraux as his Minister of Culture, and the provision of local Maisons de Culture or Arts Centres very much on the pattern recommended in England. Though the Scandinavian countries too have devised ingenious systems of cultural subsidy, the other great new source of patronage has been advertising, which not only became the principal employer of artists and the best-paid market for writers, but the main independent (i.e., non-state) sponsor, customer or patron of radio, television and the press. With this has gone a new and not wholly uncorrupting concept of culture as a form of national, industrial and even personal public relations.

Everywhere the audience for the arts has grown with the extension of secondary education and of literacy itself (a particular concern of the Educational, Scientific and Cultural Organization set up by the UN in 1945), as well as the wartime appetite for spiritual relief and the decline of the churches as a satisfactory provider of it. The mechanics of cultural dissemination have p 230 (90) changed to keep pace: paperbacks on the model of the English Penguin Books, international co-production schemes making art books available more cheaply, the 33 r.p.m. long-playing gramophone record (from about 1948), the state- or foundation-sponsored picture exhibition touring several countries—such things are all new since 1945. Any development in the arts is now instantly known about in every country whose cultural mechanisms remain reasonably free, while, thanks to air transport, artists, performers, musicians and architects can move across oceans and hemispheres as never before. To the new problem of leisure, which has come to preoccupy politicians as automation takes over and hours of work decrease, the arts are now a relevant and accessible answer, not least because an apparent decline in the technical standards demanded in some of them makes it simpler than ever for the spare-time do-it-yourself man (following such eminent examples as Churchill and Eisenhower) to practise an art as well as consume p 230 (89) it. Above all, of course, there is the new medium of television, which in twenty years has galloped across the world, bringing the techniques of the documentary film movement, the writings of the new playwrights and the personalities and ideas of advanced artists in a variety of media into millions of homes. Visual images consequently are today accepted quite as easily as verbal; the whole balance of word and picture in the scale of human communication p 231 has tilted. As for the cinema, the effect of TV has been to strip it (97–99) of its earlier role as purveyor of pap to the mass audience, instead emphasizing its status as an art that can be studied and practised as keenly as any other.

There has been one other great change in the framework: the development of internationally acknowledged cultures in former colonial countries. This is not just a matter of archaeology—though there have been revelations like the international exhibitions of pre-Colombian art or the discovery of the mysterious Ife bronzes in Nigeria—but reflects the growth of a national self-consciousness, expressed often in the language the colonists left behind. Besides

Latin America, where a whole crop of new writers made their mark in the 1950s, the non-white peoples now appeared on the scene, first with the French-language African novelists and the poets of L. S. Senghor's *Anthologie de la nouvelle poésie nègre et malgache* (1948), then with the new novelists of India, the first important West Indian writers and, by the late 1950s, the Nigerians and other Africans writing in English. Despite the doctrine of *négritude*, formulated by Sartre in his introduction to Senghor's anthology ('the sole great revolutionary poetry in our time'), the French language and literary tradition, with Claudel and Surrealism as powerful models, has proved more cramping than the English, which such writers could manipulate in their very diverse ways. The other arts have been slower to evolve, the finest of the new buildings, for instance, like Corbusier's at Chandigarh, being designed from outside. But indigenous literatures became a force in many of the young countries, to be absorbed into the educational system or acquire a publicly critical or publicly representative political role.

The combination of a new modernist orthodoxy in the West with a vastly enlarged audience and new means of instant dissemination meant that outside Russia and China the great modern pioneers came to be universally accepted, infecting even the other Communist countries, which largely retained their new cultural independence after the upheaval of 1956. During the 1950s the modern movement thus started to become loaded with the most conventional, official and even academic distinctions, Corbusier and Gropius being given the RIBA gold medal and Stravinsky that of the Royal Philharmonic; while more recently Moore has had the OM, Ionesco and René Clair have entered the Académie Française and Beckett has received the Nobel Prize. In schools and universities curricula have changed to match: literature courses now embrace the very latest trends, while the international style of architecture, the serialism of Schönberg and the Bauhaus preliminary course are taught to students in many countries. It is not simply that culture itself has moved up in the universal estimation but the very notion of an avant garde has somehow been canonized and made official. The academic teaching against which the moderns revolted has been recognized to be sterile; the critics and politicians who attacked them to be ludicrous or even criminal. The inference then is that originality and extremism are *ipso facto* good, so that any restraint on them has to be thrown off. Hence the permissiveness of much of today's teaching and criticism, and the unsure judgment of the new official patrons, who too often find themselves supporting, rewarding or disseminating work that at bottom they dislike. Hence too the slightly obsessional concern with censorship, which in no Western democracy is now in fact a serious handicap to the artist. The new apparatus demands extremes, and the way to them must be made smooth.

Postwar avant gardism

Postwar avant gardism then has taken several main forms, often pursuing some idea thrown up thirty or forty years earlier in the development of the modern movement and using it as the basis for a whole new trend. Thus the concept of the Absurd, which led out p 231 of Existentialism to the theatre of Beckett (*Waiting for Godot*, 1952), (100) Ionesco and Pinter, though it may have owed its appeal to the meaninglessness and blank despair at which, like Francis Bacon's new and powerfully expressive paintings, it was felt to point, seemed to hark back also to the inconsequentialities of Dada and the early Surrealists, or to Iwan Goll's Expressionist farces. The Abstract Expressionisms of the New York School of painters headed by Jackson Pollock took off from the earliest pre-1914 p 226 abstractions of Kandinsky, while displaying the same visible (77) frenzy of pictorial gesture as could be seen in such figurative Expressionists as Soutine, or earlier still in Van Gogh. The Lettrists in Paris and the Brazilian concrete poets of the 1950s, who were alike in their concentration on the appearance and sound of words or individual letters, had been preceded along this track by Marinetti, the Dadaists and Schwitters. Serialism in every art owed an obvious debt to Schönberg and Webern; the kinetic artists to Calder and Moholy-Nagy; the closely related 'op' art through Vasarely to the Abstraction-Création group; the New p 232 York 'minimal' artists of the 1960s to the 'black on black' and (103) 'white on white' paintings of Rodchenko and Malevitch. Even that balancing act between art and non-art which provides the main interest of so many recent works can be traced back to Duchamp's adaption and exhibition of such 'ready-made' articles as a bottle stand or a urinal—or rather to the fuss which critics and museum directors made about it.

Such experiments have been followed up in a very different spirit and under different conditions from those in which they were originally undertaken. The apparently eccentric gesture, like the painter Yves Klein's exhibition of an empty gallery in 1958, is now staged in the full limelight of publicity with the aim not so much of alienating the bourgeois as, however contemptuously, attracting him. To certain critics it is no longer the final work that has to be appreciated and judged so much as the scheme underlying it; in other words they admit that a good deal of art is better fun to interpret than to experience. Along with this new emphasis on art as process—very visible in the way the French 'new novelists' of the 1950s used the novel to discuss the actual writing of the novel— goes the treatment of art as an act: not merely as gesture but as a more or less unique performance, like the instant pictures which Georges Mathieu has painted in public. Indeed, over the whole range of the arts there has been a trend towards the theatrical, so that Happenings, as originated in New York by Allen Kaprow and others at the end of that decade, were an extension of painting and sculpture; poetry readings, with or without jazz accompaniment, began to draw a new kind of mass audience (e.g., the 6,000 who filled the Albert Hall in 1965); environmental design concentrated increasingly on making spaces for things to happen in; while the German-American neo-Dada concerts of the early 1960s became remarkable for horseplay rather than any interesting sound. In all this, there is a strong element of the expendable and ephemeral, deliberately exploited in the Swiss kineticist Jean Tinguely's prodigally ingenious self-destructive machines, which has infected even such static institutions as museums. Any public exhibition today is expected to be not so much an arrangement of items as a succession of more or less startling events.

Another reason why so many earlier avant garde ideas have been able to develop into substantial new schools is that technology has supplied the missing methods and materials needed to make them work. Today the painter has acrylic paints that can be applied over large surfaces as easily as distemper; the sculptor has a variety of transparent or bright-coloured plastics with which to make inflatables or multiples or blobby extrusions; the book designer and the concrete poet have web-offset and photo-setting to liberate their pages; the film-director has cinemascope and excellent colour; the architect finds that, half a century later, the wildest projects of Tatlin or Finsterlin or the Futurist Sant'Elia can be made to stand up. Around 1950 the tape-recorder became a commercial proposition, revolutionizing the audible arts much as photography had earlier revolutionized the visual. Henceforward the actor, the linguist and the poet could not only study and refine their own sounds but test, mix and superimpose them in new combinations, with stimulating results for radio drama and the kind of sound poetry originated by Marinetti. Above all, the composer was suddenly faced with limitless new opportunities, for given the necessary (expensive) equipment, as provided in 1951 by Pierre Schaeffer's electronic studio at the French state radio and the corresponding Cologne studio used by Stockhausen, he was free *f 14* to combine natural or chance sounds (musique concrète) or create pure electronic music using whatever frequencies and harmonics he might wish, without regard for traditional rules of temperament or the capabilities of musical instruments and their performers. The mathematical abilities demanded by the second of these approaches tied it immediately to the intensive development of serialism following Webern's death in 1945: formal, microstructural permutations were now devised for every element of the musical work, including time and dynamics. New systems of musical notation resulted, and from 1957 the computer was brought in, first to churn out compositions following the conventional rules, and then, as programmed by original composers like Yannis Xenakis and Peter Zinovieff, to execute new and extraordinarily intricate sequences and combinations.

This and its probable uses in film animation and the layout and

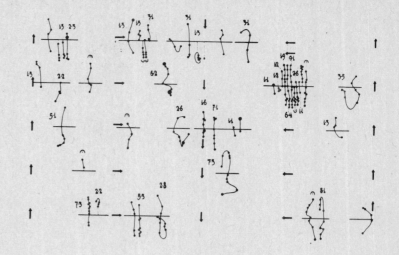

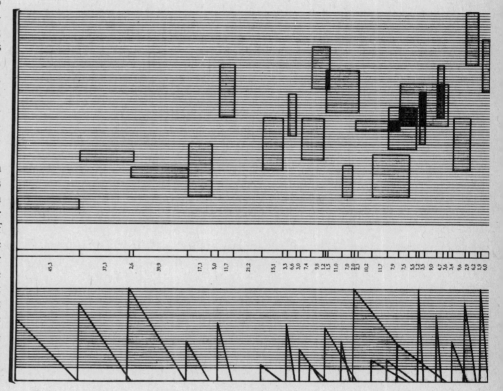

New musical techniques require new methods of notation. Above: section from the percussion part in John Cage's 'Atlas Eclipticalis', in which pitch is indicated vertically, duration by the figures. The work consists of 96 parts, not all of them necessary for a performance. Each instrument is amplified electronically. Below: part of the electronic score of Stockhausen's 'Studie II'. Frequencies are drawn along the top area, duration is indicated by the central area and volume in the bottom. (13, 14)

printing of texts appear to be the most fertile areas for the computer in the arts, though it will certainly also have a revolutionizing effect on all thought, through its application to information storage, classification (e.g., lexicography), cataloguing and searching. At the same time its seemingly inhuman capacities have come as an added stimulus to unpredictability of performance, as already seen in the Happening and the art of personal gesture. Quasi-philosophically linked to the mathematics of random numbers, to Heisenberg's indeterminacy principle and the relaxing doctrines of Zen Buddhism, a new belief in pure chance has seized artists in every field, as seen most conspicuously in the 'cut-up' writing of W. S. Burroughs (with its random collage of words) and the musical events of John Cage. The latter in particular have in- *f 13* fluenced others like Stockhausen and Boulez to bring about some kind of marriage between chance and planning, leaving areas for improvisation or accident as did the action painters with their casual splashings, the Surrealist poets of the 1930s with their 'automatic writing' and the great jazz musicians with their jam sessions and individual choruses on set themes. There is here a general reaction not only against the computer, which in the late 1960s became the occasion for something like a new Luddism on the part of the young, but against all the mechanical perfection now achieved in the reproductive arts: the exactly timed broadcast, the glossy photograph, the smoothly shot film, the hi-fi recording of the flawless performance, all artificially achieved by clever piecing-together and the elimination of error. It is in this context that one must see the 1960s concern with the total, all-excluding aesthetic experience, whether chemical or psychedelic, and its elevation of such sensual pioneers as Burroughs and Henri Michaux into semi-mystical figures.

p 228–9
(80–85)

Many of these elements have come together in the pop arts, which in some ways constitute the major movement of the past fifteen years. For they alone seem to reflect a direct concern on the artist's part with the changed society in which he lives—with the imagery of advertising, with the new mass audience and its freer acceptance of aesthetic innovations—and they have done so while assimilating many of the new approaches and techniques. Like so much else this trend began with the painters, who, starting in New York and London in the second half of the 1950s, abandoned non-figuration and took up the iconography of everyday commercial life (from detergent packets to comic strips) to make collages and combinations on more or less Dadaist lines. At the end of that decade the folk-song revival combined with American rock-and-roll, a crude and noisy jazz offshoot, to throw up English pop music, which was based geographically on Liverpool and tech-nically on the electrically amplified guitar. By 1964 the four-man

p 230 (88)

Liverpool group called The Beatles was sweeping the world with its songs, inspiring the commercial radio stations to pour out non-stop programmes of similar sound. Its members later turned to drugs, to Indian mysticism (and the influence of Indian music), to flirtations with Happenings and indeterminacy and non-art. But the barriers which they had broken remained down: between provincialism and the world, between 'serious' and popular art, between performer and audience. Not only the painters but the poets moved in through the gaps, rather as the singer Georges Brassens had done in the 1950s in France, to find a new area where verse employing current imagery could be at once original and immediately effective; the East German Wolf Biermann is perhaps the best-known example. Likewise certain films of Jean-Luc

p 231 (98)

Godard use advertising references and balloons of dialogue to make their point, besides depending on a strong element of improvisation. In all this there seems to be a development of the relationship between the arts and society such as is much less evident in other postwar trends.

Since the middle of the century our view of the modern move-ment has shifted. Not only are we remote enough in time to look at it more historically, but once the unprecedentedly venomous counter-attack of the 1930s and 40s had been beaten off there was no longer the same justification for treating its achievements in the old uncritical, crusading spirit. Admittedly there are still those, including not only philistines but some scholarly historians of the arts, who distrust the whole process and hate what they think it stands for: nihilism, fragmentation, loss of faith, contempt for humanity. However if there is an element of doubt today in the majority attitude to this 20th-century renaissance it is much more likely to arise from the problems involved in its acceptance and establishment. What are the chances of its renewing its energies and advancing further, and where, in the vast confused welter of artistic activity in today's crowded and closely interlinked world, are the vital indications of this to be sought? Perhaps nothing has made the strength of its 19th-century roots appear more clearly than the death of nearly all the great 20th-century pioneers. At the time of writing, Chaplin, Pound and Picasso alone survive, and they, like Corbusier, Braque, Schönberg, Stravinsky, Joyce and Matisse, were born and very largely educated before 1900. Nobody alive comes near to matching them in originality, stamina or breadth of influence. If we can look at the crucial revolutionary years with a certain detachment it is partly because we seem to have reached an interregnum.

Yet there is still a lot to be done to consolidate the pioneers' achievements, and ideas which they turned up in passing remain to be properly explored. What has been much less intensively cultivated so far is the collective aspect of such undertakings. For the arts today are no longer, on the whole, personal demonstrations by great individuals but team operations involving a number of specialists and communicated to the public by intermediaries, often through a complex and costly apparatus which only the community can provide. This is where the second wave of pioneers in the 1920s is of such importance, for men like Eisenstein and Brecht—or Gropius of the earlier generation—then proved able to fuse many individual contributions in realizing their vision, and could feel that in doing so they were helping to transform society. Admittedly such an achievement is much more difficult today, when even the newer media like radio and television have deve-loped their own hierarchies and can no longer be turned upside down by an individual; nor is doing so now seen as part of the artist's job, which is commonly thought to be centred rather on himself. But if the modern movement is not now to run into the sand it needs to come back to its concern not just with the self, but with every aspect of our living. Contrary to what is so often believed—at least in advanced Western countries—the 20th-century arts are not primarily a substitute religion, or a leisure-time hobby, or an index of national well-being, or some form of occupational therapy, or a protective shield against the dirty world of policemen and pollution, or an endless television show about an eccentric family. Like language, like education, like thought itself, they reach into everything we do.

XI HORIZONS OF THE MIND

Ideas and beliefs behind the modern world

ANTHONY QUINTON

'We feel that there is an inner kinship between
the attitude on which our philosophical
work is founded and the attitude which presently shows
itself in entirely different walks of life—
in artistic movements, especially in architecture.
It is an attitude which demands clarity
everywhere, but which realizes that the fabric of life
can never be quite comprehended.'

RUDOLF CARNAP, 1928

'The world is all that is the case.

The world is the totality of facts, not of things. The world is determined by the facts, and by their being *all* the facts. For the totality of facts determines what is the case, and also whatever is not the case. The facts in logical space are the world.'

It is no doubt dangerous to draw any close parallel between positivist philosophy and abstract art. No one would suggest that Paul Klee had read Wittgenstein, still less that he had understood him. Yet there is a curious thread of sympathy between the clear, definite, inhuman lines of a picture like Klee's *Calmly Daring* (opposite) and Wittgenstein's 'picture' of the world as an assembly of 'facts in logical space'. They exist in the same intellectual climate. 'Art does not reproduce the visible,' said Klee, 'it renders visible'. 'There is indeed the inexpressible,' said Wittgenstein, 'this *shows* itself. It is the mystical.' And with the famous last sentence of the *tractatus* we can be sure that Klee would have agreed: 'Of what one cannot speak, of that one must keep silent.' (1)

1930. y4. gewagt wägend

The system-builders: 20th-century philosophy has divided into two main camps, corresponding roughly to Continental Europe and the English-speaking world. Metaphysical system-building retains its hold on the former, logical analysis on the latter. For **Martin Heidegger** (left) the world is *our* world, conditioned by our experience of it, and this experience can itself be conditioned by our own voluntary choices. The supreme choice is our attitude to death. It is this emphasis on the individual *using* the world instead of merely perceiving it that has made him so potent an influence on Existentialism. (2)

Benedetto Croce (upper right) interpreted human progress in terms of the 'spirit', in which intuition and aesthetic feeling are more fundamental than reason. Like Hegel, he saw history—not science—as the key to the understanding of man. (3)

Karl Barth (right) led theology away from its tendency to rationalization and back to its roots in revelation and mysticism, stressing the 'unknowability' of God and the necessity for an 'act of faith' analogous to the Existentialist 'act of choice'. (4)

Jean-Paul Sartre (far right) took Heidegger's philosophy of choice and made it both more systematic and more emotional. Absolute freedom, rather than the acceptance of rules, becomes the basis of Existentialist morality. (7)

Oswald Spengler (right) replaced Hegel's linear, or rather zigzag, theory of history by a cyclical one. Brilliantly summarizing the essential qualities of the great civilizations, he traced a pattern of growth and decay that applied to our own as to any other age. (5)

Arnold Toynbee (right) looked for a remedy where Spengler had merely diagnosed the disease. In the process of challenge and response which forms every civilization he saw the means whereby man can escape being the helpless object of historical processes. (6)

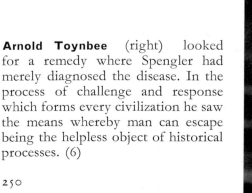

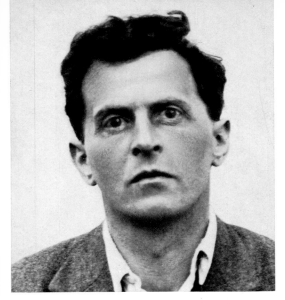

The rationalists: the empirical tradition of Britain and America, with its demarcation of disciplines and distrust of mysticism or metaphysics, has led to the virtual abandonment of many subjects (religion, psychology, morals and art) which are still living issues for Continental philosophy. **Bertrand Russell** (right) concentrated on the logic of mathematics and on the analysis of scientific knowledge. (10)

Ludwig Wittgenstein (upper left) devoted the first half of his career to constructing an abstract theory of language in which propositions were 'pictures' of facts and logic therefore an infallible mirror of reality. Later he came to reject this view utterly and to hold that language is an infinitely adaptable medium of communication in which 'meaning' corresponds to 'use'. (8)

Max Weber (left) offered a theory of history that avoided both Marx's tendentiousness and Spengler's obsession with parallelism. He saw history as a process of increasing rationalization, leading first to capitalism and then to the bureaucratic state. (9)

Karl Popper (far left) proposed a new and fruitful definition of a scientific statement—not that it is verifiable but that it is refutable. He has also contributed to political philosophy by his attack on the so-called 'closed societies' of Plato, Hegel and Marx. (11)

G. E. Moore (left) appealed to common sense and 'the language of ordinary men' as criteria for judging philosophical theories, asserting, for instance, that we 'know' the external world exists without need of further proof. (12)

A. J. Ayer (far left) introduced logical positivism from the Vienna Circle to Britain. The doctrine held that any statement neither true by definition (mathematics and logic) nor verifiable by observation (science) was nonsense. (13)

William James (left) together with C. S. Peirce founded 'pragmatism', a philosophy which gave up as hopeless the idea of 'proving' truths and asked only, on the analogy of scientific hypotheses, 'Does it work?'. (14)

251

By canonizing Marx Russian Communism effectively prevented any further development of Marxist thought. The most interesting thinkers after Lenin's death were either exiles like Trotsky or non-Russians. Gramsci in Italy, Lukács in Hungary, and Kolakowski in Poland drew attention to the attempted substitution of party discipline for the economic forces that Marxism postulates. More recent controversy with China has been chiefly dogmatic in character, turning rather on degrees of orthodoxy than on questions of interpretation. (15)

Within the Church the tendency has been towards a 'liberalization' of the liturgy combined with unyielding conservatism in faith and morals. Right: an open-air mass in Poland, complete with all its traditional colour and ceremony; and (top) a more austere celebration, reflecting Pope John's '*aggiornamento*' ('bringing-up-to-date'). In the Protestant north not only the liturgy but doctrine also has been pared down to an essential minimum, until with Bonhoeffer and Tillich Christianity becomes either a private experience or an ethical programme. (16, 17)

The science of the mind can truly be claimed as a 20th-century innovation, stemming from the work of Sigmund Freud around 1900. His postulate that our behaviour is governed neither by reason nor by accepted emotions but by subconscious desires, sexual in origin, of which we are unaware had a tremendous impact not only on philosophy but on almost every aspect of humane studies, from literary criticism to criminology. Hostile reaction was so strong that the early psycho-analysts formed a sort of closed brotherhood. Right: the 'committee' as it existed in 1922—(standing) Otto Rank, Karl Abraham, Max Eitingon, Ernest Jones, (sitting) Freud, Sandor Ferenczi and Hanns Sachs. By this date the original circle had begun to split up into heretical sects preaching views for which Freud gave no authority. (18)

Alfred Adler (above) substituted for Freud's *libido* the urge to power, born of a desire to compensate for feelings of inferiority, though both agreed on the crucial importance of experiences in early childhood. (19)

Carl Jung (above) applied Freud's theory of symbols to mythology, finding there proof of a 'collective unconscious'. Jung's goal was spiritual enlightenment, his criteria mystical rather than scientific. (20)

Freud's popular image was either that of the sexual liberator urging us to throw off our inhibitions, or that of the explorer of the dark, primitive and dangerous areas of the psyche. (21, 22)

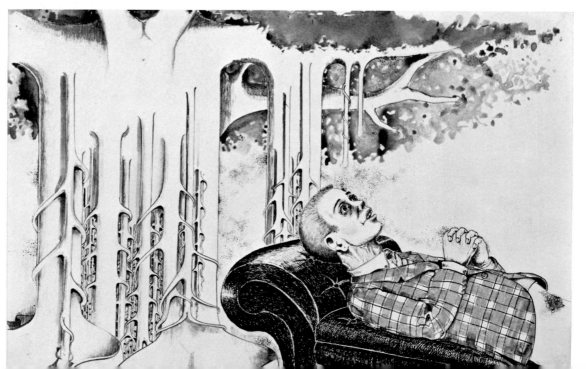

To influence conduct by old-fashioned methods of rational persuasion was an ambition that persisted, and persists, in spite of the determinism implicit in psychological theory. Indeed, the years before 1914 were prolific in schemes for the improvement of mankind.

Georges Sorel rejected the determinism of both Marx and Weber, arguing for a less bureaucratic, more heroic, society, which in some ways opened the door to Fascism. (23)

The Fabians, led by Beatrice and Sydney Webb and Bernard Shaw (above), worked patiently for a rationally organized socialist society, free from Victorian taboos and middle-class hypocrisy. (24)

Albert Schweitzer (right) won fame first as an early 'demythologizer' of Christianity, and then as a sort of secular saint concerned to preserve personal values in an increasingly depersonalized world. (25)

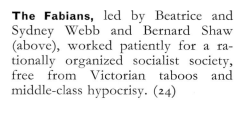

The leaders of revolt: Herbert Marcuse (right) and (below) a pseudo-naive painting of French left-bank intellectuals; they include Raymond Duncan, in the toga, and, on the right, Genet, Greco and Sartre. (26, 28)

Noam Chomsky, the author of a highly original theory of language combining psychology, semantics and philosophy, is also a distinguished leader of the American New Left. (27)

'**Anguish** *is precisely my consciousness of being my own future . . . There exists a specific consciousness of freedom and this consciousness is anguish . . . The freedom which reveals itself to us as anguish can be characterized by the existence of that* nothing *which insinuates itself between motives and act . . . I apprehend my freedom as being the possible destroyer in the present and in the future of what I am.'*

Links between art and philosophy, as we have seen, are generally tenuous, but between Expressionism and Existentialism it is possible to see connections of a more definite kind. Sartre in 'Being and Nothingness,' quoted above, makes anguish a philosophical concept. Frits van den Berghe in 'Genealogy' (opposite) makes it a pictorial symbol. Both share a discernably common ancestry in 19th-century writers and artists, and both demand not only intellectual understanding but imagination and moral involvement. (29)

Ideas and beliefs
of the twentieth century

ANTHONY QUINTON

IN THE 19th century Europe completed its domination of the world. On one level this was a matter of imperial power. On the less obvious level of influence and example, of culture and ideology in the broadest sense, European dominance of the world was even more total. Those of the great Eastern cultures that were not wholly extinct were torpid, and the two nations which were to become the major 20th-century political powers—Russia and the United States—were still intellectual dependencies of western Europe.

The 20th century saw the decline of Europe's political domination, yet Europe continues to preserve her leading position in the realm of ideas. In this respect Europe can be more or less identified with Britain, France and Germany. For a variety of reasons, amongst them economic backwardness and the intellectually autocratic nature of the Church, other European nations such as Italy and Spain have made only marginal contributions to this century's stock of ideas and beliefs. America and Russia, in their different ways, have been clients of the western European mind and have still to achieve an intellectual maturity and autonomy proportionate to their physical strength. Even the most up-to-date young revolutionaries of the United States have installed a German refugee, Herbert Marcuse, in the role of first and most coherent intellectual hero. On the other side of the fence the elements of revisionist life in Marxism, which the Russian state works so hard to extinguish, are derived from an Italian, Gramsci, a Hungarian, Lukács, and a Pole, Kolakowski.

p 255 (26)

In this study of the ideas and beliefs of the 20th century I shall divide its first seventy years into three sections, separated from each other by the wars of 1914 and 1939. In each section I shall consider philosophy, that is to say the prevailing ideas about thought and knowledge, then religion and science, the two great modes in which men have sought to understand the world as a whole, then the ideas about human nature which take their theoretical form in psychology and their practical form in morals and, finally, the ideas about society that are theoretically expressed in history and the social sciences and are practically formulated in politics and ideology.

BEFORE THE FIRST WORLD WAR

Philosophy: the attack on idealism

A striking feature of 20th-century thought is the sharp division between the philosophy of the English-speaking world and that of continental Europe. It was much less marked when the century began than it has since become. In Britain and America a form of Hegelian idealism largely prevailed, in Germany neo-Kantianism was dominant. Both schools held mind to be prior to nature in the sense that they saw nature as largely a construction of the mind and both saw philosophy as giving a higher, completer, more genuine kind of truth than natural science, though where the neo-Hegelians took philosophic reason to surpass and correct science, the neo-Kantians took it to be the source of science's indispensable presuppositions.

Around 1900 both of these idealist orthodoxies came under attack from philosophies of a realist or objectivist character. In England Moore argued for the literal reality, independent of the mind, of the material world, and Russell for the absolute truth of

p 251 (12)

the propositions of mathematics. In Austria Brentano, followed by Meinong, Twardowski (in Poland) and Husserl (in Germany), also asserted the objective, independent reality of the objects of thought and perception. At this stage there were close affinities between what were to become the remote and largely opposed schools of analytic philosophy and phenomenology. Moore's careful inquiries into the independent reality of the objects of perception owed as much to the kind of attentive introspection that Brentano held to be the proper method of philosophy as to the scrupulously literal attention to the precise meaning of philosophers' statements that was soon to become his principal method of analysis. The refutation of idealism that he published in 1903 supports its crucial distinction between the *act* of perception, which is mental, and the *object* of perception, which need not be, by an appeal very much in Brentano's spirit to the introspectible facts of mental life. In the same year Russell, in his great *Principles of Mathematics*, rediscovered the main theses of the brilliant but neglected Gottlob Frege. Russell held, as Frege had done, that logic and mathematics form a single deductive system, all of whose constituent propositions are necessarily and absolutely true and refer to an independently existing realm of timeless abstract entities. About the same time, in his *Logische Untersuchungen*, Husserl announced his conversion, under Frege's influence, from his earlier, psychologistic conception of mathematics, to one which took mathematical entities to be mental in nature. There was also a close similarity between the ethical theories of Moore and of Brentano's school. Both took values to be objective existences, known by a special, intuitive faculty of the mind.

p 251 (10)

The two objectivisms soon began to diverge. Moore turned from introspective analysis to common sense as a criterion of truth, and from elaborate self-description to examination of the precise meaning of words as a philosophical method. A number of factors led Russell away from his initial Platonism about mathematics. The discovery of a contradiction in the set theory that established the link between logic and mathematics, an instinctive repugnance to the congestion of the universe with real but non-actual entities that Platonism entailed and, above all, the influence, in the years just before 1914, of his remarkable pupil Wittgenstein all led him to conclude that the necessary truths of logic, mathematics and philosophical analysis itself are analytic or conceptual, not descriptions of a Platonic realm but only elucidations of the terms that figure in them.

p 251 (8)

A very different reaction against idealism opposed not its subjectivity but its intellectualism, its concentration on Mind, in a detached, impersonal sense, rather than on the actual minds of concrete striving people, actively engaged in preserving themselves as embodied beings in a more or less hostile world. One version of this was the pragmatism of James and Dewey in the United States. For them thought and knowledge are not abstract things in themselves but aspects of the activities of living men. The goal of thought is not contemplative truth but the facilitation of action. Beliefs and theories are human constructions and must be appraised in the light of their contribution to the fulfilment of human purposes. The truth, James said, is what works. Bergson also resisted the intellectualism of the idealists. For him the intellect is an instrument that abstractively carves up the continuous flow of

p 251 (14)

reality to make it practically manageable. In itself the world is a process, not an array of objects, and can be apprehended as it is only by intuition. Bergson's idea of real, experienced time as an indivisible continuum corresponds to James's idea of consciousness as a stream, not a sequence of atomic ideas.

The unifying theme of these activist, voluntarist philosophies is the provisional and conventional nature of our intellectual endeavours to make sense of a world which is in itself an inarticulable process. They emphasize the hypothetical nature of science and the dependence of our theories of the world on our concrete, practical needs and interests. The idea that our whole apparatus of concepts is a tissue of convenient fictions is encyclopedically developed in Vaihinger's *Philosophy of As-if* (1911). In James, Bergson and even more in Bergson's eccentrically brilliant disciple Georges Sorel, a crucial element is the falsity, or at least unproved character, of determinism. James wrote with feeling about the stuffiness of the Hegelian universe in which there is an explanation for the inevitability of everything. The real world is too large and various to be caught in the net of our rigid mental constructions. Sorel went so far as to hold that only what man has made himself, machines and experimental situations, is deterministic; nature itself, independent of man, is a field of chance and unpredictable variety. There is something of the same impatience with intellectualist rigidity in the work of Croce whose four-volume *Philosophy of Spirit* was published between 1902 and 1917. Croce was the most important Hegelian of the century but a very idiosyncratic one. An idealist in holding that participation in the activities of the mind is the criterion of reality, he rejected the idea of any final system of philosophical truth. Spirit, which is all the reality there is, is constantly developing, by the kind of fruitful conflict of which Hegel's dialectic is an image. It is essentially historical and so philosophy, as the self-consciousness of spirit, is in the end identical with history.

Croce's dynamic, historicist revision dominated Italian intellectual life until very recent years—Croce was a learned and productive polymath in all the humanistic disciplines—and had some influence in Britain. But the new movements contemporary with him were much more influential. The realism of Russell and Moore inaugurated analytic philosophy, which in due course absorbed the most gifted successors of the pragmatists. Husserl's phenomenology came to be the theoretical substructure of recent European Existentialism. Bergson's philosophy led to the massive evolutionary systems of Alexander and Whitehead but it was more widely significant in the form of Sorel's irrationalistic activism, which despite Sorel's conception of himself as a man of the Left, provided a philosophical fig-leaf for the nakedness of Fascism. By 1914 the division between the English-speaking philosophical world's conception of its subject as the analysis and justification of objective scientific knowledge and the European conception of philosophy as an inquiry into the inner life of the concrete, active individual was already clearly apparent.

The impact of Einstein

The influence of science on society is exercised on two quite distinct levels. On the one hand scientific theories affect the ideas of men about the world and their place in it, on the other the applications of science transform the conditions of human life. At any given moment the sciences that have one of these effects seldom have the other. In the 19th century evolutionary biology took over from physics the role of chief scientific provoker of new general ideas. It played a large part in the social thinking of the latter part of the century and had some effect on philosophy, first through Spencer and then, more interestingly, through the pragmatists. Both physical and biological science greatly transformed the conditions of life throughout the 19th century: physics through industrialization and railway transport, biology through scientific medicine and the hygienic practices associated with it. In the present century these transformations have accelerated with the multifarious applications of oil and electricity in production, transport, communication and the often fruitful but disturbing complication of everyday life. Above all there is the hyperbolic raising of the stakes involved in general war by the invention of nuclear weapons.

But natural science has been less powerful as a stimulator of ideas than it has in any period since Galileo put into practice that particular combination of precise observation with mathematical reasoning that is the method of modern science. There have been large changes in the body of physical and biological theory and laymen as well as speculative scientists have drawn many general inferences from them. But the greatest impact on the thinking of the age has come from sociology and psychology, disciplines whose truly scientific status has not yet been fully established. The greatly increased technicality and complication of natural science may be one reason for this fact. But perhaps a more important one is that the final authority of physics and biology about the extra-human world is now generally recognized. The chief problem of our age in the field of ideas is that of the extent to which the methods by whose application the natural sciences have achieved their authority are applicable to man and society.

Nevertheless a revolution took place in physics in the first decades of this century as great as the 17th-century revolution that culminated in the work of Newton. Its first event was the discovery in 1899 by Max Planck of the quantum of action, the fact that radiation, which had always been conceived as a continuous stream, was really particulate in nature. Another striking advance resulted from further investigations into the fine structure of matter. The 19th century had seen the establishment of the theory that different chemical substances are composed of molecules which are themselves combinations of atoms, each atom being of one of the ninety-two elements. The next penetration into the inner structure of matter, in which J. J. Thomson took a leading part, showed each atom to be made of a positively charged nucleus or proton and a number of negatively charged electrons, the number varying with the element in question and serving to explain quantitative differences between different kinds of atom. Rutherford advanced a persuasive model of the atom as a minute solar system, with its nucleus as the sun and its electrons in planetary orbits around it. This model satisfied Kelvin's requirement that every physical theory must be capable of a mechanical realization. After 1918 this intuitively simple conception of matter dissolved as a host of new kinds of fundamental particles had to be admitted and as their behaviour ceased to be pictorially intelligible.

The first major departure from the intuitable was Einstein's special theory of relativity in 1905. In 1887 the Michelson-Morley experiment showed that the speed of light is the same in whatever direction it is emitted from the earth into space and thus that either the earth is stationary in the ether or, more plausibly, that the ether does not exist. This finding undermined the Newtonian concept of absolute space since it removed any fixed point of reference in relation to which all the material contents of space could be said to move or be at rest. The main implication of Einstein's special theory is that the interval between two events is not objectively divided into definite spatial and temporal components but will be allocated differently to space and time by differently situated observers. A conception of the positional arrangement of natural happenings as relative and even conventional took the place of Newton's idea of absolute space and time as a receptacle for all physical events.

Einstein's theory lent force to the conviction of the more expert philosophers of science of the period—Mach, Poincaré and Duhem—that the scientific picture of the world is not a determinate representation of the independently existing structure of things but is rather an intellectual construction, chosen from alternatives by reason of its economy and simplicity, which does not literally describe reality but makes contact with it simply by furnishing symbolic instruments for predicting future observations on the basis of present ones. On a naively popular level Einstein's relativity was supposed, with only the most tenuous warrant, to underwrite a general 'relativism', a denial of all objective truth. But although this was unjustified two general assumptions of the Newtonian concept of nature had been put in question. The discovery of the electrical constitution of matter seemed, as Russell put it, to make matter less material, and relativity seemed to rebut the claim often made on behalf of physics that it describes the objectively ultimate nature of the world.

While the newest developments in physics had an anti-materialist

p 255 (23)

p 250 (3)

p 20

tendency theologians were constrained by prevailing confidence in the all-sufficiency of science as an account of nature to adjust the body of doctrine it was their task to interpret so that it did not clash with the findings of science. In the years before 1914 theology was dominated by the notion of Christ as a supreme ethical teacher, a notion which strenuously underplayed the supernatural claims made on his behalf. This modernist emphasis, as in such theories as that in his career on earth Christ had only the knowledge that a natural man could have, extended the diluting process begun by Hegel. It had a positive purpose as well as defensive advantages. The churches were increasingly concerned with their social responsibilities, with the succour of the poor and the oppressed, the victims of a competitive industrial society. Catholic thinkers reanimated the medieval condemnation of usury and the Anglican church was enlivened by a current of Christian socialism.

On the dogmatic rather than pastoral level the most discussed innovation of the period was the account of Christ and the early church given in Albert Schweitzer's *Quest of the historical Jesus*. Schweitzer contended that Christ on earth was wholly a natural man, that he and his first followers were all convinced that the end of the world was imminent and that the ascetic morality they

Who is falling, who is standing on the ground? Which is up and which is down? The way in which the viewpoint we choose conditions our picture of the world is the basis of this drawing by Hans-Georg Rauch. (1)

embraced was an *Interimsethik* ('interim ethic'), a purifying preparation for the shortly expected Last Judgment and not a general rule of life for the inhabitants of a continuing world. Modernist criticism of the miraculous elements in Christianity was frequent. The Catholic church endeavoured to suppress it. But the leaders of Anglican Protestantism largely accepted it, so that Ronald Knox could reasonably suggest that its theologians set about their work with the question: how much will Jones swallow?

Freud and after

Freud was without doubt the most important thinker of the first half of the 20th century. In the years before his break with Jung in 1914, the first of many such rifts, he moved on from the treatment of neurotic disorders, initially hysteria, to the construction of the main outlines of his theory of human nature. The social applications of this theory were to come later. While doing this he built up the psychoanalytic movement, and until the war the force of his own personality along with the unifying hostility of outside critics served to hold it together. After 1914 the movement came to be increasingly riven by heresy and schism while the fading away of external hostility led to the often eclectic absorption of elements of its doctrine into psychiatric practice generally. By the 1920s it was becoming part of the general culture of the age.

Freud's investigations, first of neurosis, then of dreams, the 'psychopathology of everyday life', jokes and works of art, issued in a radical rejection of the idea that man is the rational pursuer of desires of which he is immediately and infallibly conscious. In the first place, the real motivating factors of human conduct are almost wholly unknown to the agents who are driven by them. It follows that the apparently rational justifications people give of their conduct are largely rationalizations, impositions of an intelligible but false pattern on that fragment of their mental lives that is consciously available to them. Secondly, Freud maintained that the basic force behind human conduct is libido or sexual instinct, even in the very earliest phase of life (although he was later to add a destructive instinct of aggression to it). Man develops mentally by the moulding of this diffuse force into socially acceptable forms. This largely takes place in the first years of life, under parental influence. A man's first sexual object is his mother and the emotional conflict with the father for the monopoly of her affection that ensues constitutes the Oedipus complex. The rest of a man's life is determined by the structure of impulses established at the beginning of his career; the working-out of the intimate dialectic of family life can always be discerned in the style of subsequent, apparently autonomous activities.

There is a double determinism in this account of human nature. In the first place the fundamental desires are unconscious and cannot be brought to the surface without elaborate therapy. Secondly, the main lines of a man's personality are fixed long before he has come to anything like the age of reason and are fixed so rigidly that only palliative adjustments are subsequently possible, and even then only through great and costly effort. This was a very explosive charge to lay at the root of man's conception of his real nature and its theses of the unconscious domination and infantile stabilization of character seemed to rule out the entire agenda of progressive reformism.

Yet the decade and a half before 1914 was a heyday of enthusiastic meliorism which was as untroubled by the impending catastrophe of general war as it was by the thought of Freud's radical demolition of its basic assumptions about human perfectibility. In England Shaw and Wells kept alive the spirit of Samuel Butler. They combined a libertarian morality like his with the Fabian ideal of a perseveringly rational reorganization, above all in the interests of efficiency, of all political and economic institutions. Their prime target, like Butler's, was the respectable, acquisitive, hypocritical, Victorian middle-class male. In protest against his moral tyranny they demanded the emancipation of women, children and the poor. They called for the removal of Victorian sexual taboos and for freedom and equality of the sexes. They ridiculed patriotic emotion at a time when it was about to achieve its most terrible and destructive expression. Shaw endorsed various forms of progressive crankiness, condemning the eating of meat and vaccination. They and many like them displayed an intellectualist optimism as open and

p 254 (18)

f 2

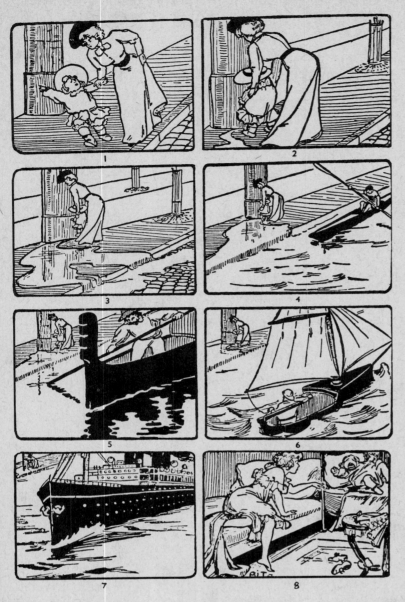

This sequence of drawings was discovered by Ferenczi in the Hungarian journal 'Fidibusz' and was at once seen as a perfect example of Freud's theory of dreams. The young mother, asleep, hears the child's cries but, not wanting to wake up, subconsciously constructs an elaborate fantasy. (2)

vigorous as that of the Enlightenment at its most extreme. In their view, human suffering and frustration were unnecessary, the products of habitual fear and ignorance, which could be removed by the diffusion of clear ideas about the possibility of human satisfaction and by co-operative effort for the removal of irrational institutions and customs. On the eve of 1914 a similarly-minded thinker, Norman Angell, argued that war is economically absurd and therefore impossible. These ideas found public expression in active movements for pacifism, feminism and vegetarianism.

Interpretations of history

At the turn of the century both thinking about society and political ideology were of three main kinds. The idealist doctrine of history and the state that derived from Hegel took the form of nationalism, imperialistic in Britain, aggressively patriotic and expansionist in Germany. On this view the nation is the prime reality in human affairs and the role of the individual is to submerge himself in service to the state. Secondly, Enlightenment ideas persisted in the earnest, scrupulous and comprehensive version of Mill, inspiring, despite his doubts, the completion of the liberal achievement of legally establishing men's natural rights by the full realization of effective democracy. Liberal and radical parties, emphasizing personal and democratic rights respectively, endeavoured to curb the aristocratic second chamber in Britain and to reduce the wealth and social power of the church in France. Thirdly the ideas of Marx, much diluted on account of the failure of his predictions of capitalist crisis to mature, together with the exigencies of parliamentary responsibility, underlay, at some depth, an increasingly reformist

and democratic socialism. Conservatism of the traditional kind was intellectually barren, and politically effective only when in nationalist or imperialist disguise. In Britain Disraeli had extended the franchise and exploited the idea of empire. The aftermath of that unsuccessful imperial venture, the Boer War, brought conservatism down in Britain as disastrously as the Dreyfus case discredited the French right. In Germany no substantial, politically active liberal centre separated the patriotic and authoritarian right from the large body of the moderately socialist left.

The authoritarian nationalism of Wilhelmian Germany rested on an idealistic theory of the nature of history and the *Geisteswissenschaften* that can ultimately be traced back to Hegel, even if neither Hegel's name nor any of his specific doctrines were honoured in Germany at the beginning of the century. Hegel had, too ambitiously, propounded an idealist theory of the world as a whole in which philosophical reason interpreted all reality in spiritual terms. His unacknowledging successors, the school of 19th-century German historians, led by Ranke, were content with a partition in which the order of nature was remitted to the empirical methods of natural science while the order of spirit—man, history and society—was held to require quite different procedures for study. Nature, on this view, is a mechanism, a field of externally related particulars, which can be grasped by the analytic understanding. Spirit, however, is organic, an internally related system which yields up its secrets, the forms and ideas embedded in it, only to a kind of intuitive perception. In Ranke's own work analysis and intuition were both present: analysis in his painstakingly detailed research, intuition in his romantic conception of the total significance of the story.

The intellectual autonomy of the spiritual world studied by history and the cultural sciences was most fully elaborated by Dilthey, from 1883 onwards, though with greatest effect in the decade before his death in 1911. Where Hegel had demoted natural science below the level of true knowledge, Dilthey admitted its validity as knowledge but held it to be confined in its legitimate application to the non-spiritual, natural aspects of reality. In man's study of himself the methods of natural science are inadequate. Human actions are not all observable surface; they have a meaning that can be grasped only by a kind of sympathetic intuition, what came to be called *Verstehen* (understanding) as contrasted with the mere *Erklären* or explanation found in natural science. Furthermore, Dilthey maintained, the intuitive significance of human actions is not something fixed and objective; it is relative to the knowledge and assumptions of the investigator, is virtually timebound. Dilthey was fully aware of the sceptical implications of his historicism and he was oppressed by them. The problem was the theme of massive studies of *Historismus* by the historians Troeltsch and Meinecke. At the same time Croce was developing a more buoyant and optimistic version of the essentially spiritual nature of the subject-matter of history.

The tradition of progressive liberalism was active in this period, as the early careers of Shaw and Wells suggest. Their Fabian socialism continued the radicalization of liberal politics beyond the point to which John Stuart Mill had carried it, but in the same leftward direction. Just as Locke's liberalism had been progressive in his own age but became a defence for established social and economic privilege in 18th-century Whiggism, so, by 1900, the radicalism of the 19th-century Utilitarians had become something like an apologia for unrestricted capitalist acquisition. Towards the end of his life, Mill recognized this misuse of his intellectual inheritance, encouraged as it was by Spencer's evolutionary endorsement of uninhibited competitive struggle, by introducing some mildly socialistic elements into his *Political Economy*. Reflective liberals at the turn of the century, like Hobhouse and Hobson, added to the customary liberal agenda a concern for the victims of capitalist class-division, for the poor, the sick and the unemployed, which became politically effective through the work of Lloyd George. The Fabians, with their idea of the rational transformation of society by a skilled socialist élite working through constitutional procedures, made this programme the centre of their policy.

Marxism, in the industrially developed countries for which it was intended, had since Marx's death become almost wholly non-revolutionary. The exact opposite of his dire predictions for capitalist society had been realized; despite occasional crises the condition of the industrial proletariat was constantly improving, governments were beginning to intervene to guarantee the workers' welfare, their unions were legally recognized and were securing perceptible improvements. Socialist parties were playing a significant part in parliamentary life.

The exception was Russia where an antique style of autocracy persisted that made few concessions to the spirit of the age and, despite the emancipation of the serfs, the economic condition of the masses remained desperately low. In Russia socialism remained revolutionary, above all in the person of Lenin who, in the frenzy of intellectual production that preceded his seizure of power in 1917, worked out a detailed theory of revolution which he took to require the formation of a rigidly disciplined and doctrinally expert vanguard party, to supply the deficiences of Marx's nebulous account of how the next and final stage of history was to come about.

Post-Hegelian patriotism in Germany, Fabianism and welfare-state liberalism in Britain and a reinvigorated and revolutionary Marxism in Russia were to dominate the political life of the world until after the Second World War. But for an anticipation of the major social and political issues of the present time, the problem of the technological society, destructive both of the individual and his environment, and the problem of the modernization of the economically undeveloped majority of the world, social theories of less immediate application must be considered. Perhaps the most importantly original social thinker of the 20th century is

p 251 (9)

Max Weber. Best known for his critique of the Marxist account of the rise of capitalism, in which he argued that Calvinism, with its emphasis on individual effort and responsibility, was as much cause as effect of the great economic changes of its age, he maintained that for our time the chief tendency was towards the permeation of all levels of social life by the kind of rational thinking characteristic of natural science and the consequent domination of society by bureaucratic élites, in place of the traditional, hereditary, quasi-divine monarchs or heroic tyrants of the past.

Another critic of Marxism, who accepted much of Marx's sociology but rejected its alleged socialist implications, was Pareto. He held that organized society is inconceivable without an élite, and contrasted the rational, logico-experimental method by which an effective élite would secure its control with the basically irrational determinants, the 'residues' or instinctive sentiments and the 'derivations' or rationalizations of these sentiments, which determine the conduct of the mass of the population. Pareto believed that élites alternated between lion-like stolidity and foxy deviousness. Other comparably Machiavellian élitists were Mosca, theorist of the political class, and Michels, propounder of the iron law of oligarchy.

Second only to Weber as an inspirer of modern sociological theory is Durkheim. The first university teacher of social science in France, he began as a positivist in the style of Comte. Unlike Weber and Pareto he offered no general theory of society, but concentrated on particular problems: the division of labour, primitive religion, suicide. He came to the conclusion that religion is the cement of social solidarity, to worship God is really to worship the social whole on which one depends. In his work the search for the functions of social institutions in maintaining the viable equilibrium of society (functions that are typically unrecognized by the individuals involved), which has been such an important feature of modern sociology, is prominent. For all Durkheim's enthusiasm for the liberal French republic his functionalism has conservative implications which have become more obtrusive in the work of his successors. In Durkheim's own work this takes the unexplicit form of a cultural critique of the isolating, specializing effect of modern society on its members.

p 255 (23)

A very different Frenchman, Georges Sorel, was the most colourful social theorist of the years before 1914, often to the point of absurdity. A disciple of Bergson and an opponent of determinism, as has been mentioned, he discarded the theoretical apparatus of Marxism while happily endorsing what he, rather idiosyncratically, took to be its practical aims. He was intensely hostile to the type of cautious, bureaucratic society which Weber had predicted and

Sorel saw developing around him. He argued against it for the necessity of heroic virtue, which could only be manifested by the still unregenerate and unmechanized proletariat who could be inspired to great historic achievements by such exciting poetic myths as that of the syndicalists' general strike. Sorel's rejection of the consumer ethic now seems more apt than it did half a century ago. Torpid decadence, in his view, is the social equivalent of entropy in the physical world; it can be overcome only by the active will, inspired, not by theory, but by myths capable of engaging the passions. His irrationalistic activism and his emphasis on heroic virtue prefigure some aspects of Fascism, although Fascism was the ideology of the petty bourgeois class he thought most devitalized. Marxism, institutionalized in the Communist world, has developed in a direction precisely opposite to the one he hoped for.

BETWEEN THE WARS

Philosophy: positivism versus metaphysics

Wittgenstein came to Cambridge to study with Russell in the years just before 1914. Their relationship soon became one of reciprocal influence. For Wittgenstein the outcome was his *Tractatus Logico-Philosophicus*, for all its cryptic obscurity the most influential philosophical book of the last half-century. Philosophy, he says, is the logical clarification of thoughts and, since all thought is linguistic, philosophy is in essence a critique of language, a theory of the conditions under which language possesses meaning and is capable of expressing thought. This has since become the governing assumption of philosophers in the English-speaking world. Wittgenstein held that a factual proposition must be a picture of the world or a collection of such pictures, when, for instance, it is general in form. The propositions of logic and mathematics are not pictures but identities, tautologies, more or less disguised definitional truisms which express permissible inferences from one factual proposition to another. The truth of 'all bachelors are unmarried' consists in the validity of inferring 'he is unmarried' from 'he is a bachelor' and both depend on the fact that being unmarried is part of the meaning of 'bachelor'. Assertions that are neither factual nor conceptual are senseless, in particular judgments of value and the propositions of metaphysics and theology that purport to refer to a transcendent world.

p 251 (8)

In Russell's middle years he advanced a doctrine of logical atomism that was a less uncompromising version of Wittgenstein's position. It identified the basic, pictorial propositions of Wittgenstein's system with subjective reports of immediate experience and argued that analysis could display all acceptable statements as reducible to these metaphysically neutral elements. The world is a system of events and the task of philosophy is to show how all acceptable assertions can be analyzed into accounts of the way in which these events are related. At the end of the 1920s both Russell and Wittgenstein moved away from philosophy (to school-teaching in both cases) at just about the time that their ideas had inspired a group of mathematically and scientifically oriented philosophers in Vienna to form themselves into a school, that of logical positivism. Carnap, Schlick and Reichenbach were the leaders of this systematic endeavour to establish the uniquely acceptable character of mathematical and scientific beliefs by applying the techniques of modern logic to them. Their main polemical instrument was the verification principle which holds that, unless it is merely analytic and conceptual, a statement can have meaning only to the extent that it is correlated with a set of possible experiences which would verify it. Carnap's *Logischer Aufbau der Welt* gave an outline sketch of the analysis of all acceptable concepts in terms of immediate sense-experience. Russell and Whitehead's *Principia Mathematica*, published between 1910 and 1914, provided the positivists with an unprecedentedly refined analytic instrument and the chief formal logicians of the period, Tarski and Gödel, were associated with the Vienna Circle. Logical positivism soon became an international movement. Ayer brought it to Britain where it soon took hold. In Poland there was an analogous, if less polemically combative, movement, led by Kotarbinski and Ajdukiewicz, and there was another in Scandinavia. In the United States a new generation of pragmatists, of whom the most dis-

p 251 (10)

p 251 (13)

tinguished was C. I. Lewis, himself a productive formal logician, expressed converging views, and the dispersion of the logical positivists from Europe by Nazism brought most of the leading figures to the United States and a fruitful continuation of their careers.

Both in Britain and America positivism remained something of an opposition movement until the Second World War. Only the brilliant but isolated R. G. Collingwood kept idealism alive in Britain by developing Croce's ideas that history and philosophy are in the end identical, that history is a re-enactment of the thoughts and experiences of others in the past and that art is the expression of imaginative intuition and not a means fabricated for ends of amusement or instruction. The reigning philosophical orthodoxy was a continuation of the point of view Russell and Moore had worked out before 1914, although Russell and Moore themselves had moved on from it to something like positivism and to an anticipation of the linguistic philosophy of the post-1945 period respectively. The reigning doctrines in the United States were pragmatism—in the form given to it by Dewey which saw the scientific method of thinking, as interpreted by pragmatism, as the key to the solution of all human problems—and a kind of realism. Loosely associated with the latter was the lonely, distinguished figure of Santayana who propounded a sceptically mitigated version of Platonic realism as a basis for his extensive critiques of what he saw as the prevailing irrationalism of contemporary culture. In the large metaphysical systems of Alexander and Whitehead the ideas of Hegel and Bergson were combined with the findings of the new physics. These imposing constructions had little effect on the course of thought inside or outside philosophy.

In continental Europe two older systems of thought had impressive exponents. Ernst Cassirer continued the neo-Kantian inquiry into the conceptual and symbolic machinery with which the human mind attempts to understand the world, and produced many massively erudite interpretations of the philosophy of the past. Hartmann returned to the old tradition of constructive ontology with something of the comprehensive ambition of the the great rationalists of the 17th century. But the two kinds of philosophy that were to prove most lively and influential were the phenomenology of Husserl and the Existentialism of his pupil Heidegger.

Husserl elaborated the technique of introspective examination of consciousness he had learnt from Brentano into a fully-fledged method, phenomenology, which, by abstracting from all assumptions about the external relations of the phenomena directly present to consciousness, reveals the essences or logical structures that inform these phenomena. The task of philosophy, for the phenomenologist, is the detailed scrutiny and elucidation of the essences that are embedded in consciousness; it is an 'eidetic science', along with logic and mathematics, and is presupposed as the foundation of all the ordinary factual sciences. Logical positivists shared this view that philosophy is, along with logic and mathematics, an *a priori* discipline, but the meanings which they, nominalistically, took to be the products of linguistic invention, the phenomenologists regarded as independently existing abstract entities. Husserl's rather generalized applications of the phenomenological method to the self and its experiences issued in the end in an arid and schematic kind of idealism, in which the objective reality of the mind's objects, which Brentano had stressed, is forfeited as they coalesce with the consciousness to which they are present. Husserl's method proved to be more fruitful than this apparently retrograde use of it. In the work of the vigorous Scheler a phenomenology of ethics in which values are seen as the structural essences of human emotions yields detailed and perceptive descriptions of complex states of mind.

Husserl's aim was to arrive at a pure, non-empirical way of examining reality as it is given in experience. In his hands the instrument he forged remained impersonal; its field of application was consciousness in general. Heidegger employed it to produce a much more dramatic account of the human situation in his *Sein und Zeit* in 1927, the book from which Existentialism principally derives. Where Husserl confined himself to the mind's cognitive activities and Scheler investigated the structure of the emotions

for a relatively circumscribed ethical purpose. Heidegger fastened on extreme emotional conditions of anxiety as an indication of man's real situation in the world. Man finds himself in a world which is not of his making and which owes such form and significance as it has to what he confers on it by the exercise of his will. The natural world consists of objects-for-us, things conceived in their capacity as tools. The deep, objectless anxiety that arises from man's contemplation of himself and his condition is a fear of the death or non-being that will inevitably overtake him. In the face of it a man can resolve to live authentically, acknowledging his prospect of annihilation and the purely voluntary nature of his choices, or he can lapse into inauthenticity, into the state of trivial anaesthesia of the spirit that comes from immersing oneself in the socially habitual interests and practices of everyday life. Heidegger advocated a kind of heroic atheism, an attitude to life in which men, recognizing their tragic situation, choose their own fates.

p 250 (2)

The philosophical split between the English-speaking world and continental Europe is still not complete in the work of Husserl. He shared the positivist view that philosophy is an impersonal, cognitive, *a priori* investigation of meaning, even if he had a different conception from theirs of the objects of the investigation. But with the dramatic, personal, emotional application that Heidegger gave to the phenomenological method the two philosophical worlds moved towards a diametrical opposition. Reaching its greatest intensity of mutual incomprehension and disdain in the years immediately after 1945, where it may be seen as reflecting the experience of those who had undergone Nazi occupation and those who had not, it is still very much a fact of intellectual life.

New models in science and religion

The revolution in physics of the first decade of the century continued for a while between the wars. In the earlier period both the substantiality of matter and the independence of space and time had been undermined. The dissolution of the basic concepts of classical physics was carried further, first by Einstein's general theory of relativity which interpreted the gravitational properties of matter as a manifestation of the geometrical properties of the space in which it was placed, and secondly by the new developments in quantum mechanics which seemed to imply that causality does not prevail at the level of the ultimate constituents of the physical world. Now that the basic Newtonian repertoire of space, time, substantial matter and causal determinacy had been transformed out of recognition, the commonsensically materialist account of physical science as a realistic description of nature seemed to be discredited.

Rutherford's model of the atom had left the ultimate constituents of matter pictorially intelligible. But Bohr's attempts to develop the model ran into insurmountable difficulties, and in the quantum mechanics of Heisenberg in 1925 the attempt at a mechanical explanation of the fine structure of matter is abandoned. Quantum mechanics, as expounded by Heisenberg or, more abstractly still by Dirac in 1930, is simply a system of equations which serves to connect experimentally observable facts with their observable outcome but has no descriptive implications about the mechanism behind the relationships it covers. One difficulty for a mechanical interpretation of the new physics is the anomalous behaviour of light: in some circumstances it behaves like a stream of particles, in others like continuous waves. Another arises from Heisenberg's uncertainty principle which rules out the discovery of both the position and the momentum of an electron. The conventionalist philosophy of science, the idea that scientific theories are not descriptions but calculating devices, seemed triumphantly confirmed.

Quantum physics reduced the behaviour of electrons only to statistical laws which treated them in the mass and not as individuals. The behaviour of an individual particle is unpredictable, it can only be assigned a probability on the basis of proportional regularities of aggregates. Most physicists took the view that the statistical laws of quantum physics are the ultimate laws of nature which cannot be derived from deeper laws of a deterministic sort, although Einstein dissented from this acceptance of ultimate indeterminacy. This expert consensus encouraged the idea that the scientific determinism which had usually been taken to be inconsistent with free will and thus with moral autonomy and responsibility was now superannuated and that there was no conflict between the findings of science and man's most cherished beliefs about himself. But this revival of spiritual self-confidence was widely agreed, on second thoughts, to be premature. At the comparatively macroscopic level at which human action is to be explained determinism still prevails.

Advances in astronomy revived cosmology as a genuinely scientific discipline, as a theory of the physical world as a whole. The earth and the solar system were now agreed to be somewhere near the edge of a flattish galactic system of stars. Beyond it in space lies a vast, but still finite, array of other such galaxies. Physical nature, it appeared, is finite in size. It was also affirmed, on good evidence, that the galaxies are all moving outwards and away from each other. From the velocity and directional properties of this expansion it was possible to calculate that some thousands of millions of years ago the material now spreading outwards was all concentrated at a particular point, in the form of a massively heavy particle whose explosion was the birth of the universe. Techniques for dating the age of matter, both on the earth and coming to it from outside, gave results broadly commensurate with these calculations of the age of the world.

The dematerialization of matter, the apparent breakdown of causality and the prevalence of the idea that scientific theories are not realistic descriptions of the world encouraged some popular theological speculation of an idealistic sort, an activity to which scientists of a religious turn of mind themselves contributed. But much more influential on technically expert theology than any changes in science was the historical disaster of the First World War with its evidence of the destructive irrationality of advanced societies and its refutation of the belief in inevitable progress.

The theological response to this apocalyptic shock was the neo-orthodoxy that first emerged within German protestantism but soon spread more widely. This movement was associated with the rediscovery of the 19th-century Danish philosopher Kierkegaard. Kierkegaard scornfully rejected Hegel's genial and optimistic dilutions of religious dogma and proclaimed an Augustinian message of the remote and unintelligible majesty of God and, correspondingly, of the baseness and dependency of man. The most important of the crisis theologians was Karl Barth, a Swiss, who first attracted attention in 1921 with his commentary on the epistle to the Romans. Barth's main aim was to reverse the humanizing, anthropocentric current of religious thought in the two preceding centuries, its constant endeavour to submit revelation to the critical scrutiny of human reason and to interpret God's actions in the light of human moral ideas. For Barth the essential fact about man is that he is an imperfect, fallen creature, whose reason is as defective as his will. In direct opposition to the liberal protestantism of late 19th-century theologians like Ritschl and Harnack, Barth argued that religious truth is revealed to man only through grace; the word of God must surpass any human efforts of critical domestication. He took his stand on the intrinsic certainty of faith and disdained the apologetics of rational theology. Christianity, in his view, can only destroy itself by compromising attempts to satisfy the canons of secular reasoning.

Emil Brunner advanced a less extreme kind of fideism, though he agreed with Barth that theology and philosophy are wholly distinct. God is not an object that we know of by way of an inference; he is a person whom we encounter. Brunner connected the objectifying, quasi-scientific character of the rational theology he repudiated with the depersonalizing influences of technological society and of the totalitarian state which is that society's extreme political realization. The social implications of neo-orthodoxy were drawn out by Reinhold Niebuhr, the main American associate of the school. Emphasizing the political relevance of the doctrine of original sin Niebuhr argued for a 'Christian realism' about society and its history which affirmed the tragic rather than progressive potentialities of social change.

Although they were fideists, in elevating faith above rational proof, the neo-orthodox were not fundamentalists; they did not uphold the literal veracity of the Bible as the direct word of God. In the works of Bultmann a programme of demythologization is undertaken in which the Bible is taken to be not a literal narrative

p 250
(4)

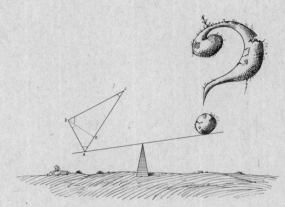

Two of Steinberg's endlessly thought-provoking symbols—the paradox of relative truth and the balance between neat abstraction and untidy reality. (3, 4)

but a mythical representation of the metaphysical conditions of human existence in the world. Bultmann borrowed Heidegger's concept of authenticity and put it to Christian use. His programme, with its likeness to Hegel's interpretation of religious dogma as imagery, stopped short at the Incarnation, the mystery of God's entrance into the world in the person of Christ.

Even the chief Catholic thinker of the period, Jacques Maritain, was constrained by the Existentialist mood of the age to wear the Thomism, to which his allegiance committed him, with a difference. Originally a pupil of Bergson, he set himself, after his conversion, to the task of reinterpreting the Catholic faith as articulated by Aquinas in contemporary terms. While endorsing Aquinas's intellectual proofs of God's existence he also argued for a non-inferential ground for belief in God, taking the form of a direct intuition of the absolute being of God.

The general retreat from liberal rationalism is nowhere more evident between the wars than in theology. The theologians' conception of man was a more resonantly personal and emotional version of the limited view of man's rational autonomy put forward by secular social theorists; their abandonment of historical optimism was in conformity with that of the cyclical philosophers of history; their notion of the dejected and inevitably sinful nature of man is close to the picture of human existence painted by the Existentialists and, more dourly, by Freud.

Psychoanalysts in schism

After the 1914 war the original unity of the psychoanalytic movement was lost. The three most notable of Freud's early adherents, Jung, Adler and Reich, went their very separate ways. Freud continued with his project of using the methods of natural science, as he conceived them, to prove the essential irrationality of human nature and its basic energies. In this second stage of his reflections Freud added a further primal instinct, aggression, to the sexual libido he had originally seen as the basic human motive. His conception of the structure of human personality settled into its final, tripartite form. Man is composed of the *id*, the unconscious reservoir of instinctual energy, the *ego*, which seeks self-preservation, and the *super-ego*, the Freudian equivalent of conscience, an unconscious redirection of part of a man's primal aggressiveness against himself, a by-product of the emotional dependencies of early life.

By this stage Freud's interests had broadened out from the clinical field to embrace the whole domain of society and culture.

In a series of works he argued that religion is a wish-fulfilment dream, that culture originated in the guilt induced in a primeval horde of jealous sons by the act of slaying their father and that the restraints of civilization are a price that must be paid if man's aggression is to be kept within tolerable bounds. Civilization is itself to some extent a kind of collective neurosis, a systematic renunciation of instinct. There are narrow limits to the possibilities of human happiness.

The apostasy of his disciples must have seemed to Freud to be a confirmation of his theory about the original rebellion of the sons against the domineering father. Jung and Adler repudiated his idea of the central place of sexuality; Reich, on the other hand, went even further than Freud in maintaining the universal significance of sex, but he did not share Freud's pessimistic anti-utopianism.

p 254 (20) For Jung sex was only one element in libido which for him was vital energy in general. He held that beside the personal unconscious, with its stock of repressed and simply forgotten material, each human mind participated in a great collective unconscious. In Jung's view the spiritual distress of modern man could be relieved by re-establishing a connection with this super-personal flux of mentality which would achieve a balance between the elements of personality. Mystical religion was one very non-Freudian path that Jung recommended for the purpose. The problems of the person are to be overcome by a more or less mystical transcendence of finite personality.

p 254 (19) Adler did not, like Jung, generalize Freud's account of man's basic energies, but replaced sexual appetite by love of power. Using the phenomenon of compensation for organic defects as a model, Adler argued that an analogous process of mental compensation for inferiority was the key with which to understand human mental life. A man's character is the instrument he devises for the maintenance of his self-respect. He may succeed, he may overcompensate and become a domineering nuisance, he may hide from his failure by retiring behind illness from the competitive struggle. Beside Freud's and Jung's, Adler's theories have a reassuringly common-sense flavour.

Reich followed Freud in tracing mental ill-health to the repression of sexual instinct but he took society at large, rather than the immediate family, to be the repressing agent and he believed that social reform was more important than individual treatment as a remedy for mental disorders. Sexual freedom, and in particular orgastic fulfilment, is the condition of a balanced and healthy life. He held that neurotic conditions are correlated with states of bodily tension, the physical effect of dammed-up sexual energy, which can be relieved by manipulation. In his last and wildest speculations he came to believe that the sexual energy which an individual must release in orgasm if he is to remain healthy is to be found outside human beings or animals as a vital force permeating the world.

Popular thinking derived an ethic of sexual liberation from Freud that was remote from his own cautious ambivalence about human instincts but was quite close to the ideas of Reich. The 'Freud' of common acceptation taught that unhappiness is neurotic and that neurosis is the direct result of sexual repression. Thus, if men are to be happy, their sexual instincts must be given free play.

p 254 (21, 22) This cheerfully superficial reading of the message of psychoanalysis was a leading moral theme of the 1920s. Traditional, 'Victorian', sexual restraint was seen as the chief and most easily removable obstacle to human well-being, and improved contraception and more emancipated women helped to encourage practical conformity with this teaching.

p 251 (10) Russell's writings of this period on sexual morality representatively express the prevailing liberalism about the subject and do so in a more reasonable and judicious way than the frenzied insistence on the central place of sex in human life to be found in the fiction of D. H. Lawrence. What Russell saw as an obvious implication of rational thought about the human condition, Lawrence favoured as an ecstatic escape from the prudential restrictions of rationality. Freud's doctrine that character is formed in the earliest years of life influenced thinking about education. The general tendency was hostile to authoritarianism and oppressiveness. Rousseau's notion of the teacher as the fosterer of natural growth was affirmed in opposition to the conventional

Following Pavlov, behaviourist psychologists hold that if the human mind is to be studied scientifically it must be measurable. (5)

view of the teacher as the dominating shaper of plastic human material. A host of progressive, experimental schools tried to put these ideas into practice. In America Dewey's milder permissiveness, with its pragmatic defence of active learning and self-discovery, permeated the country's whole educational system.

While psychoanalysis, identified with psychology in the public mind, was having its greatest influence on general ideas about morality and education, academic psychology had finally established itself as an autonomous science. The two disciplines were independent. In the late 19th century Wundt had conducted psychological investigation by the experimental methods of the laboratory and in the 20th century this type of inquiry, largely concerned with the elemental functions of the mind that men share with animals—motivation, perception, learning—was vigorously pursued. A crucial factor was the adoption of behaviourism, as a method and sometimes as a metaphysics. The academic psychologist came increasingly to confine himself to the externally observable and measurable behaviour of the human organism and *f 5* to abandon introspective examination of the facts of consciousness. The influence of Pavlov's studies of animal behaviour was important. Psychology became a science by redefining its subject-matter so as to make it amenable to the methods of natural science in their most rigorous interpretation. By the end of the period analytic philosophers were to provide this methodological resolve with a philosophical authorization by asserting that mentality is the very same thing as the dispositions of the organism to behave in certain ways.

Politics and history

p 250 (5) Spengler's *Decline of the West* was published in 1918. Its dire message of the impending collapse of Western civilization was aptly contemporaneous with the total defeat of imperial Germany. Like his more copious and professional successor Toynbee, whose massive *Study of History* appeared between 1934 and 1954, he rejected the idea of history as a single, linear, upward movement, common to the Enlightenment, Hegel and Marx, for a cyclic theory of the historical process. At the root of both systems is the large array of parallels between the present age and the declining Roman Empire in the west that Gibbon described. Under its incrustation of metaphysical paradox and startlingly juxtaposed items of evidence Spengler's thesis is simple. The history of mankind is divided into utterly distinct and separate cultures which have no influence on each other and, indeed, perilously for Spengler's project, cannot understand each other, but which all go through the same sequence of phases in all departments of cultural life and at much the same rate. For Spengler a culture has a life-cycle as definite as that of a living organism; another of his favourite analogies, the succession of the seasons, brings out the temporal fixity he ascribes to the phases of the cycle. Spengler carries through in explicit detail Hegel's powerful idea of the correlation of all aspects of a culture—its politics, its philosophy, its art, its morals and manners. Every culture begins as a heroic, epic-writing, agricultural society. At the next stage aristocrats rule and the individual artist emerges. In the autumnal phase centralizing monarchies preside over the expansion of commerce and the intellectual tone is one of sceptical enlightenment. At last, winter comes with massive cities, tyrannic Caesars, plutocracy, materialism, esoteric art and great wars. This is the age, Spengler maintains, in which we live.

p 250
(6) Toynbee knew too much to produce a scheme as neat and rigid as Spengler's. But the general upshot of his comparative study of civilizations is not all that different. He allows for more civilizations than Spengler does—more than twenty in fact—he admits relations of influence and dependence between them, he emphasizes religion as the chief formative factor where Spengler had spoken more vaguely of an ethos and an associated conception of space. A basic disagreement with Spengler is about determinism. Toynbee believes that it is possible for Western civilization to avoid the fate to which its predecessors succumbed and looks to a religious revival to stave off disaster. Our civilization is now going through its 'time of troubles', a condition from which past civilizations have partially recovered through the emergence of a universal state. The nemesis of such states in the past has been their failure in creativity: the massive integration of the social system has always extinguished the initiative of individuals.

Academic historians were indifferent or hostile to these expansive speculations. Namier, the most influential British historian of the period, in effect denied the influence of general ideas in history by reducing it to the biographies of people in prominent positions. For him, individual psychology is the key to historical understanding, and he was prepared to draw on Freud for the purpose. He and many others worked to undermine the genial oversimplifications of the Whig interpretation of history, which saw it as a progressive realization of the ideals of the Enlightenment. In the United States, a generation of historians were engaged, under the influence of Charles Beard, in a comparable task of purifying the account of their country's development from similar accretions of liberal myth. The conscious pursuit of realism by historians took the form of careful inquiry into the material interests of historically important people and has a slight affinity with Marxism. But historical materialism proper was fruitfully put to work by those, like Bloch in France, who concerned themselves with the social and economic background to the political surface of history.

In the sociology of this period there was nothing to compare with the large systems of Weber and Pareto. The most significant innovation here was the creation of the sociology of knowledge, first by Scheler, and then, with more systematic thoroughness, by Mannheim, in his *Ideology and Utopia*. Mannheim's work, like Weber's, was a reaction, by no means wholly negative, to Marxism. Marx had divided the superstructure, whose character he took to be determined by the economic organization of society, into two levels: one of the formal institutions of law and the state, the other of ideology broadly conceived, the whole array of beliefs and assumptions widely prevalent in a society. Mannheim rejected Marx's rigidly economic account of the determinants of belief but fully accepted the view that the beliefs of an age are determined by factors outside the intellectual reasons offered in justification of them and set out to investigate these causal relationships in detail. Aware that by including the whole range of men's intellectual activities within the scope of his principle of the relativity and dependence of beliefs he was putting his own theories in logical peril, he argued that the beliefs of the 'free-floating' intelligentsia, a class with no fixed, limiting interests, could aspire to objective validity. After his flight from Nazism to Britain, Mannheim applied himself to another problem, that of devising a method of social planning without which, he argued, democratic societies could not withstand the impact of the totalitarian states.

Later sociologists have continued Mannheim's line of investigation, but even more significant for them has been the development of functionalist anthropology by Malinowski and Radcliffe-Brown. Functionalism, both as a method and as a kind of ideology, had been anticipated in the work of Durkheim. Inevitably the student of society, if he is to discover anything new, must discover facts about the causal relationships of institutions which are not recognized by those who participate in them. His concern with function is a concern with the real contribution an institution makes to the over-all stability and solidarity of a social system and this may be something very different from the accepted rationale for the institution that prevails in the society. The ideology of functionalism, prefigured in Durkheim's emphasis on solidarity, is based on an organic conception of the social system in which the welfare of the whole takes precedence over that of its parts and the preservation of a working arrangement is taken to be more important than any hypothetical improvement. Thus functionalism is implicitly hostile to social change, particularly if it is large and revolutionary. It takes stability and equilibrium to be the criterion of a society's health. The more the hidden complexities of the social system come to be recognized the more dangerous it seems to tamper with it.

But although social science was becoming committed to the inevitability of gradualism, the revolutionary tradition of Marxism still persisted. In Russia, from the time of Lenin's death in 1924 and the eclipse of Trotsky, it became intellectually ossified. The role of intellectuals under Stalin was to provide an apologetic camouflage in the language of Marxism for the substantially un-Marxian p 252
(15) developments of Soviet society: the persistence of inequality, the authoritarian state, the abandonment of internationalism. Outside the reach of the Russian political police a genuine Marxian tradition showed some signs of life. Writing in Mussolini's prisons Gramsci obliquely criticized the continuing descent of Communist society into an authoritarian tyranny. With Lenin's authority for doing so, he rejected the notion of the absolute causal primacy of economic factors and stressed the libertarian promise of Marx's doctrine as a whole. Lenin, by giving the Party with its disciplined will and theoretically expert reason a vital role in revolution, had reintroduced mental factors into the essential causation of social change. Gramsci developed the implications of this tactical move and so did Lukács in his early *History and Class-Consciousness* in 1923.

On the level of practice Marxism achieved its highest level of influence in the non-Communist world in the 1930s. The economic depression that began in 1929 was of a depth and severity that seemed to confirm Marx's prediction of the impending breakdown of capitalism. Liberal democratic governments seemed powerless to handle it and the Fascist regimes that replaced them in many countries seemed an obvious pathological symptom, a last resource of bourgeois desperation. With the emergence of Fascism the battle-lines were drawn. With all the older ideologies discredited and in retreat, the children of light confronted the children of darkness. An entire generation, the most intelligent of those who came to maturity in the 1930s between the United States in the west and Poland in the east, was permeated by Marxist convictions. Many joined the Communist Party, many more accepted the Marxist view of the historical situation and its applications in all fields of cultural life: its rejection of religion, its social realist programme for art and literature. Circumstances were propitious for the popular front line to which Stalin committed the Communist Party with the emergence of the threat of Fascism. The turning-point in this involvement of a generation with Communism came with the Spanish Civil War where the real nature of Russian Communism was revealed in its brutal suppression of its popular front allies. The Nazi-Soviet pact of 1939 completed the process for all but the very hardest core of zealots and even these ranks were to be further thinned by the colonialist extravagances of postwar Russian policy in Hungary and Czechoslovakia.

In the 1930s conservatives in western Europe retreated into a frightened nationalism or approached, with more or less distaste and apprehension, the Fascists whose hostility to Communism was attractive but whose character as a totalitarian mass movement, with elements of socialism in its ancestry, repelled. Liberals, having lost confidence in the capitalist system and horrified by the rise of Fascism, allowed themselves to be drawn into popular front alliances with the Communists. Yet at this time in economics, the master-science of liberal-capitalist social theory, Keynes was devising a doctrine which made the Depression intelligible and showed how it could be overcome. In 1936 his *General Theory of*

Employment argued against the assumption of classical economics since Adam Smith that in a fully competitive economy all the factors of production offering themselves for employment would in fact be used. It is not the amount saved from consumption that determines the level of investment but rather investment that fixes the level of incomes at that point where the amount of saving needed to cover it is forthcoming. But the level of investment can be readily influenced by the government's control of the rate of interest through the supply of money. The cure for the crisis of capitalism was the opposite to that which had actually been adopted. The governments which had cut their expenditure should have inflated their national economies by incurring budget deficits. This was to be the corner-stone of capitalist economic planning in the post-1945 period. It vindicated a much larger degree of government intervention in the economy than *laissez-faire* doctrine had ever envisaged but still fell far short of socialism.

Fascism, a more ruthless tonic for the declining spirits of capitalist Europe, drew on a large array of intellectual influences: German nationalism, Sorelian irrationalism, élite theory, charlatanic doctrines of racial superiority, the Hegelian conception of society as an organism, Nietzsche's doctrine of the superman. But it produced no serious and articulate theory of its own. Its leading principles were the absolute supremacy of the nation over its individual citizens, the need for racial purity and the need for a heroic leader as the incarnation of the national will. It was the residuary legatee of all those doctrines from Nietzsche to Sorel that made will and the struggle for power the essence of human life.

The theoretically articulate Right of this period favoured the Fascists' harsh 'realism' about human nature, in opposition to what it saw as liberal sentimentalism about human perfectibility, and also its stress on hierarchy and inequality. But its élite was not aristocratic and as a mass movement it menaced the high culture that the theoretical Right saw it as its most important role to protect. Leading defenders of culture against democratic vulgarization and urban materialism were T. S. Eliot, Santayana and Ortega. It has often been noticed that most of the major literary figures of the age were fairly far to the right. Yeats, Wyndham Lewis and D. H. Lawrence, as well as Eliot, were scornful of liberalism and detested Communism, as were Montherlant and the Action Française group of writers in France. In the case of Ezra Pound anti-semitic obsession and personal instability led to a full commitment to Fascism.

One tendency in right-wing criticism of urban democratic culture in this period which was only marginally political saw Spengler's megalopolis, with its egalitarian abandonment of standards and its commercial or fashionable values, as the principal focus of the decline of civilization. In the earlier work of the critic F. R. Leavis there is a proclamation of the virtues of the traditional, rural social order that has affinities with the affirmation, by a group of poets in the United States, led by Ransom and Tate, of the aristocratic virtues of the old, agricultural South against the urban commercialism of the cosmopolitan North. A mild, eclectic critique of the impoverishment of life in urban, industrial society is to be found in the copious writing of Lewis Mumford, an anticipation of more recent and more strenuous denunciations of technological society from the New Left.

In general the period between the wars saw a polarization of ideology to left and right, both perhaps being agreed that the existing social order of western Europe, liberal, democratic, urban and capitalist is in an advanced state of decline, contains little that is worth saving and needs a radical transformation. At the same time the chief lesson of 20th-century social theory was being more firmly asserted, that the possibilities of radical social change are at once limited and hazardous.

SINCE 1945

Philosophy: language and action

The division between the philosophy of the English-speaking world and that of continental Europe has reached its extreme in the period since 1945. Communication between the two has been slight and it is not unreasonable to regard the two kinds of philosopher as engaged on quite different undertakings: on the one hand

a logical investigation of human knowledge and the language in which it is expressed, and on the other an inquiry, of a less disciplined and more imaginative sort, into the nature of human existence. There is another, less profound, division among the philosophers of the English-speaking world, which could also be seen as a separation of spheres of interest rather than of doctrines. In Britain since 1945 and at least until the 1960s the prevailing philosophical movement has been the linguistic philosophy of Wittgenstein, Ryle and Austin. It derives from Moore rather than Russell and concentrates on the ordinary thought and speech of ordinary men. In America the emphasis has been that of European logical positivism, most of whose leading exponents settled there, on formal logic as an instrument for the investigation of mathematical and scientific knowledge. Quine and Goodman are the critical continuators of the work of Carnap and, despite their modifications of his teaching, agree with him that, in Quine's words, 'for us philosophy of science is philosophy enough'. But both the British philosophy of ordinary language and the American philosophy of science have had adherents in the other country. There are many followers of Wittgenstein in the United States, while no account of the philosophy of science could omit Popper who has worked in Britain since 1945.

Linguistic philosophy has much in common with logical positivism and in both Wittgenstein played a crucial part, but they are still very different. Both see philosophy as an analysis of language with the negative aim of revealing the linguistic or conceptual confusions that underlie metaphysics. But where positivists take formal logic to be the instrument of analysis, the linguistic philosophers deny it this role. For the positivists the propositions of mathematics and natural science are the ideal form of thought and speech, but for the linguistic philosophers that status is reserved to the ordinary language that men understand first and best and in terms of which all other uses of language have to be explained to them.

Wittgenstein returned to philosophy in the 1930s and soon came to reject the doctrines of his own *Tractatus*. Language, he came to believe, is not a calculus but a very complicated array of devices for all sorts of communicative purposes besides bare assertion, and meaning is not a pictorial relation between language and the world but rather a socially established custom. The task of philosophy is to make explicit the rules embodied in these customary practices, not for their intrinsic interest but to dispel the puzzlements and paradoxes to which erroneous, precipitate assumptions about the rules of language give rise. In much the same way as Moore, Wittgenstein took conflict between the findings of philosophical reflection and some obvious truth of common sense, some sceptical argument against ordinary beliefs, to be the indicator of conceptual disorder. The main specific problem to which he applied this new idea of philosophy was the scepticism about other minds that seems to follow from the Cartesian idea that only the owner of a mental state can have direct knowledge of it.

In his *Philosophical Investigations*, published in 1953 soon after his death, he argued that the language in which we talk about mental life, our own or other people's, is and could only be public. A similar view was expressed with great force and fewer qualifications in Ryle's *Concept of Mind* in which the dualism of mental and physical is utterly rejected. For Ryle, to talk about mental life is to talk about the dispositions to behaviour of human organisms, whether one is talking about oneself or someone else. There is only one world, that of things, including people, in space and time and accessible to the senses. A major support for dualism has always been the theory, never abandoned by Russell and Moore, that the immediate objects of perception are private impressions in the mind of the perceiver. Austin brought his incomparable delicacy about nuances of meaning to the detailed criticism of the arguments on which this persistent conviction is based. Austin also reinforced Wittgenstein's insistence on the many non-assertive or non-descriptive uses of language by producing a general theory in which assertion was placed in a system of different kinds of speech-acts.

Wittgenstein and Austin were both hostile to general principles in philosophy: Wittgenstein because he thought them either obvious or simply false, Austin because he thought most such

p 251 (8)

principles rested on an over-simplified conception of the field to which they applied. Under their influence linguistic philosophy was a matter of tackling highly specific problems. More recently, notably in the work of Strawson, it has become more ambitious. Strawson sought to give an explanation of the very general primacy that reference to things and persons has in any language or conceptual scheme that we know of or can readily conceive.

Where linguistic philosophers dismissed the formal rigour of positivism as spurious and its systematization of language and knowledge as unrealistic, a basically metaphysical distortion of linguistic actuality, the philosophers of science critically continued the work of the positivists. Quine in America and Popper in Britain each rejected a central positivist thesis: Quine the sharp distinction between analytic and empirical statements, Popper the assumption that science is derived from observation by a procedure of inductive generalization. Quine argued that linguistic convention and sense-experience, which positivism assigned separately to a proprietary kind of statement, are involved in the acceptance of every kind of belief. No statement is immune from revision and all our beliefs form a single logically connected system. We should be as pragmatic about the truths of logic and immediate experience as it is generally admitted we should be about our theoretical hypotheses. For Popper scientific knowledge is never absolute and final.

p 251
(11)
It grows by imaginative conjecture and is controlled by refutation. We do not so much accumulate truth as steadily eliminate falsehood. What distinguishes science from metaphysics is that its theories are falsifiable and the heart of scientific work is the active attempt to falsify them and improve on them. They can be arrived at in the first place only by creative imagination, all observation must be guided by theoretical anticipations, it cannot mechanically yield theories on its own as the proponents of induction suppose. The important wider applications Popper made of his account of the growth of knowledge will be considered later.

Philosophy in the English-speaking world was lively within its circumscribed professional bounds but it was criticized for avoiding humanly interesting issues in ethics and politics, and its concern with sophisticated technicalities was often attacked as trivial and scholastic. European philosophy, however, was exposed to no such objections. In particular the Existentialism derived from the early work of Heidegger by Sartre, Merleau-Ponty and, at a greater remove and on a more popular level, by Camus, answered
p 250
(7)
the widely expressed demand for a philosophy of man. In *Being and Nothingness* Sartre presented his own emphatic version of Heidegger's distinction between human existence and the contents of the rest of the world. Man is being-for-himself, all else is being-in-itself. His freedom is absolute, fraught with anxiety and desperately liable to bad faith. The human individual is a self-creating being who freely chooses his own nature by acts of pure decision. This dramatic dismissal of the tendency of the age towards social and psychological determinism about human nature had been encouraged by the heroic possibilities of the Resistance years and, for all its sombre aspects, offered hope to those committed to the idea of reconstructing man and society. Soon after the war Sartre made his own basic political decision, to align himself with the international proletariat, and, though highly critical both of Marxism and the Communist Party, became a political ally of the Communist movement. Despite his discreditable involvement with Nazism Heidegger dominated German philosophy after the war. The phenomenology which had been the theoretical background of his early work flourished in Sartre and, even more, in Merleau-Ponty. In the latter's meditations about the phenomenon of perception he held that man is not a pure consciousness but an embodied subject, dialectically related to the world around him which he neither passively contemplates nor constructs but rather endows with meaning on the basis of his interactions with it.

While Sartre incorporated a Marxist political allegiance into a basically Existentialist view of the world there was also a reciprocal movement of influence. Marxists, conscious of the inhumanity of Communist practice and stimulated by the revival of interest in Marx's early more philosophical and more humanistic thought, in which capitalism's chief fault is its denial of freedom to man rather than its material exploitation of him, began to address themselves to the problems of the human individual. In the work

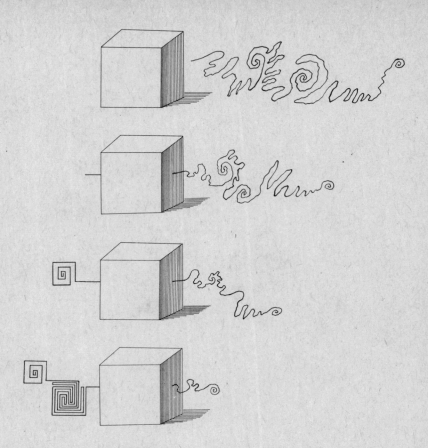

Order imposed, or everything that can be said can be said clearly—another Steinberg cartoon. (6)

of Schaff and of the more independent and profound Kolakowski the concern of the early, more Hegelian Marx with alienation, an essentially spiritual injury done to man by the workings of capitalism, is the starting-point for a more libertarian kind of Marxism in which the ultimate justifying goal is not the state power of Communist societies but the passage of man from the kingdom of necessity to the kingdom of freedom. These themes were brought into the area of philosophical debate in the West with the emergence of the New Left in the 1960s.

Matter, mind and God

The most important achievement in natural science since 1945 has been in biology, in the discovery of the physico-chemical structure of the postulated mechanism of heredity. With this discovery of the DNA molecule any remaining ground for belief in a radical difference of kind between living and non-living matter was removed. More generally it provided a favourable climate, together with less spectacular progress in working out the neurophysiology of the brain, for a revival of scientific materialism, always a minority movement in philosophy, which had been shaken by the departures from materiality in the account of matter given by the quantum physicists. In the late 1930s Carnap and the logical positivists had argued for the unity of science, both as regards the universal applicability of its methods and the derivability of its concepts and theories from concepts of and statements about ordinary material things. Even Popper, for all his doubts about the received account of the nature of scientific method, accepted these theses about the unity of science. In Poland Kotarbinski had argued between the wars that the only existences that need to be countenanced in our conception of the world are material bodies in space and time: everything else that we can usefully refer to can be defined in terms of them. This point of view now spread more widely.

For the first half of the century the standard philosophical reaction to the large departures made by physics from the traditional conception of matter, time and space had been to interpret physical theory non-descriptively as an instrument for prediction. More recently the older realistic interpretation of the ultimate and not directly perceptible constituents of nature as genuine physical things has been reaffirmed. In the spirit of Einstein's hostility to the idea that quantum physics is the final level of scientific explanation both philosophers, such as Popper, and physicists, such as

Bohm, holding science to be incompletable, take its theories to be, as they seem, a literal account of the fine structure of the world.

The phenomenon of mind, whose immateriality is central to the Platonic and Cartesian tradition that has always been the philosophical orthodoxy of the West, is the main stumbling-block to materialism. The progress of neurophysiology encouraged the hypothesis that to every mental state a distinguishable condition of the brain would be found to correspond, and in the past few years a number of philosophers, the Australian 'central state materialists' and also Quine in the United States, have come to hold that the mental state and its cerebral correlate are the very same thing, conceived in different ways, just as a lightning-flash is literally identical with a discharge of electricity. The mental states which linguistic philosophers had defined in terms of behaviour, the new materialists attributed to inner, neural and still largely unknown causes.

There were various kinds of resistance within philosophy to the materialist conception of man, as one kind of natural object among others, amenable to the methods of science. Even linguistic philosophers, despite their behaviourist analysis of mind, held that human actions were not natural events that could be causally explained since they have reasons rather than causes. Wittgenstein's theory of action implies that there can be really no such thing as a science of man, psychological or sociological. Existentialists, of course, even when atheistic, were much more radically opposed to materialism. Their conviction of the absoluteness of the distinction between man and everything else in the world is a more intense and dramatic dualism than that embodied in the tradition of Plato and Descartes.

Since 1945 theology has continued to draw heavily on Existentialism, the source of much in Protestant neo-orthodoxy between the wars. The element of desperation in Barth's fideism was more open and unconcealed in the work of Bonhoeffer which became influential after his death at the hands of the Nazis at the age of thirty-nine. In his view secularization has now wholly displaced religion as a cultural force. But this does not mean the end of Christianity; rather it clears away all the familiar, more or less idolatrous obstacles that institutional religion has put in the way of man's encounter with Christ. Christianity is not in essence either an institutional allegiance or a transcendent metaphysics; it is a personal experience to be sustained by the secret discipline of prayer.

In the later writings of Tillich there is a more genial, nebulous discarding of excess theological baggage. Faith is simply the ultimate concern that all but the most vapid and trivial of men must experience. A personal God is just a symbol of the Ultimate that is the object of this concern, an apt one since personality, human existence is man's primary point of contact with reality, certainly much more adequate than idolatrous, secular conceptions of the ultimate, a state, a party or a class.

Tillich's extreme etherealization of the content of Christian faith comes near in its effects to the more direct, less diaphanous reinterpretations inspired by analytic philosophy, more specifically by the linguistic philosophers' recognition that there are other uses of language besides the verifiable assertion to which alone positivists accord significance. This line of thought led to the very radical conclusion that religious utterances are not statements claiming truth but are disguised ethical resolutions, moral imperatives addressed to oneself. With this, Christianity ceases to be a matter of belief strictly so called and becomes a moral policy.

The limits of rationality
Since 1945 academic psychology has finally settled down as the scientific study of behaviour, a co-operative, cumulative undertaking, conducted with the full rigour of scientific method. In its inquiries the continuity between human and animal behaviour is assumed and the attempt is made to develop theories that apply to all the higher types of organism. In general, psychology conceived in this way concentrates on the more elemental aspects of human behaviour such as learning and perception. Hull sought to present the theory of learning with the kind of logical explicitness and articulateness to be found in geometry or physics.

A representative and influential figure of the period has been

Skinner, the psychological ally of the more scientistic philosophers, who has applied a rigorously behaviouristic method to a wide range of mental phenomena, including the learning and use of language. He has made it a principle to avoid postulating any internal mechanisms between the observable stimuli which impinge on organisms and the observable responses that the organisms make to them. In so far as psychologists of this school admit that there are intermediating factors between stimulus and response they look to the physiology of the nervous system to supply them, for these are as much accessible in principle to public observation as the circumstances and manifestations of behaviour that they connect. This methodological abstemiousness in no way undermined the confidence of behaviourists in the applicability in practice of their findings. Skinner himself went so far as to sketch a fictional utopia in his *Walden Two*, an account of a community whose members' behaviour had been conditioned to bring about complete social adjustment.

Greek philosophers had designated rationality as the distinguishing attribute of man, and for the Greeks there was an intimate connection between rationality and the ability to use language. Recent behaviouristic psychology of language had supposed that the mastery of language is something that is acquired by a straightforward conditioning process. It seemed to follow from their account of the matter that there would be no great difficulty in devising mechanical methods for the translation of one language into another. But the hopes entertained about this obviously useful project were frustrated in practice and were soon subjected to a deep-seated theoretical critique by Chomsky. Broadly speaking there was a widely hostile response to the behaviouristic conception of man as a machine. Yet technical developments in which complex human activities of calculation were duplicated or even improved upon by such pieces of electronic machinery as computers lent force to the behaviourist position.

Chomsky's critique of behaviourism was all the more effective for being made from as uncompromisingly scientific a standpoint as the behaviourists' own. His starting-point was the fact that every language-user can construct and understand sentences that neither he nor anyone else has come across before. The rules of the generative grammar that underlie this creative power, which practically all human beings manifest very early in life, are vastly more complicated than behaviourism suggested. Chomsky drew a distinction between the deep and surface structure of language and inserted the complexity involved between them, arguing that although all languages had the same deep structure, their surface structures were bewilderingly various. An inference he drew from these grammatical inquiries was that the human mind had elaborate innate dispositions which are common to the whole species. This conclusion had a threefold significance: it was a deliberate departure from the programmatic empiricism of the behaviourists; it conflicted with the relativistic theory advanced by some influential students of language which held that languages, and thus the conceptions of the world associated with them, could differ so fundamentally as to be radically untranslatable; and it gave some support to the moral conviction of the unity of mankind which may be thought to inspire Chomsky's furious hostility to American policy towards people of other races outside and inside its borders. Chomsky, the most intellectually distinguished member of the New Left, came from just that scientific élite whose amoral use of scientific knowledge was one of the New Left's basic targets.

The psychoanalytic side of the study of the human mind also developed in a manner that was highly critical of the moral and political *status quo* in the West. At a time when the psychoanalytic profession generally had come to be as normal a supplier of service to better-off Americans as the practitioners of physical medicine there arose a line of fundamental criticism of the assumptions under which psychiatrists were carrying on their work of adjusting people to their society. Norman O. Brown went on from the last speculations of Freud about the neurotic character of civilization and sought to correct them in a utopian way. Freud had seen the achievement of genital sexuality as a condition of maturity. Brown held that the problematic nature of human personality, its aggression, its inability to come to terms with the fact of death, could be overcome by re-establishing the continuity between man and

p 255 (27)

The modern cure of souls: 'Either he thinks he's sinned and is coming to you, or he hasn't managed to and is coming to me.' (7)

nature that is present at the stage in very early life where what Freud called 'polymorphous perversity' reigned. Brown drew heavily on the work of another speculative psychologist, Eric Erikson, whose imaginative exploration of the anxieties generated in the child's acquisition of an identity amounted to a critique of the oppressiveness of society's methods of upbringing and education. A comparable utopian Freudianism to Brown's is associated with the social doctrines of Herbert Marcuse. Most extreme of all is R. D. Laing, who with great insight listened to the broken utterances of schizophrenics which had hitherto been dismissed as anguished babble, and concluded that it is rather society than those whom it sequesters as lunatics that is mad.

p 255 (26)

At the end of the war the experiences of the Resistance on the continent of Europe provided an answering response to the call of Sartre for a morality of commitment. But in the 1950s two factors encouraged a widespread return from principled involvement with public issues to a life-style of private pleasure and fulfilment. On the one hand the record of Stalinism, confirmed by its continuing policies, produced an unusually complete measure of political consensus. At the same time the remarkable recovery of Western societies, in which capitalist production was guided by the state and its social failures compensated for by large-scale welfare programmes, brought about an increase of relative affluence which restored confidence in the mode of organization of society. The character-structure of the period was delineated in Reisman's account of the 'other-directed' personality, the individual whose aim is to adjust, to get on well with his fellows, who designs his style of life in conformity with the fashions authorized by commercial advertising and who seeks to enjoy the opportunities society provides for him rather than to change it in accordance with ideal principles to which he is committed in the manner of the older, 'inner-directed' type of man.

A new generation coming to maturity in the 1960s took affluence for granted. Its members had no memories of depression and war and so none of their elders' suspicions of ideological principle. Prosperity and widened educational opportunities made a kind of bohemianism that had formerly been a privilege of the few available to the young *en masse*. For it was through the bohemian symbols of colourful and elaborately decorative or elaborately debilitated clothing, along with drug-taking, orgiastic rituals and other techniques of defiance that they expressed their hostility to the society their elders had prepared for them. At the front of their minds was not its technological profuseness but its technological constraints and menaces. They saw mixed-capitalist society as a

dehumanizing machine and rejected its liberal-individualist ideal of self-perfection for more communal, or even tribal, notions of fulfilment.

Industrial society and its future

In the years just after the war there was a reaction against large-scale theories of historical change which drew its emotional strength from the idea that such prophetic doctrines are the intellectual foundation of totalitarianism. The kind of certainty about the future claimed by Spengler and Marx was seen as a ready justification for the ruthlessness of totalitarian societies, Fascist or Marxist, in ensuring the compliance of their members to the supposedly known requirements of history.

Collingwood's attack on the notion of a general science of history came out posthumously in 1946. Identifying the kind of historical metaphysics he opposed with the positivist assumption that all inquiries should follow the methods of science, he argued that human actions, as embodiments of reason, cannot be systematically brought under causal law. In Popper's attack on historicism, as he called it, it was rather false views about the methods of science that were held to blame. Thus, paradoxically, Collingwood used Hegelian premises to discredit one of Hegel's most important projects, and Popper applied his findings from the study of science, in particular that science grows through human creativity, to set limits to the application of its methods. Berlin, like Popper, saw doctrines of historical inevitability as in fundamental conflict with liberalism, but rested his objection to them on their incompatibility with the moral autonomy of man.

p 251 (11)

In the actual practice of history, rather than reflection about it, the influence of Marxism persisted, even if it was, to a large extent, Marxism as a method of historical understanding and not Marxism as an ideology. Generally the retreat from merely political history continued. Sociology, economics and geography were laid under contribution to enlarge the scope of historical explanation beyond the area of purely personal desire and decision. The unification of the world brought about by modern techniques of communication led to an increase of interest in the history of non-European peoples.

Sociological theory was dominated by Americans, in particular by Parsons, in whom functionalist emphasis on social equilibrium was expressed in abstractly theoretical terminology, and by Merton. The assumptions of functionalism, above all that social conflict was a pathological state and not at once the normal case and the essential source of social change, were challenged by Mills, a lively but superficial Marxist. His own concept of the power élite prepared the way for the prevalence in the vocabulary of popular dissent of the notion of the Establishment.

In the early 1940s a number of social theorists had reflected on the failure of Marx's social prophecies to mature. At a popular level there was Burnham's thesis that it was a managerial and not a proletarian revolution that was bringing capitalism to an end. Burnham went on, by way of a strenuously 'realistic' Machiavellianism, derived from Pareto, to become an embattled defender of American capitalism. Schumpeter went beyond the recognition that capitalism had failed to succumb in accordance with Marx's predictions because its new styles of organization had improved the condition of the workers and had brought into being a large new technical and managerial class with a strong interest in its continuance. He held that the entrepreneurial function was now being institutionally rationalized along the lines indicated by Weber and he described a neo-capitalism of great corporations which are in a position to take over the tasks of investment and innovation and to deprive them of risk. Aron's concept of 'industrial society' was the culmination of this line of thought, a concept that is exemplified both by the neo-capitalist welfare states of the West and the planned economies of the Communist world. In both, the productive relations, which Marx had seen as the basic causal factor in social change, lodge ultimate power in a technically rational Weberian bureaucracy.

The notion of industrial society as the underlying structure of all economically advanced nations played some part in supporting both the thesis of inevitable convergence between the West and the Communist world and the idea that society's self-understanding is sufficiently advanced for ideological myth to be dispensed with. In the work of thinkers like Dahl, political science achieved something very close to complete freedom from ideology: it became a pure and neutral description of the ways in which power is distributed and used. In the English-speaking world it was often asserted, with more or less enthusiasm, that political theory in the traditional manner was dead, as a consequence of the putting into practice in the social sciences of the positivist distinction between the scientific and the normative. Only a rather solitary Marxist, the Canadian Macpherson, argued that the premises of liberal-individualist social theory, derived from Hobbes and Locke, were not absolute truths but embodied questionable moral assumptions, appropriate to the possessive market society in which they were adopted.

In Europe, however, a more ideological style of social theory prevailed. Camus and Hannah Arendt (a German living in America) based impassioned defences of classic liberalism on a more or less Existentialist basis. Its insistence on the person which led Sartre to fellow-travelling with the Communist Party, led them, more consistently, to a vigorous reaffirmation, on wholly new grounds, of the values of the Enlightenment. The most striking development in anthropology in the postwar years, the structuralism of Lévi-Strauss, was also European, and its ideological potential was soon realized. Lévi-Strauss sought to interpret the features of the customs and institutions of primitive societies that seemed most particularly primitive and irrational to the observer from an advanced society as serving a real purpose, an essentially communicative or linguistic one, in the lives of the societies in question. There is an analogy between this and the work of Chomsky: both theories support the idea of the essential unity of mankind as against the flattering convictions of progress and superiority generally entertained in the technically advanced West.

The defeat of Fascism and the continuing and now universally recognized brutality of Stalin's Communism awoke the Left in western Europe and America from the illusions that had made the popular front possible. Popper derived from his critique of historicism a doctrine of gradual reform by small and gradual steps

that in its repudiation of large-scale schemes of social transformation had much in common with the firmly unregenerate individualism of Hayek and Oakeshott's revival of Burke's belief that politics is a matter of experienced skill not of abstract rational theory. Even social democrats looked to Schumpeter rather than Marx for an understanding of the possibilities of social improvement.

But if the Marx of *Das Kapital* was disregarded, interest awoke in the 1950s in the earlier, more humanistic and philosophical Marx with his doctrine of alienation and his insistence on creative freedom, rather than material equality, as the goal of socialism. The early Marx was a tactical necessity for the heretical leftist intellectuals of eastern Europe as a warrant for the theological propriety of their revisionism. For the western New Left, who took up where the eastern revisionists were compelled to leave off by state power, it served to rescue Marx from the moral pollution to which his Russian exponents had submitted him. For some time the chief inspirer of the New Left was Herbert Marcuse, one of a group of metaphysically inclined Marxist thinkers in Germany in the 1930s who combined a Hegelian version of Marxism, in which economic determinism was removed from the foreground, with an interest in Freud. In recent years Marcuse's thought has turned from utopianism to a resonant despair, induced by what he sees as the irresistible power of a revived capitalism to induce a spurious satisfaction by a profusion of material advantages in the masses that it basically, and in a more spiritual sense, exploits and oppresses.

p 255 (26)

Marcuse is the leading Marxist contributor to a swelling chorus of denunciation of technological society. Its material benefits are held to be bought at the cost of a thoroughgoing dehumanization in which men are absorbed into organizations, dominated by the apparently advantageous technical processes they have initiated without a realization of their indirect effects. Most extreme and uncompromising of these protesters is Jacques Ellul. Their theme of the seemingly irreversible tendency to pollution of the natural environment, waste of resources, trivialization of work and degradation of the city, an over-all syndrome of deterioration produced by the autonomous mechanism of material production, has come to be the fundamental thesis of radical dissenters, as being the underlying source of the more specific political offences of imperialism and oppression of classes and minorities which call forth the demonstrative energies of dissent.

There is one prominent exception to this widely diffused desperation about the future: Marshall McLuhan, the Canadian theorist of communications. McLuhan sees mankind at a major turning-point in history. The period that Marx calls capitalist he calls 'linear' or 'print-oriented'. It is the epoch of the printed book, privacy, individualism. We are, in his view, now passing into a new tribal epoch, in which the whole planet is brought, by the agency of electronic communications, with their instantaneous transmission of knowledge from any part of the world to any other, into a single 'global village' where a new, physically intimate, depersonalized style of essentially communal living will prevail. At times McLuhan protests his personal fondness for the older order, but the bewildering jocularity of his account of the next stage of history seems full of enthusiasm. The lack of consecutiveness in much of his reasoning is at least congruous with his thesis that consecutive reasoning has had its day. Whatever its value as a general prophecy, his new tribalism is an apt enough description of the life-style of the more adventurous and excited members of a generation younger than his own. In at once predicting and endorsing it he has at least identified the crucial issue between the generations, that of the preservation of the unique, rational, self-conscious human individual, which under all differences of doctrine has hitherto been the assumed definition of the nature of man since Greek philosophy and Christian theology combined in the formation of the Western mind.

XII SCIENCE COMES OF AGE

Achievements . . . and responsibilities

STEPHEN TOULMIN

'The way in which the persecution of Galileo has
been remembered is a tribute to the quiet commencement
of the most intimate change in outlook which the
human race had yet encountered.
Since a babe was born in a manger, it may
be doubted whether so great a thing has
happened with so little stir.'

ALFRED NORTH WHITEHEAD

The coming of age of science

has been among the most distinctive features of the 20th century. The programme proclaimed in the 17th century—to arrive by hypothesis, observation and experiment at an understanding of nature's laws and an ability to manipulate them for man's advantage —has been put into practice and has abundantly yielded the results that Francis Bacon had predicted. Yet, along with its achievements as a means of discovering new truths about the physical universe, there have emerged also new perils and responsibilities, as the very scale of intellectual and technological success has revealed the limits of Man's own world.

The history of science goes hand in hand with that of technology. Today, as research is geared to attack particular problems, and as new knowledge comes increasingly to depend upon their solution, scientific advance in many fields is a straightforward consequence of improvements in the technique of investigation. The new worlds of the immensely large and the minutely small which have been revealed in this century are due to a very great extent to modern telescopes and microscopes. Both extremes are illustrated opposite.

The Mount Palomar telescope (large picture), begun in the early thirties, was until recently the most powerful optical instrument in the world. The pyrex mirror disc, nearly seventeen feet in diameter, the largest single piece of glass ever cast, took ten months to cool and then several years of careful polishing to give it the required precision. Mounted in its movable cradle and installed in the observatory on Mount Palomar, California, it has enabled astronomers to see more than twice as far into space as had been possible previously.

The electron microscope (inset) reveals objects which are too small for any magnification to make optically visible. It operates by directing a beam of electrons, with a wavelength less than that of light, at an object (this is happening in the vertical tube), and the pattern thus obtained is projected on to a screen rather like a television picture. This instrument, the Emma-4, combines electron microscope with X-ray micro-analyser. (1, 2)

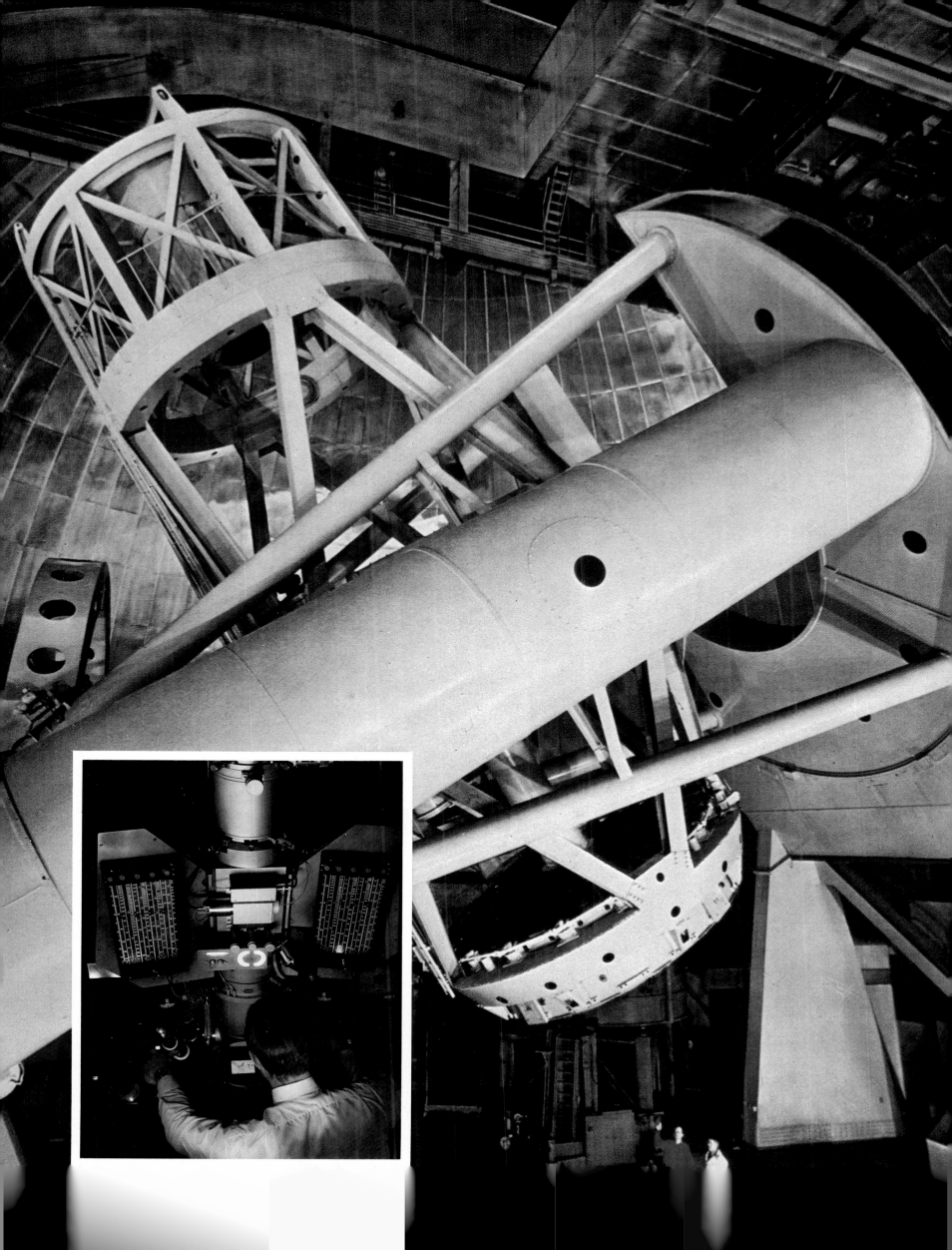

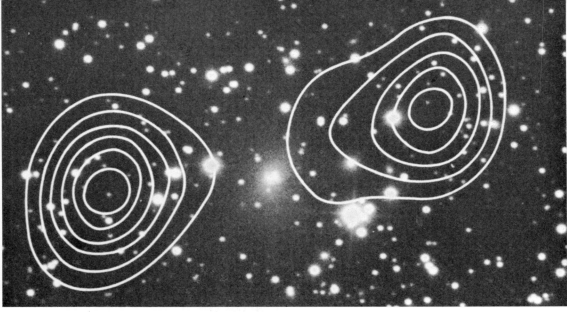

A new eye, the radio telescope, which 'sees' radio emissions instead of light, is giving astronomers a novel picture of the universe. The Crab nebula (above left) is the remains of a stellar explosion which took place about 3 000 BC — its light was observed by Chinese astronomers when it reached the earth some 4 000 years later, and its radio 'noise' is still being picked up. Above right: a radio contour-map of Cygnus A; strangely, the strongest radio emissions do not correspond in position with the visible. Below: the radio telescope of Jodrell Bank, England, the largest steerable instrument in the world. (3–5)

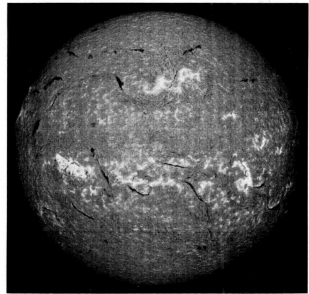

Our sun has been measured, analyzed and photographed by astronomers until its main structure and the source of its energy are fairly well understood. In the red light emitted by its hydrogen (left) it looks like a solid sphere. It is in fact a mass of gases 864,000 miles in diameter, producing immense amounts of light, heat and ultra-violet radiation through the fusion of hydrogen to form helium. (6)

Our galaxy, the Milky Way, is a disc-shaped spiral of stars, about 100,000 light-years in diameter, rotating on its own axis. Our sun, with its attendant planets, is located towards the rim of the disc. We see part of it, edge-on (below), as a belt of pale light across the night sky. (7)

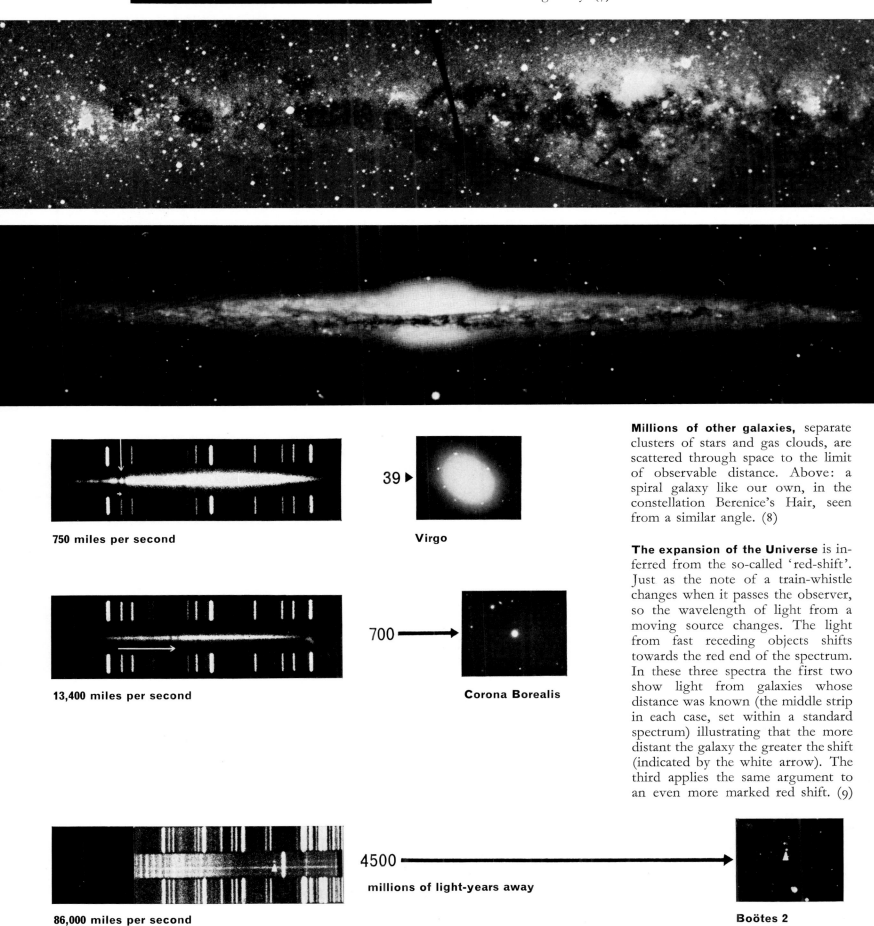

750 miles per second

39 ▶

Virgo

13,400 miles per second

700

Corona Borealis

86,000 miles per second

4500 ⟶ **millions of light-years away**

Boötes 2

Millions of other galaxies, separate clusters of stars and gas clouds, are scattered through space to the limit of observable distance. Above: a spiral galaxy like our own, in the constellation Berenice's Hair, seen from a similar angle. (8)

The expansion of the Universe is inferred from the so-called 'red-shift'. Just as the note of a train-whistle changes when it passes the observer, so the wavelength of light from a moving source changes. The light from fast receding objects shifts towards the red end of the spectrum. In these three spectra the first two show light from galaxies whose distance was known (the middle strip in each case, set within a standard spectrum) illustrating that the more distant the galaxy the greater the shift (indicated by the white arrow). The third applies the same argument to an even more marked red shift. (9)

The components of matter are now seen in a way totally different from that prevailing before 1900. No longer does it make sense to ask for a 'model' of the atom. According to Rutherford it consisted of a positively charged nucleus with negatively charged electrons orbiting round it. Using relatively simple apparatus (left) he found that the nucleus of a nitrogen atom could be broken up by bombarding it with a form of radioactive energy called Alpha rays.

Below: the modern apparatus for doing roughly the same thing — the two-mile long Stanford accelerator, California. Here electrons are accelerated by means of magnetic 'boosters' to nearly the speed of light before colliding with and shattering the nuclei of stationary atoms and releasing energy. (10, 11)

Atoms at peace: the first self-sustaining nuclear chain-reaction was achieved in 1942, using uranium. By insulating the reacting material and carefully regulating the rate of fission, the energy released can be used as a source of heat and thus of industrial power. Left: a French nuclear power station at Chinon. (12)

Atoms at war: if the chain-reaction is allowed to proceed unchecked, the result is the almost instantaneous fission of all the uranium, or plutonium, present—an explosion millions of times greater than dynamite (above). In 1945, the so-called 'fall-out' of radioactive material, with its long-term biological effects, had been only dimly foreseen but the destruction of all life on earth became a distinct possibility. Left: the physicist J. Robert Oppenheimer with General Leslie R. Groves at the site of a test-explosion. The Bomb brought the worlds of science and politics into a sombre and guilt-ridden alliance. (13, 14)

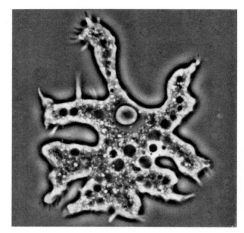

The component of life, the single cell, had been glimpsed in the 19th century. What has been added in the 20th is a deeper knowledge of its internal structure and the way in which different kinds of cell are designed for specific functions. Above: the single all-purpose cell of the amœba, one of the most primitive of animals. Below: a section through a plant cell, showing the chloroplasts, the long striped structures which enable the plant to use the sun's energy to manufacture food. (15, 18)

Inside the cell a network of parts keeps the system functioning and self-perpetuating. In this yeast cell (below), the two large oval areas in the centre are the all-important nucleus and a fluid-filled vacuole, the smaller ones the mitochondria, the main energy-generators of the cell. (16)

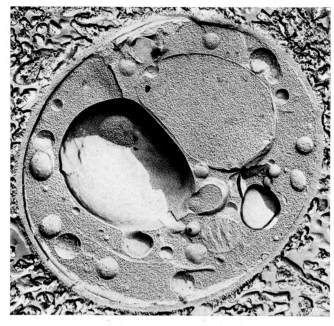

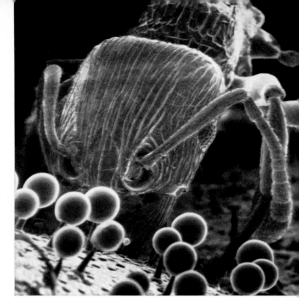

Complex co-operation between bodily parts makes possible that division of labour which characterizes the higher forms of life. Here, the scanning electron microscope has opened up new worlds in biology as well as in physics. Above: the head of an ant, caught among the sticky-tipped hairs on the leaf of an insectivorous plant. (17)

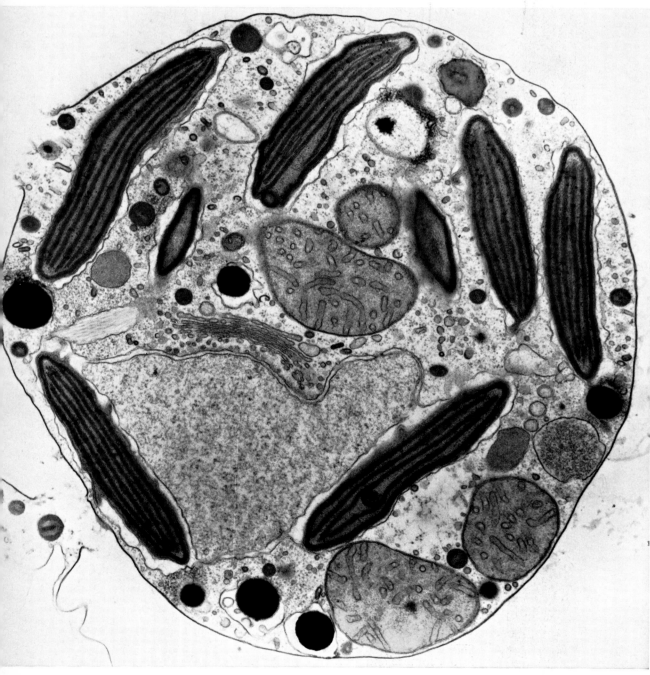

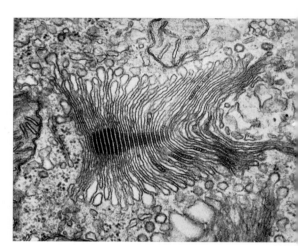

Specialization: three examples of cells, or parts of cells, which perform single precise functions. Above: the mysterious Golgi bodies, which help to process protein and carbohydrate within the cell. Below: red blood corpuscles, entire cells devoted to carrying oxygen through the body. Bottom: rows of muscle cells, working in unison to translate nerve impulses into physical movements. (19–21)

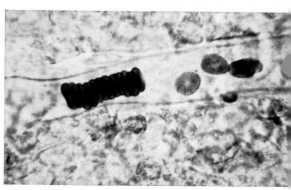

The breakthrough came in 1953 when two young biochemists at Cambridge were able to demonstrate the structure of DNA. James Watson and Francis Crick, shown here with a DNA model, together with Maurice Wilkins won a Nobel Prize for their work in this field. (23)

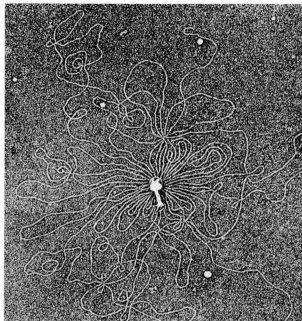

The DNA molecule of a virus, the bacteriophage, so elementary that it has been called, facetiously, 'a naked gene', is shown above, magnified 90,000 times. The chain has been broken and scattered as it burst, and would normally be coiled up inside the bacteriophage, the white object in the centre. Below: sections of DNA corresponding to genes in the process of manufacturing new chains of nucleic acid. (24, 25)

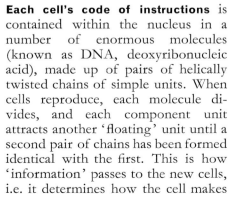

Each cell's code of instructions is contained within the nucleus in a number of enormous molecules (known as DNA, deoxyribonucleic acid), made up of pairs of helically twisted chains of simple units. When cells reproduce, each molecule divides, and each component unit attracts another 'floating' unit until a second pair of chains has been formed identical with the first. This is how 'information' passes to the new cells, i.e. it determines how the cell makes its immense variety of proteins. Only within the last twenty years have scientists succeeded in understanding its structure and so gained new insight into bodily growth and the inheritance of characteristics from one generation to the next (each characteristic being correlated with a section of a DNA molecule). This model (above) shows a minutely small part of a DNA molecule, each sphere representing one atom: carbon, nitrogen, oxygen, phosphorus and hydrogen. (22)

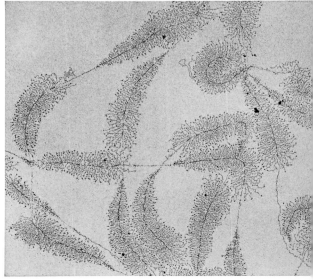

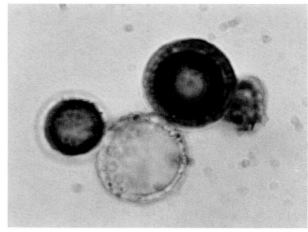

The origin of life was a subject which 19th-century scientists could debate only speculatively. Now at last an approach can be made on the basis of experiment. Dr S. L. Miller (left) has recreated in the laboratory the probable atmospheric conditions on the Earth millions of years ago, and exposed it to the radiation and electrical discharges which are likely to have been present then. On analyzing the result he found amino acids, the basic 'bricks' of protein. Again in the right conditions, these simple 'proteinoids' can be made to form 'microspheres' (above) which have many of the characteristics of cells, and can even grow and reproduce. Below right: the earliest evidence of life, a fossil alga, 2000 million years old. (26–28)

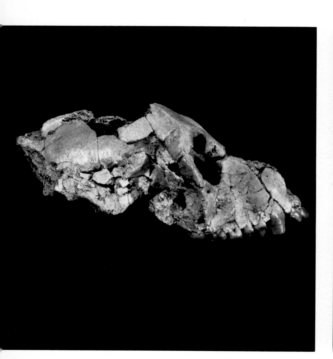

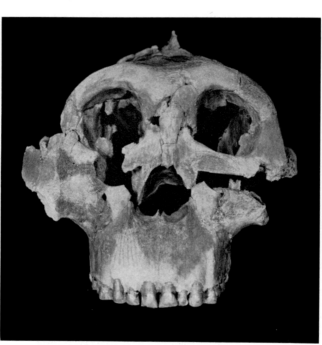

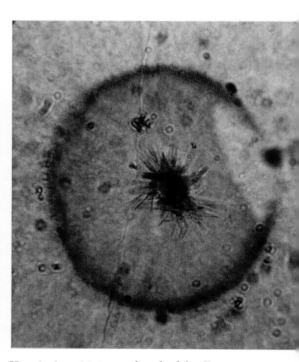

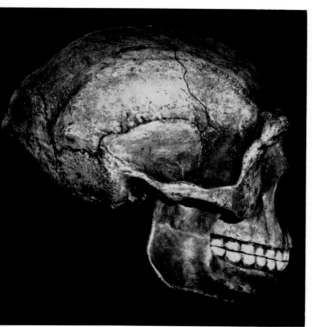

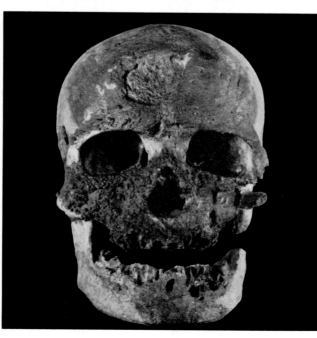

Man before history, sketched by Darwin in the last century, can now be seen in far more detail. On the left are four skulls which illustrate human evolution between about 30 million and 20,000 years ago. All were discovered during this century. Top left: *Aegyptopithecus* (lower jaw missing). More like a monkey than an ape or man, the creature had a tail and large projecting teeth. Top right: *Australopithecus* (nearly 2 million years old), walked upright on two legs and may have used pebbles as tools. Lower left: Pekin Man, a mere half million years old, made tools of his own and cooked his food. Lower right: Cro-Magnon Man, first example of *Homo sapiens* whose palaeolithic culture created the cave paintings of France and Spain, another surprise discovery of this century. (29–32)

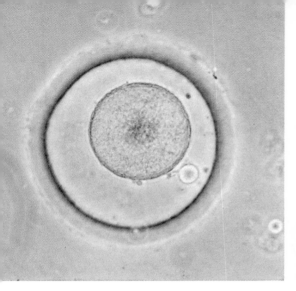

Man before birth can today be photographed in fascinating detail, so that embryology has become almost a new science. The human egg (above) is a cell a seventh of a millimetre in diameter, consisting of a nucleus which contains half the number of chromosomes (the dark patch in the middle) present in the mother's cells. These will join with those carried in the sperm to form the genetic complement of the offspring. In the cytoplasm is stored food for the growing embryo. Right: an embryo in its seventh week, just over one centimetre long, with paddle-like hands and tubular brain. (33, 34)

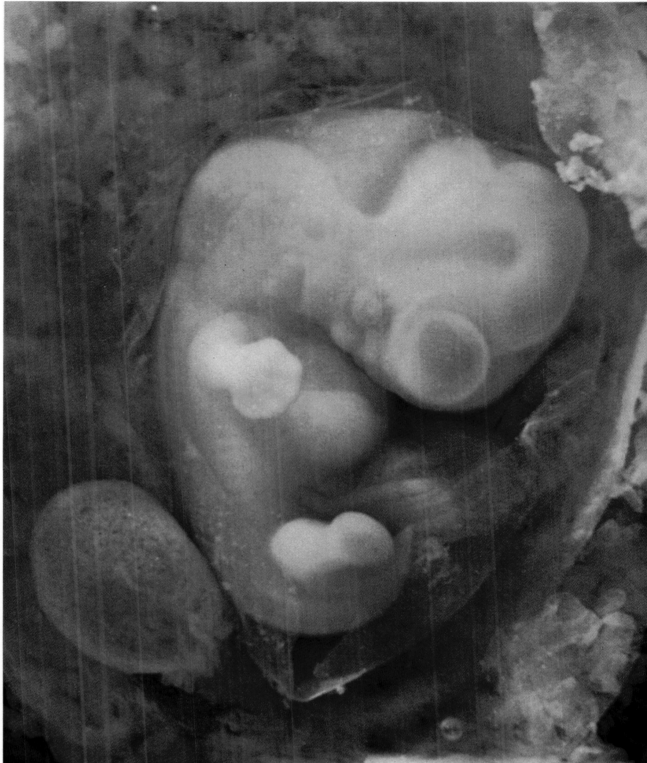

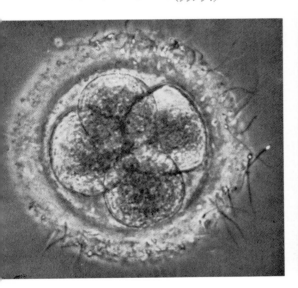

Fertilization in a test tube for human eggs has now been achieved. Above: the fertilized egg has already divided twice to form four cells. As yet these eggs do not survive for long, reaching only about the 64-cell stage. Further growth outside the womb has been achieved for the early stages of other embryos, but still only for short periods. Of these two rat embryos (right), the one on the left has been cultured in an incubator, that on the right has grown normally within the mother. (35, 36)

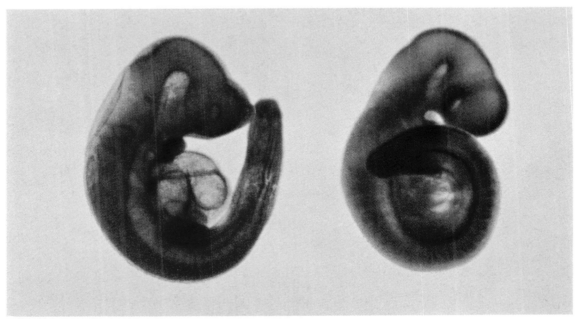

The scientist's responsibility for the direction in which modern life is developing grows daily heavier, as governments lean for advice upon experts, and as every new acquisition of knowledge is more and more rapidly put to use, or misuse. Here one is strictly entering the realm of technology, the subject of the next chapter, but on these concluding pages are shown a few of the most dramatic ways in which the scientist can wield powers of good and evil. Subjected to the pressures of governments which pay for his research, and the conflict between his loyalty to truth and freedom of expression and his political obligations as a citizen, how are his final choices to be made? In no other century has the seeker after knowledge been placed in so fateful and yet so ambiguous a position.

From understanding to control is a short step. By planting minute electrodes inside the brain, particular groups of brain cells can be stimulated, producing particular kinds of behaviour. In the photograph above, the normally domineering leader of a colony of monkeys, seen in the centre, has had radio electrodes fixed to his brain, which when switched on render him peaceful and friendly. One of the weaker monkeys has learned the secret and, on the left, turns on the switch himself. (37)

Exploring the mind through the brain: the old dichotomy between mental and physical events is no longer so absolute, as closer and closer correlations are established between thoughts and other mental activities on the one hand and the electrical and chemical behaviour of the brain on the other. Left: electro-encephalograph recordings being taken during sleep. (38)

New wheat for the world's hungry has resulted from Dr Norman Borlaug's researches (left), which have taken twenty-five years of his life. By combining different strains, he and his team produced a variety that can be grown in countries like India, Pakistan and Mexico, where normal wheat would not flourish. 'The plants of the world,' said Dr Borlaug, 'have a lot of wonderful genes in them, if you can just find and combine them.' (39)

Chemical pesticides and fertilizers have a long history, though the 20th century has employed them on a scale previously unknown (right: spraying vines from the air in Switzerland). Recent research suggests that the law of diminishing returns operates here, and that the long-term solutions must be biological rather than chemical. (40)

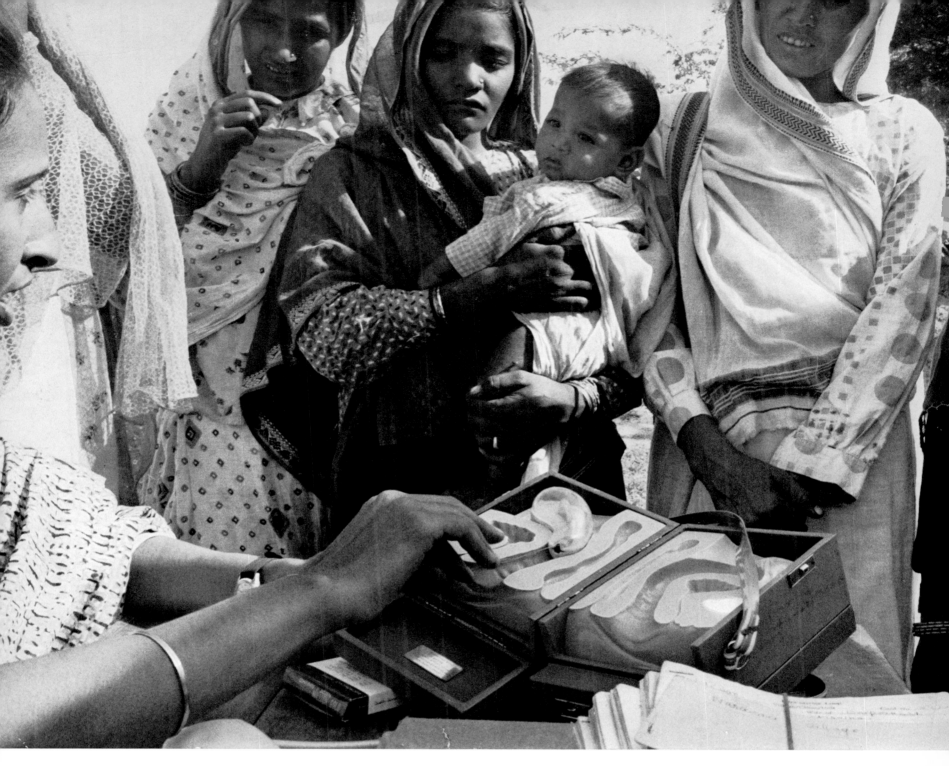

Controlling birth: Indian women (above) being instructed in the 'loop' type of contraceptive. (41)

Controlling death (right): mass immunization is capable of conquering epidemics. New jet injectors, using pressure instead of a needle, are quicker and completely painless, in spite of the young victim's expression. (43)

Making war on nature (left): defoliated trees in Vietnam, after treatment by the American air-force to deprive the enemy of cover. (42)

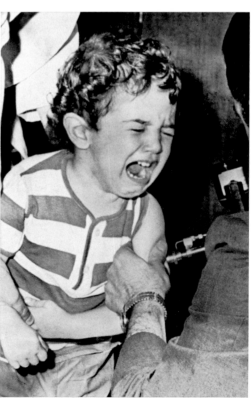

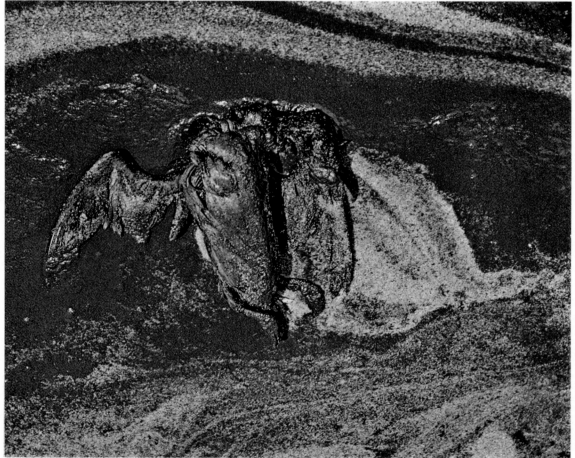

The dangers of progress have only recently forced themselves on world attention. While the Victorians polluted the atmosphere of their cities with coal smoke, modern technology discharges its own more harmful effluents. Air and water are becoming overloaded with nitrates and phosphates, some of them added to agricultural land as fertilizers and thence finding their way into rivers and lakes, some absorbed into rainfall from the exhaust fumes of petrol engines. (44)

The accidents of progress: a dead sea-bird, washed up on the oil-polluted beaches of Cornwall after the *Torrey Canyon*, a giant tanker, had broken up and spilt her cargo into the sea in 1969. Disasters like this may perhaps be foreseen and prevented; the main long-term dangers to the environment come not from the failures but from the *successes* of modern technology. 'We have become enticed into a nearly fatal illusion,' wrote a prominent scientist, 'that we have at last escaped from the dependence of man on the rest of nature.' (45)

Achievements . . . and responsibilities

STEPHEN TOULMIN

A DREAM that comes true never takes, in actual fact, the precise form it had when first conceived. The conditions of real life impose a dozen requirements and limitations that the initial conception did not allow for; and their effects can change the very quality of the dream. So, in its realization, the conception may end by creating almost as many problems as it solved, and may even take on, in some respects, something of the character of a nightmare.

The programme of modern science was worked out in the 16th and 17th centuries by Galileo Galilei and Francis Bacon, René Descartes, Isaac Newton and their colleagues. Between them, these men conceived of a new kind of 'natural philosophy', which was intended to reform the method of men's intellectual operations, and—almost incidentally—to transform their practical lives also. The method was to be mathematical and experimental: renouncing older authorities and 'idols', and refusing to place any reliance on scholarly tradition or verbal argumentation. (As the Royal Society of London put it, in their chosen motto: *nullius in verba*.) It was also to be open-minded and systematic: building up a general picture of the workings of nature that could be rationally convincing to any man, since it respected only the authority of human reason and the evidence of impartial observation. And it was to transform men's practical lives, because a recognition of the real 'forms, qualities and relations' in the natural world was seen as the first necessary step to controlling them. True power could be founded only on genuine knowledge: once this was achieved, men would at last be able to determine their own material conditions. Let the Tree of Know-ledge grow high enough, and the men who lived off its fruits, and in its shade, could fashion a new manner of life for themselves.

Few of men's collective dreams have been more completely realized than this one, even though its fulfilment has had to wait for three centuries. We in the 20th century grow up into a world that our 17th century forefathers conceived for us. By the systematic use of mathematical and experimental methods of investigation, our predecessors have indeed achieved a new understanding of the natural world—constructing their new picture of nature around concepts and theories whose implications have stood up repeatedly to critical analysis and observational testing. Adoption of these new theories has, as they foresaw, demanded a new modesty about our traditional ideas, and a readiness to look at nature in ways that were frequently novel, and even paradoxical. And our reward has been just what Francis Bacon foretold. Knowledge has bred power. In coming to understand the workings of nature, we have multiplied our command over them.

Seen from close to, however, the new world of science has proved to be both richer in texture, and more difficult to handle, than its original prophets foresaw. What our forefathers saw as a bright and distant prospect turns another darker face to those who inhabit it. Both in intellectual and in practical terms, man's relationship to nature is more ambiguous than the men of the 17th century guessed. Instead of studying the natural world as 'rational on-lookers', and manipulating it as we please, we in fact view nature (it now appears) *from within*; and all our interventions are liable to rebound on us in unexpected ways. Intellectually, our knowledge of natural processes is a unitary complex, within which one can no longer distinguish sharply between the respective contributions of man the observer, and of nature the observed; while the neuro-

logical mechanisms involved in our sensory perception and rational understanding—and so our 'thoughts'—are rapidly be-coming objects of scientific scrutiny like any others. The practical blessings of applied science, too, have been purchased only at the cost of new and unforeseen side-effects. The same antibiotics that have made killer diseases harmless have provoked, in response, the appearance of resistant strains of infection, and have also given rise to quite unintended political and spiritual crises. Efficient, world-wide death control makes birth control an inescapable issue. The same nuclear energy that might make the Sahara bloom creates un-equalled military hazards. And the better we understand the work-ings of our own minds and bodies, the more we lay up for ourselves what Gordon Rattray Taylor has described as a 'biological time-bomb': the more, that is we create the possibility of manipulating and changing human beings themselves, for ill as well as for good.

p 283 (41, 43)

We have found out how to achieve practical command over nature, and so to fashion the world after our desires; but, as the price of this knowledge, we are having to develop new kinds of moral and political self-understanding and self-command. So the 17th-century dream of a scientific Earthly Paradise is 'coming true' in the form of a 20th-century Garden of Eden, in which the Tree of Knowledge continues to bear, even-handedly, both good and bad fruit.

The seventeenth-century programme . . .

As contrasted with the ideas of earlier epochs, the view of nature inherited by the 20th century—the view that has been the common property of scientifically minded Europeans throughout the last three hundred years—had three leading features. It was an *optimistic* view, which placed no external limits on man's ability to understand and control the operations of nature; it was an *ordered* view, which saw all the objects and processes of the natural world as conforming to a common, unchanging specification, and governed by a com-mon, unchanging system of laws; and it was a *mechanistic* view, which interpreted the entire physical cosmos as a self-contained chain of interlocking mechanisms—a vast and perfectly designed gear-train from the hand of the Divine Clockmaker, as the stock 18th-century image depicted it. This was, at any rate their view of the material world, governed by physical causality: by contrast the rational activities of mind were generally thought of as exempted from the causality of the world-machine.

All three features were novel ones. If we leave aside a very few rationalistic thinkers in antiquity, such as the Stoic philosophers, the natural world had been regarded in previous centuries as a mere stage-setting, whose material props could be manipulated, arbi-trarily and unpredictably, by a *dramatis personae* of divine powers: the important thing was the cosmic drama played out on that stage. Furthermore, most Christian thinkers before 1600 thought of the providential drama of the Fall and Redemption as having an overall time-scale of some ten thousand years at the outside.

The new scientific picture, foreseen, if not actually inaugurated, by Francis Bacon, opened up the material world to human under-standing and control, by treating it as a single orderly system. In the new picture the image of God as a providential agent, continually intervening in the affairs of his Creation, was displaced by an image of God as the Divine Architect, who had laid down the original specification for the order of nature and set it going in the beginning, according to laws of his wise contrivance. The course of history need no longer be regarded as unpredictable in principle: given, at any time, the positions and velocities of all the material particles in the natural world (as Laplace was to argue) a calculator of unlimited power could, in theory, use the laws of physics to foretell the whole subsequent sequence of events.

Finally, the orderliness of nature was, on this new view, the orderliness of a vast machine. Where earlier philosophers had thought of the cosmos in animistic or organismic terms—talking of it (e.g.) as a unitary Organism governed by a World-Soul—the whole pattern of scientific thought, from the mid-17th century right up into the 20th century, was to be dominated by metaphors drawn from mechanical engineering. 'Is the Divine Watchmaker so incompetent,' Leibniz quizzed the Newtonians in the 1710s, 'that he has to step in from time to time, to adjust and mend his own Creation?'; and, two hundred years later, we find scientists like Wilhelm Ostwald and theologians like Dean Inge, equally, concerned with the question whether thermodynamics implies that the 'cosmic machine' is ineluctably 'running down'.

On this optimistic, orderly and mechanistic world-picture, the founders of modern science based their double dream. By systematic intellectual innovation, men could discover the laws governing the operation of the cosmic mechanism, and so come to understand nature; and, by systematic practical innovation, they could exploit that understanding so as to turn it to their own welfare. There was no built-in assurance that the world would work out to man's benefit, without any effort on his part, and without his choosing to make it do so. The guarantees of providence were thus replaced by the maxims of self-help. But there was no built-in obstacle to man's self-improvement, either. Once men were convinced that, both intellectually and practically, they could make themselves the masters of nature, it was only a matter of time and industry before they would do so. United by this conviction, there grew up that famous alliance between science, capitalism and the protestant ethic, with which scholars like R. H. Tawney and Robert Merton have made us familiar, and which has done so much to shape the modern world.

. . . and its twentieth-century fulfilment

To see how this 17th-century programme has been fulfilled in the 20th century, we must recall, first, the intellectual content of natural science seventy years ago. By the 1890s, the overall theory of nature sketched by Newton at the end of his *Opticks*, nearly two hundred years before, had apparently been confirmed and elaborated in all its major details. The outcome was the system of physical ideas that, in scientific circles, came to be known—significantly—as 'classical' physics and chemistry; and the compactness and self-consistency of this system were such that, for the moment, the fundamental theoretical work of science seemed to have been completed.

True, a few unsolved problems and anomalies remained to be dealt with, but in general terms the system appeared to be final. In theoretical physics, three 19th-century achievements had made a particular impression, and had helped to reinforce this sense of finality. In the theory of matter, Clausius and Maxwell had demonstrated that chemical 'atoms' and 'molecules', invoked by Dalton to explain the facts of chemical combination and dissociation, could be identified with the minute physical 'particles' whose energy of motion explained most of the phenomena of heat and temperature. This identification seemed to confirm one of the primary elements in the classical Newtonian system: namely the 'solid, massy, hard, impenetrable, movable Particles' into which Newton supposed that God had 'form'd Matter in the Beginning'. And Maxwell himself shared Newton's belief, arguing that the molecules of the ninety-odd distinct chemical elements were permanent constituents of the world as God made it—'perfect in number and measure and weight,' with 'ineffaceable characters impressed on them' by the Creator. (By 1900, of course, Becquerel and the Curies had begun to study the phenomenon of radioactive transmutation; but this discovery had not yet shaken a general faith in the stability of material atoms.)

Meanwhile, in an even more important piece of work, Maxwell had demonstrated also that the phenomena of electricity, magnetism

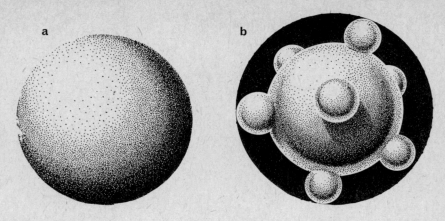

and optics were simply so many species of a single genus: without exception, it appeared, those physical phenomena that were not explained in terms of the properties of material atoms could be explained as effects of 'electromagnetic radiation', and Heinrich Hertz had even shown how such electromagnetic waves could be generated and detected artificially. (In 1900, Marconi was hard at work turning this discovery to practical use.) In this way, Maxwell apparently confirmed the other primary element in Newton's system: namely, the 'vibratory motions in the aether' by which the 'hard, massy Particles' supposedly interacted. (Once again, of course, there were some notorious problems about this hypothetical 'aether'; but in the 1890s many physicists could still regard these as marginal.) Finally, the work of Helmholtz and Boltzmann had shown how the two chief branches of physics—the theory of material atoms, and the theory of electromagnetic waves—could be brought together and unified under the principles of 'energetics': i.e. what we now know as the two laws of thermodynamics. So (it seemed) three basic and definitive truths had been established for certain. Matter was composed of Atoms, Radiation of Waves, and both alike obeyed the Conservation of Energy. Ultimately—many scientists in 1900 would have been tempted to add—that is 'all we know in physics, and all we need to know'.

By comparison, the biological sciences were less far along the road to completion, though there was little in them to raise doubts about the fundamental physical world-picture. Physiology and biochemistry were making a good start, thanks largely to the balanced and clear-headed methods of Claude Bernard, while a first rough

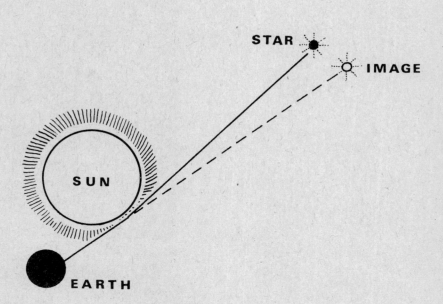

Einstein's theory of relativity postulated that light had mass and would therefore be affected by gravity. This was not easy to verify in practice, but on 29 May 1919 a total eclipse of the sun enabled astronomers to measure the deflection of light from a distant star as it passed through the sun's gravitational field. It was found that the star's apparent position differed from its real position by about $1\frac{1}{2}$ seconds of arc, thus confirming Einstein's prediction. (1)

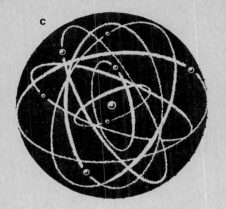
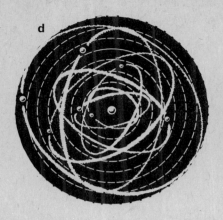
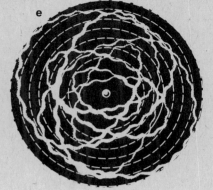

The history of atomic theory is a progression from the simple, easily visualized model of Democritus to the almost wholly abstract modern concept. (a) Democritus put forward a picture of the basic component of matter as a minutely small solid sphere. This held the field until the 19th century. (b) J. J. Thomson (1897) proposed the 'currant bun' model— negative charge-carriers embedded at geometrically regular intervals in a solid positive nucleus. (c) Rutherford, by 1911, was forced to the conclusion that the atom was mostly empty space, and proposed a model in which the *electrons 'orbit' the nucleus like planets in a solar system. (d) Two years later Bohr restricted the electrons to certain 'permitted' orbits from which they could move only by 'quantum jumps'. (e) De Broglie (1924) inter-preted the orbiting particles as waves. (f) The modern picture, worked out by Schrödinger, Born and Heisenberg, goes further, speaking simply of 'areas of probability'; these can only be represented symbolically, as clouds varying in thickness according to the degree of probability of the electron's existing within the area. (2)*

conception was being arrived at of the psychological functions performed by different internal structures within the brain. (Even Descartes had expected a mechanistic physiology to explain the causes of our passions and emotions, and had attempted to exempt from causality only the rational functions of the mind.) Mean-while, the status of the individual 'cell' had been established, as the material unit of living organisms, and its main internal compo-nents—nucleus, nucleolus, chromosomes etc—had been recog-nized and named, though in 1900 the significance of cell-division for genetic inheritance was still largely mysterious. (Mendel's work was just about to be repeated and rediscovered.) There remained one other isolated intellectual peak in biology, which was still a highly contentious topic among thinkers of all kinds, and had not yet been integrated into the main fabric of science: viz. Darwin's account of the origin of species as the historical outcome of variation and natural selection. The first theological anxieties aroused by Darwin's theory had been quieted, by Asa Gray and others, but some grave scientific problems remained unsolved. It was clear, for instance, that a Darwinian history of organic life on earth must take for granted a time-span of several hundred million years; yet William Thompson, Lord Kelvin—the Grand Cham of British physics in the 1890s—had calculated that the earth's surface was uninhabitably hot as little as twenty-five million years ago. Else-where, the accepted history of the physical world conformed more closely to good Newtonian principles. Apart from the little matter of Mercury's perihelion, the internal motions of the planetary system obeyed Newton's laws of dynamics and gravitation per-fectly, while all serious problems about the earth seemed likely to yield, in due course, to intelligent application of the same familiar physical and chemical laws.

'Classical' science dissolves

Between 1900 and 1914, there was a dramatic change. This 'classical' picture crumbled at every point; though the full extent of the damage was not appreciated until after the First World War. Any textbook of general physics today describes how the fundamental dichotomy of Newtonian physics—between particle-like matter and wave-like radiation—was broken down, as material particles and electromagnetic waves respectively turned out to have com-plementary, wave-like or particle-like properties; how the ninety-odd classical types of 'hard, massy, unchangeable' atoms were replaced by so many different 'sub-atomic' configurations, made up from three much smaller and more 'elementary' particles—protons, electrons and neutrons—only for the number of such 'elementary particles' to burgeon, in turn, so that by now several hundred are *f 1* known; and how Einstein's two theories of relativity compelled a fundamental reappraisal even of the laws of Newtonian dynamics— with the anomalous motion of Mercury acting as one key witness in support of the newer theories. Intellectually, one may say, scarcely a

single fundamental feature of the Newtonian picture survived unscathed the conceptual changes that physics underwent during the first half of the 20th century.

By 1940, however, the intellectual situation had in many respects been more than redeemed. The new theories of quantum mechanics and relativity gave an account of the mechanism of nature in which yet more comprehensive laws, applied to simpler and more universal structures, accounted in exact detail for a vaster range of physical phenomena than the classical system had ever embraced. Since 1945, several further major steps have been taken, and scientists have achieved something resembling a fresh 'classical synthesis': although the Newtonian ideas have been largely abandoned, there have been notable gains in the process. Not only have the physical sciences achieved a greater unity, power and scope than they had on the classical view. In addition, the biological sciences have reached, during the 20th century, the same kind of conceptual maturity as physics and chemistry; and the realms of Matter, Life and Mind, which were for practical purposes—and even, in some respects, as a matter of principle—dealt with separately in earlier centuries, are rapidly coming to be recognized as three related aspects of the same natural world.

We must touch briefly on a few of the most significant intellectual novelties in 20th-century science. Since 1900, physicists have— first and foremost—been exploring the interstices, and the impli-cations, of the new sub-atomic world opened up by J. J. Thomson, *f 3, 4* Ernest Rutherford and Nils Bohr in the years before 1914. The initial thoughts about the quantum theory put forward by Max Planck in the closing weeks of 1899 led by 1926–27 to the fully-fledged theory of quantum mechanics, as formulated by Heisenberg, Schrödinger and Dirac, and the story of this development forms one of the most creative and adventurous phases in the history of physics. At certain points, there are by now hints that even quantum mechanics may be only a transitional theory; yet, in itself, the intellectual command provided by the resulting theory has given us the means, not just of accounting for sub-atomic and nuclear phenomena, but—more important—of building up a unified theory applicable to material systems of many kinds, by bringing to light the forces that maintain matter in the solid state (the liquid state is still, largely, a blessed mystery) by integrating the concepts of chemistry with those of physics (through Debye's quantum theory of valency) and by moving effectively, through biochemistry, into the biological sphere also.

It was, in fact, a speculation thrown out in Erwin Schrödinger's brilliant popular essay, *What is Life?*, that put J. D. Watson on the trail that led to the new science of molecular biology. Before 1900, Auguste Weismann had argued cogently that the extraordinary stability of genetic inheritance from generation to generation— the Habsburg nose, for instance, reappearing recognizably down the centuries, despite all the hundreds of cell-divisions involved in the development of each individual—must have some molecular basis in the living cell. Yet, at the time, there was no way of discovering what this basis was. Only since 1950 has it been possible to bring together ideas and techniques from biochemistry and quantum theory, X-ray crystallography and computer analysis, to decipher the inner structure of genes and chromosomes, and by now molecular biology has gone a long way towards elucidating the internal processes of cellular development and cell-division. As a result, we can say for certain that one crucial link between physics and biology—between the physico-chemical mechanisms of the inanimate realm, and the physiological processes of the animate realm—lies in the detailed structure of certain key 'macro-molecules', notably those of the so-called 'nucleic acids'. Meanwhile, at the other end of the scale, astronomers also have been gaining new insights from the quantum theory of atomic structure, together with its Siamese twin, the quantum theory of radiation: in this way they have begun to understand, with a new detail, the major phases in the astronomical evolution of stars and galaxies, and to speculate about the emergence of the whole visible cosmos from a possible cataclysmic event some ten thousand million years in the past.

During the 20th century, the biological sciences have likewise been developing a new coherence and unity. At the present time, a concerted attack is under way on the internal microstructure and operation of the brain, focussed on questions that could not even be posed until the leading concepts of contemporary physics, biochemistry and molecular biology were available. As Darwin always hoped, the gravest scientific objections to the theory of evolution have also lost much of their bite: Joly's work on the formation of mountain-ranges, for instance, has made it clear that the surface temperature of the earth is continually being maintained at an even level by internal radioactive heat-sources, so that the thermal history of the earth need no longer be confined within Kelvin's restricted limits. As a result, the theory of organic evolution is no longer at loggerheads with physics. On the contrary, contemporary neo-Darwinism has gained important new links with the rest of science, and these have added immensely to its intellectual authority. To begin with, Darwin's general, qualitative arguments about the possible effects of natural selection have been put in an exact mathematical form. Beginning with J. B. S. Haldane and R. A. Fisher, population geneticists have analyzed the precise relations to be expected in different environments between mutation-rates, selection-pressures etc., and the results of their analysis have set at rest most of the scientific doubts about natural selection as a mechanism of speciation. In addition, the creation of 20th century genetics as an experimental and theoretical science, by William Bateson, T. H. Morgan and their successors, has filled in the missing intellectual links between evolution theory and cell biology; and these links, in turn, have made it possible to raise once again, in a manageable form, older speculative questions about the physico-chemical origin of living organisms on the earth. Urey, Calvin and others (at any rate) have begun to show how, in the primitive terrestrial atmosphere of ammonia and carbon dioxide that existed before the appearance of life, the crucial chemical substances of which cells are composed (proteins, amino-acids etc.) could have been formed and begun to accumulate as a result of familiar natural processes. All of this is, up to now, understood only in a very sketchy and tentative manner; nevertheless, a new history of life on our planet is already in sight, based on the unified ideas of population genetics and molecular biology, ecology and biochemistry.

The new synthesis

In many respects, this new 20th-century synthesis may still seem at first glance, to be modelled on the same pattern as its classical predecessor. Physicists still talk about the world of nature (for instance) in terms of 'particles' that are governed by 'laws of nature', and that form different configurations or 'compounds' at different times. Yet, at another level, the new picture differs profoundly from the old. None of today's 'particles' have unlimited lifetimes—some of them, indeed, last for a mere million-millionth of a second; nor can we so readily think of the 'laws' of physics today as divine edicts. In such differences as these, we see the other side to the contemporary intellectual situation in science. To put the point

concisely: during the 20th century, developments within their own disciplines have obliged scientists to come to terms, once again, with historical and philosophical considerations that the classical 19th-century system could afford to ignore.

Philosophically speaking, both quantum mechanics and relativity have reintroduced into the heart of physics epistemological questions that Descartes and Newton temporarily evaded. Once we move on to the microphysical level of elementary particles and sub-atomic processes, it becomes impossible any longer to draw a clear distinction between the activities of the observing scientist, together with his measuring instruments, and the properties of the system that he studies. Man and Nature, the knower and the known, the procedures of observation and the processes observed, are linked together in complexes which can no longer (it seems) be divided up sharply, even in theory. On the one hand, we have the empirical 'observations' which provide scientists with their raw material; on the other hand, we have the theoretical 'concepts', 'calculi' and 'frameworks of interpretation' into which those observations have to be fitted; but it is no longer possible, on either level, to separate out absolutely those aspects of any phenomenon that reflect the activities of the observer from those others that reflect the properties of the object under observation.

If, within contemporary science, we can still draw a valid philosophical distinction between the respective contributions of man and nature, this will cut along a different line. It is not a Cartesian distinction between the observing mind and the external world it contemplates. Rather (as Hertz and Planck were already arguing) it is a Kantian distinction between the framework of purely formal structure which the creative activity of the scientist contributes to the theories and concepts of a science, and the specific relations and values of the empirical variables, which can be determined only by actual observation of nature. The consequent reorientation is one important aspect of 20th-century physical theory, and it is still going on: certainly such men as Albert Einstein, Werner Heisenberg and David Bohm have contributed to physical science, as much by deepening its epistemological analysis, as by devising more revealing experiments or more ingeneous mathematical methods.

In brain physiology and neuroscience, intellectual positions that were bastions of 17th-century scientific philosophy are likewise under siege. Where T. H. Huxley epitomized the central preoccupation of late 19th-century biology as the problem of *Man's Place in Nature*, Charles Sherrington rightly characterized the leading topic of 20th-century physiology in the phrase *Man on His Nature*. The shift is significant. As we learn to understand better the structure and operations of the central nervous system, it becomes harder to treat as an axiom of scientific procedure the conventional 17th-century dichotomy between causal mechanisms, typical of the physical world of matter, and rational thoughts, typical of the psychological world of mind. It is no longer plausible, for example, to suggest that any part of the human brain will prove (like the pineal gland for Descartes) to be exempted from the otherwise-general laws of physical and chemical action. Rather, it must now be supposed that Man's rational activities call into play corresponding mechanisms and processes in the brain just as much as his emotions and passions; and our current knowledge of these processes (especially, the current observations of Sperry on 'split-brain' subjects) make it doubtful whether one can establish any unitary association of consciousness, rationality or even speech with some single location in the brain.

Historically speaking, too, 20th-century scientists have reached a position very different from that of their classical predecessors. We can see now that all the basic principles of the 17th-century programme for science were, in fact, radically a-historical. Descartes himself scorned historical knowledge as lacking in intellectual seriousness, and he would concede rational adequacy only to a mathematically-based science. Newton, Boyle and their Protestant colleagues assumed that true natural knowledge must be knowledge of the unchanging material structures and mathematical laws that God had impressed on the world at the Creation. For Newtonian physicists as much as Cartesian philosophers, the very intelligibility of the natural world was bound up with the fixity of its basic laws and structures. To all the founders of modern science,

p 279
(22)

p 280
(26)

p 282
(38)

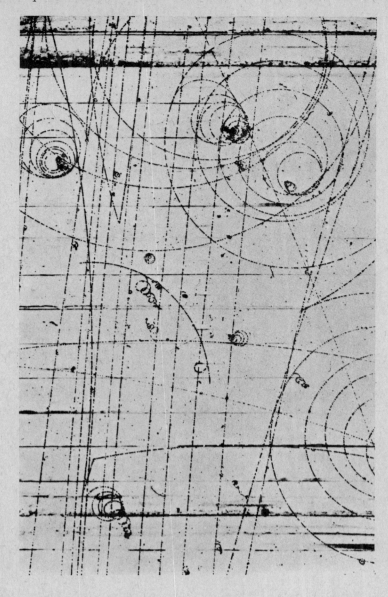

Sub-atomic particles cannot be seen, but their bubble tracks can be photographed as they travel at immense speeds through a liquid. In this print and diagram a number of particle-divisions—either through collisions with other particles or decay—are shown. At A, for instance, one particle splits into two, one (negatively charged) being deflected to the right, while the other (positive and therefore leaving no trail of bubbles) goes on to B, where it splits into three more positive particles, each of which splits into two negative ones at C, D and E. (3, 4)

then, the order of nature was a timeless order, changeable—if at all —only by the decision of God who created it.

At the outset, this unchanging cosmic mechanism comprised not only the universal laws of motion and gravitation, and the general forms of the ultimate particles of matter, but also many specific features of the world: the structure of the solar system, the frame of the earth, the natures of different organic species, and even the forms and structures of our bodily organs. Only gradually, during the subsequent two hundred years, did astronomy, geology and zoology succeed in developing an authentically historical dimension—and, in each case, this happened only after an intellectual struggle. Even then, Laplace's omniscient calculator was frequently invoked to prove that this historical aspect was, in principle, secondary and derivative. To this day, indeed, mathematically-minded thinkers often find difficulty in taking the historical element in Darwinism seriously, and they are sometimes as unwilling as Descartes would have been to allow Darwinian explanations the full title of 'science' or 'knowledge'. So it is worth reminding ourselves explicitly, here, just how completely the a-historical fixity of the original scientific world-picture has, by now, been eroded. On the contemporary scientific view, it is not the earth and its organic species alone that have acquired a history. According to Hoyle, the chemical elements too have a 'life-history', being evolved in the furnaces of new stars; none of today's 'elementary particles' of matter has the immutable character of Newton's 'particles' and Maxwell's 'molecules'; and some physicists (e.g. E. A. Milne and P. A. M. Dirac) have even suggested that certain of the laws of nature may themselves have varied systematically, from one cosmic epoch to another. At this point, historical categories have finally penetrated the central core of the earlier, a-historical world-picture of science.

At the beginning of the modern era (in short) it seemed as though man could set himself apart from the external, historically-change-

less order of the natural world, and study it with the eye and mind of a detached rational observer. In the 20th century, we have been learning that this Olympian posture is impracticable. Man is himself a part of the natural world, and he must study its workings from within: his own scientific investigations form an inextricable element in the natural happenings on which they are intended to throw light. Man and nature together are, furthermore, caught up in a single nexus, having a history of its own: in the last resort, therefore, the order of nature can no longer—as Descartes and Newton believed—be separated either from the process of history that changes it, or from the activities of the mind that studies it.

Science and society

Similar complexities and ambiguities have affected 20th-century science in its other, outward-looking roles: as a social and political influence. In terms of sheer magnitude, the institutional and professional story of 20th-century scientific work may again look like the triumphant culmination of three centuries of continuous development. A figure is often quoted (has, indeed, already been quoted in this book) that, of all the scientists who have ever lived, nine out of ten are alive today. This statistic is, technically, irrelevant. Given the exponential growth of scientific activity throughout the modern era, the same statement was equally true in 1770 or 1870: the 'doubling period' for the growth of scientific activity has been steady, at about fifteen years, since the early 18th century. Nonetheless, in view of the absolute numbers involved, this figure is impressive. But it is of still greater significance that, just recently, the unchecked 'epidemic' spread of natural science has reached a point at which scientific research begins to be a serious factor in the financial and manpower budgeting of nations: in the most highly-developed industrial countries, for instance, the total cost of research and development now accounts for between 2% and 4% of the gross national product. For every full-time scientist working in

f 3, 4

Europe or the United States in 1900, as a result, there are today two or three dozen actively engaged on research in universities, research institutes or industrial laboratories all over the world.

One consequence of this great increase in 'scientific manpower' has been a rise in the amount of team-work in science. Particularly where investigations require large and complex apparatus, a single research project may now involve the collaboration of three, five or even ten scientists, and a glance at the scientific journals will confirm how far 'multiple authorship' of scientific papers has increased in recent years. Another consequence has been a new degree of intellectual specialization in science. Nobody today can be an acknowledged expert throughout an entire broad field like physics. On the contrary, there are by now professional divisions between such finely differentiated sub-disciplines as cosmic-ray physics, high-energy particle physics and nuclear-shell theory, and a man who can speak with authority even about the whole of atomic physics will be reckoned versatile. This specialization has its disadvantages, but it has greatly sharpened the immediate cutting-edge of science. Any self-contained group of scientific problems may thus be under attack, independently, by half-a-dozen research teams in (say) Japan and France, Russia and America; the twenty, fifty or hundred-odd men who are really masters of each sub-discipline form an international fraternity or 'invisible college'; and their mutual respect and emulation ensure that the problems of the sub-discipline are kept under continuous analysis and attack. Supported by the patronage of government and industry, and by the expansion of colleges and universities, 20th-century scientists have thus built up institutionalized professions and developed formal career-structures such as the amateur scientists of earlier centuries never knew.

Yet, paradoxically, this very success has begun to impose on scientists external restraints of a new kind, that they can no longer avoid. For instance: it has now become, for the first time, a question of practical politics what fraction of the total national resources is to be devoted to natural science, and how this amount should be divided up between enquiries of different kinds. Even in planning their own work, therefore, scientists can no longer hold themselves aloof from politics, or treat their professional activities as essentially detached and a-political. In 1900, this social change was scarcely imagined, even by scientifically-minded visionaries like H. G. Wells. At many universities, original research was still an activity that gentlemen-professors of science happily paid for out of their own pockets. (The costs were not heavy: science was still in the era of sealing-wax and string, and the wages of a professional glass-blower were likely to be the only major item.) Nor was the real potential of applied science yet seen, outside the boundaries of those few industries that had been the first technological creations of science—like the German dyestuffs and explosives industry. When the United States entered the First World War, in 1917, the American Chemical Society is said to have offered the Army Department the professional services of its members, only to receive in reply a polite message, saying, 'Thank you very much, but we already employ a chemist.' The great period of applied science, and science-based industries, was in fact to begin only after the Second World War, and particularly after 1950.

Right up until 1940, the social pattern of scientific work remained what it had become in the course of the 19th century. Academic scientists, for the most part, felt overriding loyalties to their chosen intellectual problems, and they preserved their autonomy by refusing to consider direct grants-in-aid from public funds or industrial firms. (The British Department of Scientific and Industrial Research, set up as a result of experience during the 1914–1918 war, had limited resources, which were chiefly used to strengthen nationally-important sectors of industry.) As late as 1937, Ernest Rutherford could declare that the work being done by his research team at the Cavendish Laboratory, Cambridge on sub-atomic structure and artificial transmutation, was—thank God!—of no conceivable practical use to anyone. (To complete the irony, one of Rutherford's most distinguished pupils, John Cockcroft, was later to take charge of the British programme for developing atomic energy and atomic weapons.) And throughout 1939, under the shadow of Hitler's War, the scientific community of Britain was debating, in scandalized tones, an outrageous book

p 276 (10)

just published by a red-haired young Irish Communist crystallographer, called John Desmond Bernal, on *The Social Function of Science*. This book preached a whole string of dreadful Marxist heresies: e.g. that the funds for natural science should come from the central government, and should be allocated with an eye to political and social benefits. In response, men like Michael Polanyi and John Baker denounced these infamous encroachments, and a Society for Freedom in Science was established to resist them.

On the twenty-fifth anniversary of the publication of Bernal's book, many people were surprised to find that most of its heresies had become innocent commonplaces. As a result—as Stevan Dedijer pointed out—the 'science policy' planks of the US Republican and Soviet Communist Party platforms had become indistinguishable. Nowhere were Bernal's maxims more rigorously applied than in America. In Washington, the support of scientific research had become, by the mid-1960s, a major governmental concern, watched over by a whole network of federal offices and agencies—from the President's personal Science Adviser down, through the co-ordinating Office for Science and Technology, to working agencies like the National Science Foundation and National Institutes of Health. In turn, the officials of the august Bureau of the Budget were attempting to tackle the 'allocation problem' in science, and to develop 'criteria of choice' for deciding between rival scientific claimants for public support. (After 1965 this debate went sour, as a casualty of the Vietnam War; but the questions that it raised will continue to be important ones from now on.) Meanwhile, in other industrially-developed countries, similar agencies have begun to arise—a Council on Scientific Policy here, a Ministry for Scientific Research there—while, in Europe, the successful example of the internationally-funded European Centre for Nuclear Research (CERN), outside Geneva, has carried the debate onto a wider plane still. So if, in its intellectual programme, the world of 20th-century science remains in many respects the world that Bacon and Newton prophesied, in its social organization and impact it is, more clearly, the world foretold by Bernal.

The transition from the monastic science of the 1920s and 30s to the socially-committed—or, at least, politically-implicated—science of the 1960s can be studied, as it affected the very lives of Rutherford's colleagues and pupils. During the Second World War, the beastliness of Nazism did what the advocates of Marxism could never do: it enrolled the scientists of Cambridge and Manchester, Berkeley and MIT in government-sponsored research. At first, the major scientific effort went into electronics. The scientific instrument of defence that cancelled out the numerical advantage of Hitler's air-force was radar, and work on radar attracted budding physiologists like Alan Hodgkin and future radio-astronomers like Bernard Lovell, as well as many of Rutherford's young atomic physicists. Later, the highly secret Manhattan project, with its British associate at Harwell, drew off many of the nuclear scientists into the development of the first atom-bombs. By the summer of 1945, with Hiroshima and Nagasaki obliterated, the age of scientific innocence was over.

p 302 (19)

Science and the state

Just how completely it was over, the scientists directly involved did not at once recognize. After the war, they went back to their universities and tried to take up their old lives, but the demands of the outside world were now too strong. Within a few years, it was at last clear to them all that the wartime marriage of science and politics was irreversible. Some of them were still able, in good conscience, to act as government employees or advisers; others constituted themselves into a kind of critical Greek chorus, speaking through the *Bulletin of the Atomic Scientists;* others again, like J. Robert Oppenheimer, tried at great personal cost to reconcile conflicting loyalties, to their new national duties and to their older supra-national ideals. And for some a fresh escape from this dilemma appeared, in the exciting and apparently constructive world of 'science-based industry'.

p 277 (14) f 5

The success of radar and the atom-bomb project had shown what might be achieved, in favourable circumstances, if high-grade scientists collaborated in an organized way to devise solutions of technological problems. Both wartime activities now bred peacetime successors. For a time, the prospect of cheap and unlimited

The struggle between pure science and military advantage has been a feature of the 20th century which has no parallel in previous ages. (5)

p 276 (12) energy from controlled atomic reactors aroused enthusiasm in several countries, and national governments supported medium-scale efforts to develop atomic power-stations for generating electricity. Institutionally, these first atomic-energy programmes were organized as continuations of wartime research, and subsequent development has been taken over by the heavy electrical industry, without major structural changes. On the electronic front, however, matters went very differently. The miniature radio-valves, printed circuits and transistors, developed in succession for use in compact radar and communication equipment, made possible other devices and techniques with a hundred new sorts of practical p 302 (18) applications—electronic computers being only the most striking and familiar. Many of these applications were far outside the experience of existing industrial firms, and they could be exploited only through the active involvement of research scientists whose primary connections were still with universities; many of them, too, called for little capital outlay in the early stages of development; and the result was that, given enthusiasm, some managerial talent and quite a minor investment, a few professional scientists—especially in the United States—were able to launch brand-new and successful light industries, in which the key personnel all had PhDs in science or engineering, and the chief stock-in-trade was a supply of innovations in scientific technology. (Three well-known examples are Land's Polaroid Corporation and van der Graaf's High Voltage Engineering, both established on Route 128 outside Boston, and Varian Associates of Palo Alto, California.)

Alongside these new firms, which drew their strength directly from the university community—being organized by and around p 276 (11) scientists, to work on science-based techniques—the scale of scientific research within universities was also continuing to increase: both because the sheer number of working scientists was growing, and because some of their projects were demanding apparatus of a size and cost unheard-of before 1940. Memories of the Manhattan project had—quite literally—given university scientists big ideas. E. O. Lawrence's pre-war 'cyclotron' was now eclipsed by a dozen new and larger designs for particle accelerators; scientists working in other fields began to expect comparable equipment; the possibility of further 'national programmes', of research on radio-astronomy (say) or on oceanography, became a realistic topic of discussion. In a phrase, the age of Big Science had arrived. With it, there arrived also a new style of community and institution. Inevitably, firms and laboratories whose activities were dominated by the ideas emerging from their research departments ended up with different internal structures from traditional heavy-industrial production firms. At the same time, the research centres, laboratories and institutes involved in all this large-scale scientific work—whether industrial or academic—drew technical and supporting staff into themselves, as well as requiring normal housing and supplies, until they began, in the USA particularly, to form the nuclei of entire 'research towns'. (In one such US community, 60% of the children in the local school-system have fathers with PhDs). As a result, the research town promises to be as typical a social phenomenon of the late-20th century as the mill-town was of the mid-19th century.

In this respect, 20th-century science is once again developing in ways foreseen neither by Bacon nor by Marx. The founders of modern science saw clearly enough the kinds of power that improved scientific understanding could bring with it, but they could scarcely recognize how deep would be the longer-term social consequences of those powers. Here too (we can now see) their view of the scientist's role was too detached. Lacking a proper conception of the ways in which social structure, technology and economic organization interact, they assumed that the scientists could bring their inventions and discoveries *to* society, as contributions to human welfare, without affecting the structure *of* society—still less, becoming personally involved in its reorganization. To begin with, the social impact of scientific innovation was indeed only marginal and indirect. The first generations of scientific-minded industrial entrepreneurs—men like Josiah Wedgwood, the potter—learned what they needed from their scientific contemporaries, without drawing them, as scientists, into the organizational structure of their firms. The social consequences of the first Industrial Revolution could, therefore, not be attributed directly to the effects of science: rather, it was the growth of capital investment, and the development of the new forms of economic organization, that progressively undercut the political power of the old dynastic regimes. And writing in the middle of the 19th century, with a sharp eye for the significance of economic power, Marx and Engels regarded economic relations—naturally enough—as fundamental to society. They in turn, could hardly foresee that, eventually, intellectual power might begin to play as significant a part as economic power in social and political affairs.

Yet this is—arguably—what we can now see happening in the industrialized countries. In science-based industries, technological innovations are no longer marginal factors in the growth of production: they are the very *raisons d'être* of those industries, and the whole production and marketing policies of the companies concerned depends upon the new scientific possibilities worked out in their research departments. In this new kind of enterprise, economic decisions for once have to wait on intellectual ones, rather than *vice versa*. With the rapid spread of automation and computers into more traditional branches of industry, a similar pattern is beginning to develop there also. Research is ceasing to be the mere servant of commercial and financial policy, and is becoming something more like an equal partner. As a result, we are witnessing (in Dedijer's phrase) 'the subversion of economic materialism by science', with scientific ideas ceasing to be the 'ideological superstructure' and helping to shape the 'economic base'. Intellectual innovation is, thus, having as drastic an effect on the patterns of social and industrial organization established in the 19th century as the rise of industrialism itself had on the dynastic system earlier.

The dilemmas of progress

Nor have the direct results of scientific technology, for that matter, been the unmixed blessing that its prophets hoped. Quite apart from all longer-term social consequences, many of the practical developments that 20th-century science has made possible have had unwanted side-effects as striking as their intended effects. Some of

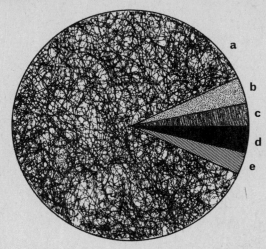

Recipe for a Los Angeles smog. The total amount of pollutants pumped into the air in a single day is nearly 14,350 tons. Most of it (a) comes from the fumes of internal combustion engines. The rest is (b) organic solvents, (c) combustion of fuels, (d) petroleum and (e) other materials. (6)

these consequences were, presumably, not only unforeseen but unforeseeable: for instance, the 'radar-assisted collisions' recognized by marine insurers as due to errors of judgment in the use of radar-navigational aids. Others were predicted a century or more ago: for instance, the danger of overpopulation described by Thomas Malthus, which has become a matter of serious political importance only during the last two generations. As for the most pervasive of these consequences—namely, the problems concerned with the preservation and control of our terrestrial environment—these were hinted at in a few 19th-century anti-Utopias, such as Anatole France's *Penguin Island*, but nobody recognized in time how protean they would be, or how rapidly and drastically they would make themselves felt: in particular, how the increasing flow of urban and industrial waste-products (car exhausts, factory effluents, even simple domestic trash) would upset the biochemical and ecological balance, both in the atmosphere and in rivers and lakes. So a situation was created in which, by 1969, the United Nations itself was ready to accept a motion by the Government of Sweden—which has reason to complain of atmospheric pollution originating in Britain and Germany—calling for international action to counteract environmental damage and declaring that this is now a greater threat than atomic war to the survival of human life.

p 284
(44, 45)
f 6

However one regards this extreme view, the form of the problems involved is revealing. Industrially as well as intellectually, the prophets of modern science assumed that men could exploit their scientific understanding in controlled and isolated ways, without producing uncontrolled and undesirable by-products. They thought of human action, as they did of human observation, as taking place on so small a scale that its side-effects would, in practice, be negligible. In actual fact, the scale of industrial activity and urban development is now so great that for the scientific technologist—as for the Heisenbergian 'observer'—the act of intervening in the world is forever producing unintended consequences, which modify the conditions of his original problem in unpredictable ways. Here, as in quantum mechanics, we are again having to learn the same new lesson: that human actions are just one element in complete interlocking systems—in the present case, the delicate systems of natural checks and balances by which the conditions of life first came into existence on this earth.

So, on every level, the problems of pure and applied science are now more closely interwoven with social and political problems than earlier scientists either imagined or desired. Evidently, the benefits of science can be used to improve the quality of human life comprehensively, only if we adapt the organizations and institutions of society to take advantage of the new possibilities that it creates. This fact has had two further consequences for the practice of politics and administration. Constructively, one notable development in the years since 1950 has been the widespread acceptance of 'research' as a necessary function of government departments, industrial managements and international agencies. If one claims this new type of social research, directed at immediate practical

problems, as a further example of 'applied science', there is a good historical reason for doing so. Its methods are, largely, those first devised during the Second World War by natural scientists attached to naval, military and airforce operational headquarters, for the purpose of appraising and comparing (e.g.) different convoy tactics, artillery control systems, or bombing methods. Out of the experience of that wartime work there have grown up all the techniques of operational research, computer simulation and technological forecasting; and many of the men actually involved in today's policy research organizations and institutions (such as the Rand Corporation at Santa Monica) learned their arts in the course of wartime operational research.

At the same time, this development too is creating fresh embarrassments of its own. The more that social problems and choices come to turn on technical issues—the more that political decisions depend on a detailed analysis and evaluation of alternative courses of action, and on an understanding of all their complex consequences—the more difficult it becomes to maintain effective democratic control over the executive operations of government. For lack of sufficient information, both ordinary citizens and national legislatures are finding it increasingly difficult to scrutinize government decisions in a relevant and effective way. So the growing influence of scientific methods on public affairs is, in part, responsible also for institutional innovations in the organs of government and representation: e.g. for the establishment of special committees of Parliament or Congress, to keep a detailed watch on the different technical aspects of national affairs—health or agriculture, astronautics or atomic energy.

The scientist's life

How have all these changes—both intellectual and social—affected the life of the scientist in the 20th century, as compared with earlier times? For the few supremely talented individuals, they have done so scarcely at all: for the majority of professional working scientists, they have done so profoundly. After all, William Whewell only invented the word *scientist*—as a counterpart to *artist*—as recently as 1840; and the term became the name for a recognized group of professional occupations only at the turn of the 20th century. So, before 1900, the 'life of the scientist' still meant—by and large—the very varied lives of as many very different individuals: Galileo at Pisa and in the villas of the Medici, Stephen Hales in the garden of his rectory at Teddington, Franklin at his Philadelphia printing-press and as American representative in Paris, Darwin on the voyage of HMS Beagle and later closeted at Downe. If, on the other hand, we talk of the 'life of the scientist' meaning a particular mode of life, career-structure and social function, we can do so only in reference to the last hundred years.

In their external circumstances, the few outstanding individuals probably have been, and will be, as personal and unpredictable in every century. At the core of their lives, the most original scientists are as 'inner-directed' as (say) a Michelangelo or a Beethoven: seeking the opportunity to pursue their novel trains of thought wherever it can be found, and exploiting that opportunity—whatever it may be—with a single-minded application. The Galileos of the world have a way of finding their Medicis and, having found them, of accepting without a second thought the social standing and political influence reflected from this distinguished patronage; yet they continue all the while, at the centre of their minds, pondering the same problems that preoccupied them before. So likewise, in the 20th century, Albert Einstein could be a glory of the Kaiser Wilhelm Institut in Berlin, or of the Institute for Advanced Studies at Princeton; but, in those prestigious positions, his efforts were still directed at the same group of theoretical issues that he had been writing about in 1905—his *annus mirabilis*—when he had been earning his living as an inspector in the Swiss Patent Office. A man like J. B. S. Haldane, again, will always have the capacity to turn himself, not only into a splendid political polemicist, but also into a penetrating theoretical biologist with all the freshness and versatility of the inspired amateur, at the same time as completing a full-scale classical education at Eton and Oxford. (His ode to cancer, written out in India during the last weeks of his life, was a characteristic mixture of courage and intellectual brilliance: my own last recollection of him is at a dinner in Broadcasting House, at the time of

Suez, reciting from memory hundreds of lines of Latin verse by A. C. Swinburne and W. E. Gladstone.) Yet such exceptional individuals as these are, of course, no more 'typical' now than they ever have been, and their number certainly does not increase in direct proportion to the total number of working scientists. Rather, they represent the tip of a pyramid, increasing (it has been suggested) more nearly as the fourth-root of the total—so that sixteen times as many working scientists are needed in order to support twice as many 'geniuses'.

If anything, then, that vast majority of working scientists must be taken as 'typical' of 20th-century science, and their mode of life is quite new. In the late 20th century, the apprentice scientist can choose from an unprecedented range of professional opportunities and established careers. Teaching, government service, industry: what shall he go for? His education as a scientist—say in geology—equips him for a dozen lines of work, most of them still unknown in the year 1900: oil-prospecting in Papua for an international corporation, geological surveying for the government of Jamaica, research and teaching at the university, writing or producing scientific programmes for television. And, as he moves up his career ladder, he may well come to have a wider influence of a sort that scientists, as such, could not expect in earlier times. As an academic, he may be president of a professional institution with ten thousand members, or succeed in winning one of the supremely-coveted Nobel Prizes: from director of research, he may become managing director of his firm, or move into the higher administrative ranks of his government department. Either way, he may end up as a Presidential Adviser or Life Peer, or as the head of a United Nations agency with worldwide functions. In all these ways, the new possibilities of the scientific life reflect the novel ways in which science is woven into the social fabric of the 20th century.

Though the 20th century has had its share of profound new theoretical insights, it has not been much different at this level from the previous three centuries: on every other level, the sheer massiveness and professional organization of scientific work have had their effect. To summarize the peculiar character of 20th-century science in a single phrase, ours is not so much a century of *genius* as a century of *scale and organization*. Who then—we may ask—is this 'professional scientist', this New Man? Certainly, the hundreds of thousands who qualify for that occupational classification nowadays are not so many Galileos; nor do they live the sparkling, intellectual, country-house life that Viviani depicts Galileo living at Arcetri. In some respects (it is true) the professional scientist today does preserve the same pattern of life as all creative workers: the same alternation between concentrated bursts of work, long past midnight, and periods of fallow depression, the same inner-directed intellectual detective work—even, the occasional *Eureka*. Yet, just because he is more likely than not employed in a large organization using expensive apparatus and plant, with a budget for which he is accountable to others, his life will inevitably be more regulated by the clock, and more subject to routine, than that of his predecessor for whom scientific research was a pastime, an avocation or a purely personal mission.

To some extent, again, the contemporary scientist's exact choice of problems to work on, and lines to follow up, will be for himself to determine, since he will have been employed in the first place as a man trained to exercise his own judgment in this choice. Yet, just because the benefits of applied science are at last appreciated in the way that Francis Bacon hoped, the options between which his choice is made are more likely to be restricted by the external needs, demands and functions of the organization within which, or through whose patronage, he is working. Just because the 20th century is in so many ways an age of applied science, therefore, the life of the professional scientist is that much the more like the life of all his fellows. As scientific research has lost its monastic character, and been integrated into the other activities of society, so too have the lives of the scientists engaged in it.

The professionalization of scientific work has had incidental effects, also, on the scientists at the apex of the pyramid. Among themselves, these men will complain about the new pressures of 'administration' and about the temptations that, in middle age, divert 'sound men' out of the single-minded life of dedicated research into organizational work, public service and popularization.

Man, the moon-sick being: a German allegory of the space-programme. (7)

In the age of Bacon, science was popularly associated with magic, and it is an association that has never completely disappeared. Modern science fiction is a strange combination of genuine knowledge, which often anticipates research, and primitive levels of fantasy. (8)

(Arguably, of course, these burdens are a measure of their success.) To the onlooker, the unintended influences of professionalization on the character of scientific work appear more significant. With sub-disciplines proliferating, it is harder for any one man to be a Maxwell or a Darwin—to take a critical look at the concepts governing a whole field of science, and to propose a radical reconstruction of its theoretical principles. This fragmentation of science is often reinforced, particularly in the United States, by the career-structure and rewards of the professionalized life. Where research is financially dependent on short-term grants and academic advancement requires a steady record of publications, there is an inescapable pressure to get quick results and a temptation for academic scientists to work on small, easily-soluble problems, rather than on longer-term issues calling for years of reflective research and analysis. In this respect the more conservative institutions of Europe probably still provide a better environment for some more fundamental kinds of scientific work than do those of America, where too small a proportion of scientific institutions provide—like the Rockefeller University in New York City—the conditions for long-term, reflective scientific innovation.

Along with this increased pressure for publication and quick results, there is also a growing scope in the new scientific professions for the kinds of internal political manoeuvring to be found in all large-scale human institutions. As science becomes more worldly, all those presidencies and chairs, editorships and research directorships that are its positions of power and influence cease to be the unlooked-for rewards of disinterested achievement, and become that much the more citadels to be bargained over, fought for or stormed. By now, at any rate, there is no longer any pretence that such politicking does not take place in science, or that the institutions and organizations within which pure scientists work are —by some miracle—havens of unanimity and disinterestedness of a kind unknown in other spheres of human life. For a time, it is true, episodes like that described in C. P. Snow's *The Affair* were still regarded as products of a novel-writer's heated imagination. Scientists who knew of similar episodes in real life felt entitled to hush them up, or brush them aside, as wholly-untypical lapses from a general standard of spotless virtue. We owe our more balanced acceptance of the common humanity of scientists, not least, to Jim Watson's delicately-malicious chronicle of the early days of molecular biology, *The Double Helix;* but we still lack a definitive *Microcosmographia Scientifica*, which would match F. M. Cornford's *Microcosmographia Academica* by codifying the rules and practices of the competitive scientific life.

p 279
(23)

Finally—and most important—the new involvement of science in the problems of human welfare and society has thrust the 20th-century scientist back into the arena of moral choice and ambiguity. The older, monastic science could be pursued single-mindedly, simply because it recognized only one single virtue. (For many earlier scientists, this was perhaps part of its charm.) As long as scientific enquiries were entirely 'pure' or 'academic', a passion for truth could be its own sufficient justification, and the discovery of truth its own undoubted reward. In the 20th century, scientists have at last had to come to terms, not just with the ideal of truth, but also with the reality of power. As the changing nature of their work has brought them into closer contact with the rest of human life, so— to use a phrase from Don K. Price's book, *The Scientific Establishment*—they have found their problems moving along 'the spectrum from truth to power'; and the ethical choices facing them in their work have become correspondingly more complex.

For many years to come, the moral and spiritual conflict of the 20th-century scientist will, no doubt, be personified by the figure of J. Robert Oppenheimer. By intellectual standards, Oppenheimer was no Galileo: before the Second World War, he had shown himself an inspired teacher, but his greatest contribution to physical theory was the rather minor 'Born-Oppenheimer approximation'. It was his appointment as director of the Manhattan project that cast him—politically speaking—in the role of a 20th-century Galileo: precipitating him into deep personal, political and moral conflicts for which he was not fully prepared, and to which he responded with all the human passions, strengths and weaknesses that were read by Bertolt Brecht into Galileo's life also. Yet the most compact statement of the 20th-century scientist's new moral dilemmas perhaps remains a remark made, not by Oppenheimer himself, but by his colleague Bainbridge, as he watched the mushroom cloud rising from the first experimental atom-bomb: 'We are all sons-of-bitches now!'

Throughout the 20th century, accordingly, the programme for science conceived as an intellectual possibility, three hundred years earlier, has continued to control the ideas and activities of natural scientists; and in many ways the scientific world-picture of the 1970s appears simply to be the fulfilment of that intellectual programme. As for the technological ambitions of Francis Bacon and the early Royal Society: during the 20th century these have been fulfilled to an extent that would take their breath away. Yet this is only one side of an ambiguous picture. The very process of fulfilling the 17th-century programme has obliged us also to recognize its limitations. We have had, in that process, to square the intellectual and practical ideals inherited from Bacon and Newton with social and historical realities that men have learned to appreciate only more recently; and in the scientific sphere, these social and historical problems have turned out to be just as intractable as elsewhere. At times, indeed, it has almost seemed that History was revenging itself on a Science that had attempted to deny it.

If taken naively and at its face value, the 17th-century scientific world-picture has proved to be thoroughly a-historical, while the practical hopes that were based on it grossly underestimated the social consequences of their own fulfilment. As men have moved progressively into the new scientific world during the last seventy years, the social and historical dimensions missing from the original vision of science have re-entered the perspective; and with them also the shadows. On every front, the successes of the scientific movement have brought it up against its own unforeseen side-effects. Intellectually, the 20th century has seen a revival of philosophical and historical issues at the heart of scientific thought. Socially, it has seen scientific research lose its earlier monastic character, and natural science itself become, for the first time, a serious factor in national and international politics. Finally, as individuals, scientists have found themselves at last compelled to face the question whether knowledge for its own sake is, in all cases, an undoubted good. As a result, the unmixed optimism of earlier times is no longer an appropriate attitude for natural scientists, and a necessary sense of moral tragedy has re-entered their professional lives.

XIII A WORLD TRANSFORMED

Industrial and technological advance

JOHN MADDOX

'It is an illusion to think that, because we have
broken through the prohibitions, taboos and rites that
bound primitive man, we have become free.
We are conditioned by something new:
technological civilization.'

JACQUES ELLUL

'**The Age of Technology**'
by the German artist Max Schulze-Sölde, 1925, conveys something
of the ambivalence which 20th-century man feels towards technology—on the one hand impressed by the grandeur of its
achievement, on the other apprehensive about the changes, often
unintentional, that it makes to the quality of life. The most
pressing problems of the world today, many of which loom large
in other parts of this book—overpopulation, pollution, the
disturbance of ecological balances—are those which have arisen
not as a result of technology's failures but of its triumphs.

This chapter looks at the way in which the discoveries of science
are applied to the solution of particular problems, and how those
solutions are made available nationally or commercially. It is a
story that lies behind much of the political and economic history
that has formed the subject of earlier chapters, and in the long
perspective of the future it will probably be seen as the single most
important aspect of our century. (1)

Builders of the future: Thomas Alva Edison, John Burroughs (a writer on natural history), Henry Ford and Harvey Firestone (President of the Firestone Tyre and Rubber Co.) photographed in 1918 against one of the oldest sources of power, a water-wheel. Above right: Count Ferdinand von Zeppelin with one of his airships. (2, 3)

The telephone, which spread rapidly in America during the 1880s, was introduced to Europe on a commercial scale in the following decade. By 1913 (above: an exchange at Posen, Germany) it was already semi-automatic. (4)

Electricity, well understood in the 19th century, formed the basis of many new technologies of the 20th (see p. 302–303). Below: a hydro-electric station at Trostberg, Germany, 1913. (6)

Wireless soon made itself indispensable in a variety of ways, from telegraphy at sea (above, in 1912) to political oratory. The first English party-leader to use broadcasting was Stanley Baldwin in 1924 (below left). By the thirties (below right) it had become a major weapon of Nazi propaganda. (5, 7, 8)

The first airplane (above left) flew on 17 December 1903, when the brothers Wilbur and Orville Wright lifted their frail craft off the ground. Development was surprisingly slow until the First World War (above: early bombing methods) showed its strategic value. (9, 10)

Ford's assembly line was a major breakthrough in the application of technology to industry, making possible the mass-manufacture of a complex machine at costs far below those of his competitors. These photographs (left and below) show the factory at Detroit about 1925. (11, 12)

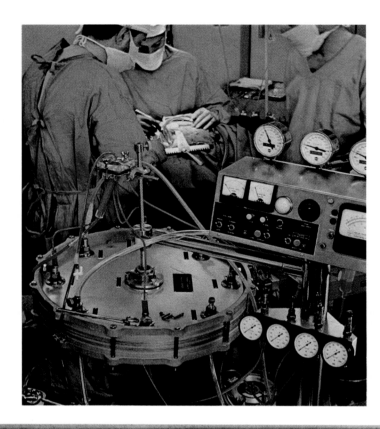

Modern medicine is also the product of the trilogy science-technology-industry, each as vital as the other two. The heart-lung machine (left) takes over the patient's blood, supplies it with oxygen and pumps it back into the body. (13)

The giant forces of modern industry come to life in the Mexican painter Diego Rivera's frescoes in the Institute of Fine Arts, Detroit. In the centre is Ford's assembly-line, with steering-wheels being fitted on to the chassis of cars. Rivera shows all the stages of manufacture and all social grades, including the managers and a crowd of bourgeois visitors who have come to watch. (14)

Without the jet engine no aircraft could fly much faster than 450 miles per hour. Although it had been invented in the mid-thirties, it was the war which provided the incentive to develop it. The aircraft shown here (left), the US bomber B-52, powered by four pairs of jet engines, is carrying a new type of spacecraft without wings, which is launched in mid-air, goes into a steep dive, and lands by utilizing the air-resistence in a landing-flare. Below: the General Electric GE4, a recent American engine. Bottom: the Anglo-French Concorde, first supersonic passenger airliner. (15, 16, 17)

The miniature world of electronics also grew largely from wartime demands. Computers were developed to enable anti-aircraft gunners to hit fast-moving targets. Left: a section of the 'memory' of a modern computer. Each disc contains 'information' (i.e. 'Yes' or 'No' to a specific question) which determines the way in which the current in the wires is directed. The square in the centre (a 'monolithic chip') is a reduced version of a whole circuit, about 1/16 of an inch across. (18)

Hydro-electric stations remain one of the cheapest sources of power. This (below) was the world's largest in 1967, at Bratsk in Russia. (22)

Fibres by the mile are run off from the machines of the Dangevpils mill in Russia (top). Synthetic chemistry can now provide substitutes for almost any substance occurring in nature. The modern assembly-line in the lower picture is at the Fiat works, Italy. (20, 21)

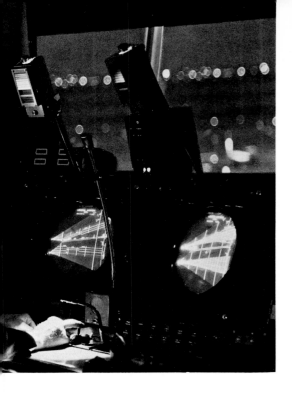

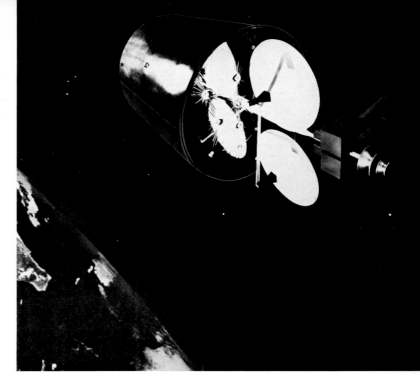

To detect hostile aircraft Britain evolved radar, a technique for using radio waves of very high frequency to 'reflect' on solid objects. It is now an essential part of air-traffic control at busy airports (left). (19)

The 'spin-off' from the space-race has produced a number of useful inventions, of which one is the communications-satellite (right). It can focus its power into two spotlight 'beams' and point them in the direction needed, carrying television signals round the curved surface of the earth. (23)

The largest ships are no longer passenger liners, but oil-tankers. Below: launching the giant 'Caterina M' in June 1969. (24)

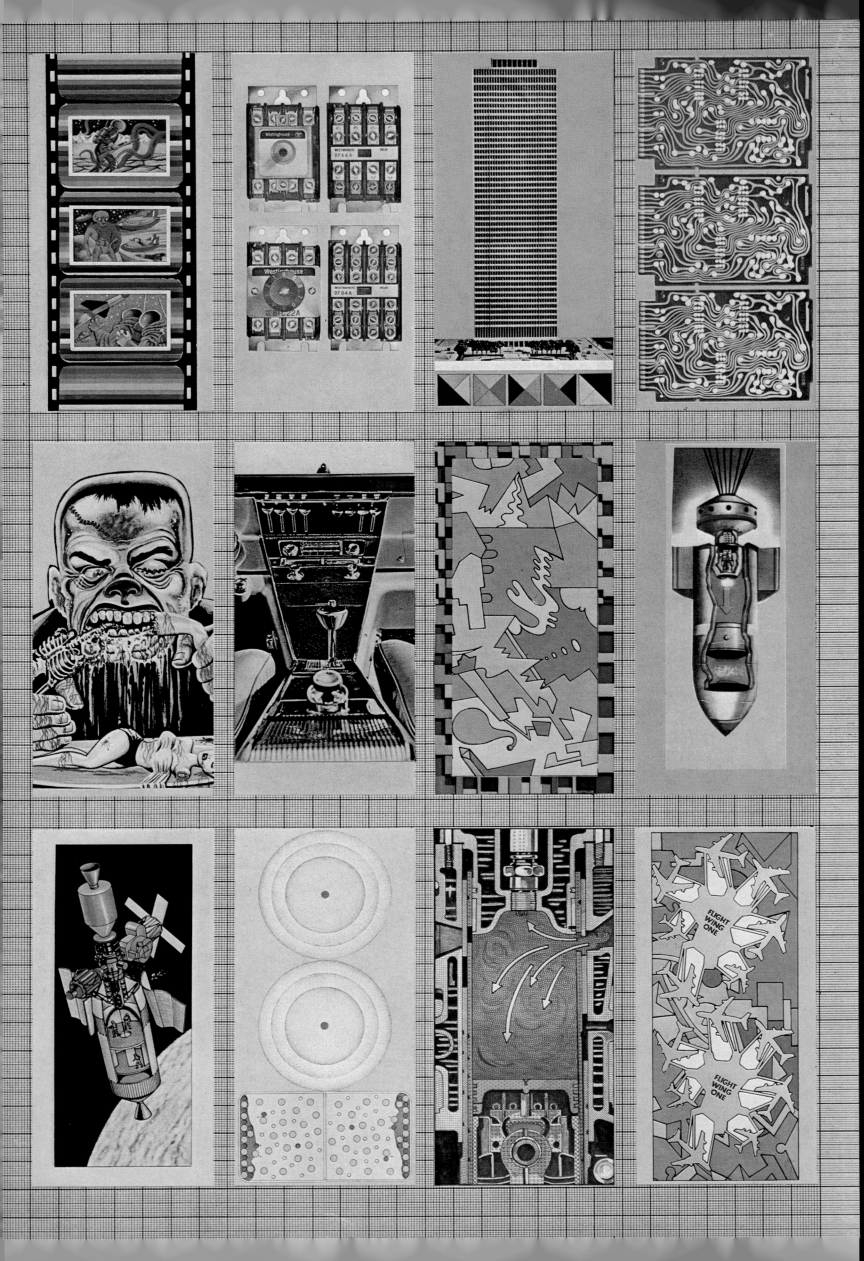

Industrial and technological advance

JOHN MADDOX

MODERN TECHNOLOGY began with the Industrial Revolution. That was the period during which the foundations were laid for a great many industries still essential for the working of industrial societies—steel, railways and heavy chemicals, for example. More important, the Industrial Revolution was itself characterized by the way in which technical innovations were deliberately exploited for economic gain. The mill-owners of Lancashire in the 19th century, for example, were every bit as careful with their calculations of the potential benefits of new machinery as are modern technologists in their attempts to calculate potential benefits of, say, a new source of power or a new type of aircraft. Now as in the Industrial Revolution, the essence of technology is the interplay between technical invention and economic exploitation.

The pace of industrial change in the past few decades may have been rapid enough to discomfit and even affront large sections of the population, especially in those countries in which the pace of change is most rapid, but it is hardly more remarkable than the changes brought about in western Europe by the Industrial Revolution more than a century ago. The growth of the British steel industry in the early 19th century is a good indicator of the pace of change. Between 1825 and 1850, for example, the output of pig iron from blast furnaces in Britain multiplied five times. Between 1850 and 1870, the length of the operating railway tracks in Britain increased from 6,000 miles to 18,000 miles (and the output of pig iron doubled again). The output of Bessemer steel, an invention of the mid-century, increased from 225,000 tons a year in 1865 to more than 1,000,000 tons a year a mere twelve years later. (The steel industry of France, with a slower start, multiplied by eight in these same twelve years.) These changes of scale are in every way comparable with the growth of more recently created industries, with the electronic computing industry a possible exception.

Sources of the Industrial Revolution

A small number of mechanical inventions were necessary ingredients of the Industrial Revolution. The steam engine was all-important. Techniques for mining coal at depth were also important, and were curiously symbiotic with the development of the steam engine. Automatic textile machinery, driven first by water power and then by coal-fired steam engines, provided not merely a means of saving labour previously employed on spinning and weaving but a device for increasing the output of the British textile industry and for reducing its production costs to the point at which all competition was swept aside. Thus the British economy was able to grow quickly and at the same time to maintain a favourable balance of trade with the outside world. Beginning in the 1830s, railways began to spread out over the surface of the British Isles, and three decades later there were if anything too many of them. Heavy chemicals underwent several important transformations during the Industrial Revolution, chiefly in the processes available for the manufacture of alkalis (themselves the raw materials for making soaps) but the seeds of the modern chemical industry were sown only much later in the 19th century. Innovations in metallurgy were more important, especially the refinement of blast furnace techniques and the development of the Bessemer furnaces.

Much of what counted as progress in the decades before 1900 consisted of the slow and steady improvement of the basic principle by careful engineers each bent on making a more efficient and more commercially profitable machine. Stephenson's *Rocket* may have been a rudimentary device in comparison with the giant locomotives that were hauling heavy trains over great distances by the end of the century, but the principle was substantially the same. The technology of the classical Industrial Revolution was almost entirely empirical. Radically new machines or processes were usually the product of the resourcefulness of a courageous and persuasive inventor. The first railway locomotives, for example, were innocent of what is now called industrial research, while the analogue of what is now called development was the construction of a prototype and the patient attempt to make it work. The habit of making a close analysis of an engineering problem came only with hindsight and with the need to squeeze the greatest economic potential out of a piece of machinery by means of careful attention to design.

In circumstances like these, it is not surprising that the technology of the 19th century should have come to seem a dramatic business. Bridge builders became heroes. Railway engineers became tycoons and even politicians. Nobody could be sure what technical innovation would next transform his way of life, yet the pace of change seems to have been sufficiently rapid for the gap between ordinary people's expectations and their rewards never to be dangerously wide. And in spite of the sombre conditions of many of the new industrial slums, 19th-century Britain seems to have been able to keep alive a robust and even noisy optimism.

On the mainland of Europe and in the United States, the course of the Industrial Revolution seems to have been similar in principle but often significantly different in detail. Both in France and Germany, the process of change was later to begin than in Britain, but just as rapid in the end. Both countries were able to profit from their late start by reaping the benefits of hindsight. In the United States, it remains something of a puzzle that the early decades of the century, in what was still largely a rural economy, should have been so rich in industrial innovations of all kinds. One persuasive view is that the acute labour shortage of the early decades of the 19th century provided a sharper incentive than in Europe for the replacement of muscles by machines. It is also clear, however, that geography had an important part to play in the development of the railway system and in the rapid and vigorous exploitation of methods of communication such as the electric telegraph. The mechanization of farming was also an important goal, the source of a great many types of agricultural machinery still in use.

Comparisons like these suggest that until the last quarter of the 19th century, technology seems mostly to have rested on the radical innovations that made possible the classical Industrial Revolution. To be sure, there were important improvements of technique. The scale of industrial operations also multiplied enormously, so that rural nations were turned into industrial nations within the span of a century. By the closing decades of the 19th century, however, technology was largely what it would have been predicted to be by some prophet of the 1830s, yet the sheer success of the operation seems to have left not merely a powerful

The spread of telephones revolutionized business life, but of course depended on a sufficiently long list of subscribers. A whole series of advertisements like this appeared in newspapers around 1900. (1)

industrial base in many countries but a sense of confidence in the processes of industrial change. The scene was set for the second of the three great periods of innovation in modern technology, and for the beginnings of the 20th century as such.

Currents of progress: electricity, the telephone, radio

The technology of the 20th century springs from a spate of inventions and innovation in the closing decades of the 19th century which is, in its way, as remarkable as any similar period before or afterwards. Landes has called this period the Industrial Revolution's 'second wind'. As at the beginning of the century, this period was marked not by the steady improvement of existing processes but by the creation of entirely new industries. In this sense, the history of technology in the 20th century begins in the 1880s.

The growth of the electricity industry, much delayed, was the starting point for many later innovations, and the starting point of the electrical industry was the development of a method of generating worthwhile amounts of electricity using some mechanical machinery as a source of energy. Although Faraday had demonstrated in 1831 the way in which a magnet moving within an electrical circuit will stimulate the flow of an electrical current, the construction of a practical machine for making electricity by this method turned out to be surprisingly difficult. A part of the trouble seems to have been indifference to the potential benefits of electricity generated by electromagnetic machinery—it seems not to have been recognized with sufficient clarity that methods of converting mechanical energy into electrical energy could produce much larger amounts of electricity than could be stored in the electrical storage batteries widely in use from the beginning of the 19th century. It is also plain, however, that turning Faraday's notion of electromagnetism into a practical machine for making electricity from mechanical energy (a dynamo) was intellectually much more difficult than, say, the embodiment of Watt's observation of a boiling kettle into a working steam engine.

What this implies is that the dynamos (driven by steam engines) which came into service in the 1880s were made possible only because of the careful understanding of the interaction of electrical currents and magnetic forces which had been accumulated in universities and engineering factories in several European countries but especially Britain, Germany and France. Haphazard though this work may have been, the fact remains that for the first time an important step forward in the development of technology was seen to rest on a profound intellectual understanding of a complicated physical phenomenon. By accident but through necessity, a marriage had been arranged between technology and science.

The applications of the new sources of electricity are significant, if only because they show how the course of technical development depends not merely on the technical capabilities of innovations but on the historical context in which they are introduced. To begin with, dynamo electricity was used for public or domestic

lighting. In London and New York, public generating stations were commissioned in 1882. (One Philadelphia department store had installed arc lamps lit by electricity from a dynamo a good five years earlier, but this seems to have been more a novelty than a practical device.) In the event, however, the spread of electric lighting seems to have been more rapid in the United States than in Britain, chiefly because the British gas-making industry was more efficient and thus more strongly competitive with electricity than the American. With the development of electrical motors for turning electricity back again into mechanical energy, other applications followed. By 1895, the first electrified railway line was in operation in the United States. By the turn of the century, the foundations had been securely laid for the development of the electricity generating industry which is now responsible for a substantial part of each industrialized nation's capital investment and for the diversity of applications of electric motors without which the 20th century would be unrecognizable.

p 298 (6)

The closing decades of the 19th century also saw the development of two innovations in telecommunications which have set their stamp on the 20th century—the invention of the telephone and the use of radio waves for broadcasting. The first telephone was exhibited by its inventor, Alexander Graham Bell, at the Centennial Exhibition in the United States in 1876 and, after some years of dispute about the ownership of the patent, telephone systems spread quickly through the United States. The United States was the natural ground for the commercial exploitation of telephones as means of communication, and the growth of telephone networks in American cities was especially rapid. Elsewhere, the pace of growth was more leisurely.

The successful development of the telephone differed from that of earlier devices with an important effect on the economy of industrial societies by its dependence on a complicated study of the conversion of electrical signals into sounds carried out in Germany by the physicist Helmholtz. In due course, this study was the basis of the microphones used in telephone systems and in broadcasting both for converting the energy of speech into the oscillations of an electric current, and for converting electrical signals into sounds. The development of the telephone is thus a splendid but early example of the way in which basic scientific research can provide the means for the foundations of a new technology. In the earlier innovations of the Industrial Revolution, the understanding of natural phenomena on which the new devices were based was often less explicit and much more empirical.

f 1 p 298 (4)

The development of radio broadcasting is a similar case. To begin with, the recognition that radio waves should exist was predicted theoretically by Maxwell in the 1880s and confirmed soon afterwards by the German physicist Herz. The problem was how to make use of this intrinsically scientific discovery for practical purposes and by the turn of the century a great many people were engaged on this endeavour. As it happens, the first piece of research carried out by Ernest Rutherford at the Cavendish Laboratory, Cambridge, was an attempt to transmit radio waves through the atmosphere. In the event, the first practical system was that developed by Marconi, who first sent radio signals carrying speech across the Atlantic in 1901.

These first long-distance transmissions were spectacular in themselves but not sufficient as guides to how radio transmitters and receivers might be made into commonplace pieces of machinery. For the first decade of the 20th century, the outstanding problem was that of devising some method by means of which radio waves from some distant place might be detected, and the signal carried by them—the electrical representation of the sound of a human voice, for example—might be extracted. To begin with, the devices for doing this job were exceedingly unreliable. Eventually, it became plain that the most hopeful way of doing this would be to rely on the electronic valve (or 'tube' in the United States)—a device which could serve as a detector of the signals carried by radio waves because of its capacity to allow electricity to pass through it in one direction only, and which could also be used in conjunction with other electrical components to amplify the weak signals thus extracted from a radio wave. (Conversely, in transmitters, the same or similar valves could be used for loading on the radio wave transmitted the electrical representation of a signal to be broadcast.) But even when the importance of the electronic valve was evident by the end of the first decade, it was clear that the devices then in use were not reliable.

p 298 (5) The eventual development (by 1912) of a suitable electronic valve differs from the other technical innovations of the period in its dependence on the scientific understanding of the movement of electricity in gases which had been formulated in the previous decade by academic scientists. Indeed, the rational understanding of the working of the electronic tube would not have been possible without the demonstration in 1897 by J. J. Thomson of how electricity can travel through a vacuum in the form of electrified particles of matter called electrons. The electronic valves which eventually provided the backbone for the construction of radio receivers and transmitters owed much to the work of academically trained physicists, the American Langmuir almost the chief among them.

The search for workable components for radio equipment created patterns of industrial development which were at the time unique and which were models of developments to come much later on. For one thing, the first decade of the radio industry was preoccupied with the attainment of a goal defined not so much in technical as in functional terms—the object was to devise a reliable device for processing radio waves in both transmitters and receivers. There were in principle several possibilities from which to choose, while all the industrial companies concerned were well aware that the prize for success would be a commanding lead in a new industry certain to be commercially profitable. The result was the emergence of the modern pattern of industrial research, the use of teams of technically trained people to put flesh on the bones of abstractly defined objectives. To set out to perform some previously defined function by the selection of some scientific principle and the development of a technical device based upon it is naturally a more sophisticated concept than the thorough exploitation of some known piece of scientific understanding as in, for example, the development of the electrical generating industry at the end of the 19th century.

New power from oil and steam

The threshold of the 20th century was also remarkable for the way in which there were developed several important sources of mechanical power, the most spectacular of which was the internal combustion engine which, in its turn, made possible the automobile industry and heavier-than-air flying machines. This again was an innovation which sprang from an explicit understanding of the principles by means of which the energy of chemicals and vapours can be converted into mechanical energy. The internal combustion engine, after all, is analogous to a steam engine in which the source of power is not a vapour at high pressure but, rather, a gas at high pressure produced *in situ* by the combustion of a hydrocarbon fuel. The middle decades of the 19th century, dependent as they were on steam engines for the production of power, were understandably preoccupied with the need to construct engines of the most efficient design, which in turn provided an incentive for the development of theoretical understanding of the conversion of one form of energy into another, the science of thermodynamics. This, in turn, provided the conceptual framework within which new engines could be built.

The first successful internal combustion engines were built and installed in the late seventies, first of all in Germany, using coal gas as a fuel. The potential advantages of using petroleum as a fuel were already plain, but the heavy oil available in the 1880s, and similar in many ways to the material used nearly a century later as fuel oil, could only be manipulated with difficulty. After a decade of unsuccessful development, a workable oil engine was manufactured in Britain in the nineties by Ruston and Hornsby, and towards the end of the century, in 1897, the first diesel engine was manufactured. This design, efficient and practical, was the clearest embodiment of the thermodynamic principles after which generations of Victorians had striven. In due course, however, diesel engines burning heavy oil were in competition with petrol engines based on the lighter fractions of petroleum—for many purposes, particularly in the production of comparatively small amounts of mechanical power, the latter were preferable, but their

widespread use was only possible after the development of reliable carburettors in the last few years of the century.

The invention of the first flying machines—the Wright brothers first covered a few hundred yards on 17 December 1903—was another culmination of several decades of experiment, in this case much of it comparatively empirical. Through much of the 19th century, attempts had been made to design efficient gliders and a great deal was learned about the construction of aircraft by means of kite-flying experiments with suitably designed wings. The most successful attempts to lift weights and people by means of kites involved constructions on the box kite principle, which goes some way to explain why the first aircraft devised by the Wright brothers was a biplane in which the wings were put together much as in a kite. Eventually, of course, the men who made the first flying machines were driven to acknowledge that monoplanes would be more efficient than biplanes—the problem was as much a problem of mechanical construction as of the provision of lifting surfaces. Although the turn of the century also saw the invention of the p 298 (2) Zeppelin—a development of the power-driven lifting balloon tried out in the closing decades of the century—it was the powered aircraft that cast its spell (some would say shadow) on the 20th century.

In this productive period, the development of the steam turbine by C. A. Parsons must have seemed almost a superfluous innovation. The incentive was the need somehow to design a method of driving the rotating shaft of electric dynamos. Steam engines were not capable of driving the rotating machinery at a speed great enough to produce electricity economically, with the result that intermediate trains of gears were necessary, so that much of the mechanical energy generated by the steam engine was lost in friction. The steam turbine was a device by means of which a jet of steam at high pressure was forced past a series of blades mounted on a rotating shaft much as the wind flows past the vanes of a windmill. As with the other innovations of this formative period, the efficiency and indeed the economic viability of the steam turbine developed by Parsons in the years after his first patents in 1884 stemmed from an understanding of the scientific principles on which devices of this kind might function. In the event, steam turbines turned out to be the workhorses of the growing electricity-generating industry of the 20th century, the most effective means of providing ships with large amounts of power in a compact space and thus with speed and, in due course, the models on which the gas turbine of the 1940s was constructed.

Towards the end of the 19th century, the chemical industry too was transformed by a series of discoveries which changed it from a producer of industrial raw materials used on a very large scale to a manufacturer of chemicals with much more precise uses—dyes and even pharmaceuticals. The roots of this transformation lie in the discovery by W. H. Perkin in 1856 of the chemical called mauveine, the first synthetic dyestuff. Throughout the second half of the 19th century, Perkin and his competitors abroad, particularly in Germany, were hard at work in the search for dyestuffs and other materials made frequently from the coal tar obtained as a by-product in the manufacture of coal gas. The culmination of this competition was the development of synthetic indigo in 1897, by which time the increasingly sophisticated chemical industry was hard at work in the manufacture of explosives, fertilizers and the extraction of some of the rarer metals, the use of which was increasingly important in the refinement of the metallurgical industries.

The recognition that the scientific understanding of the natural world could help with the transformation of industry served also as an inspiration to those who argued that scientific education was a necessary preliminary for industrial strength. This is why, throughout western Europe and the United States, the turn of the century saw a great preoccupation among educators with the need to provide young men and women with a training in the sciences and in engineering. This, after all, was a period in which the University of Cambridge first established university departments in chemistry and physics. Before long the universities of Europe and the United States began to turn out substantial numbers of graduates in scientific subjects. This pool of talent turned out to be of great value when eventually the First World War began, and when it became necessary to hasten the natural pace of development in several fields of industry. In the chemical industry, the consequences were more immediate; the great chemical companies, spurred on by the success with which Nobel had been able to manufacture explosives, established their traditions of linking scientific research directly with the process of innovation. And the consequences of these educational innovations for the technological history of the mid-century were profound.

The early history of 20th-century technology is nevertheless industrial history and not a record of invention. There grew up during this period several new industries—electricity generation and aircraft construction, for example. In many circumstances, the new industries of the 20th century were interlocking industries. Both automobiles and aircraft were made possible only by the availability of light petrol engines. Steam turbines serviced both electricity generators and fast ships. But there is little doubt that the most significant of all the new industries was that of motor vehicle manufacture, which cast its spell on the imaginations of ordinary people, which contributed enormously to the pattern of the economy in industrialized nations and which transformed the habits of whole sections of industry.

Mass production: the age of Henry Ford
By the turn of the century, the industrial dominance of the United States had already been clearly established. The reasons why this should be are by no means understood. Undoubtedly, the chronic shortage of labour in North America throughout the 19th century had provided a continuing incentive for the imaginative use of machines. The richness of North America in raw materials for industry, particularly newer materials such as petroleum, must also have helped to make North America the most innovative of industrial nations at the beginning of the 20th century. To begin with, however, the most pregnant development was not an invention but the development of a technique—that for manufacturing the components of complicated machines with such precision that entire machines could be assembled from what were called 'interchangeable parts'. This was a technique to which many people had aspired throughout the 19th century, chiefly so as to avoid the difficulty and the expense of ensuring that each machine manufactured would consist of parts which had been carefully fitted together after manufacture by necessarily empirical adjustments of size and shape. The first applications of the technique, halfway through the 19th century, were in the manufacture of rifles in the United States. In due course, the same techniques were used, towards the end of the 19th century, in the manufacture of domestic articles such as sewing machines as well as for the assembly of the machine tools which themselves were used in the manufacture of interchangeable parts. Throughout, the incentive—particularly in the United States—was the saving of labour. The result was first of all the manufacture of cheap motor cars by Henry Ford, the spread of the technique of mass production throughout manufacturing industry, and the beginning of what is now called production engineering.

In the closing years of the 19th century, in Britain, the United States and France, the manufacture of motor vehicles had been carried on by a host of back-street companies and workshops. Ford set up his first plant in Detroit in 1902 and by the diligent application of the technique of precision manufacture, interchangeable parts and production line assembly was able to market the first Model T Ford in 1908. By the mid-twenties, such a motor car cost $300, much less than the real cost of comparable vehicles (if such were) elsewhere in the world. By that time, the Ford Motor Company had sold more than 15 million Model T Fords. By 1930, there were 26 million motor vehicles registered in the United States, five times as many as in the whole of Europe put together. The motor car industry had come to play an important role in the national economy, consuming sixteen per cent of steel production in the United States and contributing such a large part to the Gross National Product of the country that the health of the motor car industry was at once an index of national prosperity and the determinant of it.

The technical developments which sustained the growth of the motor vehicles industry were at once daring and humdrum. There

p 298 (2)
p 299 (11, 12)

has been no essential change in the construction of motor vehicles since the first petrol-driven vehicles made their way gingerly about the roads of Europe and North America in the nineties. From the beginning, however, each manufacturer and his engineers have contributed improvements to the basic concept of how a steerable chassis resting on four wheels should be driven from place to place by an engine. The crude electrical systems of the early motor vehicles were rapidly improved. Starting motors were eventually introduced and thus liberated motorists from the need to start their engines by hand. Transmission systems were improved and made more flexible. Mechanical gearboxes eventually became but one of the means by which power could be transferred from the engine to the driven wheels. But the most common improvements of design were comparatively unspectacular—better steering, better suspension, even better paintwork. It is common to scorn the notion of technical devices 'developed by committee', but the modern motor vehicle is itself the embodiment of a whole sequence of minor innovations contributed by an army of engineers, many of them unknown.

In one strictly technical sense, the development of the motor vehicle influenced industry in a way in which, much more recently, the aerospace development programmes of the United States and elsewhere have functioned. For the search for improvements in the design of motor vehicles was frequently synonymous with a search for materials that would permit lighter components and thus a more efficient use of the propulsion system. For, if the function of a motor vehicle is to carry people or goods from place to place, why not reduce as far as possible the dead weight that must be propelled along as well? One effect of considerations like these was to put the metallurgical industries under pressure, and the 1900s saw the beginning of a vigorous but continued search for alloys of steel and other metals that are stronger, weight for weight, than more old-fashioned materials. Coupled with other pressures of a similar kind, especially from the aircraft industry in the twenties and later, this tendency ensured that the metallurgical industries would be well provided with skilled technical people capable of carrying on the search for ever stronger metals. That is a striking example of how the young motor vehicle cast its shadow forward over the decades that followed.

The growing motor vehicle industry managed to establish a pattern of industrial organization in which many other industrial enterprises of the early decades of the 20th century were cast. The sheer scale of the enterprise ensured this. In the United States and later in Britain, the irreducible function of the motor manufacturers themselves was the assembly of finished parts. The manufacture of individual components was often however entrusted to smaller and somewhat specialized manufacturing companies, partly for the sake of economizing in capital investment and partly so as to lend flexibility to the organization of assembly lines. One immediate result, however, was to spread the exacting standards of manufacture required of an assembly process dependent on the bringing together of interchangeable parts throughout a large part of engineering industry. Another was to familiarize engineering industry as a whole with the cost-consciousness of the motor vehicle manufacturers—a knowledge which led both to the practice of requiring that engineering designs should satisfy explicit and exacting economic criteria and also to the techniques of work study.

One particularly beneficial consequence of the rapid growth of the motor vehicle industry was the incentive which it provided for the development of machine tools beyond the point reached in the closing decades of the 19th century, when the principles had already been established that automatic ways of shaping metals could be devised if only the necessarily imprecise hands of a technician could be replaced by mechanical means of holding the workpiece and moving it mechanically against the cutting edge of a tool of some kind. In the United States, especially, electric motors quickly made their appearance as the driving force for the early machine tools. In this as in many other respects, Europe lagged conspicuously behind. In the United States, however, the concept had already been formulated of the way in which it might eventually be possible to link together machine tools of various kinds in such a way as to provide largely automatic sequences of

p 299 (11, 12) p 300 (14)

The two World Wars brought nothing but good to technology. Between 1914 and 1918 not only were important advances made in motor vehicles, *aircraft and radio, but the way industry was organized was put on a new, national scale. (2)*

machine tools for the manufacture of quite complicated devices. The foundations of automation were, in other words, laid in the 1900s in the motor vehicle factories of the United States. Very quickly it was evident that the benefits of such techniques consisted not merely of reproducibility and thus of interchangeability but of cheapness and good design as well.

The pattern of industrial organization established by the motor vehicle industry was itself also a determinant of the character of later industrial innovation. For much of the 20th century, manufacturers have sought to recreate the circumstances in which production engineers can apply the lessons they have learned from Detroit. On the whole, the results have been worthwhile. The result is that now the manufacturing plants that produce machines as different as domestic refrigerators and electronic computers depend as far as may be possible on the techniques first applied in a rudimentary fashion to the manufacture of the first motor vehicles. Is it too fanciful to think that the same pattern has led naturally to the way in which large industrial enterprises manufacturing several different products—conglomerates as they are called—tend to be organized into hierarchic interlocking manufacturing plants related to each other as are the different parts of an assembly line?

Among the other new industries of the 20th century, the aircraft industry was much less quickly turned into a giant. One of the puzzles of the early years is that the United States, which had so vigorously seized upon the motor vehicle as the essential ingredient of a gigantic enterprise, was comparatively neglectful of the significance of the first flight by the Wright brothers, Wilbur and Orville. In the first five years of this century, the event caused just as much excitement in Britain and France as in the United States, with the result that there sprang up a whole series of more or less amateur construction enterprises, often under the auspices of owners of garages only recently set up (or converted, from stables) to cater for the motor cars then making their appearance on the roads. British companies, eventually with the support of the British government, were commendably but uncharacteristically

p 299 (9)

quick to become involved. In retrospect, it is sobering that the aircraft industry should have had a much less powerful effect on the pattern of the rest of industry than had the motor vehicle industry, but until the outbreak of the First World War its operations were conducted on a very small scale, while the techniques for the construction of the first aircraft were not in themselves demanding enough to stretch the aptitudes of manufacturing industry. For several years, wood and oiled silk were the raw materials for airframe construction.

The impetus of war

Motor vehicles, aircraft and radio were all destined to play an important part in the First World War. For much of Europe, this was the incentive needed to ensure that the American experience in motor vehicle construction would be emulated. Technically, the First World War was most significant of all for the design of aircraft, which were enormously more sophisticated by 1918 than at the beginning of the war. And military experience demonstrated that radio communications were certainly a practicable and most probably an economical method of spanning distances between people. In short, the war lent reality to what had previously been something of a novelty. With the exception of the strictly military developments—ranging from the deployment of tanks and poison gas to the naval use of torpedoes and submarines—the chief technical consequence of the First World War was the acceleration of the development of three industries barely twenty years old by the end of the war.

p 299 (10)

In institutional terms, however, the First World War provided the first proof of the importance of technical development to the conduct of public business by governments, and it is no accident that in Britain, the United States and elsewhere many of the institutions still active in the regulation of technology date from this period. In Britain, the government established at this time a Department of Scientific and Industrial Research intended somehow to bring together the talents of technical people from the universities and industry and the technical needs of government.

f 2

From this point, it seems also to have been accepted that governments would have to retain a continuing responsibility for the support of technical development in industries strategically as important as the design of aircraft. The recognition of this principle may in the long run have been more important than the impetus provided for the faster development of the new industries most directly involved in the conduct of the war.

The new industries not directly relevant to the military conduct of the First World War necessarily grew more steadily, and are the more simply indicative of the growth of technological industry as such. It was during this period, in the then industrialized nations, that the crude rule of thumb was established that the rate at which electricity is consumed doubles every decade. In the early years of the century, the causes of this rapid increase of demand for electricity are easy to identify. This, after all, was the period during which manufacturers were replacing steam engines (used to drive machine tools, for example) by electric motors (but it remains a cause for complaint that British manufacturers were slower to move in this direction than their competitors in the United States). This was also the period in which the textile industry was replacing steam power by electric power, but again more rapidly in the United States than elsewhere. And electrically driven domestic machinery was coming into service. Moreover, to the extent that a great part of the extra demand for electricity in the early decades came from those who sought a more convenient source of light than coal gas, the increasing demand for electricity was a measure of the increasing prosperity of industrialized nations. The fact that the simple rule that the demand for electricity doubles every decade has not yet been falsified in countries such as those of western Europe and North America (but the rate of growth is faster in developing countries) is a natural phenomenon in its own right.

The technical means by which the electrical generating industry, in Britain, the United States and elsewhere, has been able to meet the growing demand for electricity is a striking illustration of the character of one kind of technical progress. At the turn of the century, the generating capacity of a typical dynamo would rarely exceed a few thousand kilowatts. Such a plant could provide domestic lighting for quite a large community, but would be inadequate for most of the industrial uses now commonplace. In principle, to be sure, there is no reason why the electrical engineers concerned with the design of generating plant at the turn of the century should not have leapfrogged over the decades to construct generating equipment ten or even a hundred times as powerful as the machinery they built. Certainly the generating machines producing 30,000 kilowatts of electricity which came into service in Britain in the early forties, and the steam turbines needed for driving them, could have been built within the framework of the technology of the early twenties. Two separate kinds of considerations helped to restrict the pace of growth, however. First, with necessarily expensive capital equipment, the risks of excessively rapid jumps ahead would have been too great for the empirical engineers by then in charge to have accomplished easily. Second, the demand for electricity could grow only as quickly as potential users could install the equipment necessary for consuming electricity.

Between the beginning of the 20th century and the great Depression of the early thirties, technological development brought about great changes not merely in the pattern of industrial and economic activity but in the character of personal life in industrialized societies. So much is beyond dispute. In Britain, for example, the growth of the motor vehicle industry was accompanied by the steady decline of coal mining (a large exporting industry before the First World War), textiles (or at least cotton spinning and weaving) and industries such as tinplate making. Why should this be? The truth is, of course, that there are limits to the capacity of any country to be up to date in all technologies at all instants of time. Indeed, it is inevitable that the prosperity won by new technologies will by itself increase the difficulties of those industries which are the more labour intensive and thus the more exposed to competition from abroad. In the years immediately after the First World War, industrialized nations everywhere began to learn that there is often a painful price to pay for economic progress.

p 298 (6)

The twenties: technology marks time

The decade immediately following the First World War seems from this distance, however, to have been a decade in which several important lessons were unlearned. No doubt the aftermath of the war and the acute shortage of capital which accompanied it were largely responsible. The result, however, seems to have been that the twenties were almost ostentatiously unconcerned with innovation as such but only with the further exploitation of what was known already. In Europe, at least, this was a time when the universities more or less marked time, as if it had been forgotten that the exciting developments of the early 20th century had been made possible only because of the way in which scientific understanding of the natural world had thrown light on the way in which industrial problems should be solved. And such technical development as there may have been tended to be exploited less efficiently or less vigorously than might have been the case, possibly for lack of capital. This, for example, was a time when the builders of aircraft were more optimistic about the future than the airlines supposedly in business to make money by operating passenger aircraft.

In the twenties, the most cheerful tale is that of the radio industry, as much a mushroom as any ingredient of the Industrial Revolution. In Britain, for example, the number of licensed radio receivers doubled from 1·1 million in 1924 to 2·2 million in 1926. As with the development of the motor vehicle industry in the 1910s, moreover, the widespread use of radio created industries consisting of assembling manufacturers surrounded by networks of components suppliers. By the early thirties, the economic importance of the radio industry in western Europe was even within sight of that of the motor vehicle industry. Technically, throughout this period the designers were hard at work with attempts to increase the frequency at which radio equipment would function well, chiefly because they were aware of the need somehow to make the fullest use of the way in which extremely short radio waves can in suitable circumstances be made to travel great distances around the Earth. Guided by the understanding of radio propagation provided by the scientific laboratories, this effort was eventually to become the foundation for a whole series of modern developments.

p 298 (7, 8)

In sum, however, the period finishing with the Depression is something of a disappointment. The innovations of the last few years of the 19th century had provided the ingredients for what might have been a second industrial revolution. The century started splendidly, and the Edwardian optimists were entirely right to be as cheerful as they were. But the First World War and its aftermath were more a distraction than a stimulus, and the twenties were comparatively arid. To be sure, technology made steady progress, chiefly by the addition of minor if important innovations. Just as the United States had seized the opportunities of the new century more vigorously than European nations, so the United States survived the First World War in better condition. For industrialists in Britain, perhaps the most sombre consideration was the relative improvement of the condition of German technology in the years after the First World War. For everybody, however, it should have been disappointing that industrialized societies should have been induced by the war and the twenties to overlook the importance of the liaison between science and industry so fruitfully demonstrated at the end of the 19th century.

The Second World War: radar, the jet-engine, the Bomb

If the First World War put technology to sleep, the threat of the second brought it to life again. The preparations for the Second World War, with which a great many scientists, engineers and politicians were concerned in the late thirties, laid the foundations for a great deal of contemporary technology. Four chief lines of development, begun in the thirties, were especially influential for the course of later events.

The development of radar, originally a method for detecting the approach of hostile aircraft, has for example contributed since the Second World War to the development of telecommunications in several important ways. The first radar sets were natural developments of the techniques evolved by radio engineers for sending beams of radio waves in specified directions. The higher

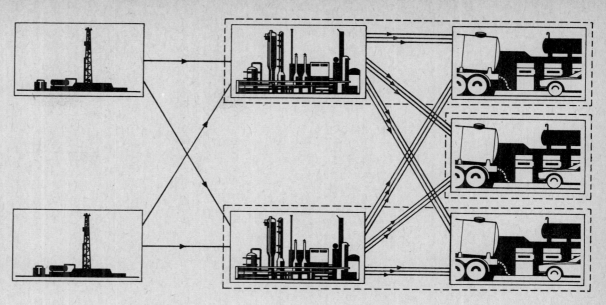

One of the ways in which computers aid industry is by working out the cheapest and most efficient routes from source to market. This simplified diagram shows the choices open to an oil company with two sources of supply, two refineries and three marketing areas. The data fed into the computer would cover such points as supply capacity, cost of transport, work-programme at the refineries, and estimated market-demand; and the result would say which of the twelve possible permutations should be preferred. A real-life example (e.g. B.P. oil) could involve over 8,000 items of information.(3)

the frequency (or the shorter the wave length) of the radio waves, or the larger the aerial, the narrower the beam could be. The notion that it might be possible to use such a narrow beam of radio wave to sweep the sky as if it were a searchlight, reflecting radio waves from metallic objects such as aircraft, was simple enough. In the late thirties, the practical problems were those of manipulating radio waves of the highest possible frequency and of devising some method sensitive enough to detect the radio waves reflected from an aircraft or some similar object. Although the enthusiasm of those in Britain and elsewhere engaged on projects like these in the late thirties was able to wring usable designs out of the theoretical calculations, it was not until the early forties that a team of scientists in Britain developed a practical method of producing intense sources of radio waves with a wavelength of 10 cm or so, less than a tenth of the wavelength of the radio waves first used for the detection of hostile aircraft. During the Second World War, this development and those which sprang from it led to the design of a whole armoury of new weapons systems—radar sets sufficiently small to be carried in aircraft and therefore valuable as means of letting military aircraft operate at night. A related development was that of fuses for bombs and anti-aircraft shells that would detonate an explosive charge within some predetermined distance of the target, thus enormously increasing the effectiveness of such devices.

The radar devices developed during the war are now, of course, essential parts of most systems for the regulation of air traffic, civil as well as military. The fact that beams of radio waves with a wavelength of 10 cm down to a few millimetres can be pointed in comparatively narrow pencils from one place to another has also, in the past decade, provided a convenient vehicle for telecommunications. Such a team of radio waves can carry simultaneously the equivalent of several hundred telephone conversations or even several television broadcast signals (each of which may be the equivalent of five hundred or so ordinary sound radio broadcasts). The result has been that microwave transmission has become a convenient way of handling telephone messages in bulk and of carrying television signals from one place to another, especially in circumstances in which other methods of communication are impractical—where, for example, it may be necessary to span rough terrain with telecommunications or to use an earth satellite as an intermediate repeater station. In the same way, the techniques developed during the Second World War for manipulating radar signals have become important ingredients of the technology of modern electronics. So as to be able to recognize radar waves reflected from aircraft, methods were needed for sending out bursts of radar waves lasting for only exceedingly short intervals of time—a millionth of a second or so to begin with but now very much less than that. Familiarity with the techniques for making pulses of radio waves has now led to the use of similar techniques in fields as different as telecommunications and the design of modern electronic computers.

p 302 (19)

p 302 (18) Electronic computers, which came into their own in the sixties, owe their origin in modern times to the preparations for the Second World War. One of the practical problems of defence

against air attack was, for example, that of aiming anti-aircraft guns in such a way as to increase the likelihood that an anti-aircraft shell would hit its quickly moving target. Both in Britain and in the United States, the development of devices like these was quickly recognized to be equivalent to the development of machines for carrying out all kinds of mathematical calculations. The first equipments of this kind were in fact what are called analogue computers in the sense that they simulated electronically and mechanically the mathematical relationships that exist between the known course of a fast moving aircraft and its likely position at some point in the future. Machines of this kind had indeed been developed for scientific purposes (and only incompletely) in the years immediately before the war by people such as Professor D. Hartree at the University of Manchester. Their existence during the Second World War led not merely to the development of more sophisticated analogue computers in the years after the Second World War but also to the development of the theory of cybernetics—the properties of machines which can simulate sentient processes and which are also closely concerned with control of processes as different as the movement of muscles in the limbs of animals and the guidance of complicated assembly lines for the mass production of, say, motor cars.

The preoccupation of Second World War governments with the problems of air defence provided one of the most urgent incentives for the development of jet engines—devices able to convert the energy of low grade petroleum fractions into motive power just as steam turbines were developed for generating electricity and for driving ships at the turn of the century. The first jet engines were constructed in the mid-thirties by Mr F. Whittle, but were regarded seriously as potential sources of power for aircraft only on the eve of the Second World War. In the event, the development work turned out to be long and expensive, with the result that aircraft driven by jet engines appeared only towards the end of the war. In short, the jet engine and the technology of modern civil aircraft which has flowed from it owes the speed of its development to the urgency of preparations for the Second World War but contributed very little to one side or the other. Only when the war had finished did jet engines become the power plants of the generation of military aircraft which dominated military strategy for two decades after the war, and which eventually (by the mid-fifties) provided the means of driving civil aircraft. It goes without saying that the suitability of jet engines for high-flying fast civil aircraft is by now so obvious that if they had not been developed for military reasons during the war, they would since have found civil patrons attracted by commercial opportunities. That said, there is no question that the development of jet engines and of modern civil aircraft would have been much more leisurely if there had been no war. It is perhaps relevant that aircraft would not be able to travel much faster than 350 miles an hour or so if jet engines did not exist. Certainly, supersonic speeds would be quite out of the question.

p 301 (15–17)

Of all the developments of technology during the Second World War, however, there is no doubt that the development of atomic energy is the most spectacular. This was the technical feat that set its stamp on the postwar world. The tale of what happened under the umbrella of the Manhattan Project is not merely one of the signs of the cleverness of those concerned but is also one of the most important sources of the postwar belief, itself an echo of Victorian optimism a century earlier, that technology can move mountains.

When the first proof was obtained, in 1938, that atomic nuclei of materials such as uranium can be split into two parts by the impact of an atomic particle called a neutron, there could be no certainty that an important weapon would emerge from this academic discovery. The belief that it might was, to begin with, entirely founded on theoretical arguments. Although by 1942 enough was known about the processes by means of which neutrons interact with atomic nuclei such as those of uranium to provide some assurance that a nuclear bomb would actually function, nobody was sure, in the three years that followed, that the plans which had been made would suffice for the making of a usable weapons system. Would the fissionable uranium turn out to be pure enough for a usable bomb? Would it be possible to carry the weapon in then existing aircraft? And what would be the effect of the weapon on the unfortunate people against whom it would be directed? The Manhattan Project is remarkable for the way in which it represents the triumph of technological optimism.

p 276
(13)

However sombre may be the shadow that nuclear weapons have cast on the postwar world, there is no question that they represent the most striking proof that goals which are in principle attainable are in practice within the grasp of those prepared to spend the time, the effort and the money. That belief is as much an exemplar of the postwar world as nuclear fission itself.

In the circumstances, it is perhaps surprising that those concerned with the development of weapons during the Second World War were comparatively unconcerned with the possible civil applications of their work, and in particular with the possibility that nuclear energy might become a source of power for the manufacture of electricity. Only towards the closing stages of the war did this goal become explicit. Only gradually, in the five or six years after the war, did people begin to appreciate that fissile materials such as uranium might be not merely useful adjuncts to existing sources of power of all kinds but prime sources of energy in fuel in their own right. By the early fifties, however, the first small nuclear reactors for turning the energy of uranium into heat had been constructed. By the mid-fifties, the foundations of the new technology had been almost completely laid—internationally, the United Nations held its first conference on the peaceful uses of nuclear energy, in the United States President Eisenhower launched the 'Atoms for Peace' programme and in the United Kingdom the government published what is plainly in retrospect

p 276
(12)

a most ambitious and unrealistic plan for the construction of nuclear power stations of various kinds.

So is it the case that wars such as the Second World War are such powerful stimulants of technological developments that there should be more of them? This question, of course, is a jibe. But it is a proper question to ask why the Second World War should have been such a powerful incentive. To begin with, the beginning of the war found that in the United States as well as Britain there was more technical and scientific skill than commercial industry could usefully employ, with the result that the new programmes of military development were able to recruit helpers from the universities and even the high schools in large numbers. Second, the universities themselves had begun to appreciate, especially in the United States, the need for a closer link between themselves and other agencies of public life, the military and the industrial estates. Third, by the beginning of the Second World War, it had become apparent that the old-fashioned distinction between pure science and applied technology had become an anachronism. Already it had become clear that some of the great successes of engineering technology were the products of scientific discoveries. Especially in nuclear physics, there were by then plenty of examples to show that even the progress of pure science could only be sustained by continuing technical development.

The Second World War was also, however, important for the institutions concerned with technical development which it created. This was the point at which governments and government depart-

ments began to acknowledge that technical objectives could be attained by gathering together teams of people prepared to work on common problems on an interdisciplinary basis. In the United States, several public laboratories remain now as monuments to the time during the war at which such common enterprises were established—the great laboratories originally concerned with nuclear weapons at Oak Ridge, Livermore and Los Alamos, but also the aircraft laboratories at Langley and the naval research laboratories in Washington. In Britain, this was also the period which saw the setting up of the Royal Radar Establishment (originally the Telecommunications Research Establishment) at Malvern, yet another source of innovation in the years after the Second World War. One way and another, it is now clear, the Second World War created not merely the belief that all things are possible but the means by which a great many of them could be and are still being attained.

Modern technology: the dilemmas of success

The Second World War finished with a conviction among technologists that all things are possible and with a profound sense of disquiet among technologists and their public about the implications of innovation, especially about nuclear weapons. The conflict between optimism and pessimism about technology has now become its most obvious attribute, perhaps because it has become increasingly difficult to win economic and social advantages from innovation.

Military technology projected forward for almost exactly two decades the technical prowess of the Second World War. Although the nuclear weapons dropped on Nagasaki and Hiroshima were the equivalent of 20,000 tons of high explosives, it quickly became possible to make much larger weapons and also weapons much more easily adapted to the delivery systems available at the end of the war, principally propeller-driven aircraft. From the beginning, however, it was also clear that still more powerful nuclear weapons could be devised by a combination of fissionable material such as uranium and other material such as hydrogen, the atoms of which release energy not by being split in half but by being fused together. The thermonuclear weapons which stemmed from this principle, the first of them in 1954, were as much as a thousand times as powerful as the weapons dropped on Hiroshima and Nagasaki. Although, immediately after the war, there was a case for saying that the coming of atomic weapons had not changed the essential character of war but merely its destructiveness, thermonuclear weapons (possessed by both the United States and the Soviet Union in the second half of the fifties) have profoundly influenced military strategy.

To begin with, thermonuclear weapons, by posing a threat against the large centres of population on a quite unprecedented scale, have made possible the strategy of deterrence and, it is fair to say, the stability provided by mutual deterrence as well. But the coming of thermonuclear weapons has also made more urgent the search for other delivery systems than aircraft. In the years since the Second World War, the strategic capacity of countries such as the United States and the Soviet Union, not to mention Britain and France (two other nuclear powers), has been determined much more by the availability of delivery systems than by the mere possession of nuclear explosives. The result has been an urgent search by the larger military powers for more efficient means of delivering powerful weapons at distant targets, which explains why both the United States and the Soviet Union (followed more recently by countries such as France and Japan) have spent large sums of money on the development of rocket systems, one of the most exacting branches of technology. The fact that long-range missiles have within fifteen years been designed so as to deliver weapons within a hundred yards or so of a target 5,000 miles or more away is a measure of what is being accomplished. It is fair to say that such technology itself springs first of all from early work in Tsarist Russia and in the United States on the theoretical design of rockets and from the development of rocket missiles in Germany during the Second World War. The successful development of military rockets in the fifties and sixties, however, has rested almost entirely on the electronic systems of guidance now available, and by this standard the rocket systems now deployed by the United States and the Soviet Union are as different from the German V-2 rocket as are supersonic aircraft from the biplane in which the Wright brothers flew.

Both nuclear weapons and their up-to-date delivery systems have been the springboard for important commercial developments. Nuclear fission has, for example, become the principle on which the nuclear power industry is founded. Ever since the mid-fifties, industrialized nations have been making plans for the generation of electricity from thermal energy released by fission of uranium or, in some cases, thorium. For much of this time, the optimism of the engineers and scientists that their devices could be made to yield supplies of electricity cheaply and easily has been accepted as an ingredient of fuel policy in industrialized nations. Nobody denies that nuclear reactors will in due course be needed to take up the vacuum that will be left when fossil fuels price themselves out of the market. It is only fair to say, however, that the cost of developing commercial nuclear power has been greater than first anticipated, that the optimistic forecasts of the engineers have frequently been falsified by events, and that nuclear power, while now competitive, is still very much in its infancy. What seems to have happened is that the obvious applications of this new technique for generating power have been harder and more expensive than they might have been.

The commercial development of rockets has been similarly spectacular but disappointing. Given accurate rockets and sufficient power, earth satellites (the first of which was launched in 1957) were inevitable. From that point on, the question has been what use could be made of these devices. Scientific research, of course, has benefited enormously from the anxieties of public authorities in the United States and the Soviet Union to find some use for rockets and satellites. Weather forecasting has benefited from the availability of photographs of cloud cover above the Earth, although here it is hard to know what would have happened if orthodox meteorologists had been given an opportunity to spend the same amount of money in another way. So far the most striking, but in itself almost a sufficient, proof of the value of Earth satellites has been the building of communications satellites for linking p 303 (23) distant stations by telephone or television. At the same time, both the United States and the Soviet Union have been able to launch men by rocket into space and even to the Moon, which has naturally prompted much talk of space travel. The chances are, however, that fifty years from now the attempts recently made to move people beyond the atmosphere of the Earth will seem as rudimentary as did the first flights of the heavier-than-air machines.

But is not high technology like this of value as a spur to other kinds of more useful activities? This is one of the questions repeatedly advanced as a justification for activities like these. For much of the past decade, both the United States and the Soviet Union have put forward arguments like these, and there is no doubt that projects for building important military systems or for sending people to the Moon serve as valuable organizing principles in the mobilization of technical effort. To be sure, what is called in the United States the spin-off from such projects is hardly sufficient to justify their cost, but there have in recent years been suggestions that what matters is not the direct benefit from projects p 92 (36) such as the American programme for landing people on the Moon but the sense in which they enormously increase the sophistication of the goals at which industrial companies can aim. The other view, now becoming apparent in many ways, is that by putting industry in such a forcing house, growth is stimulated in artificial directions. It is no accident that the industries created by military technology in the decades after the Second World War are those in which people are most inclined to doubt the necessity of the supposed association between industrial activity and prosperity.

Since the Second World War, the industry to have benefited most from the continuing preoccupation with military affairs is electronics and the application of electronics. One of the reasons why the German V-2 rockets were inaccurate was that their designers could not devise ways of mounting with the warhead means of guidance comparable in accuracy with those available to aircraft. A part of the trouble was the lack of sufficient awareness of the problems of how to control rocket systems when these were inevitably subject to all kinds of inaccuracies—motors not burning

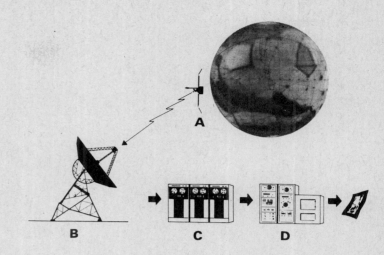

A major achievement of the US space programme has been the pictures of Mars sent back by Mariner in 1970. The signals from the space-craft (A) were so faint—one thousand-billionth of a watt—that they had to be amplified at the receiving station (B) before being co-ordinated by a computer (C) and transferred to film on a converter (D). (4)

uniformly, for example—but it is also plain, with hindsight, that the greatest single deficiency in the V-2 rocket was that of a method of responding mechanically to fluctuations from ideal performance with enough speed for corrective action to be taken. Only when it was possible to incorporate in a rocket system miniature electronic computers able to undertake these tasks could accuracy be assured. (The first versions of long-distance military rockets left the computers on the ground, which entailed a two-way radio link between the rocket and its base.) Needless to say, the benefits of electronic control were evident not merely in military applications but in all kinds of civil fields as well.

In the years immediately after the war, great energy was spent with some effect on the design of conventional radio valves for electronic tubes capable of operating at frequencies much higher than those in use before the war and also capable of being designed on a very much smaller scale. Ultimately, however, rapid progress was only possible by the invention of transistors (in 1948), which replaced necessarily bulky valves or tubes by pieces of solid material capable of handling electronic signals of ever greater frequency so long as they were made ever smaller. For one thing, transistors and the elaborations of them now available have made it possible to compress electronic equipment into a much smaller space than had previously seemed possible. The objective of making a piece of electronic apparatus as complicated as a piece of nervous tissue and no bigger is still impracticable but not completely out of the question. Second, the arrival of transistors has fitted in well with the development of digital electronic computers which differ from the analogue machines used for anti-aircraft guidance in the Second World War by being concerned more with counting than with measuring. Digital computers promise now to bring about a more profound change in the temper of modern life than anything since the invention of the steam engine, nuclear power and its military and civil applications notwithstanding.

Electronic computers began slowly. By the end of the war, a few rudimentary machines had been built, as much to demonstrate the ways in which brief bursts of electrical energy could simulate numbers as to perform useful work. Even by the mid-fifties, very little had been done outside the universities to apply the technology of the computer to commercial and industrial operations. For much of the time, military interest in activities like these was a continuing incentive to innovation, and by the early sixties the computer industry was growing rapidly, confidently and prosperously. By now, computers are at once cheaper, smaller and more powerful than the first designers imagined. The pace of development has been such that those most eager to make use of computers have nevertheless found the conceptual difficulty of doing so to be almost insuperable. This, certainly, is the spirit in which the common cry among the systems analysts who dance attendance on the machines is that few people are yet using computers efficiently. Most probably the complaint is true. And it is also clear that there are many technical developments still to be exploited—electronic computers functioning near the absolute zero of temperature for example. Nobody should be surprised if electronic computers give modern society its characteristic stamp thirty years from now.

Since the Second World War, the chemical industry has also flourished more luxuriantly than the dyestuff makers of the turn of the century would have imagined possible. By the thirties, Bakelite had become widely used for the first synthetic resin or plastic. By the mid-forties, a wide range of synthetic plastics had been designed by chemists concentrating their energies on the value to be wrung from ways of combining simple chemical molecules into long and complicated molecules, similar in many ways to those occurring naturally in substances such as wool, hair, rubber and the like. Synthetic rubber, indeed, was a wartime necessity in Germany and the United States. After the war, synthetic materials were developed to match the properties of and even to substitute for materials such as cotton, rubber, silk and even wool. The same substances turned out to be valuable as substitutes for glass, several metals and even ancient materials such as wood. The synthetic chemists and the chemical engineers who turned their theories into chemical processes are now able to think of designing materials whose properties are almost specified in advance, and are able to do this with a great variety of starting materials. Petroleum and its products are already being used for making materials as different as polythene and animal feeding stuffs. It is not entirely beyond the bounds of possibility that old-fashioned materials such as coal will one day be converted into butter.

The chemical industry has also been the source of a new industry ancillary to medicine. The starting point was the development of antibiotics academically in the thirties and industrially in the forties. Penicillin was the first of the antibiotics, and the technology which made possible its use in the treatment of disease was that for growing large quantities of a fungus on an industrial scale—the fungus happens to secrete the antibiotic as part of its ordinary activity. The uses of penicillin and the other antibiotics obtained from similar fungi are a technology in themselves by now. The antibiotics are not by now the only synthetic chemicals used widely for the treatment of disease—pharmaceutical chemists have learned how to manufacture not merely substitutes for natural hormones (valuable in the treatment of diseases in which for genetic reasons the natural hormones are absent) but also means of controlling fertility (by mimicking the physiological activity of natural hormones) as with the Pill. *Prima facie*, there is no limit to the extent to which the still young pharmaceutical industry, and the part of the chemical manufacturing industry which imitates life by making materials of biological effectiveness, can continue to broaden their activity. Undoubtedly, the discovery in the past few years of how living things replicate themselves and of how cells grow, divide and multiply will be, in due course, the foundation for industries which manufacture synthetic enzymes for carrying out specific chemical operations (such as photosynthesis), for substituting for natural foods and even for making good the deficiencies of genetics, at least in those unfortunate individuals born with genetic defects

p 339
(5)

of one kind or another. It does not follow from this that all the nightmares of the science fiction writers will come true—the chances are that the easiest jobs for the biologists to tackle are those whose consequences are beneficial.

The technology of medicine is also remarkable for the pace with which it has developed since the war. The use of drugs for treating disease is straightforward application of chemistry in medicine. The manipulation of bits and pieces of the human frame is another matter. In the years since the Second World War, techniques for keeping hearts alive without continuing support from the body and of keeping bodies alive without the presence of their hearts have for example demonstrated the ease with which surgeons can hope to reassemble intact creatures from their several parts. There remain, however, enormous obstacles to the kinds of medical engineering frequently recited in the textbooks of science fiction, not the least of which is the simple chemical identity of individuals with dissimilar genetic origins. The transplantation of organs from one person to another may be the most dramatic aspect of modern medicine but it is also the least important. What now matters is not so much the application of a few advanced techniques in medicine to a few people but the development of methods of making full use of all kinds of medical techniques, most of them much less spectacular.

p 300
(13)

The contrast in modern medicine between spectacular methods of treatment and the problem of how best to organize medical resources so as the most efficiently to care for a whole population somehow epitomizes the problem of modern technology—how to reconcile the great leaps forward which excite the imagination with the need somehow to attend to humdrum problems such as the improvement of national prosperity and even the maintenance of washing machines or motor cars. Linked with this is the problem which causes most public anxiety—how to make sure that the available resources are spent in such a way as to keep a proper balance between innovation in unknown fields and the proper application of what is known already. One of the attributes of the past few years has been the tendency to suppose that the balance is already upset. In the United States, for example, gloom about pollution of the environment and its potential consequences for human life has been rife. Elsewhere, there are fears that innovations such as supersonic aircraft or the possible applications of molecular biology may upset the previously delicate balance of nature. On the whole, fears tend to be exaggerated because they spring from the belief that what is possible will certainly come to pass—the belief engendered by the technologists of the Second World War. But the more serious scandal is that there are several fields in which the perfectly ordinary application of familiar technology is under-exploited. This, for example, is as true of the way in which the British electricity industry in 1970 was rightly pilloried for lax design of modern equipment and of the way in which too many purchasers of electronic computers fail to appreciate the importance of using them sensibly. There is, it is true, a danger that governments by entirely neglecting the need to strike a proper balance between innovation and application might make technology useless and pervert society. It is at least as likely that technology will be less valuable than it might be because it is badly understood or even feared.

p 284
(44, 45)

XIV WORLD TRADE AND FINANCE

The changing balance of economic power

ANDREW SHONFIELD

*'Economic history has always been in part
the story of international competition for wealth . . .
The Industrial Revolution gave this competition
a new focus—wealth through industrialization—
and turned it into a chase. . . . No-one wants to stand
still; most are convinced that they dare not.'*

DAVID S. LANDES, 1969

In wealth, as in military and political power,
Europe dominated the world of 1900. The three leading European countries, Britain, France and Germany, exported two-thirds of the whole world's manufactured goods. Their nearest competitor, the USA, was in fact the largest *producer* of such goods, but consumed most of them in the home market.

For Europe, the first fourteen years of the century were the end of the *belle époque*. It was the high point of upper bourgeois prosperity. European capital went abroad; the world's goods came to Europe. The great stores of Paris, London and other cities were stocked with an unparalleled profusion of wares and there was ample money to buy them. Shown opposite are three views of the Bon Marché, Paris, in 1900, by Félix Vallotton. 'Les Grands Magasins du Bon Marché' was founded in 1852 as a small haberdasher's shop in the Rue de Bac. Under one of its original partners, M. Aristide Boucicaut, it expanded phenomenally, first along one side of the street and then (1924) along the other as well. (1-3)

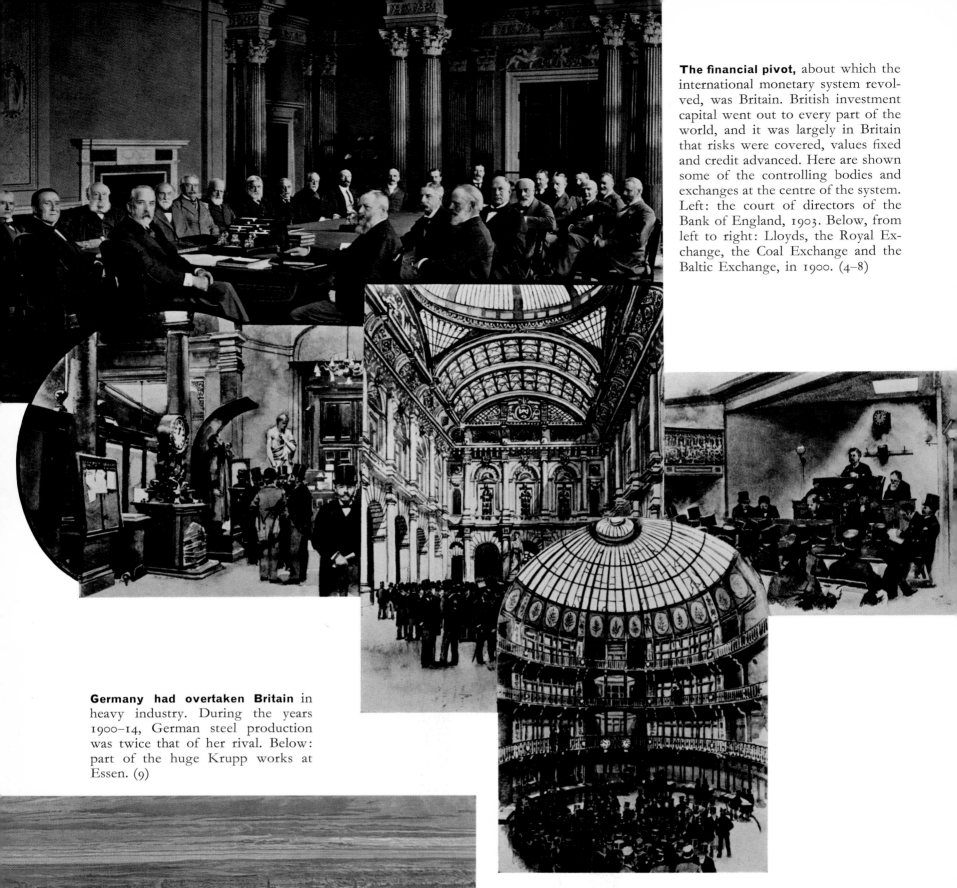

The financial pivot, about which the international monetary system revolved, was Britain. British investment capital went out to every part of the world, and it was largely in Britain that risks were covered, values fixed and credit advanced. Here are shown some of the controlling bodies and exchanges at the centre of the system. Left: the court of directors of the Bank of England, 1903. Below, from left to right: Lloyds, the Royal Exchange, the Coal Exchange and the Baltic Exchange, in 1900. (4–8)

Germany had overtaken Britain in heavy industry. During the years 1900–14, German steel production was twice that of her rival. Below: part of the huge Krupp works at Essen. (9)

Laissez-faire, the basis of orthodox capitalism, was resented when foreign goods seemed to be competing on the home market. Below: a British protest of about 1900. (10)

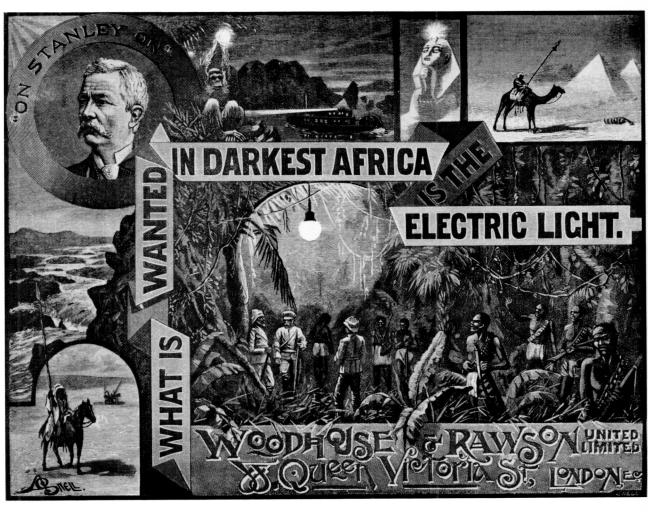

A British trade empire encircled the world, filling it with manufactured goods of every description, including many which were the fruits of businesses established abroad on British capital. The advertisements of this time (above and right) betray a self-satisfied belief that to export products of this kind was more or less the same as exporting civilization. (11–14)

In the land of plenty: Harrods store, London, (left) began in 1848 when Mr Harrod opened a grocer's shop in the then unfashionable Brompton Road. New buildings went up in 1895 and 1902. (15)

The Great Crash, sparked off by the collapse of the New York stock market, came after ten years of erratic postwar fluctuation and desperate attempts at control by the world's bankers. Below left: Ben Strong, Governor of the Federal Reserve Bank of New York, and Montagu Norman, Governor of the Bank of England. Centre: *Dies Irae, October 29,* by James N. Rosenberg. Below right: investors anxiously watching the latest quotations on the San Francisco stock market, 1931. (16–19)

'**Frozen Assets**' (left) was the Mexican painter Diego Rivera's allegory of New York in the slump. The 'assets' are her skyscrapers, her port (symbolized by the cranes and the line of workers waiting for the 'El'), her people—asleep in one of the 'municipal piers' opened to accommodate the unemployed—and finally her gold: all 'frozen' in helpless immobility. (20)

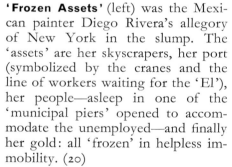

France was not seriously affected at first, but by 1931 (right) there were queues of unemployed at the free-food centres. (21)

In Germany (right), which suffered more than any other European country, the slump was a major factor in the Nazis' rise to power. The poster in this photograph, 'Our last hope, Hitler', is actually the one reproduced on p. 61. (22)

The United States had set off the chain reaction by calling back European loans, thus abolishing the market upon which American business largely depended. In New York (left) the dole queues lengthened. Relief began to come only with F. D. Roosevelt's New Deal programme (see p. 85) of increased public spending at home. (23)

The second postwar period, from 1945 onwards, has been like the slump in reverse, with American money flowing into, instead of out of, Europe, and the European countries co-operating instead of setting up barriers against each other. The US-financed Marshall Plan (left) spanned the years 1948 to 1952, and was later continued as the Organization for European Economic Development. (24)

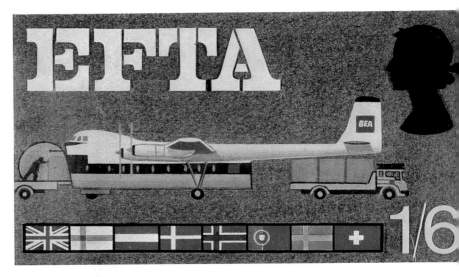

EFTA, the European Free Trade Association, was formed in 1959 to reduce tariffs between industrial countries, but did not aim at economic, still less political, integration. The members are Britain, Iceland, Austria, Denmark, Norway, Portugal, Sweden and Switzerland. (25)

Western prosperity was more widely shared over the whole of society in the second half of the 20th century than ever before, leading to a great and continuing boom in consumer goods. This in turn created new patterns of buying and selling, the development of the 'supermarket' (right, in America) and of the 'shopping centre' (far right, in Sweden), which may be compared to the great stores of sixty years ago shown earlier. The cutting of tariffs had the effect of filling these new shops with goods from other countries. (26, 29)

The European Common Market (left) embarked in 1958 on the progressive integration of the economies of its member states, France, Germany, Italy and the Benelux countries. Among the aims laid down in its founding document, the Treaty of Rome, were 'an ever closer union of the peoples of Europe' and 'an accelerated rise in the standard of living'. (27)

Foreign products such as automobiles are widely imported into countries which have flourishing industries in the same products themselves. These advertisements drawn from different countries all feature a similar type of 'people's car' and make their appeal mainly to the taste for foreign makes. (28)

The paradox of poverty in the midst of wealth remains as sharp in 1971 as it was seventy years before, but the 'two nations'—rich and poor classes in the same society—have been replaced by the 'two worlds', the developed and the developing countries, both expanding industrially and economically but at wildly different rates. Sometimes the two worlds meet, as at Hong Kong (above), where the 20th century is only a few hundred yards from the Middle Ages. (30)

The changing balance of economic power

ANDREW SHONFIELD

AT THE START of the century the world economy was overwhelmingly Europe-centred. The big three European countries, Britain, Germany and France, together accounted for two-thirds of all the world's exports of manufactured goods. Britain alone supplied one-third of the total. The biggest exporter of manufactures outside Europe, the United States, sold somewhat less than the smallest of the big three, France. Even at the end of the great boom which continued, with brief interruptions, from the early 1900s until the outbreak of World War I, when United States production went ahead very fast indeed, the predominance of Europe in international trade had not been seriously challenged.

The changing balance: Europe and America

This was in spite of the fact that the United States had taken the lead as the world's largest producer of manufactured goods several years before the end of the 19th century. It took a long time for the facts of American economic power to be fully understood in Europe, even after they had become blatantly apparent. Already before World War I the great gap between the productive performance of the average worker on the two sides of the Atlantic had been firmly established. In 1914 American productivity in manufacturing is estimated to have been twice the average European level. Even after the 1914–18 war there was no general appreciation of the fact that the United States had moved far ahead of Europe in the mastery of the new technologies, especially mechanical engineering and motor transport, on which industrial power had come to depend. In the 1920s there was a widespread disposition to believe that world conditions would, sooner or later, return to normal, and then Europe would once again be on top. People tended to blame the unfair advantage that the Americans had gained by coming late into the war, coupled with the slow rehabilitation of the European battleground, for the delay. The evidence of a different, more scientific approach to the problems of industrial organization, of production methods which gave the average American industrial worker significantly higher wages than his opposite number in Europe, did not impress.

It was not until they experienced the aftermath of World War II that the Europeans finally grasped the full extent of the changed relationship between themselves and the United States in the balance of world economic power. The Marshall Plan (1948–52) which provided, largely in the form of a free gift, the wherewithal for the rehabilitation of Europe's destroyed or damaged industrial plants was a unique demonstration of the capacity of the world's richest nation to sustain another continent without sacrificing the increase in its own living standards. It was an oddly delayed reaction. Apart from a certain stubbornness in clinging to the preferred Euro-centred vision of the world economy, there were some incidental factors which helped to obscure the realities of the United States position. First of all in the 1920s, when the US had emerged as a major exporter of manufactures, on a par with Britain and Germany, its policies failed to reflect an awareness of its relationship with the international economic system. There was no sense of permanent commitment, and in the early years of the League of Nations there was a deliberate abstention from its efforts to bring some order into international economic relations. It was as if the Americans continued to believe that they were a world

p 323
(27)

unto themselves—and that the other world would have to take them or leave them as best it could. They were not going to consider how their commercial policies, for example on external tariffs, fitted or failed to fit the needs of other nations. They continued to maintain a high tariff, while they achieved large export surpluses year after year, simply because heavy protection was thought to be in the interest of the industries of the United States. And they chose to raise their already considerable tariff wall to unprecedented heights right in the midst of the Great Depression, in 1930, when other trading nations were making a last desperate effort to halt the rapid spread of import restrictions by introducing a 'tariff truce'—an agreement that for the time being there would be no further increases in import duties.

Meanwhile the financial mechanism which had allowed the United States to export so much and import so little, based on a continuing flow of American investment funds to Europe, had broken down. The new tariff could not help the US balance of payments. There followed a period lasting until World War II when the American economy performed worse than that of any other major economic power. Its capacity to manage its own affairs, let alone to provide economic leadership to the rest of the world, seemed very limited.

The changing balance: Europe and Russia

It was at this stage that the enlarged economic significance of the other major non-European power, the USSR, became manifest. The old Russian Empire in the last year before World War I had been responsible for a little over 5% of the world's manufacturing production. By the late 1930s the share of the USSR—on a somewhat smaller territory—had risen to more than 18%. In part this high proportion reflected the failure of the capitalist nations of the West to use their available manufacturing capacity and labour force to anything like their full extent. The United States in particular was producing in 1938 one-tenth less than it had done ten years before. Russian industrial production had in the interval multiplied itself several times over.

These were the years of Stalin's first two Five-Year Plans, of the forced collectivization of agriculture, and of vast capital investment in Russian heavy industry. By the end of the period, just before World War II, the full range of the productive apparatus of a modern industrial state was in place. Of course this was not just the work of ten years; the Russian industrial base inherited from the Tsarist regime was neither so primitive nor so narrow as the Bolsheviks subsequently liked to make out. The twenty years before World War I had been a period of rapid industrial progress. Indeed it can be plausibly argued that if circumstances had been different and Russia had been able merely to continue to advance after 1914 at the same pace as it had reached during the previous decade, without the disruption of war and revolution, it would by the second half of the 1920s have become a substantial industrial power. As it was, industrial output had barely climbed back to the pre-World War I level by the time that the Soviet Government decided to launch the first Five-Year Plan in the late 1920s. Even so, the pace of industrial advance which followed was spectacular by any standard. According to the best available estimate, industrial production increased from 1928 to 1938 at an average annual

p 228
(12)

p 156
(27, 28)
rate of 12–13%. The Japanese during the 1950s—again a delayed postwar recovery operation—managed to match this; but it is hard to find another comparable case. That the achievement was bought at very high cost in terms of peasant misery, agricultural inefficiency, low wages, and an extremely authoritarian management of industry, supplemented by forced labour drawn from prison camps, is clear. But if the object was to create a largely self-sufficient economy with the capacity to sustain a major war, that object was fulfilled: the USSR took second place after the United States as a producer of manufactures, having surpassed Britain and Germany during the 1930s.

By the middle of the 20th century, the effect of two long and destructive wars fought on European soil, combined with the great reinforcement of the productive resources of the two major non-European nations, had been to alter the world balance sharply in Europe's disfavour. Yet if the matter is looked at from another viewpoint, that of the loss of Europe's advantages—first as an early starter in the process of industrialization, which gave it a quasi-monopolistic position in the markets for many manufactured products at the end of the 19th century, and second as the centre of imperial power controlling sources of supply and outlets for the sales of its goods stretching across Asia, the Middle East and Africa—it is remarkable how the weight of Europe once again asserted itself in the world economic system during the period following World War II.

The changing balance: Europe and the world

The mid-point of the century turned out to be a poor vantage point from which to judge the relative stature of the main actors in the international economy. In 1950 Europe appeared excessively diminished. By contrast, the primary producing countries outside the North Atlantic area appeared to have achieved a gain in their economic bargaining power: the prices of the commodities which they sold had gone up more than those of the manufactured goods which they bought. This was seen at the time as another factor making for Europe's impoverishment: it would henceforth have to surrender a larger volume of its output in order to obtain its raw materials and foodstuffs from the rest of the world. It was even suggested by some Marxist analysts that it was only European imperial power, reflected in the management of the economies forming its overseas empires, which had in the past artificially turned the terms of trade against the underdeveloped countries. This, it was held, had in turn robbed these countries of the resources required to start the process of industrialization; they were starved of capital because they were being compelled to sell their products too cheaply. Let the advanced industrial countries of Western Europe look out! The end of colonial empires would start a race with the newly industrializing nations in which the Old World would soon be overtaken.

Matters turned out differently, partly because the process of industrialization and the creation of a modern economy involve a much more profound and wide-ranging reorganization of society than this theory suggests. Of all the countries of Asia, Africa and Latin America only one, Japan, compassed the task in the course of this century—and even in that case the essential changes had begun several years earlier. The exceptional character of the Japanese case became fully apparent only after World War II. Japan's powers of rapid adaptation to adverse economic circumstances—the loss of its main markets and sources of supply in Asia and the decline of world trade in textiles on which its export industries had heavily depended—were such that it was able, in little more than a decade and a half, to alter its basic industrial
p 157
(29)
structure and create the world's largest shipbuilding industry, backed by a steel industry which was next in order of size to that of the US and the USSR. Meanwhile its national income grew to be larger than that of any West European nation and was exceeded only by the two super-powers.

The evidence since the end of the European empires overseas does not suggest that colonial rule was, in general, a decisive obstacle to rapid economic advance in Asia and Africa: it may have hindered the development of particular lines of production in particular places, but it gave powerful assistance to the development of new products in others. This is not to say that the economic

effects of imperialism were neutral. It is merely to record the discovery which followed World War II that the causes of economic backwardness are multiple and complex; the removal of alien political rule does not of itself liberate economic forces which quickly convert backward countries into serious competitors of their erstwhile masters. The recognition of this fact was clearly reflected in the changing attitude towards economic aid for the underdeveloped world. Originally envisaged by the newly independent countries as a transient need, it had come to be seen by the end of the 1960s, both by them and by the Western donor nations, as a much more fundamental requirement, likely to persist till the end of the century.

There was some loss of captive markets by European industry; but again this was a process which had begun earlier and had already gone far before Europe began to lose its colonies. The outstanding case was Britain's market for cotton textiles in India. This was probably the most valuable captive export market that any nation ever had; just before World War I when cotton textiles were much the biggest single British export, India bought nearly 40% of the total British output of cloth. But the evolution of trade during the following quarter of a century showed that India was much less closely tethered to Lancashire than envious textile merchants in other countries, as well as Lancashire itself, had supposed. By 1924 the rapid rise of an indigenous textile industry in India, partly financed by British capital and run by British management, had halved British cloth exports to this market. By the 1930s the decline had gone much further, assisted by the Indian Government's measures to protect the domestic industry during the Great Depression; in 1937 the Indians had reduced their imports of British cotton cloth to 10% of the pre-1914 volume—and that was a decade before India achieved political independence. The Indian textile case is only the extreme example of a general trend towards import substitution which proceeded in the non-industrial countries outside the North Atlantic area during the high tide of European imperialism after World War I. Steel output was actively fostered in these overseas territories, particularly in the areas of white settlement in the British dominions—and to such good effect that European exports of steel to the rest of the world were less in the late 1930s than they had been in the period just preceding the war. The world's consumption of steel had meanwhile gone up by 75%.

Why was it that Europe did not suffer more permanent damage in the second half of the century? From 1950 onwards, against the expectations of the immediate postwar period, the terms of trade moved continuously in Europe's favour: the value of the manufactured goods which made up its exports steadily increased in relation to the primary produce that they bought from the rest of the world. The Europeans also became less dependent on overseas supplies of raw materials and food, as their own output of synthetic materials and of agricultural produce increased. More efficient methods of production meant that they used less and less raw material per unit of manufactured goods than before. And the nature of the products on which they concentrated their main industrial effort changed too: the areas of most rapid growth, engineering and chemicals, were not great users of imported raw materials. As to the loss of overseas markets through the process of import substitution, the very development of new productive capacity there to make goods that were previously imported led to a vast demand for the products of the most advanced technology, in the form of machines and precision instruments and the new materials produced by the chemical industry, of which Western Europe and the United States were the main suppliers.

Thus part of the answer lies in the ability of the West European countries to regain their technological lead over the rest of the world, outside the US and the USSR. They were also able, in the course of the two and a half decades following World War II, to reassert a substantial and independent economic power *vis-à-vis* both the Americans and the Russians. As indicated earlier, this seemed an improbable outcome to most observers when they surveyed the postwar economic scene at mid-century. That it occurred was chiefly due to Europe's special position as an international trader. The two super-powers were nations for whom foreign trade had always been a marginal element in the total

In the years before *1914 Germany was competing with Britain in overseas investments, as well as in industry. This painting shows the Berlin Stock* Exchange in *1902. German capital went mainly to other European countries, but also in part to North and South America. (1)*

complex of economic activity; even after the expansion of their trade in the years following World War II, exports for both of them represented less than 5% of their total output. Both nations had been dominated by the experience of the expanding internal frontier; big business, whether it involved the state or large-scale private enterprise, was primarily the business generated at home. By contrast, many of the European nations were used to earning up to one-quarter of their national income through sales abroad, and some of the smaller ones as much as one-third and more. For them the dynamic business was traditionally export business. The 1930s had been a gloomy interlude when the Europeans had lost their economic bearings. Given the postwar opportunity provided by the expansion of international trade, they were admirably placed to exploit their special advantages.

This was especially true of the smaller nations of Western Europe, those whose economies were most dependent on export earnings. There had been a steady build-up by these countries throughout the century of a series of export specialities, like watches and chemicals from Switzerland, ball-bearings and electrical machinery from Sweden, steel from Belgium; they had shown a striking capacity to hold their own in international competition with nations endowed with a much wider industrial base. It was their performance in terms of sheer salesmanship, their sensitiveness to the needs of foreign markets, their quick response to changing demands, their systematic approach to the problem of mobilizing relatively slender resources to the maximum effect, which gave them their advantage. These smaller European countries—'small' in the sense of their economic resource base rather than by the measure of territory or population (Italy for instance is included in this category)—prospered greatly in the first two decades of the second half of the century. So that even though

the big three of Western Europe, Britain, Germany and France, lost their position of overwhelming dominance in world trade in manufactured goods, with their share of total exports reduced from over 60% before World War I to a little over 40% in the late 1960s, the rest of Europe made up much of the lost ground. This progress was especially marked in Western Europe; but among the smaller countries of Eastern Europe too, where economic development (other than in Czechoslovakia and East Germany) had previously lagged markedly behind the West, there was also a growth of industrial exports, chiefly directed towards the markets of the Soviet bloc. All in all the nations of Europe, excluding the USSR, were still jointly responsible for around two-thirds of the world's exports of manufactures.

A considerable portion of this trade consisted of exports from one European nation to another; intra-European exchanges have during most of this century been one of the dynamic elements in the development of world trade. The smaller nations have been especially active traders with one another. But a large part of their exports of specialities has been destined for distant markets; and so have the sales of manufactures by Britain, Germany and France. Intra-European trade during the period following World War II was, besides, an important element in reducing the dependence of continental Western Europe on overseas sources of supply. From the late 1950s onwards, the balance of payments of this area with the rest of the world was in heavy surplus; and this resulted, first, in a large transfer of gold from the United States into European reserves and, later, in a large and rapid accumulation of dollar liabilities by the US to Europe. With the emergence of Western Europe as a large-scale creditor of the United States the relationship which had ruled ever since World War I was reversed. It was a reversal which was visibly reflected in the changed balance of power in the international organizations like the GATT (General Agreement on Tariffs and Trade) and the International Monetary Fund responsible for the formulation of collective world policies on trade and finance. The United States was still by far and away the most important single voice in these bodies; but it had ceased to dominate them as of right.

FOUR PHASES

The economic history of the 20th century up to the end of the 1960s divides itself into several distinct sequences which conform closely with the main divisions of its political history. There is, first, the period of extremely rapid economic growth and high employment up to 1914. This is followed, after World War I, by a sharp break in the secular pace of economic progress; it lasts a couple of decades during which the system of international economic relationships, which had previously been taken for granted, fails to function. World trade advances haltingly, when it advances at all. Since the mechanism of international adjustment cannot be relied upon to work, nations increasingly turn inwards and conduct their domestic economic affairs largely in disregard of their external repercussions. The closing years of the inter-war period provide the classic illustration of the working of beggar-your-neighbour policies. Then, after World War II, the carefree growth of the early years of the century is resumed, but at an even faster rate than in the years before 1914. World trade in manufactures expands even more rapidly than the increase in industrial production. There are the beginnings of institutionalized forms of international collaboration, notably in the Western industrial world, which aim to use the techniques of voluntary agreement among nations to replace the automatic mechanisms of adjustment which served the international economy well, but too brutally, in the early years of the century.

There is one addition to this threefold division of the period in which major economic change seems to proceed largely independently of political events. This is the Great Depression and its aftermath, beginning in 1929 and lasting to the outbreak of World War II. Since this is in some ways the outstanding economic occurrence of the epoch, from which so much else, including arguably World War II, stemmed, it is treated separately in what follows.

I. 'La belle époque'

This, the label attached to the first period, the decade or so before World War I, can hardly justify itself in any other terms than those of material prosperity; in terms of its politics, its aesthetics, its popular sentiment, its social relationships, there was little which would seem, in retrospect, to justify singling out this as *the* 'belle époque'. But for the Europeans who experienced it, if they had some money or possessions, it was remembered subsequently as an era of exceptional ease and of opportunity. So it was. It was in some sense the apogee of bourgeois society. The middle classes which had been kept at the periphery of society up to the beginning of the 19th century had gradually edged their way in, and now stood unmistakably at the centre. National frontiers were open and people and money, as well as goods, moved more easily than ever before. The export of capital from Europe proceeded on a vast scale. As much as half of Britain's total annual investment during the decade before World War I consisted of capital sent overseas. French foreign investment was only second to the British in volume; here, too, ventures abroad, particularly in Russia, seemed to attract the investor more readily than humdrum business activity at home. Even Germany, while maintaining a higher ratio of investment at home than Britain or France, managed to export increasing amounts of capital during the years just before the war, directed particularly to central Europe and southern Europe. There was also some German investment in South America, previously regarded as a British preserve, and in the United States. By 1914 German long-term foreign investment was equal to as much as one-third of the British total.

The United States sent very little capital abroad. It was, on the other hand, an enormous recipient of foreign workers, as well as foreign money. This was the high point of the great migratory movement from Europe overseas. It is estimated that in the first two decades of the century 25 million Europeans emigrated—twice as many as in the previous forty years—and that over half of them went to the United States. This represented a sizeable addition to the US population, which by 1913 was just short of 100 million. The Americans engaged in a fury of investment activity in the effort of absorbing these extra millions of immigrants. Merely to house them, often in slum conditions, and to provide the transport to move them to the places where work was available involved vast expenditures. However it would be wrong to think of the United States at this stage as staggering under a load of social investment commitments. It was able to absorb the shiploads of immigrants from Europe chiefly because its industries were expanding faster than those of any other country. This is the period when the giant American corporation emerges into full public view—and becomes the centre of political controversy about the dangers of the over-mighty subject who is able to act as a state within the state.

Other migrants from Europe went to the British dominions, chiefly Canada and Australasia which added a couple of millions each to their populations by this means, and to Latin America. The three elements in the great exodus, men, money and trade, moved in unison. The investments, particularly in the areas of settlement in the Southern Hemisphere, provided the basis for the production of food and raw materials which were marketed back in Europe. During these years the terms of trade were favourable to the primary producing countries; the rising income which they received for their products allowed them to spend freely on imports of manufactured goods chiefly from Europe.

And at the centre of the system was Britain—by far the largest exporter of goods, the biggest supplier of investment capital abroad, a wide-open and expanding market for all manner of imports but more particularly for imports of agricultural produce, against which other countries were trying to protect the home producer by means of tariffs. Britain was also the financial pivot on which the international system rested. Traders would take the risks attendant on new enterprises in remote markets because they could find in London people who would finance the venture with the minimum of fuss, discounting the risks to a nicety on the basis of expert knowledge and at competitive rates. Moreover there was no need to worry about the currency in which the proceeds of such international transactions would materialize. Sterling was readily exchangeable for gold, and if the transaction was handled through London and denominated in pounds there was a clear assurance that the proceeds could be exchanged into any other currency as the need arose. There was no need to insure, as later generations have had to, against the risks of exchange depreciation. Not only sterling but all the major currencies maintained firmly fixed parities in terms of gold. If a country ran into trouble with its balance of payments and its currency weakened, this showed up directly in the shipment of gold to make payment to its creditors. As its reserves of gold were reduced, the whole money base of its economy contracted. Bank credit became scarce and dear; business became more difficult; employment fell—and the process of deflation continued until the country concerned was able to restore its competitive position, either by an improvement in its trade balance or by pushing up interest rates high enough to attract fresh credits from abroad.

This is a simplified account of a mechanism which was both sensitive and complex. It allowed nations to operate with remarkably low reserves; the Bank of England at this time maintained a gold reserve of less than £50 million. The condition for operating with such a small reserve was that at the slightest sign of trouble on the international front caused by any temporary fluctuation in the country's balance of payments, the authorities would act promptly and forcefully to restore the external position, regardless of the effects on the domestic economy. It was a harsh world in which national economic policy was to a large extent an epiphenomenon of the international monetary system. But on the other hand there was the advantage that the system could be relied upon to work; and the real elements which sustained the movement of resources around the world, the investment decisions, the migration of people, the exchange of goods in international trade, were made to fit snugly together. No wonder it was widely held as an article of faith that you could not better the invisible hand of the

The normal left-wing reaction to the Depression was to blame the business-man. George Grosz's drawing of 1932 shows the familiar capitalist exploiter, bloated with factories, indifferent to the workers' sufferings. (2)

capitalist economic process; it did not even seen blasphemy to identify it with the hand of God.

For Britain, however, in spite of appearances, the system was not pure gain. Few people saw clearly at the time that the obsessive concern with the development of the country's external assets had as its counterpart the relative neglect of domestic industrial growth. There was no necessary connection between these two things, but as it turned out the main thrust of investment interest was directed to enterprise abroad. Indeed during the Edwardian period, when Britain's economic position as an industrial producer and world trader seemed so strong, the industrial lag was especially pronounced. In relation to the performance of its main competitors abroad, the British level of domestic industrial investment and the growth of industrial productivity was probably never again, either in the period between the Wars or following World War II, so poor as at this time. There was some malaise intermittently expressed by a minority of observers. Britain was too obviously lagging in certain industries behind her nearest rival on the continent of Europe, Germany. The established British lead in world iron and steel production had already been lost in the 1890s first to the US and then to Germany; but it was the relative rates of growth of the German and British steel industries in the subsequent period which were especially disturbing. The average output of British steel was less than half the German during the period 1900–14. In the newer technologies of chemicals and electrical machinery Germany had well before this achieved a clear lead. As a general indicator of the level of industrial development across a wide range of manufacturing industry, the production of sulphuric acid for home consumption serves: it shows Britain in 1900 with a production still nearly twice that of Germany. By 1913 the German production was 50% greater than the British. When the two countries went to war with one another in the following year, Germany had become an industrial power on a scale that Britain could no longer match.

Various reasons have been advanced for this striking reversal of positions. For a long time Britain had preserved the advantages of its early start in the industrial revolution; other nations industrialized, but the British capacity for continued technological innovation kept it a step ahead. Then in the early years of the 20th century Britain's capacity to innovate seemed relatively to diminish. One contributory factor was surely Britain's relative neglect, in comparison not only with Germany but with other countries of Western Europe, of technical and scientific education. Another

p 318
(9)

was the ability of Britain to earn its living comfortably with the products of an older technology; it was not under pressure to move ahead in the advanced technologies, because it found that it could sell exports, in much greater volume than anyone else, derived essentially from the industries of the early industrial revolution—textiles, railway equipment, coal. Its investments in overseas markets gave it a dominant position as a supplier of traditional capital equipment. There were also trading privileges, formal and informal, in Empire markets.

However, the picture of a country sustaining itself by its trade and investments in a politically protected fief is misleading. Only 30% of British exports went to the colonies and dominions, and they absorbed less than half of British overseas investment. Perhaps the underlying weakness of Britain's industrial position would have revealed itself soon enough if the period of peace had been extended beyond 1914; certainly the German traders and industrialists were confident of their ability to overtake the British as the world's leading exporter. As it was, the reality was obscured during the succeeding decades by two wars and their aftermaths and by the Great Depression, when the British economy performed relatively well compared with its main industrial rivals. Britain's decline as an industrial power only became fully evident some time after World War II, during the 1960s.

II. The period of maladjustment, 1918–29

Economic policy in the years following World War I reflects an entirely new mood, a mood based on a deep scepticism about a whole range of assumptions in regard to international economic relations which had previously been taken for granted. Yet there was also a propensity to believe that if only the appropriate set of switches could be found and operated the world could somehow be transformed intact into its pre-1914 pattern. Politicians seemed to behave at times like severely deprived children trying out half-remembered gestures belonging to an earlier happier time. When gestures failed—for example at the time of the return to the gold standard in the mid-1920s when Britain insisted, at considerable cost to itself, on precisely the same rate of exchange as had ruled before the war—those responsible grew characteristically resentful and destructive in their behaviour. If the international system failed to work as it used to, then too bad for international collaboration! Other methods which disregarded the interests of the international community were the obvious remedy.

This reaction belongs especially to the second half of the inter-war period, after the world economic crisis of 1929. The first half was occupied by a very slow recovery in Europe—much slower than after World War II when the destruction was far greater—and then from about 1925 onwards by the start of a boom and a rhythm of expansion that at least began to remind businessmen of prewar conditions. World trade picked up and some new essays in international collaboration were tentatively launched. The high point was probably the World Economic Conference of 1927 which tried to mobilize support for a wide-ranging programme of tariff reduction. But the mood of resistance was too strong, and, when the short-lived prosperity of the late 1920s collapsed into the slump, European import duties on finished manufactures were still 50% above the average prewar level. They then rose vertiginously.

What had gone was the sense of great opportunity in international trade which had dominated the phase of rapid industrialization of the western world until 1914. Instead the mood of business and of governments expressed itself increasingly in the slogan: 'What we have we hold!' What they had was, first of all, the home market, around which they built constantly higher and thicker walls, and, secondly, privileged access to certain export markets which they endeavoured to enlarge and to consolidate. The latter advantage was the subject of great resentment by those European nations, like Italy and Germany, which had very few, or no colonies. There was a tendency to exaggerate the value of colonial markets as a prop to the economies of European imperial powers. On the whole they served as useful make-weights in a slump, rather than as engines of industrial growth in the mother country.

The British example might suggest that something more than this was involved, and it was the British example which tended to dominate the thinking of politicians and the influential journalism about economic imperialism. But the British case was a quite unusual one; it was exceptional as to the sheer size of its empire, in which about one-quarter of the inhabited territory of the world was included, and as to the great demand for imports of relatively sophisticated manufactured goods which went with the high incomes of the original colonies of white settlement, the imperial dominions. These countries, though representing a very small proportion of the total population of the British Empire, provided more than half of the Empire market for British exports. Britain's circumstances were also unusual in the sense that British policy had continued to cling to the ideal of free trade much longer than anyone else, so that when it finally introduced a general tariff in the early 1930s it had something *new* to bargain with in the endeavour to obtain preferred entry for its manufactured goods in overseas markets. It exploited this new bargaining counter in the establishment of the Imperial Preference system under the Ottawa Agreement, 1932, but might have exploited it, and indeed did so later on, to make some favourable trade bargains with nations outside the Empire. Finally there was the highly unusual circumstance that Britain was a vast import market, much the largest in the world, for food and agricultural produce. This provided the basis of reciprocal advantage, particularly for the dominions, on which the Imperial Preference system was built.

We shall have occasion to refer to the rise of the preferential system of trading in connection with the debacle of world commerce in the 1930s. The 1920s were in some ways a prelude to the grand failure that followed. There was a failure to provide the conditions for a revival of intra-European trade, which had for a long time been one of the mainstays of the world trading system (and became so again after World War II); there was a failure to clean up the financial aftermath of war, either of the reparations, which continued to be demanded from Germany right through the decade, or the war debts to America, which continued to be claimed long after it; lastly, there was a fundamental failure to adjust the European economy, on which the health of the international trading system largely depended, to changes in world supply and demand. The war itself had given a great impetus to the development of new industrial centres overseas, which were well equipped to supply themselves with the staple manufactures previously bought from Europe. Meanwhile there was a rapid growth of demand for the products of the newer technologies, notably in motor vehicle manufacture and in other forms of engineering, and European industry was slow to respond to this. The United States had a decisive advantage as an exporter in these new fields, and so captured a greatly enlarged share of the diminished volume of world exports of manufactures.

Why Europe was quite so unresponsive to these changed conditions is not clear. There was the obsessive concern with the world before 1914: it continued to provide the model of a 'normal' world. This may have made for a slow reaction to the new. There was also the absence of a rapidly expanding internal market to provide the incentive for new industrial investment and change. The contrast with the United States was striking. Sluggish investment was one of the reasons for the slow European recovery from the war. And Europe's weak economic performance in turn affected the primary producing countries in the rest of the world: their production capacity had expanded considerably in response to wartime needs and it would have required a considerable increase in the demands of the importing countries to absorb the rise in world agricultural output. The glut of supplies brought down agricultural prices, and that reduced still further the purchasing power of the primary producing countries in international trade. This was again the opposite of the market situation ruling before the war when the relative prices of manufactured goods and primary products had moved in favour of the latter. When the great slump came at the end of the 1920s, its most obvious and also its most stubborn feature was the crisis of agricultural overproduction.

European industry certainly suffered from under-stimulation. It was not only the export industries that were weakened in the process. There was an 'inertia in the renewal of capital equipment', as Svennilson says in the survey of the period issued by the Economic Commission for Europe, extending to public utilities like electricity (in competition with gas) and the railways (in competition with road transport), as well as in steel, shipping, cement and chemicals. The whole of the inter-war period was 'a prolonged transformation crisis of the European economy'. He concludes: 'Europe was suffering from arterio-sclerosis of an old-established, heavily capitalized economic system, inflexible in relation to violent economic change.'

Political factors aggravated the trouble. The creation of new national states after World War I increased the length of national frontiers with customs barriers built into them by some 12,500 miles in Europe, and the number of separate customs units from 20 to 27. Because of the widespread assumption that war among these European states was at some stage quite likely to break out, governments deliberately set out to achieve a high degree of national self-sufficiency. If costs were in consequence higher and living standards lower than they need have been, that was an inconvenience which had to be borne. The experience of World War I had brought home the risks that were taken by any nation which allowed itself to become heavily dependent on others for the supply of goods and services that were essential to its economy. Pleas for a more rational international division of labour, which were intermittently made, came up hard against this fact of political life. It became increasingly apparent that a general political settlement leading to a measure of trust between the nations of Europe was a pre-condition for the re-establishment of an effectively functioning international economy. In default of this the major nations proceeded to exploit their political relationships with particular states in order to establish their own privileged economic hinterlands.

III. The Great Depression

The immediate cause of the great slump, which lasted from 1929 to 1933 and at its lowest point brought down the industrial production of the world by some thirty per cent, was the collapse of the stock market in New York. The loans from the United States which had sustained European economic activity, at a time when Europe's external balance of payments was weak, were suddenly called back. In an attempt to overcome the ensuing crisis in their external balance of payments the European countries engaged in a massive economic deflation at home. Each aggravated the problems for the others. Collectively, they bought less and less, and, as the chart below shows, the value of world trade fell steadily month after month for more than four years; by early 1933 it was down to a *f 3*

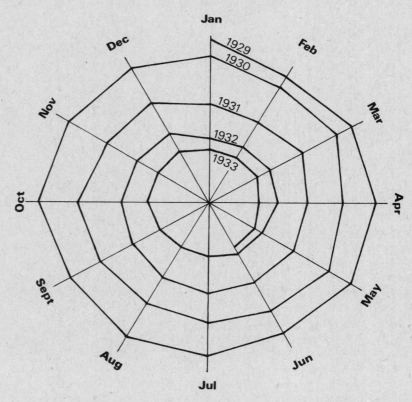

The slump: world-trade month by month, 1929–33, showing how the value contracted in a vicious spiral. (3)

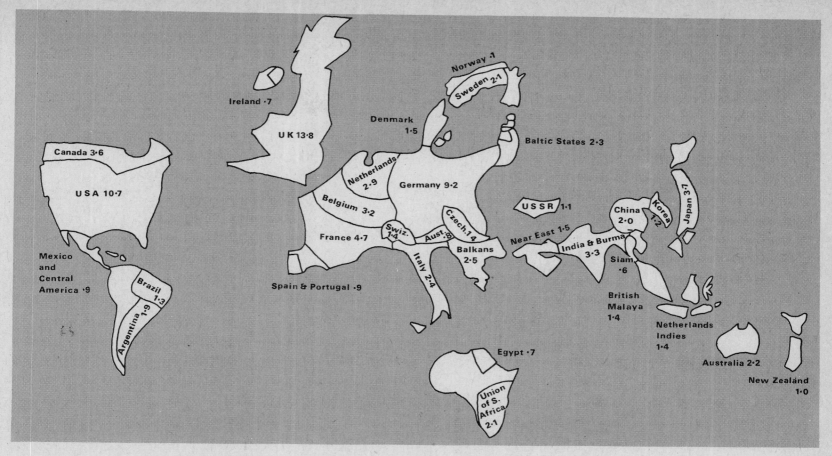

In this map the size of each country is determined not by geographical area but by its share of world trade in 1938. (4)

meagre one-third of what it had been before the onset of the slump.

p 321
(21–23)
Meanwhile in Europe and North America the number of officially registered unemployed—which even so left out much of the unemployed agricultural labour—rose to a total of 30 million. In several Western countries a quarter of the industrial working population was idle. The misery of the agricultural population does not lend itself to this sort of statistical measurement; it was acute. Agricultural stocks had risen as a result of the good harvests of 1928 and 1929, and when the break came prices plunged downwards. At the bottom of the depression, food and other agricultural products were selling on average at one-quarter of the prices that farmers had obtained in the mid-1920s.

p 320
(16–19)
Although the collapse on Wall Street started the chain of events leading to the Great Depression, there were more profound causes which help to explain both its extraordinary intensity and its duration. One was the primitive level of economic knowledge available to those who were trying to manage the crisis; and this was combined with an instinct, derived from unquestioned rules of private business morality, which, when faced with any national economic difficulty, assumed that the proper answer must be to cut back public expenditure. There were, in any case, inhibitions about interfering with a machine which was widely supposed to work best when untouched by human hand. Many of the essential mechanisms which determine the level of activity in a modern economy were little understood, and the key statistical data which could have provided early warning of changes in underlying economic trends were not collected on a systematic basis. Hunch ruled. Another factor was the failure of the international community to give administrative expression to its collective interests. The United States was, as indicated earlier, entirely unprepared politically to engage in the effort of international collaboration. Russia was treated as outside the community of nations; its government was in any case wholly absorbed in its internal battle with the peasantry over the forced collectivization of the land and in the first Five-Year Plan of industrialization. France's policies during the worst of the slump were chiefly concerned with preserving its extremely large reserve of gold, at whatever cost in terms of lost production and trade. The French central bank was particularly unhelpful in international matters, and the bank's views seemed largely to dominate the French Government. By contrast, the Bank of England and the US Federal Reserve System worked for a while closely together. But once the crisis took hold this relationship weakened too.

What was lacking was any spirit of international give-and-take. Thus the smaller nations of Europe which were heavily dependent on foreign trade were especial victims of the slump; but when Belgium and Holland tried to palliate their problems by forming a customs union Britain objected. Similarly Germany and Italy raised objections to the scheme for a customs union among the small nations of the Danubian Basin. Only the big nations were able to go ahead and make their exclusive trading arrangements with client states.

The outstanding case, both in terms of the scale of the operation and of its impact on world trade, was the system of Imperial Preference established by the British Empire. When Britain introduced its Import Duties Act in 1932, imposing for the first time a basic minimum tariff on all imports, and then signed the Ottawa Agreement a few months later, this was an event of a major symbolic character. It marked the deliberate retreat from the principle of unrestricted international trading by the nation which had been for nearly a century its leading exponent. Britain had in the previous year retreated from the system of unrestricted international payments when the pound sterling was declared to be no longer freely convertible into gold. In 1933, when the World Economic Conference which assembled in London failed to produce anything to replace the old machinery of international economic order, there was nothing left but for each nation to take cover as best it could.

It was not that Britain had stuck rigorously to the practice of free trade before all this; it had intermittently tried to exploit its imperial advantage. However, the fact remained that before the Great Depression less than 20% of all the imports coming into Britain—which was much the biggest import market in the world—paid any duty at all. In the end, what persuaded Britain to depart from her traditional policy in favour of a closed imperial system was the evidence of the growing dependence of British export trade on the markets of the dominions and colonies. As Britain's share of world exports declined during the 1920s the proportion going to Empire markets rose, until it was nearly half.

The Imperial Preference system was successful in helping the British industrial recovery in the 1930s, which occurred sooner and took effect more rapidly than in other major industrial countries. It also secured a larger share of the British import market for the products of Empire countries. But it did nothing to ease the problem of world-wide agricultural over-production: the big Empire producers of grain in temperate zones and of tropical commodities in Africa and Asia were still faced with the problem of finding an outlet for their staples beyond the empire. As part of the effort to manage markets so as to maintain the prices of these vulnerable agricultural products, Britain took the lead in organizing various international commodity restriction schemes. The United States, in particular, bitterly resented both the Imperial Preferences, which put American traders at a disadvantage in selling to Empire markets, and the way in which British political influence was used to enforce a higher price for certain commodities imported by the US than it would otherwise have paid.

p 85
(13, 14,
17)

Slowly and painfully from 1933 onwards the industrial nations began to emerge from the Depression. The United States had the worst experience. As part of President Roosevelt's New Deal a variety of novel economic programmes were introduced, aimed at the creation of new jobs and at raising the depressed domestic price level. There was a great outpouring of Federal funds for these purposes on a scale never contemplated before. Nevertheless the American economy strikingly failed to gather momentum. After a brief recovery in 1936–37 it slumped again in 1938 when unemployment rose to nearly 10 million. Business confidence was never restored to the point where private investment was undertaken once again on the scale required to sustain employment at anything like the pre-Depression level. On the other side the Federal Government, after its series of initial emergency measures in 1933–34, never intervened boldly enough and with sufficiently large resources to provide an effective substitute for the missing stimulus of private investment. It was in turn influenced in its cautious policies by the widely felt suspicion of the American business community that the motives behind any government intervention in the economy were likely to be hostile to private enterprise. It is true that the Roosevelt administration in its first years did introduce a number of major reforms which subjected commerce, and financial organizations in particular, to much closer surveillance than they had been accustomed to. But neither the president nor most of the reformers seriously doubted that in a prosperous US economy privately owned business and capital would continue to play a major role. Still, the popular myth among businessmen was enough to do the damage. Thus the ideological opposition to the New Deal, the emotional hatred which it engendered among traditional business leaders, probably played a significant part in holding back American recovery.

Elsewhere government intervention in what had hitherto been regarded as the sacred preserves of the private enterprise economy became habitual. It operated on an extensive scale in primary producing countries like Australia and New Zealand and in Latin America, as well as among the industrial nations of Europe. This was one of the beneficial by-products of the Great Depression; governments were in consequence much better prepared after World War II to take active charge of the process of economic recovery. They were also, in the interval before that, able to mobilize their economic resources for the purpose of waging war much more effectively than during the 1914–18 conflict. The outstanding performance in this latter respect was that of Britain.

IV. The postwar world

It would be hard to find a sharper contrast of mood than that between the ways in which the nations approached the problem of organizing the world economy after the two World Wars. As we have seen, the years following World War I were dominated by a mood of diffused nostalgia for what came to be regarded as a golden age of international economic relations. After World War II there was an almost ferocious *anti-nostalgia*. The politicians and officials concerned may have disagreed about many things, but they were united in their conviction that they had to create something different from what had been. It did not matter if some of the schemes proposed looked very strange and new.

They still shied away from profoundly radical proposals, such as that put forward by Keynes to the financial conference of the Allied nations on postwar reorganization at Bretton Woods (1944) for the establishment of an International Clearing Union, which would have replaced gold by a single internationally managed currency. But even in this case the central idea was not entirely lost; it was revived in a modified form in the late 1960s in the scheme for the creation of a new form of international money (the so-called Special Drawing Rights) under the control of one of the two world organizations which came out of Bretton Woods, the International Monetary Fund. (The other organization was the World Bank.)

It is not claimed that the plans of those concerned with postwar reconstruction showed consistent wisdom and foresight. They often got things wrong. For example, there was a fundamental misapprehension on the part of the United States about the speed with which it would be possible to rebuild a normal world in which trade moved without restriction and currencies were freely exchanged with one another. More generally, there was a tendency to over-estimate the time that it would take to bring world production back to a high peace-time level and to underestimate the time required to put the international economic system back into full working order. Having been disappointed in the early hopes of removing restrictions on international trade and payments, the Western nations swung to the other extreme and tended to exaggerate the fundamental character of the world shortage of US dollars. This was seen as the main cause of the continuing disequilibrium in international payments, caused by the rest of the world's inability either to earn enough dollars or to attract dollar investment, and it was widely regarded either as permanent or as likely to last a very long time. So that, when in the late 1950s the external balance of payments of the United States visibly shifted to a continuing and substantial deficit, there was a reluctance, which lasted for some years, to proceed to the new measures required by the changed situation.

However, what can reasonably be claimed for the international economic arrangements of the postwar world is that they gave rise to robust international institutions which were constructed with enough flexibility to adjust to changing circumstances. Thus the World Bank, whose main task had been envisaged as the financing of postwar reconstruction, became by the 1960s the dominant international body providing aid for underdeveloped countries. The Organization for European Economic Co-operation (OEEC), started in 1947 as a body to formulate Europe's recovery programme on the basis of the US-financed Marshall Plan (1948–52), was still functioning in Paris more than twenty years later with a change of title (to OECD). It had become the forum in which the West Europeans and the Americans, together with the Japanese, tried to work out common positions on scientific policy, international payments, aid to underdeveloped countries, and other world-wide problems. Its new name, Organization for Economic Co-operation and Development, adopted in 1961, reflected the changed emphasis of its work, as well as of its membership, which now included non-European nations like the United States and Japan. Aid for economic development was intended to be a major preoccupation of the OECD member nations during the 1960s; by the end of the decade they were supplying over $12,000 million annually, in the form of public and private capital, to the underdeveloped countries.

The GATT (General Agreement on Tariffs and Trade), established in Geneva in 1947, was perhaps the outstanding example of the adaptive power of institutions. Set up originally as a makeshift device for coping with a number of postwar trading problems, until a full-blown world trade organization could be established, it survived to preside over a series of multilateral tariff-cutting sessions of an unprecedented scale and complexity. These culminated in the so-called Kennedy Round of negotiations, 1964–67, which reached agreement on a series of cuts that would bring the level of tariffs on manufactured goods in the industrial countries down by an average of one-third by the early 1970s. By that time most of the import duties on manufactures in the Western world would have been reduced to a historic low of around 10%.

The internal economic policies of the Western industrial nations were also subjected to certain pressures towards conformity with one another. The process was more gradual and subtle than in the international supervision of external trade and payments. In the sphere of external relations the objective was clear from the beginning: the new regulatory agencies, the International Monetary Fund, GATT, OEEC, would systematically build up a body of international economic law, to which the actual behaviour of states would more and more conform. What was not foreseen

After World War II the productive power of the industrialized countries increased at a greater rate than that of the underdeveloped ones, with the result that the gap between the two became wider. Low's cartoon of 1946 shows Lord Beveridge trying to measure the distance from the US grain surplus to the starving Third World. (5)

was that a by-product of the incessant argument and bargaining among the Western industrial countries over a constantly expanding range of subject matter would be a certain creeping convergence in their domestic economic policies. The early postwar years were full of the sound and fury of the great debate on the new techniques and objectives of economic policy—full employment (which was believed by some to involve governments in entirely new methods of managing the economy that were barely compatible with a liberal international policy); economic planning and the role of the 'welfare state'; the new-fangled techniques of employing the annual budget on Keynesian lines as an instrument for keeping the level of overall economic activity at some predetermined high level, rather than as a device for balancing the government's business accounts. However, once the period of immediate postwar reconstruction was over by the end of the 1940s, it was gradually found that there was less difference in practice than had been supposed between a state which expressed a doctrinal devotion to 'full employment' (in the British/Scandinavian style) and another which confined itself to the pursuit of a 'high employment' policy (in the continental-European style). The common conviction came to be established in Europe by the late 1950s that a rate of unemployment of more than 2–3% of the working population was evidence either of a failure of policy or of some profound maladjustment in the economic structure of the country concerned. In the 1960s, the number of unemployed in most West European countries was below the lower of these two figures. In the US President Kennedy's Democratic administration which took office in 1961 adopted, for the first time in American history, a full employment target, based initially on the 4% figure. US unemployment remained at or slightly below this figure for most of the 1960s.

Similarly, economic planning, in the sense of a set of policies based on comprehensive forecasts of the supply and demand for key resources projected some years ahead, became commonplace in the 1960s. At the same time some of the excessive claims of the early postwar planners to be able to control events in detail were gradually surrendered. Budgetary management of the economy also came to be widely practised, not least in the United States. There were still important differences between political parties, as well as between nations, about the significance to be attached to these new aspects of economic policy. But much of the ideological heat had gone out of the argument over the issues of principle. Government finance was accepted as being inevitably a much larger factor in the economies of the capitalist countries of the Western world than it had ever been before. Taxation took a far

higher proportion of the national income, and there was a massive and continuing transfer of resources, presided over by governments, from the prosperous to the disadvantaged members of society.

All this helped to maintain economic activity at a more stable level than in the past. West European governments had at their disposal more effective instruments for damping down economic fluctuations, and they began to use them with increasing skill in the 1950s. The United States followed suit in the 1960s.

In the countries of the Soviet bloc, economic growth during the period following World War II was maintained at a high level. Progress was, however, confined to the industrial side; Soviet agriculture continued to lag. And in industrial development priority was given to the 'heavy industries', so that it was in engineering and metal manufacture that the most rapid advances were made. The dominant economic position of West Germany in Western Europe was paralleled by East Germany in Eastern Europe. Although trade among the members of the Soviet bloc expanded rapidly, there was little integration of their economic activities. A joint economic organization, COMECON, was established in Moscow in 1949, but it was not endowed with effective powers. Meanwhile there was suspicion and opposition on the part of individual member countries towards policies aimed at a more rational division of economic activity, which seemed likely to make them permanently dependent on another member of the bloc for the supply of any important industrial product. The effective integration of rigidly planned economies such as those of the Soviet bloc necessarily would have required the joint formulation of major investment programmes, and these did not materialize. The flow of trade within the bloc continued to be closely constricted by a series of bilateral agreements among pairs of members.

By contrast, in Western Europe economic integration based on the removal of trade restrictions and tariffs went ahead fast. The Treaty of Rome setting up the European Common Market of France, Germany, Italy and the three Benelux countries, came into operation in 1958; by 1968 all import duties on industrial goods traded between member countries had been removed, and a common external tariff with the rest of the world established. The Common Market had introduced a measure of joint management of the economic affairs of member countries in the field of agriculture, where common prices for individual commodities were established and the European Commission in Brussels made responsible for managing the market in agricultural produce, in taxation and in matters like the control of monopolies and restrictive practices.

p 323 (27)

The European Free Trade Association (EFTA) based on the Stockholm Convention, 1959, which brought together the other advanced industrial countries of Western Europe, plus Portugal, did not have economic integration as its primary purpose. Its aim

p 322 (25)

Britain's attempts to enter the European Common Market occupied years of negotiation. Here De Gaulle, the sentry, faces a Mr Wilson weighed down with the Commonwealth, military commitments overseas, and a balance of payments deficit. (6)

was simply to provide the benefits of free trade in industrial products among a group of countries which were excluded from the trading advantages of membership of the European Common Market. Although EFTA started later it completed the gradual elimination of its industrial tariffs earlier than the Common Market, in 1967. It also found itself progressively involved, through the process of securing equal treatment for the trading interests of all member states within the group, in the collective formulation of certain economic policies.

The experience of the two West European regional organizations in the 1960s, by contrast with that of the Soviet bloc, suggested that free trade was a more powerful instrument of economic integration between countries than the more deliberate action of governments faced with the problem of dovetailing their national plans with one another. The West European experience also contrasted with the slow and laborious progress of the Latin American Free Trade Area, based on the Treaty of Montevideo, 1960, and with the failure of the new states in Africa to form, or even to maintain existing regional associations in which goods and services could be exchanged freely. In Africa, and in Asia too, the tendency was towards the reinforcement of the economic frontiers between states, whereas in Western Europe they were becoming more permeable. The contrast reflected in part differing political attitudes of the states concerned towards their neighbours. But that was not all. Economic conditions during the 1950s and 1960s were extraordinarily favourable to Western Europe. With a background of full employment, rising living standards, good terms of trade for Europe's manufactures, and a steadily increasing volume of international trade, European nations were ready to take the risks attendant on free trade within regional groups which they might otherwise have eschewed.

The gap in living standards between the Western industrial world and the less developed countries of Asia, Africa and Latin America widened markedly in the period following World War II. It was not due to a decline in the productive power of the latter group of countries; on the contrary their production increased more rapidly than ever before. But the rise in the standard of living was held back by the exceptionally rapid growth of their populations. The economic and political environment of the underdeveloped world was about as unfavourable as it could be to the introduction of the new forms of international collaboration which the Western nations had laboriously been learning to practise, after several false starts, in the second half of the 20th century. When an attempt was made to subject the problems of economic underdevelopment to systematic international action under the aegis of the United Nations Conference on Trade and Development (UNCTAD) in 1964 the results were meagre. UNCTAD became a permanent organization; but its first attempts to secure a measure of co-ordination in the economic policies of the underdeveloped countries were not encouraging.

At the end of the period under review the traditional problem of 'the two nations', the rich and the poor, within the industrial societies of the West had given way to the problem of 'the two worlds'. And the great majority of the earth's population were inhabitants of the poor world. The individual citizen of that world contemplating his lot at the start of the 1970s might well feel that the great economic engine of the 20th century, with its proved capacity for making a vast mass of people richer than had ever been thought possible before, had somehow passed him by. Looked at from his standpoint the main achievements of the 20th century to date had been to multiply the number of his fellow citizens requiring to be fed without giving rise to famine, and to make the wealthy industrial countries of the West less dependent on the products that he could most readily sell to them.

p 324 (30)

XV MAN, FREEDOM AND THE FUTURE

Patterns of social and political change

REINHARD BENDIX

'*I sit at the roadside.*

The driver is changing a wheel.

I do not like where I have come from.

I do not like where I am going.

Why am I watching the wheel-change

With impatience?'

BERTOLT BRECHT, 1953

World overcrowding

which faces the human race now for the first time, gives a new dimension to every social and political problem. More than ever before, men are dependent upon one another, forced into closer and closer proximity, their lives more and more tightly regulated to make society function at all. This has generated psychological and other tensions of which the 19th century was only dimly, or prophetically, aware. The individual easily sees himself dominated by forces outside his control. The Spanish artist Juan Genovés, whose *Focus* is reproduced opposite, can depict humanity as a panic-stricken crowd seen through the lens of a telescope or spot-lit by a searchlight beam, an object of pity but as helpless as a colony of ants. (1)

The rate of population growth rises more steeply every year. During many millennia world population grew slowly until it reached one thousand million in 1825. Then the pace quickened. The two thousand million mark was passed in 1930, three thousand million in 1960... The reasons are complex and vary from region to region. At present the steepest rises are in Asia (the babies, left, are in a Tokyo hospital) and South America, where improved medicine and more food ensures that more people survive and have children.

A corollary of population-growth is increased urbanization, leading to a near breakdown of housing, water supply, sewage facilities, etc. Below left: one of the shanty towns outside Brasilia, where, in the shadow of the new government departments, thousands of the poor live in huts covered with sacking. Below: the water problem in Calcutta. Fifty million gallons a day are needed; every source has to be exploited, so that cholera and intestinal diseases are rife. Population continues to rise; the problem gets worse.

Far right: the endless proliferation of the modern city—Tokyo from the air. (2, 3, 4, 6)

ORALE
KONTRA
ZEPTION
MEDICA

The answer: voluntary limitation of population. Of the many methods now in use, 'the pill', which affects the female reproductive cycle so as to prevent fertilization, is one of the most effective. But at present it is too expensive for poor countries like India. (5)

Population growth from 1750 to 1950, showing both the total world population and the growth by continent. The figures for 1950 appear as a section on the right edge. (7)

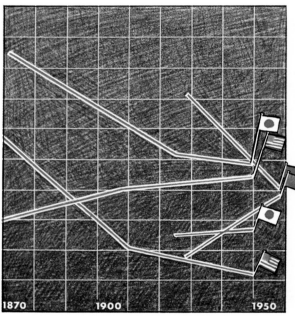

Urbanization: the height of each skyscraper corresponds to the percentage of population in each continent living in cities (that is, towns of 20,000 and over) in 1960. (8)

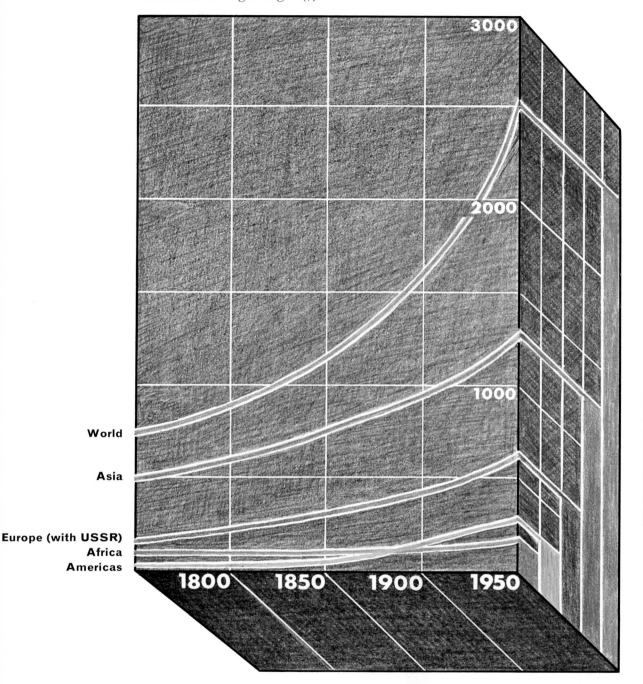

World

Asia

Europe (with USSR)
Africa
Americas

3000

2000

1000

1800   1850   1900   1950

How the labour force has undergone redistribution in the USA, Russia and Japan is shown in the diagram above. The green lines stand for agriculture and the red for industry. In all three countries, the percentage in agriculture has dramatically declined, while that in industry has risen. (10)

A different aspect of world population emerges if we compare not the absolute figures for each continent but the percentages of the total that each represents. In this diagram, each division stands for 10%. It is then clear that, although the population of Asia is increasing in absolute terms more than any other continent, the *percentage* of Asians in the world remains almost stable at about one half. (9)

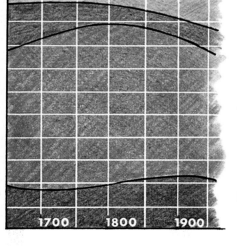

Americas

Africa

Asia and
Australasia

Europe

1700   1800   1900

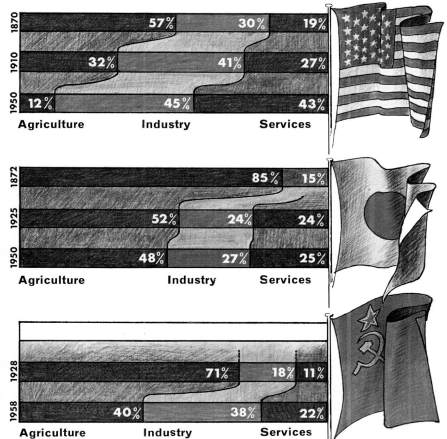

The pattern within each country is set out in these three diagrams, where the numbers in agriculture, services and industry are shown as percentages of the total labour forces. (11)

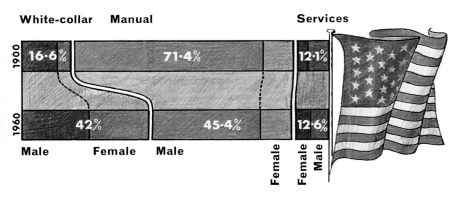

The contrast between 1900 and 1960 is here represented in more detail for the USA. The total force is divided into white-collar, manual and service workers, and each subdivided into male and female. These figures are broken down still further in the statistical table on p. 351. (12)

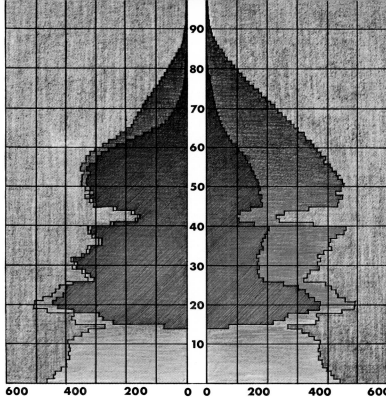

In a single country, West Germany (without Berlin), the events of the first sixty years of this century can be made vivid by a diagram such as this. It shows the age-structure on December 31st, 1959. Ages are represented on the vertical scale, population figures in thousands horizontally, men on the left, women on the right. The darker area in the middle denotes men and women in employment. Beginning at the bottom, there are nearly 500,000 babies of each sex. The sharp reduction in numbers of 14- and 15-year-olds reflects the drop in the birth-rate during 1944–45. Another such drop in those aged 28 or 29 corresponds to the Depression years. Soon after the age of 30 the number of men declines more sharply than that of women; this is explained by the losses of men who were aged between 18 and 50 during World War II. Another 'bite' at age 40–44 shows the drop in the birth-rate during 1915–19. A second, though by now less acute, deficiency of men between the ages of 60 and 72 reflects the losses of World War I. (13)

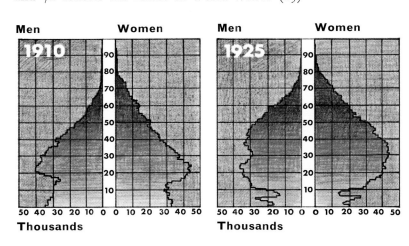

The city of Berlin is shown in a similar way in these four diagrams. Again, figures are in thousands. Here the fluctuations are due not only to the drops in birth-rates (which naturally travel up the chart through the age-levels) but also to immigration (e.g. of people aged around 30 in 1939) and the crippling losses of World War II. In 1945 there were only a few thousand men in their twenties left in the city. (14)

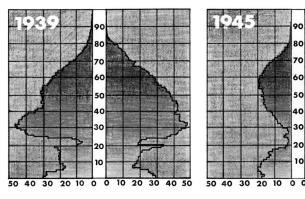

Mass politics, whether of the left or the right, rely on basically the same psychological approach: absolute loyalty to a single party and the submerging of the individual in a crowd activated by a single will. To express that will and to mobilize the whole people is the mission of the party. No phenomena are more ominously characteristic of the 20th century than propaganda — the manipulation of public opinion — and the mass rally.

Left: a typical Communist poster, produced in Poland in 1955, presenting the conventional symbol of the party as the steersman of the state. Right: a rally at Pyongyang, capital of North Korea. Over 40,000 students and children took part in a pageant on the theme, 'The Korean people rise up to repulse the US imperialists' armed aggression and defend freedom in the fatherland'. (15, 16)

The Nazis were the greatest political showmen of all. A rally such as that held at Nuremberg in 1936 (below) was skilfully designed not only to weld party members into a unity, but also, through film, to impress the rest of the world. To those immune to such techniques, like the artist Magnus Zeller, the Nazi State (below right) was a new Moloch, a frightful idol to which Germany was sacrificing her own children. (17, 18)

The city of the 20th century has created a quality of life which, whether welcomed or feared, has no precedent in earlier centuries. Much modern literature and art can be seen as concerned with the psychology of the city dweller and his reaction to its peculiar stresses.

'Golconda' (right) by René Magritte: ▶ a strange dream-like painting which conveys the individual's isolation in the closed and private world of city apartments, the 'lonely crowd' of modern urban life. (21)

'Street Noises Invade the House' (above) by the Italian Futurist Boccioni brings out the dynamism of modern urban existence, 'the exuberance of action'. (19)

'Métro Station Opéra' (below) by a Dutch Sunday painter, Van Genk, also sees the crowded city — Paris — as a source of stimulation and excitement. (20)

'Dwellings': L.S. Lowry makes the industrial north of England his subject (below right). Sombre and bleak to the outsider, it retains a strong sense of community. (22)

Social division threatens many Western states from within, often as a direct consequence of egalitarian and welfare measures. Groups previously excluded from political life demand a revision of their status. Three such groups are women, Negroes and young people.

Women obtained many civil rights (e.g. to their property after marriage or to the franchise) during the 19th century, though the position varied from country to country. In Britain they were granted the vote only in 1919 after vigorous agitation led by Mrs Pankhurst (right). Revolutionary totalitarian regimes have often made a point of placing the same burdens on women's shoulders as on men's, (below: Russian women working at the Kharkov electrical works). Today, the so-called Women's Liberation Movement (below right) is concerned with attitudes rather than laws. (23–25)

Negroes in the USA formed a socially inferior class ever since slavery. The battle against school segregation is in process of being won; that against unfair discrimination goes on. (26)

Youth confronts the law when the existing system seems to offer no legal means of influencing decisions. Protests against university government have easily overflowed to protests on wider political issues. Left: Paris, May 1968. (27)

347

Wholesale rejection of modern civilization and all its values has been a small but significant feature of recent history. Beliefs in the efficacy of science or technology, in the perfectibility of man, in reason itself, are being seriously questioned. Pop festivals (above: the Isle of Wight, 1970) attracting immense crowds, reinforce the sense of belonging to a culture within a culture. Groups like this in Crete (left) have almost succeeded in returning to the Stone Age. Artificial as such attempts may be, they represent a crisis of confidence in the way in which society is developing. (28, 29)

Patterns of social and political change

REINHARD BENDIX

Two THIRDS of the 20th century are now past. In the period since 1900 the speed and diversity of change seem unprecedented. The late 1960s witnessed a rising sense of uncertainty especially in Western societies. To the contemporary observer the future appears more impenetrable than ever. But the present century is accessible to him, as other centuries are not. The question is whether social change during this century is basically different from that of earlier historical periods. I believe the answer is yes.

P 340-1
(7, 8)

P 341
(10)
f 1

Since 1900 world population and world urbanization have shown an accelerated growth for which there is no parallel. Now Asia and Latin America rather than Europe and North America are the areas of most rapid growth. In most industrialized countries the 20th century has also witnessed the decisive shift of the labour force out of agriculture; only in England did this shift occur much earlier. Other occupational shifts have been equally distinctive: the declining importance of unskilled labour, the rise of managerial, technical and white-collar occupations, and the employment of women. These characteristic changes of the 20th century will be surveyed in the first part of this essay.

The second part deals with an outline of political changes. In this century the social and political institutions of Western societies have been transformed through the simultaneous growth of mass politics and the welfare state, the rise of Bolshevism and Fascism, and the great contention between democratic and totalitarian tendencies. On a still larger scale the world of empire of the years before 1914 has been superseded by the world of rich and poor nations since World War II.

The social changes surveyed in the first sections of this chapter suggest that the theories of the 19th century have become inapplicable to the experience of the 20th. These Western European theories conceived societies as self-contained and integrated, a condition approximated by some countries before the turn of the century. Today these assumptions are invalid. Our world has become one in the sense of interdependence. With modern communications and the division of the world into super-powers and satellites, events anywhere can have instant repercussions everywhere. Also, the civic integration of the working class, which so preoccupied the 19th century, is no longer the major issue even in the industrially developed societies. It may be contrasted with major civic problems of the 1960s in order to underscore the basic difference of the 20th century.

Population: the world pattern

World population stood at one thousand million in about 1825, at two thousand million in 1930 and at three thousand million in 1960. It took millennia to reach the 1825 figure, 105 years to reach the 1930 figure, but only 30 years to reach the 1960 figure. Before 1930, world population grew at a rate between 4% and 7% each decade. Since 1930 it has increased at a rate between 14% and 20%. The general cause of accelerating population growth is clear. Modern medicine and sanitation have wiped out epidemics. Increased agricultural productivity is capable of sustaining a much larger population. Accordingly, death-rates have declined rapidly, while birth-rates have stayed high. Only when birth-rates begin to fall, will the rate of growth decline, and then only gradually.

Population growth mirrors a key problem of social change in the 20th century. To see this we must compare the history of industrialized countries with the present experience of countries that are economically underdeveloped. Take England and Wales, the pioneers of industrialization. In a period of 175 years (from about 1780 to about 1955) the English birth-rate declined from 37 to 16 per 1,000, and the death-rate from 25 to 4 per 1,000. Average life expectancy increased from 40 years in 1850 to 53 in 1900 and 70 in 1955. Other industrialized countries show comparable patterns. Death-rates declined first as a result of improved sanitation, hygiene, and the development of modern medicine. As more infants survived, the most compelling reason for large families—to ensure their continuity—lost ground. Gradually, motives for the curtailment of reproduction gained. As industrialization provided people with new opportunities, early marriage and the cost of raising children appeared as obstacles to personal advancement and security.

Now take India by way of contrast. Prior to 1920 her crude birth- and death-rates were 47 and 40 per 1,000 respectively. (Note that these figures are considerably higher than those for England in 1780.) In the decades since 1920 the Indian birth-rate has declined somewhat, probably to 44 per 1,000. In the same period her death-rate has declined to about 20 per 1,000. Whereas India's population grew by 11% in the 1920s, it increased by 21% in the 1950s. A 20% increase in a single decade is higher than any rates of increase recorded for Western European countries in the last century and a half. Nor is this Indian figure the most extreme. In the 1950s the population of Ceylon reached an increase of 34%, and countries like Taiwan, Malaya and Costa Rica had similar rates of growth.

In the countries of Asia and Latin America nothing has led as yet to a major decline in reproduction. But in a few decades the death-rates have declined to one half or less of their former level, a point reached by a country like Sweden only after 130 years. The result is clear. The average growth of the world's population has become very uneven, with Asia and Latin America contributing a large share of the increase. As Kingsley Davis has stated:

> The demography of the non-industrial countries today differs in essential respects from the early history of the present industrial nations. . . . Today, non-industrial populations are growing faster and at an earlier stage than was the case in the demographic cycle that accompanied industrialization in the 19th century.

The reasons for this difference are in dispute. Some argue that the falling death-rate in non-industrialized countries is due to a slowly rising standard of living increasing the people's resistance to disease. In this view public health measures and modern medicine merely assist an economic development that is under way. It is hoped this development will eventuate in a declining birth-rate and a diminished rate of growth, as it did in Europe. Others regard this as wishful thinking. Medicines and public health measures have had a quick effect. But it takes decades to achieve a rapid rate of economic growth and limit family size in response to new opportunities. In the industrialized countries the people's reproductive behaviour has come to fluctuate with business conditions, but in non-industrialized countries (as is again shown by Kingsley Davis) the correlation between population growth and annual gain of per capita income is negligible. In some measure the issue can be resolved only in the future. But it is clear now that formerly unquestioned values such as health and a long life can be problematic, even tragic, in their results when they contribute unwittingly to population growth unmatched by economic advance.

World urbanization is a recent phenomenon. Between 1900 and 1960, the number of people living in cities of 100,000 and over increased from 75 to 525 millions, or from 4·7% to 17·5% of world population. The population of all cities of 20,000 or more grew from 14% to 25%. This means that amid general urban growth, the larger cities have grown most rapidly. In the period 1920–60 the world's population increased by a factor of less than two, but urban population (cities of 20,000 or more) by a factor of three.

p 340 (8)
Regional differences are pronounced in respect to the number of urban residents and their rate of growth. In 1960 Europe (without the USSR) had the largest *number* of residents in cities of 20,000 and over, followed by East Asia, South Asia, Northern America, the Soviet Union, Latin America and Africa in that order. However, this ranking by total number obscures divergent *rates* of growth as well as the divergent proportions of the urban sector in the entire population. Europe's urban population was 41% of its total population in 1960. This urban sector had grown by 18% in the preceding decade. By contrast, East Asia's urban population was only 20% of total population, but the urban rate of growth was 52%.

Thus, in the older industrialized regions of the world, the urban sector represents a high proportion of total population, but the urban rate of growth is relatively low. So many people have already migrated from the land in some countries, that city growth slows down. Some cities grow no more than the general population. In the newer industrialized regions, like the Soviet Union, and to a lesser extent North America, the urban sector is already large but its rate of growth is still high. The pattern is reversed in the non-industrial regions of Asia, Latin America and Africa; the urban sector is small, but its rate of growth very high.

This urbanization of economically underdeveloped countries today differs from the past urbanization of industrialized countries. In the past the growth of cities required an enormous influx of people from farms and villages, because urban employment opportunities increased rapidly while death-rates were higher in the cities than in the countryside. That influx continued even after sanitation had reduced the high urban death-rates. In the United States 27 millions migrated to the cities between 1920 and 1959, with the result that the farm population declined from about 32·5 million to 20·5 million. If only the families dependent on agriculture are counted, the farm population is down to 12·9 million, or 6·8% of the US population. Today, in the economically underdeveloped countries, the towns and cities also grow very rapidly. But while public health measures have lowered their urban death-rates, their urban birth-rates are almost as high as in the rural areas.

In Latin America and many countries of Asia, urbanization occurs primarily as a result of a rapidly rising population, not because of rural–urban migration. Between 1927 and 1963, Costa Rica's urban population almost trebled, but only 20% of that increase was due to rural influx. In Switzerland between 1850 and 1888 urbanization resembled that of Costa Rica, but there rural–urban migration accounted for 69% of the growth of towns. Thus, non-industrial societies face the grave dilemma that their rapid urbanization does little to alleviate the simultaneous growth of the rural population. Underemployed farmers are crowding the land, while the growing cities are dotted with shanty-towns of squatters eking out a life of stark deprivation.

Figures on population growth and urbanization reflect the growing discrepancy between rich and poor countries. Where economic advance is slow, public health measures preserve life at the expense of well-being: population grows faster than per capita income. Under these conditions urbanization is not accompanied by a rapid rise of industry and of national income, as it was in 19th-century Europe. In South Asia, for example, the growth of cities has occurred together with slow industrialization and, still worse, with a relative stagnation of agriculture. In 1952–56 (using the figures quoted by Gunnar Myrdal) South Asia's volume

of agricultural output at 100 compared with 580 for Europe and 1,780 for the United States. Since economic improvement is so often assumed to be a part of industrialization, it is well to remember the crucial importance of a corresponding revolution in agriculture.

The proportion of the labour force employed in agriculture is a convenient measure of the transformation of societies in the 19th and 20th centuries. Shifts out of agriculture indicate not only the growth of the labour forces in all other sectors of the economy, but also—if indirectly—the rise in agricultural productivity. In America one farm worker's labour fed seven people in 1900, but thirty-three people in 1965. Great Britain, as the oldest industrialized country, has the longest record of shifts out of agriculture. The proportion of her labour force in agriculture was already as low as 35% in 1801, fell to 9% by 1901, and to 5% by 1951. Countries which industrialized later may be compared with these bench-mark figures. The United States had less than 50% of her labour force in agriculture before the turn of the century, whereas for Japan that change occurred after 1925 and for the USSR during the 1930s.

In these and other industrialized countries the labour force shifted first into industrial employments (mining, manufacturing, construction, power and light utilities, transport, communications) and, as these became more labour-saving, into services (trade, finance, real estate, personal business, domestic, professional or government employment). These shifts between major branches of the economy were made possible by a second industrial and by a scientific revolution.

In the last decades of the 19th century the early age of steam and coal were superseded by the age of steel and electricity, of oil and chemicals. As shown elsewhere in this volume the decades at the turn of the century witnessed an economic and technical breakthrough of major proportions, followed in short order by development of air transportation, radio and television. Yet all of this seems dwarfed by what is happening now. In the past few decades science has grown into a mass collective endeavour. Eighty to ninety per cent of the scientists who have ever lived, are alive today. Atomic energy, the electronics industry with its transistors, computers and automated devices, and now the development of space travel involve not only a profusion of technical innovations, but a concerted national effort. There is good reason to believe that today we are in the midst of a scientific and technological revolution which is qualitatively different from what went before.

p 298–9 (2–12) p 302–3 (18–24)

These headlong advances are reflected in the changing occupational structure. In the United States between 1900 and 1960, the share of wage-and-salary earners in the labour force increased from 75% to 93%. This also means a decline in the proportion of self-employed from 25% to 7%. Increasingly, the individual is obliged to become a functionary in large organizations, although in some aspects this was already true some sixty years ago.

f 1
Fig. 1 indicates the changed occupational structure of the United States and may show the direction in which industrial societies are advancing. In the past sixty years, mounting technical complexities have required an increasingly skilled labour force. A dwindling proportion of farmers and unskilled workers (8 and 9) are a contrast to the more or less steady proportion of skilled workers (6 and 7). Yet the losses of the first category are so great that manual workers as a whole declined by more than 30%. Meanwhile, white collar workers have increased by the 30% that the manual category has lost. The 'technostructure' (J. K. Galbraith) requires personnel at the technical, managerial and clerical levels, and all three categories have doubled, quadrupled, or even increased ten-fold. The share of women in all white-collar occupations has increased greatly, although their subordinate role persists. A disproportionate number of typists and sales personnel are women, while a disproportionate number of managers and officials are men. And among professional and technical workers most women are probably laboratory assistants and other subordinate technical personnel.

The occupational shift towards greater skill required better education and more of it. All strata of the population have been affected by this. Among those aged seventeen, high school students increased from 6·4% to 76·2% between 1900 and 1967. Among

Selected Occupational Group	Share of Occupational Groups in Total (per cent)			Share of Females in Occupational Group (per cent)	
	1900	**1960**	**1967**	**1900**	**1960**
1 Professional, technical and kindred workers	5·7	12·2	13·3	35·2	38·1
2 Managers and officials	0·8	5·8	10·1	0·4	14·4
3 Clerical and kindred workers	4·0	16·0	16·6	24·2	67·6
4 Sales workers	6·0	8·0	6·1	17·4	36·4
5 White collar workers (lines 1–4)	**16·6**	**42·0**	**46·1**	**24·5**	**45·7**
6 Craftsmen, foremen and kindred workers	14·1	15·4	13·2	2·5	2·9
7 Operatives and kindred workers	17·1	21·5	18·7	34·0	28·1
8 Non-skilled labourers except farm and mine	16·6	5·9	4·8	3·8	3·5
9 Farm labourers and foremen	23·6	2·6	2·1	13·6	17·3
10 Manual workers (lines 6–9)	**71·4**	**45·4**	**38·9**	**14·0**	**15·7**
11 Service workers except household	4·8	9·6	10·2	34·3	52·4
12 Household workers	7·3	3·0	2·4	96·6	96·4
13 Service workers (lines 11–12)	**12·1**	**12·6**	**12·6**	**71·8**	**63·0**

The occupational structure of workers in the United States in 1900, 1960 and 1967, showing the increase in the percentage of white-collar employees. Sub-totals are printed in bold type. (1)

those aged eighteen to twenty-one, the number of students in higher education has increased from 2 to 6·3 millions between 1946 and 1967, and is expected to reach 9·6 millions by 1977. In a twenty-one year period the proportion of these college students has doubled from 22% to 46% of every 100 persons aged eighteen to twenty-one.

The effect of this educational advance has been pervasive. In the civilian labour force, among those aged twenty-five or more, the proportion of those who completed high school rose from 46% in 1957–59 to 55% in 1965–66 and is expected to reach 66% by 1975. This massive development of education has had a substantial effect on productivity. For the period 1929–57 national output per worker increased by 56% and estimates attribute two-fifths of that rise to the increasing education of the work force. Gross National Product in the United States grew from 103 thousand million dollars per year in 1929 to 789 thousand million in 1967. During the same period all expenditures for education increased from 3·2 million to 54·6 million, or from 3% to almost 7% GNP. Between 1900 and 1965 income increased 32 times, but the labour force producing that income increased only 2·7 times. Clearly, the shift out of agriculture, away from unskilled labour and towards white-collar work has been accompanied by rapidly increasing productivity and a greatly increased demand for higher levels of education in the work force. These indicators are important clues to social change in the 20th century.

People and power

The historical turning-points of this century have been cataclysmic. Since 1900 there have been two world wars, each ending with a Communist revolution. In the fifty years since the Bolshevik Revolution of 1917, Soviet Russia has built up an industrial society and a new world empire. Since 1949 China has begun a similar effort, although her internal consolidation and external role are still in the future. Together the two Communist giants encompass almost one third of the world's population. The years since Hitler's rise to power in 1933 have brought the decline of European empire, the rise of the United States as an industrial and political world power, and the proliferation of national regimes around the world. Since 1945, 51 newly established sovereign nations have been recognized as members of the United Nations,

increasing the total from 71 to 122. World affairs have been dominated by the contentions between Russia and the United States for political, military and technical superiority. In Europe and the Far East, Germany, Korea and Vietnam have been divided. America, Russia and now also China compete for spheres of influence in Asia, Africa and the Middle East. And since the 1940s the hazard of nuclear destruction casts a pall over every move.

Changes in the internal structure of societies have been no less momentous. The two world wars destroyed whole segments of the population and caused massive migrations, especially in Central Europe. Figures 2 and 3 show the displacement of populations, while the population pyramid for the Federal Republic of Germany reflects the casualties of these wars and the shortages of births resulting from them, as well as from the Great Depression of the 1930s. In 1960, 25% of the population in the Federal Republic consisted of migrants from other parts of Europe. Perhaps countries like Russia and China were ravaged to the same extent, but we lack comparable statistical information.

f 3, 4 p 341 (13)

The political structure of Western countries was transformed by these upheavals. National organization for modern war, the Bolshevik and Fascist regimes of the inter-war years, and the economic depression of the 1930s led to the political mobilization of great masses of people. To an extent such mobilization was anticipated already by developments preceding World War I.

Until the 1870s the franchise was restricted to owners of property, and parliament was an assembly of dignitaries from the upper strata of society. In the United Kingdom, for example, even the Reform Bill of 1867 extended the franchise to only one out of thirty persons. In the absence of the secret ballot, election results were manipulated by the ruling oligarchies. These conditions changed with the introduction of universal manhood suffrage in France and the German Empire (1871), Switzerland (1874), and other countries following suit in the 1890s or later. (In European settlements like the United States or Australia the extension of the franchise occurred earlier.) Note that in most of these cases women received the franchise in the years following World War I, some fifty years later than men, even though they had become a considerable part of the labour force.

The extension of the franchise was the political expression of a changing concept of the lower classes in Western societies. In the 19th century and amid rapidly advancing industrialization pauperism had been considered the overriding social problem. It was attributed to personal failure in life's struggle for survival. In England, a franchise restricted to owners of property meant second-class citizenship for the five out of six adult males who could not vote. This second-class position was reversed by the extension of the franchise—in England from the introduction of the secret ballot in 1872 and the Third Reform Bill of 1884, to universal suffrage in 1918. During the same period the identification of poverty with degradation was abolished step by step through an extension of the welfare principle. The children, the old, the sick, and the unemployed were gradually extracted from the category of pauperism by measures designed to provide an assistance that did not carry the stigma of second-class status.

The gradual abolition of second-class citizenship for the vast majority of the population brought in its train a decline in the politics of notables so characteristic of the 19th century. The mass democracy which took its place required political parties which could organize mass participation in the electoral process. In Europe and the other countries which modelled themselves after her, this took the form of permanent membership organizations. These parties imposed a discipline on all functionaries and representatives of the party and catered to the diverse interests of the members through a multitude of affiliated organizations. In the United States, party organizations were permanent only at the level of an oligarchic leadership which undertook to organize a mass following in every electoral contest.

Party policies can be confirmed or altered in broad outline only during periodic elections. But the details that really affect the individual citizen are hammered out in the long intervening periods, through parliamentary debate and committee work, through legislation and administrative implementation. At these levels politics had been largely a matter of personal influence during the 19th century, involving family relations or social contacts among a relatively small group of the privileged. Here also, the politics of notables has been superseded, not, however, by mass democracy, but by a politics of organized interests. Although the transactions of parliament and of administrative agencies are related to electoral politics, they are more immediately influenced by those segments of the public capable of organizing and representing their interests to legislators and officials. As government functions expand, so do the efforts to influence policy.

No simple measure of that expansion is available. The size of public employment and government purchases can only serve as a gross index, since government influence extends far beyond its own direct operations. In the United States, in 1966, public employment had reached 14·4 million out of a total labour force of 72·8 million persons, with government purchases of goods and services reaching a total of 154·3 thousand million out of a Gross National Product of 743 thousand million dollars. Since roughly one-fifth of all employed persons and of all purchases involve public authority directly, the transactions of parliament and of government agencies have become too important to be left to politicians and officials.

Moreover, governmental decision-making is not the exclusive domain of legislators. Policy decisions and control of implementation become the concern of administrators and experts in the many cases in which legislators depend upon and use advice for political ends, or avoid political choices by recourse to 'knowledge'. In addition, the work of government has been delegated since World War II to what one writer has called 'the quasi non-governmental organization'. This means that private organizations of many types are engaged in research and production under public contract in fields in which the government does not want to operate directly. It is little wonder that organized interests have been mobilized to exert pressure on government when public decisions are made. Such mobilizations must be considered a public response to modern government, much as mass political parties were a response to the universal franchise.

Democratic and totalitarian regimes

The structural changes here reviewed—the political mobilization of the people and the transformation of decision-making—can be analyzed at a more abstract level as a basis for the consideration of totalitarian regimes below. To do this it is useful to distinguish direct democracy from representative government, or the plebiscitary from the representative component of democratic government—a distinction originally formulated by Ernst Fraenkel. The term 'plebiscite' refers to the direct vote on an important public issue by all qualified electors of a community. Where qualifications are at a minimum, all adult members of the community would participate directly in the decisions of public authority. Plebiscitarian rule assumes that the public interest is identical with the public will, and that this will is unified enough for effective public action and ascertainable through direct vote on all major issues. In this view minorities or special interests interfere with the untrammelled formation of public opinion. Even a system of parliamentary representation appears as an inadequate substitute for public decision-making, or direct democracy. Public authority should thus be based on a continual plebiscite, as in periodic public opinion polls which would extend the universal franchise to the periods between elections. In practice, such mobilization has occurred, not through periodic polls, but through one-party regimes which carried the principle of political participation by everyone to its logical conclusion.

In a representative government all important public issues are voted upon only by those who have been elected to perform this function by the qualified voters of a community. Such a government will take account of majority opinion whenever possible, but it does not assume that the public interest is identical with the public will. Rather, the public interest, hypothetical as it is, will be preferred to a public opinion that can change quickly and is frequently uninformed. Parliament is the model of representative government, although with the expansion of government functions administrators of particular agencies also respond to the

publics they serve and in a sense represent them. Moreover, with the devolution of parliamentary functions, the distinction between public and private often becomes so blurred that even agents of organized interests claim to be representatives in a quasi-public sense. Such agents have been elected by a private constituency and represent its interests. They pervert the idea of representation when they claim to speak in the name of the public.

Modern democratic governments are an interplay between these two principles. Universal franchise is the model of plebiscitary rule. The direct democracy of the town hall meeting is applied to national affairs, although in practice it is combined with the idea of representation. Parliament is the model of representative government. Representation has an affinity with oligarchic rule, although in practice it is frequently responsive to public opinion. How can this interpretation be related to the wars and dictatorships mentioned at the beginning of the previous section?

Modern wars and dictatorships are radical applications of the plebiscitary principle. They are so extreme, however, that government by the people is turned into its opposite. In practice, no regime ever conducts its affairs by means of continual plebiscites. Instead, when public issues are decided by direct vote of all adult citizens, the regime becomes one of mass acclamation on staged public occasions. No individual interest is permitted to obstruct the popular will and in its name all people and resources are mobilized. Thus plebiscitary rule has an authoritarian as well as a populist side. But this authoritarian meaning is given a semblance of popular rule by construing the actions of government as a direct decision of 'the people', with no representative bodies intervening. p 342–3 (15–18)

In the era of mass politics and democratic ideals government by public consent has a powerful appeal. Thus, wartime governments may issue decrees curtailing or suspending partisan politics, but they are likely to proceed as if a universal consent had been given. And the decrees themselves are limited usually to the duration of the war. On the other hand, dictatorships are regimes of perpetual emergency, real or simulated. To meet such emergency, such regimes begin with the destruction of parliamentary institutions. The dissolution of the Constituent Assembly by the Bolsheviks in 1917, or the Reichstag fire of 1933 exploited by Hitler, marked the beginning of a para-military destruction of all independent organizations, no matter how non-political. To a modern dictatorship, every organization that is independent is also political. p 62–3 (17–26)

These first steps result in a continuous mobilization to achieve the national task. In an effort to describe the resulting regimes comprehensively, Professor Robert Tucker refers to 'revolutionary mass movement regimes under single party auspices'. Although such regimes differ in many respects, they also have much in common. Their overthrow of an 'old regime' fulfils the first task of their ideological mission. This overthrow is a plebiscite in action, the result of a mass movement against the Establishment. The spearhead and ruling force of the mass movement is the single party. To achieve the necessary unity and drive, the party organizes for political combat by controlling all other organizations of the society. In this way the party claims to express the will of the people, and to act on the basis of a continual plebiscite. As Professor Tucker observes:

> In practice this means the enlisting of masses of people in the activities of trade unions, youth, professional, and other organizations that are formally non-party in character but operated under party guidance and supervision via directorates from top to bottom in which disciplined party members predominate. A large proportion of the population is thus drawn into the whirlpool of guided public life, and many may derive an experience of political participation that was denied them under the old regime.

The price of this mobilization is high. It has been estimated that some 20 million people perished under the Stalinist regime in Soviet Russia. A locational map of German prisons, Gestapo commando posts, and concentration camps under the Nazis shows the country covered from one end to the other. And the baffling Great Proletarian Cultural Revolution in China appears to have

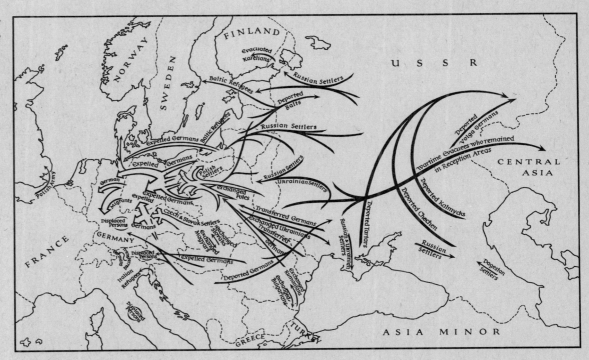

Population shifts in Europe and the USSR, 1918–39. These were brought about partly by the First World War and the preceding Balkan wars, partly by forced deportations, and partly by economic factors (e.g. the migration of Italian workers to France). (2)

Flights and transfers of population in Europe and the USSR produced by the Second World War. (3)

been similarly extensive, although we do not know at what human cost. The point is that total mobilization can be achieved only by the destruction of all independent organizations which could mediate between the central power of the state and the individual. By representing a particular segment of society each of these organizations would jeopardize the claim of the single party to represent the people as a whole.

These characteristics of 'revolutionary mass movement regimes' have proved compatible with quite divergent cultural and historical traditions. The Bolshevik regime was the first full-scale example, coming to power in 1917 following the protracted agonies of Russia's participation in World War I. As a single-party regime in an economically backward society, the Bolsheviki initiated the industrialization of the whole country. This fact destroyed the 19th-century notion that rapid economic growth could only be the product of a free market and private initiative. Bolshevism thus appeared as a threat to economically advanced countries in which this conception was widespread. And the defence against this threat encouraged the rise of Fascist movements in many European countries.

In Italy and Germany, these movements established regimes of the far Right. This proved that the techniques of mass mobilization and single-party rule could also be used in industrially advanced countries. Where national crises are severe enough to arouse people's anxiety and jeopardize the functioning of institutions, Fascism can rise to power on the claim that the national interest

demands a clean sweep of conventional politics, of the 'Establishment' or *das System*, as Hitler put it. This extremist possibility did not end with Hitler's and Mussolini's defeat in World War II. In the last third of the 20th century it is a likely threat, where mounting problems at home and abroad polarize the political community and thereby undermine its institutional framework.

The organizational similarities between Bolshevism and Fascism (or rather between Stalinism and Hitlerism) should not obscure the differences between them. At the ideological level they are a world apart: a universalist materialism and a belief in progress on one side, a racist romanticism and belief in war and national superiority on the other. But in practice, both regimes are nationalist in the extreme. Both are dedicated to advance their country by a civic simulation of perpetual combat against external and internal enemies, a continuation of war by quasi-peaceful means. These common elements of totalitarian regimes have replaced absolute monarchy as an alternative model of rule which competes with Western democracy.

p 342–3 (16, 17)

In the second half of the 20th century all the countries of the so-called Third World face the double task of developing a sense of national identity and achieving rapid economic growth. For that purpose nationalist authoritarian regimes have tended to borrow whatever served their immediate ends: from the Bolshevik version of the Marxian tradition, from the national socialist anti-democratic orientation of Fascism, as well as from the older liberal, Christian and racist ideology of the colonial past. In

Europe the rise of Bolshevism and Fascism signalled the transformation of 19th-century political structures. But in Africa and Asia the ideas of European liberalism inspired nationalist movements of independence from Western domination. The mass-movement regimes of Europe and these independence movements in many parts of the world combined nationalism with plebiscitarianism, mostly at the expense of democratic institutions. An account of social change in the 20th century must summarize how these developments have changed the character of world politics.

World powers

In 1900 European population represented one fourth of world population, having grown by 51% since 1850. The beginning of this century marked a highpoint of European dominance. Her share in world trade amounted to 65·9%. World production had been increasing rapidly and Europe contributed the lion's share of it. Between 1870 and 1900 production of coal had trebled; between 1850 and 1900 production of iron ore had increased tenfold; between 1860 and 1900 production of petroleum had increased more than 200 times. In 1900 Western Europe produced 54% of the world's pig iron compared with 34·8% for the United States and 7·1% for Russia. Europe's share in the world's manufacturing production was more than 40% in 1913.

This period of industrial growth was also one of imperial expansion. The opening of the Suez Canal in 1869 was followed by English and French colonization in Africa. The 1880s and 1890s witnessed European advances in Asia, including Russia's penetration of Siberia and of the inner Asian frontiers of China. From 1876 to 1914 colonial powers of the world annexed eleven million square miles of territory.

Within Western European societies themselves, pauperism had been the major social problem of the 19th century. It was the result of rapid industrialization and urbanization. Increasing wealth seemed the answer to pauperism. At the same time workers grew aware of their second-class status and this made citizenship the major political problem. Extension of the franchise established equal citizenship and seemed an effective answer to the workers' protest. Both answers appeared readily available in nations enjoying a rising standard of living at home and increasing power abroad. Economic growth at home was linked with political and military expansion abroad. Propagandists of 'social imperialism' no longer exhorted the poor to remain content with their station in life, as the evangelists of the early 19th century had done. Instead, they sought to enlist the poor in a common national endeavour of overseas expansion. Rich and poor would benefit alike, at the expense of the 'inferior races'.

Yet European predominance in the decades since 1880 was at the same time the passing of the European age. A period of strident self-confidence also witnessed growing uncertainty and despair. As John Lester has noted, the praise of life lived to the fullest was increasingly marred by doubt that life was worth living. In 1905 Edward Carpenter wrote that 'we are dying slowly and surely of Unbelief—and there can be no deadlier disease'. In the midst of unprecedented material achievements and imperial power, writers of sensibility noted the undercurrents of the age with profound scepticism. At the turn of the century Europe was already undergoing the transformations which have led to the world of the second half of the 20th century. Demographic and economic indicators tell that story in one way. A changed international setting and an altered sensibility do so in other ways.

From 1900 to 1950 European population fell from one-fourth to one-fifth of world population. More important, her rate of growth in the decade 1950 to 1960 was down to almost one half of the world average, whereas in that decade Asia's population increased almost twice as fast and Latin America's almost three times. By 1960, 56% of the world's population and its greatest potential for growth were found in Asia. Europe, the USSR and North America together encompassed only 28%. In the field of economic growth the passing of the European age was as clearly marked. In 1800 Europe's share in world trade had been 75% and in 1900 65%. By 1956 it had gone down to 43%, a decline of over 20% in five decades. In 1900 Western Europe produced 54% of the world's production of pig iron, but by 1959 her production

was down to 30·4%. Simon Kuznets has compared the productive capacity of several European countries with those of the United States, Russia and Japan. While England and France, for example, increased total production by more than six times the initial level a century ago, the United States and Japan increased total product thirty-four times. If the current growth-rate of the Soviet Union is extrapolated for a century, she would have increased her total product seventy-four times the initial level.

The implications of these developments were anticipated by some. In the 1830s, Tocqueville foresaw that the rise of Russia and America would overshadow Europe. In the 1880s the English historian J. R. Seeley declared that, once Russia and the United States were mobilized by steam, electricity, and a network of railways, European states like France and Germany would be dwarfed. For its time Seeley's insight was remarkable for the inclusion of Russian industrialization as a major factor in the changing balance of power. To less prescient observers, the rising imperial role of Russia and the United States remained hidden. In the case of Russia, Bolshevism was largely seen as a threat to the social order of other countries, not as the ideology of a world power. Russia was too preoccupied with her internal development to appear plausible as the future centre of an empire. The United States became deliberately isolationist after her participation in World War I, and would not join the League of Nations. But these appearances of isolation were shattered by World War II.

The alliance between England, France, the United States and Russia, the domination of the postwar world by the two super-powers, the revolution in China in 1949, and finally the rise to political prominence of a large number of newly sovereign countries have all shaped a world in which Europe has lost her former pre-eminence. Divested of her empires, Europe faces great spiritual difficulties. There is not much left of the confidence which still prevailed in 1900, despite the fact that material achievements of industrial societies are very much greater today than they were at the turn of the century. There is a deep chasm between European cultural tradition and the legacies of depredation which five centuries of Western expansion have left behind. None of the glories of European culture can undo or allay those legacies. In her decline from world eminence, Europe must come to terms with this fact. It is easier, of course, to evade this dilemma, and instead view the super-powers as the twin dangers to civilization. While Russia and now China are seen in the image of an undifferentiated mass of humanity menacing the individual, the United States is seen as a world in which the soul is sacrificed to the machine. Yet the contemptuous rejection of other cultures is not an effective defence of one's own. Indeed, the massive critique of things Russian and American is a form of European self-righteousness, an arrogance coupled with anxiety, as the Swiss writer Karl Schmid has put it.

While the dream of Europe as the cradle and centre of civilization is not easily relinquished, the two super-powers face burdens of their own. None of the achievements of the United States can efface her guilt in the enslavement and persecution of Negroes. A century after the Civil War, the problem of integrating this submerged tenth of the nation is as unsolved as ever. Nor has American history prepared her people to handle the responsibilities of world power at a time when the United States has become the unwitting heir of Europe's earlier imperial role. There are signs that American democracy will be tested severely, if unresolved problems at home and abroad further polarize the easily aroused segments of the population, on the Right and the Left. Meanwhile, Russia has celebrated the fiftieth anniversary of the Bolshevik revolution (1967). The momentum of her successful industrialization is a tremendous source of national power and internal legitimacy, despite the horrors of Stalinism. But this achievement is marred by the unresolved problems of economic organization, the continual persecution or harassment of ethnic and national minorities, the fitful but pervasive suppression of thought, and perhaps above all the stultifying mediocrity of a top-heavy bureaucracy. It is marred also by Russia's mounting imperial problems with restless satellites in the west and a hostile Communist regime of 700 million Chinese in the east. The United States and Russia thus face the last third of the 20th century with an enormous technical

Groups of countries by per capita income

			$1,000 and over (a)	$575 to 1,000 (b)	$350 to 575 (c)	$200 to 350 (d)	$100 to 200 (e)	Under $100 (f)
General	1	Number of countries, 1958	**6**	**11**	**14**	**13**	**14**	**10**
	2	Population (millions)	216·7	396·8	183·8	226·2	171·5	667·6
	3	Per capita income, 1956–58 ($)	1,366	760	431	269	161	72
Urbanization	4	Per cent of total population in urban areas (recent census)	68·2	65·8	49·9	36·0	32·0	22·9
	5	Per cent of population in communities of more than 100,000, about 1955	43	39	35	26	14	9
Mortality	6	Expectation of life at birth, 1955–58 (years)	70·6	67·7	65·4	57·4	50·0	41·7
	7	Infant mortality per 1,000, 1955–58	24·9	41·9	56·8	97·2	131·1	180·0
Food consumption	8	Per cent of private consumption expenditures spent on food, 1960 or late 1950s (36 countries)	26·2	30·5	36·1	37·6	45·8	55·0
	9	Per capita calorie consumption, latest year (40 countries)	3,153	2,944	2,920	2,510	2,240	2,070
	10	Per cent of starchy staples in total calories, latest year (40 countries)	45	53	60	74	70	77
Energy consumption	11	Per capita kilos of coal equivalent, 1956–58	3,900	2,710	1,861	536	265	114
Education	12	Per cent of population, 15 years and over, illiterate, 1950	2	6	19	30	49	71
	13	Per cent of school enrolment to four-fifths of the 5–19 age group, latest year	91	84	75	60	48	37

Table comparing living conditions in countries grouped according to per capita income. Examples from the six categories are (a) USA and most of the former British Dominions; (b) most European countries; (c) Eastern Europe, Japan; (d) Portugal, Spain, Latin America; (e) the Middle East and most of Africa; (f) China, India, and most of Asia except Japan. (4)

civilization, a materialist culture that alienates their educated élites, and a host of problems that cannot be solved either by American anti-Communism or Soviet anti-Americanism.

In addition, the Western world has come to be haunted by the stark discrepancies between rich nations and poor. A glance at the accompanying table should not lead one to the view that the gulf between rich and poor nations is new. But the new political independence of poor countries and the remaining scars of colonialism together have made this gulf a potent issue. The poor countries are also the coloured nations, so that their hostility to rich nations is frequently joined with anti-Western sentiments born of colonialism and racial discrimination. Thus the legitimacy of rich nations is questioned, because they are also Western and white and as such a reminder of exploitation and inequality. An apparent exception like Japan is only used to demonstrate that in fact the coloured people are superior and their poverty is un-justified. Such feelings are widespread in the second half of the 20th century. They greatly aggravate the domestic problems of many societies of the West. For racial minorities and youths the poor nations of the world are a symbol of the injustice perpetuated by 'the Establishment', past and present, and hence a reason to attack its legitimacy.

Societies in transition
Nineteenth-century theories of society do not explain this crisis of legitimacy in the midst of affluence, nor do they deal with the civic integration of minorities. Such problems will beset us for the rest of this century. We have no comprehensive theory to analyze them, but even in its absence we can take a measure of our time by finding why the old theories are inapplicable.

Note that all such theories are a product of Western thought, as is the idea of a scientific study of society. These theories were developed in societies which had pioneered the industrial and democratic revolutions of the modern world and these revolutions occurred at the centre of world empires. It is not surprising that such theories depicted societies as self-contained units and focussed their attention on the division of labour within these units. This division was considered the major determinant of social classes and social change. Several variants of this model developed. Liberals emphasized the rise in productivity and market exchange as by-products of the division of labour. Conservatives empha-sized the division of society into status groups, each with its rights and duties defined as parts of the whole. Radicals saw that division

in terms of conflicts between exploiters and exploited. Each of these perspectives emphasized what the other two neglected, but none of them attended to considerations that have since proved important.

Nineteenth-century theorists neglected the international setting of societies and the existence of groups formed on the basis of sex, age or ethnic identity, rather than on an economic basis. The importance of boundaries for the economy and the nation-wide division of labour made it plausible to consider 'society' in isola-tion from other societies. It also seemed clear that being a citizen politically and being a member of society were two aspects of the same reality. Tacitly, these theories identified the term 'society' with the nation state. This identification has proved faulty. To analyze some of the urgent problems facing us today, it will be useful to examine the range of facts which come into view when these 19th-century assumptions are called into question.

Nineteenth-century theorists treated society as if it were an island, isolated from countries beyond its shores and without effect upon them. To be sure, these theories took some notice of the international setting. Liberal theory was concerned with inter-national trade. Conservative theory emphasized the inequality of nations as a natural outgrowth of power politics. Radical theory construed international affairs as a continuation of the national class struggle by other means. Yet these considerations remained only peripheral extensions of the idea that the division of labour within society is the main determinant of stability and change. Nineteenth-century theories neglected the manifest historical importance of the diffusion of techniques and ideas.

After some four centuries of European expansion it seems paradoxical to think of societies as if they were self-contained units. This idea neglects the fact that societies around the world have suffered massive dislocation due to conquest or economic de-pendence. It also neglects the fact that the industrial and demo-cratic revolutions in England and France towards the end of the 18th century were emulated by other countries. Conquest and economic expansion as well as industrial techniques and demo-cratic ideas have made the world one. Yet it is in this world that the idea of 'society as an island' has come into prominence.

True, the earliest European expansion had a rather superficial impact upon the non-European world. But the economic and political revolutions of the 18th century became an instant object of attention, since they promised to relieve poverty and secure freedom. Both English industrial advance and French democratic ideas provided models to imitate or even to rival. And since England and France were world empires, imitation also seemed to imply a promise of national power. The attempt to emulate 'the West' was already notable in Eastern Europe during the 18th and 19th centuries, but has become more prominent still in the 'under-developed' countries of the 20th century.

The diffusion of techniques and ideas gives special importance to the educated élite, which had little or no place in theories that judged social groups in relation to the division of labour. Already at the end of the 17th century, the German philosopher Leibniz advised Peter the Great to adopt advanced Dutch techniques of commerce and craftsmanship but avoid the painful errors which are the lot of the pioneer. Since then, the world has become divided into societies that have achieved high levels of industrialization, and others which have not but are trying against great odds to build up their economies. The breakthrough by the 'Western' countries has been witnessed from afar by men to whom the backwardness, autocracy, or instability of their own country appears still more intolerable by comparison.

Standing thus uneasily between modernity and tradition, men of letters do not remain estranged witnesses of a materialist civilization as they have so often in Western Europe. Instead, they try to become the intellectual and political leaders in the drive towards modernization. There are those who want their country to progress by imitating the more advanced countries. Others emphasize the well-springs of strength in their own culture. Both are aware that the attractions of Western wealth and power pose a threat to the native tradition. The ambivalence of these views corresponds to the cultural and institutional divisions within these countries. For a small number of people have adopted ideas and practices from abroad, while the mass of the population is still beholden to native traditions.

The social and political problems posed by this division are intractable. In the 19th century, the autocratic regimes of Eastern Europe or the Far East were attempting to cope with them. These were strictly regimes of notables. They sought to regulate society by government edict and a corresponding bureaucracy. In 1861, when Tsar Alexander II decreed the emancipation of the Russian serfs, he remarked to Bismarck in an interview: 'God only knows what might be the ultimate outcome of the current transaction between peasants and landowners, if the power of the Tsar was not strong enough to give an unconditional guarantee of leader-ship.' This absolutist approach required the government to regulate not only a gradual increase in legal equality, but also social relations arising from inherited privilege, from economic relations, and from the religious, ethnic, and linguistic divisions of the population. We know today that many autocratic regimes failed in their attempt to superintend the transition to the modern world.

The problems of these autocracies and of the now emerging nations can be compared with the rise of the European nation states. Generally, the European nations began their development with a unification and centralization of governmental functions and an extensive diminution of group differences. This was a gradual development. The new states of the 20th century face a more difficult task, because through imitation they have accelerated change, making it even more unmanageable. And from the start they are confronted with economic competition from already developed countries. Most of the newly sovereign countries arose from movements of independence which appealed to all the people, and accordingly established regimes based on a universal franchise. Thus they began their political existence with the full complement of democratic institutions developed in Western Europe. But to achieve national identity and economic growth a national government appears indispensable. And under the conditions of the new states such a government is difficult to establish and maintain with any degree of stability. As Clifford Geerts has shown, notions like state or citizenship still mean little to people whose social ties remain bound up with blood, race, language, locality, religion or tradition. Universal franchise and the modern press encourage the public manifestation of these social ties so that most modern political devices tend to conflict with a national realization of collective aims. Thus, in the new states the divisive

tendencies of traditional society are intensified by just those nationalist and democratic developments which in 19th-century Europe led to a greater degree of national unity.

Three excluded groups

Yet this unity of Western nation states, limited as it was, is now threatened from within. Social divisions other than those of class had existed all along, but in the 1960s they have become political issues. Nineteenth-century theory had assumed that a society encompasses all the people living in the territory of a nation state. However, the meaning of this assumption was limited in various ways. Liberal theory tended to account only for people directly involved in exchange relations, thereby excluding economic dependants of all kinds. Conservative theory tended to account for all people by virtue of their social status, but then placed dependants of all kinds in an inferior position. Nor could conservatives do much with people like intellectuals or foreigners whose status was unclear, or with categories like legal equality or citizenship which applied to everyone. Radical theory tended to account only for people directly involved in employment relation-ships and encompassed all others by subsuming them under the categories of exploiters and exploited. The 20th century has wit-nessed the social and political emergence of groups which these 19th-century theories left out of account: women, racial minorities, youths, the aged, intellectuals and others. Each of these groups poses problems peculiar to itself in relation to the larger issue of citizenship. With reference to the industrialized nation states I shall discuss the first three groups as segments of the population which were omitted by, or dissatisfied with, the successful develop-ment of national citizenship.

Women were the first of the excluded groups to demand a change of status. Under the influence of the French Revolution they had obtained many civil rights during the 19th century: liberty of person, freedom of speech and thought, the right to own property and to conclude valid contracts. But political rights were denied them. During the last decades of the 19th century a movement for the emancipation of women came to the fore. The right to vote and to stand for an elective office was granted, but only gradually. In some countries, like Switzerland, women are denied political rights to this day. In the field of social rights the record is mixed. Since women were economic dependants for much of the 19th century, they were considered proper objects of welfare measures designed to protect them against the most extreme hazards of exploitation and insecurity. However, as they increased their participation in the labour force, women ceased to be considered automatically as dependants and frequently could obtain public assistance only on the same basis as men, perhaps an equivocal gain.

Here the contrast between the new states and the nation states of 'the West' is especially striking. Where the ties of blood and tradition remain strong, the position of women is not only that of economic dependants but of social inferiors. In this setting only men have rights. Yet just here the winning of national indepen-dence brings with it the full range of political rights, not gradually but all at once. The full range of social rights, while also granted, remains on paper. Thus, in the new states, women often remain in their age-old position of social inferiority. Little can be done to ensure them a minimum degree of welfare, but they now have the right to vote and stand for elective office, unlike some women in Europe who still have to win these rights.

The emancipation of women remains an unresolved problem. For even where it has gone the farthest in terms of civil, political and social rights, it has not resolved the inherent paradox of equalizing the conditions of those who are different by nature. Liberal theory believed the emancipation of women resolved when it advanced their equality of rights before the law and on the market place. But this did nothing to eliminate the social bias against women. In a large number of occupations women are discriminated against to this day. They often receive less pay than men for the same type of work. Nor can formal equalization alter the special role of women in the family. Where women remain in the labour force by staying single or making arrangements for their children they must compete with men as equals. That com-

p 346
(23–25)

petition can have a lacerating emotional effect. And one may wonder what the emotional effects on women are in countries like the Soviet Union, where official doctrine holds them to be equal and where, in the absence of occupational choice, they must shoulder the same burdens as men.

The case of racial minorities is similar to that of women in some respects. Gunnar Myrdal noted some years ago that prejudice against Negroes and women was remarkably alike. Both are reputed to be mercurial, childlike, of lesser intelligence, and both suffer from some of the same disabilities like less pay for equal work, employment in menial occupations, greater risks of dismissal and others. But these parallels of prejudice and social inferiority do not go to the heart of the problem.

p 347
(26)
p 88
28, 29)
Racial minorities, and especially the Negro population in the United States with its history of slavery, constitute a lower class as women obviously do not. An ethnically or racially segregated lower class is a distinctive phenomenon of industrialized societies in the 20th century. It differs fundamentally from the proletariat of the 19th century in the sense that race has been added to class as the reason for a denial of civil, political and social rights. It differs also from the many countries in Asia and elsewhere, in which racial minorities represent ethnic enclaves that constitute virtually separate societies and economies. For these enclaves are not classes, but distinct ethnic communities. In the United States, ethnic communities are on the whole integrated economically and to some extent socially. By contrast, the American Negro, the Puerto Rican and Mexican-American suffer not only from the disabilities of racial discrimination generally, but constitute a special lower stratum by virtue of their exclusion from the working class.

The citizenship of racial minorities remains an unresolved problem. Members of minority groups are denied rights which are formally theirs, a condition far worse than that faced by workers in the 19th century, who could attack the clear symbols of their second-class status like disenfranchisement or the laws prohibiting trade unions. Negro Americans or West Indians in England face a social discrimination so hydra-headed that institutional changes like special guarantees of due process or of the right to vote, important as these are, do not alter their outcast status effectively.

Conservative theory with its belief in natural inequality ignored this problem, but even liberal and radical theory cannot cope with it. For the market does not provide opportunities for those who suffer from massive social discrimination. And the working class will not extend its solidarity to those who find themselves forced to work at lower rates. In this setting, it becomes the task of welfare institutions to prevent the worst deprivations. The schools must attempt to raise the skill level of these outcast groups. And while these institutions become arenas of racial conflict, the major political and economic institutions ignore the problem as long as possible and for the most part confront it only when they must.

p 347
(27)
I conclude this survey of current problems with a brief reference to the question of youth. It is not customary to consider this a problem of citizenship. However, citizenship means active participation in public affairs, and when youths come of age they acquire the formal right of participation. In the 19th century entry into citizenship did not present a major problem, because youths could join the forward movement of Western societies, whether this consisted in movements of emancipation, the settlement of continents or an imperial mission. But, as noted earlier in this discussion, there were many countries in the 19th century which did not enjoy this forward movement. Economically backward and politically repressive, countries like those of Eastern Europe witnessed progress only from afar. In such countries men of letters were often the spokesmen of a youth chafing under the prospect of careers that would only frustrate their personal and national ambitions. To these youths and to their modern peers in the countries of Asia and Latin America, a social order had first to be created in which citizenship would be worthwhile.

In the 20th century, entry into citizenship has become a critical

'March of the Noughts'—an indictment by Werner Heldt (1935) of the anonymous totalitarian state. (5)

concern in ways quite unsuspected during the 19th century. As long as the franchise was limited, the target had been clear. Demands for lowering the voting age and eliminating property qualifications were in the end satisfied, except in oligarchic regimes incapable of this adaptation. But once these demands were met, it became apparent that the right to vote was meaningful only if the values attached to that right were accepted. And this in turn depended on the credibility of the institutional structure. Once the right to vote at age twenty-one can be taken for granted, the critical question becomes whether those who turn twenty-one are committed to uphold the structure in which they have now a right to participate. In Western Europe social critics had questioned that structure throughout, but with particular insistence since the end of the 19th century. And the great writers of the 20th century have treated the ideas of liberal democracy with indifference or hostility. For youth such indifference or hostility has become a passionate concern during the great crises of our era.

In the large context sketched here, these 'generational revolts' have a logic of their own. They have occurred at the turning points of Western civilization which put prevailing assumptions in jeopardy. World War I destroyed the balance of power among states. The Great Depression witnessed the destruction of the market mechanism as traditionally conceived. And following the recovery from the ravages of World War II the 1960s have experienced a sense of crisis arising from the prospect of nuclear destruction, the world-wide confrontation of the super-powers, and the unresolved legacies of five centuries of Western expansion.

p 320–1
(16–23)

Problems of the future

What then is the prospect before youth today? No one can answer this question, but the reasons for our uncertainty are familiar. In our time the speed and diversity of change have been so unprecedented that the preoccupations of earlier decades seem already curiously old-fashioned. Who still considers it vital to discuss central planning *v.* the market principle, when partially planned economies have developed under both socialist and capitalist auspices? Who still looks to world government as the solution to international problems, when in fifty years of effort since the founding of the League of Nations only regional alliances and precariously maintained *détentes* have shown some slight promise of results. Even the horrors of totalitarian rule have dimmed somewhat, as other kinds of one-party rule have been adopted widely, although the harshness of dictatorship remains. Also,

p 33
(1)

fissures have come to divide the Communist bloc and the nuclear threat has put accommodation on the agenda of the super-powers.

In the second half of this century there are two dangers, however, which are unprecedented in their implications. One is a transformation of radical protest, the other a transformation of the belief in progress through knowledge. Both signify a great, perhaps a fatal weakening of the enlightenment tradition.

In the mid-19th century Marx had turned his back on utopianism by rejecting speculations about the future and basing present actions upon economic and historical analysis. His was a rationalist approach to capitalist society and the road of the labour movement to revolution and a socialist society of the future. Perhaps Lenin was the first to modify this rationalism by organizing the revolution in a backward country and making his Party independent of working-class support. Mao Tse-tung has carried this modification further, though his voluntarism is still limited by the insistence that the Party or the army must win and retain the support of the peasant masses. With men like Castro, Guevara and Debray and with spokesmen of the New Left this rationalist tradition of radical protest has been eroded. A secular religion based on the charismatic prestige of insurrection has taken the place of both, analysis of social conditions and the search for popular support. The Marxian belief in theory and practice has been abandoned. (On these points I am indebted to Richard Lowenthal, 'Unreason and Revolution', *Encounter*, XXXIII (November 1969), pp. 22–34.)

p 160
(40)

Equally noteworthy is the declining belief in reason within the citadel of Western science. Since the discovery of atomic energy, the prestige of science has been questioned and with it the remaining legacies of the Enlightenment. For all the indispensable knowledge that it alone can develop, science has created powers of destruction so great that agonizing questions are raised concerning the unconditional quest for knowledge. And with these questions comes a renewed concern with the large-scale alterations of the natural environment which are a by-product of headlong and heedless advances in technology. Yet science and scholarship presuppose a belief in knowledge 'for the benefit and use of life' (Bacon), a belief in the perfectability of man. They do not flourish amidst preoccupation with their own potential evil, or where doubts concerning the value of knowledge prevail. Therefore the last decades of this century may well witness a crisis of conscience, raising long-overdue questions concerning the purpose of knowledge. The prospect inspires anxiety and hope, but hardly confidence.

(Drawing by Saul Steinberg.) (6)

List and sources of illustrations

I A Promethean Age

13 1. Earth photographed from an artificial satellite, November 1967. Photo *NASA/USIS*

14 2. Illustration from *The Graphic* welcoming the year 1900. Guildhall Library, London. Photo *John R. Freeman*
3. Traffic jam on a German autobahn. Photo *Camera Press, London*
4, 6, 9. Three of a series of French printed cards showing life in the year 2000; c. 1900. Collection Professor and Mrs Asa Briggs. Photo *Michael Holford*
5. Hovercraft outside Dover harbour. Photo *Ray Warner (Camera Press, London)*
6. See 4, above
7. Elementary school child learning to write imaginatively with the aid of a tape recorder. Photo *Colin Davey (Camera Press, London)*
8. Industrialized building site. Photo *courtesy Concrete Ltd*
9. See 4, above

15 10. 'The projectile passing the moon', frontispiece to Jules Verne, *From the Earth to the Moon*, London 1876. British Museum, London. Photo *John R. Freeman*
11. Lunar spacecraft approaching command module; Apollo 11, July 1969. Photo *NASA/USIS*
12. Boeing 747 at Heathrow airport, London. Photo *Camera Press, London*
13. 'Aerial locomotive'; c. 1900. Collection Professor and Mrs Asa Briggs
14. Illustration by Albert Robida from his book *Le Vingtième Siècle*, Paris 1883. British Museum, London. Photo *John R. Freeman*
15. Man looking at portable television set (advertisement). Photo *Photographic Techniques Ltd, London*

16 16. Naum Gabo: *Linear Construction*, 1942–3. *The Tate Gallery, London*
17. Alexander Calder: *Poisson Rouge, Queue Jaune*; hanging mobile, 1968. *The Property of the Brook Street Gallery, London*

17 18. Piet Mondrian: *Composition with Red, Yellow and Blue*, 1921. Gemeentemuseum, The Hague

18 19. Albert Einstein at Saranac Lake, New York. Photo *Associated Press*
20. Mahatma Gandhi. Photo *Camera Press, London*
21. Pope John XXIII. Photo *Patrick Morin (Camera Press, London)*
22. Anna Pavlova. *Radio Times Hulton Picture Library*
23. Greta Garbo as Mata Hari. Photo *National Film Archive, London*
24. Marilyn Monroe. Photo *National Film Archive, London*
25. Charlie Chaplin. *Radio Times Hulton Picture Library*
26. Bing Crosby. Photo *National Film Archive, London*
27. Mick Jagger, lead singer of the Rolling Stones, at an outdoor concert in Hyde Park, London. Photo *Mike Charity (Camera Press, London)*

19 28. Joseph Stalin. Photo *Popperfoto, London*
29. Adolf Hitler speaking at a Nazi rally. Imperial War Museum, London. Photo *Camera Press, London*

30. General Charles de Gaulle addressing a rally. Photo *Camera Press, London*
31. Captain Robert F. Scott. Photo *Popperfoto, London*
32. Charles Lindbergh, with the 'Spirit of St Louis' after his successful solo crossing of the Atlantic in 1927. *Radio Times Hulton Picture Library*
33. Yuri Gagarin at London airport. Photo *Camera Press, London*
34. Edward, Prince of Wales (now Duke of Windsor) attending a British Legion rally at the Crystal Palace, October 1922. Photo *Popperfoto, London*
35. Ernesto Che Guevara during the battle of Santa Clara. Photo *Keystone Press Agency*
36. Joe Louis, 1938. Photo *United Press International*

20–21 37. Motor-racing at Spa, Belgium. Photo *Magnum*
38. Mexico Olympics 1968: hurdling. Photo *United Press International*
39. Brazil v. Italy: World Cup, Mexico, 1970. Photo *United Press International*

22–23 40. First World War cemetery at Gallipoli. Photo *Camera Press, London*
41. Mass grave, Belsen, 1945. *Imperial War Museum, London*
42. Hiroshima, after the dropping of the first atomic bomb in 1945. Imperial War Museum, London. Photo *Camera Press, London*

24 43. Jørn Utzon: Sydney Opera House; begun 1959. Photo *Picturepoint, London*
44. Le Corbusier: pilgrimage church of Notre-Dame-du-Haut, Ronchamp, 1950–54. Photo *Burkhard-Verlag Ernst Heyer, Essen*

27 Le Corbusier: sketch showing the building of tall point-blocks in Paris, in accordance with his *Plan Voisin*, 1925

II Peace and War

33 1. Stresemann's last speech at the League of Nations. Photo *the late Dr Erich Salomon (Magnum)*
2. (Inset) John Heartfield: *The Spirit of Geneva* ('the home of capital cannot be the home of peace'); photomontage, first version, 1932

34–5 3. *Land of Hope and Glory*, patriotic postcard, c. 1900. Victoria and Albert Museum, London. Photo *John R. Freeman*
4. Cartoon from *Simplicissimus*, Munich, 1906. British Museum, London. Photo *John R. Freeman*
5. Cartoon from *Simplicissimus*, Munich, 1906. British Museum, London. Photo *John R. Freeman*
6. A humorous map of Europe, 1914. Imperial War Museum, London. Photo *Eileen Tweedy*
7. Alex Eckener: *Floating Dock*, c. 1905–10. Städtisches Museum, Flensburg
8. Austrian war loan poster. *Imperial War Museum, London*
9. British recruiting poster by Saville Lumley, 1914–18. *Imperial War Museum, London*
10. French war loan poster by Abel Faivre, 1914(?). *Imperial War Museum, London*

35 11. *The European threshing Floor*, German

propaganda postcard, 1914. *Altonaer Museum, Hamburg*

36 12. Recruits at Southwark Town Hall, London; December 1915. *Radio Times Hulton Picture Library*
13. *US Marines on Land and Sea*, recruiting poster for World War I by S. H. Riesenberg. *Lord's Gallery, London*
14. Shell-filling shop of a British munitions factory. Imperial War Museum, London. Photo *Camera Press, London*
15. Detail of a commemorative ribbon dedicated to the German fleet; Berlin 1914. Imperial War Museum, London. Photo *Eileen Tweedy*
16. Detail of a commemorative ribbon dedicated to the Zeppelin crews, 'the youngest branch of the German air fleet'; Berlin 1915. Imperial War Museum, London. Photo *Eileen Tweedy*

37 17. British troops fixing bayonets in a trench during the Battle of Albert, before the assault on Beaumont Hamel, July 1916. Imperial War Museum, London. Photo *Camera Press, London*
18. French troops at Verdun, 1916. *The Bell of Arms Ltd, Ilkley*
19. Kaiser Wilhelm inspecting his troops in Galicia with Count Boethmer. Imperial War Museum, London. Photo *Camera Press, London*
20. British troops landing on the beach at Suvla Bay, Gallipoli, 3 September 1915. Imperial War Museum. Photo *Camera Press, London*

38–9 21. Paul Nash: *We are Making a New World*, c. 1918. Imperial War Museum, London. Photo *Eileen Tweedy*
22. William Orpen: *The Signing of the Peace in the Hall of Mirrors, Versailles, 28 June 1919*. Front: Dr Johannes Bell (signing) and Hermann Miller. Middle row: General Tasker H. Bliss, Col. E. M. House, Henry White, Robert Lansing, Woodrow Wilson, Georges Clemenceau, D. Lloyd George, A. Bonar Law, Arthur Balfour, Viscount Milner, G. N. Barnes, Marquis Sainozi. *Imperial War Museum, London*
23. Pro-Chinese Russian poster, 1932. *Kunstgewerbemuseum, Zurich*
24. *The Legionaries of Victory*, postcard issued by the Lombardy Section of the Istituto Coloniale Fascista, glorifying the Italian invasion of Abyssinia, 1935. *Archivo Achille Bertorelli, Milan*
25. Anti-appeasement poster printed in Great Britain, 1939. Imperial War Museum, London. Photo *Eileen Tweedy*

40 26. Chamberlain returning with the Munich agreement. Photo *Camera Press, London*
27. German troops entering Danzig, September 1939. Photo *Camera Press, London*
28. German troops marching into Warsaw, October 1939. *Imperial War Museum, London*
29. German troops in occupied Paris. Photo *Roger-Viollet, Paris*
30. French refugees fleeing the German advance, 1940. *Imperial War Museum, London*
31. Air-raid shelter in a Tube station, London. *Radio Times Hulton Picture Library*
32. French church in Berlin after Allied

bombing, 24 May 1944. Photo *Keystone Press Agency*

33. British forces awaiting evacuation from Dunkirk beaches, June 1940. *Radio Times Hulton Picture Library*
34. The US naval air station at Pearl Harbor after the Japanese raid of 7 December 1941. Photo *US Department of the Navy*

41 35. British pilots running to their planes during the Battle of Britain, 1940. Imperial War Museum, London. Photo *Camera Press, London*
36. Churchill outside Downing Street during the War. Photo *Popperfoto, London*
37. North African campaign: tanks in the desert, 26 October 1942. Imperial War Museum, London. Photo *Camera Press, London*
38. Ruins of Monte Cassino, April 1944. The Abbey was finally taken in May. Imperial War Museum, London. Photo *Camera Press, London*
39. Burma campaign: officer addressing Gurkha troops at the Arakan front, January 1944. Photo *Cecil Beaton (Camera Press, London)*
40. Defeat of Germans at Stalingrad, February 1943. Photo *Novosti Press Agency*
41. Allied troops landing on the Normandy beaches, June 1944. *Imperial War Museum, London*
42. Soviet troops raising the Red Flag on top of the Reichstag building, Berlin, 8 May 1945. Photo *Deutsche Fotothek Dresden*
43. US Marines raising the American flag on Mount Suribachi, Iwo Jima, February 1945. Photo *Associated Press*

42 44. Winston Churchill, Franklin D. Roosevelt and Joseph Stalin at the Yalta Conference, February 1945. Photo *US Department of the Army*
45. *Vigilance the Price of Liberty*, cover of NATO pamphlet, 1960. By courtesy of the NATO Information Service, Brussels. Photo *R. B. Fleming*
46. Meeting of the Warsaw Pact leaders at Bratislava, 1968. Photo *CAF, Warsaw (Camera Press, London)*

43 47. Cuban poster celebrating the Day of Solidarity of the Afro-American people. *OSPAAAL*
48. Frontier Patrol, Korea. Photo *US Department of the Army*
49. War scene in Vietnam. Photo *P. J. Griffiths (Magnum)*
50. Israeli troops on the Mount of Olives during the Six Day War, June 1967. Photo *Ronald Sheridan*

44 51. Ben Shahn: *Dag Hammerskjold*, 1962. Nationalmuseum, Stockholm
52, 53. Milós Ciric: *The End of War* and *The Beginning of Peace*; linocuts, 1968

46 1. T. A. Steinlen: 'C'est ici chez nous'; lithograph, 1918. British Museum, London. Photo *John R. Freeman*
47 2. Will Dyson: *Peace and Future Cannon Fodder*; from the *Daily Herald*, 1919
48 3. Alfred Kubin: *Demagogy*; pen drawing, 1939. Albertina, Vienna
51 4. George Whitelaw: 'Further Retreat is Impossible'—Berlin Radio; from the *Daily Herald*, 1944

1926 (right). Collection of The Museum of Modern Art, New York. Photo *Berbert Matter*

224 69. Gerrit Thomas Rietveld: Schröder House, Utrecht; 1924. Photo *Burkhard-Verlag Ernst Heyer, Essen*

70. Gerrit Thomas Rietveld: colour project for the interior of the Schröder House, Utrecht; 1924

71. Le Corbusier: Villa Savoye, Poissy; 1927–30. Photo *Lucien Hervé, Paris*

72. Ludwig Mies van der Rohe: Lake Shore Drive Apartments, Chicago; 1948–51. Photo *Hedrich-Blessing*

73. Le Corbusier: High Court, Chandigarh; 1952–6. Photo *Lucien Hervé, Paris*

226–27 74. Ben Nicholson: *April 1959 (Paros)*. Private collection

75. Henri Matisse: *The Snail*; 1953. Tate Gallery, London

76. Jackson Pollock: *One (number 31, 1950)*; 1950. Collection of the Museum of Modern Art, New York. Gift of Sidney Janis

77. Henry Moore: *UNESCO Reclining Figure*; 1957–8. Photo *courtesy Henry Moore*

78. Germaine Richier: *Water*; 1953–4. Tate Gallery, London

79. Mark Rothko: *Orange Yellow Orange*; 1969. Marlborough Gerson Gallery, New York

228 80. Roy Lichtenstein: "*Whaam!*"; 1963. Tate Gallery, London

81. Andy Warhol: *Campbell's Soup*; 1964. Collection Mr and Mrs Leo Castelli, New York

82. Jean Tinguely and Niki de Saint-Phalle: *Hon* (She); 1966. Museum of Modern Art, Stockholm. Photo *Hans Hammarskiöld*

229 83. David Hockney: *Typhoo Tea*; 1961. Bischofberger collection, Zurich. Photo *courtesy Kasmin Gallery, London*

84. Peter Blake: *On the Balcony*; 1955–7. Tate Gallery, London

85. R. B. Kitaj: *Cultural Value of Fear, Distrust and Hypochondria*; 1966. Courtesy Marlborough Fine Art (London) Ltd

230 86. New Victoria Cinema, London; 1929. Photo *Ian Yeomans*

87. Hans Scharoun: Concert Hall of the Berlin Philharmonic Orchestra, Berlin; 1960–63. Photo *R. Friedrich, Berlin*

88. Frame from *Yellow Submarine*, featuring the Beatles; designer Heinz Edelman, 1968

89. Four frames from a Manns Beer advertisement on English television. *Courtesy PKL*

90. Paperback books. Photo *Eileen Tweedy*

231 91. Herbert von Karajan, conductor of the Berlin Philharmonic Orchestra. Photograph by Karsh of Ottawa. Photo *Camera Press, London*

92. Benjamin Britten conducting *Peter Grimes*; February 1969. Photo *BBC*

93. Karlheinz Stockhausen

94. Scene from *West Side Story* by Leonard Bernstein, 1957: the rumble (battle between the gangs of Sharks and Jets). Photo *Camera Press, London*

95. Scene from *Symphonic Variations*, ballet by Frederick Ashton to music by César Franck. Photograph by Baron at Covent Garden Opera House, London; 1946. The dancers are Moira Shearer, Margot Fonteyn, Pamela May, Michael Somes and Henry Danton. *Radio Times Hulton Picture Library*

96. Scene from Act III of *Siegfried*, produced by Wieland Wagner; Bayreuth Festival, 1952. Photo *Festspielleitung Bayreuth, courtesy* Opera Magazine

97. Frame from *Open City* by Rossellini; 1945. Photo *National Film Archive, London*

98. Frame from *Alphaville, Une Étrange Aventure de Lemmy Caution* by Jean Luc Godard; 1965. Photo *National Film Archive, London*

99. Frame from *The Seventh Seal* by Ingmar Bergman; 1956. Photo *National Film Archive, London*

100. Scene from *End Game* by Samuel Beckett; 1958. Photo *Reg Wilson, London*

101. Yves Klein: 'Painting Ceremony' (the creation of *Imprints*). Photo *Shunk-Kender, Paris*

102. Scene from *The Winter's Tale* at the Questors Theatre, Ealing. Photo *R. W. Sheppard, courtesy Rank Strand Electric*

232 103. Victor Vasarely: *Vega Jon*; 1964. Private collection. Photo *courtesy London Arts Gallery*

104. John C. Mott Smith: *Colour Computer Graphic*; 1968. Photo *courtesy Studio International*

234 *1*. Ernst Ludwig Kirchner: program of *Die Brücke*, 1905

2. Wassily Kandinsky: design for the cover of the *Blaue Reiter* almanach; black printing only from coloured woodcut, 1911/12

235 *3*. Paul Klee: *Exotics' Theatre*; drawing, 1922. Paul Klee Foundation, Museum of Fine Arts, Berne

236 *4*. Guillaume Apollinaire: *Il Pleut*; from *Calligrammes*, 1918

5. Jean Cocteau: *Stravinsky composing 'The Rite of Spring'*, 1913

237 *6*. Jean Arp: *Der Zeltweg*; woodcut, 1919

238 *7*. Oscar Schlemmer: symbol for the 'State Bauhaus'

239 *8*. El Lissitzky: letterhead for the magazine *Veshch*, 1922

9. Le Corbusier: drawing illustrating his module, 'Modulor'; from *Le Modulor*, 1946

240 *10*. Illustration by Joseph Lada showing Schweik by the telephone, from *The Good Soldier Schweik* by Jaroslav Hašek, first published in 1930

241 *11*. Emblem of the record company His Master's Voice; from an early record sleeve

12. e. e. cummings: *Charlie Chaplin*. Collection Dr J. S. Watson

245 *13*. Section from the percussion part (no. 4) of *Atlas Eclipticalis*, by John Cage. Copyright Henmar Press Inc., New York

14. Part of the score of *Studie II*, by Karlheinz Stockhausen; 1954. Copyright Universal Music Publishers

XI Horizons of the Mind

249 1. Paul Klee: *Calmly Daring*: watercolour, 1930. *Paul Klee Foundation, Museum of Fine Arts, Berne*

250 2. Martin Heidegger. *Staatsbibliothek, Berlin*

3. Benedetto Croce, 1949. Photo *Camera Press, London*

4. Karl Barth, Professor of Theology at Basel University. Photo *Max Ehlert (Camera Press, London)*

5. Oswald Spengler. *Staatsbibliothek, Berlin*

6. Arnold Toynbee. Photo *courtesy Professor Arnold Toynbee*

7. Jean-Paul Sartre. Photo *Fritz Eschen (Camera Press, London)*

251 8. Ludwig Wittgenstein. Photo courtesy *Trinity College, Cambridge*

9. Max Weber, c. 1920. *Staatsbibliothek, Berlin*

10. Bertrand Russell at a rally in support of nuclear disarmament at Trafalgar Square, London, 26 February 1962. Photo *Popperfoto, London*

11. Sir Karl Popper, Professor of Philosophy at the London School of Economics, 1962. Photo *Professor E. H. Gombrich, by courtesy of Professor Sir Karl Popper*

12. George Edward Moore; portrait in pencil and chalk by P. F. Horton, 1947. *National Portrait Gallery, London*

13. Alfred Jules Ayer, Wykeham Professor of Logic at Oxford University. Photo *Camera Press, London*

14. William James; photograph by Alice Boughton, c. 1900. *By permission of the Harvard College Library*

252 15. May Day Parade in Red Square, Moscow. Photo *Magnum*

253 16. Celebration of mass at St Joseph's College, Minnesota. Photo *Burt Glinn (Magnum)*

17. Cardinal Wyszynsky celebrating mass in the open air. Photo *Magnum*

254 18. Sigmund Freud and the 'Committee' in Berlin, 1922. Standing, left to right: Otto Rank, Karl Abraham, Max Eitingon, Ernest Jones; seated: Freud, Sandor Ferenczi, Hanns Sachs. *Staatsbibliothek, Berlin*

254 19. Professor Alfred Adler lecturing at Schoeneberg town hall, Berlin, 1930. Photo *the late Dr Erich Salomon (Magnum)*

20. Dr Carl Jung. Photo *Karsh (Camera Press, London)*

21. John Held Jr: 'Sweet Sexteen', cover for *Life* (Chicago), 30 September 1926. *Bodleian Library, Oxford*

22. Bruno Caruso: *Psycho analysis*, 1969. *By courtesy of the artist*

255 23. Georges Sorel. Photo *Roger-Viollet, Paris*

24. George Bernard Shaw with Beatrice and Sidney Webb, c. 1930. Photo *Daily Herald*

25. Albert Schweitzer. *Staatsbibliothek, Berlin*

26. Herbert Marcuse. Photo *Marc Riboud (Magnum)*

27. Noam Chomsky, Professor of Philosophy at the Massachusetts Institute of Technology. Photo *Bill Potter (Camera Press, London)*

28. G. Patrix: *Saint-Germain-des-Prés*, 1948. Left to right: M. Boubal, owner of the Café de Flore; Raymond Duncan (seated); Boris Vian, writer and musician; Jacques Prévert, poet; Camille Bryenne, painter and poet; 'le Bonapartiste' (a local eccentric); Jean Genêt, novelist and playwright; Juliette Greco, actress and singer; Jean-Paul Sartre. In the artist's collection. Photo *Snark International, Paris*

29. Frits van den Berghe: *Genealogy*, 1929. Sabam-Brussels. *Kunstmuseum Basel and Emanuel Hoffmann-Stiftung*

259 *1*. Hans-Georg Rauch: drawing from *Dessins à regarder de près*, 1969

260 *2*. Cartoon from *Fidibusz*, Budapest

263 *3, 4*. Saul Steinberg: drawings from *The Labyrinth*, 1954

264 *5*. Riccardo Manzi: illustration from an article on psychotechnics from *Rivista Italsider*, Genoa

267 *6*. Saul Steinberg: drawing from *The Labyrinth*, 1954

269 *7*. Sempé: drawing from *Des hauts et des bas*, Paris 1970

XII Science comes of age

273 1. 200-inch Hale telescope at Mount Palomar. © California Institute of Technology and Carnegie Institution of Washington. Photo *Hale Observatories*

2. Analytical electron microscope, Emma-4. Photo *AEI Scientific Apparatus Ltd*

274 3. Crab nebula in Taurus. Photo *Hale Observatories*

4. Cygnus A radio contour map. *A. T. Moffett*

5. Jodrell Bank radio telescope. *Central Office of Information, London (Crown copyright reserved)*

275 6. Surface of the sun and solar flare (10 May 1959) photographed in hydrogen light. Sacramento Peak Observatory Air Force Cambridge Research Laboratories

7. Part of the southern Milky Way photographed in red light. Photo *Dr Arthur D. Code and Dr T. E. Houck*

8. Spiral galaxy in Berenice's Hair. Photo *Hale Observatories*

9. Illustrations of the 'red-shift'; adapted from spectrograms taken at Mount Wilson and Palomar Observatories

276–77 10. Lord Rutherford holding an alpha-particle accelerator. Photo *Cavendish Laboratory, Cambridge*

11. The 2-mile-long electron accelerator built by Stanford University, California. Photo *Stanford Linear Accelerator Center*

12. French nuclear power station at Chinon. Photo *courtesy French Embassy, London*

13. Explosion of the hydrogen bomb

14. Dr J. Robert Oppenheimer and General Leslie R. Groves. Photo *United Press International*

278 15. Free-living amœba (*Hartmanella astrontis*). Photo *Gordon F. Leedale*

16. Frozen-etched yeast cell (*Saccharomyces cerevisiae*). *Laboratorium für Elektronenmikroskopie ETH*

278 17. Stereoscan electron microscope photograph of a trapped ant on the leaf of the insectivorous plant *Pinguicula grandiflora*. Photo *Dr Y. Heslop-Harrison*

18. Section through lower plant cell showing nucleus, Golgi bodies, chloroplasts, mitochondria, endoplasmic reticulum, etc.

19. Golgi bodies in a plant cell. Photo *Gordon F. Leedale*

20. *In vivo* anatomy of a connective tissue capillary in man, as observed by vital microscopy. Photo *copyright P.-I. Branemark*

21. Striated muscle from a rabbit. Photo *H. E. Huxley*

279 22. Model of the DNA molecule. Photo *R. E. Barker*

23. Watson and Crick with DNA model. Photo *Camera Press, London*

24. E. Coli bacteriophage (T) releasing DNA molecule after osmotic shock. A. K. Kleinschmidt, New York University Medical Center. *Courtesy Elseiner Publishing Co.*

25. *Triturus viridescens*: electron micrograph of 'genes in action'. *O. L. Miller, Jr, and Barbara R. Beatty, Biology Division, Oak Ridge National Laboratory*

280 26. Dr S. L. Miller and his 'origin of life' experiment. *Courtesy Dr Stanley L. Miller*

27. Sydney Fox's protenoid microspheres; electron micrograph. *Courtesy Stephen M. Brooke*

28. Algal fossil from Gunflint rock, Ontario. *Courtesy E. S. Barghoorn*

29. Skull of *Aegyptopithecus zeuxis*. *Courtesy Elwyn Simons, Yale*

30. Skull of *Australopithecus (Zinjanthropus)*. Photo *Photo Researchers*

31. Skull of Pekin Man. *British Museum (Natural History), London*

32. Skull of Cro-Magnon Man. *Musée de l'Homme, Paris*

281 33. Human ovum, showing first polar body. Photo *Landrum B. Shettles*

34. Embryo 12 mm long in its seventh week. Photo *Erich Blechschmidt, from* Vom Ei zum Embryo *(Deutsche Verlags-anstalt 1968)*

35. Human egg fertilized in the laboratory. *Courtesy Dr R. G. Edwards*

36. Cultured and normal rat embryos of the same age. Photo *D. A. T. New*

282 37. Heterostimulation of 'boss' rhesus monkey through an electrode implanted in the amygdala. Photo *José M. R. Delgado*

38. Electro-encephalograph recordings being taken from electrodes on the head of a sleeping subject. Photo *Roche Products Ltd*

39. Dr Norman Borlaug handling selected wheat stocks at the Rockefeller Agricultural Institute in Mexico. Photo *Associated Press*

40. Helicopters spraying Swiss vines. Photo *Associated Press*

283 41. Indian women receiving instruction on methods of contraception. Photo *Holmes-Lebel (Camera Press, London)*

42. Results of 'defoliation' chemicals. Photo *Vietnam News Agency, Hanoi*

43. Measles immunization given by jet injection. Photo *Associated Press*

284 44. Smoke belching from factory chimneys polluting the atmosphere. Photo *Patrick Thurston*

45. Razorbill coated with oil. Photo *Anthony Clay (Royal Society for the Protection of Birds)*

286–87 *1*. Diagram illustrating the curvature of light. After a drawing in L. Barnett, *The Univers and Dr Einstein*, London (Collins) 1949

287 *2*. Six models of the atom; redrawn from *Bild der Wissenschaft*, November 1969

289 *3, 4*. Photograph and diagram of bubble chamber tracks. *CERN, Geneva*

291 *5*. Seles: cartoon from the Yugoslav journal *Magyar Szó*

292 *6*. Diagram analysing pollution over Los Angeles; redrawn from an article by J. R. Goldsmith in *Science Journal*, October 1969

The illustrations on the chapter title-pages have been adapted from photographs from the following sources: I *Bild der Wissenschaft*, November 1969; II Camera Press, London (p. 36); III National Film Archive (p. 63); IV Rockefeller Center, New York; V Camera Press, London; VI Magnum (p. 252); VII Camera Press, London; VIII Keystone Press Agency; IX Anti-Slavery Society for the Protection of Human Rights, London (p. 194); X Camera Press, London; XI Philip Gotlop; XII E. McQuillan; XIII IBM; XIV Philip Gotlop; XV US Department of Commerce, Environmental Science Services Administration: Coast and Geodetic Survey.

Index

Page numbers in *italic* refer to illustrations